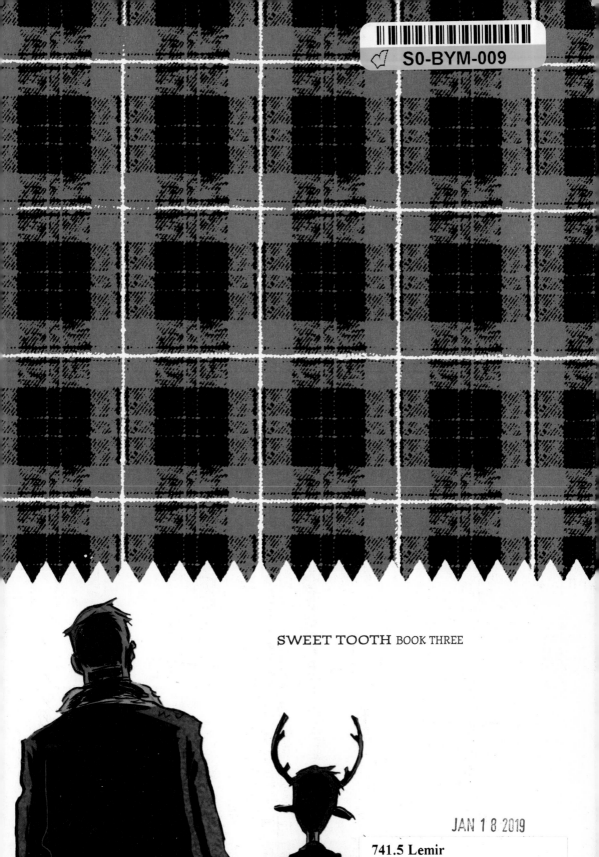

SWEET TOOTH BOOK THREE

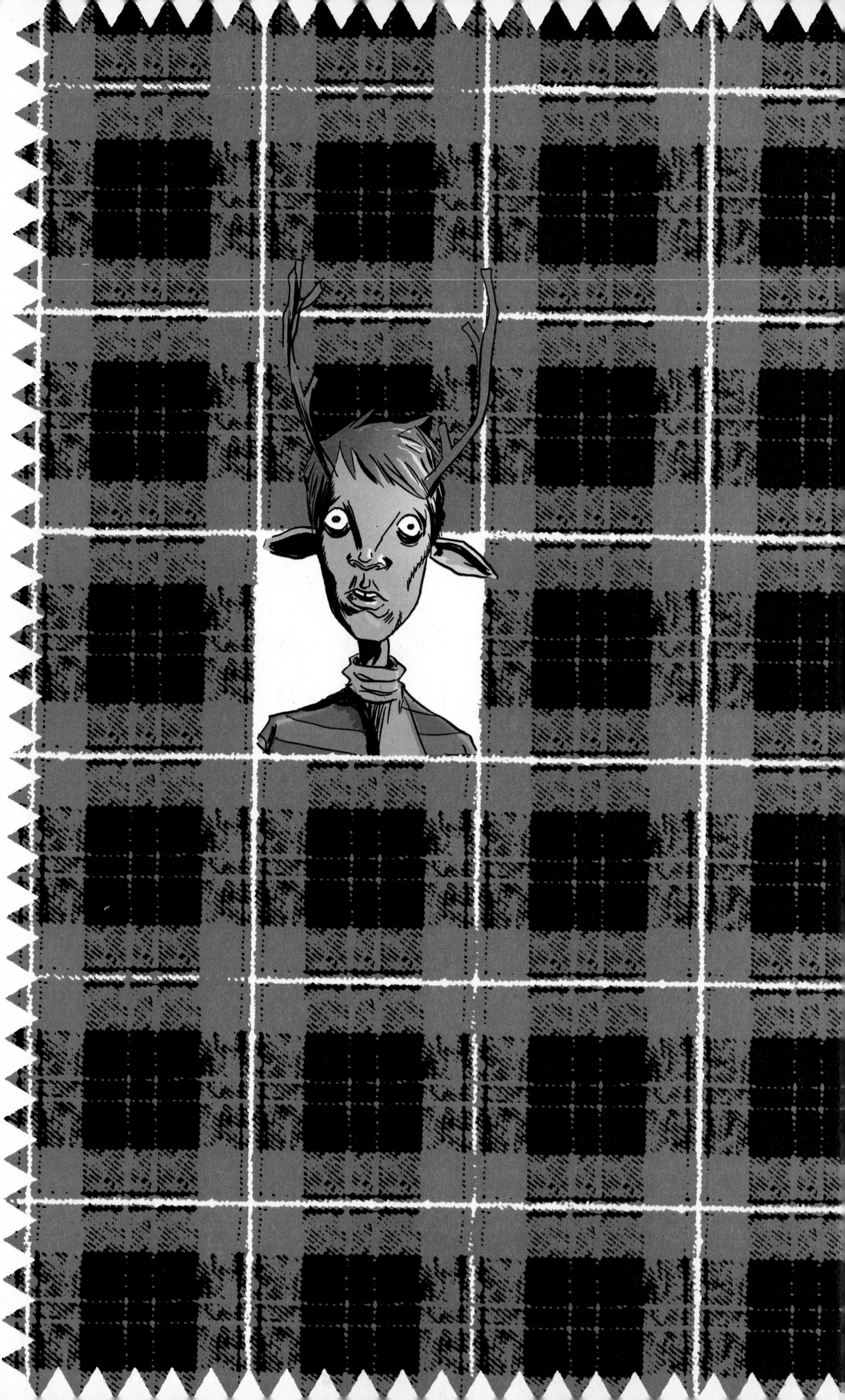

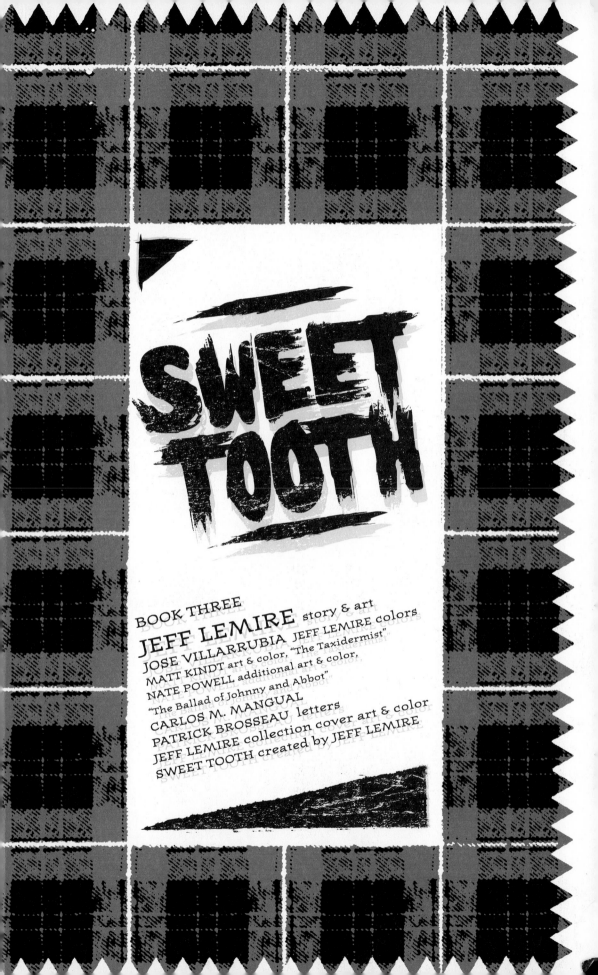

SWEET TOOTH

BOOK THREE

JEFF LEMIRE story & art

JOSE VILLARRUBIA JEFF LEMIRE colors

MATT KINDT art & color, "The Taxidermist"

NATE POWELL additional art & color,
"The Ballad of Johnny and Abbot"

CARLOS M. MANGUAL
PATRICK BROSSEAU letters

JEFF LEMIRE collection cover art & color

SWEET TOOTH created by JEFF LEMIRE

Mark Doyle Editor – Original Series
Gregory Lockard Assistant Editor – Original Series
Jeb Woodard Group Editor – Collected Editions
Robin Wildman Editor – Collected Edition
Steve Cook Design Director – Books
Louis Prandi Publication Design

Bob Harras Senior VP – Editor-in-Chief, DC Comics
Mark Doyle Executive Editor, Vertigo & Black Label

Dan DiDio Publisher
Jim Lee Publisher & Chief Creative Officer
Amit Desai Executive VP – Business & Marketing Strategy,
Direct to Consumer & Global Franchise Management
Bobbie Chase VP & Executive Editor, Young Reader & Talent
Development
Mark Chiarello Senior VP – Art, Design & Collected Editions
John Cunningham Senior VP – Sales & Trade Marketing
Briar Darden VP – Business Affairs
Anne DePies Senior VP – Business Strategy, Finance &
Administration
Don Falletti VP – Manufacturing Operations
Lawrence Ganem VP – Editorial Administration & Talent
Relations
Alison Gill Senior VP – Manufacturing & Operations
Jason Greenberg VP – Business Strategy & Finance
Hank Kanalz Senior VP – Editorial Strategy & Administration
Jay Kogan Senior VP – Legal Affairs
Nick J. Napolitano VP – Manufacturing Administration
Lisette Osterloh VP – Digital Marketing & Events
Eddie Scannell VP – Consumer Marketing
Courtney Simmons Senior VP – Publicity & Communications
Jim (Ski) Sokolowski VP – Comic Book Specialty Sales & Trade
Marketing
Nancy Spears VP – Mass, Book, Digital Sales & Trade Marketing
Michele R. Wells VP – Content Strategy

SWEET TOOTH BOOK THREE

Published by DC Comics. Original compilation
published as SWEET TOOTH: THE DELUXE EDITION
BOOK THREE Copyright © 2016 Jeff Lemire. All
Rights Reserved. Originally published in single
magazine form in SWEET TOOTH 26-40. Copyright
© 2011, 2012, 2013 Jeff Lemire. All Rights Reserved.
Vertigo and all characters, their distinctive
likenesses and related elements featured in this
publication are trademarks of DC Comics. The
stories, characters and incidents featured in this
publication are entirely fictional. DC Comics does
not read or accept unsolicited submissions of ideas,
stories or artwork.

DC Comics, 2900 West Alameda Ave.,
Burbank, CA 91505
Printed by LSC Communications, Owensville, MO,
USA. 11/30/18. First Printing.
ISBN: 978-1-4012-8565-4

Library of Congress Cataloging-in-Publication Data
is available.

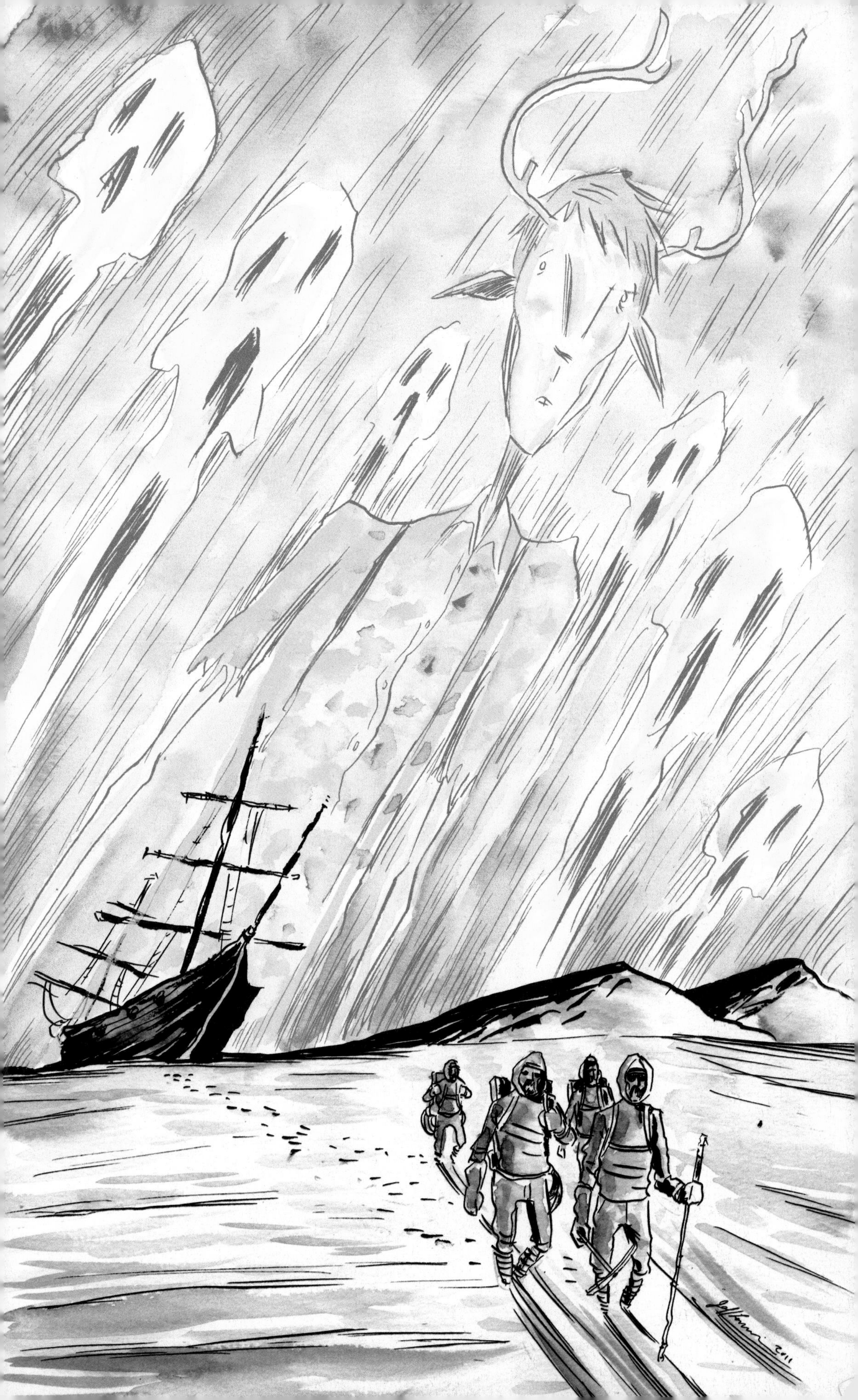

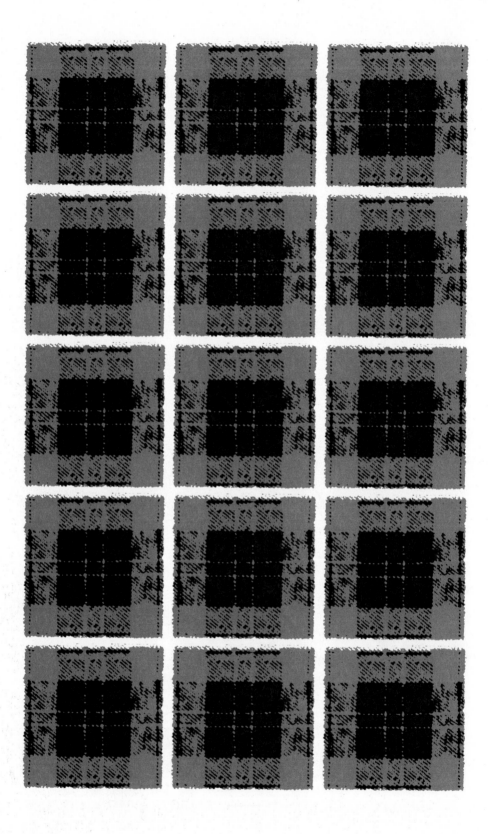

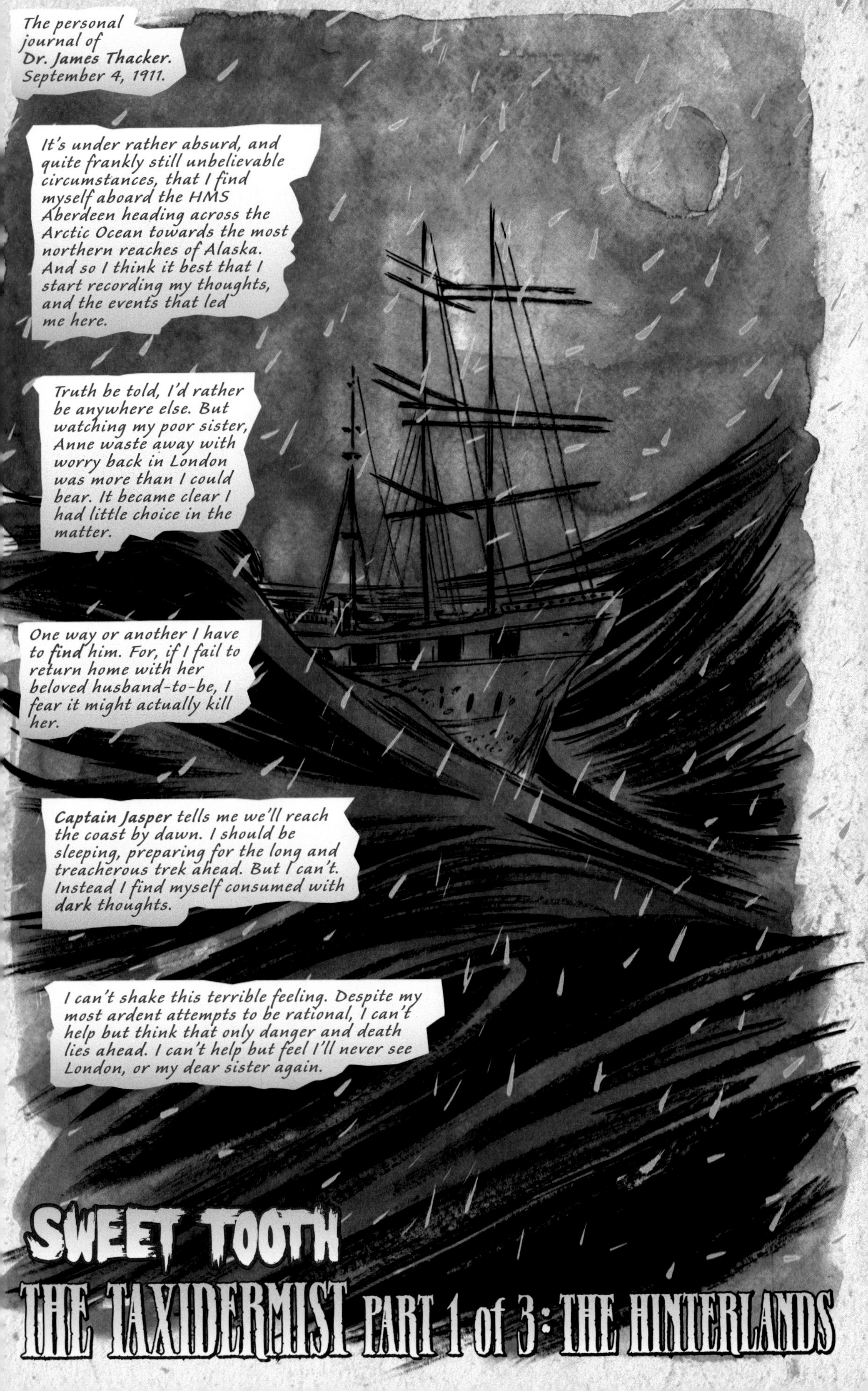
The personal journal of Dr. James Thacker. September 4, 1911.
It's under rather absurd, and quite frankly still unbelievable circumstances, that I find myself aboard the HMS Aberdeen heading across the Arctic Ocean towards the most northern reaches of Alaska. And so I think it best that I start recording my thoughts, and the events that led me here.
Truth be told, I'd rather be anywhere else. But watching my poor sister, Anne waste away with worry back in London was more than I could bear. It became clear I had little choice in the matter.
One way or another I have to find him. For, if I fail to return home with her beloved husband-to-be, I fear it might actually kill her.
Captain Jasper tells me we'll reach the coast by dawn. I should be sleeping, preparing for the long and treacherous trek ahead. But I can't. Instead I find myself consumed with dark thoughts.
I can't shake this terrible feeling. Despite my most ardent attempts to be rational, I can't help but think that only danger and death lies ahead. I can't help but feel I'll never see London, or my dear sister again.
SWEET TOOTH
THE TAXIDERMIST PART 1 of 3: THE HINTERLANDS

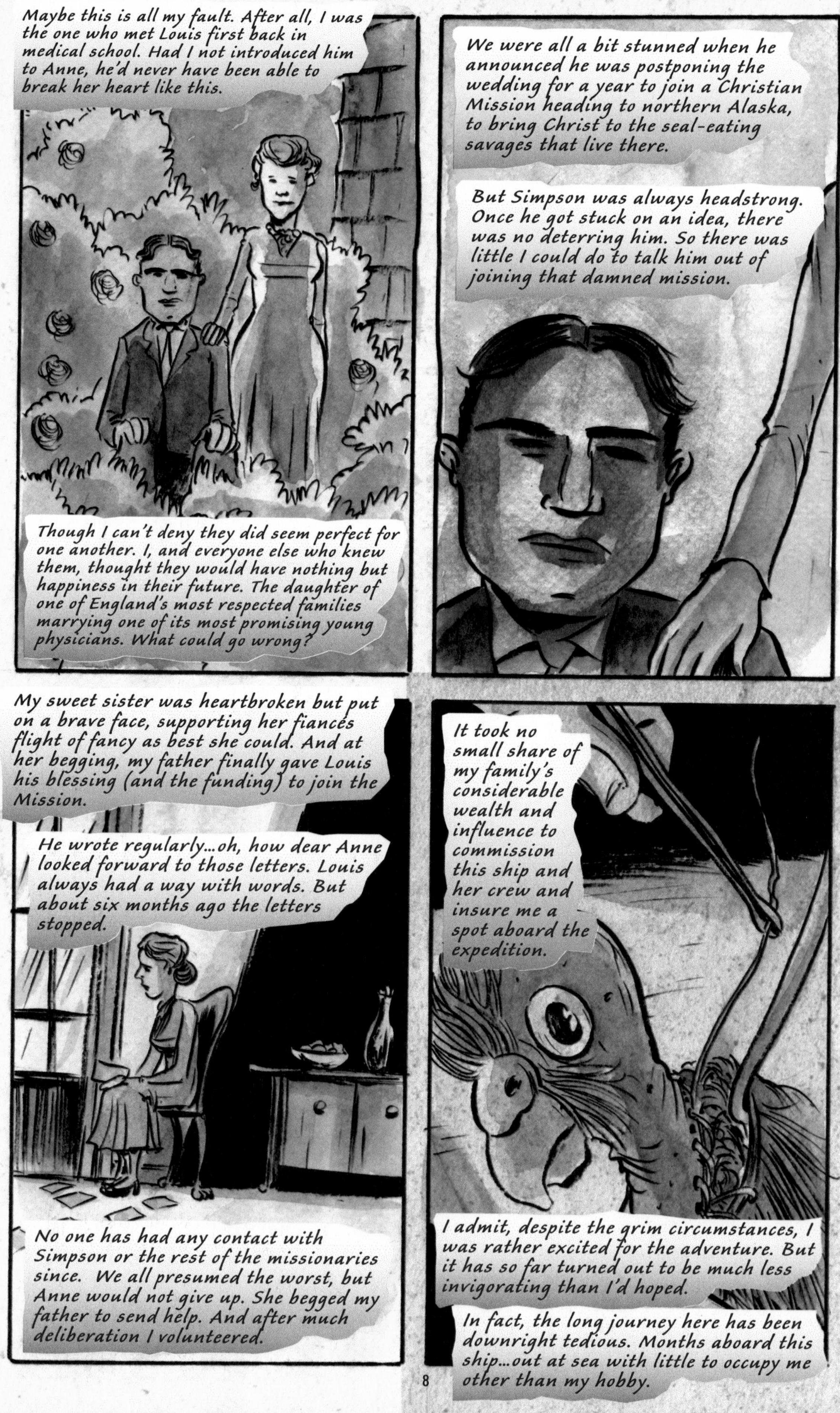
Maybe this is all my fault. After all, I was the one who met Louis first back in medical school. Had I not introduced him to Anne, he'd never have been able to break her heart like this.
Though I can't deny they did seem perfect for one another. I, and everyone else who knew them, thought they would have nothing but happiness in their future. The daughter of one of England's most respected families marrying one of its most promising young physicians. What could go wrong?
We were all a bit stunned when he announced he was postponing the wedding for a year to join a Christian Mission heading to northern Alaska, to bring Christ to the seal-eating savages that live there.
But Simpson was always headstrong. Once he got stuck on an idea, there was no deterring him. So there was little I could do to talk him out of joining that damned mission.
My sweet sister was heartbroken but put on a brave face, supporting her fiancés flight of fancy as best she could. And at her begging, my father finally gave Louis his blessing (and the funding) to join the Mission.
He wrote regularly...oh, how dear Anne looked forward to those letters. Louis always had a way with words. But about six months ago the letters stopped.
No one has had any contact with Simpson or the rest of the missionaries since. We all presumed the worst, but Anne would not give up. She begged my father to send help. And after much deliberation I volunteered.
It took no small share of my family's considerable wealth and influence to commission this ship and her crew and insure me a spot aboard the expedition.
I admit, despite the grim circumstances, I was rather excited for the adventure. But it has so far turned out to be much less invigorating than I'd hoped.
In fact, the long journey here has been downright tedious. Months aboard this ship...out at sea with little to occupy me other than my hobby.

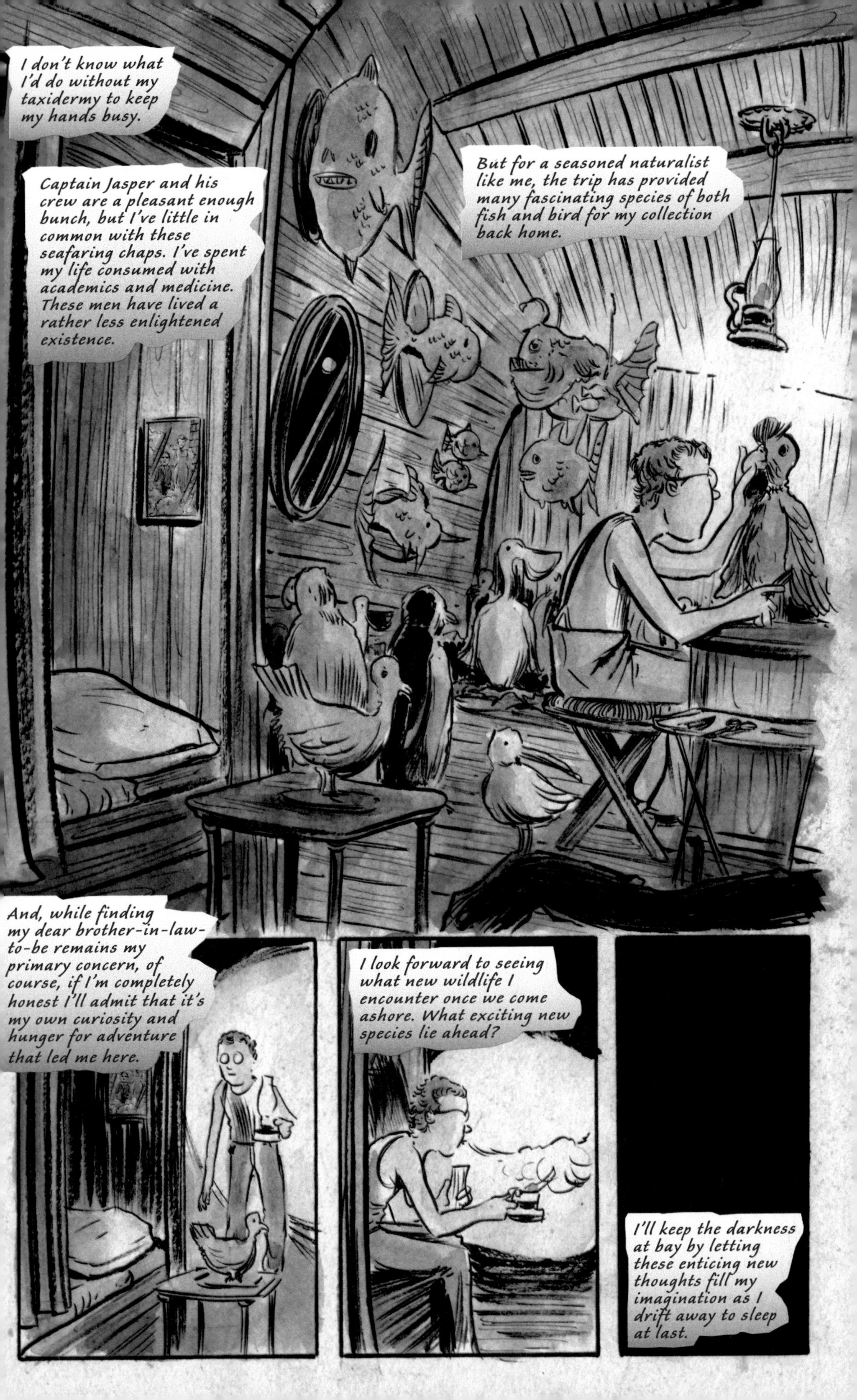
I don't know what I'd do without my taxidermy to keep my hands busy.
Captain Jasper and his crew are a pleasant enough bunch, but I've little in common with these seafaring chaps. I've spent my life consumed with academics and medicine. These men have lived a rather less enlightened existence.
But for a seasoned naturalist like me, the trip has provided many fascinating species of both fish and bird for my collection back home.
And, while finding my dear brother-in-law-to-be remains my primary concern, of course, if I'm completely honest I'll admit that it's my own curiosity and hunger for adventure that led me here.
I look forward to seeing what new wildlife I encounter once we come ashore. What exciting new species lie ahead?
I'll keep the darkness at bay by letting these enticing new thoughts fill my imagination as I drift away to sleep at last.

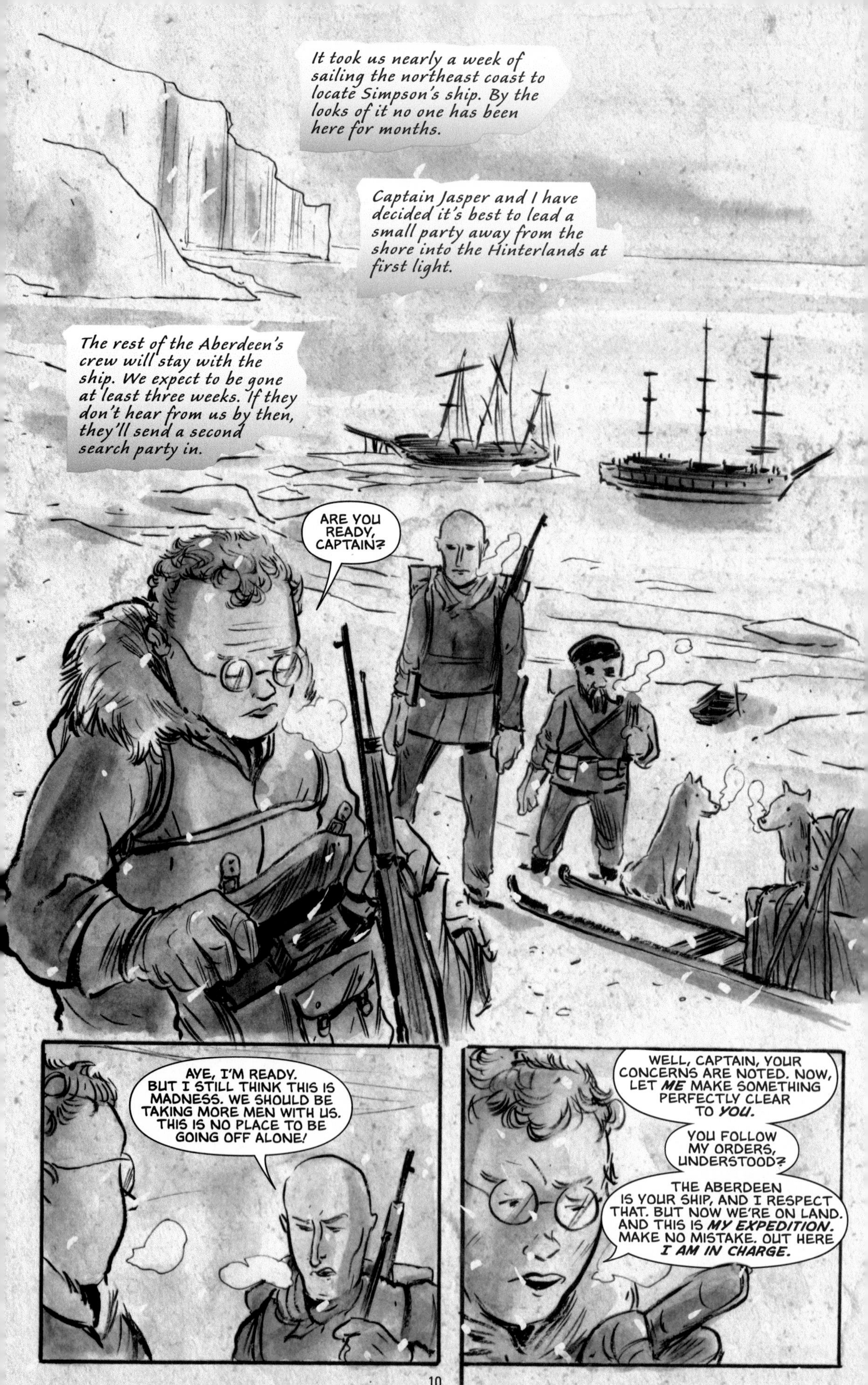
It took us nearly a week of sailing the northeast coast to locate Simpson's ship. By the looks of it no one has been here for months.
Captain Jasper and I have decided it's best to lead a small party away from the shore into the Hinterlands at first light.
The rest of the Aberdeen's crew will stay with the ship. We expect to be gone at least three weeks. If they don't hear from us by then, they'll send a second search party in.
ARE YOU READY, CAPTAIN?
AYE, I'M READY. BUT I STILL THINK THIS IS MADNESS. WE SHOULD BE TAKING MORE MEN WITH US. THIS IS NO PLACE TO BE GOING OFF ALONE!
WELL, CAPTAIN, YOUR CONCERNS ARE NOTED. NOW, LET ME MAKE SOMETHING PERFECTLY CLEAR TO YOU.
YOU FOLLOW MY ORDERS, UNDERSTOOD?
THE ABERDEEN IS YOUR SHIP, AND I RESPECT THAT. BUT NOW WE'RE ON LAND. AND THIS IS MY EXPEDITION. MAKE NO MISTAKE. OUT HERE I AM IN CHARGE.

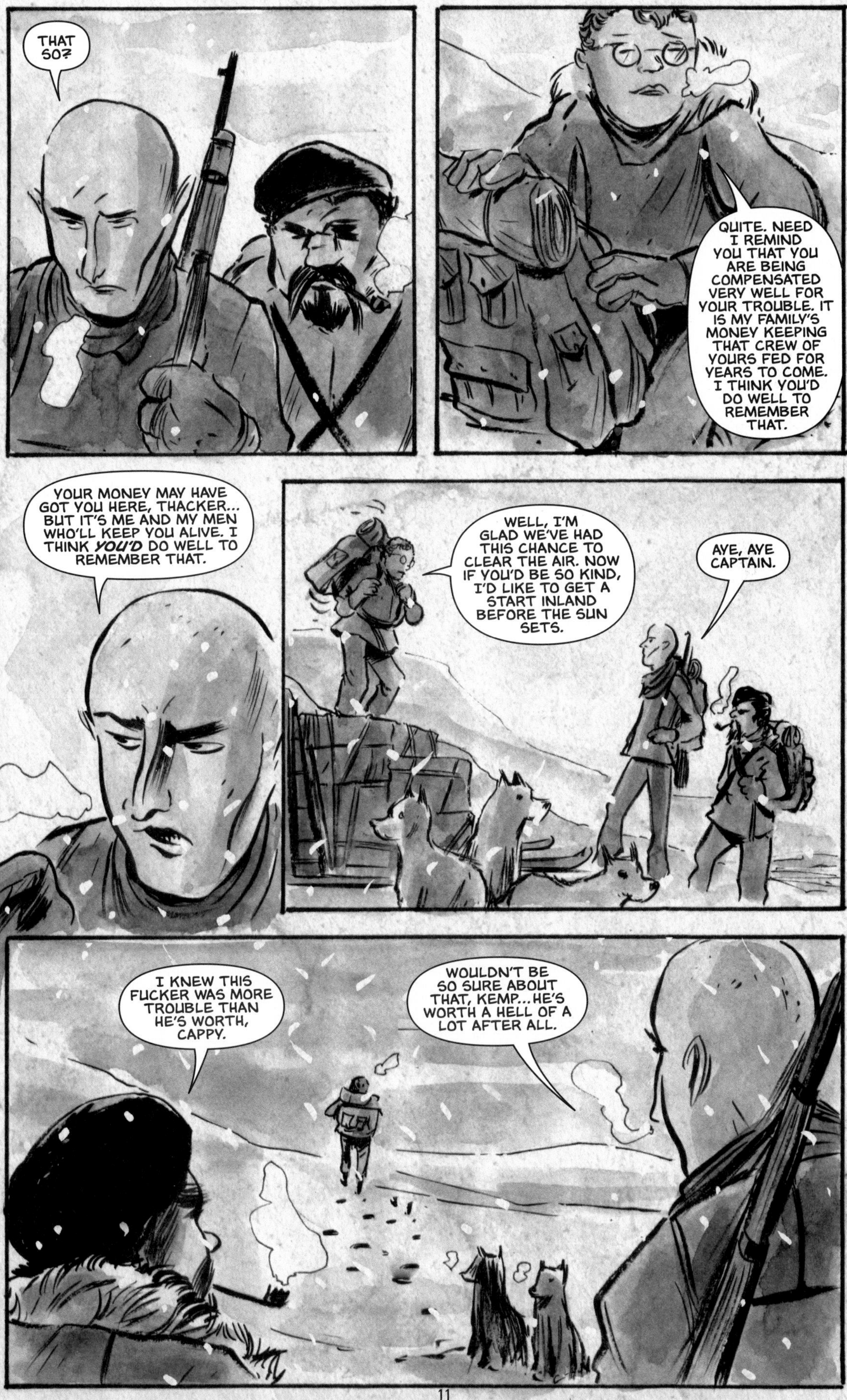
THAT SO?
QUITE. NEED I REMIND YOU THAT YOU ARE BEING COMPENSATED VERY WELL FOR YOUR TROUBLE. IT IS MY FAMILY'S MONEY KEEPING THAT CREW OF YOURS FED FOR YEARS TO COME. I THINK YOU'D DO WELL TO REMEMBER THAT.
YOUR MONEY MAY HAVE GOT YOU HERE, THACKER... BUT IT'S ME AND MY MEN WHO'LL KEEP YOU ALIVE. I THINK *YOU'D* DO WELL TO REMEMBER THAT.
WELL, I'M GLAD WE'VE HAD THIS CHANCE TO CLEAR THE AIR. NOW IF YOU'D BE SO KIND, I'D LIKE TO GET A START INLAND BEFORE THE SUN SETS.
AYE, AYE CAPTAIN.
I KNEW THIS FUCKER WAS MORE TROUBLE THAN HE'S WORTH, CAPPY.
WOULDN'T BE SO SURE ABOUT THAT, KEMP... HE'S WORTH A HELL OF A LOT AFTER ALL.

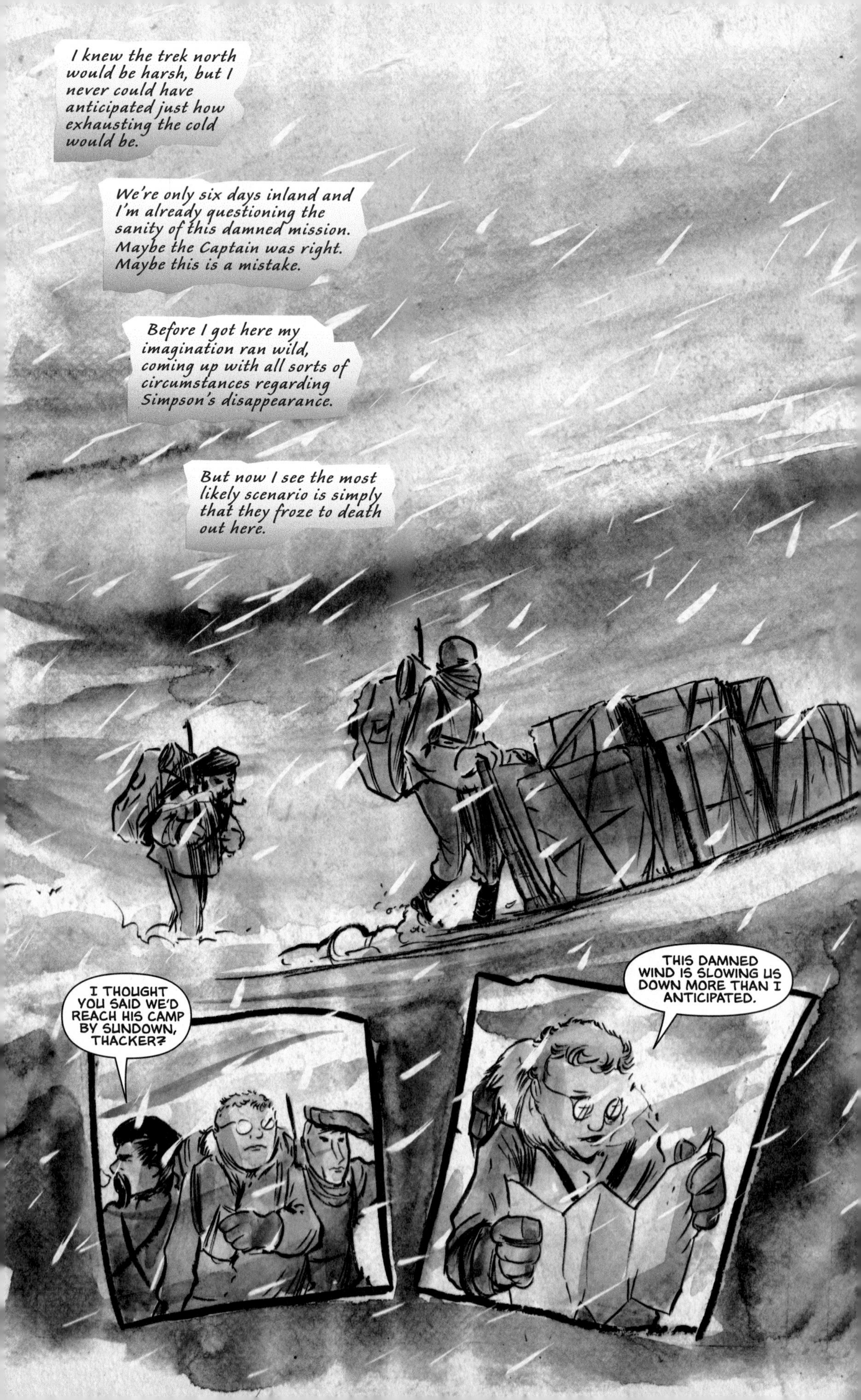
I knew the trek north would be harsh, but I never could have anticipated just how exhausting the cold would be.
We're only six days inland and I'm already questioning the sanity of this damned mission. Maybe the Captain was right. Maybe this is a mistake.
Before I got here my imagination ran wild, coming up with all sorts of circumstances regarding Simpson's disappearance.
But now I see the most likely scenario is simply that they froze to death out here.
I THOUGHT YOU SAID WE'D REACH HIS CAMP BY SUNDOWN, THACKER?
THIS DAMNED WIND IS SLOWING US DOWN MORE THAN I ANTICIPATED.

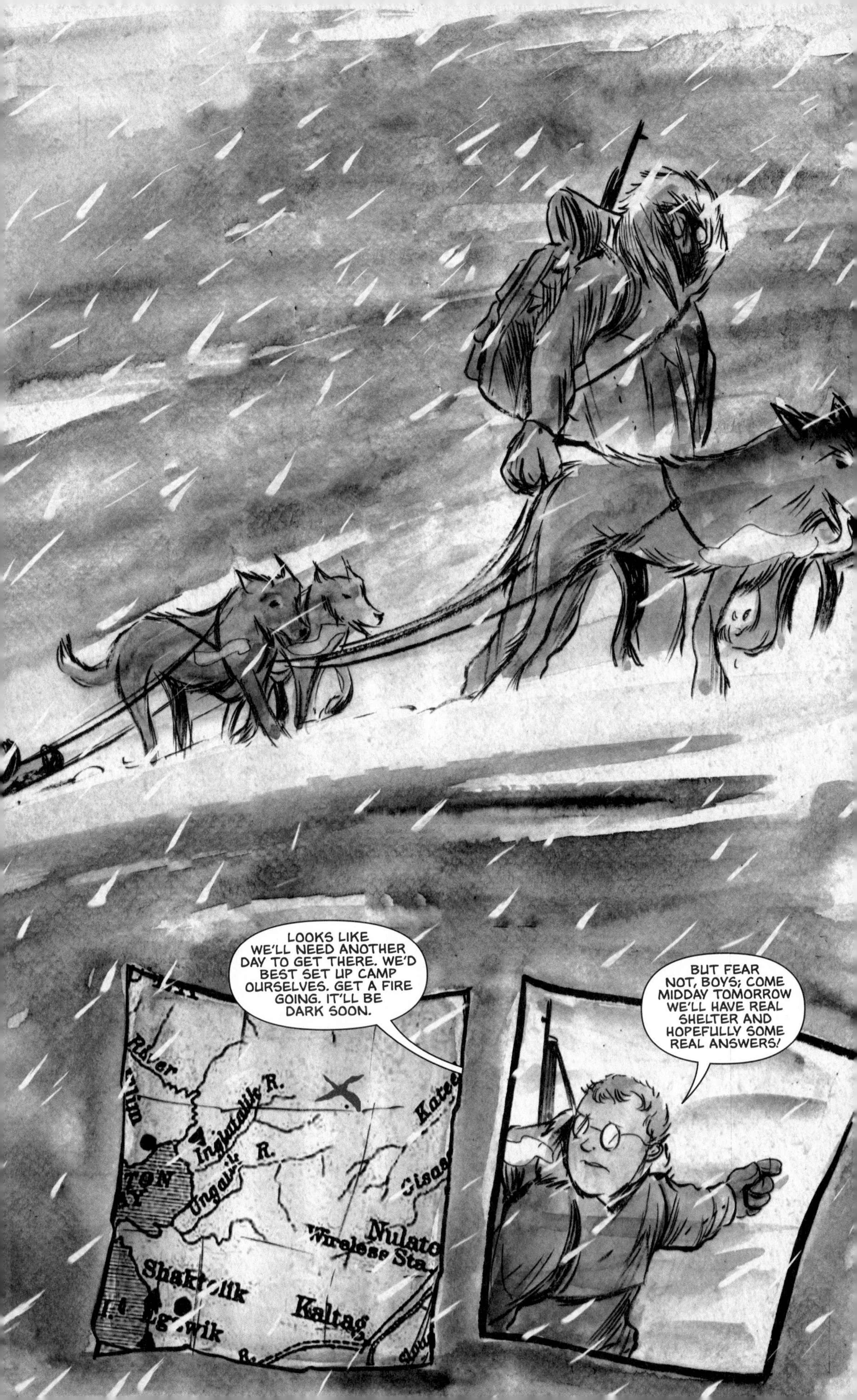
LOOKS LIKE WE'LL NEED ANOTHER DAY TO GET THERE. WE'D BEST SET UP CAMP OURSELVES. GET A FIRE GOING. IT'LL BE DARK SOON.
River
Inglutalik R.
R.
Nulato
Wireless Sta.
Kaltag
BUT FEAR NOT, BOYS; COME MIDDAY TOMORROW WE'LL HAVE REAL SHELTER AND HOPEFULLY SOME REAL ANSWERS!

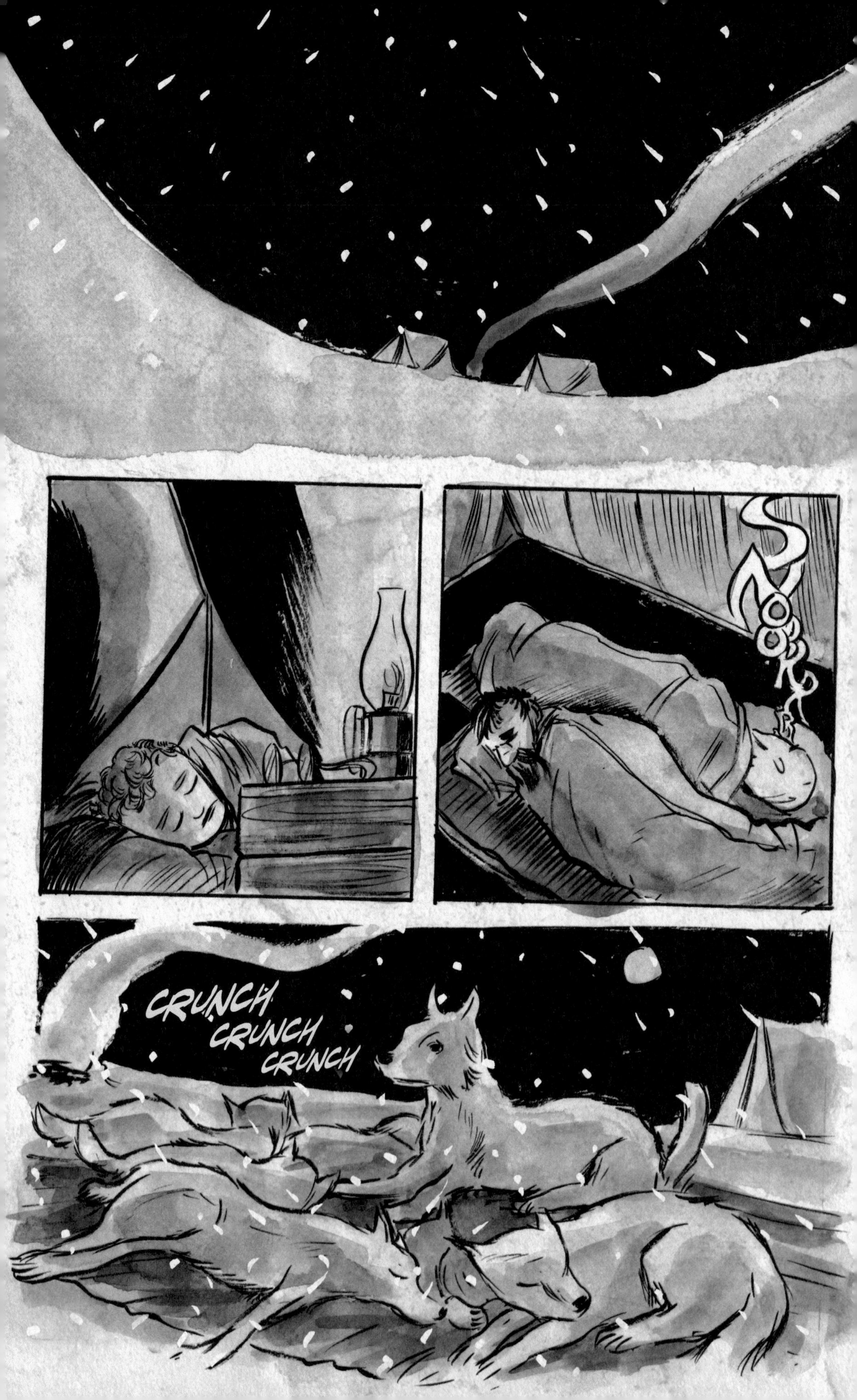
SNOOR
CRUNCH
CRUNCH
CRUNCH

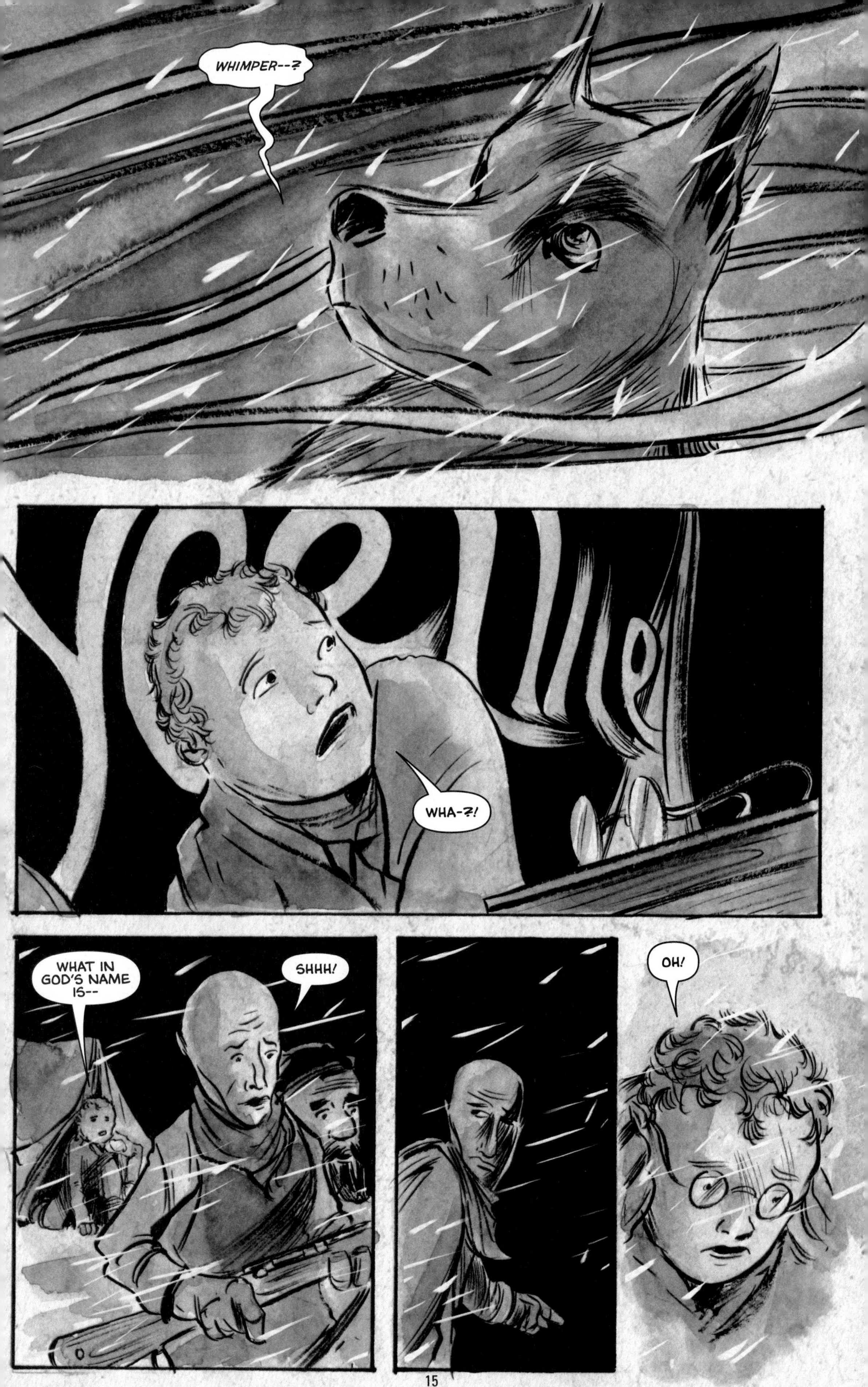
WHIMPER--?
WHA-?!
WHAT IN GOD'S NAME IS--
SHHH!
OH!

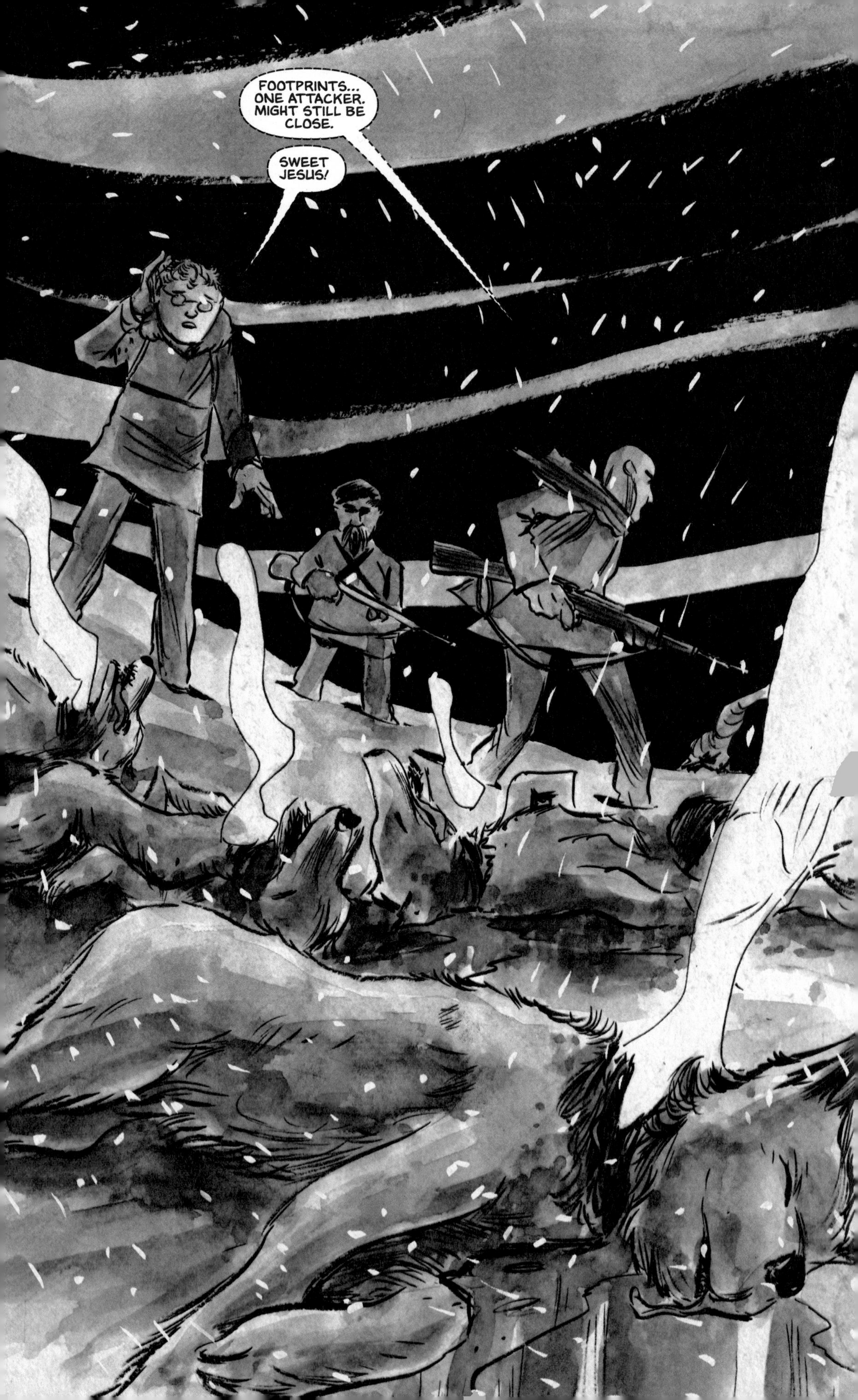
FOOTPRINTS... ONE ATTACKER. MIGHT STILL BE CLOSE.
SWEET JESUS!

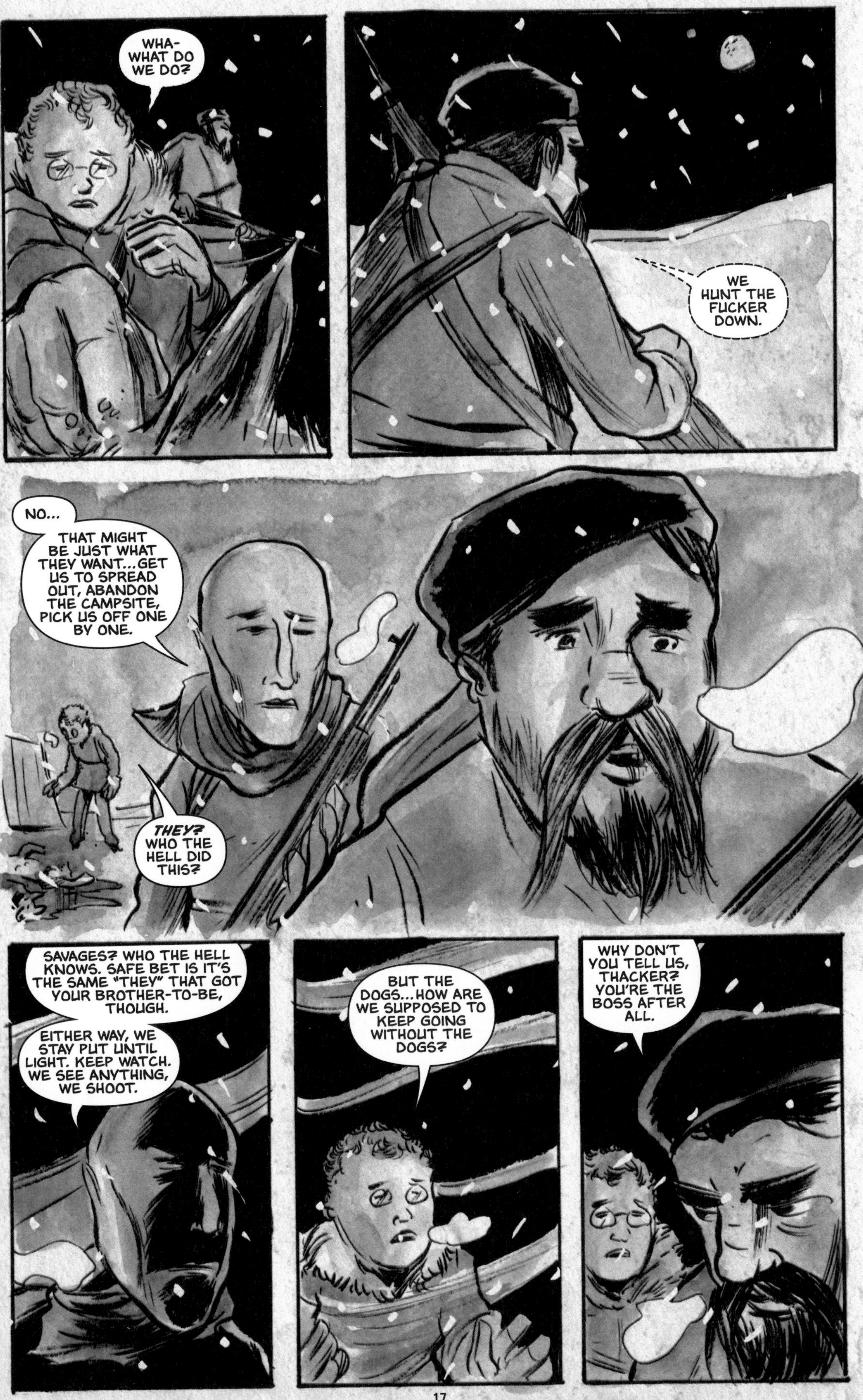
WHA-WHAT DO WE DO?
WE HUNT THE FUCKER DOWN.
NO...
THAT MIGHT BE JUST WHAT THEY WANT...GET US TO SPREAD OUT, ABANDON THE CAMPSITE, PICK US OFF ONE BY ONE.
THEY? WHO THE HELL DID THIS?
SAVAGES? WHO THE HELL KNOWS. SAFE BET IS IT'S THE SAME "THEY" THAT GOT YOUR BROTHER-TO-BE, THOUGH.
EITHER WAY, WE STAY PUT UNTIL LIGHT. KEEP WATCH. WE SEE ANYTHING, WE SHOOT.
BUT THE DOGS...HOW ARE WE SUPPOSED TO KEEP GOING WITHOUT THE DOGS?
WHY DON'T YOU TELL US, THACKER? YOU'RE THE BOSS AFTER ALL.

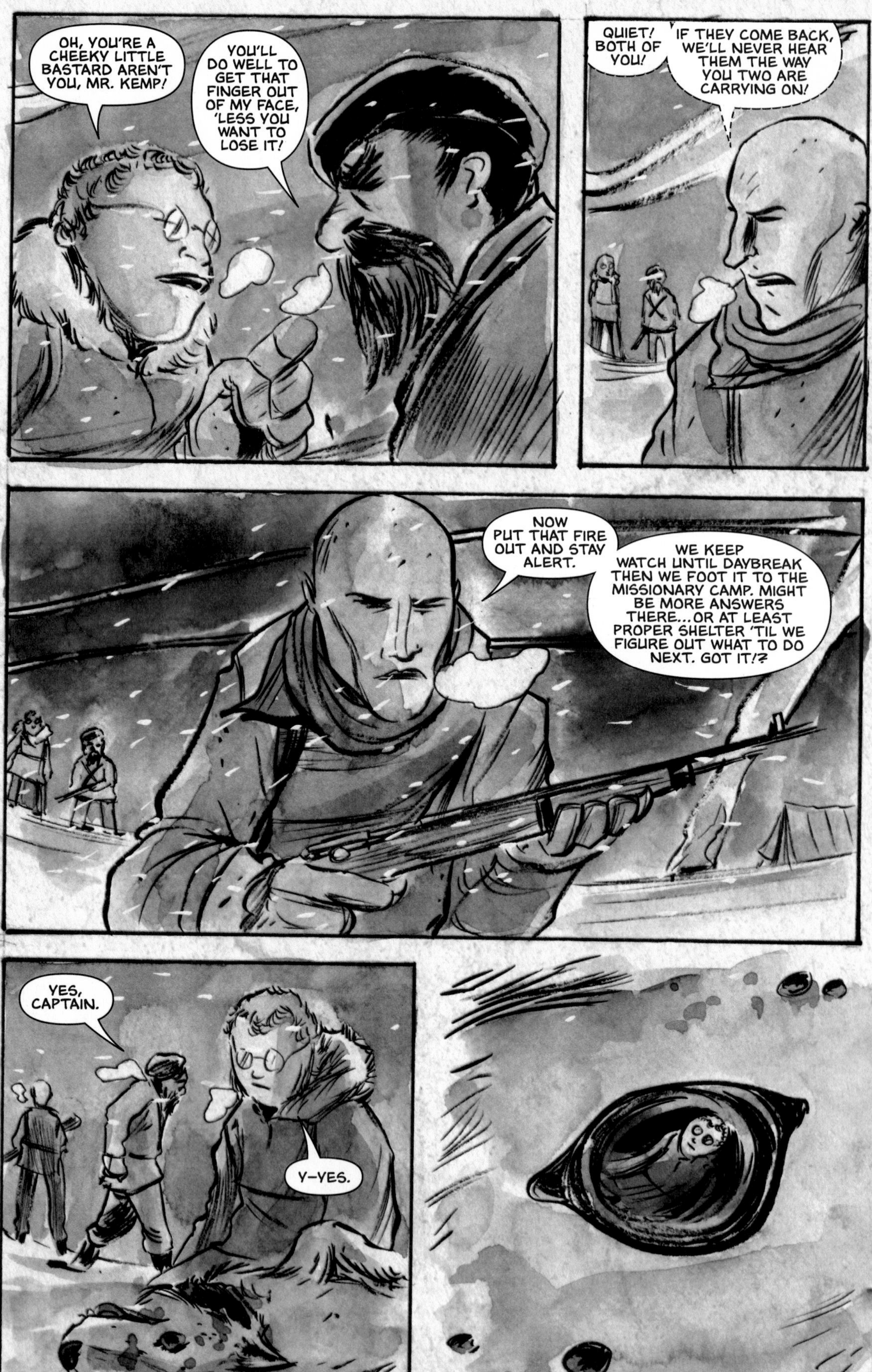

OH, YOU'RE A CHEEKY LITTLE BASTARD AREN'T YOU, MR. KEMP!
YOU'LL DO WELL TO GET THAT FINGER OUT OF MY FACE, 'LESS YOU WANT TO LOSE IT!
QUIET! BOTH OF YOU!
IF THEY COME BACK, WE'LL NEVER HEAR THEM THE WAY YOU TWO ARE CARRYING ON!
NOW PUT THAT FIRE OUT AND STAY ALERT.
WE KEEP WATCH UNTIL DAYBREAK THEN WE FOOT IT TO THE MISSIONARY CAMP. MIGHT BE MORE ANSWERS THERE...OR AT LEAST PROPER SHELTER 'TIL WE FIGURE OUT WHAT TO DO NEXT. GOT IT!?
YES, CAPTAIN.
Y-YES.

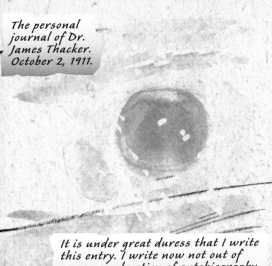

The personal journal of Dr. James Thacker. October 2, 1911.

It is under great duress that I write this entry. I write now not out of some grand notion of autobiography, but rather as a record in case we never make it back to England...or even to the Aberdeen alive.

Someone came to us in the night and slaughtered our helpless dogs.

We took watch through the night, but saw no sign of their return.

I admit I've been rather critical of Captain Jasper since this journey began, but now I find myself grateful to have him with me. He is a hard man...and if we do make it back to The Aberdeen I've no doubt it will be because he kept us alive out here.

It seems clear now that whoever is attacking us also may have gotten to poor Louis and his missionaries. But why? By all accounts the savages of these northern regions are an ignorant people, but not inherently malicious.

And why attack our dogs, but leave us unharmed? It's as if they wanted to stop our progress north. To force us to turn back, but not kill us.

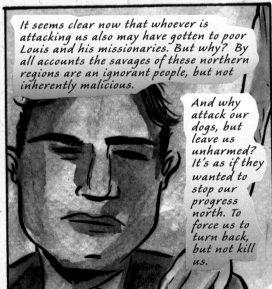

Well, whoever attacked us will soon learn that the Thackers are not easily scared off.

If anything, they've only reinforced my ambitions to uncover the truth!

October 6. We found the Missionary Camp today. And now I wish we'd never come here.

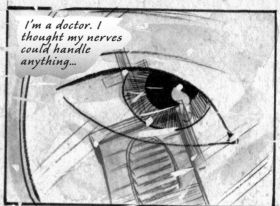

I'm a doctor. I thought my nerves could handle anything...

...I was wrong.

NOBODY'S BEEN HERE FOR A LONG TIME.

WOULDN'T BE SO CERTAIN.

TRACKS... TWO SETS. PRETTY FRESH.

KEMP, STAND GUARD.

THACKER, YOU'RE WITH ME.

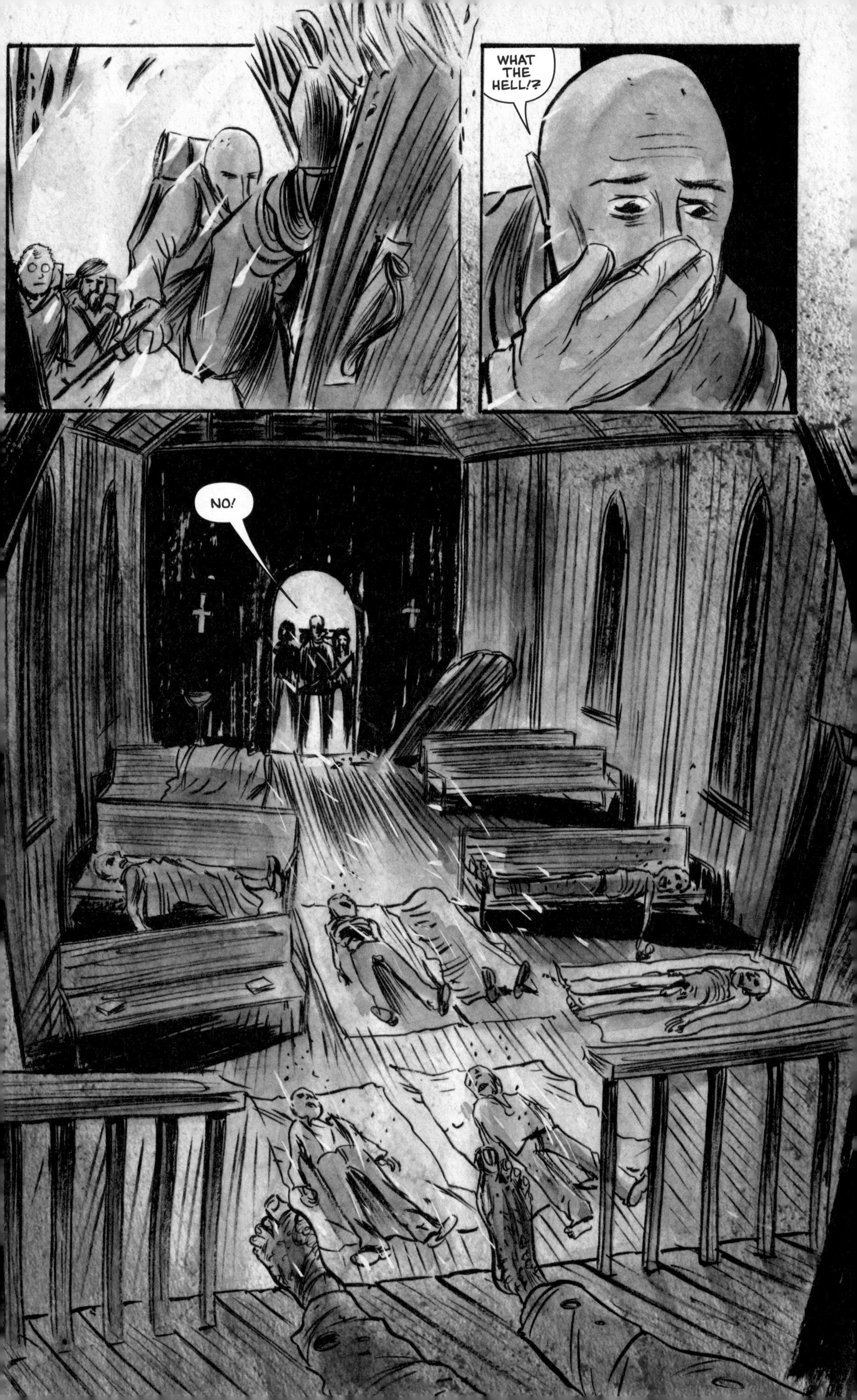
WHAT THE HELL!?
NO!

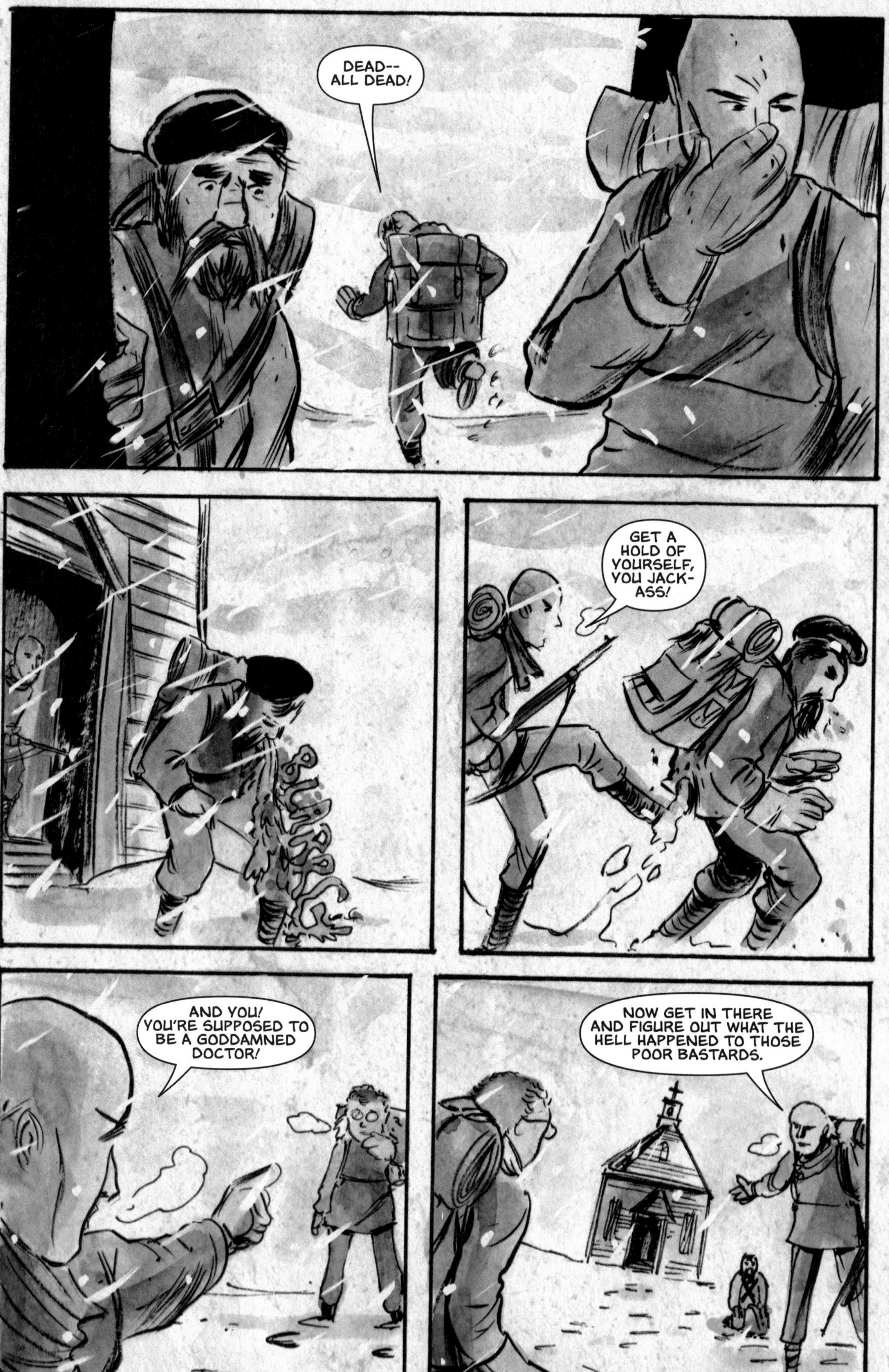
DEAD-- ALL DEAD!
GET A HOLD OF YOURSELF, YOU JACK-ASS!
AND YOU! YOU'RE SUPPOSED TO BE A GODDAMNED DOCTOR!
NOW GET IN THERE AND FIGURE OUT WHAT THE HELL HAPPENED TO THOSE POOR BASTARDS.

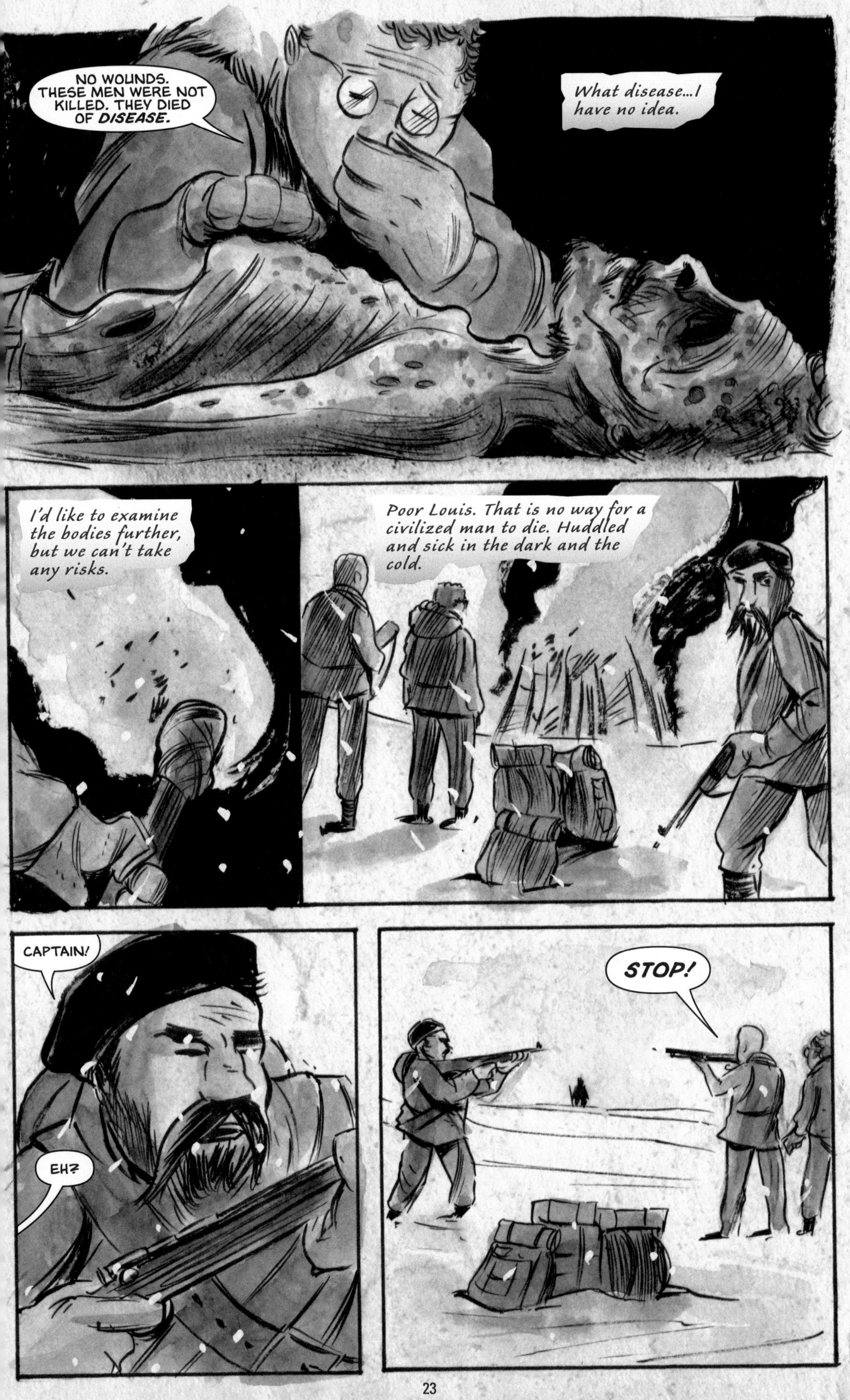
NO WOUNDS. THESE MEN WERE NOT KILLED. THEY DIED OF *DISEASE.*
What disease...I have no idea.
I'd like to examine the bodies further, but we can't take any risks.
Poor Louis. That is no way for a civilized man to die. Huddled and sick in the dark and the cold.
CAPTAIN!
EH?
STOP!

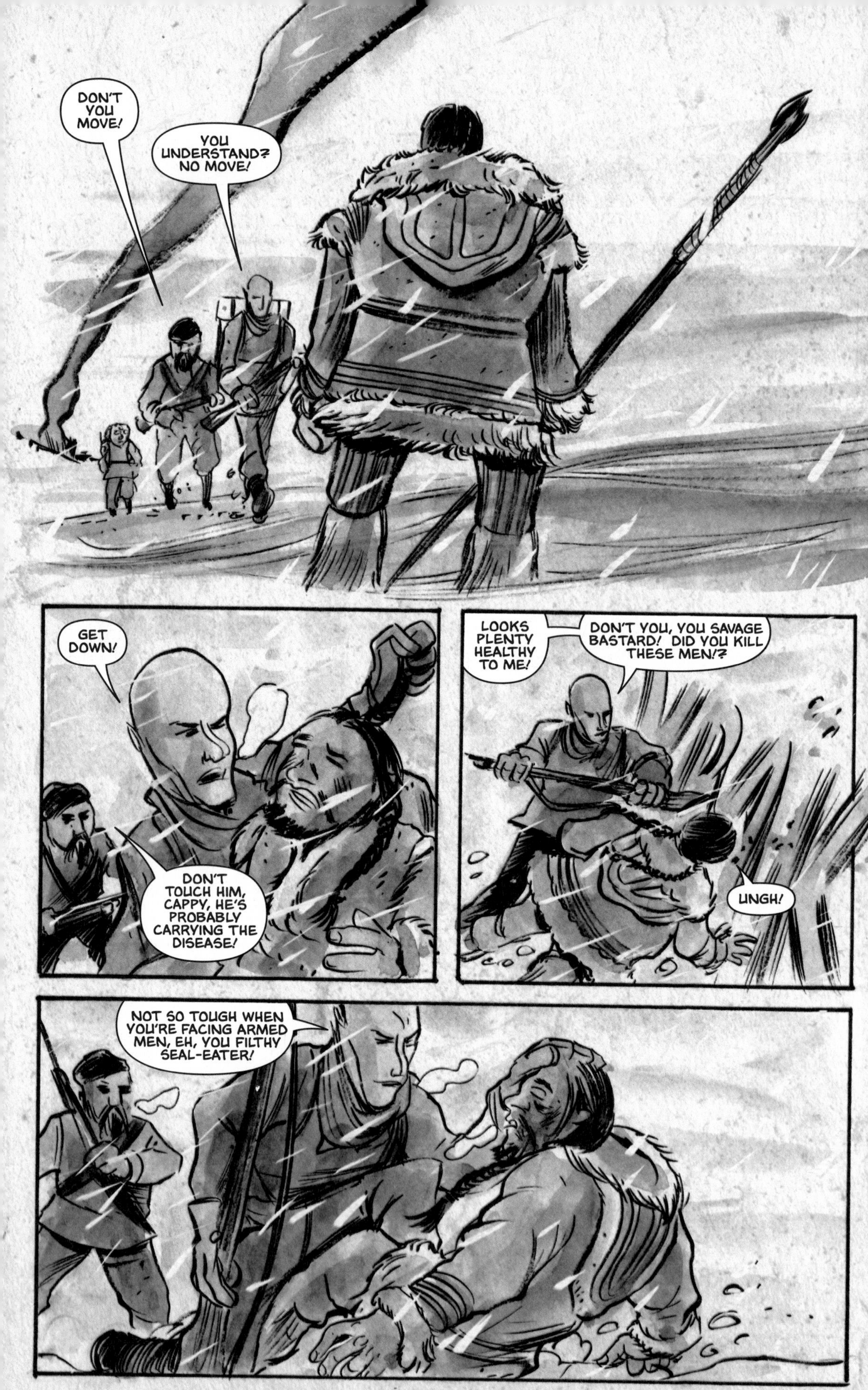
DON'T YOU MOVE!
YOU UNDERSTAND? NO MOVE!
GET DOWN!
DON'T TOUCH HIM, CAPPY, HE'S PROBABLY CARRYING THE DISEASE!
LOOKS PLENTY HEALTHY TO ME!
DON'T YOU, YOU SAVAGE BASTARD! DID YOU KILL THESE MEN!?
UNGH!
NOT SO TOUGH WHEN YOU'RE FACING ARMED MEN, EH, YOU FILTHY SEAL-EATER!

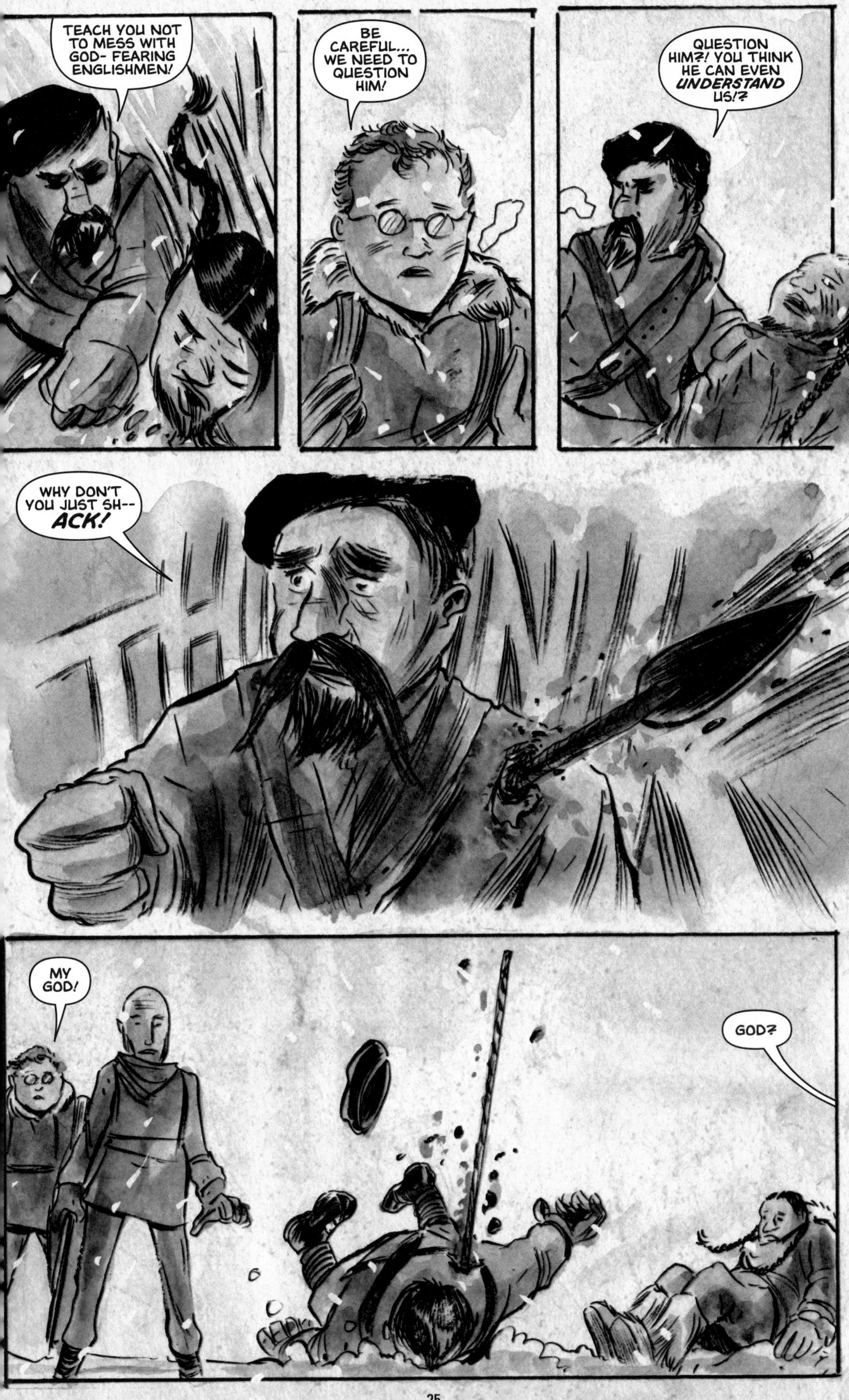
TEACH YOU NOT TO MESS WITH GOD- FEARING ENGLISHMEN!
BE CAREFUL... WE NEED TO QUESTION HIM!
QUESTION HIM?! YOU THINK HE CAN EVEN UNDERSTAND US!?
WHY DON'T YOU JUST SH-- ACK!
MY GOD!
GOD?

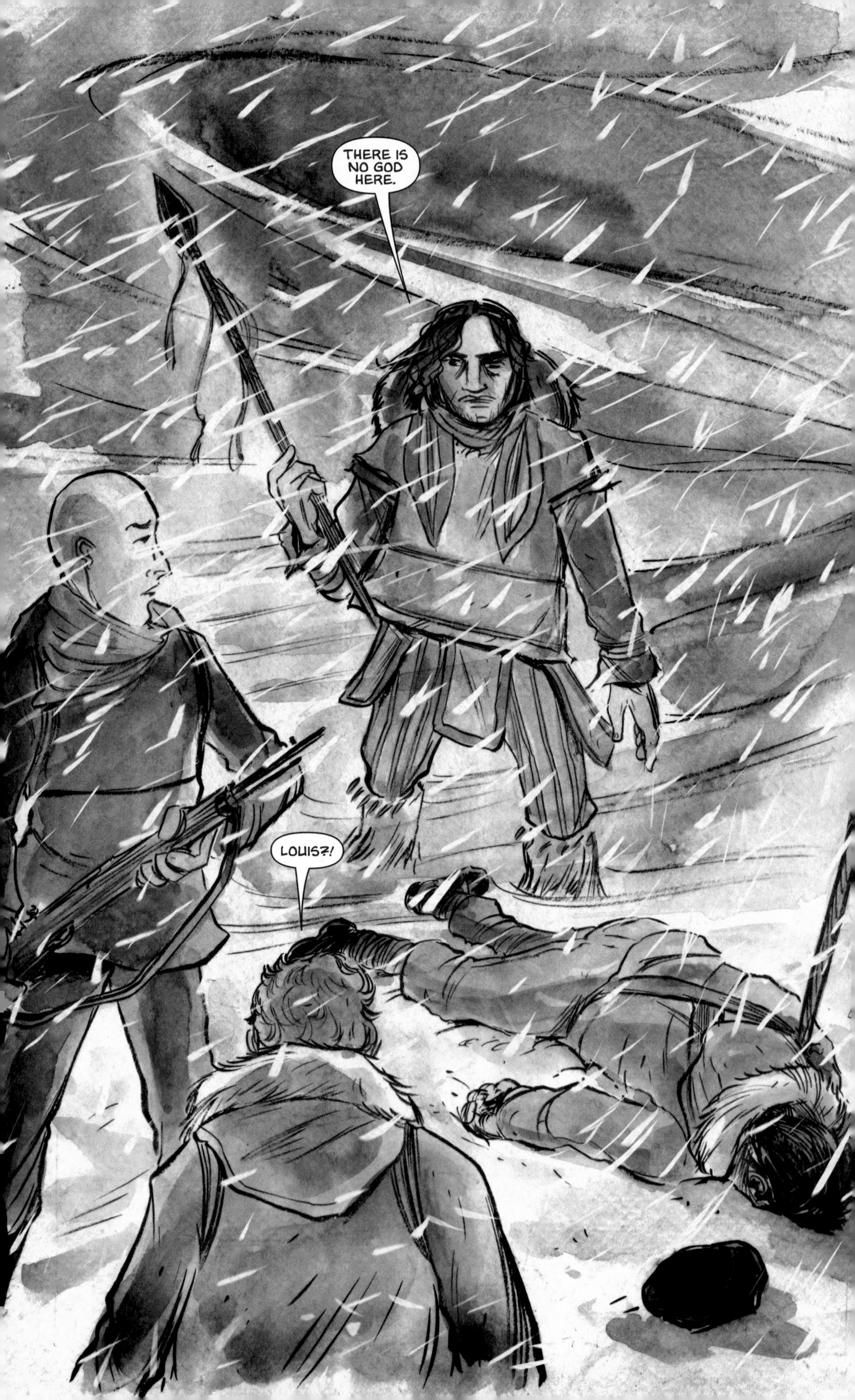
THERE IS NO GOD HERE.
LOUIS?!

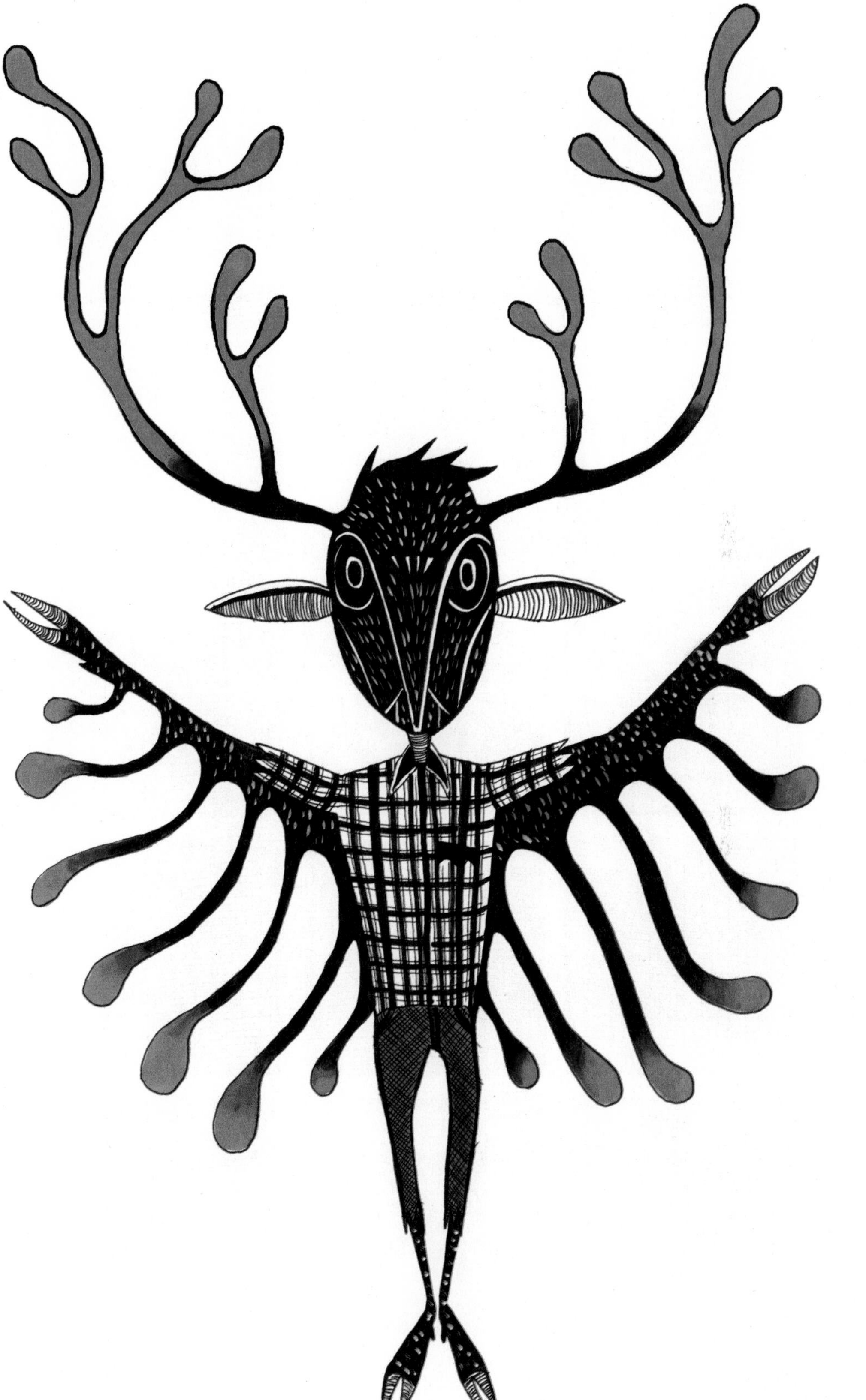

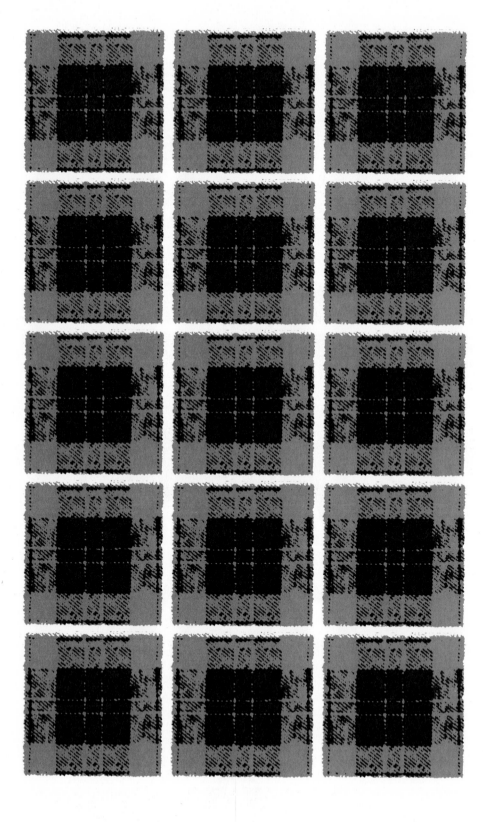

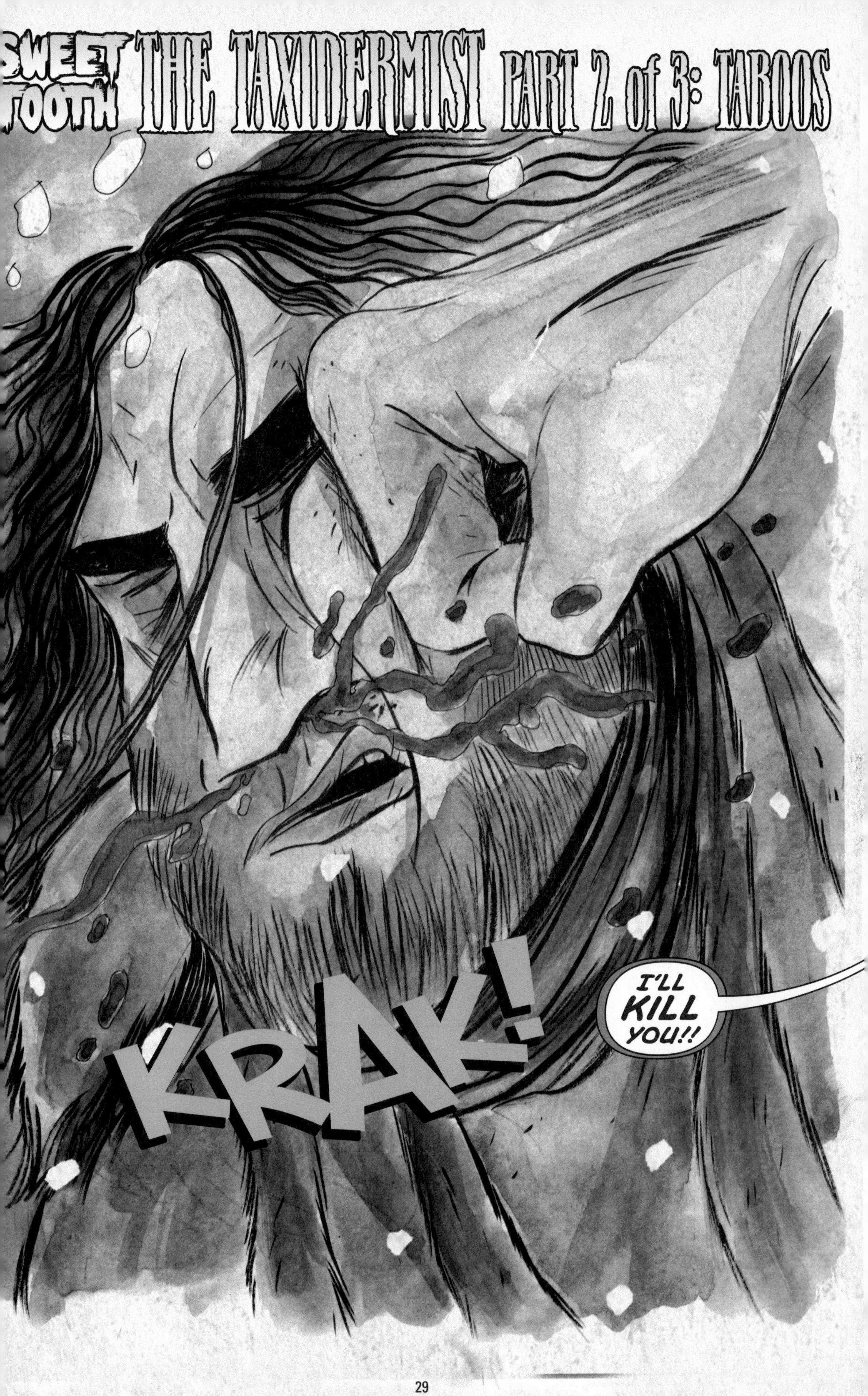
SWEET TOOTH THE TAXIDERMIST PART 2 of 3: TABOOS
KRAK!
I'LL KILL YOU!!

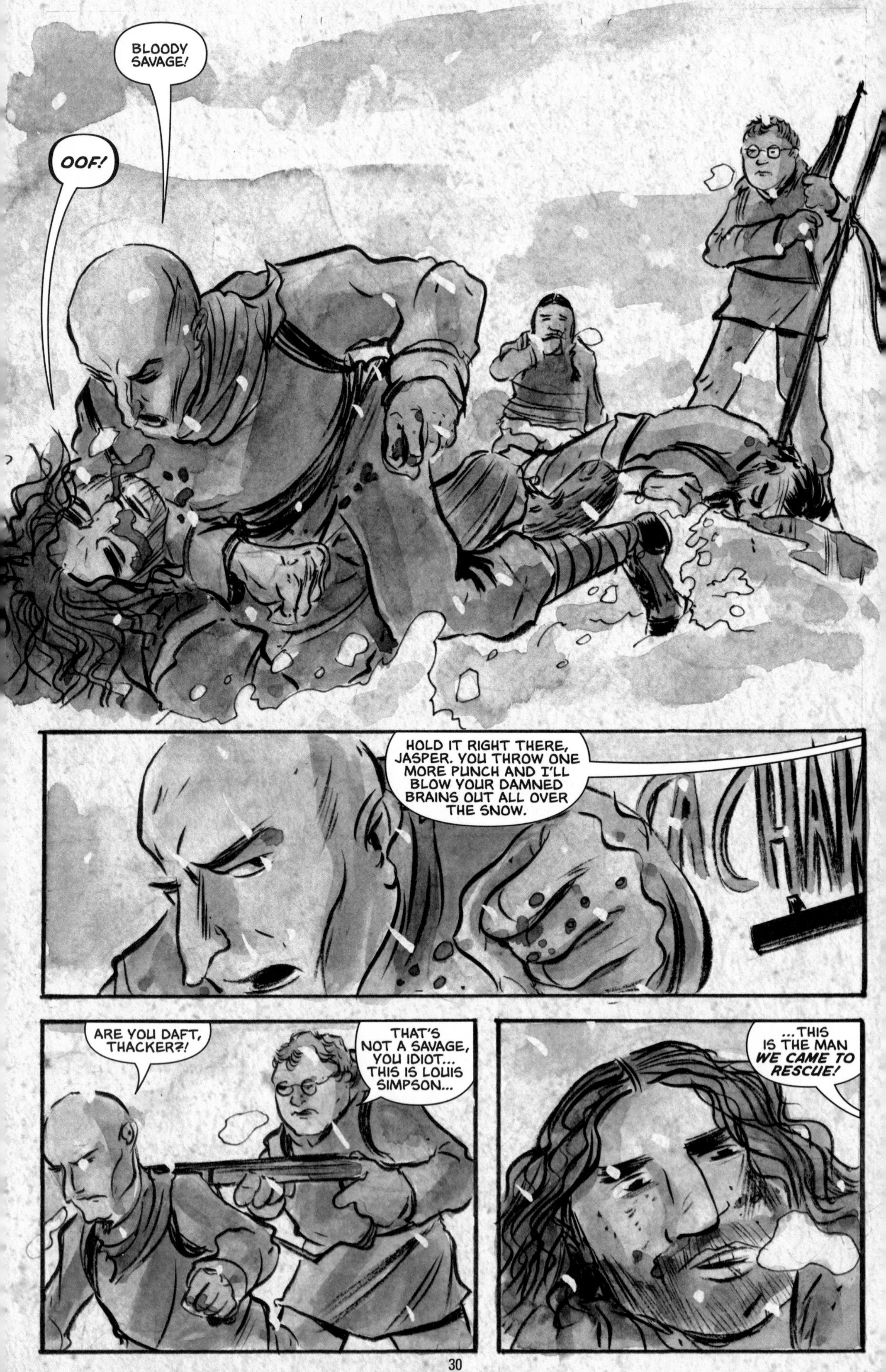
BLOODY SAVAGE!
OOF!
HOLD IT RIGHT THERE, JASPER. YOU THROW ONE MORE PUNCH AND I'LL BLOW YOUR DAMNED BRAINS OUT ALL OVER THE SNOW.
CACHAK
ARE YOU DAFT, THACKER?!
THAT'S NOT A SAVAGE, YOU IDIOT... THIS IS LOUIS SIMPSON...
...THIS IS THE MAN *WE CAME TO RESCUE!*

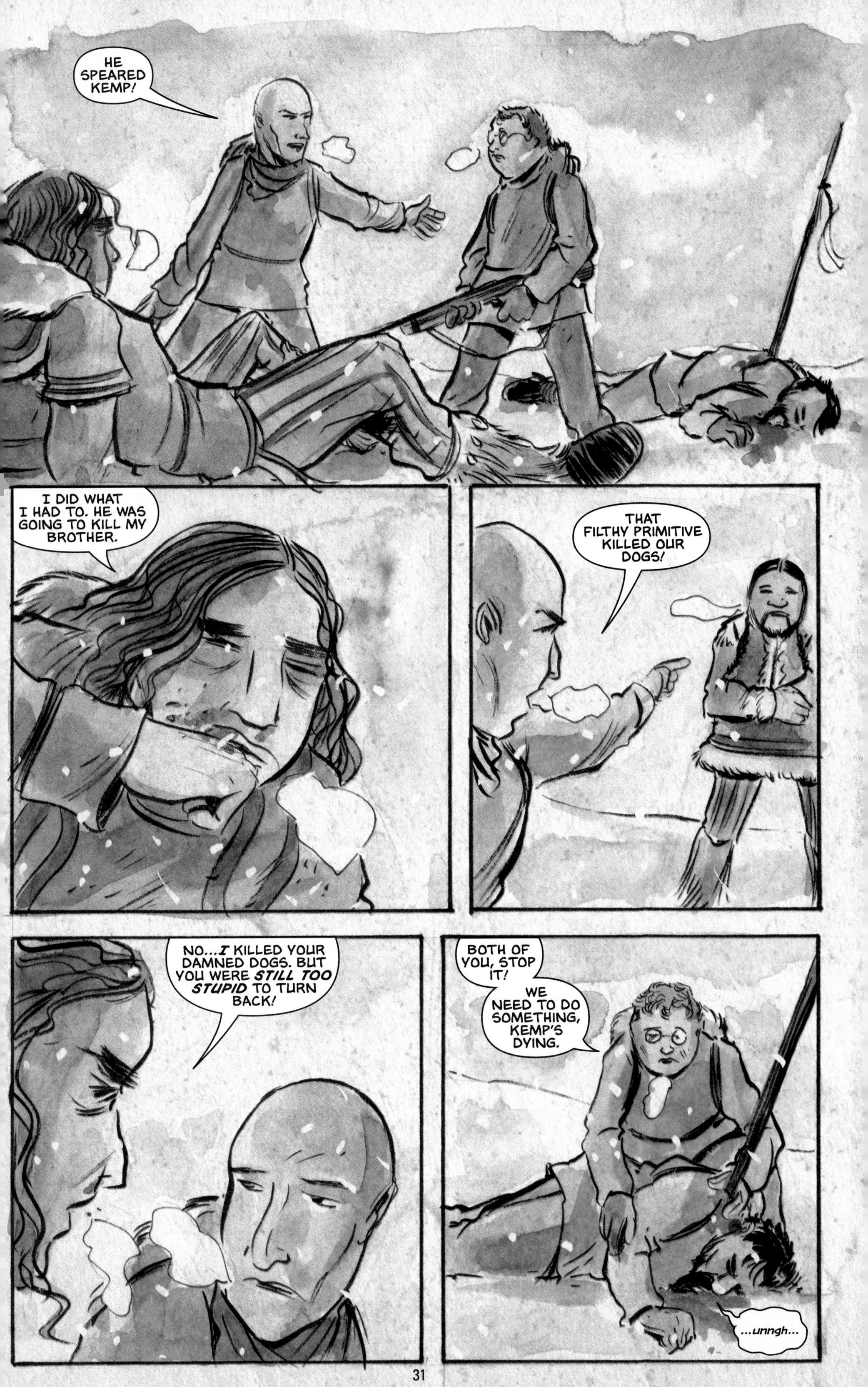
HE SPEARED KEMP!
I DID WHAT I HAD TO. HE WAS GOING TO KILL MY BROTHER.
THAT FILTHY PRIMITIVE KILLED OUR DOGS!
NO... I KILLED YOUR DAMNED DOGS. BUT YOU WERE STILL TOO STUPID TO TURN BACK!
BOTH OF YOU, STOP IT!
WE NEED TO DO SOMETHING, KEMP'S DYING.
...unngh...

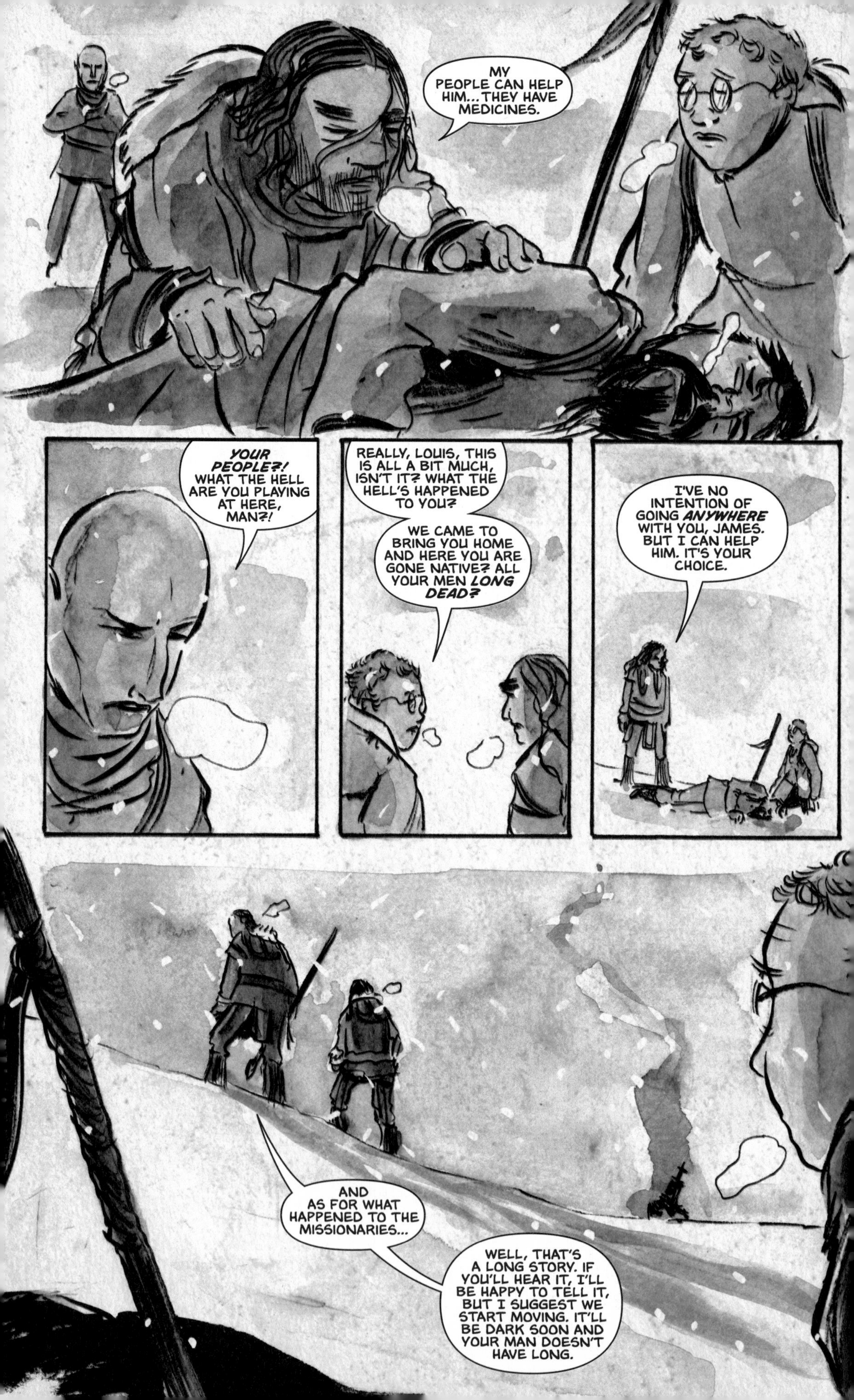
MY PEOPLE CAN HELP HIM... THEY HAVE MEDICINES.
YOUR PEOPLE?! WHAT THE HELL ARE YOU PLAYING AT HERE, MAN?!
REALLY, LOUIS, THIS IS ALL A BIT MUCH, ISN'T IT? WHAT THE HELL'S HAPPENED TO YOU?
WE CAME TO BRING YOU HOME AND HERE YOU ARE GONE NATIVE? ALL YOUR MEN LONG DEAD?
I'VE NO INTENTION OF GOING ANYWHERE WITH YOU, JAMES. BUT I CAN HELP HIM. IT'S YOUR CHOICE.
AND AS FOR WHAT HAPPENED TO THE MISSIONARIES...
WELL, THAT'S A LONG STORY. IF YOU'LL HEAR IT, I'LL BE HAPPY TO TELL IT, BUT I SUGGEST WE START MOVING. IT'LL BE DARK SOON AND YOUR MAN DOESN'T HAVE LONG.

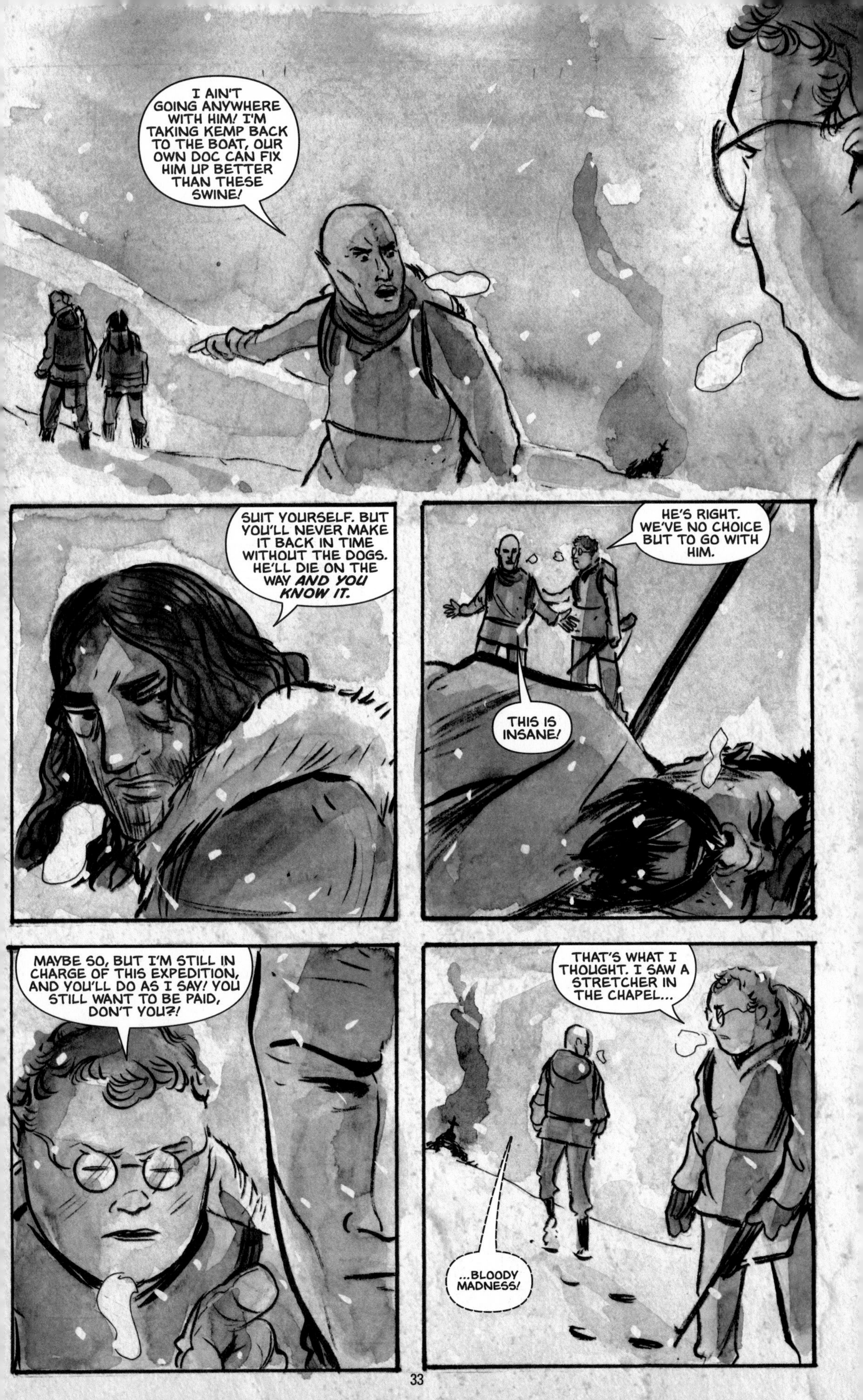
I AIN'T GOING ANYWHERE WITH HIM! I'M TAKING KEMP BACK TO THE BOAT, OUR OWN DOC CAN FIX HIM UP BETTER THAN THESE SWINE!
SUIT YOURSELF. BUT YOU'LL NEVER MAKE IT BACK IN TIME WITHOUT THE DOGS. HE'LL DIE ON THE WAY *AND YOU KNOW IT.*
HE'S RIGHT. WE'VE NO CHOICE BUT TO GO WITH HIM.
THIS IS INSANE!
MAYBE SO, BUT I'M STILL IN CHARGE OF THIS EXPEDITION, AND YOU'LL DO AS I SAY! YOU STILL WANT TO BE PAID, DON'T YOU?!
THAT'S WHAT I THOUGHT. I SAW A STRETCHER IN THE CHAPEL...
...BLOODY MADNESS!

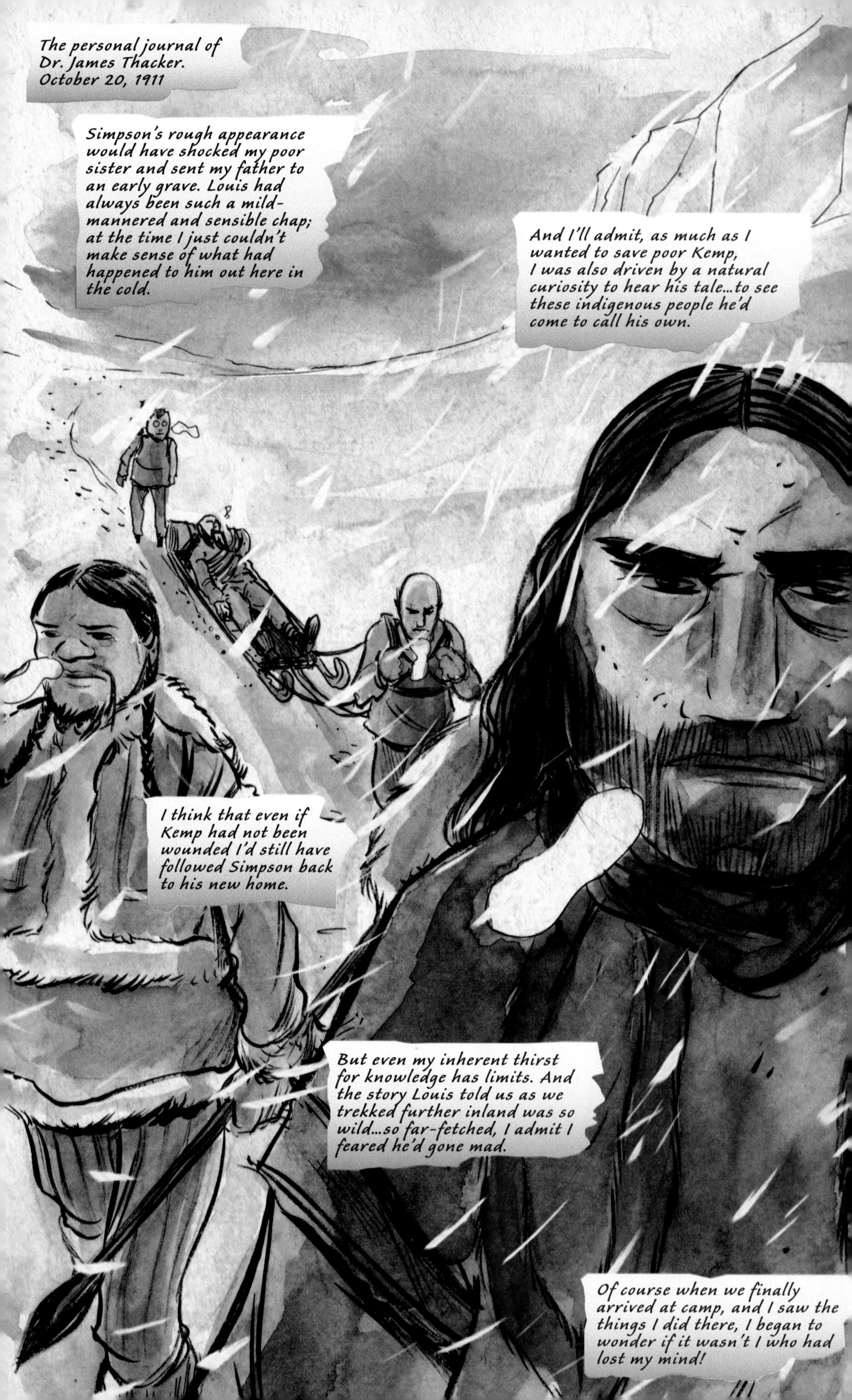
The personal journal of
Dr. James Thacker.
October 20, 1911
Simpson's rough appearance would have shocked my poor sister and sent my father to an early grave. Louis had always been such a mild-mannered and sensible chap; at the time I just couldn't make sense of what had happened to him out here in the cold.
And I'll admit, as much as I wanted to save poor Kemp, I was also driven by a natural curiosity to hear his tale...to see these indigenous people he'd come to call his own.
I think that even if Kemp had not been wounded I'd still have followed Simpson back to his new home.
But even my inherent thirst for knowledge has limits. And the story Louis told us as we trekked further inland was so wild...so far-fetched, I admit I feared he'd gone mad.
Of course when we finally arrived at camp, and I saw the things I did there, I began to wonder if it wasn't I who had lost my mind!

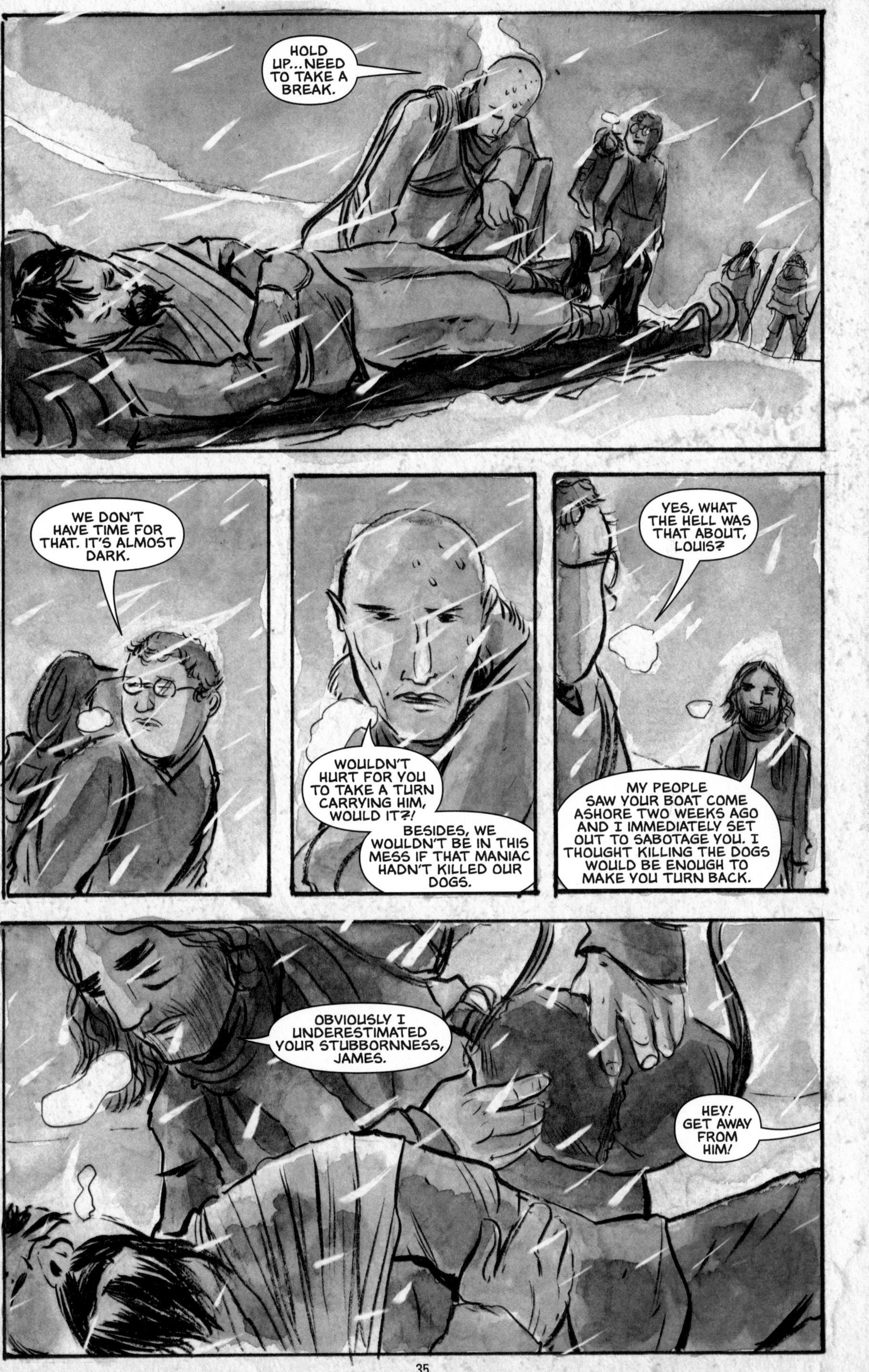
HOLD UP...NEED TO TAKE A BREAK.
WE DON'T HAVE TIME FOR THAT. IT'S ALMOST DARK.
WOULDN'T HURT FOR YOU TO TAKE A TURN CARRYING HIM, WOULD IT?!
BESIDES, WE WOULDN'T BE IN THIS MESS IF THAT MANIAC HADN'T KILLED OUR DOGS.
YES, WHAT THE HELL WAS THAT ABOUT, LOUIS?
MY PEOPLE SAW YOUR BOAT COME ASHORE TWO WEEKS AGO AND I IMMEDIATELY SET OUT TO SABOTAGE YOU. I THOUGHT KILLING THE DOGS WOULD BE ENOUGH TO MAKE YOU TURN BACK.
OBVIOUSLY I UNDERESTIMATED YOUR STUBBORNNESS, JAMES.
HEY! GET AWAY FROM HIM!

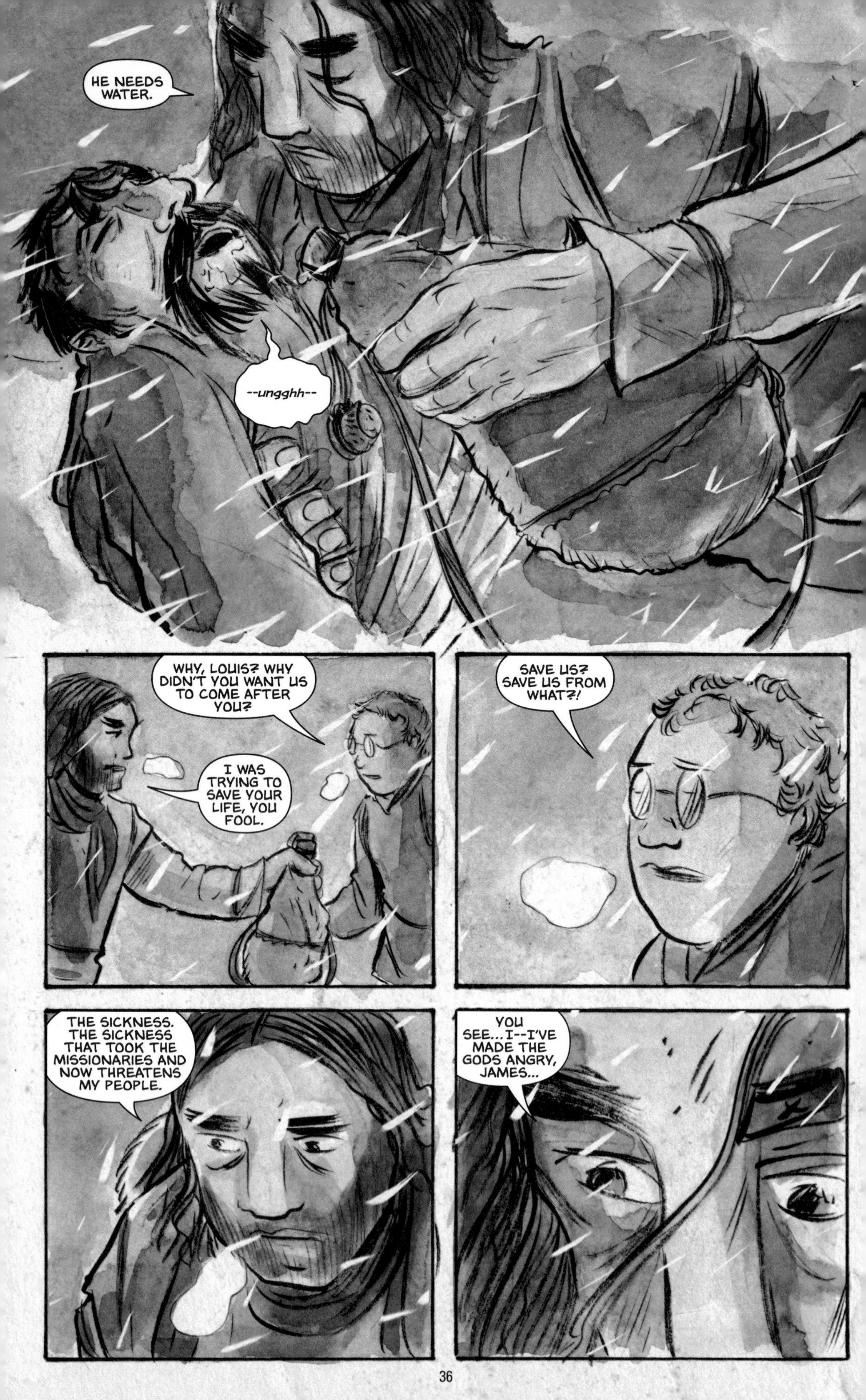
HE NEEDS WATER.
--ungghh--
WHY, LOUIS? WHY DIDN'T YOU WANT US TO COME AFTER YOU?
I WAS TRYING TO SAVE YOUR LIFE, YOU FOOL.
SAVE US? SAVE US FROM WHAT?!
THE SICKNESS. THE SICKNESS THAT TOOK THE MISSIONARIES AND NOW THREATENS MY PEOPLE.
YOU SEE... I--I'VE MADE THE GODS ANGRY, JAMES...

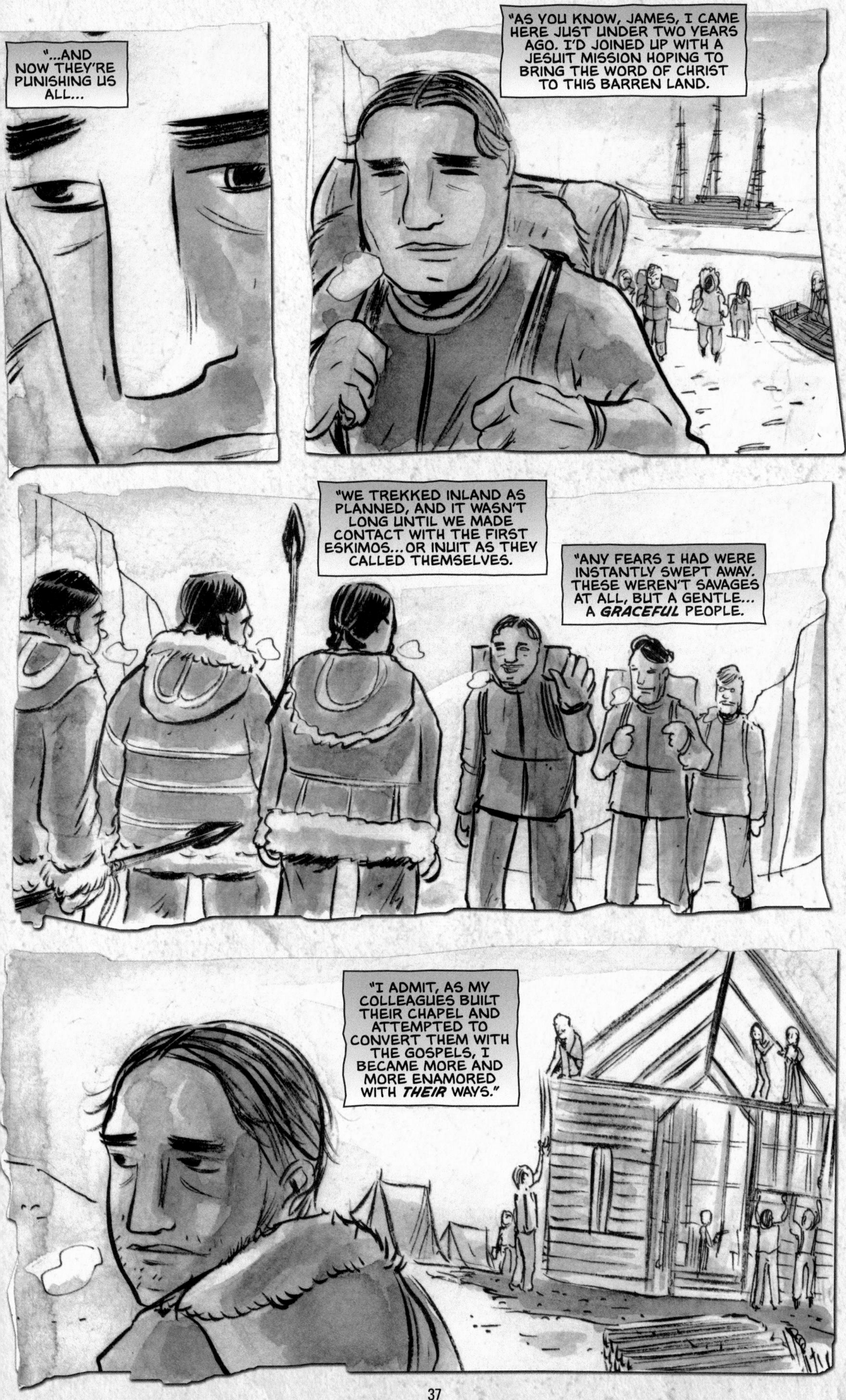
"...AND NOW THEY'RE PUNISHING US ALL...
"AS YOU KNOW, JAMES, I CAME HERE JUST UNDER TWO YEARS AGO. I'D JOINED UP WITH A JESUIT MISSION HOPING TO BRING THE WORD OF CHRIST TO THIS BARREN LAND.
"WE TREKKED INLAND AS PLANNED, AND IT WASN'T LONG UNTIL WE MADE CONTACT WITH THE FIRST ESKIMOS...OR INUIT AS THEY CALLED THEMSELVES.
"ANY FEARS I HAD WERE INSTANTLY SWEPT AWAY. THESE WEREN'T SAVAGES AT ALL, BUT A GENTLE... A *GRACEFUL* PEOPLE.
"I ADMIT, AS MY COLLEAGUES BUILT THEIR CHAPEL AND ATTEMPTED TO CONVERT THEM WITH THE GOSPELS, I BECAME MORE AND MORE ENAMORED WITH *THEIR* WAYS."

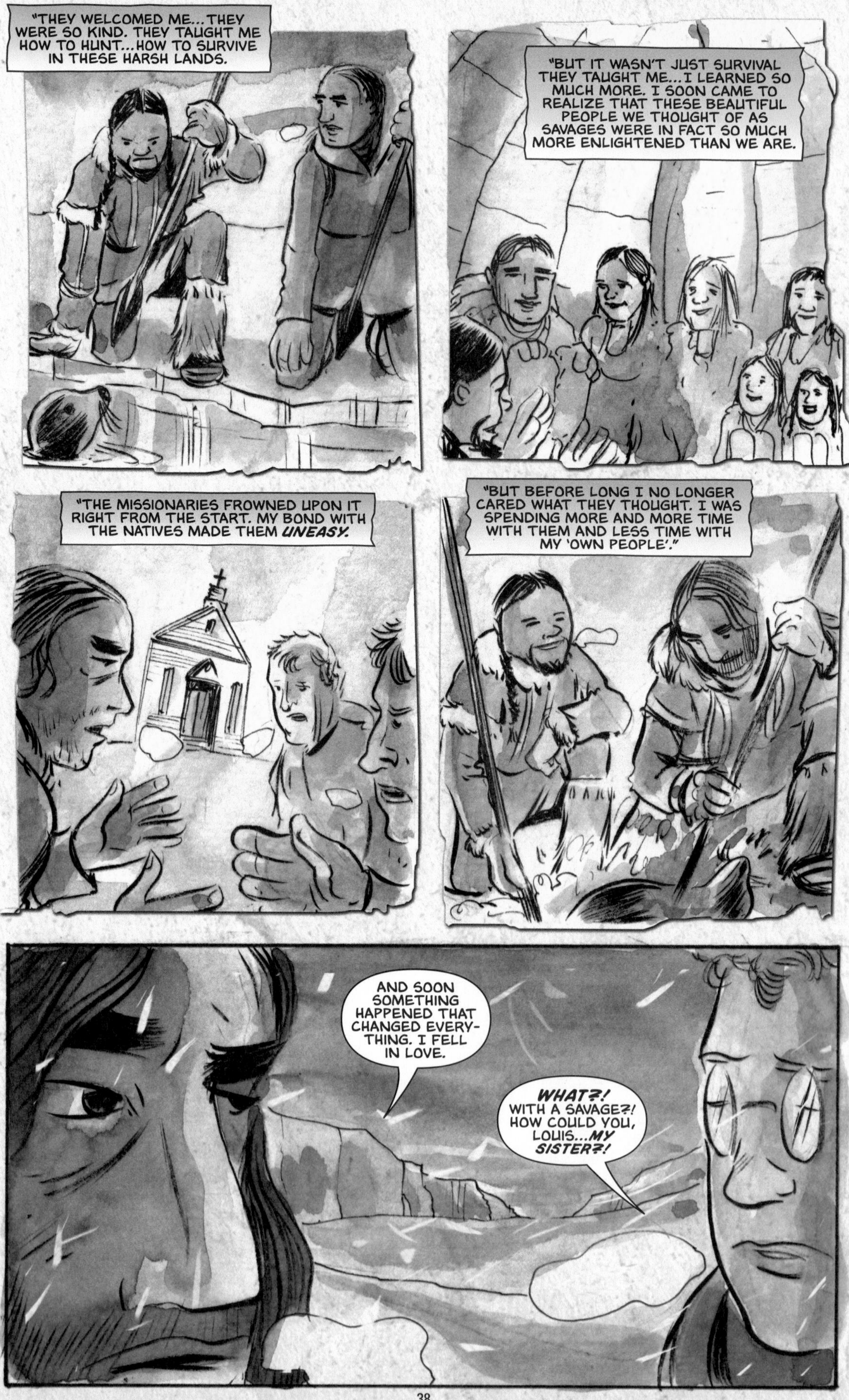
"THEY WELCOMED ME... THEY WERE SO KIND. THEY TAUGHT ME HOW TO HUNT... HOW TO SURVIVE IN THESE HARSH LANDS.
"BUT IT WASN'T JUST SURVIVAL THEY TAUGHT ME... I LEARNED SO MUCH MORE. I SOON CAME TO REALIZE THAT THESE BEAUTIFUL PEOPLE WE THOUGHT OF AS SAVAGES WERE IN FACT SO MUCH MORE ENLIGHTENED THAN WE ARE.
"THE MISSIONARIES FROWNED UPON IT RIGHT FROM THE START. MY BOND WITH THE NATIVES MADE THEM *UNEASY.*
"BUT BEFORE LONG I NO LONGER CARED WHAT THEY THOUGHT. I WAS SPENDING MORE AND MORE TIME WITH THEM AND LESS TIME WITH MY 'OWN PEOPLE'."
AND SOON SOMETHING HAPPENED THAT CHANGED EVERY-THING. I FELL IN LOVE.
WHAT?! WITH A SAVAGE?! HOW COULD YOU, LOUIS... *MY SISTER?!*

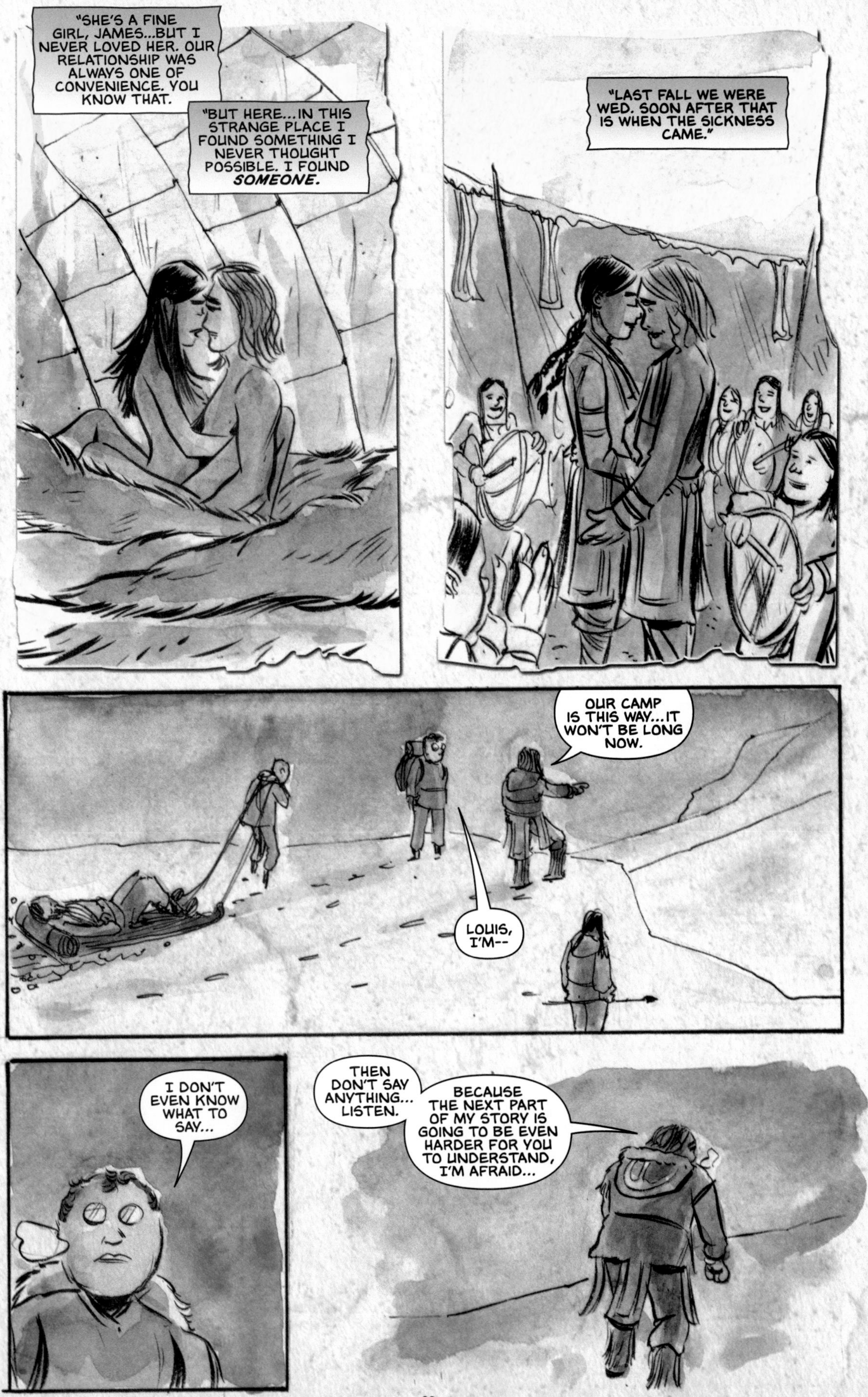
"SHE'S A FINE GIRL, JAMES...BUT I NEVER LOVED HER. OUR RELATIONSHIP WAS ALWAYS ONE OF CONVENIENCE. YOU KNOW THAT.
"BUT HERE...IN THIS STRANGE PLACE I FOUND SOMETHING I NEVER THOUGHT POSSIBLE. I FOUND *SOMEONE.*
"LAST FALL WE WERE WED. SOON AFTER THAT IS WHEN THE SICKNESS CAME."
OUR CAMP IS THIS WAY...IT WON'T BE LONG NOW.
LOUIS, I'M--
I DON'T EVEN KNOW WHAT TO SAY...
THEN DON'T SAY ANYTHING... LISTEN.
BECAUSE THE NEXT PART OF MY STORY IS GOING TO BE EVEN HARDER FOR YOU TO UNDERSTAND, I'M AFRAID...

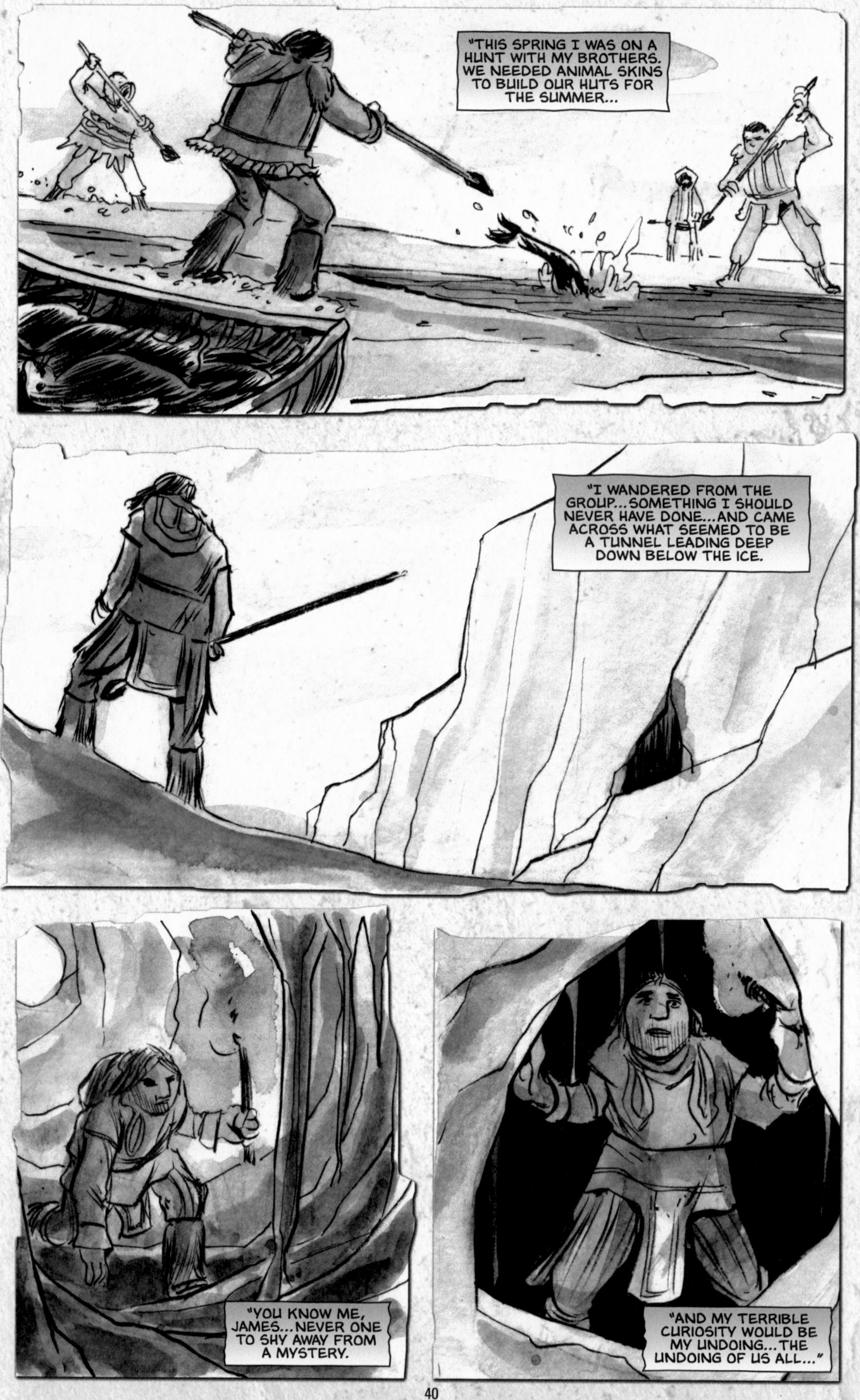
"THIS SPRING I WAS ON A HUNT WITH MY BROTHERS. WE NEEDED ANIMAL SKINS TO BUILD OUR HUTS FOR THE SUMMER...
"I WANDERED FROM THE GROUP...SOMETHING I SHOULD NEVER HAVE DONE...AND CAME ACROSS WHAT SEEMED TO BE A TUNNEL LEADING DEEP DOWN BELOW THE ICE.
"YOU KNOW ME, JAMES...NEVER ONE TO SHY AWAY FROM A MYSTERY.
"AND MY TERRIBLE CURIOSITY WOULD BE MY UNDOING...THE UNDOING OF US ALL..."

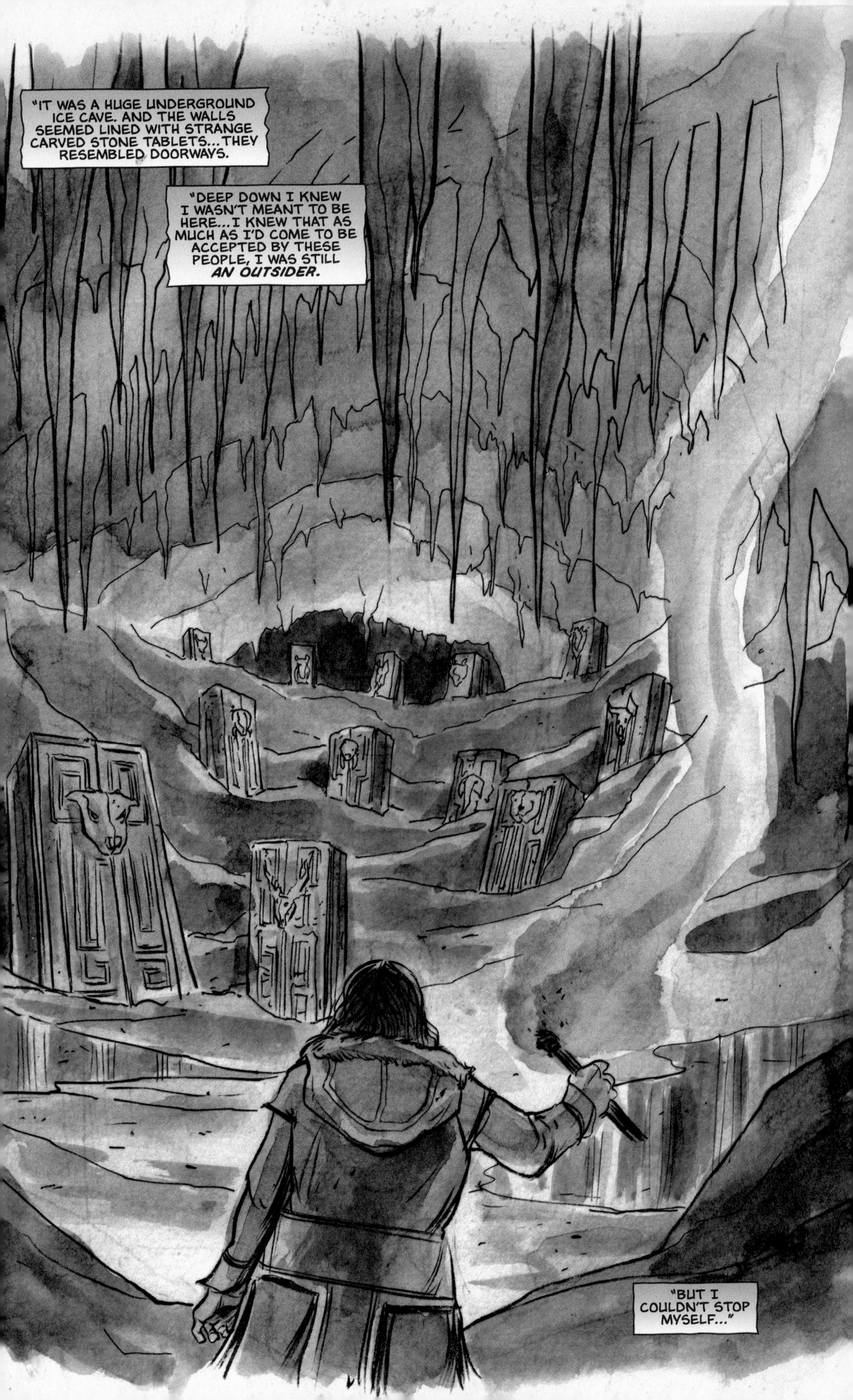
"IT WAS A HUGE UNDERGROUND ICE CAVE. AND THE WALLS SEEMED LINED WITH STRANGE CARVED STONE TABLETS...THEY RESEMBLED DOORWAYS.
"DEEP DOWN I KNEW I WASN'T MEANT TO BE HERE...I KNEW THAT AS MUCH AS I'D COME TO BE ACCEPTED BY THESE PEOPLE, I WAS STILL *AN OUTSIDER.*
"BUT I COULDN'T STOP MYSELF..."

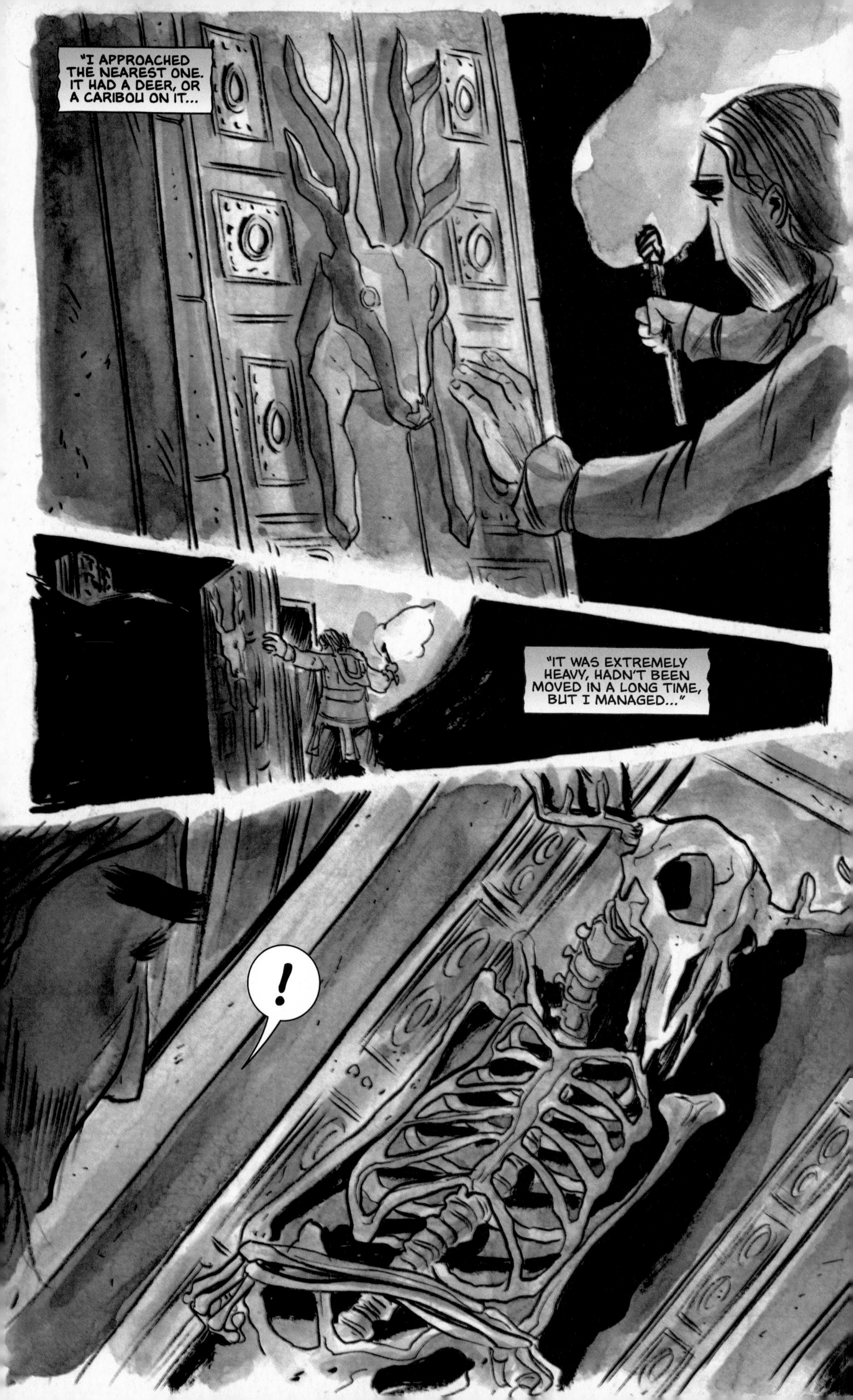
"I APPROACHED THE NEAREST ONE. IT HAD A DEER, OR A CARIBOU ON IT...
"IT WAS EXTREMELY HEAVY, HADN'T BEEN MOVED IN A LONG TIME, BUT I MANAGED..."
!

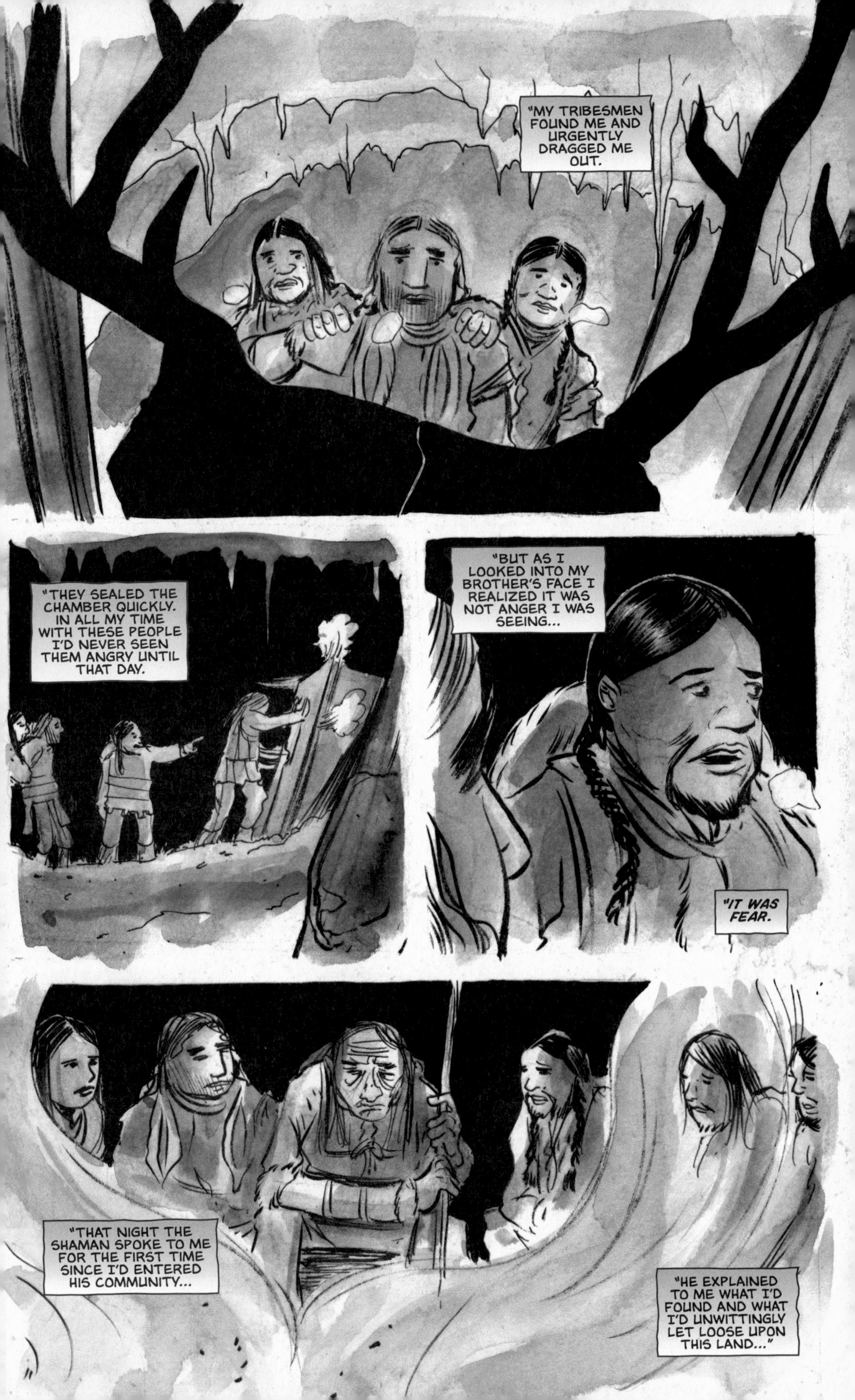
"MY TRIBESMEN FOUND ME AND URGENTLY DRAGGED ME OUT.
"THEY SEALED THE CHAMBER QUICKLY. IN ALL MY TIME WITH THESE PEOPLE I'D NEVER SEEN THEM ANGRY UNTIL THAT DAY.
"BUT AS I LOOKED INTO MY BROTHER'S FACE I REALIZED IT WAS NOT ANGER I WAS SEEING...
"IT WAS FEAR.
"THAT NIGHT THE SHAMAN SPOKE TO ME FOR THE FIRST TIME SINCE I'D ENTERED HIS COMMUNITY...
"HE EXPLAINED TO ME WHAT I'D FOUND AND WHAT I'D UNWITTINGLY LET LOOSE UPON THIS LAND..."

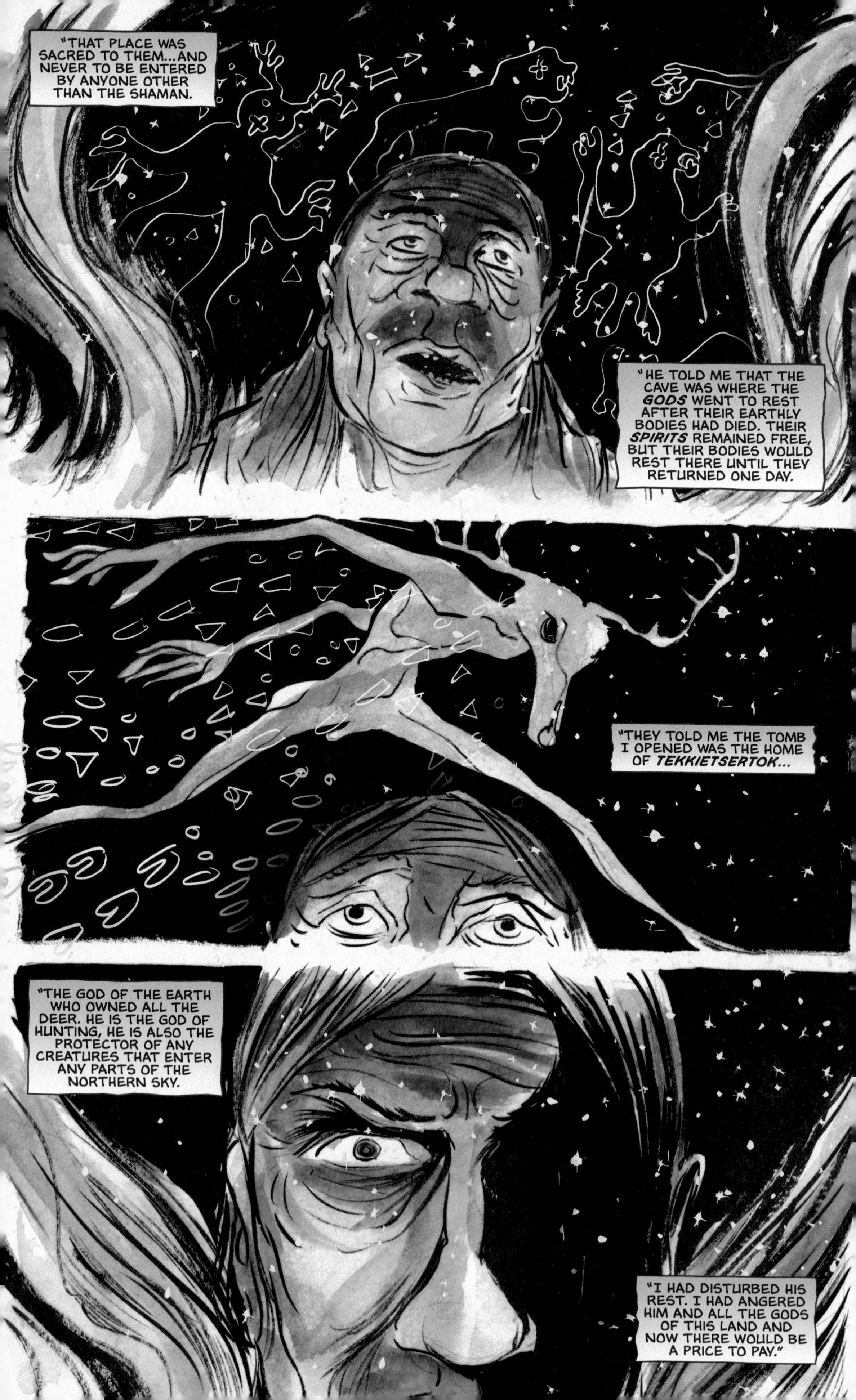
"THAT PLACE WAS SACRED TO THEM...AND NEVER TO BE ENTERED BY ANYONE OTHER THAN THE SHAMAN.
"HE TOLD ME THAT THE CAVE WAS WHERE THE GODS WENT TO REST AFTER THEIR EARTHLY BODIES HAD DIED. THEIR SPIRITS REMAINED FREE, BUT THEIR BODIES WOULD REST THERE UNTIL THEY RETURNED ONE DAY.
"THEY TOLD ME THE TOMB I OPENED WAS THE HOME OF TEKKIETSERTOK...
"THE GOD OF THE EARTH WHO OWNED ALL THE DEER. HE IS THE GOD OF HUNTING, HE IS ALSO THE PROTECTOR OF ANY CREATURES THAT ENTER ANY PARTS OF THE NORTHERN SKY.
"I HAD DISTURBED HIS REST. I HAD ANGERED HIM AND ALL THE GODS OF THIS LAND AND NOW THERE WOULD BE A PRICE TO PAY."

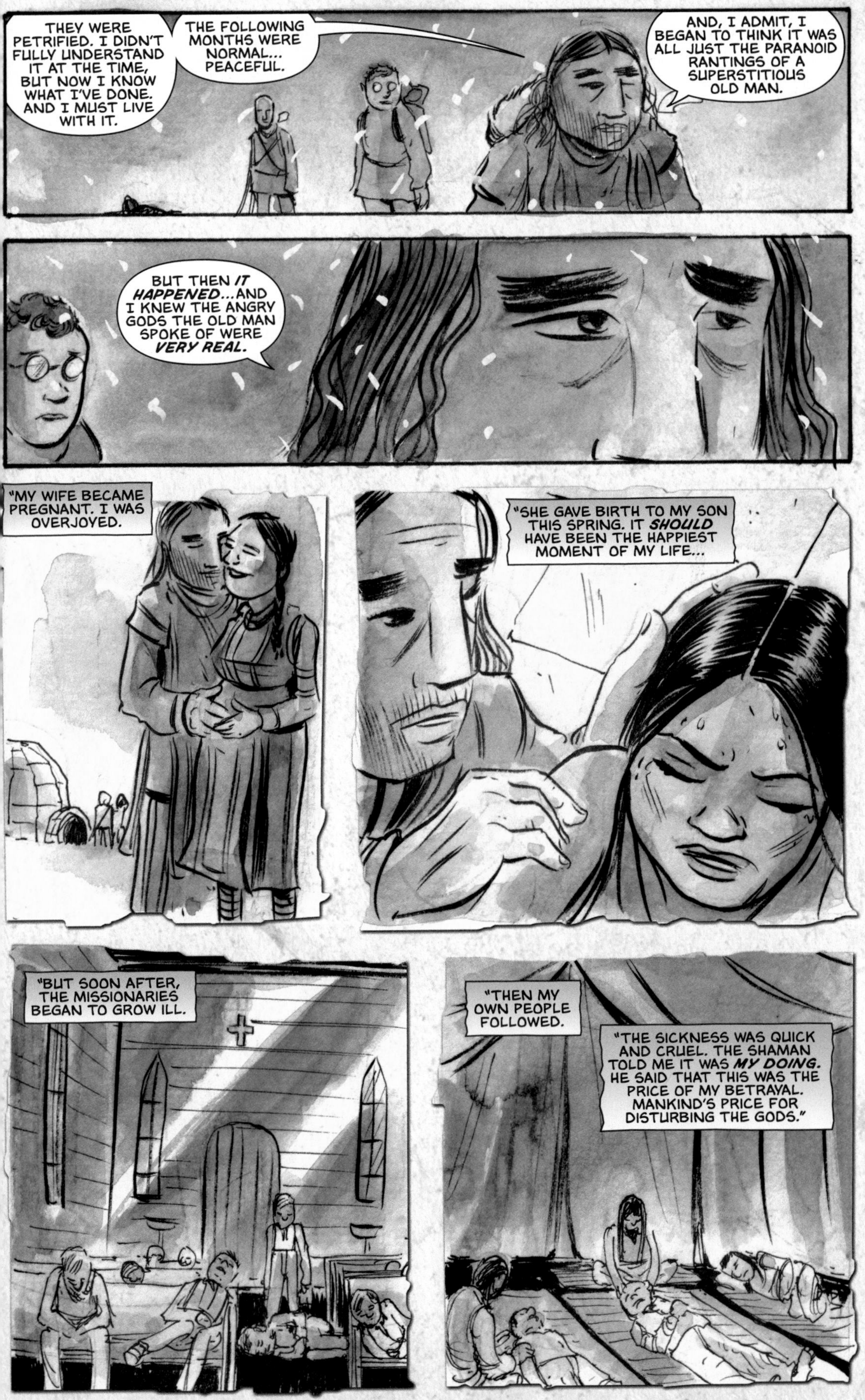
THEY WERE PETRIFIED. I DIDN'T FULLY UNDERSTAND IT AT THE TIME, BUT NOW I KNOW WHAT I'VE DONE. AND I MUST LIVE WITH IT.
THE FOLLOWING MONTHS WERE NORMAL... PEACEFUL.
AND, I ADMIT, I BEGAN TO THINK IT WAS ALL JUST THE PARANOID RANTINGS OF A SUPERSTITIOUS OLD MAN.
BUT THEN *IT HAPPENED*...AND I KNEW THE ANGRY GODS THE OLD MAN SPOKE OF WERE ***VERY REAL.***
"MY WIFE BECAME PREGNANT. I WAS OVERJOYED.
"SHE GAVE BIRTH TO MY SON THIS SPRING. IT ***SHOULD*** HAVE BEEN THE HAPPIEST MOMENT OF MY LIFE...
"BUT SOON AFTER, THE MISSIONARIES BEGAN TO GROW ILL.
"THEN MY OWN PEOPLE FOLLOWED.
"THE SICKNESS WAS QUICK AND CRUEL. THE SHAMAN TOLD ME IT WAS ***MY DOING.*** HE SAID THAT THIS WAS THE PRICE OF MY BETRAYAL. MANKIND'S PRICE FOR DISTURBING THE GODS."

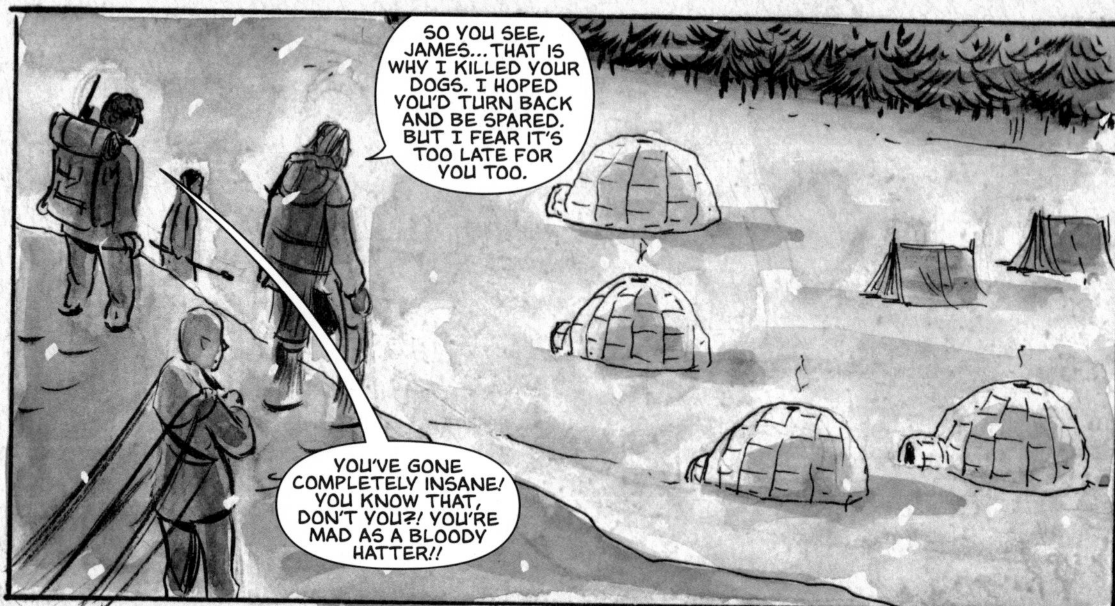
SO YOU SEE, JAMES... THAT IS WHY I KILLED YOUR DOGS. I HOPED YOU'D TURN BACK AND BE SPARED. BUT I FEAR IT'S TOO LATE FOR YOU TOO.
YOU'VE GONE COMPLETELY INSANE! YOU KNOW THAT, DON'T YOU?! YOU'RE MAD AS A BLOODY HATTER!!

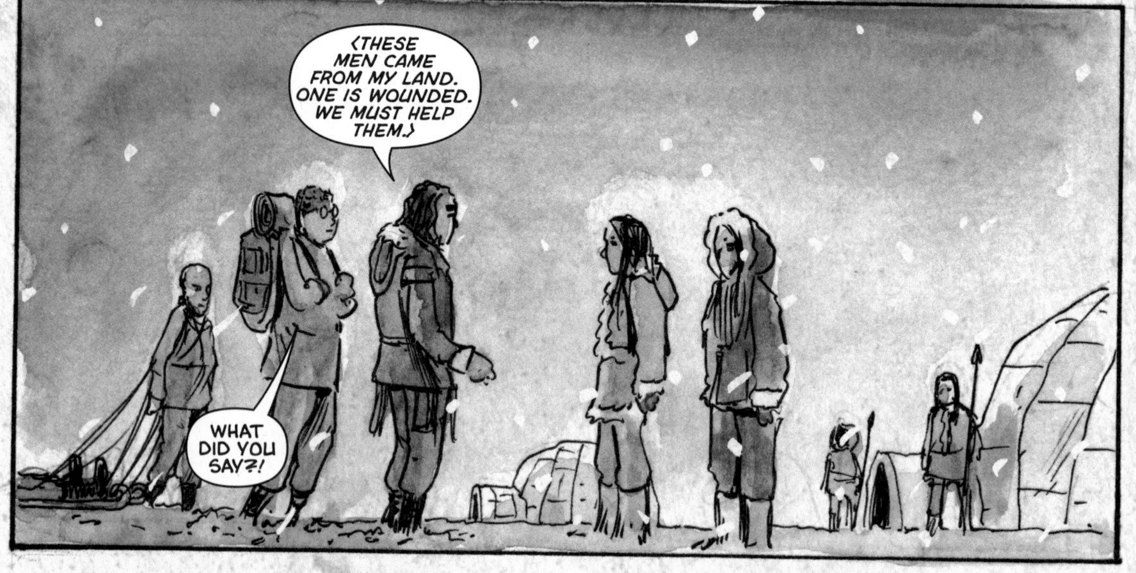
<THESE MEN CAME FROM MY LAND. ONE IS WOUNDED. WE MUST HELP THEM.>
WHAT DID YOU SAY?!

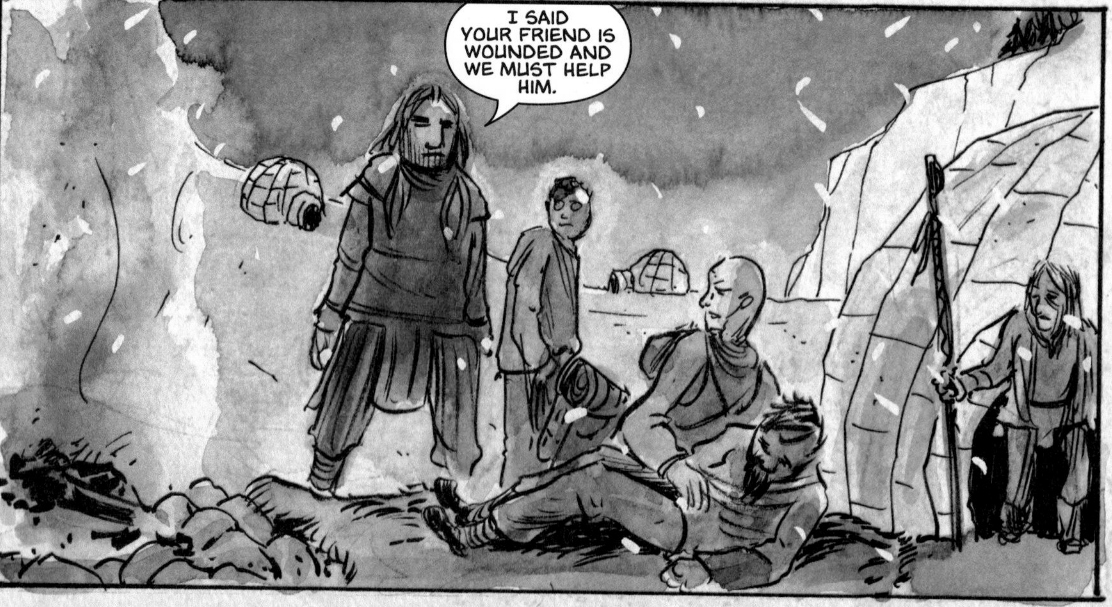
I SAID YOUR FRIEND IS WOUNDED AND WE MUST HELP HIM.

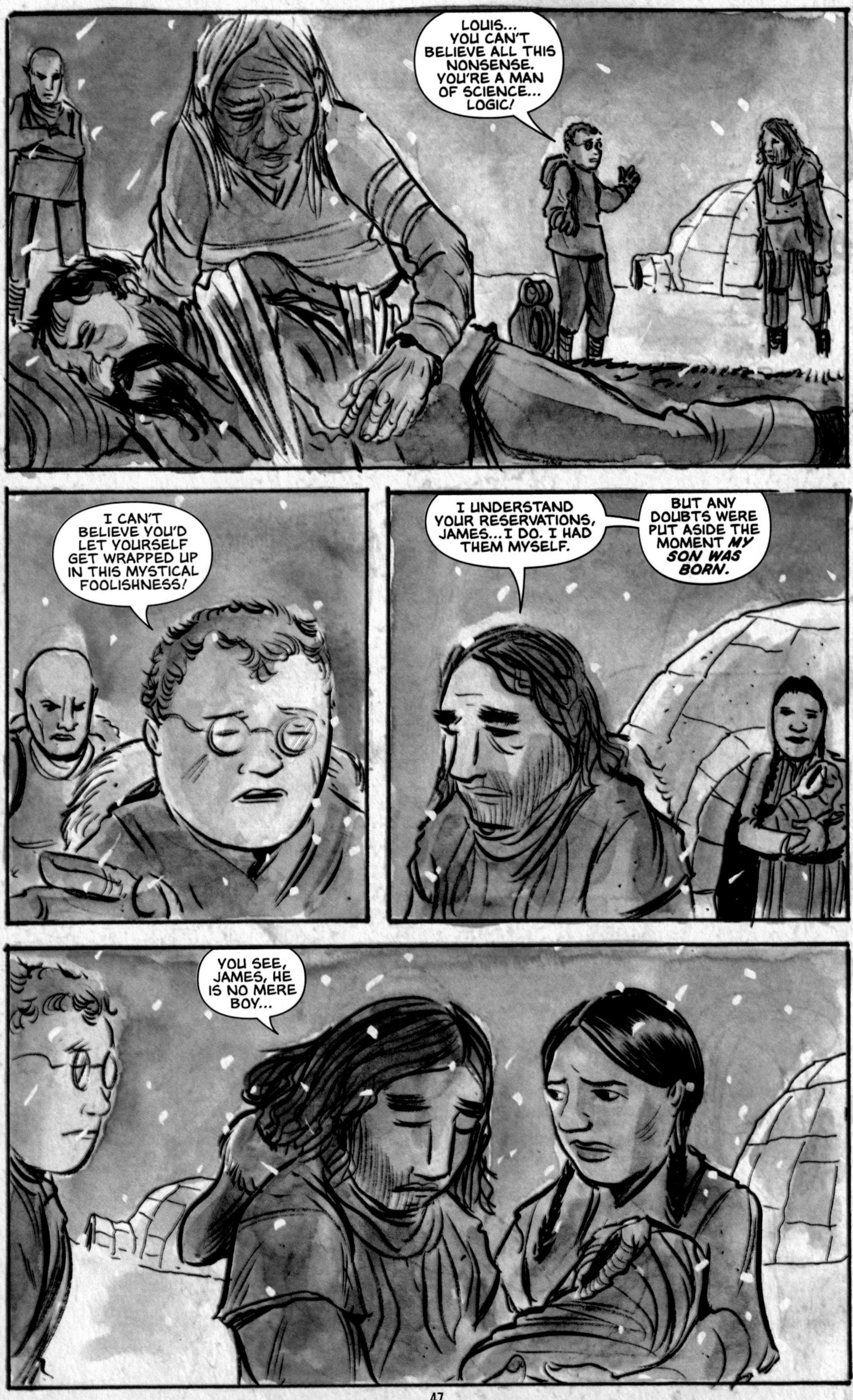
LOUIS... YOU CAN'T BELIEVE ALL THIS NONSENSE. YOU'RE A MAN OF SCIENCE... LOGIC!
I CAN'T BELIEVE YOU'D LET YOURSELF GET WRAPPED UP IN THIS MYSTICAL FOOLISHNESS!
I UNDERSTAND YOUR RESERVATIONS, JAMES... I DO. I HAD THEM MYSELF.
BUT ANY DOUBTS WERE PUT ASIDE THE MOMENT *MY SON WAS BORN*.
YOU SEE, JAMES, HE IS NO MERE BOY...

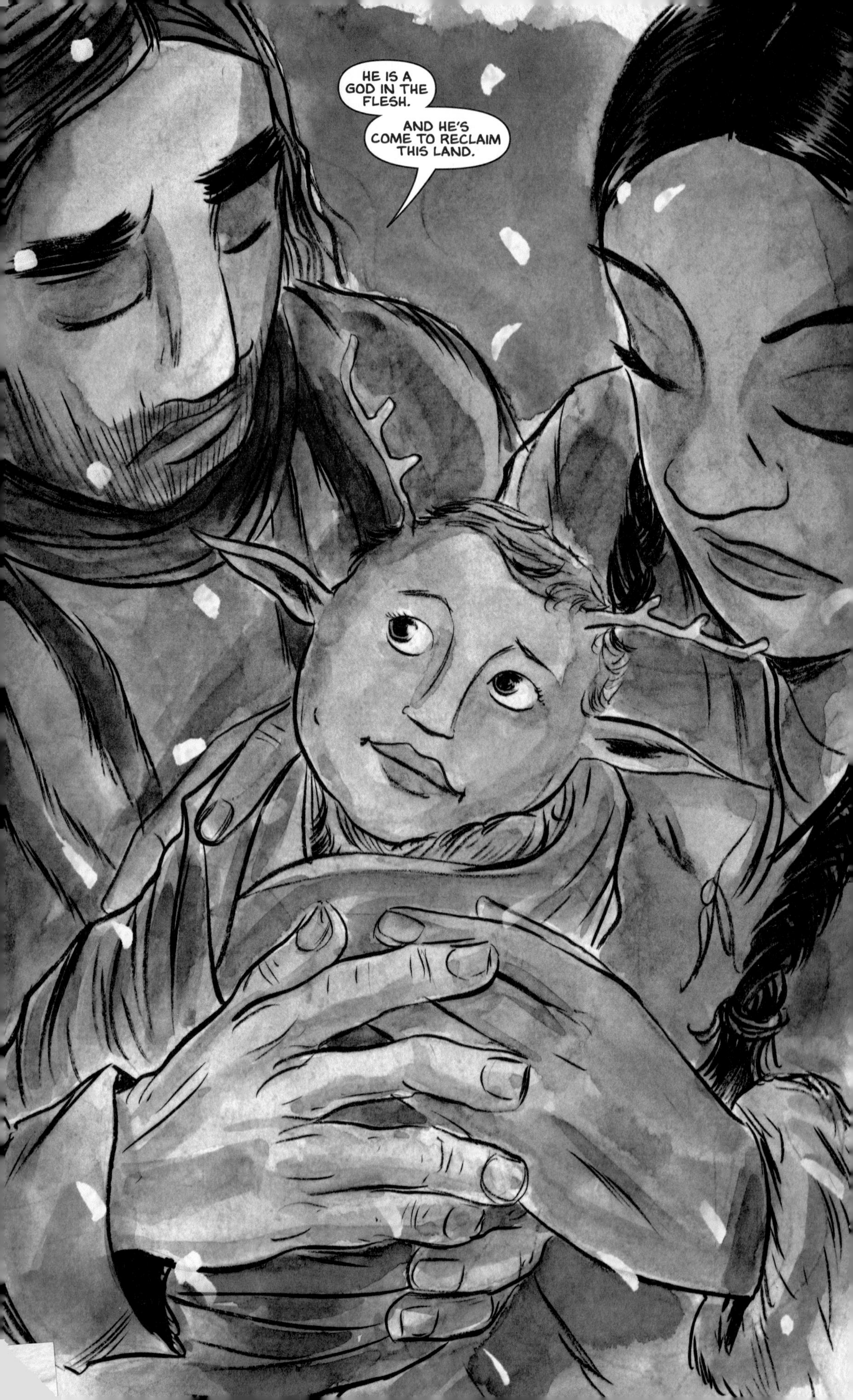
HE IS A GOD IN THE FLESH.
AND HE'S COME TO RECLAIM THIS LAND.

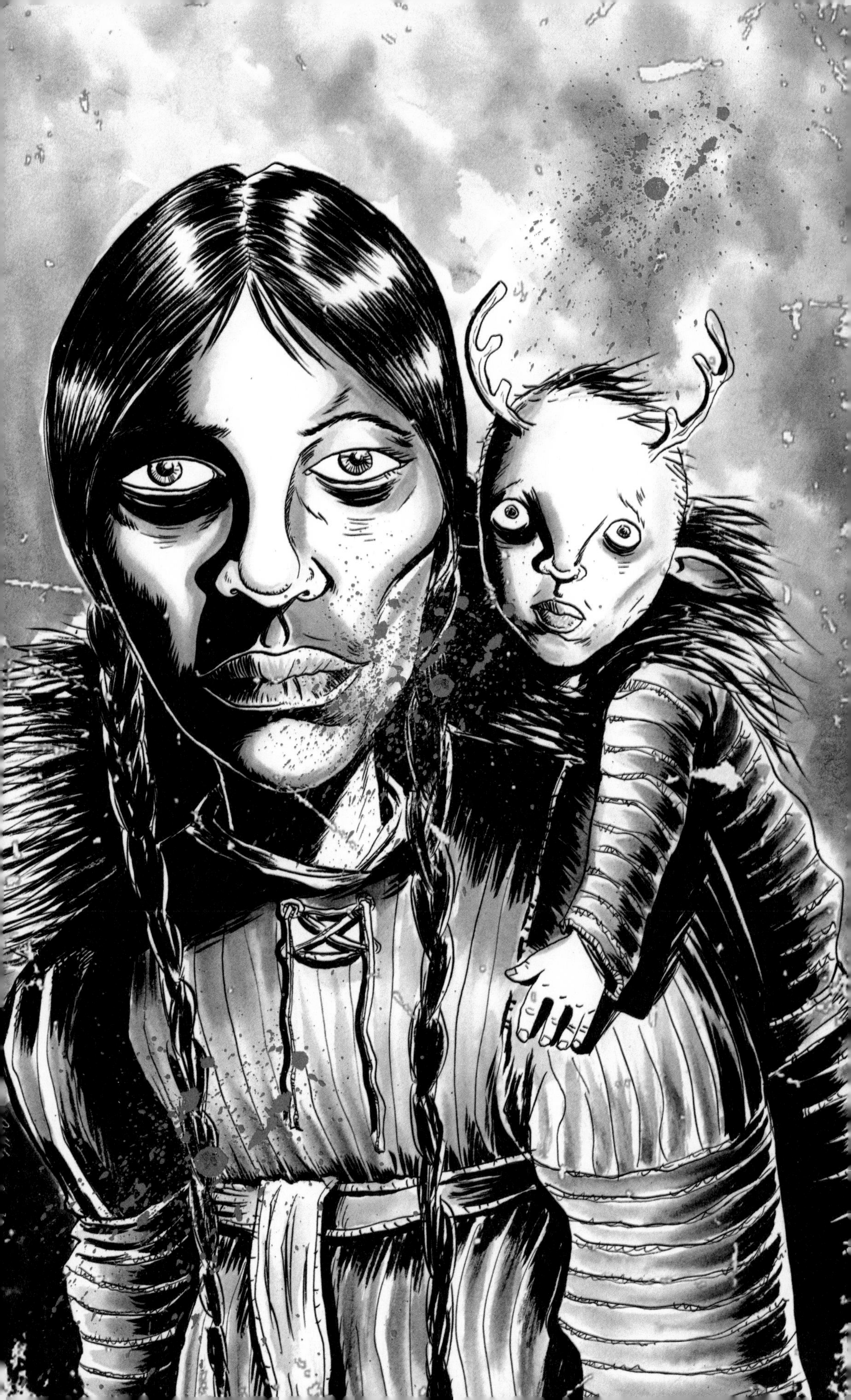

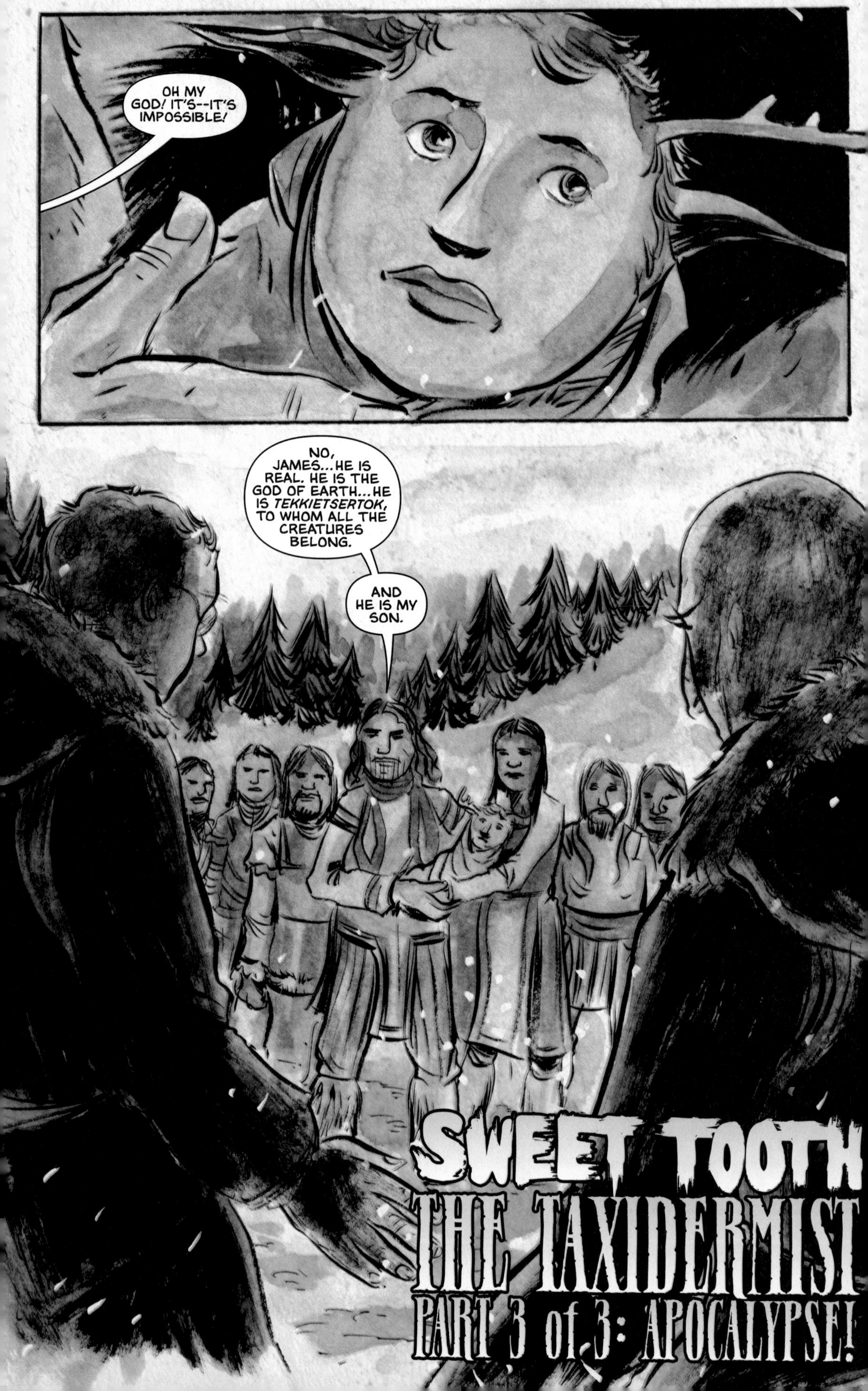
OH MY GOD! IT'S--IT'S IMPOSSIBLE!
NO, JAMES...HE IS REAL. HE IS THE GOD OF EARTH...HE IS *TEKKIETSERTOK*, TO WHOM ALL THE CREATURES BELONG.
AND HE IS MY SON.
SWEET TOOTH
THE TAXIDERMIST
PART 3 of 3: APOCALYPSE!

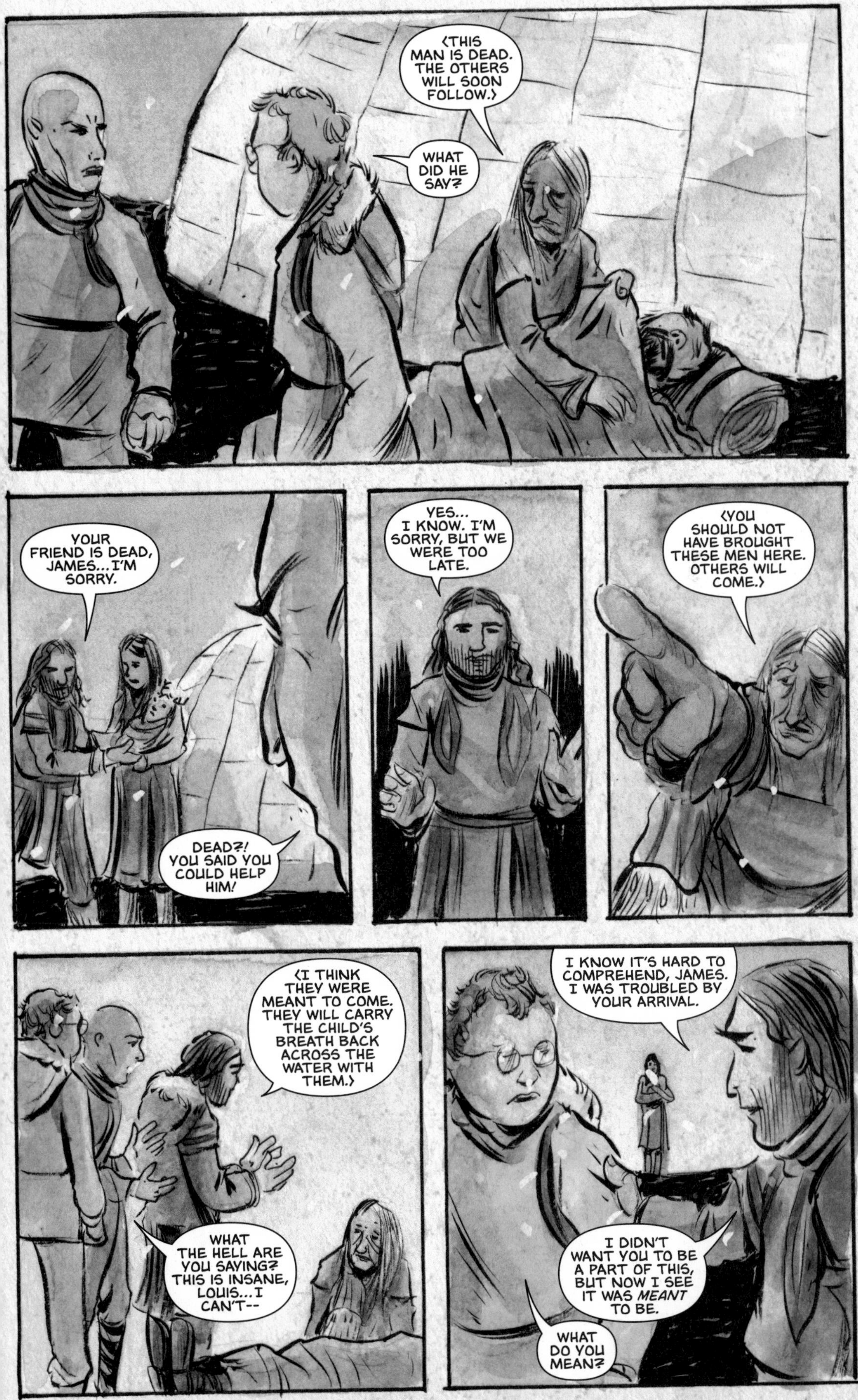
‹THIS MAN IS DEAD. THE OTHERS WILL SOON FOLLOW.›
WHAT DID HE SAY?
YOUR FRIEND IS DEAD, JAMES... I'M SORRY.
DEAD?! YOU SAID YOU COULD HELP HIM!
YES... I KNOW. I'M SORRY, BUT WE WERE TOO LATE.
‹YOU SHOULD NOT HAVE BROUGHT THESE MEN HERE. OTHERS WILL COME.›
‹I THINK THEY WERE MEANT TO COME. THEY WILL CARRY THE CHILD'S BREATH BACK ACROSS THE WATER WITH THEM.›
WHAT THE HELL ARE YOU SAYING? THIS IS INSANE, LOUIS... I CAN'T--
I KNOW IT'S HARD TO COMPREHEND, JAMES. I WAS TROUBLED BY YOUR ARRIVAL.
I DIDN'T WANT YOU TO BE A PART OF THIS, BUT NOW I SEE IT WAS *MEANT* TO BE.
WHAT DO YOU MEAN?

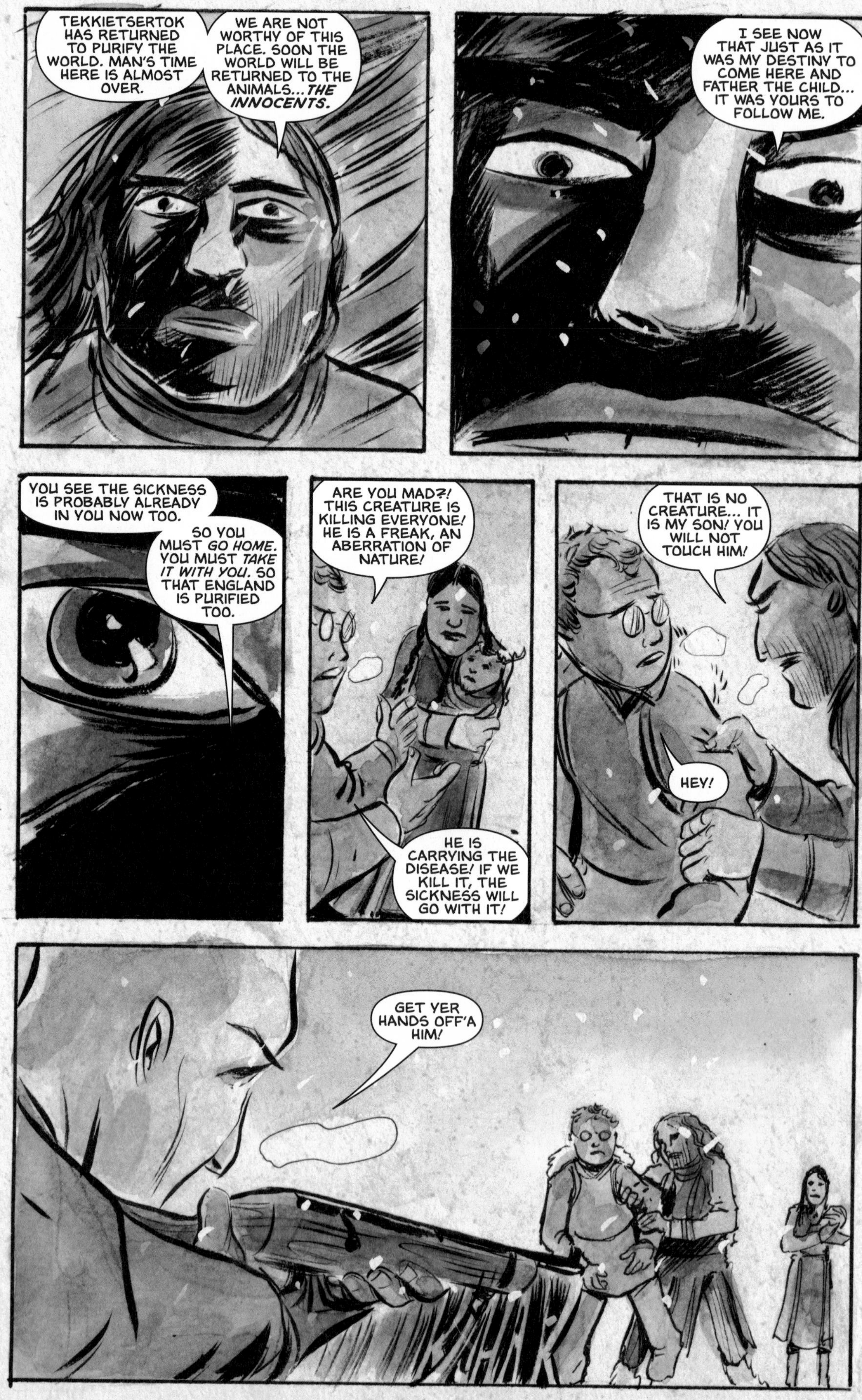
TEKKIETSERTOK HAS RETURNED TO PURIFY THE WORLD. MAN'S TIME HERE IS ALMOST OVER.
WE ARE NOT WORTHY OF THIS PLACE. SOON THE WORLD WILL BE RETURNED TO THE ANIMALS... *THE INNOCENTS.*
I SEE NOW THAT JUST AS IT WAS MY DESTINY TO COME HERE AND FATHER THE CHILD... IT WAS YOURS TO FOLLOW ME.
YOU SEE THE SICKNESS IS PROBABLY ALREADY IN YOU NOW TOO.
SO YOU MUST *GO HOME*. YOU MUST *TAKE IT WITH YOU*. SO THAT ENGLAND IS PURIFIED TOO.
ARE YOU MAD?! THIS CREATURE IS KILLING EVERYONE! HE IS A FREAK, AN ABERRATION OF NATURE!
HE IS CARRYING THE DISEASE! IF WE KILL IT, THE SICKNESS WILL GO WITH IT!
THAT IS NO CREATURE... IT IS MY SON! YOU WILL NOT TOUCH HIM!
HEY!
GET YER HANDS OFF'A HIM!
KCHAK

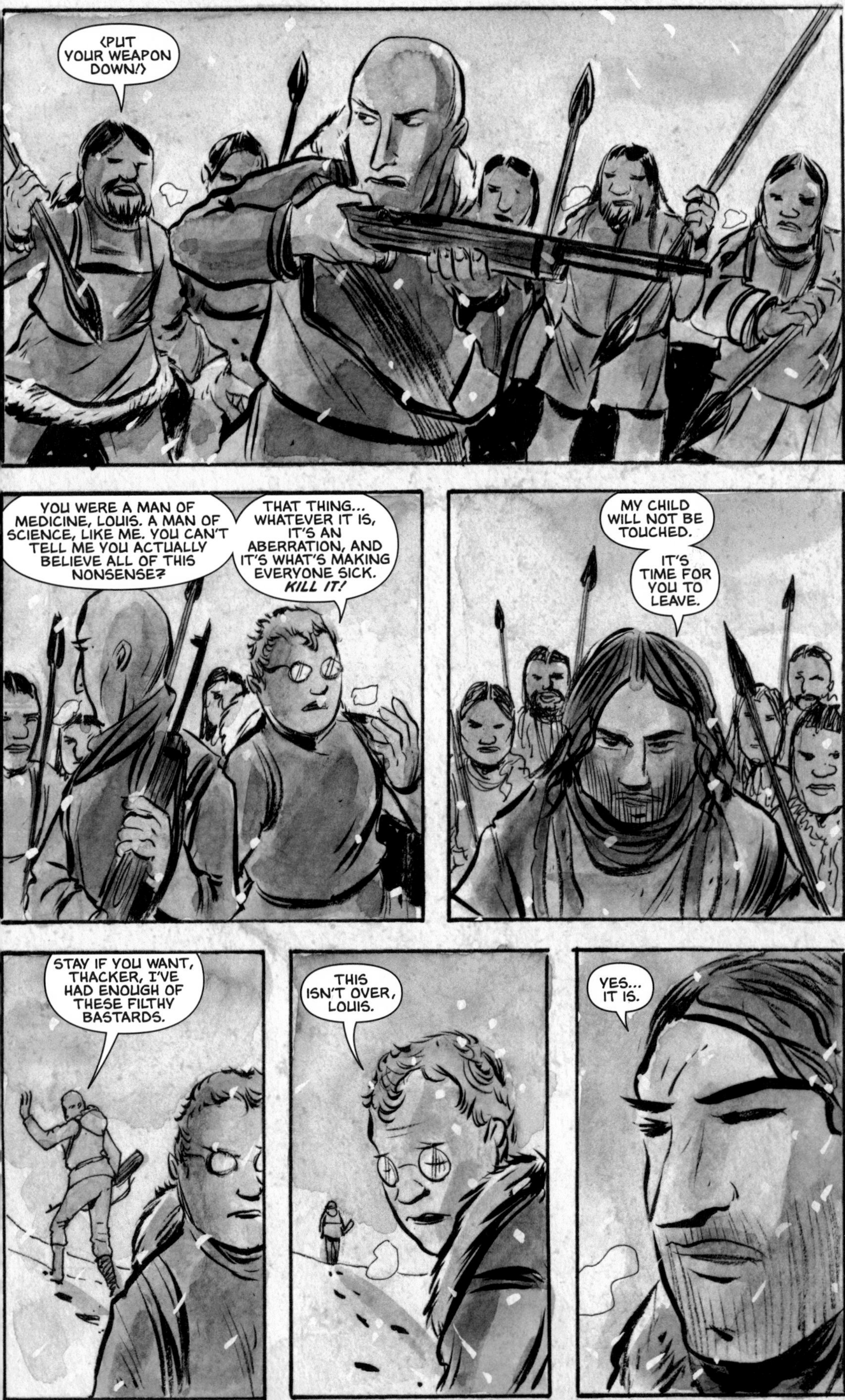

‹PUT YOUR WEAPON DOWN!›
YOU WERE A MAN OF MEDICINE, LOUIS. A MAN OF SCIENCE, LIKE ME. YOU CAN'T TELL ME YOU ACTUALLY BELIEVE ALL OF THIS NONSENSE?
THAT THING... WHATEVER IT IS, IT'S AN ABERRATION, AND IT'S WHAT'S MAKING EVERYONE SICK. *KILL IT!*
MY CHILD WILL NOT BE TOUCHED.
IT'S TIME FOR YOU TO LEAVE.
STAY IF YOU WANT, THACKER, I'VE HAD ENOUGH OF THESE FILTHY BASTARDS.
THIS ISN'T OVER, LOUIS.
YES... IT IS.

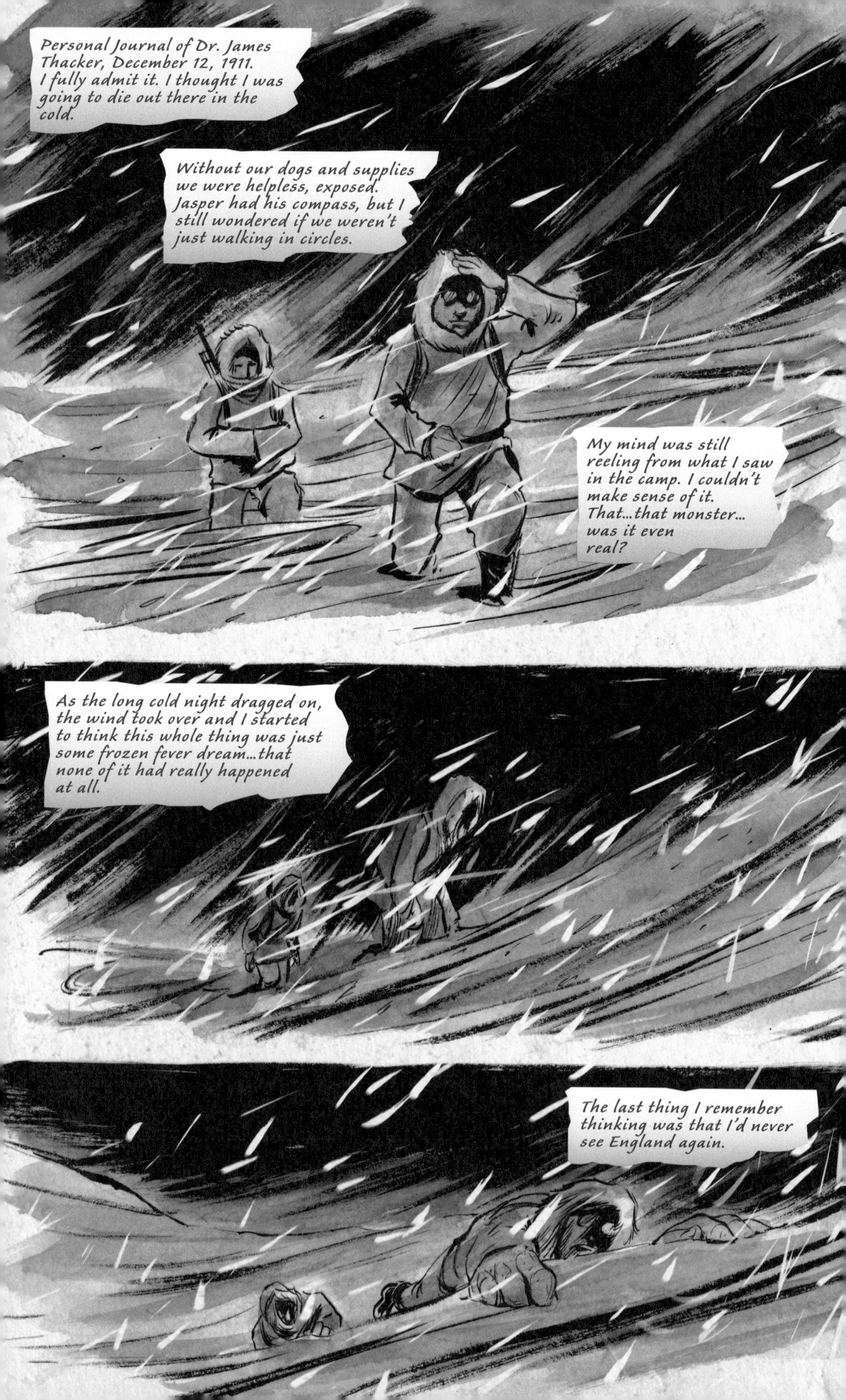
Personal Journal of Dr. James Thacker, December 12, 1911. I fully admit it. I thought I was going to die out there in the cold.
Without our dogs and supplies we were helpless, exposed. Jasper had his compass, but I still wondered if we weren't just walking in circles.
My mind was still reeling from what I saw in the camp. I couldn't make sense of it. That...that monster... was it even real?
As the long cold night dragged on, the wind took over and I started to think this whole thing was just some frozen fever dream...that none of it had really happened at all.
The last thing I remember thinking was that I'd never see England again.

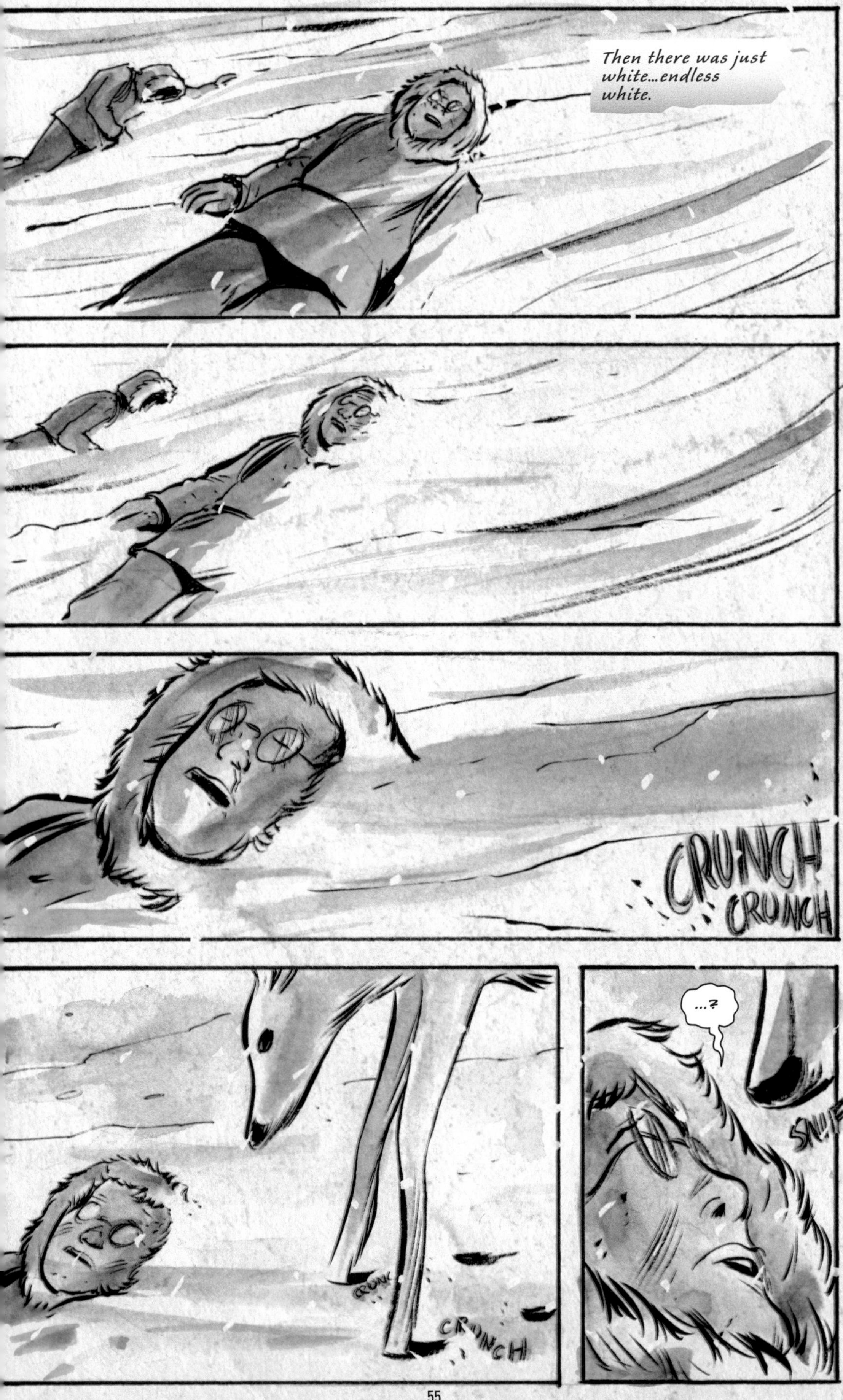
Then there was just white...endless white.
CRUNCH
CRUNCH
CRUNK
CRUNCH
...?
SNIFF

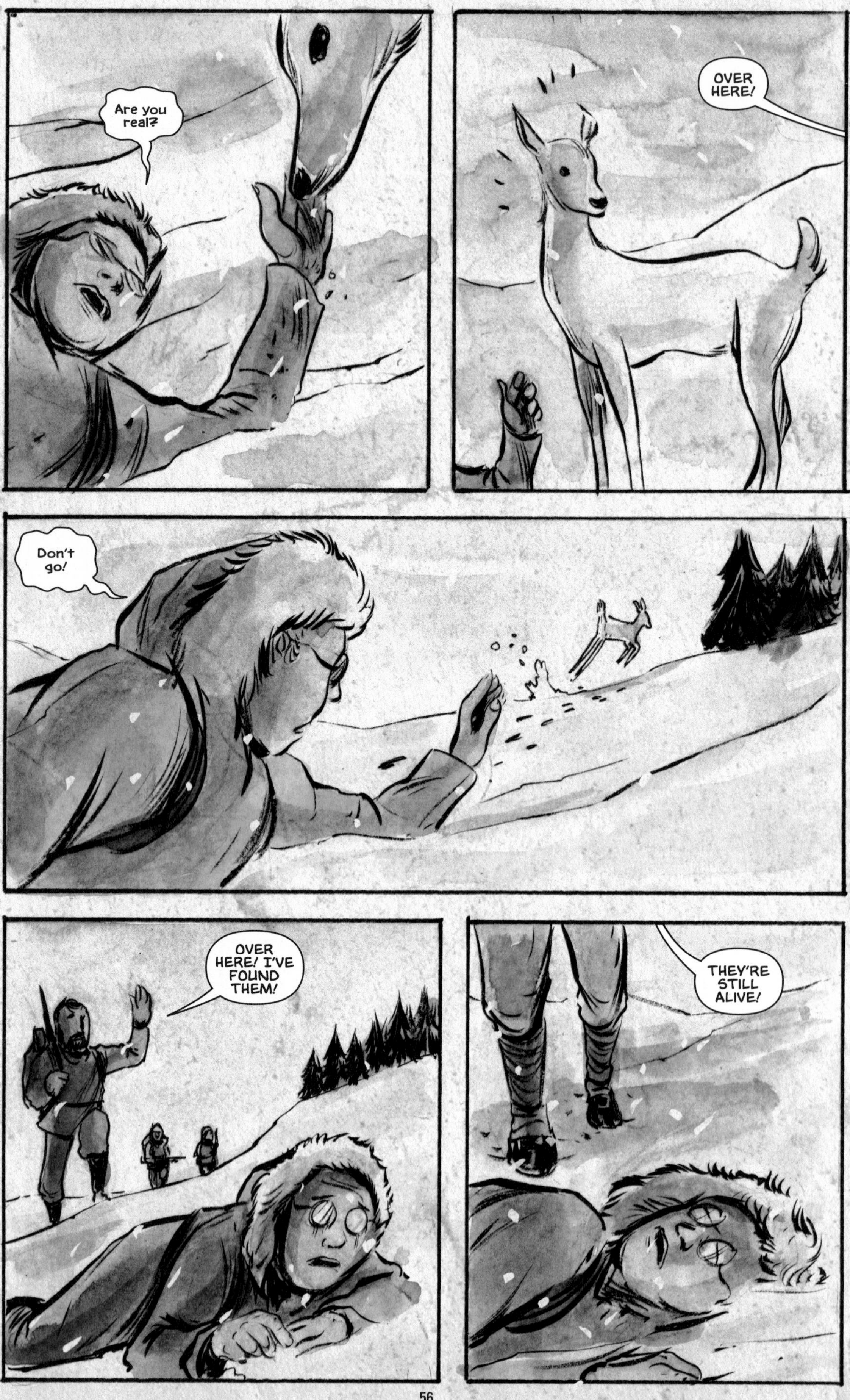
Are you real?
OVER HERE!
Don't go!
OVER HERE! I'VE FOUND THEM!
THEY'RE STILL ALIVE!

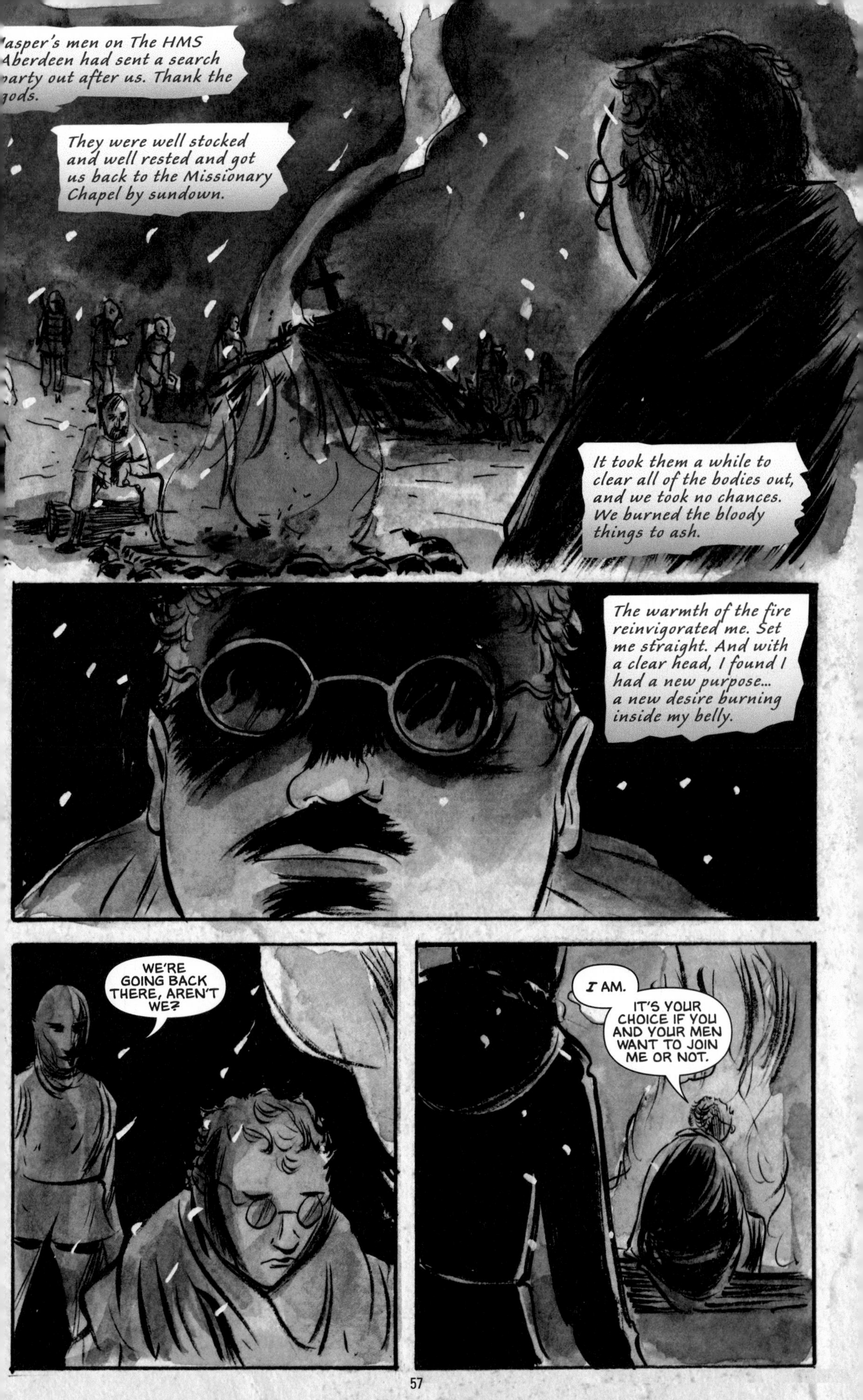
asper's men on The HMS Aberdeen had sent a search arty out after us. Thank the ods.
They were well stocked and well rested and got us back to the Missionary Chapel by sundown.
It took them a while to clear all of the bodies out, and we took no chances. We burned the bloody things to ash.
The warmth of the fire reinvigorated me. Set me straight. And with a clear head, I found I had a new purpose... a new desire burning inside my belly.
WE'RE GOING BACK THERE, AREN'T WE?
I AM.
IT'S YOUR CHOICE IF YOU AND YOUR MEN WANT TO JOIN ME OR NOT.

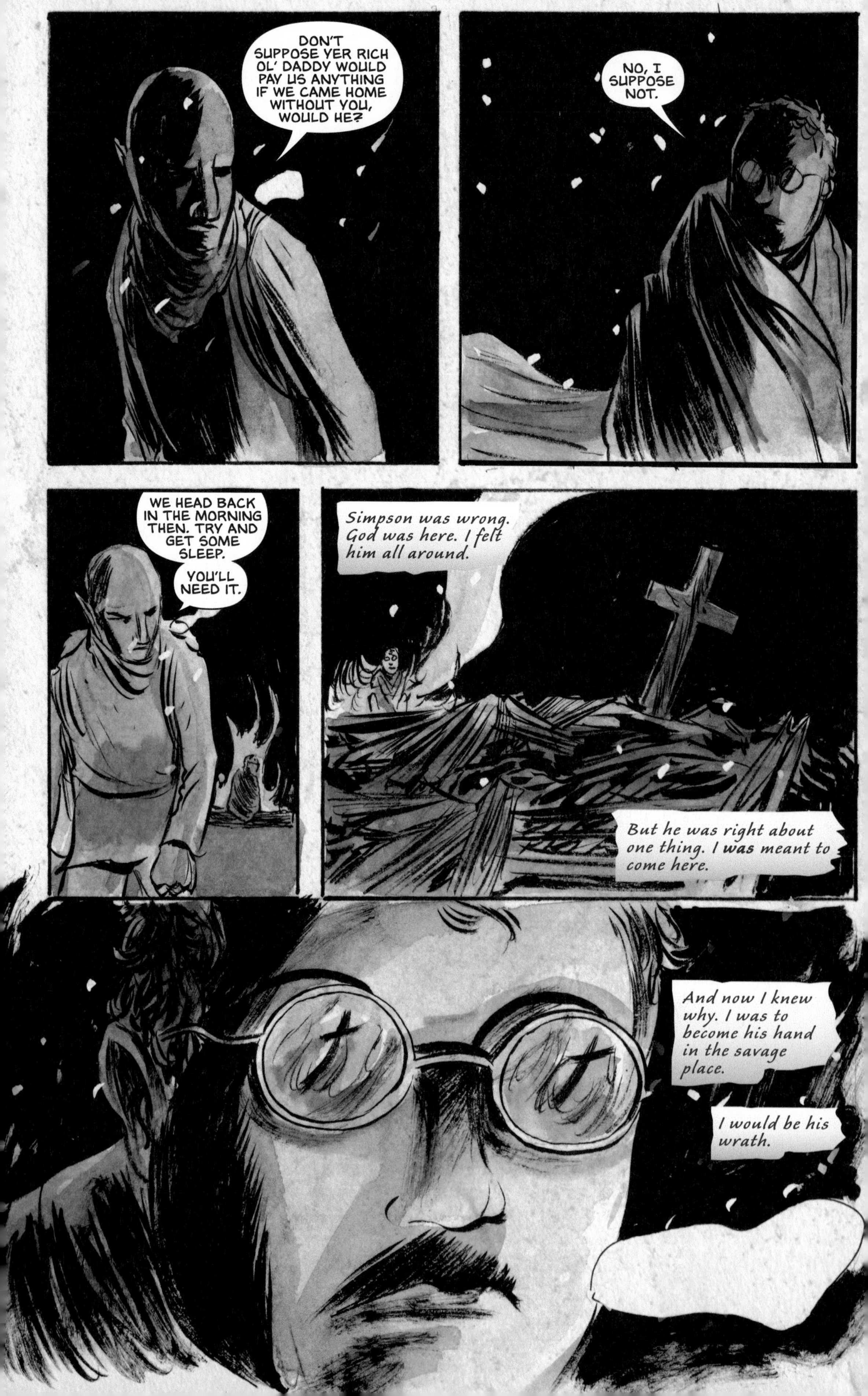
DON'T SUPPOSE YER RICH OL' DADDY WOULD PAY US ANYTHING IF WE CAME HOME WITHOUT YOU, WOULD HE?
NO, I SUPPOSE NOT.
WE HEAD BACK IN THE MORNING THEN. TRY AND GET SOME SLEEP.
YOU'LL NEED IT.
Simpson was wrong. God was here. I felt him all around.
But he was right about one thing. I was meant to come here.
And now I knew why. I was to become his hand in the savage place.
I would be his wrath.

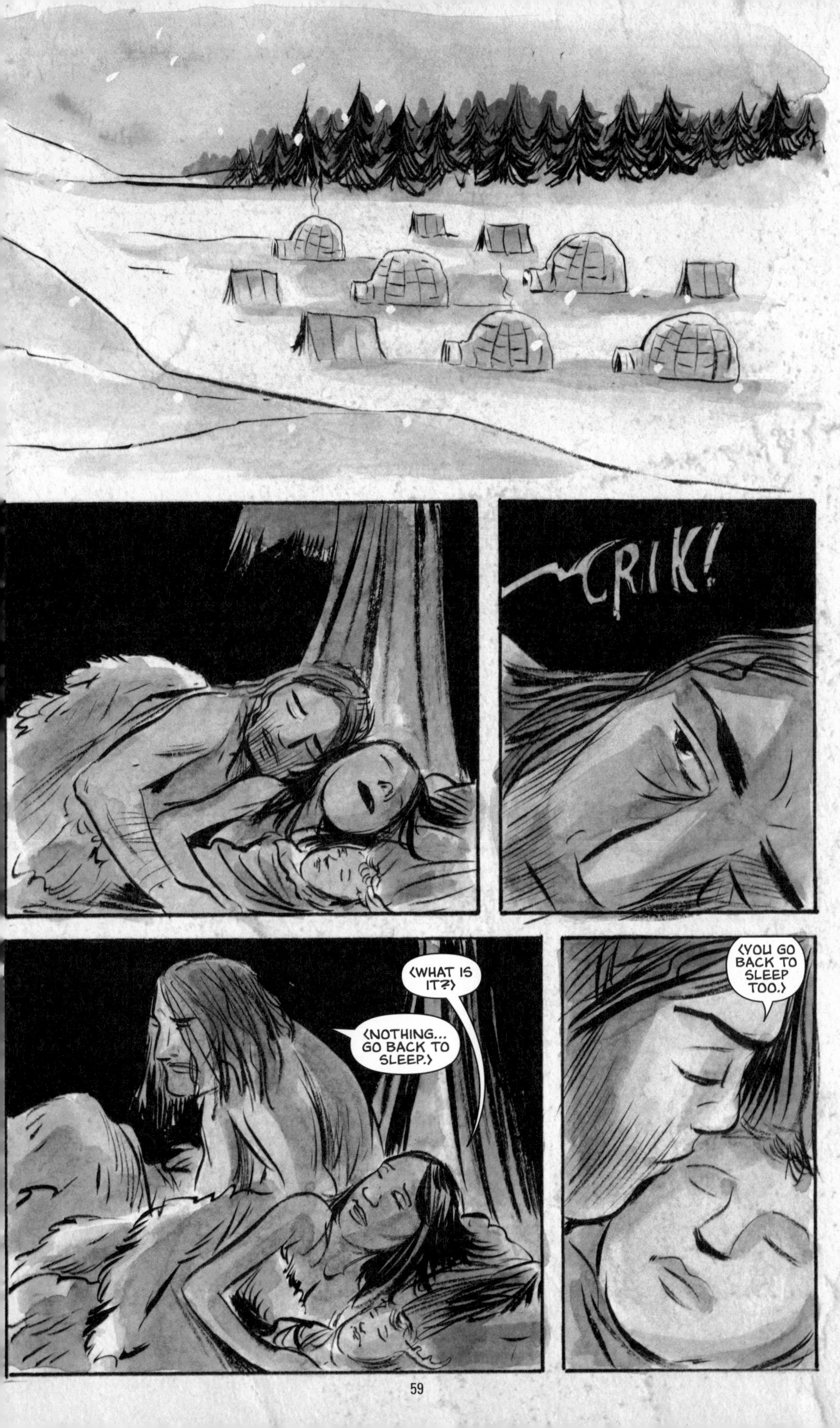
CRIK!
‹WHAT IS IT?›
‹NOTHING... GO BACK TO SLEEP.›
‹YOU GO BACK TO SLEEP TOO.›

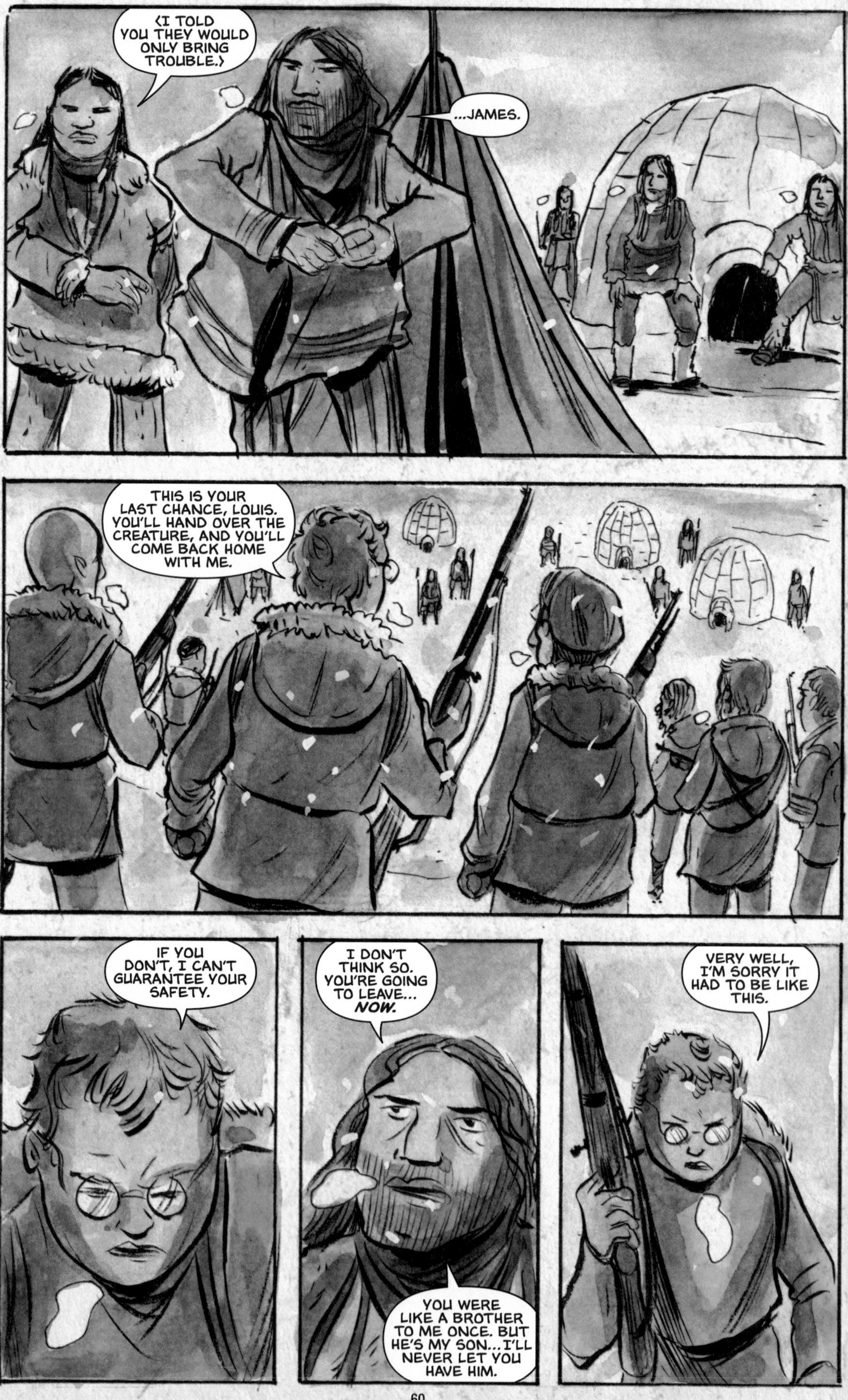

⟨I TOLD YOU THEY WOULD ONLY BRING TROUBLE.⟩
...JAMES.
THIS IS YOUR LAST CHANCE, LOUIS. YOU'LL HAND OVER THE CREATURE, AND YOU'LL COME BACK HOME WITH ME.
IF YOU DON'T, I CAN'T GUARANTEE YOUR SAFETY.
I DON'T THINK SO. YOU'RE GOING TO LEAVE... *NOW.*
YOU WERE LIKE A BROTHER TO ME ONCE. BUT HE'S MY SON... I'LL NEVER LET YOU HAVE HIM.
VERY WELL, I'M SORRY IT HAD TO BE LIKE THIS.

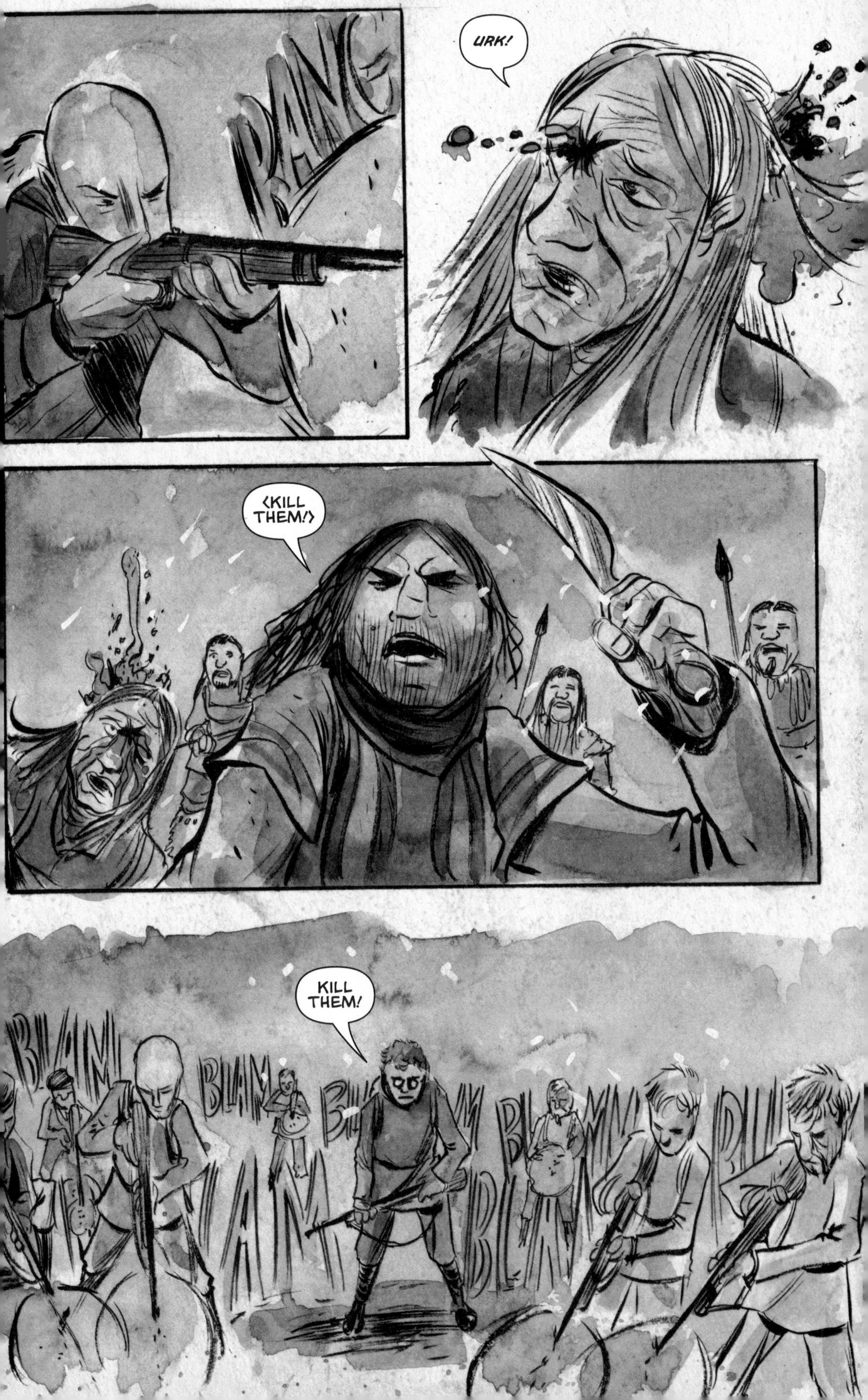
BANG
URK!
‹KILL THEM!›
KILL THEM!
BLAM BLAM

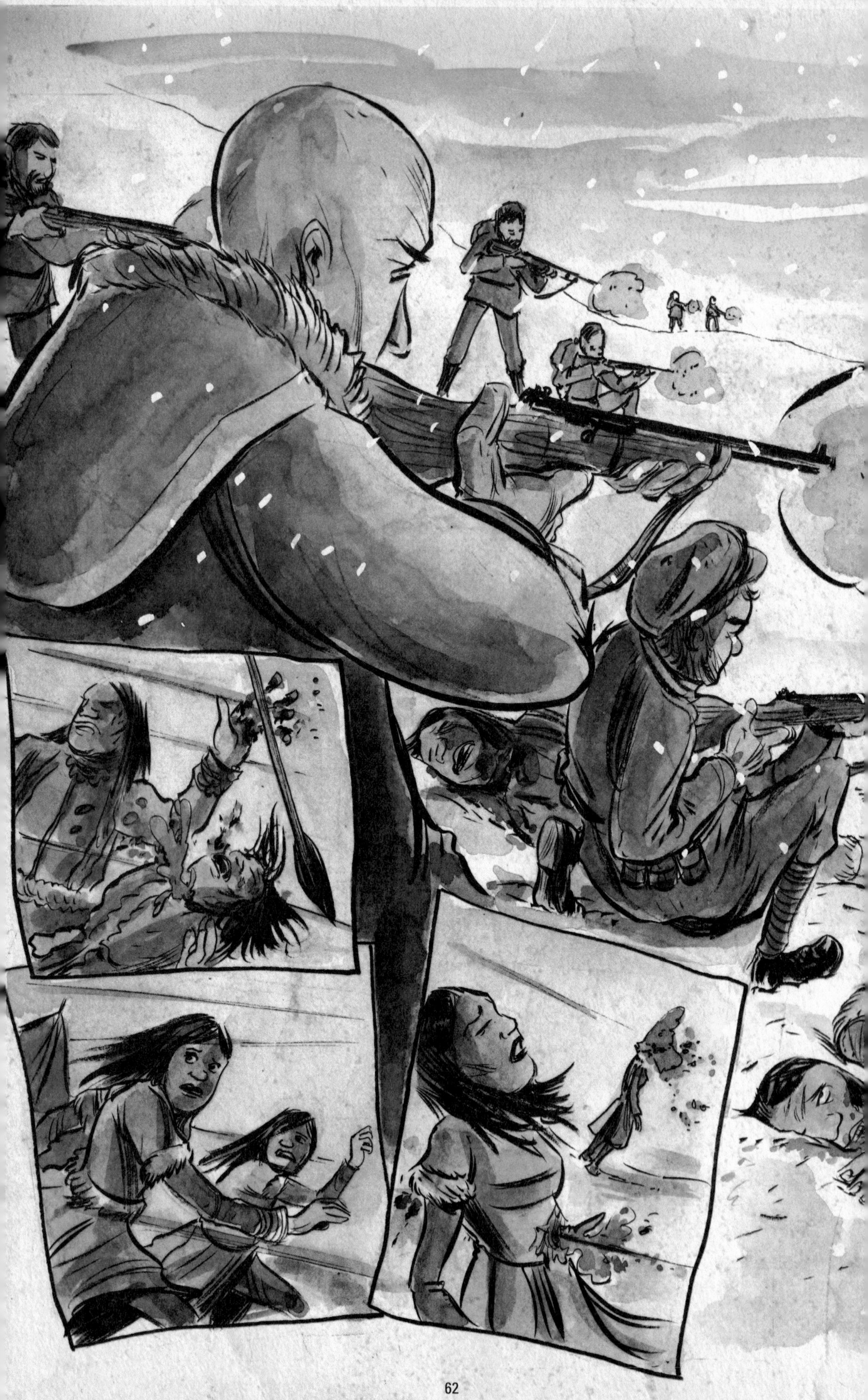

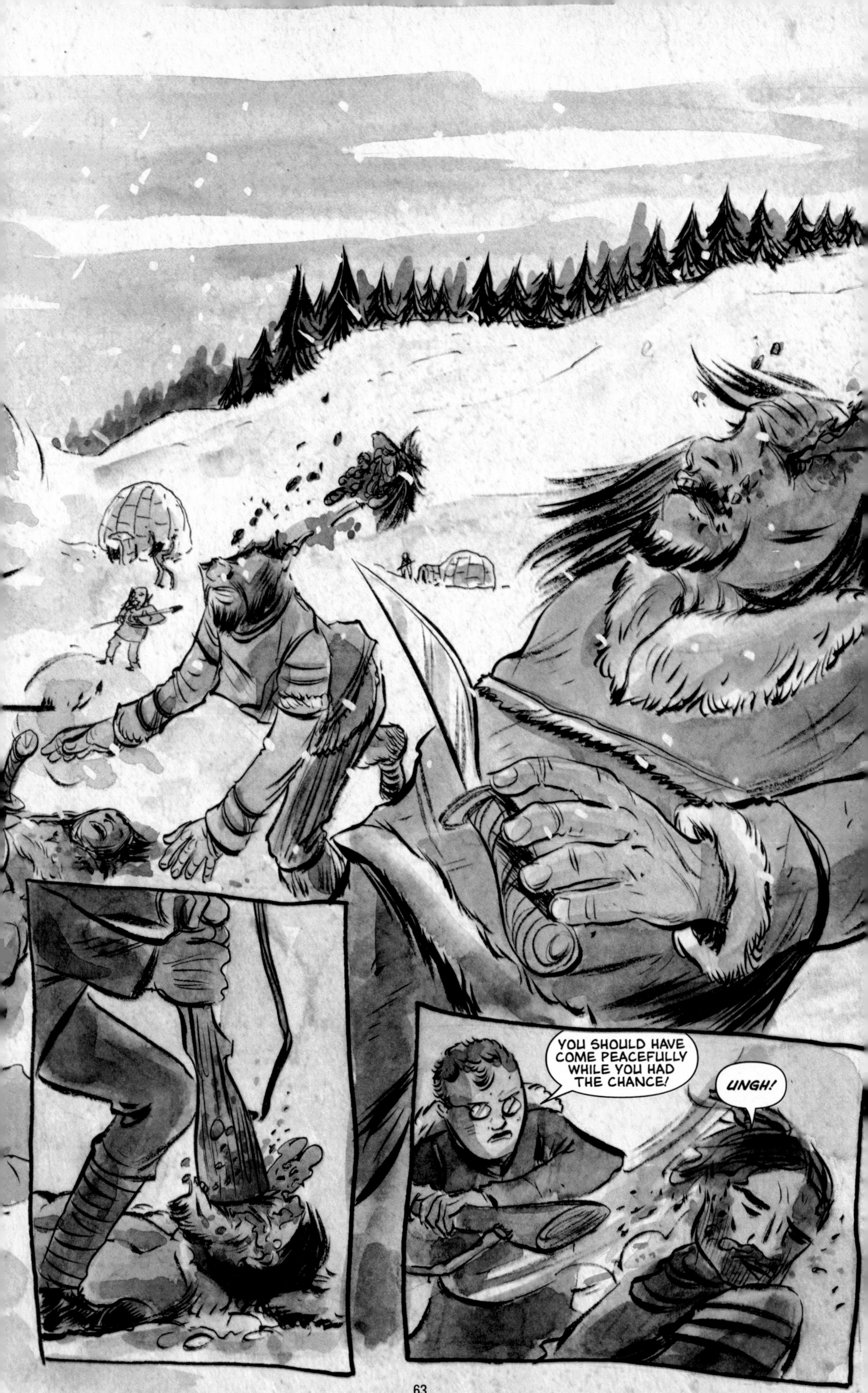
YOU SHOULD HAVE COME PEACEFULLY WHILE YOU HAD THE CHANCE!
UNGH!

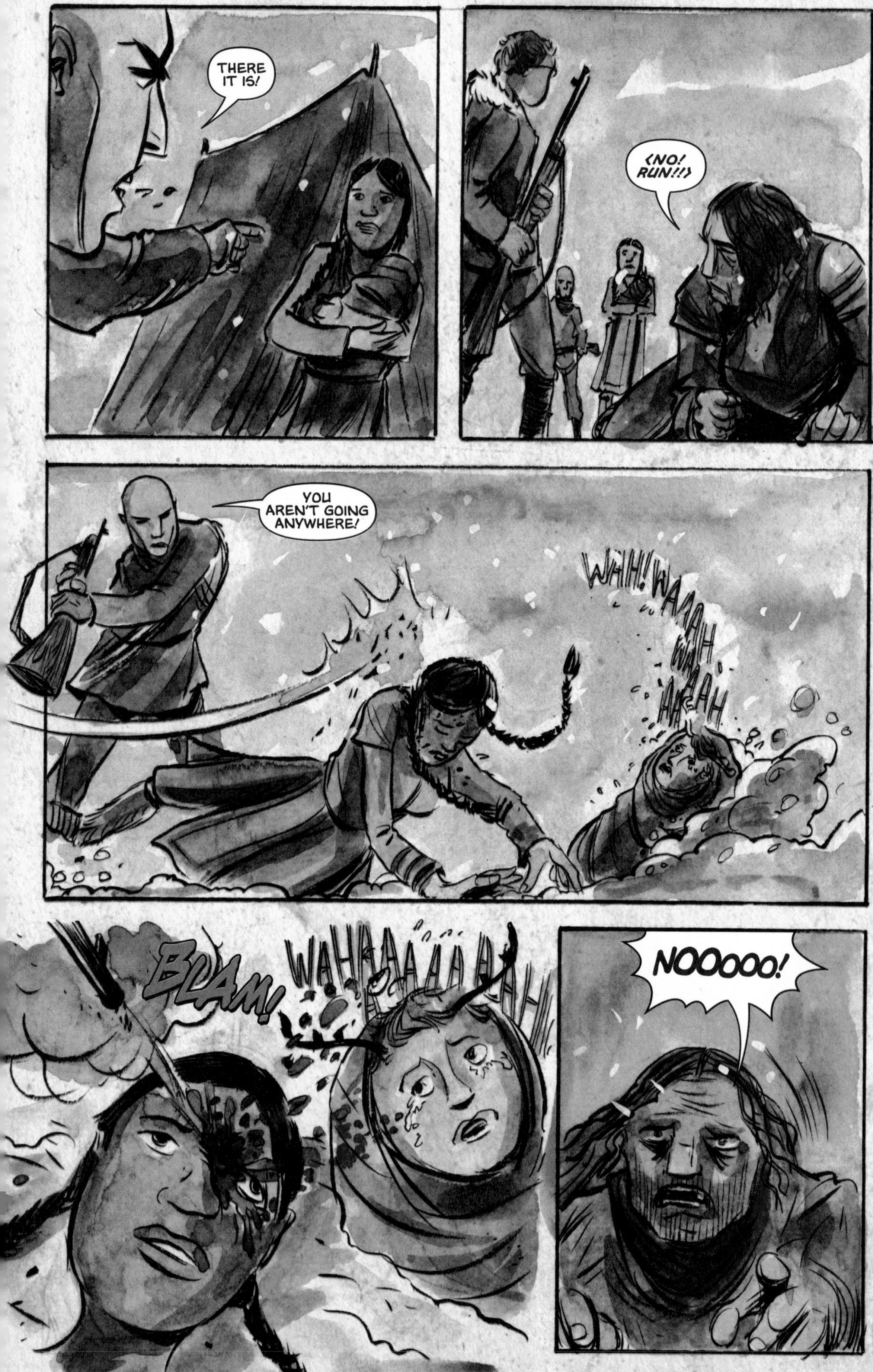
THERE IT IS!
‹NO! RUN!!!›
YOU AREN'T GOING ANYWHERE!
WAH! WAAAH WAAAH HAAAH.
BLAM!
WAHAAAAAAAH!
NOOOOO!

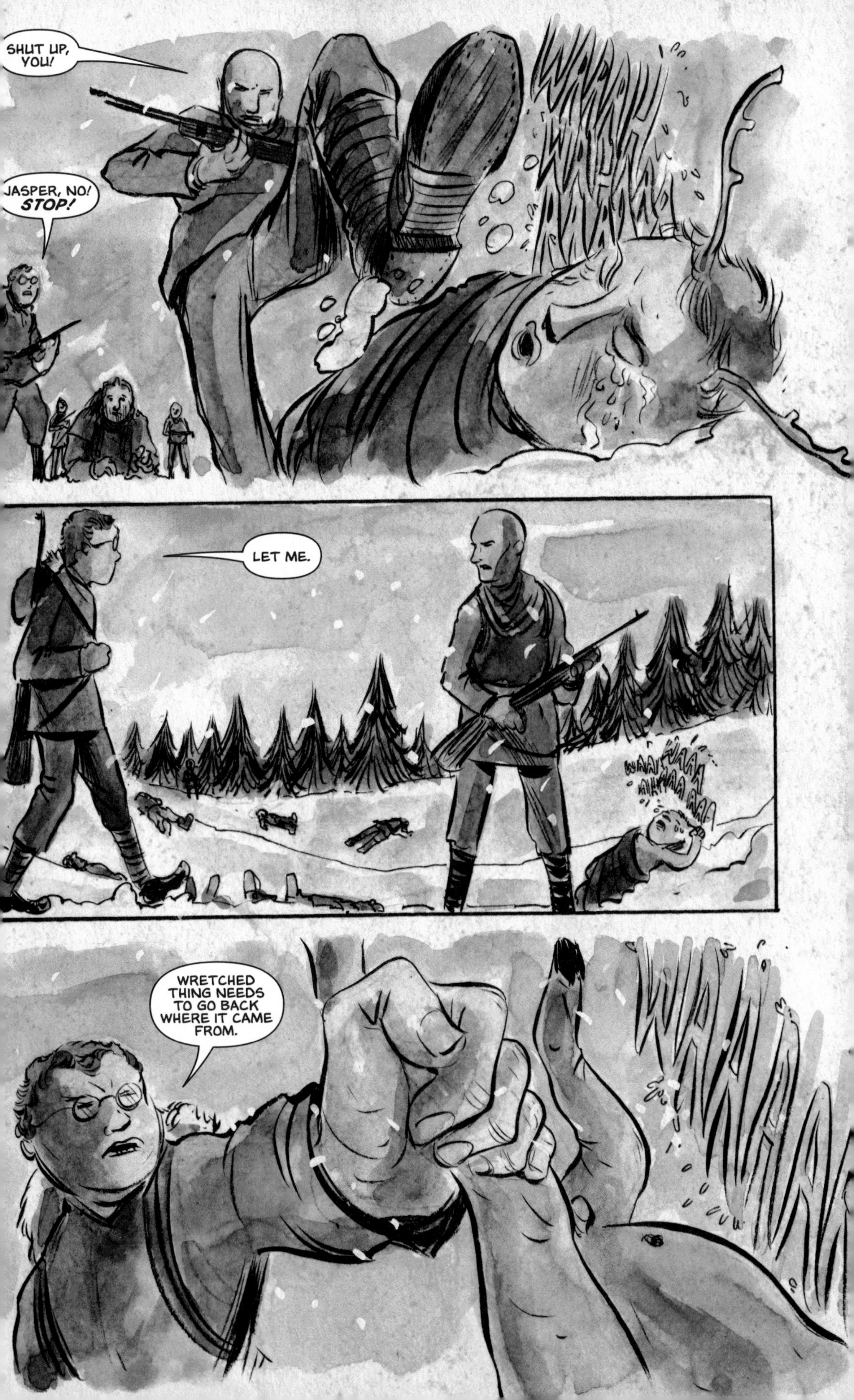
SHUT UP, YOU!
JASPER, NO! *STOP!*
LET ME.
WRETCHED THING NEEDS TO GO BACK WHERE IT CAME FROM.

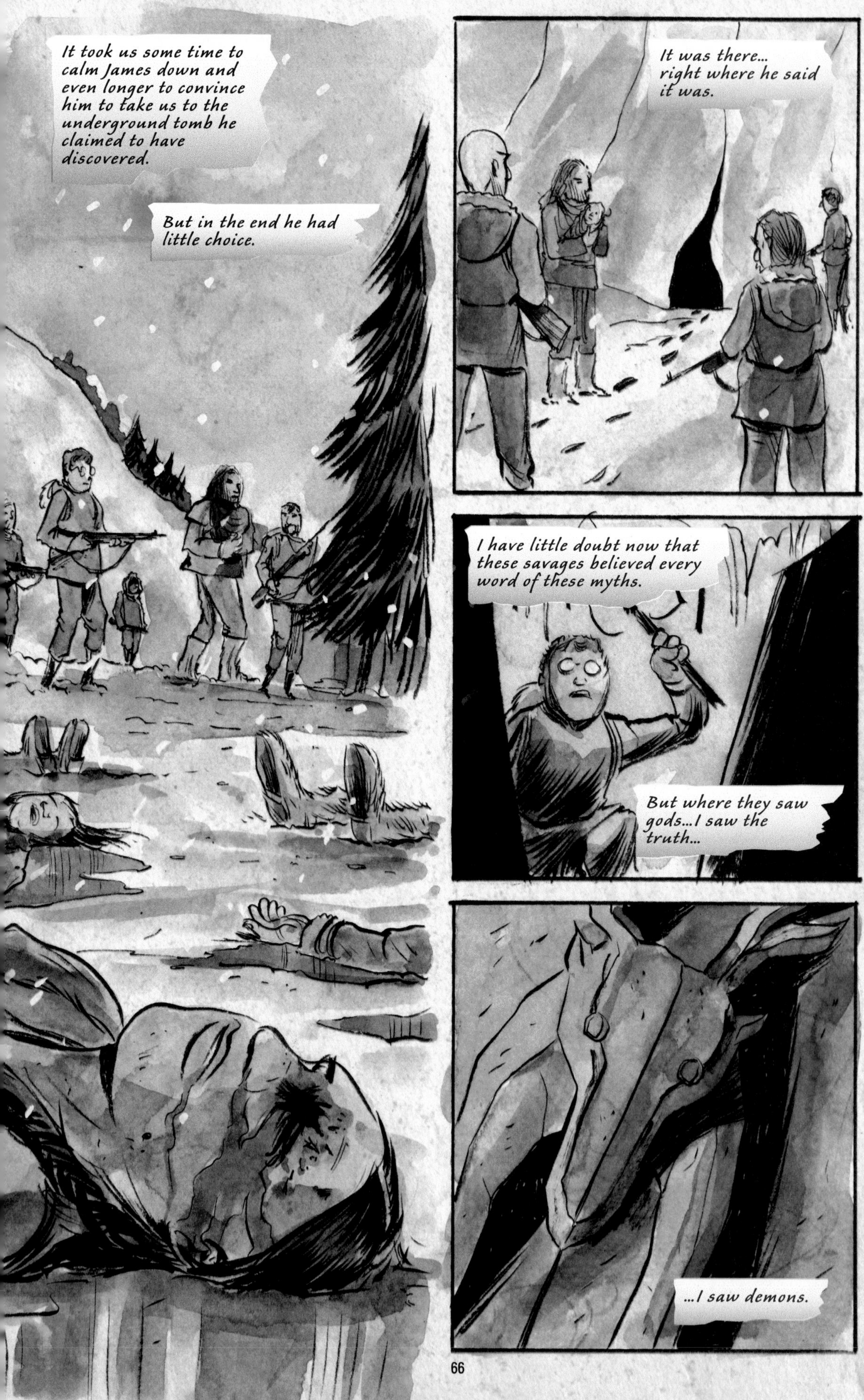
It took us some time to calm James down and even longer to convince him to take us to the underground tomb he claimed to have discovered.
But in the end he had little choice.
It was there... right where he said it was.
I have little doubt now that these savages believed every word of these myths.
But where they saw gods...I saw the truth...
...I saw demons.

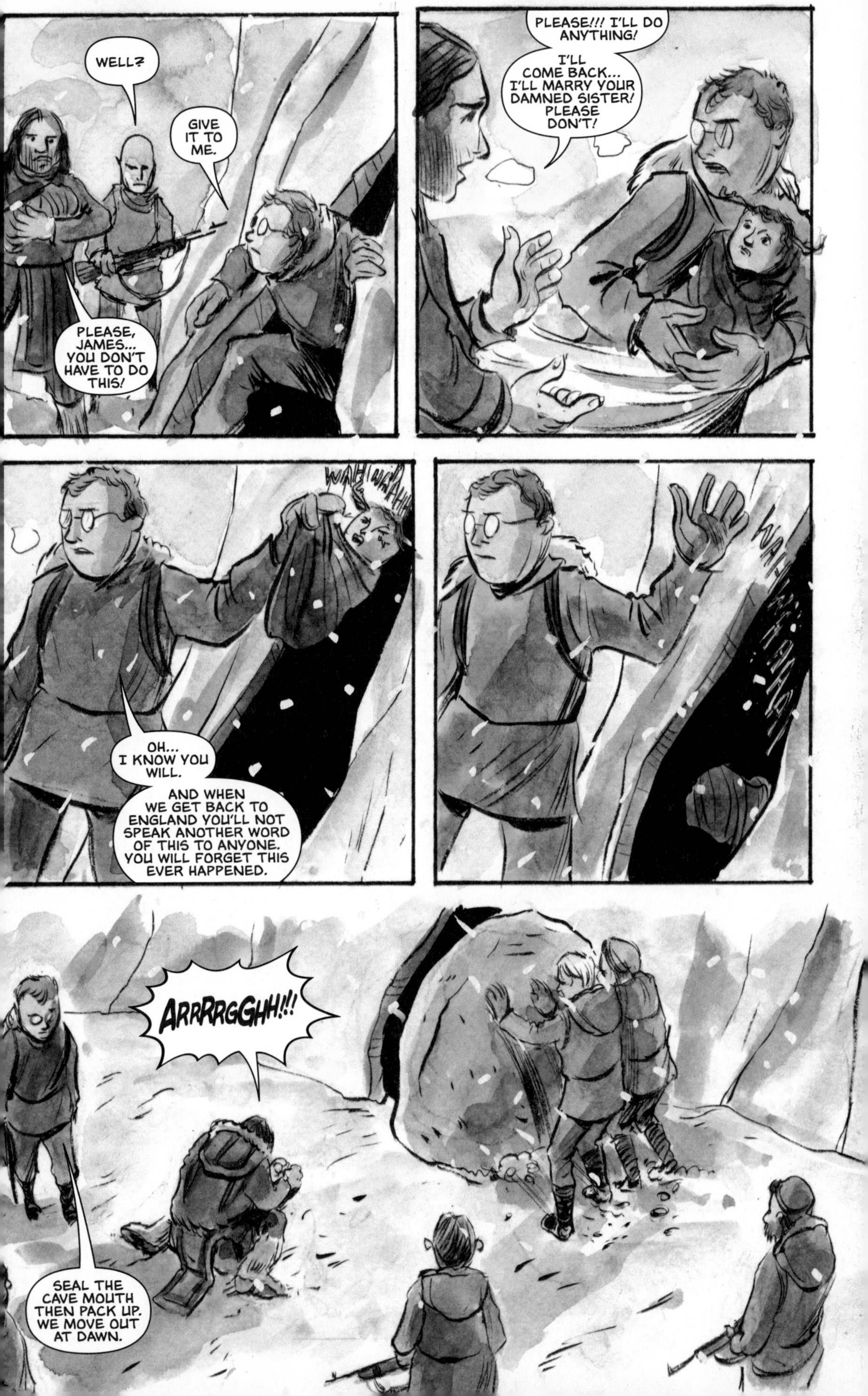
WELL?
GIVE IT TO ME.
PLEASE, JAMES... YOU DON'T HAVE TO DO THIS!
PLEASE!!! I'LL DO ANYTHING!
I'LL COME BACK... I'LL MARRY YOUR DAMNED SISTER! PLEASE DON'T!
OH... I KNOW YOU WILL.
AND WHEN WE GET BACK TO ENGLAND YOU'LL NOT SPEAK ANOTHER WORD OF THIS TO ANYONE. YOU WILL FORGET THIS EVER HAPPENED.
ARRRRGGHH!!!
SEAL THE CAVE MOUTH THEN PACK UP. WE MOVE OUT AT DAWN.

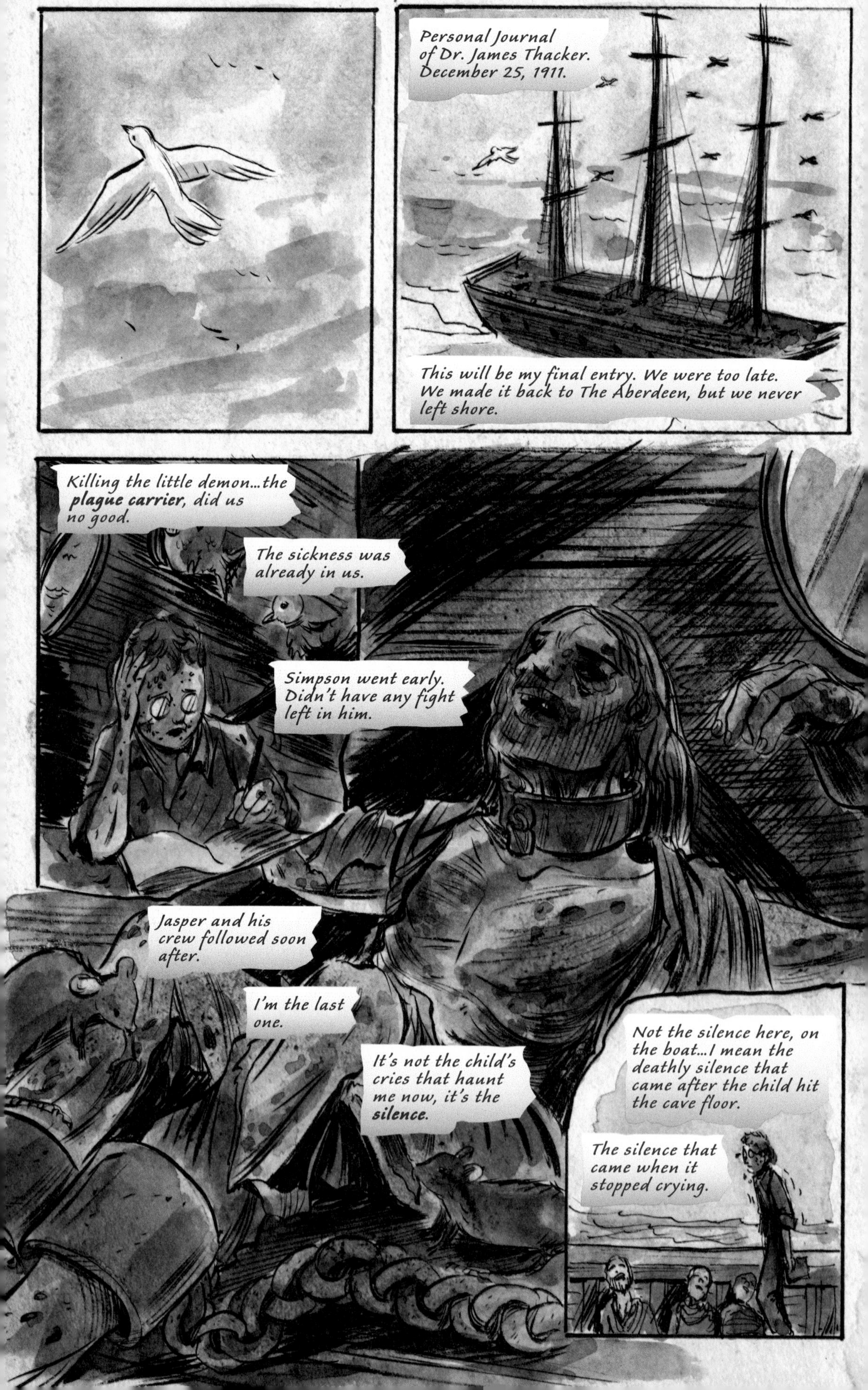

Personal Journal of Dr. James Thacker. December 25, 1911.
This will be my final entry. We were too late. We made it back to The Aberdeen, but we never left shore.
Killing the little demon...the **plague carrier**, did us no good.
The sickness was already in us.
Simpson went early. Didn't have any fight left in him.
Jasper and his crew followed soon after.
I'm the last one.
It's not the child's cries that haunt me now, it's the **silence**.
Not the silence here, on the boat...I mean the deathly silence that came after the child hit the cave floor.
The silence that came when it stopped crying.

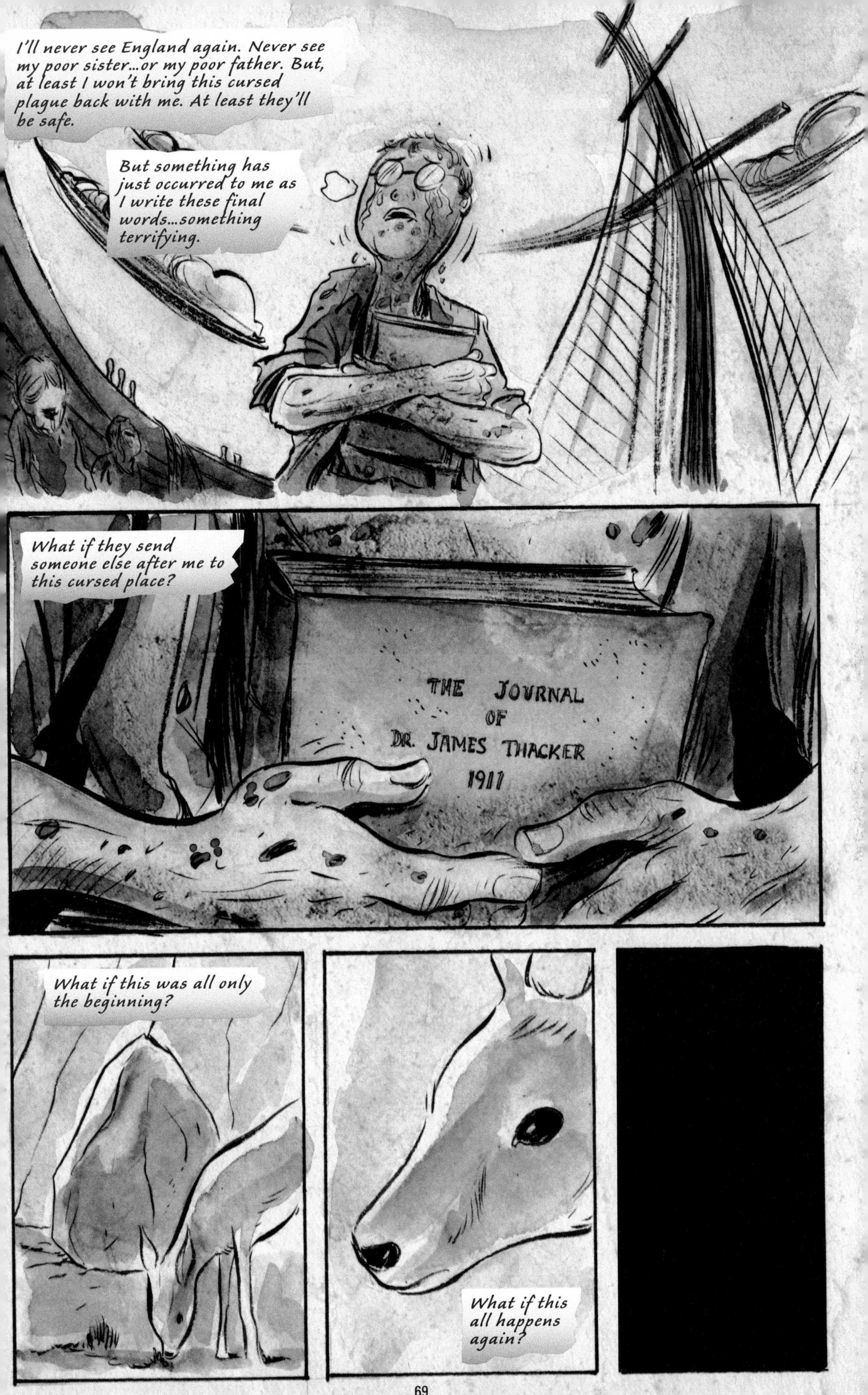
I'll never see England again. Never see my poor sister...or my poor father. But, at least I won't bring this cursed plague back with me. At least they'll be safe.
But something has just occurred to me as I write these final words...something terrifying.
What if they send someone else after me to this cursed place?
THE JOURNAL OF DR. JAMES THACKER 1911
What if this was all only the beginning?
What if this all happens again?

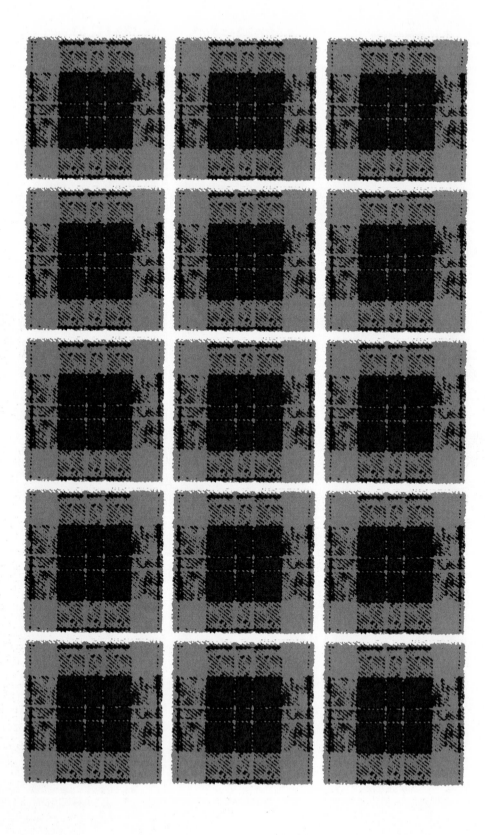

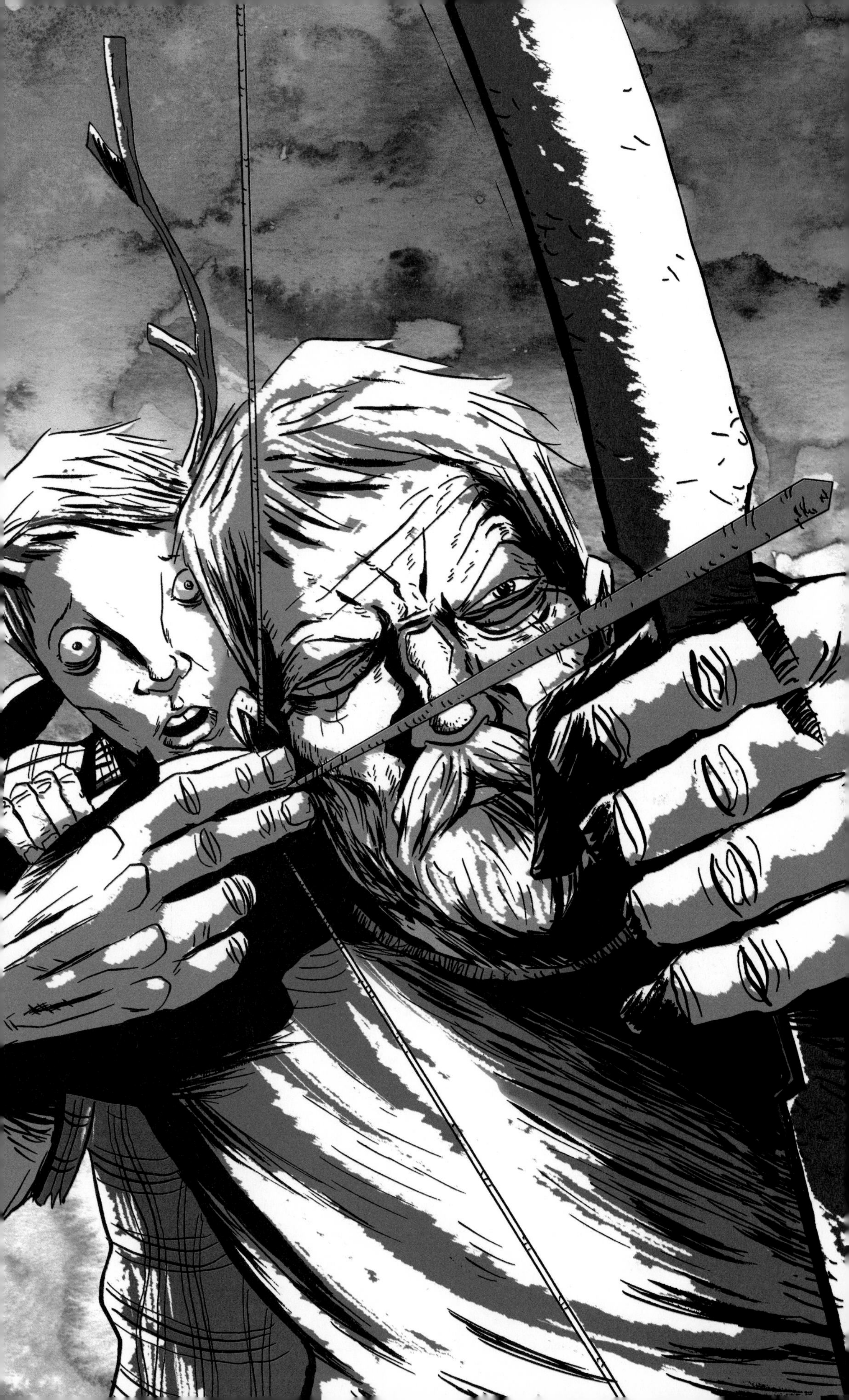

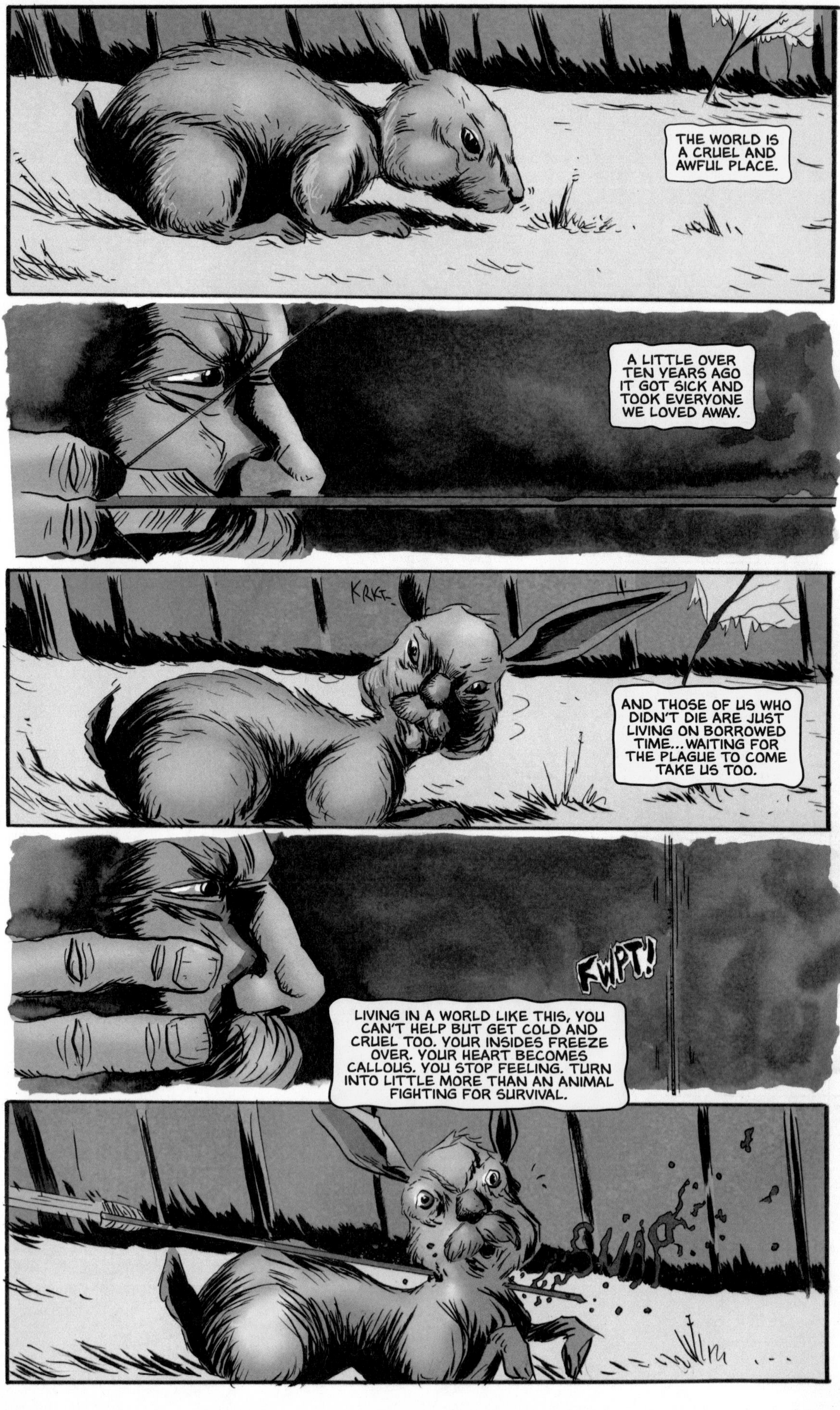
THE WORLD IS A CRUEL AND AWFUL PLACE.
A LITTLE OVER TEN YEARS AGO IT GOT SICK AND TOOK EVERYONE WE LOVED AWAY.
KRKT
AND THOSE OF US WHO DIDN'T DIE ARE JUST LIVING ON BORROWED TIME... WAITING FOR THE PLAGUE TO COME TAKE US TOO.
FWPT!
LIVING IN A WORLD LIKE THIS, YOU CAN'T HELP BUT GET COLD AND CRUEL TOO. YOUR INSIDES FREEZE OVER. YOUR HEART BECOMES CALLOUS. YOU STOP FEELING. TURN INTO LITTLE MORE THAN AN ANIMAL FIGHTING FOR SURVIVAL.
SNAP

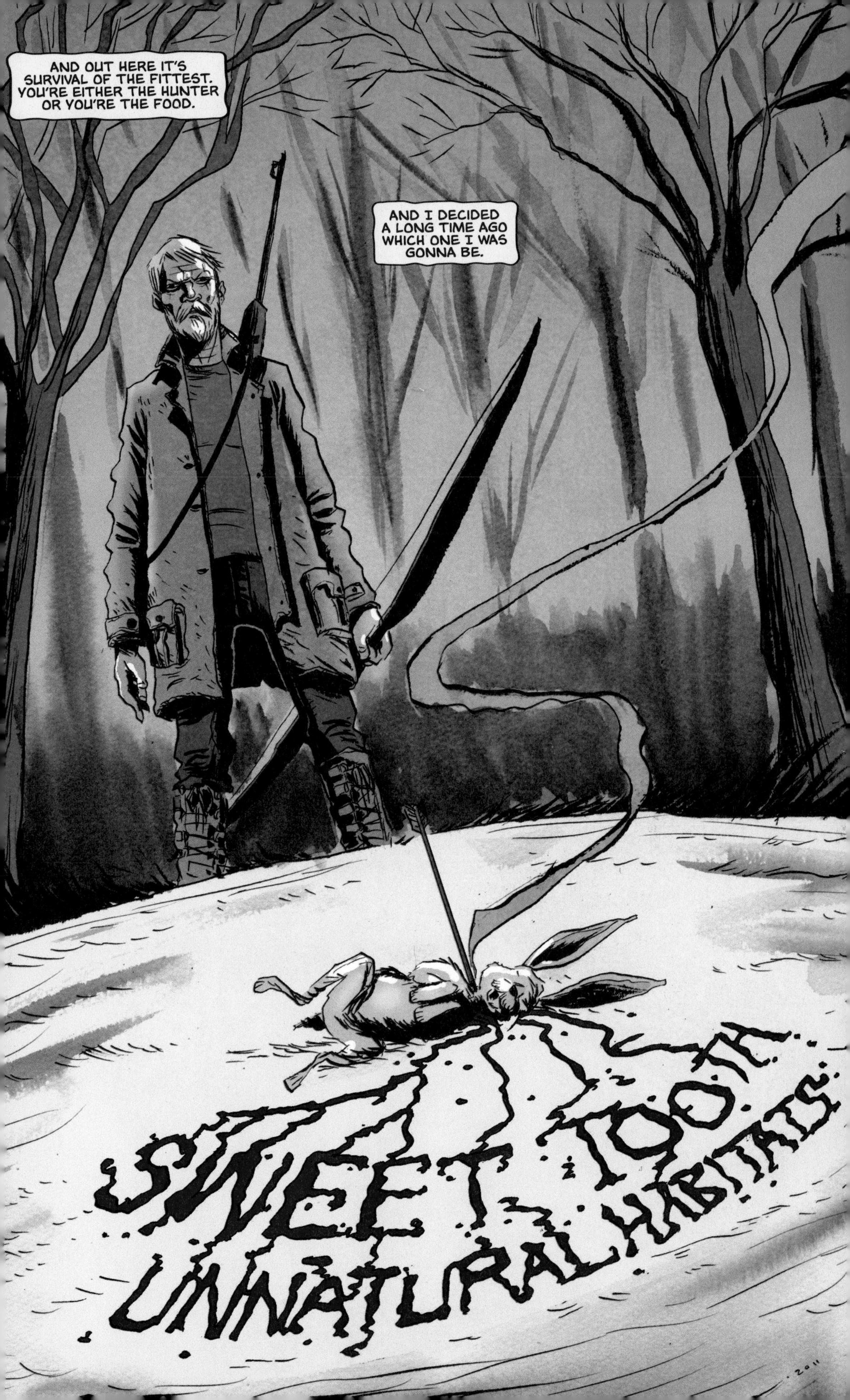
AND OUT HERE IT'S SURVIVAL OF THE FITTEST. YOU'RE EITHER THE HUNTER OR YOU'RE THE FOOD.
AND I DECIDED A LONG TIME AGO WHICH ONE I WAS GONNA BE.
SWEET TOOTH
UNNATURAL HABITATS

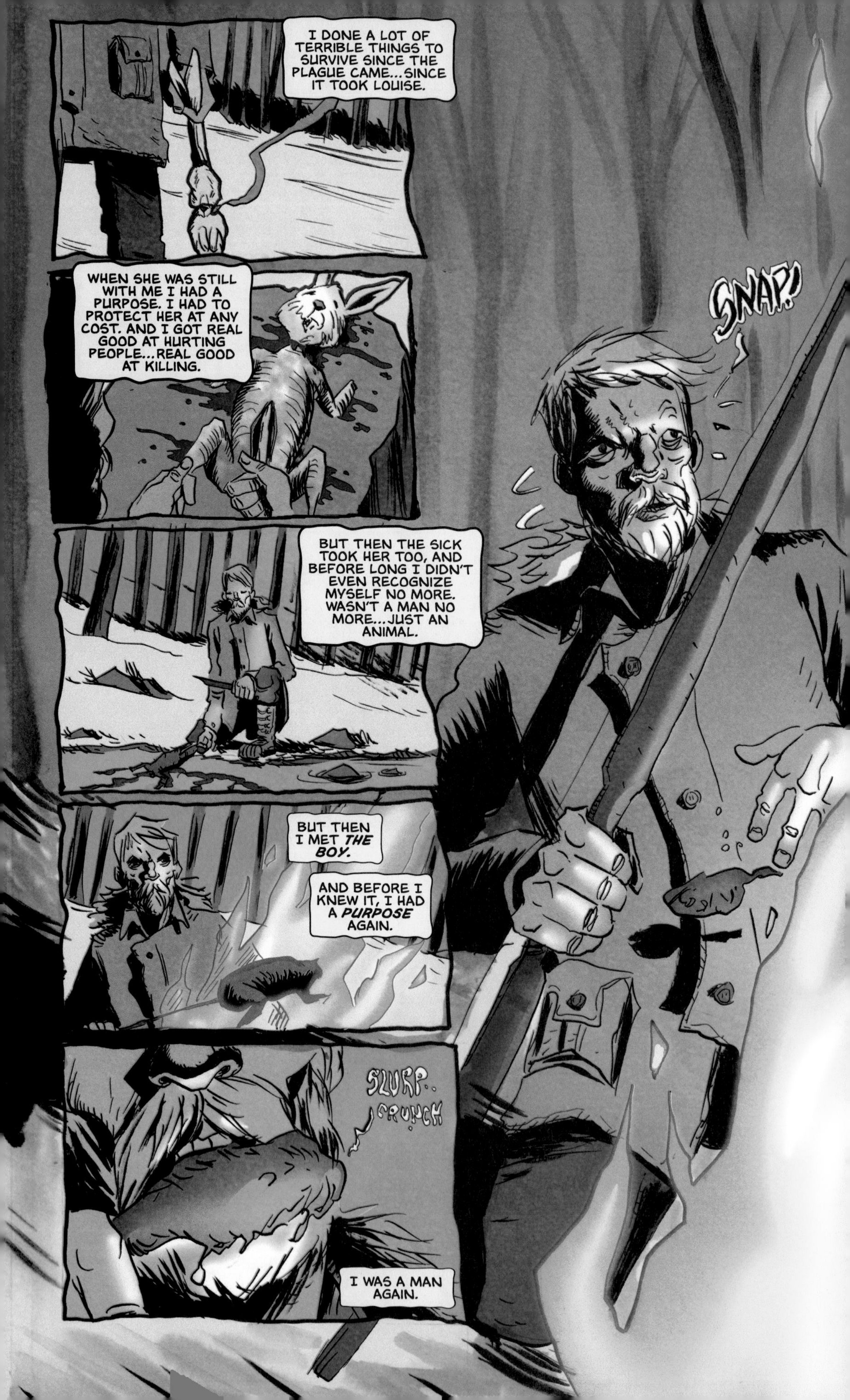
I DONE A LOT OF TERRIBLE THINGS TO SURVIVE SINCE THE PLAGUE CAME...SINCE IT TOOK LOUISE.
WHEN SHE WAS STILL WITH ME I HAD A PURPOSE. I HAD TO PROTECT HER AT ANY COST. AND I GOT REAL GOOD AT HURTING PEOPLE...REAL GOOD AT KILLING.
SNAP!
BUT THEN THE SICK TOOK HER TOO, AND BEFORE LONG I DIDN'T EVEN RECOGNIZE MYSELF NO MORE. WASN'T A MAN NO MORE...JUST AN ANIMAL.
BUT THEN I MET *THE BOY.*
AND BEFORE I KNEW IT, I HAD A *PURPOSE* AGAIN.
SLURP..
CRUNCH
I WAS A MAN AGAIN.

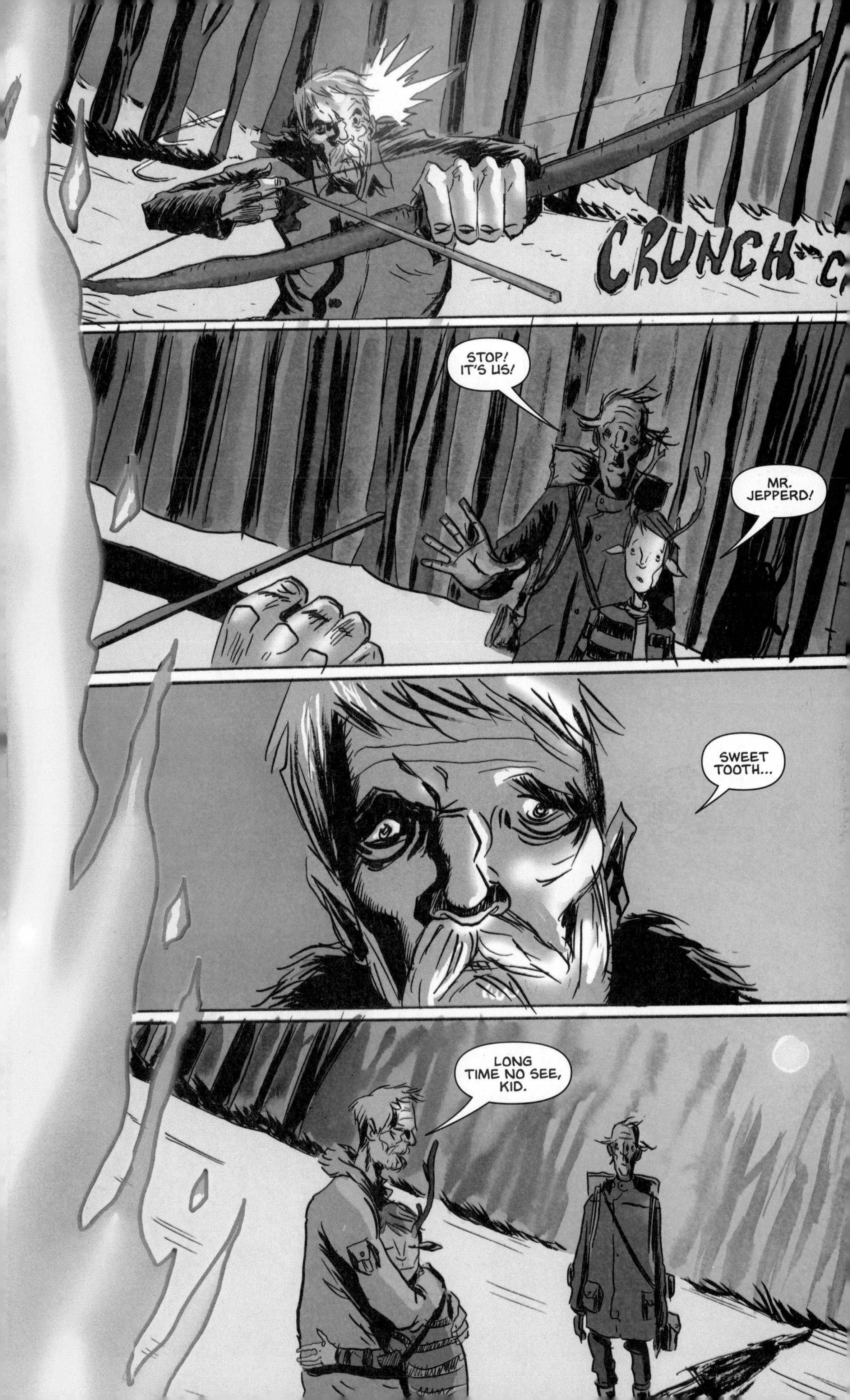
CRUNCH-C
STOP! IT'S US!
MR. JEPPERD!
SWEET TOOTH...
LONG TIME NO SEE, KID.

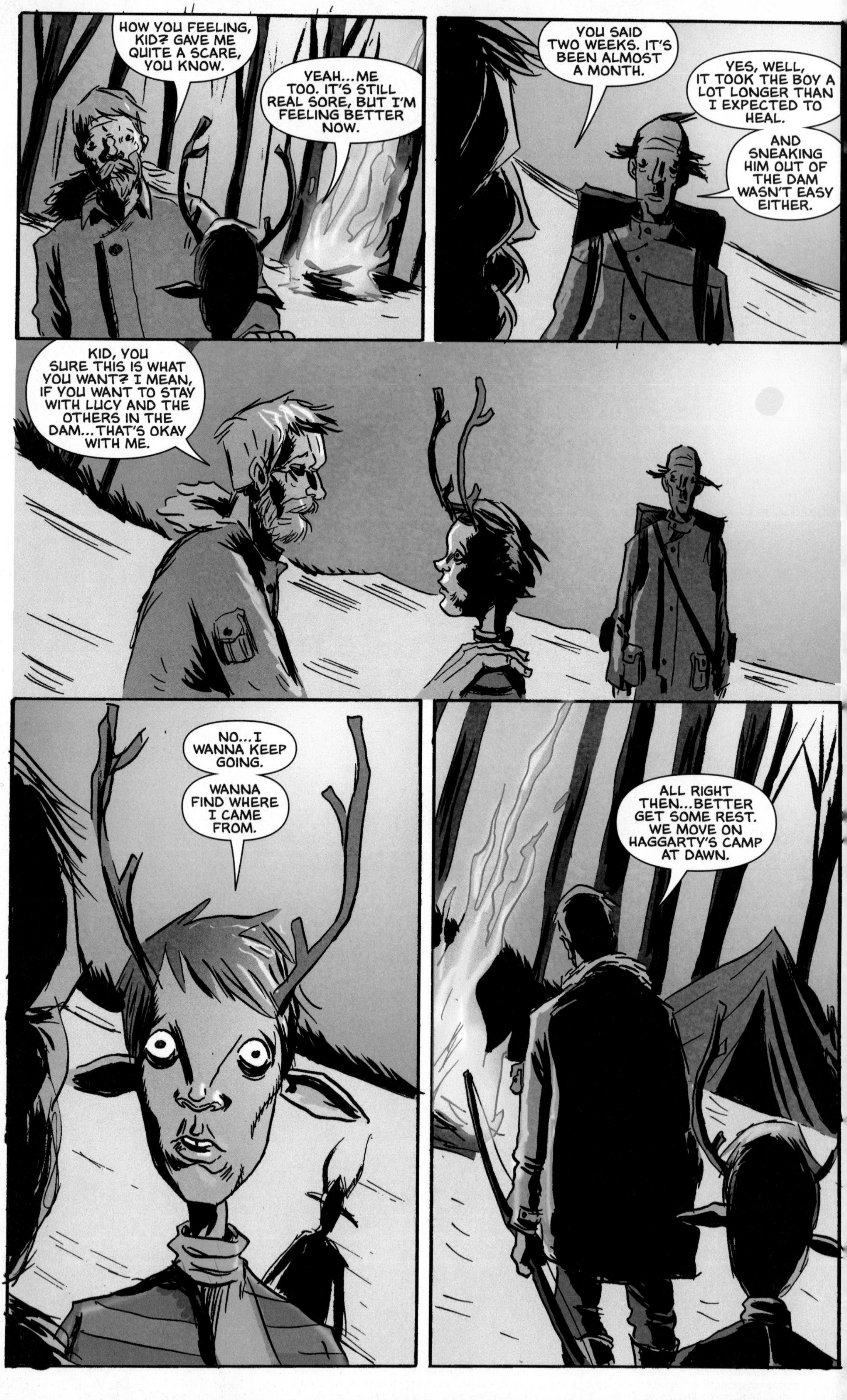
HOW YOU FEELING, KID? GAVE ME QUITE A SCARE, YOU KNOW.
YEAH...ME TOO. IT'S STILL REAL SORE, BUT I'M FEELING BETTER NOW.
YOU SAID TWO WEEKS. IT'S BEEN ALMOST A MONTH.
YES, WELL, IT TOOK THE BOY A LOT LONGER THAN I EXPECTED TO HEAL.
AND SNEAKING HIM OUT OF THE DAM WASN'T EASY EITHER.
KID, YOU SURE THIS IS WHAT YOU WANT? I MEAN, IF YOU WANT TO STAY WITH LUCY AND THE OTHERS IN THE DAM...THAT'S OKAY WITH ME.
NO...I WANNA KEEP GOING.
WANNA FIND WHERE I CAME FROM.
ALL RIGHT THEN...BETTER GET SOME REST. WE MOVE ON HAGGARTY'S CAMP AT DAWN.

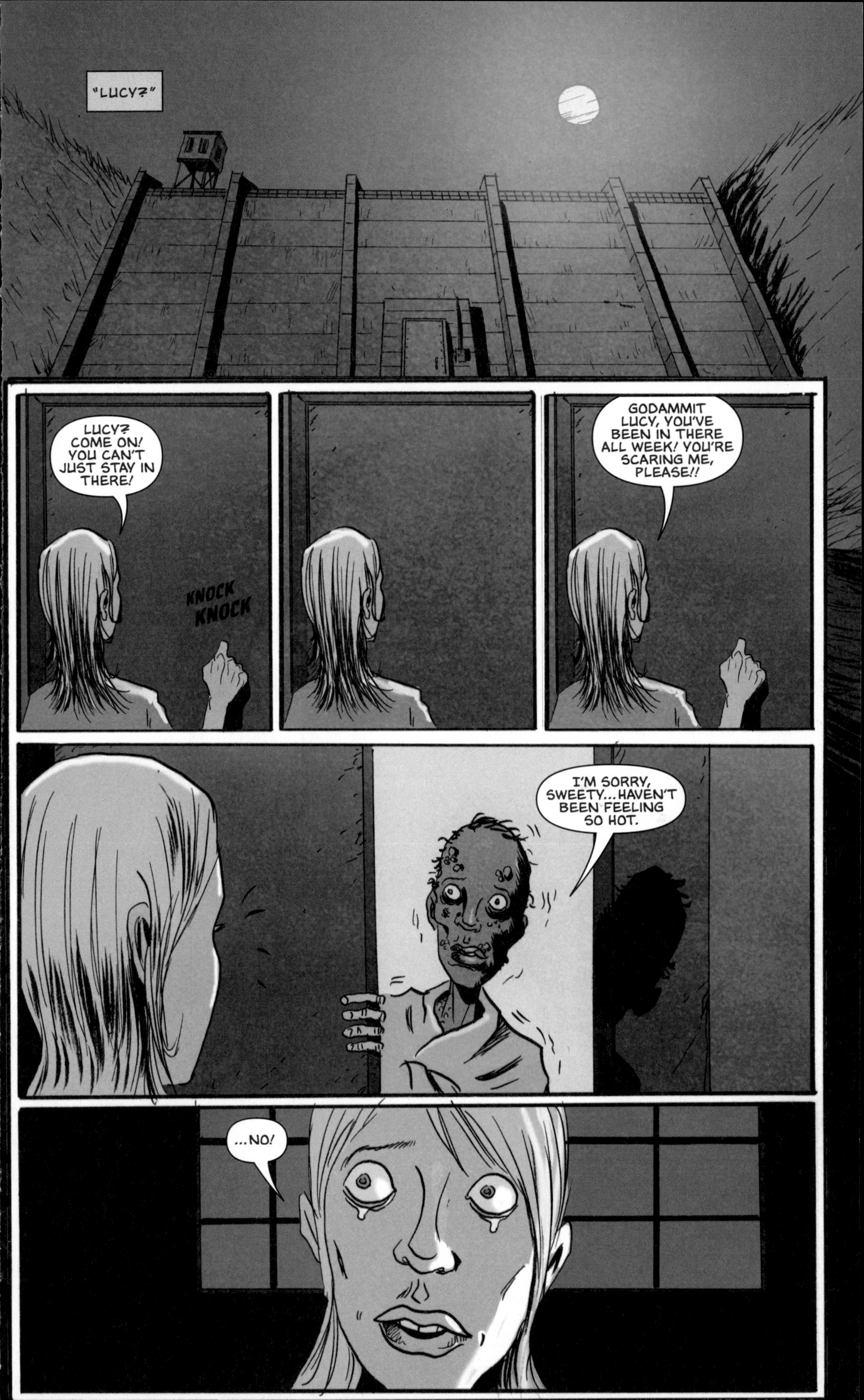
"LUCY?"
LUCY? COME ON! YOU CAN'T JUST STAY IN THERE!
KNOCK KNOCK
GODAMMIT LUCY, YOU'VE BEEN IN THERE ALL WEEK! YOU'RE SCARING ME, PLEASE!!
I'M SORRY, SWEETY... HAVEN'T BEEN FEELING SO HOT.
...NO!

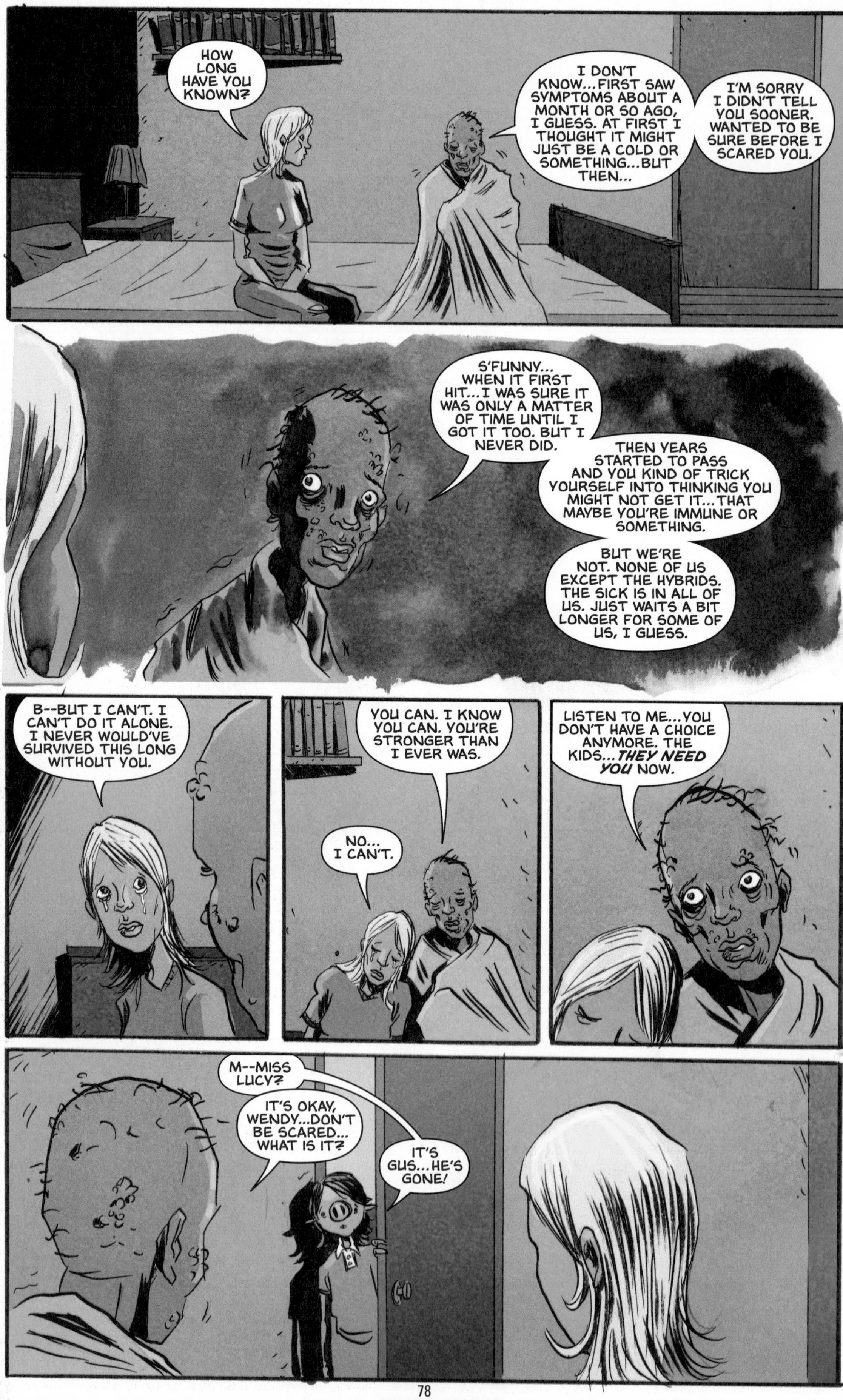
HOW LONG HAVE YOU KNOWN?
I DON'T KNOW...FIRST SAW SYMPTOMS ABOUT A MONTH OR SO AGO, I GUESS. AT FIRST I THOUGHT IT MIGHT JUST BE A COLD OR SOMETHING...BUT THEN...
I'M SORRY I DIDN'T TELL YOU SOONER. WANTED TO BE SURE BEFORE I SCARED YOU.
S'FUNNY... WHEN IT FIRST HIT...I WAS SURE IT WAS ONLY A MATTER OF TIME UNTIL I GOT IT TOO. BUT I NEVER DID.
THEN YEARS STARTED TO PASS AND YOU KIND OF TRICK YOURSELF INTO THINKING YOU MIGHT NOT GET IT...THAT MAYBE YOU'RE IMMUNE OR SOMETHING.
BUT WE'RE NOT. NONE OF US EXCEPT THE HYBRIDS. THE SICK IS IN ALL OF US. JUST WAITS A BIT LONGER FOR SOME OF US, I GUESS.
B--BUT I CAN'T. I CAN'T DO IT ALONE. I NEVER WOULD'VE SURVIVED THIS LONG WITHOUT YOU.
YOU CAN. I KNOW YOU CAN. YOU'RE STRONGER THAN I EVER WAS.
NO... I CAN'T.
LISTEN TO ME...YOU DON'T HAVE A CHOICE ANYMORE. THE KIDS...*THEY NEED YOU* NOW.
M--MISS LUCY?
IT'S OKAY, WENDY...DON'T BE SCARED... WHAT IS IT?
IT'S GUS...HE'S GONE!

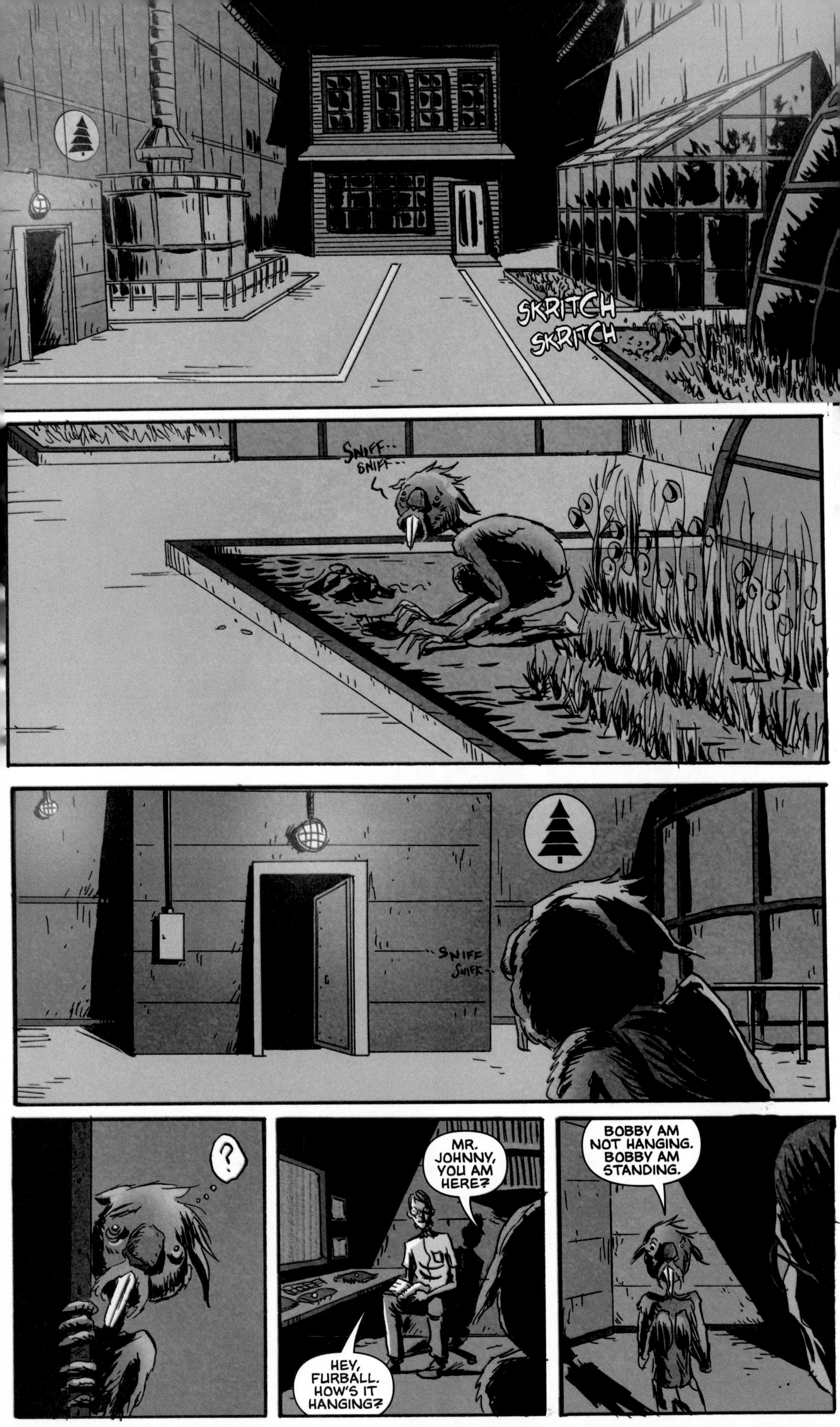
SKRITCH
SKRITCH
SNIFF..
SNIFF..
SNIFF
SNIFF..
?
MR. JOHNNY, YOU AM HERE?
HEY, FURBALL. HOW'S IT HANGING?
BOBBY AM NOT HANGING. BOBBY AM STANDING.

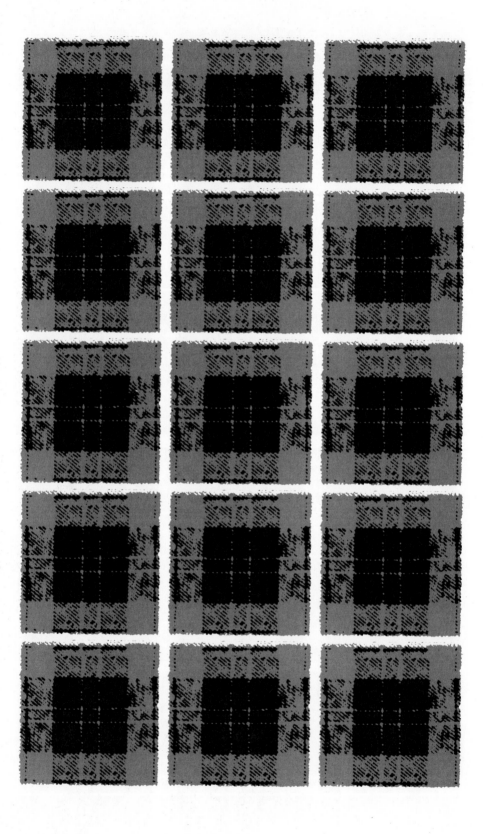

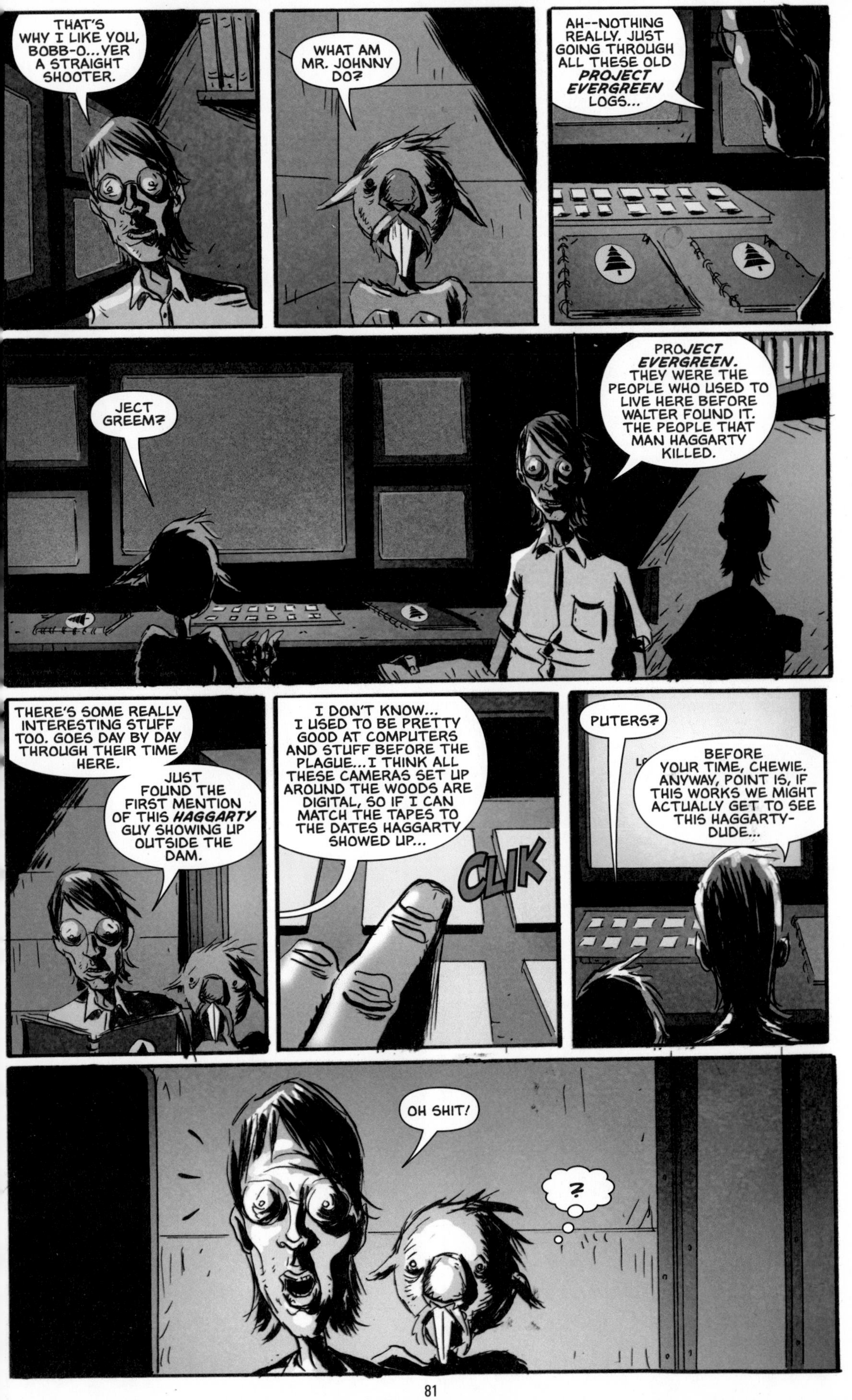
THAT'S WHY I LIKE YOU, BOBB-O...YER A STRAIGHT SHOOTER.
WHAT AM MR. JOHNNY DO?
AH--NOTHING REALLY. JUST GOING THROUGH ALL THESE OLD *PROJECT EVERGREEN* LOGS...
JECT GREEM?
PROJECT *EVERGREEN.* THEY WERE THE PEOPLE WHO USED TO LIVE HERE BEFORE WALTER FOUND IT. THE PEOPLE THAT MAN HAGGARTY KILLED.
THERE'S SOME REALLY INTERESTING STUFF TOO. GOES DAY BY DAY THROUGH THEIR TIME HERE.
JUST FOUND THE FIRST MENTION OF THIS *HAGGARTY* GUY SHOWING UP OUTSIDE THE DAM.
I DON'T KNOW... I USED TO BE PRETTY GOOD AT COMPUTERS AND STUFF BEFORE THE PLAGUE...I THINK ALL THESE CAMERAS SET UP AROUND THE WOODS ARE DIGITAL, SO IF I CAN MATCH THE TAPES TO THE DATES HAGGARTY SHOWED UP...
CLIK
PUTERS?
BEFORE YOUR TIME, CHEWIE. ANYWAY, POINT IS, IF THIS WORKS WE MIGHT ACTUALLY GET TO SEE THIS HAGGARTY-DUDE...
OH SHIT!
?

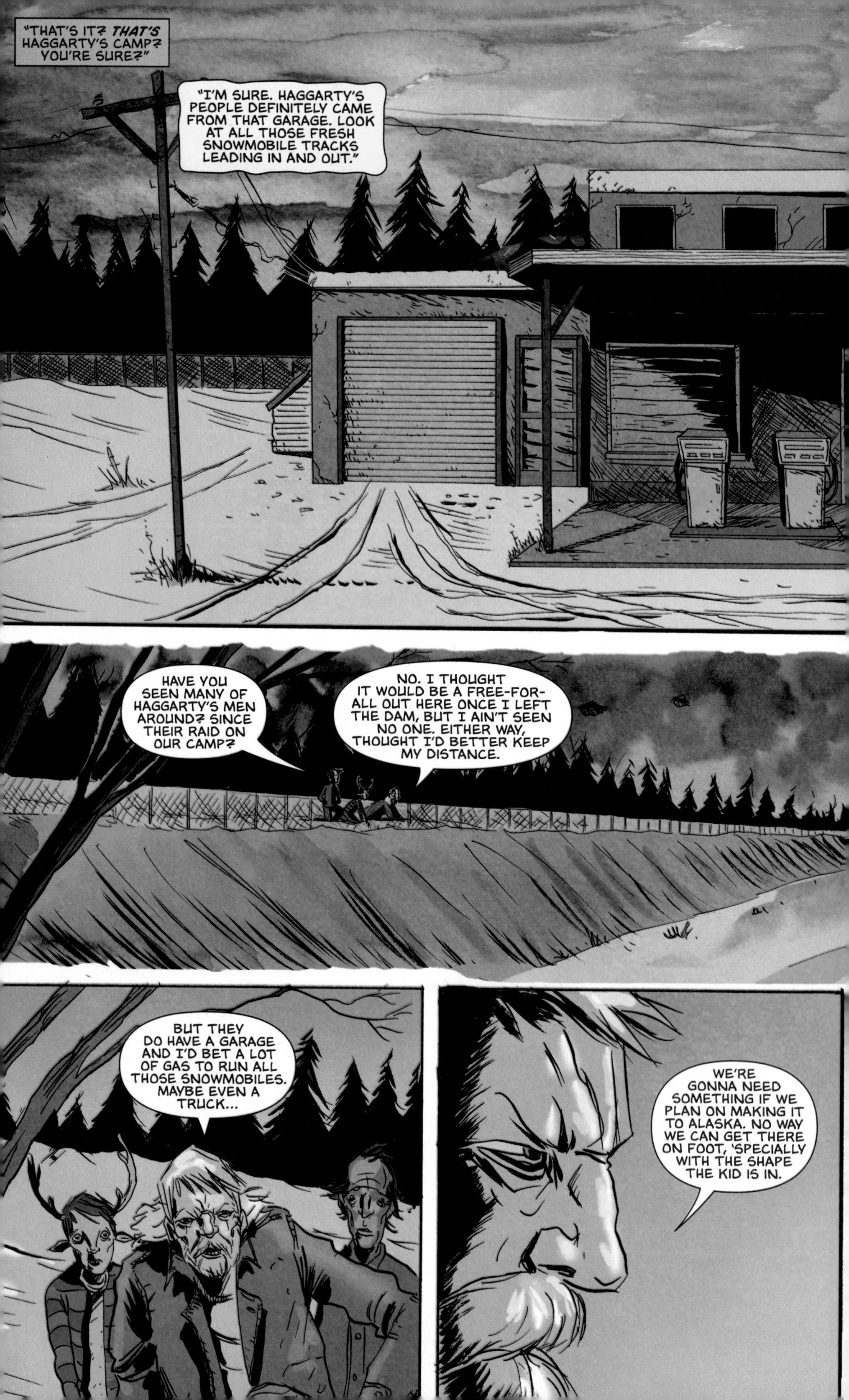
"THAT'S IT? THAT'S HAGGARTY'S CAMP? YOU'RE SURE?"
"I'M SURE. HAGGARTY'S PEOPLE DEFINITELY CAME FROM THAT GARAGE. LOOK AT ALL THOSE FRESH SNOWMOBILE TRACKS LEADING IN AND OUT."
HAVE YOU SEEN MANY OF HAGGARTY'S MEN AROUND? SINCE THEIR RAID ON OUR CAMP?
NO. I THOUGHT IT WOULD BE A FREE-FOR-ALL OUT HERE ONCE I LEFT THE DAM, BUT I AIN'T SEEN NO ONE. EITHER WAY, THOUGHT I'D BETTER KEEP MY DISTANCE.
BUT THEY DO HAVE A GARAGE AND I'D BET A LOT OF GAS TO RUN ALL THOSE SNOWMOBILES. MAYBE EVEN A TRUCK...
WE'RE GONNA NEED SOMETHING IF WE PLAN ON MAKING IT TO ALASKA. NO WAY WE CAN GET THERE ON FOOT, 'SPECIALLY WITH THE SHAPE THE KID IS IN.

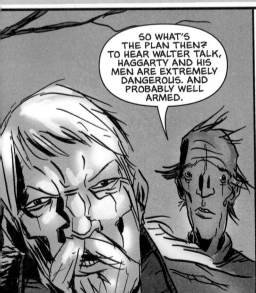

SO WHAT'S THE PLAN THEN? TO HEAR WALTER TALK, HAGGARTY AND HIS MEN ARE EXTREMELY DANGEROUS. AND PROBABLY WELL ARMED.

YEAH...WELL, WE DON'T HAVE A WHOLE LOT OF OPTIONS. I'M GOING IN, IF I'M LUCKY I MIGHT BE ABLE TO SNEAK INTO THAT GARAGE AND TAKE WHAT WE NEED.

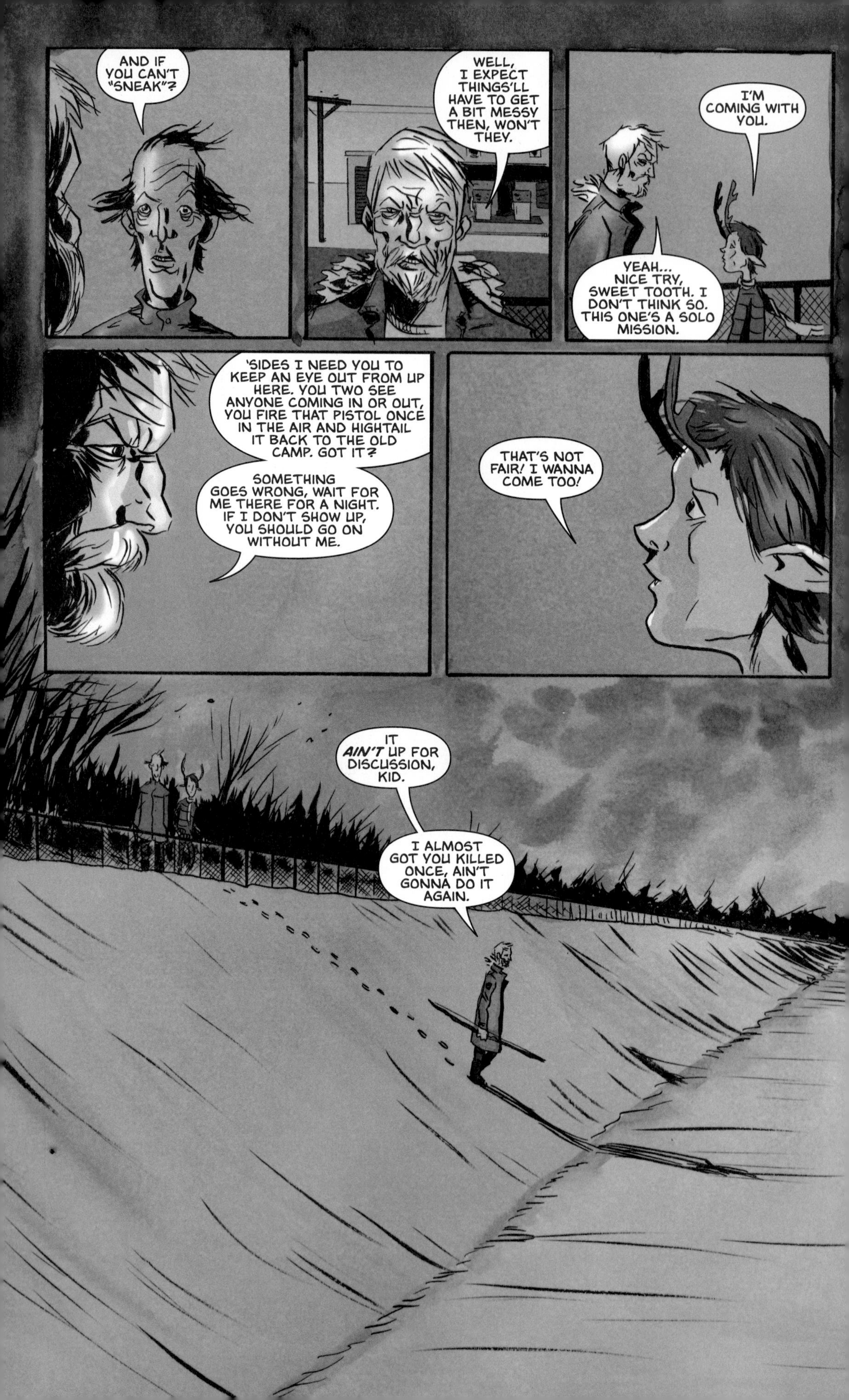
AND IF YOU CAN'T "SNEAK"?
WELL, I EXPECT THINGS'LL HAVE TO GET A BIT MESSY THEN, WON'T THEY.
I'M COMING WITH YOU.
YEAH... NICE TRY, SWEET TOOTH. I DON'T THINK SO. THIS ONE'S A SOLO MISSION.
'SIDES I NEED YOU TO KEEP AN EYE OUT FROM UP HERE. YOU TWO SEE ANYONE COMING IN OR OUT, YOU FIRE THAT PISTOL ONCE IN THE AIR AND HIGHTAIL IT BACK TO THE OLD CAMP. GOT IT?
SOMETHING GOES WRONG, WAIT FOR ME THERE FOR A NIGHT. IF I DON'T SHOW UP, YOU SHOULD GO ON WITHOUT ME.
THAT'S NOT FAIR! I WANNA COME TOO!
IT *AIN'T* UP FOR DISCUSSION, KID.
I ALMOST GOT YOU KILLED ONCE, AIN'T GONNA DO IT AGAIN.

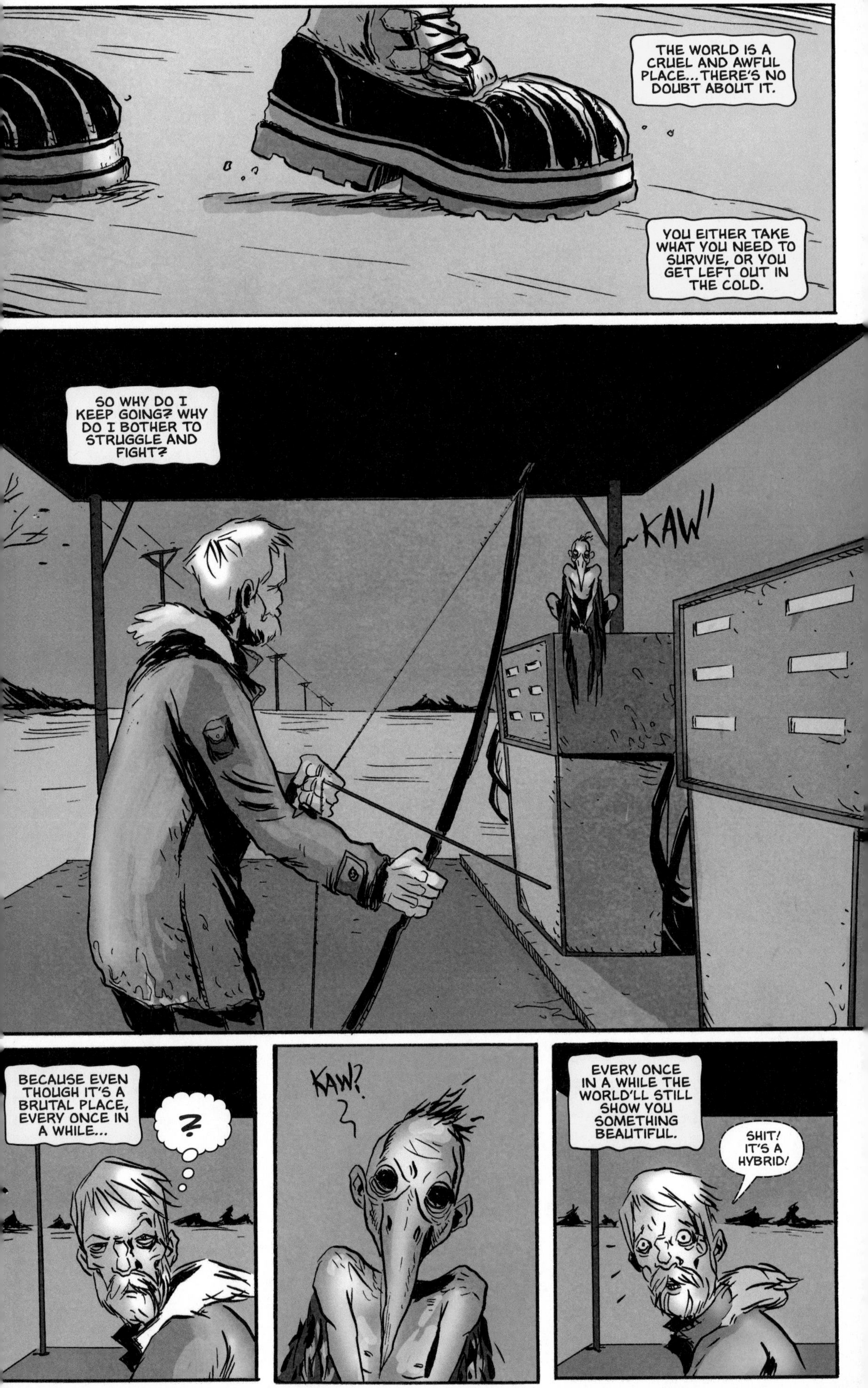
THE WORLD IS A CRUEL AND AWFUL PLACE...THERE'S NO DOUBT ABOUT IT.
YOU EITHER TAKE WHAT YOU NEED TO SURVIVE, OR YOU GET LEFT OUT IN THE COLD.
SO WHY DO I KEEP GOING? WHY DO I BOTHER TO STRUGGLE AND FIGHT?
KAW!
BECAUSE EVEN THOUGH IT'S A BRUTAL PLACE, EVERY ONCE IN A WHILE...
?
KAW?
EVERY ONCE IN A WHILE THE WORLD'LL STILL SHOW YOU SOMETHING BEAUTIFUL.
SHIT! IT'S A HYBRID!

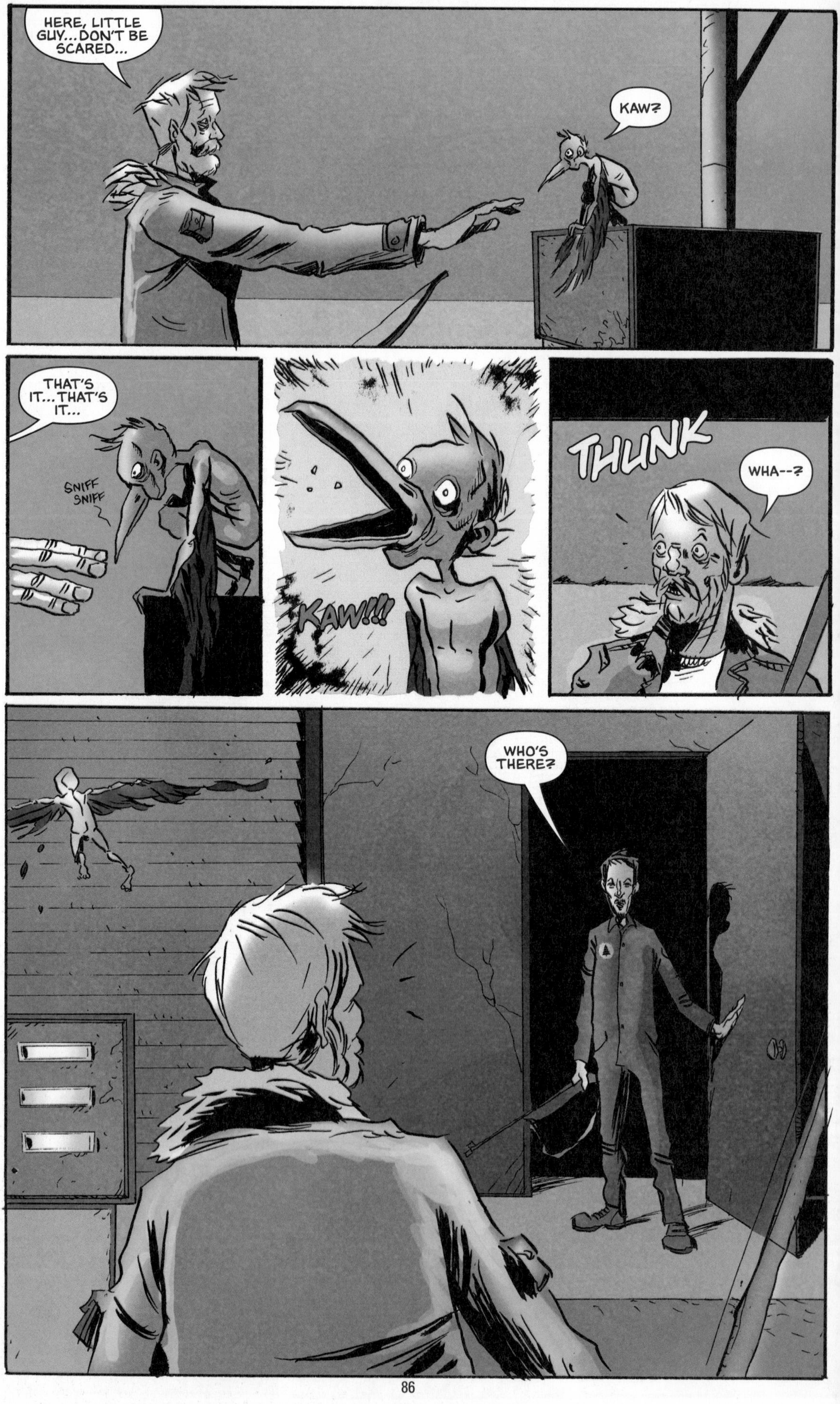

HERE, LITTLE GUY...DON'T BE SCARED...
KAW?
THAT'S IT...THAT'S IT...
SNIFF SNIFF
KAW!!!
THUNK
WHA--?
WHO'S THERE?

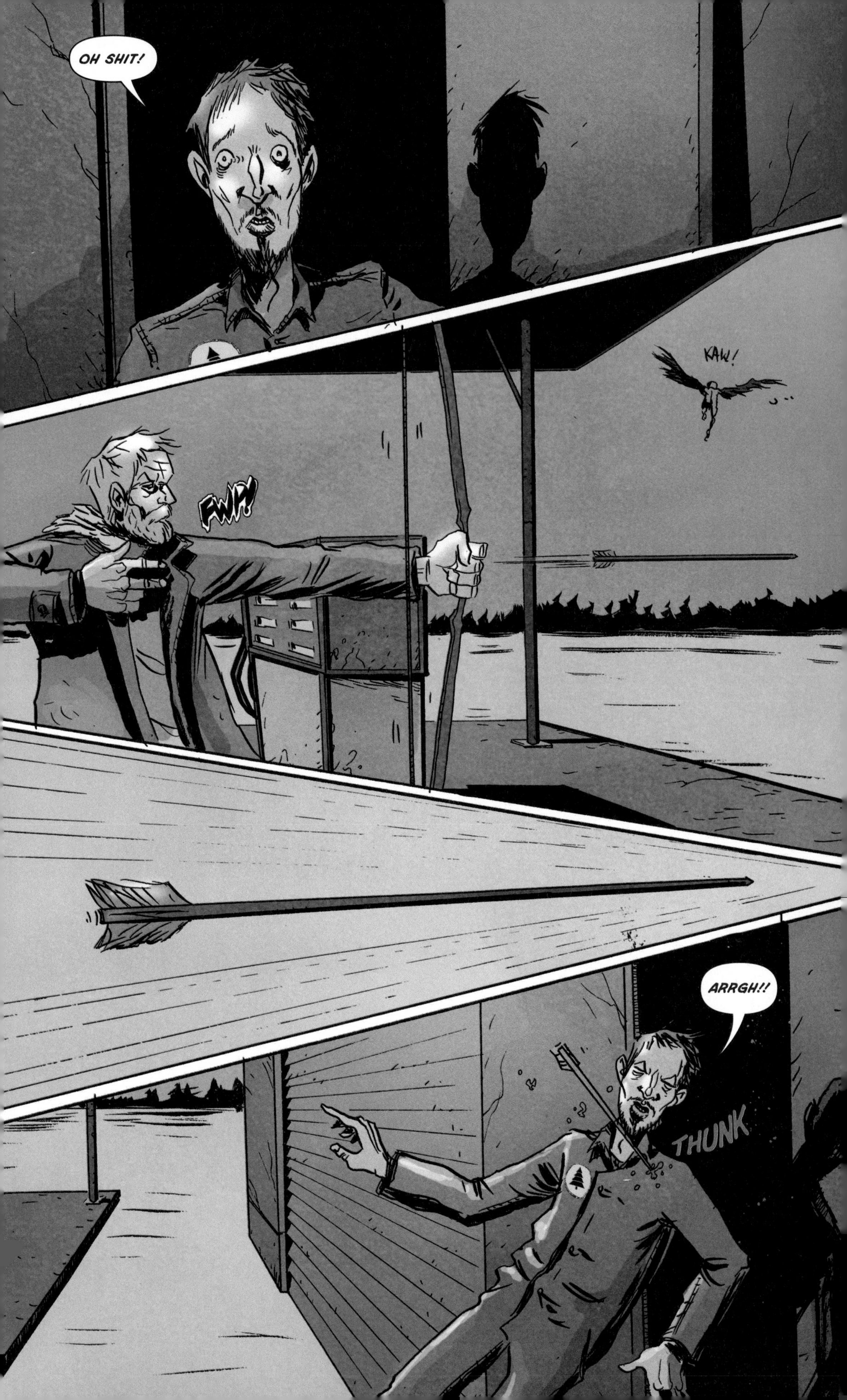
OH SHIT!
KAW!
FWIP!
ARRGH!!
THUNK

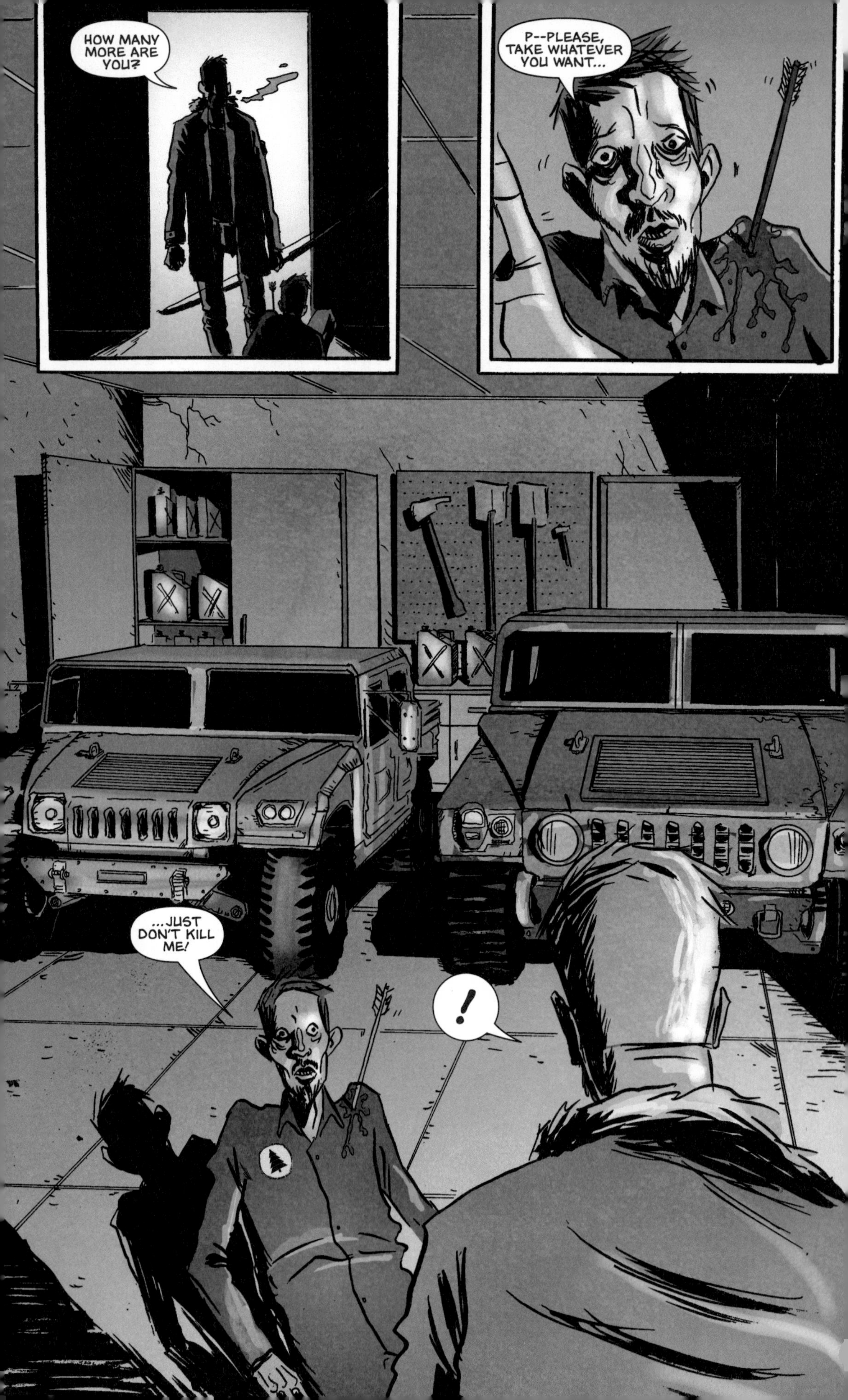
HOW MANY MORE ARE YOU?
P--PLEASE, TAKE WHATEVER YOU WANT...
...JUST DON'T KILL ME!
!

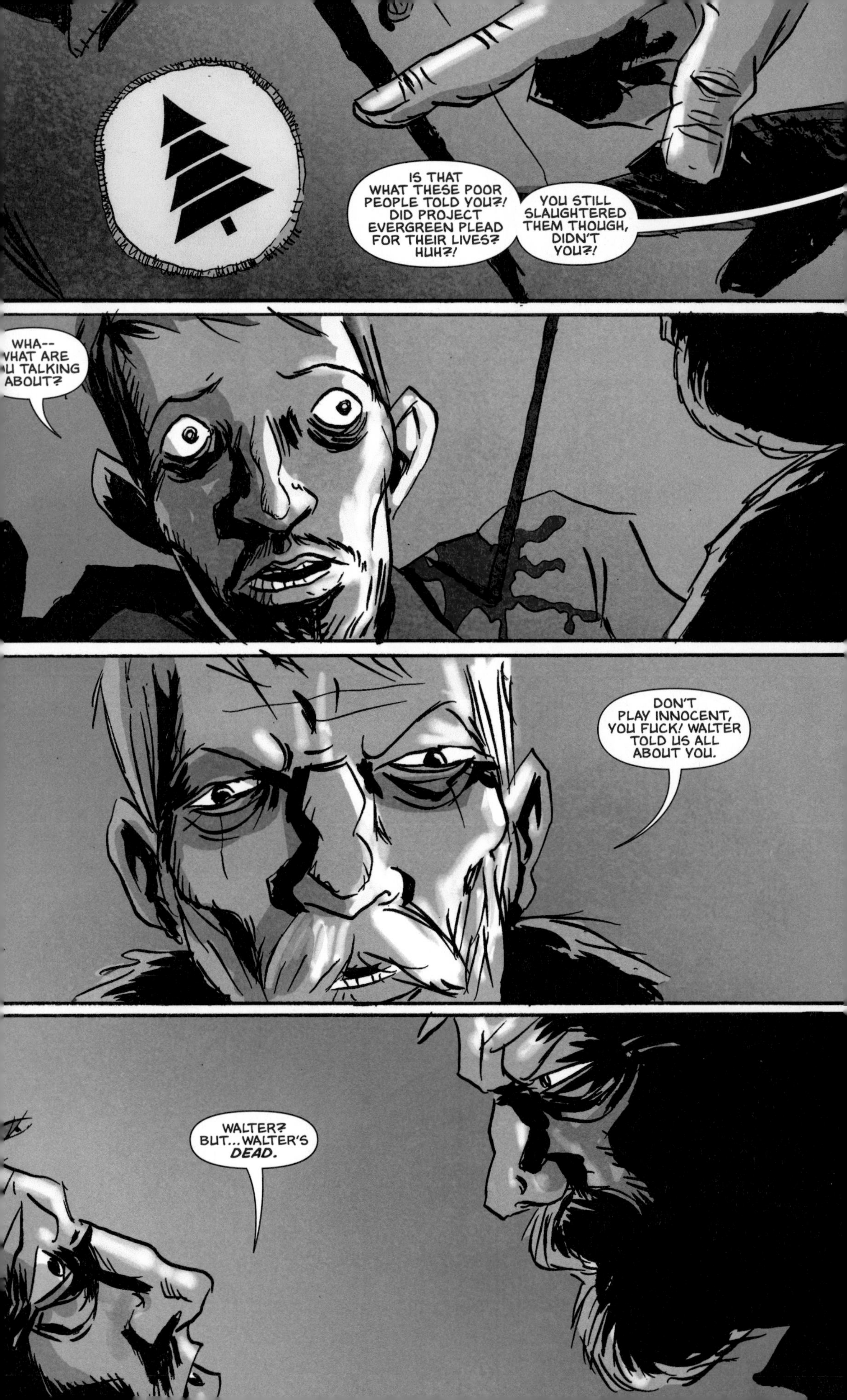
IS THAT WHAT THESE POOR PEOPLE TOLD YOU?! DID PROJECT EVERGREEN PLEAD FOR THEIR LIVES? HUH?!
YOU STILL SLAUGHTERED THEM THOUGH, DIDN'T YOU?!
WHA-- WHAT ARE U TALKING ABOUT?
DON'T PLAY INNOCENT, YOU FUCK! WALTER TOLD US ALL ABOUT YOU.
WALTER? BUT... WALTER'S *DEAD.*

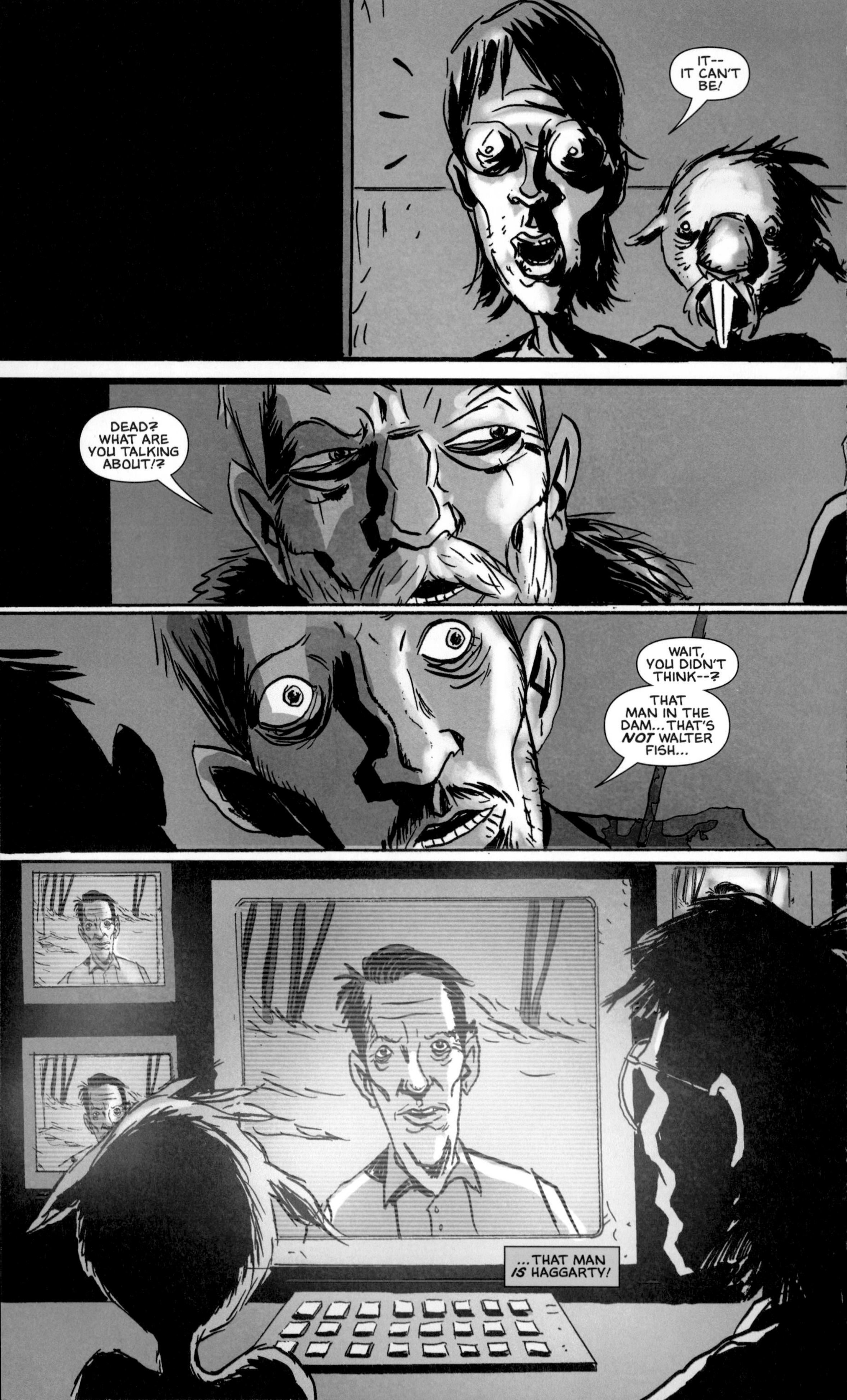
IT--
IT CAN'T BE!
DEAD? WHAT ARE YOU TALKING ABOUT!?
WAIT, YOU DIDN'T THINK--?
THAT MAN IN THE DAM...THAT'S *NOT* WALTER FISH...
...THAT MAN *IS* HAGGARTY!

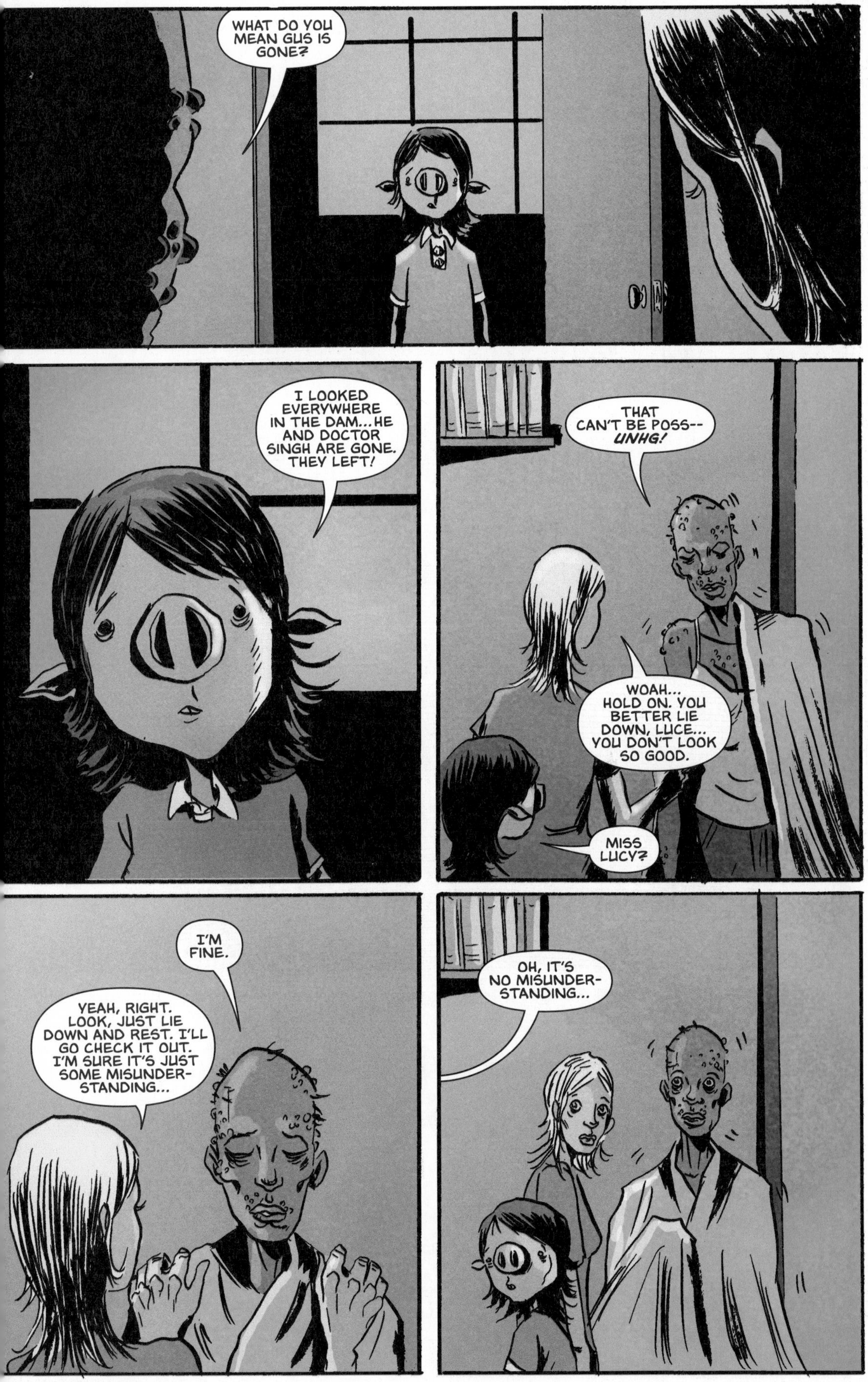
WHAT DO YOU MEAN GUS IS GONE?
I LOOKED EVERYWHERE IN THE DAM...HE AND DOCTOR SINGH ARE GONE. THEY LEFT!
THAT CAN'T BE POSS-- *UNHG!*
WOAH... HOLD ON. YOU BETTER LIE DOWN, LUCE... YOU DON'T LOOK SO GOOD.
MISS LUCY?
I'M FINE.
YEAH, RIGHT. LOOK, JUST LIE DOWN AND REST. I'LL GO CHECK IT OUT. I'M SURE IT'S JUST SOME MISUNDER-STANDING...
OH, IT'S NO MISUNDER-STANDING...

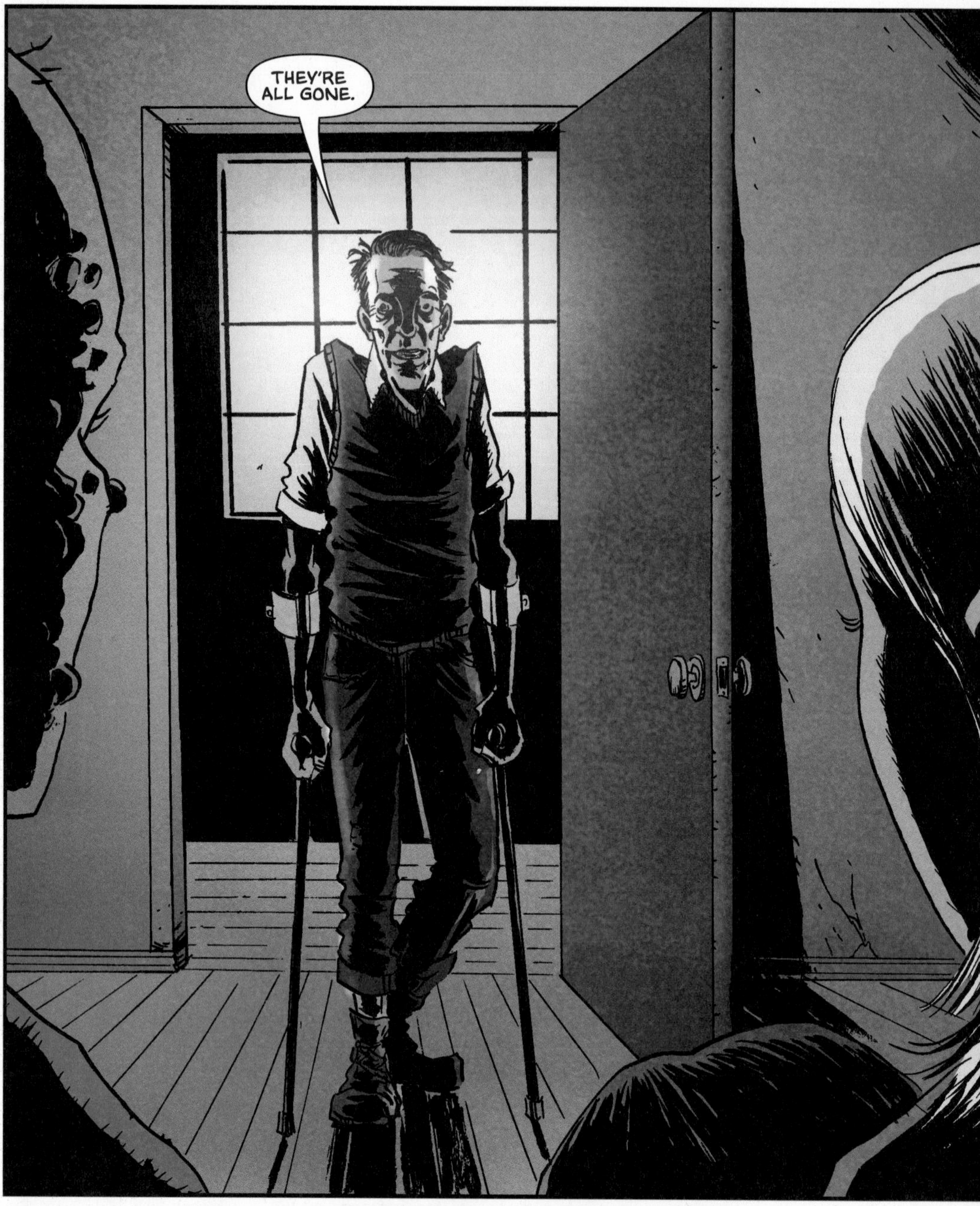
THEY'RE ALL GONE.

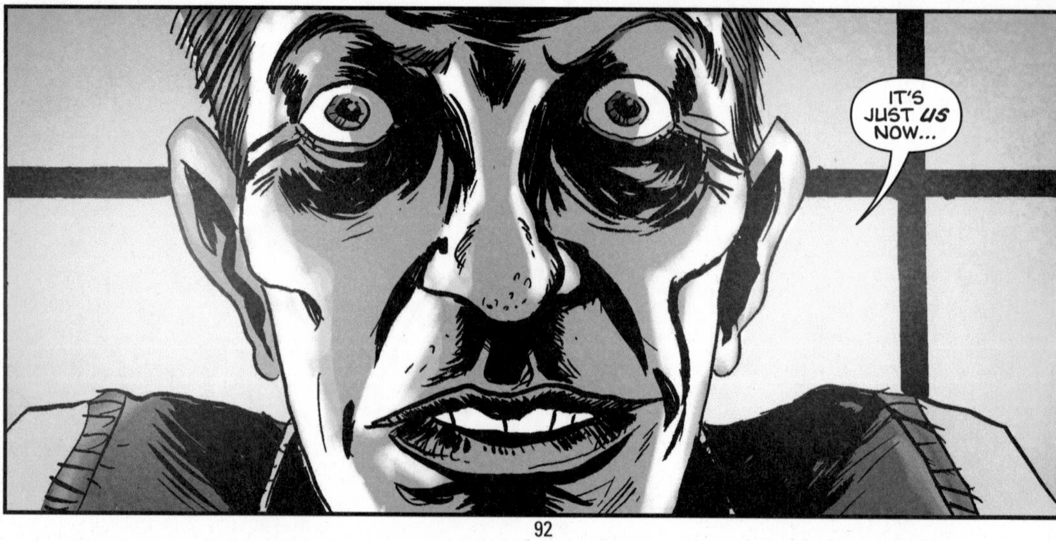
IT'S JUST *US* NOW...

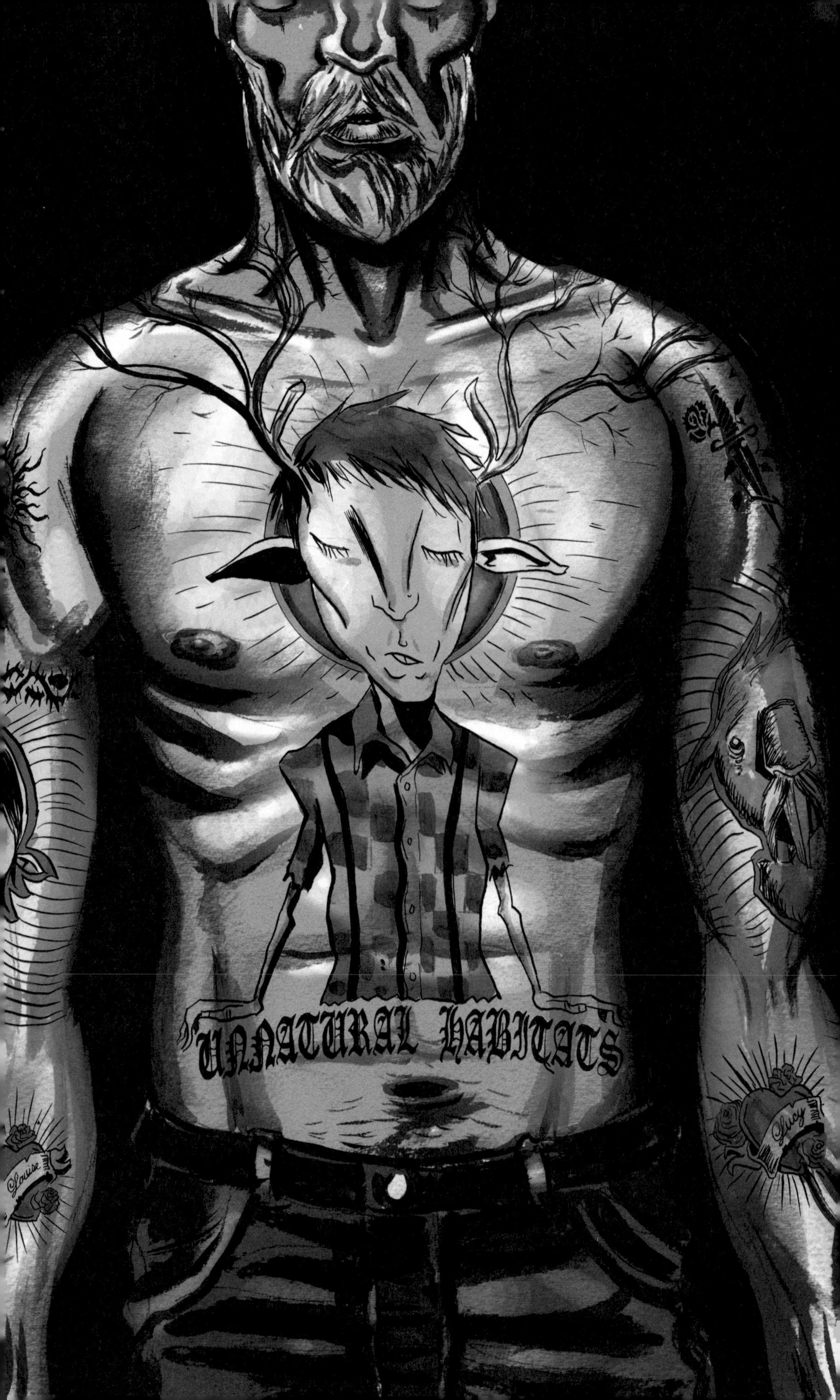
UNNATURAL HABITATS
Louise
Lucy

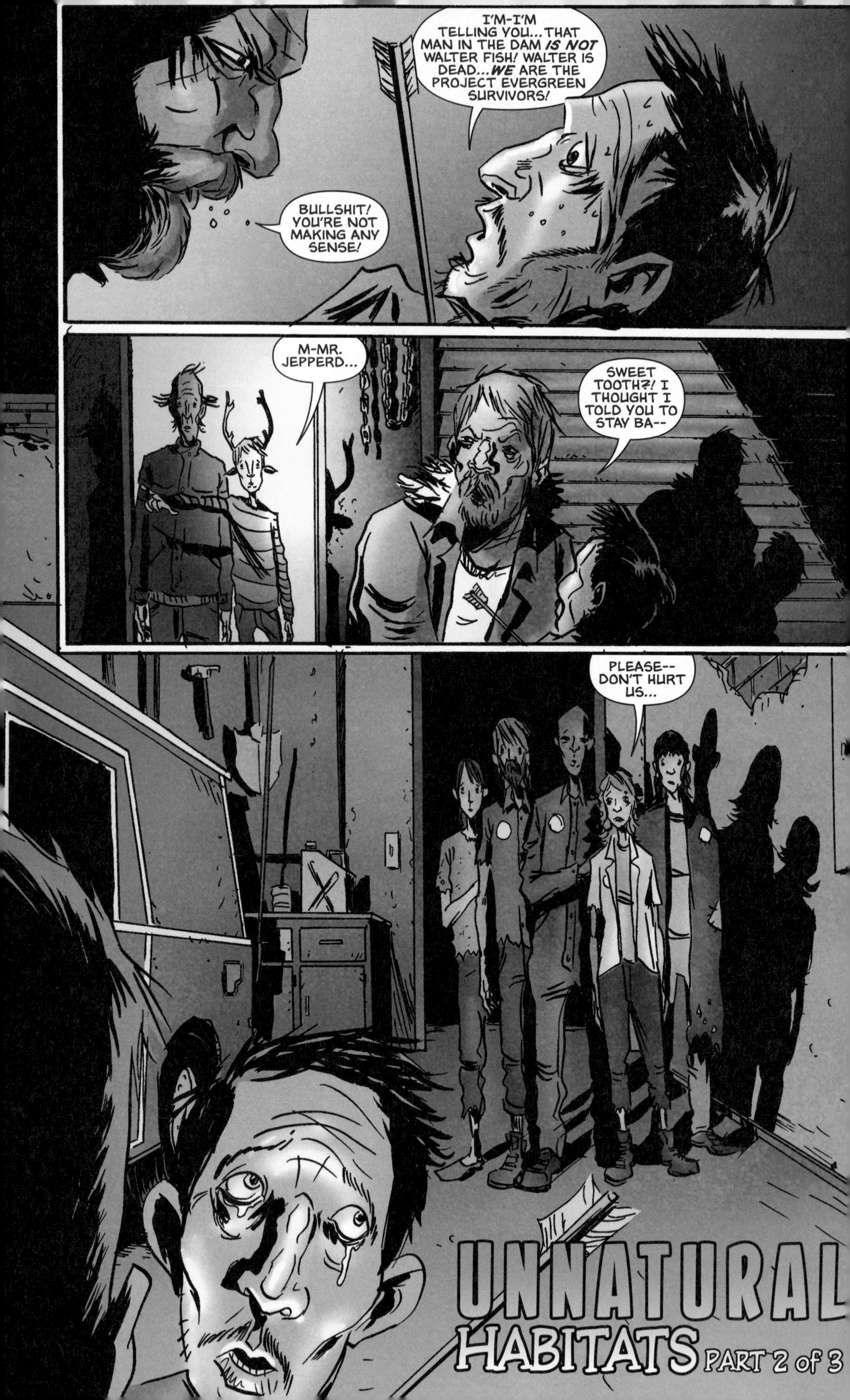
I'M-I'M TELLING YOU... THAT MAN IN THE DAM IS NOT WALTER FISH! WALTER IS DEAD... WE ARE THE PROJECT EVERGREEN SURVIVORS!
BULLSHIT! YOU'RE NOT MAKING ANY SENSE!
M-MR. JEPPERD...
SWEET TOOTH?! I THOUGHT I TOLD YOU TO STAY BA--
PLEASE-- DON'T HURT US...
UNNATURAL HABITATS PART 2 of 3

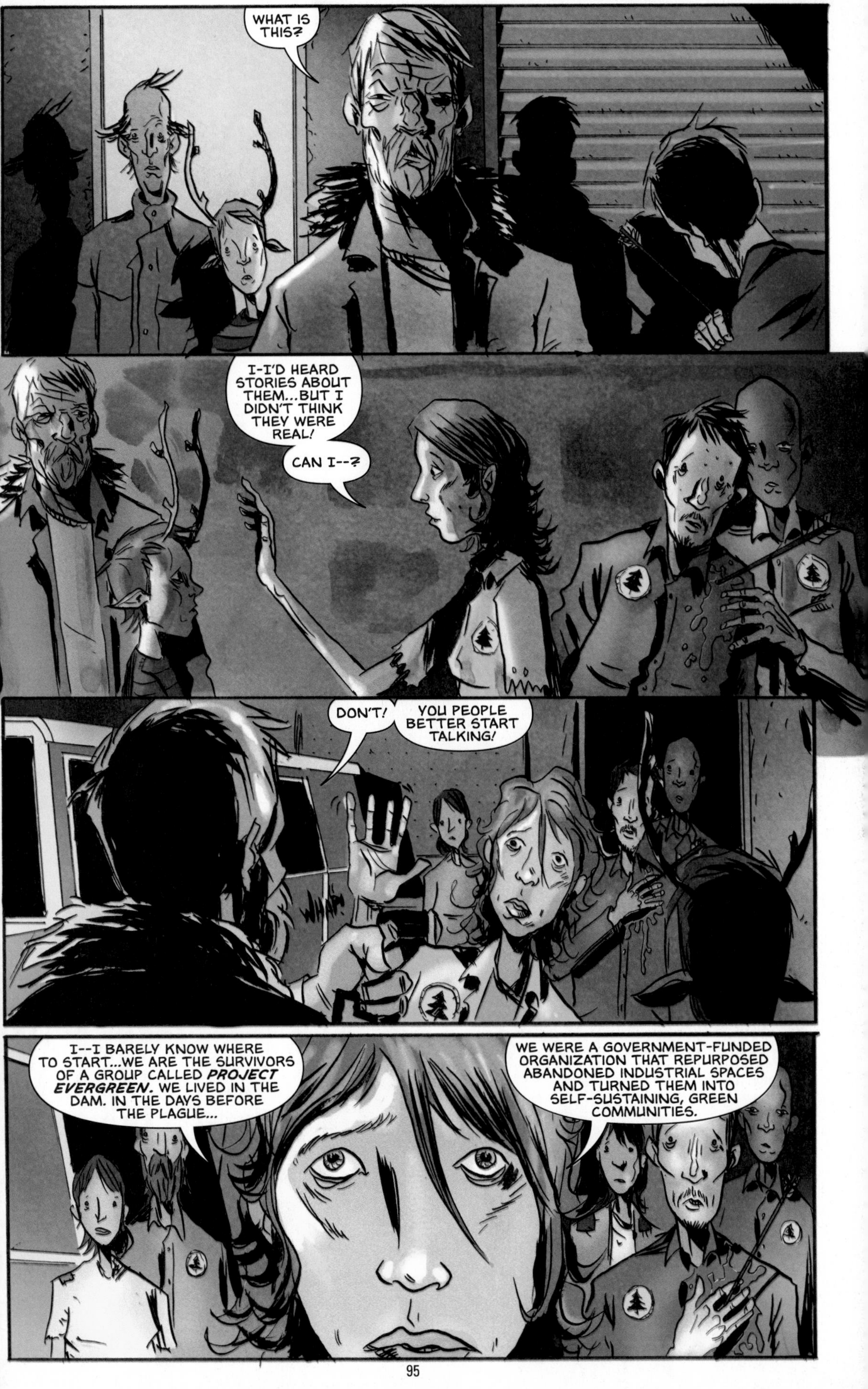
WHAT IS THIS?
I-I'D HEARD STORIES ABOUT THEM...BUT I DIDN'T THINK THEY WERE REAL!
CAN I--?
DON'T!
YOU PEOPLE BETTER START TALKING!
WHAP!
I--I BARELY KNOW WHERE TO START...WE ARE THE SURVIVORS OF A GROUP CALLED ***PROJECT EVERGREEN.*** WE LIVED IN THE DAM. IN THE DAYS BEFORE THE PLAGUE...
WE WERE A GOVERNMENT-FUNDED ORGANIZATION THAT REPURPOSED ABANDONED INDUSTRIAL SPACES AND TURNED THEM INTO SELF-SUSTAINING, GREEN COMMUNITIES.

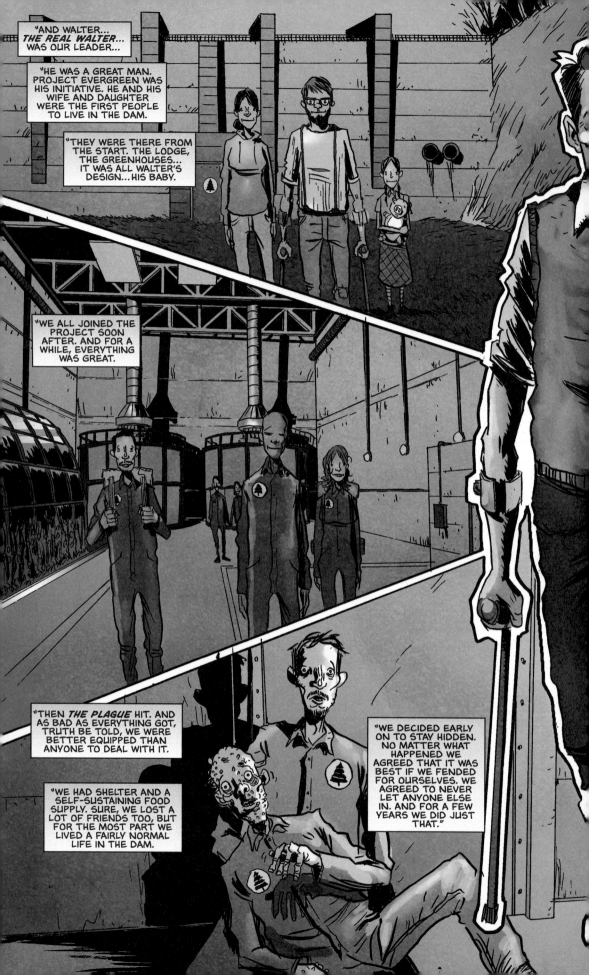

"AND WALTER... *THE REAL WALTER*... WAS OUR LEADER...

"HE WAS A GREAT MAN. PROJECT EVERGREEN WAS HIS INITIATIVE. HE AND HIS WIFE AND DAUGHTER WERE THE FIRST PEOPLE TO LIVE IN THE DAM.

"THEY WERE THERE FROM THE START. THE LODGE, THE GREENHOUSES... IT WAS ALL WALTER'S DESIGN...HIS BABY.

"WE ALL JOINED THE PROJECT SOON AFTER. AND FOR A WHILE, EVERYTHING WAS GREAT.

"THEN *THE PLAGUE* HIT. AND AS BAD AS EVERYTHING GOT, TRUTH BE TOLD, WE WERE BETTER EQUIPPED THAN ANYONE TO DEAL WITH IT.

"WE HAD SHELTER AND A SELF-SUSTAINING FOOD SUPPLY. SURE, WE LOST A LOT OF FRIENDS TOO, BUT FOR THE MOST PART WE LIVED A FAIRLY NORMAL LIFE IN THE DAM.

"WE DECIDED EARLY ON TO STAY HIDDEN. NO MATTER WHAT HAPPENED WE AGREED THAT IT WAS BEST IF WE FENDED FOR OURSELVES. WE AGREED TO NEVER LET ANYONE ELSE IN. AND FOR A FEW YEARS WE DID JUST THAT."

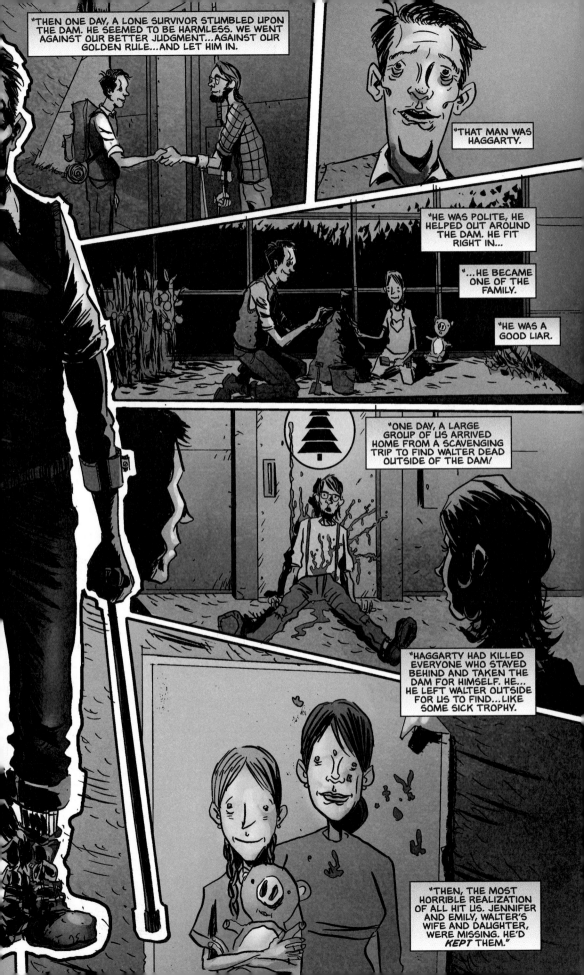

"THEN ONE DAY, A LONE SURVIVOR STUMBLED UPON THE DAM. HE SEEMED TO BE HARMLESS. WE WENT AGAINST OUR BETTER JUDGMENT...AGAINST OUR GOLDEN RULE...AND LET HIM IN.

"THAT MAN WAS HAGGARTY.

"HE WAS POLITE, HE HELPED OUT AROUND THE DAM. HE FIT RIGHT IN...

"...HE BECAME ONE OF THE FAMILY.

"HE WAS A GOOD LIAR.

"ONE DAY, A LARGE GROUP OF US ARRIVED HOME FROM A SCAVENGING TRIP TO FIND WALTER DEAD OUTSIDE OF THE DAM!

"HAGGARTY HAD KILLED EVERYONE WHO STAYED BEHIND AND TAKEN THE DAM FOR HIMSELF. HE... HE LEFT WALTER OUTSIDE FOR US TO FIND...LIKE SOME SICK TROPHY.

"THEN, THE MOST HORRIBLE REALIZATION OF ALL HIT US. JENNIFER AND EMILY, WALTER'S WIFE AND DAUGHTER, WERE MISSING. HE'D *KEPT* THEM."

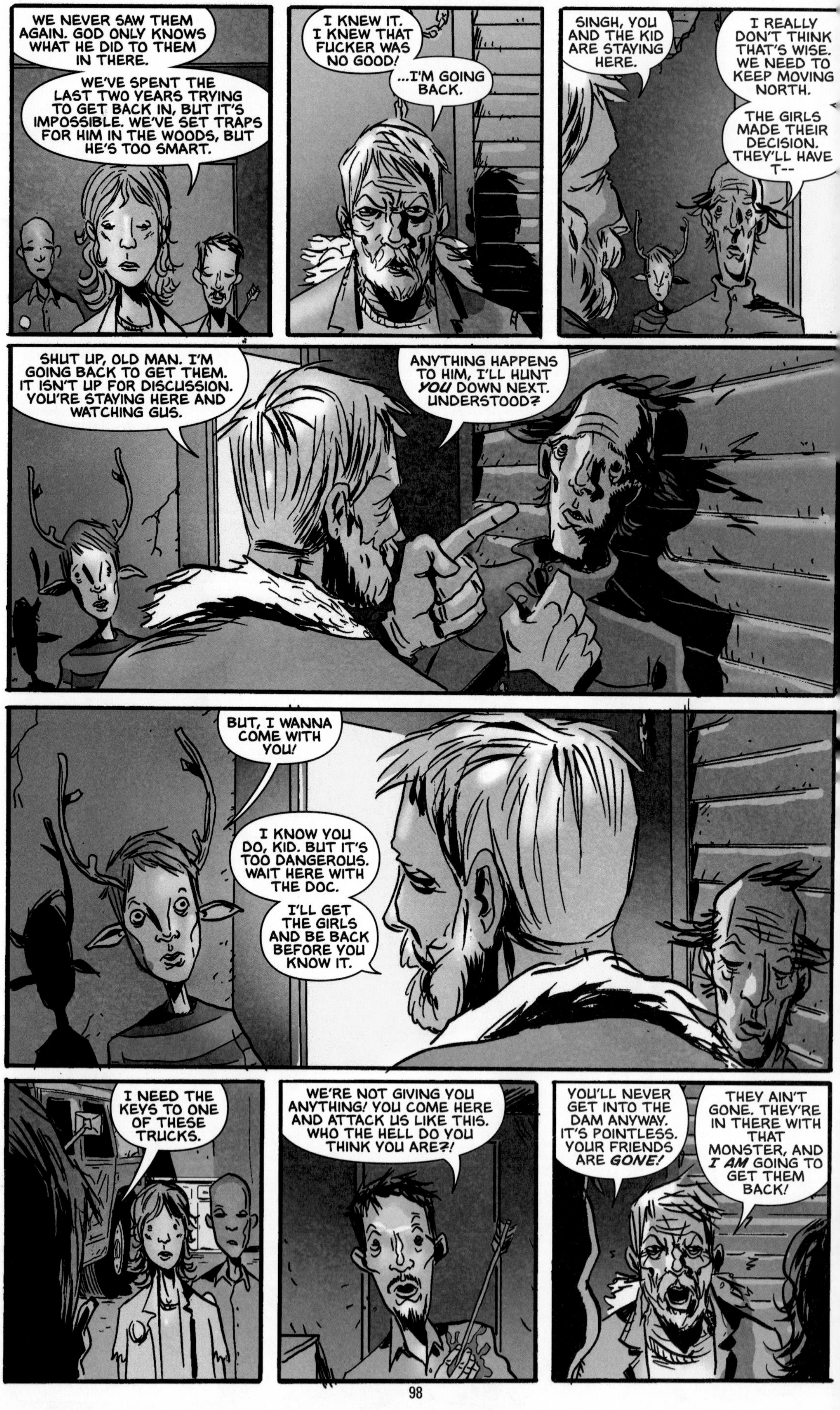
WE NEVER SAW THEM AGAIN. GOD ONLY KNOWS WHAT HE DID TO THEM IN THERE.
WE'VE SPENT THE LAST TWO YEARS TRYING TO GET BACK IN, BUT IT'S IMPOSSIBLE. WE'VE SET TRAPS FOR HIM IN THE WOODS, BUT HE'S TOO SMART.
I KNEW IT. I KNEW THAT FUCKER WAS NO GOOD!
...I'M GOING BACK.
SINGH, YOU AND THE KID ARE STAYING HERE.
I REALLY DON'T THINK THAT'S WISE. WE NEED TO KEEP MOVING NORTH.
THE GIRLS MADE THEIR DECISION. THEY'LL HAVE T--
SHUT UP, OLD MAN. I'M GOING BACK TO GET THEM. IT ISN'T UP FOR DISCUSSION. YOU'RE STAYING HERE AND WATCHING GUS.
ANYTHING HAPPENS TO HIM, I'LL HUNT *YOU* DOWN NEXT. UNDERSTOOD?
BUT, I WANNA COME WITH YOU!
I KNOW YOU DO, KID. BUT IT'S TOO DANGEROUS. WAIT HERE WITH THE DOC.
I'LL GET THE GIRLS AND BE BACK BEFORE YOU KNOW IT.
I NEED THE KEYS TO ONE OF THESE TRUCKS.
WE'RE NOT GIVING YOU ANYTHING! YOU COME HERE AND ATTACK US LIKE THIS. WHO THE HELL DO YOU THINK YOU ARE?!
YOU'LL NEVER GET INTO THE DAM ANYWAY. IT'S POINTLESS. YOUR FRIENDS ARE *GONE!*
THEY AIN'T GONE. THEY'RE IN THERE WITH THAT MONSTER, AND *I AM* GOING TO GET THEM BACK!

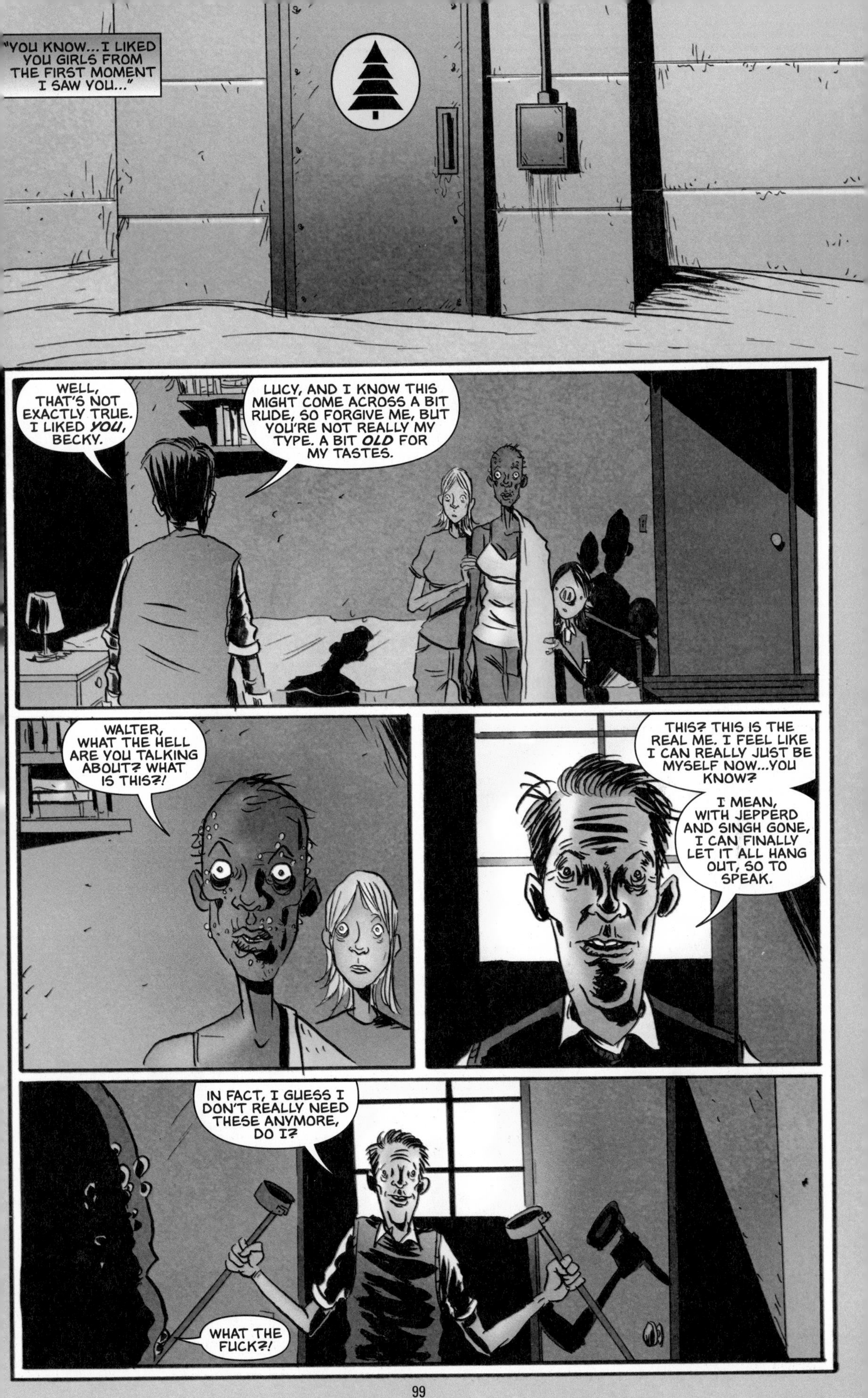
"YOU KNOW...I LIKED YOU GIRLS FROM THE FIRST MOMENT I SAW YOU..."
WELL, THAT'S NOT EXACTLY TRUE. I LIKED *YOU*, BECKY.
LUCY, AND I KNOW THIS MIGHT COME ACROSS A BIT RUDE, SO FORGIVE ME, BUT YOU'RE NOT REALLY MY TYPE. A BIT *OLD* FOR MY TASTES.
WALTER, WHAT THE HELL ARE YOU TALKING ABOUT? WHAT IS THIS?!
THIS? THIS IS THE REAL ME. I FEEL LIKE I CAN REALLY JUST BE MYSELF NOW...YOU KNOW?
I MEAN, WITH JEPPERD AND SINGH GONE, I CAN FINALLY LET IT ALL HANG OUT, SO TO SPEAK.
IN FACT, I GUESS I DON'T REALLY NEED THESE ANYMORE, DO I?
WHAT THE FUCK?!

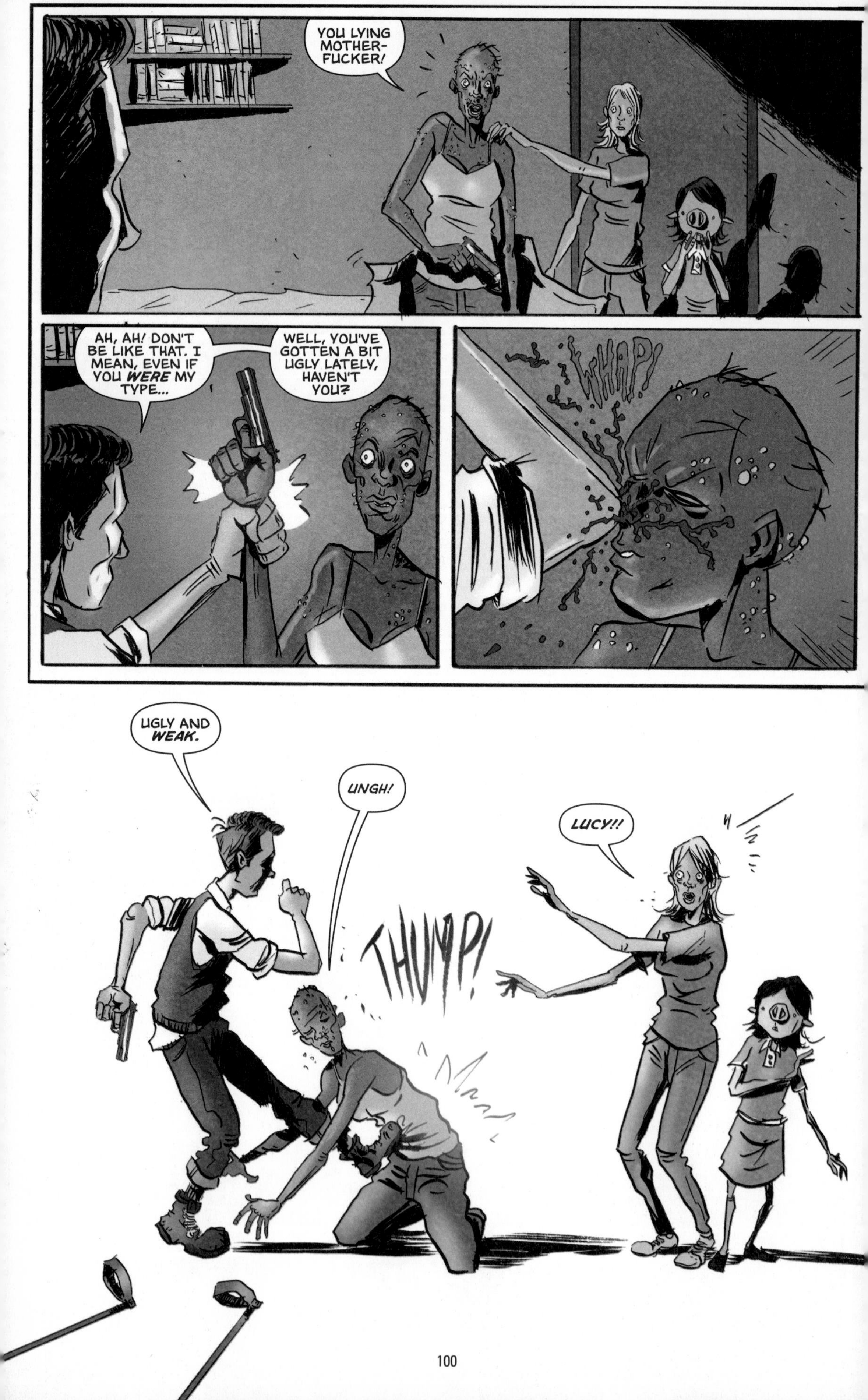
YOU LYING MOTHER-FUCKER!
AH, AH! DON'T BE LIKE THAT. I MEAN, EVEN IF YOU WERE MY TYPE...
WELL, YOU'VE GOTTEN A BIT UGLY LATELY, HAVEN'T YOU?
WHAP!
UGLY AND WEAK.
UNGH!
THUMP!
LUCY!!

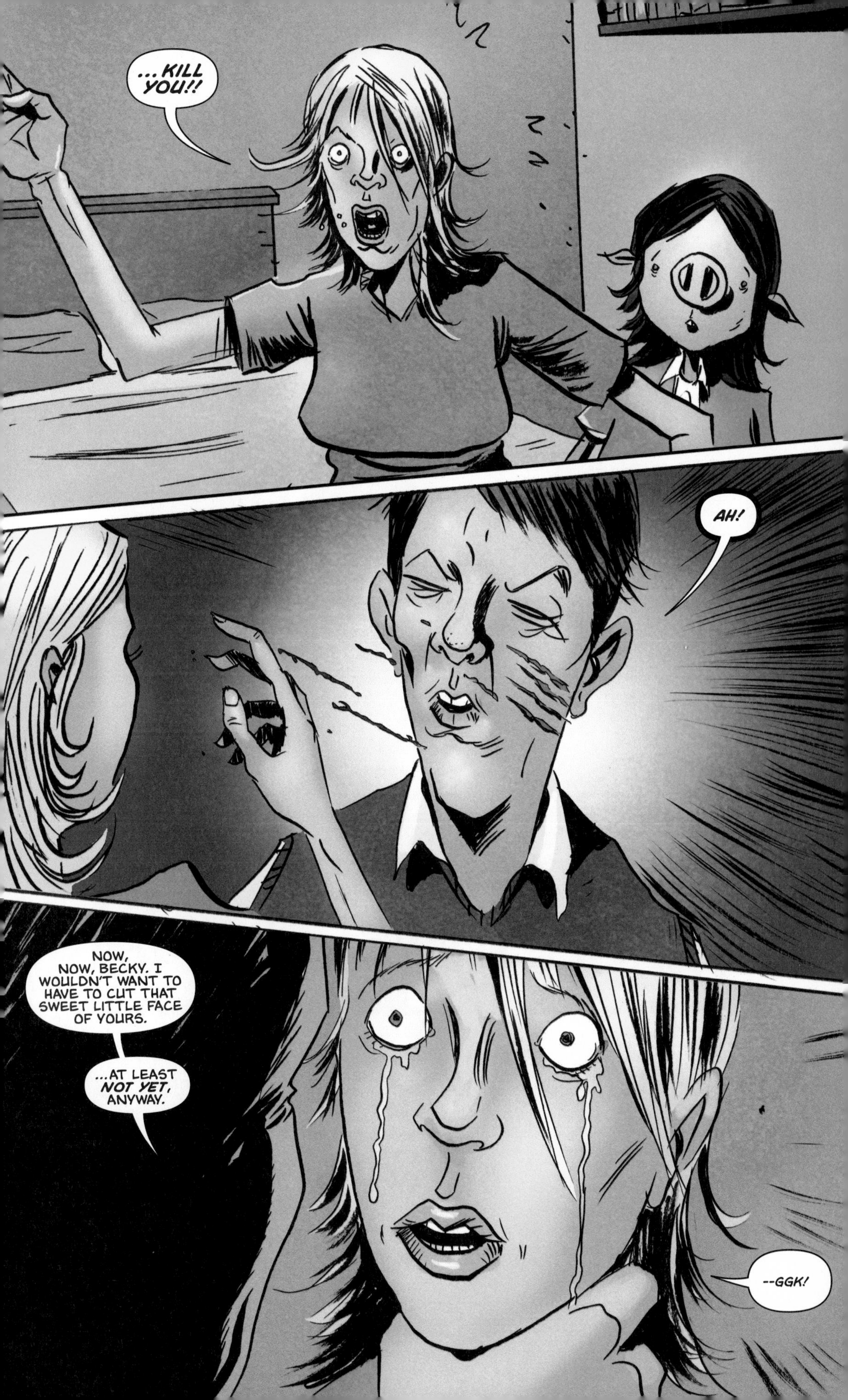
...KILL YOU!!
AH!
NOW, NOW, BECKY. I WOULDN'T WANT TO HAVE TO CUT THAT SWEET LITTLE FACE OF YOURS.
...AT LEAST NOT YET, ANYWAY.
--GGK!

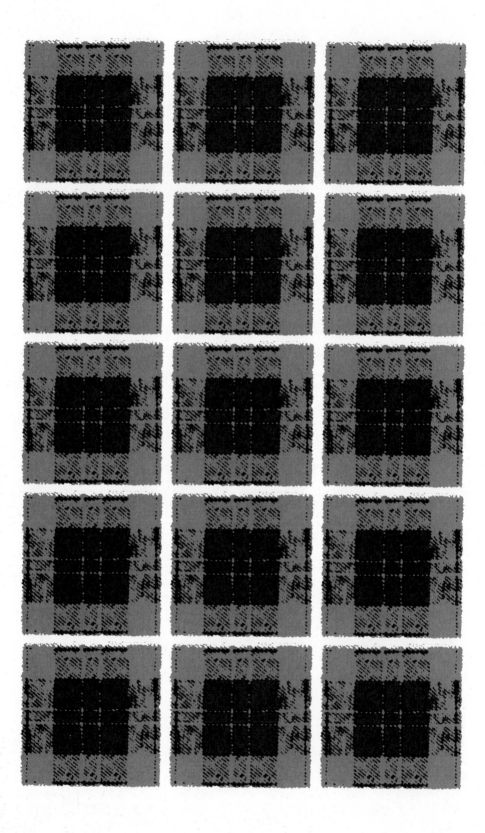

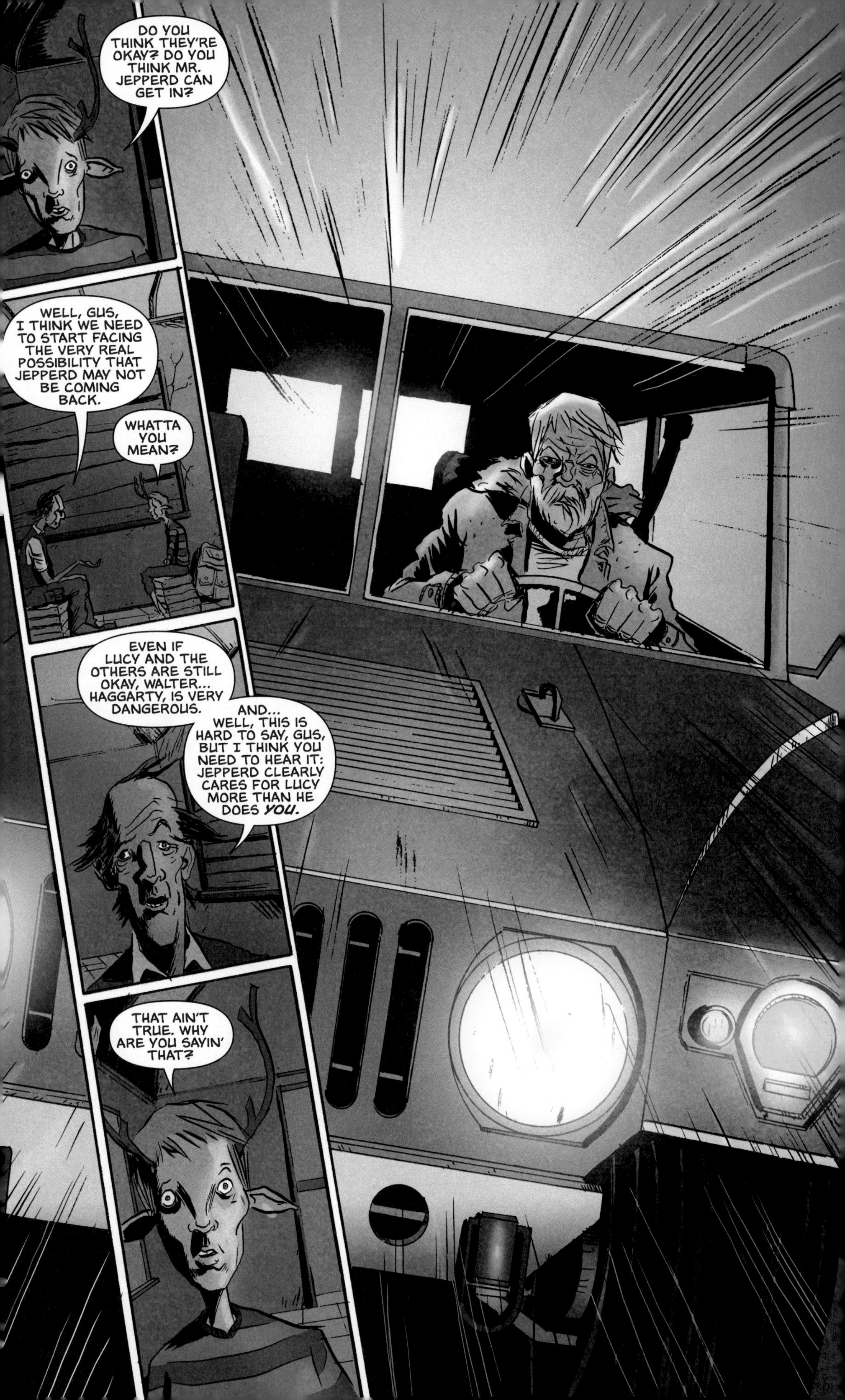
DO YOU THINK THEY'RE OKAY? DO YOU THINK MR. JEPPERD CAN GET IN?
WELL, GUS, I THINK WE NEED TO START FACING THE VERY REAL POSSIBILITY THAT JEPPERD MAY NOT BE COMING BACK.
WHATTA YOU MEAN?
EVEN IF LUCY AND THE OTHERS ARE STILL OKAY, WALTER... HAGGARTY, IS VERY DANGEROUS.
AND... WELL, THIS IS HARD TO SAY, GUS, BUT I THINK YOU NEED TO HEAR IT: JEPPERD CLEARLY CARES FOR LUCY MORE THAN HE DOES *YOU.*
THAT AIN'T TRUE. WHY ARE YOU SAYIN' THAT?

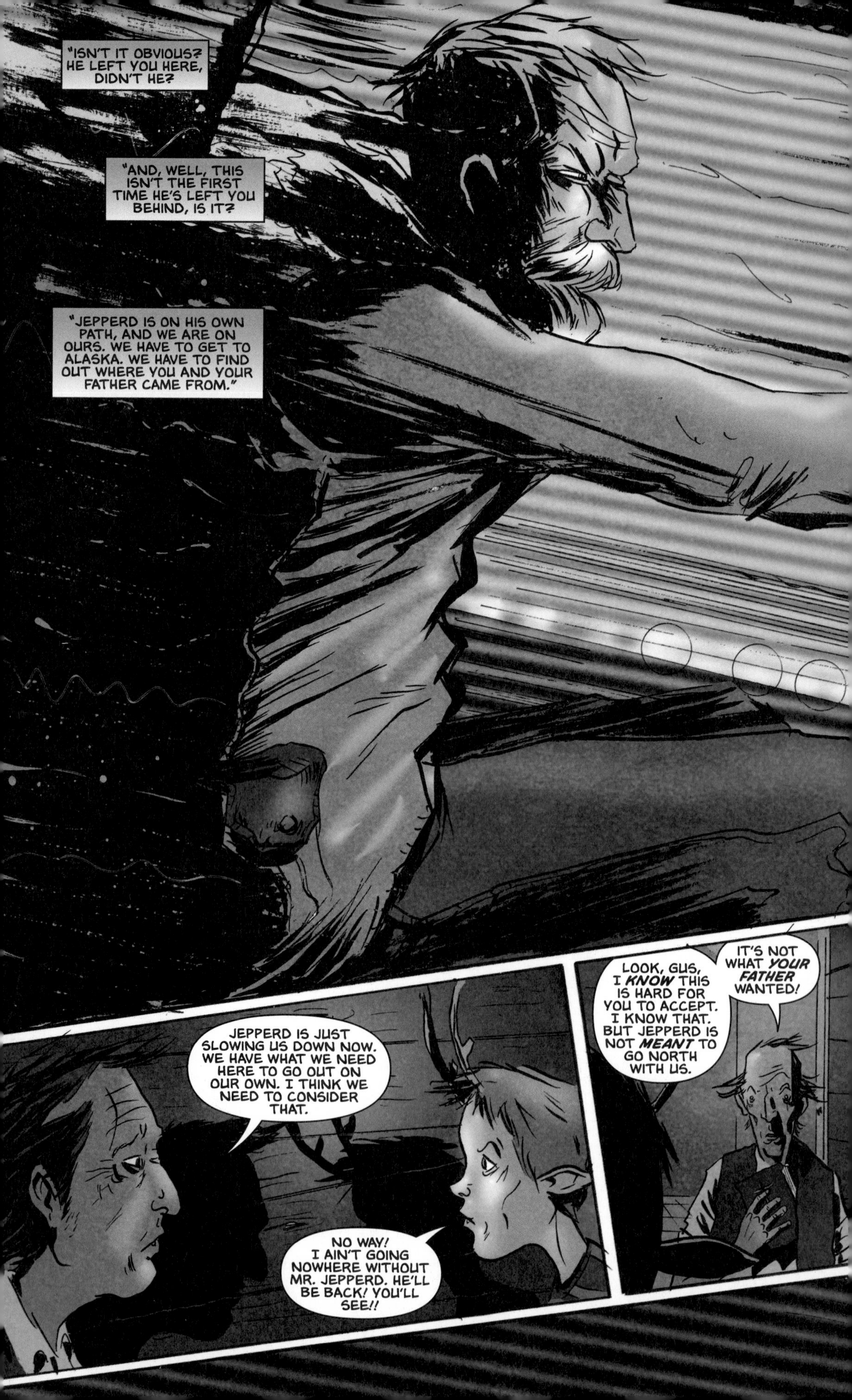
"ISN'T IT OBVIOUS? HE LEFT YOU HERE, DIDN'T HE?
"AND, WELL, THIS ISN'T THE FIRST TIME HE'S LEFT YOU BEHIND, IS IT?
"JEPPERD IS ON HIS OWN PATH, AND WE ARE ON OURS. WE HAVE TO GET TO ALASKA. WE HAVE TO FIND OUT WHERE YOU AND YOUR FATHER CAME FROM."
JEPPERD IS JUST SLOWING US DOWN NOW. WE HAVE WHAT WE NEED HERE TO GO OUT ON OUR OWN. I THINK WE NEED TO CONSIDER THAT.
NO WAY! I AIN'T GOING NOWHERE WITHOUT MR. JEPPERD. HE'LL BE BACK! YOU'LL SEE!!
LOOK, GUS, I KNOW THIS IS HARD FOR YOU TO ACCEPT. I KNOW THAT. BUT JEPPERD IS NOT MEANT TO GO NORTH WITH US.
IT'S NOT WHAT YOUR FATHER WANTED!

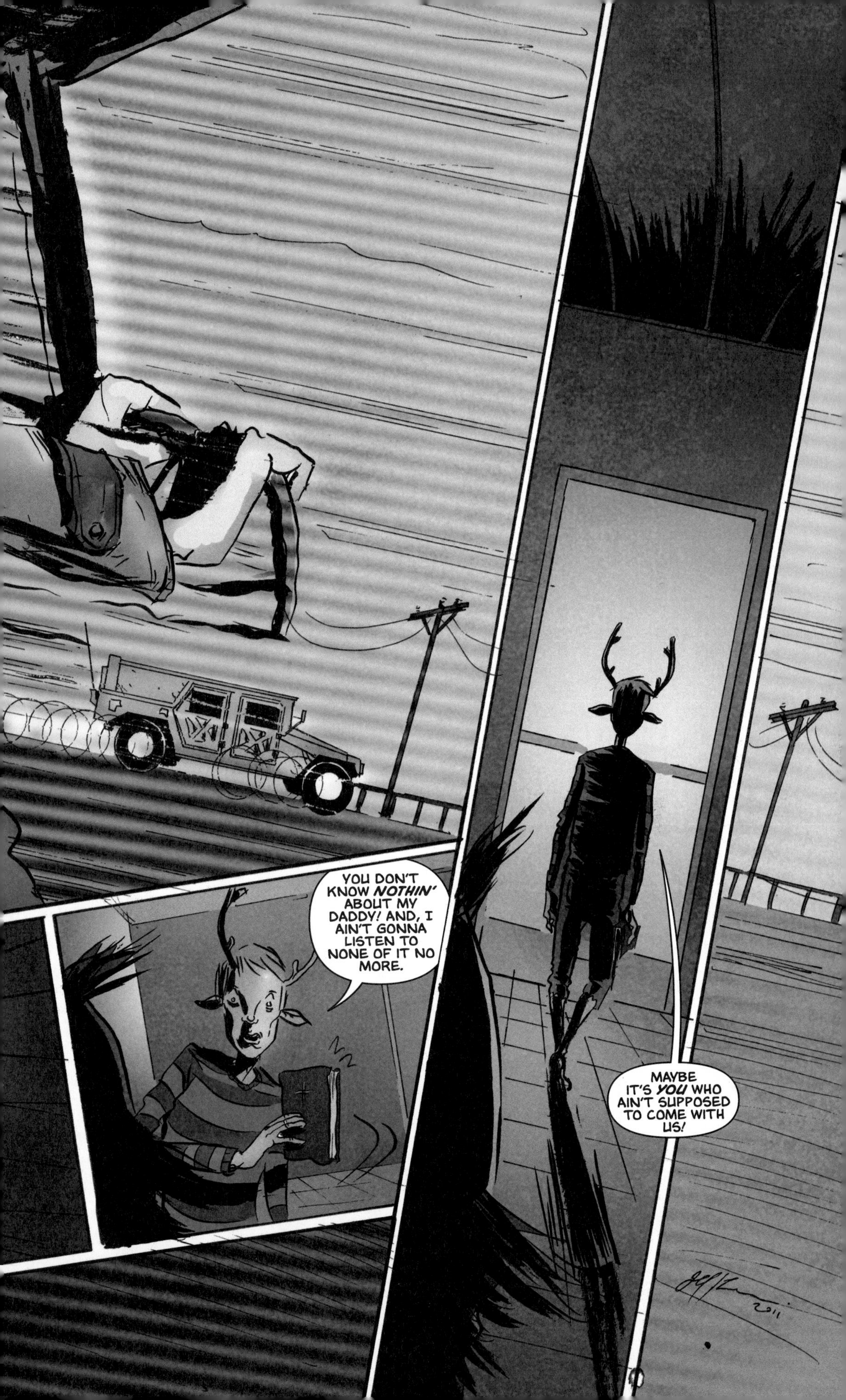
YOU DON'T KNOW *NOTHIN'* ABOUT MY DADDY! AND, I AIN'T GONNA LISTEN TO NONE OF IT NO MORE.
MAYBE IT'S *YOU* WHO AIN'T SUPPOSED TO COME WITH US!
2011

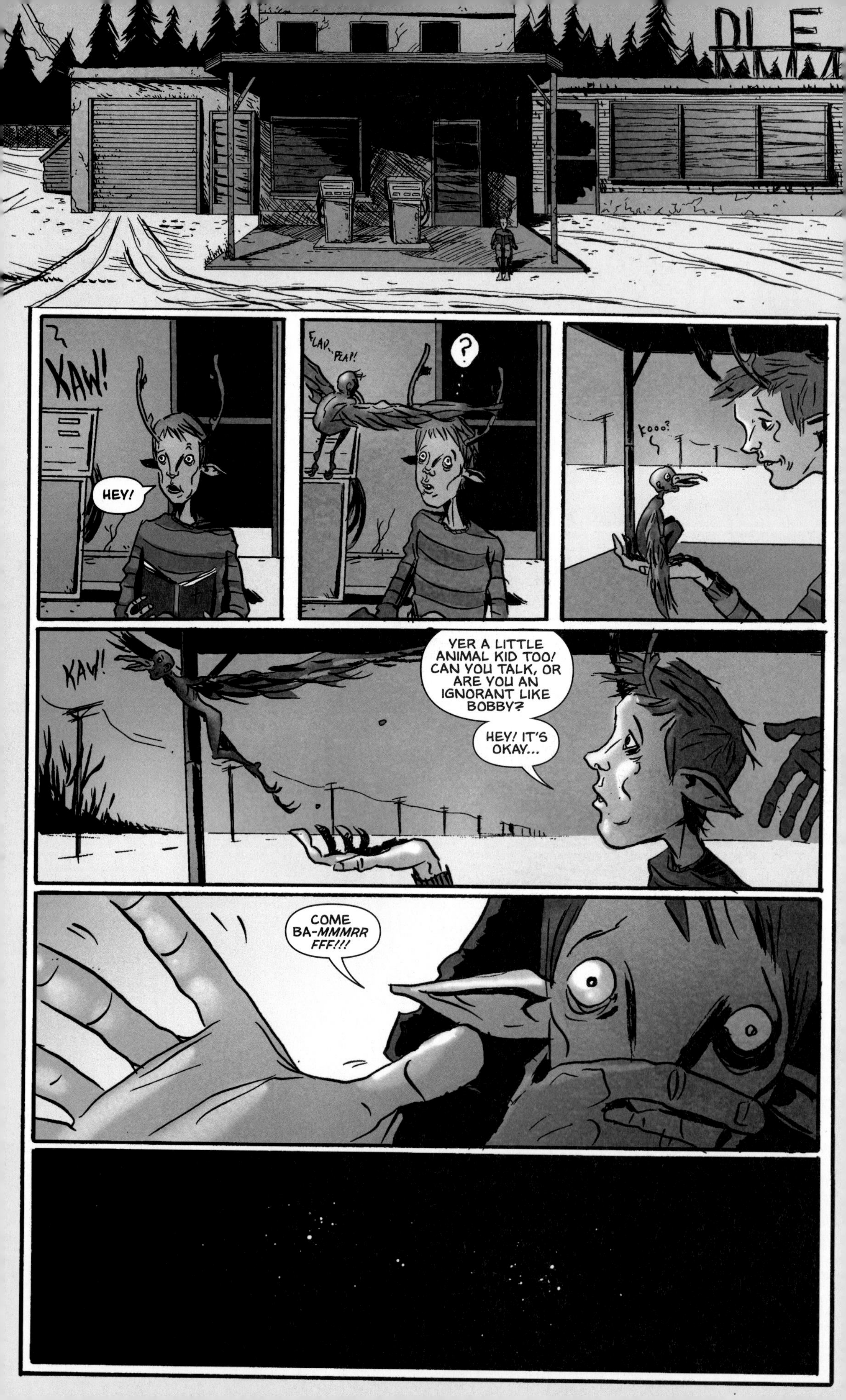
DLE
KAW!
HEY!
FLAP.. FLAP!
?
KOOO?
KAW!
YER A LITTLE ANIMAL KID TOO! CAN YOU TALK, OR ARE YOU AN IGNORANT LIKE BOBBY?
HEY! IT'S OKAY...
COME BA-MMMRR FFF!!!

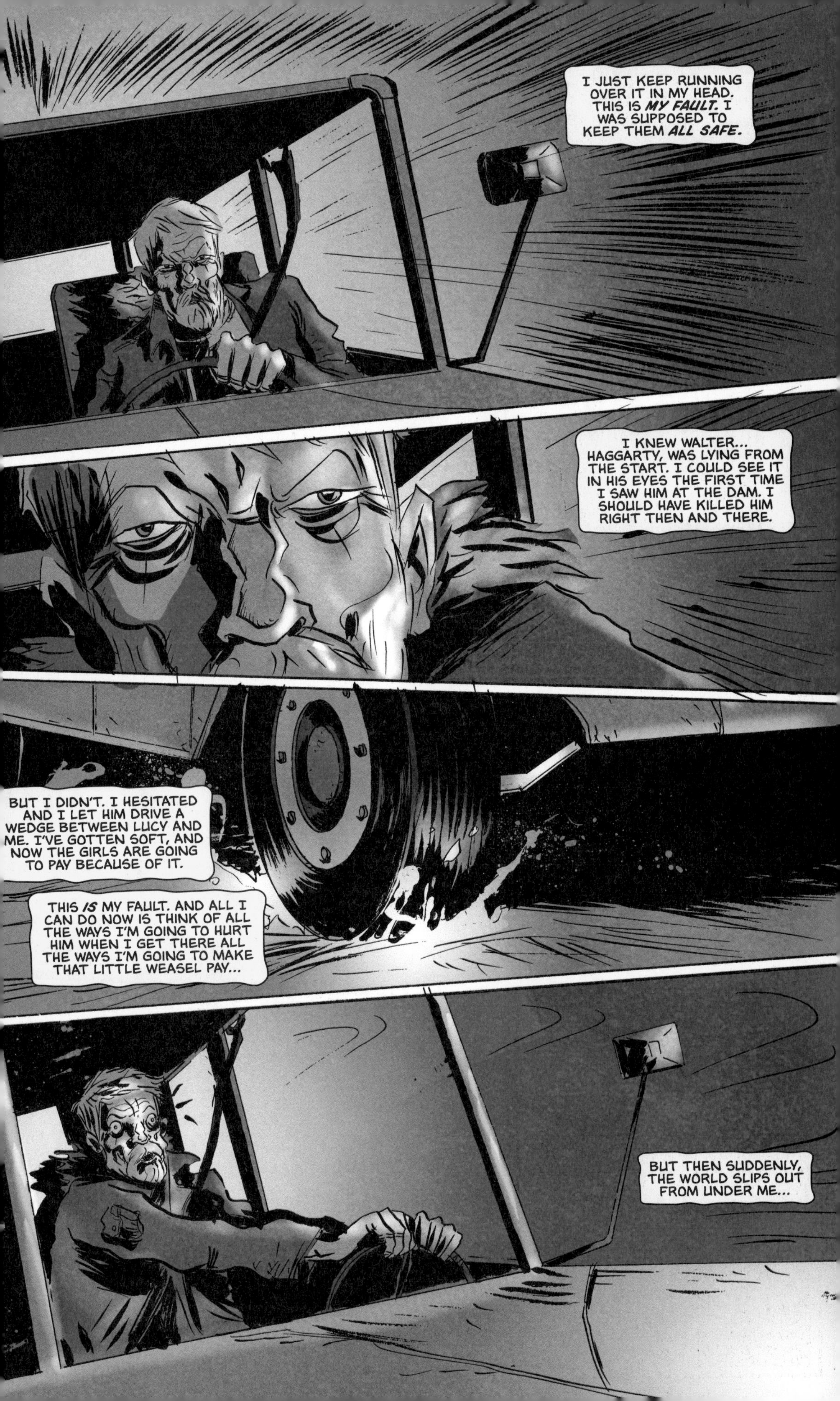
I JUST KEEP RUNNING OVER IT IN MY HEAD. THIS IS MY FAULT. I WAS SUPPOSED TO KEEP THEM ALL SAFE.
I KNEW WALTER... HAGGARTY, WAS LYING FROM THE START. I COULD SEE IT IN HIS EYES THE FIRST TIME I SAW HIM AT THE DAM. I SHOULD HAVE KILLED HIM RIGHT THEN AND THERE.
BUT I DIDN'T. I HESITATED AND I LET HIM DRIVE A WEDGE BETWEEN LUCY AND ME. I'VE GOTTEN SOFT, AND NOW THE GIRLS ARE GOING TO PAY BECAUSE OF IT.
THIS IS MY FAULT. AND ALL I CAN DO NOW IS THINK OF ALL THE WAYS I'M GOING TO HURT HIM WHEN I GET THERE ALL THE WAYS I'M GOING TO MAKE THAT LITTLE WEASEL PAY...
BUT THEN SUDDENLY, THE WORLD SLIPS OUT FROM UNDER ME...

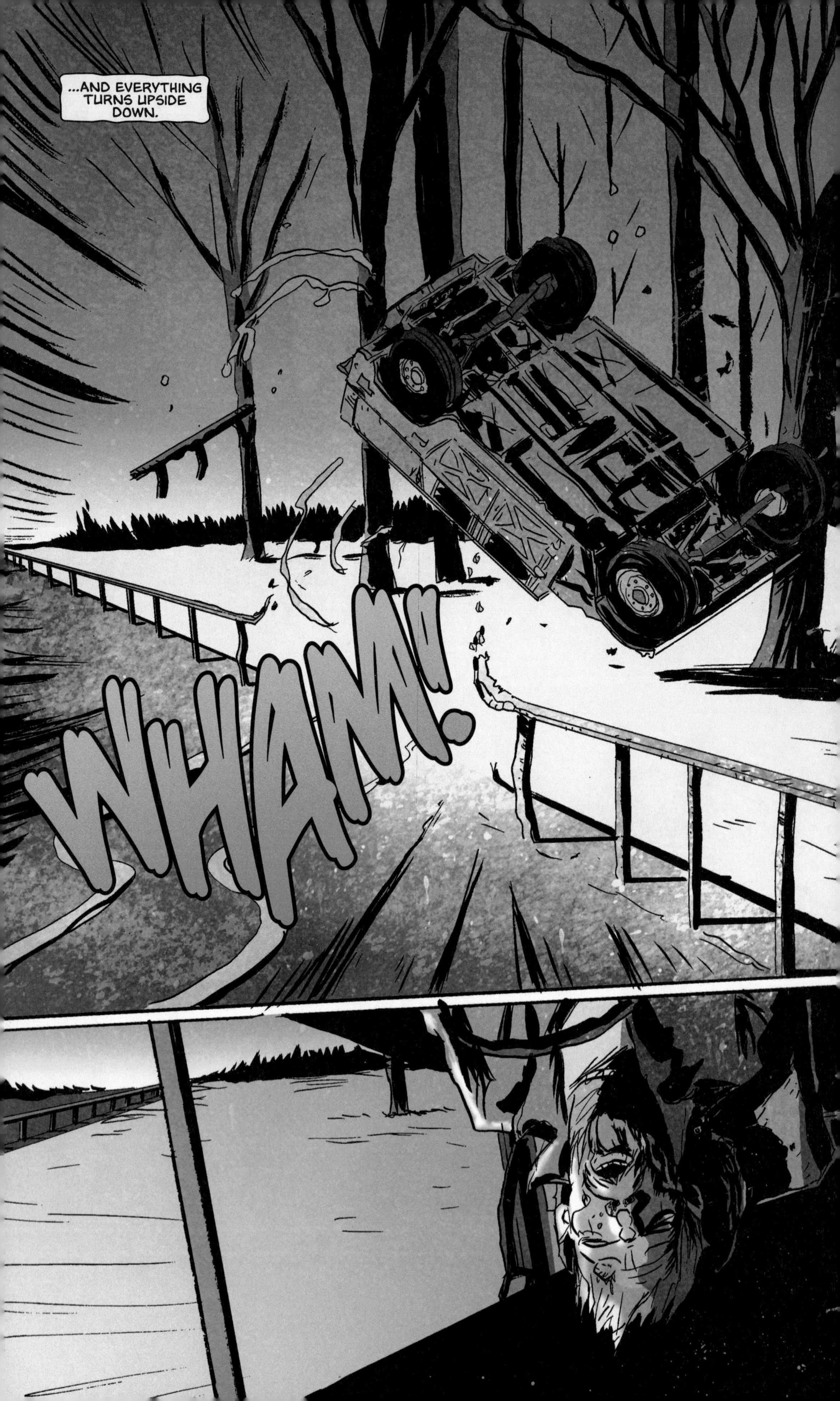
...AND EVERYTHING TURNS UPSIDE DOWN.
WHAM!

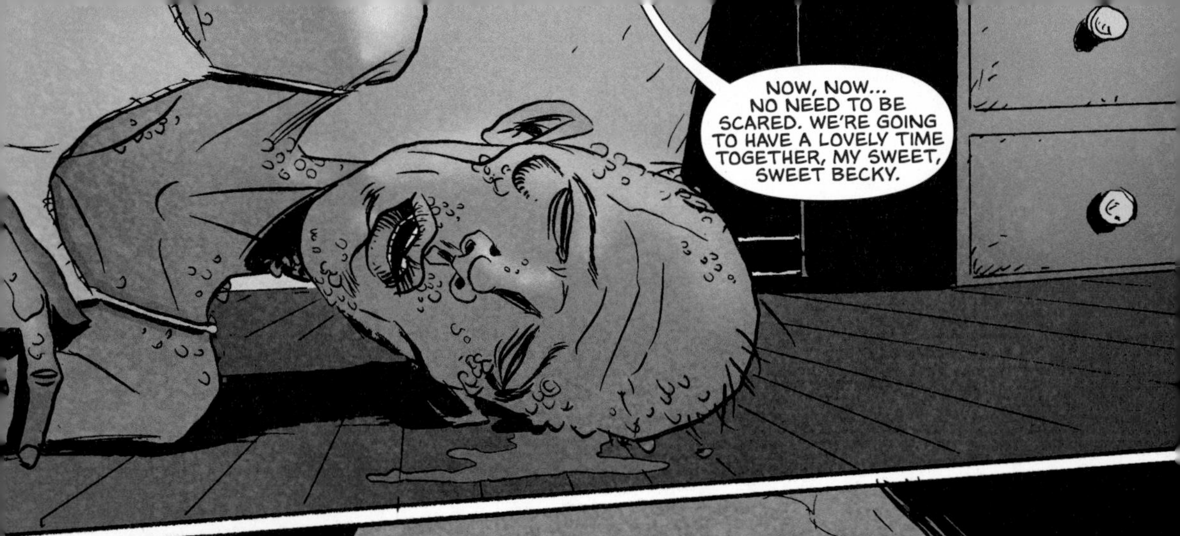
NOW, NOW... NO NEED TO BE SCARED. WE'RE GOING TO HAVE A LOVELY TIME TOGETHER, MY SWEET, SWEET BECKY.

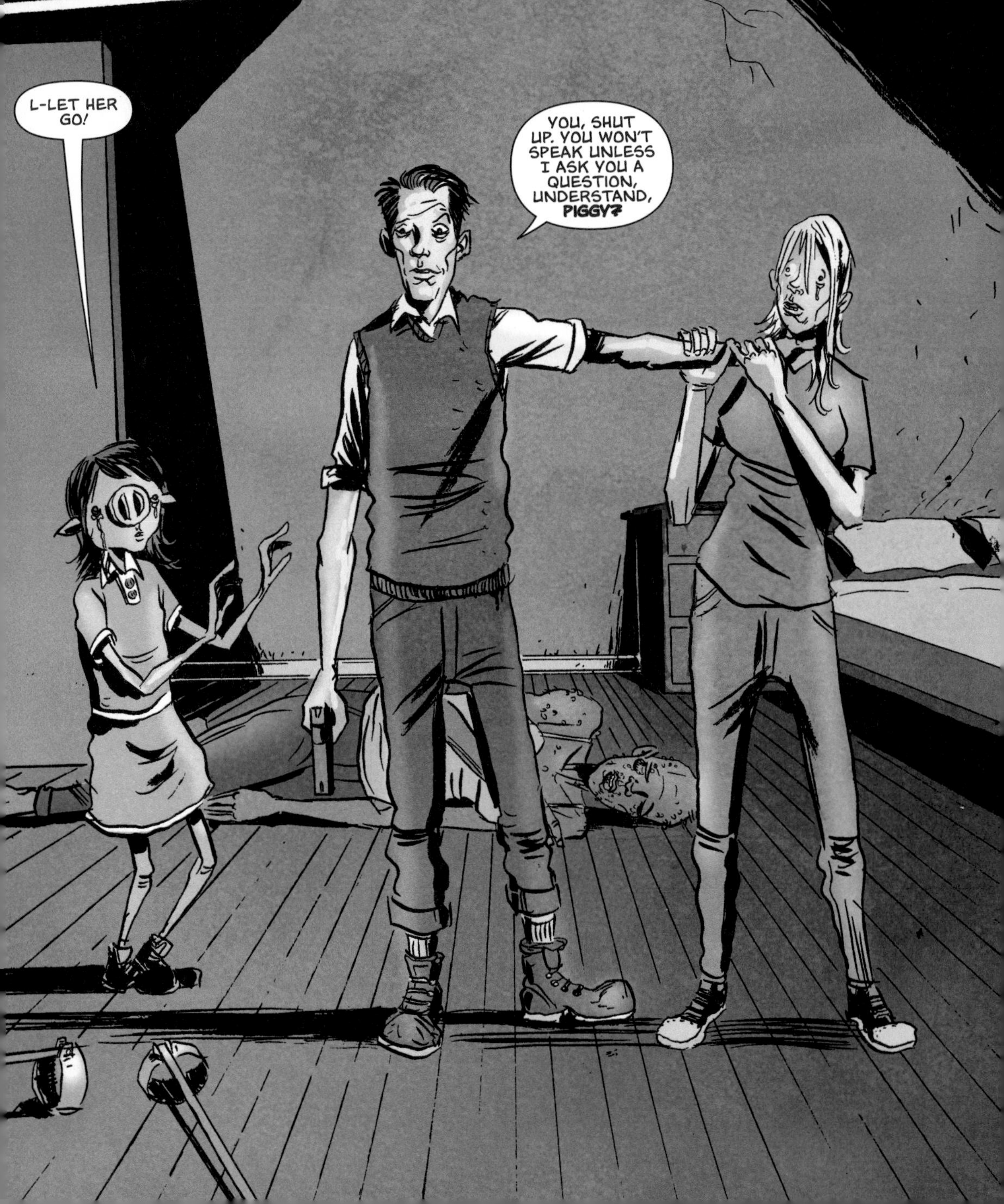
L-LET HER GO!
YOU, SHUT UP. YOU WON'T SPEAK UNLESS I ASK YOU A QUESTION, UNDERSTAND, PIGGY?

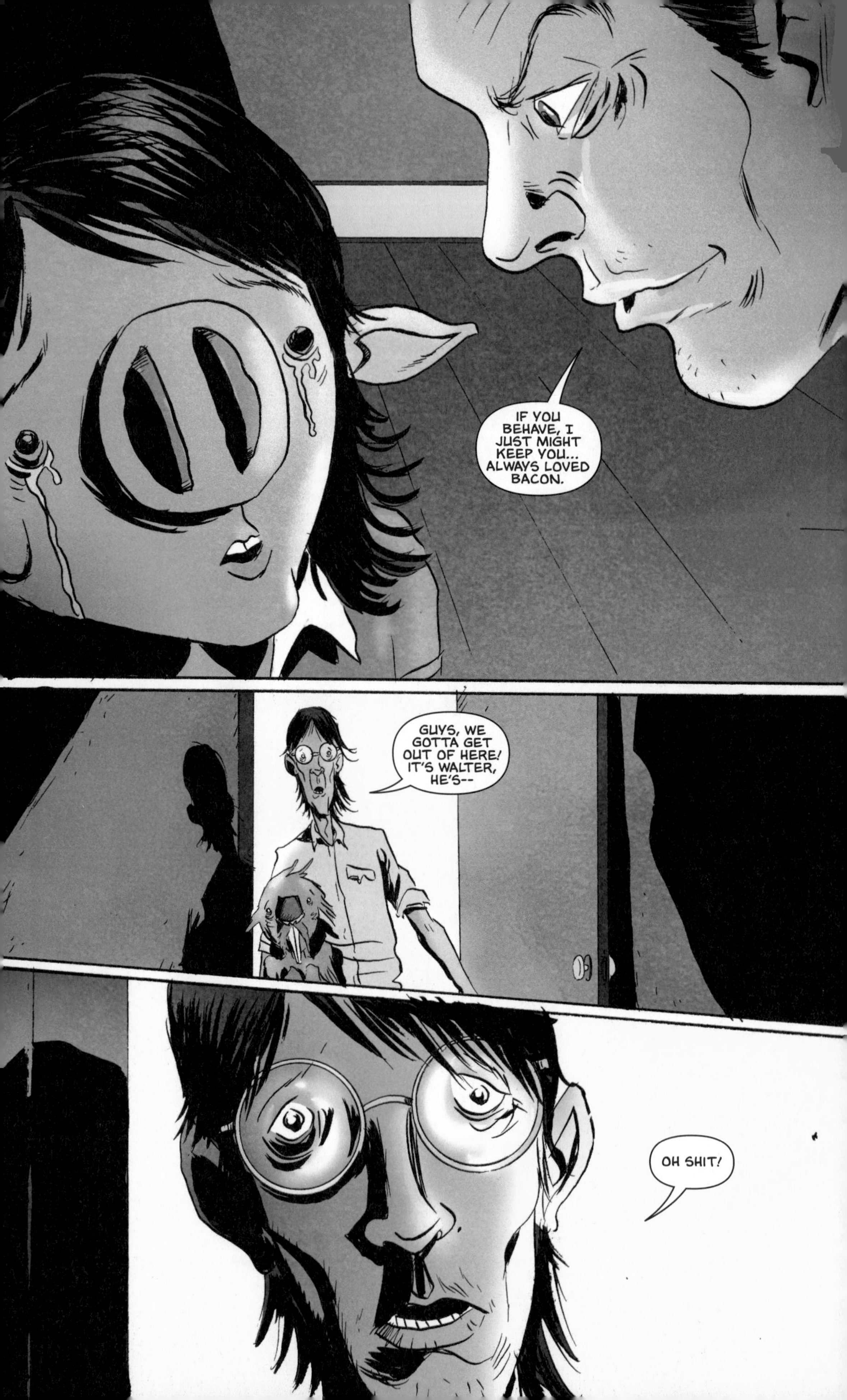
IF YOU BEHAVE, I JUST MIGHT KEEP YOU... ALWAYS LOVED BACON.
GUYS, WE GOTTA GET OUT OF HERE! IT'S WALTER, HE'S--
OH SHIT!

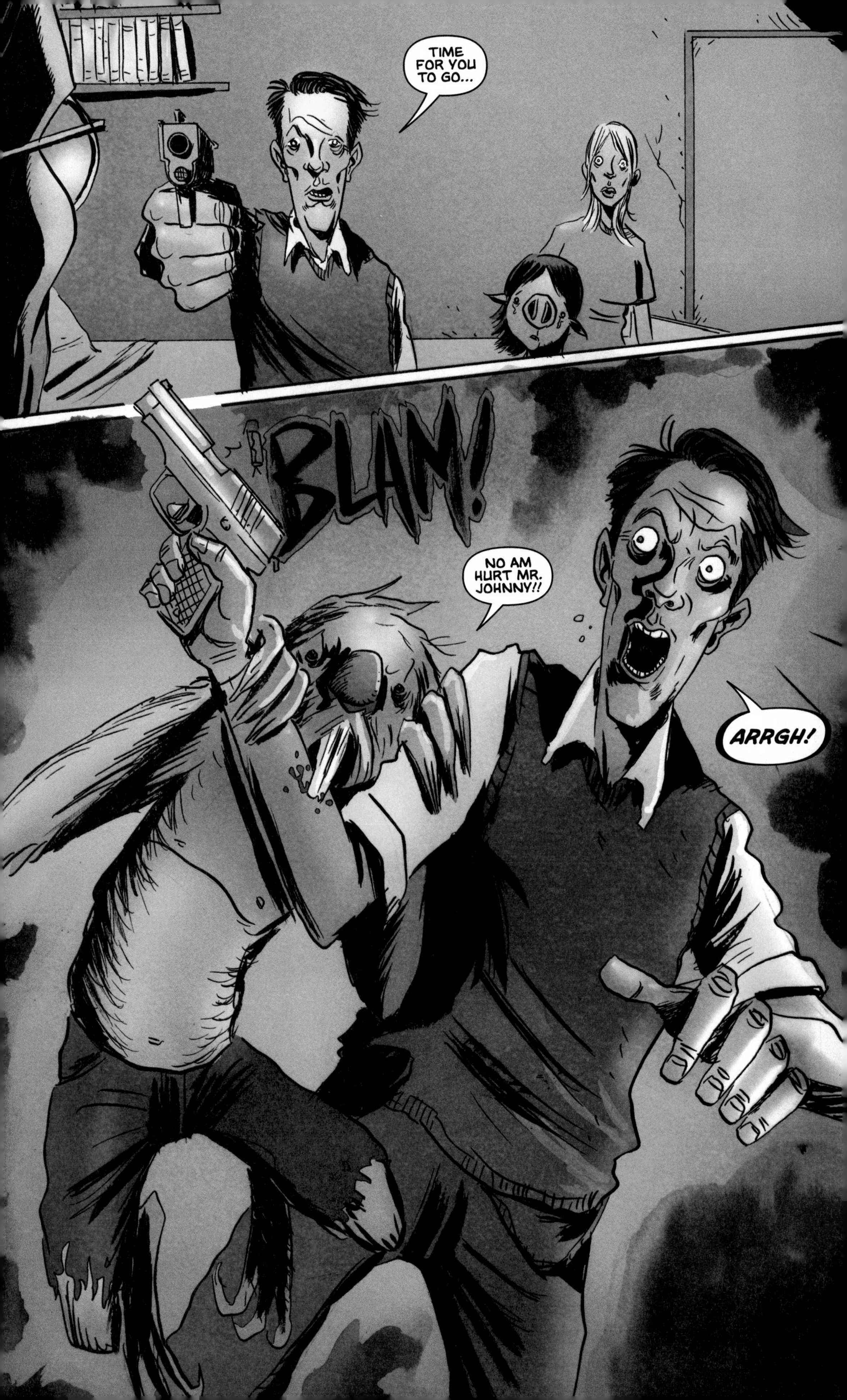
TIME FOR YOU TO GO...
BLAM!
NO AM HURT MR. JOHNNY!!
ARRGH!

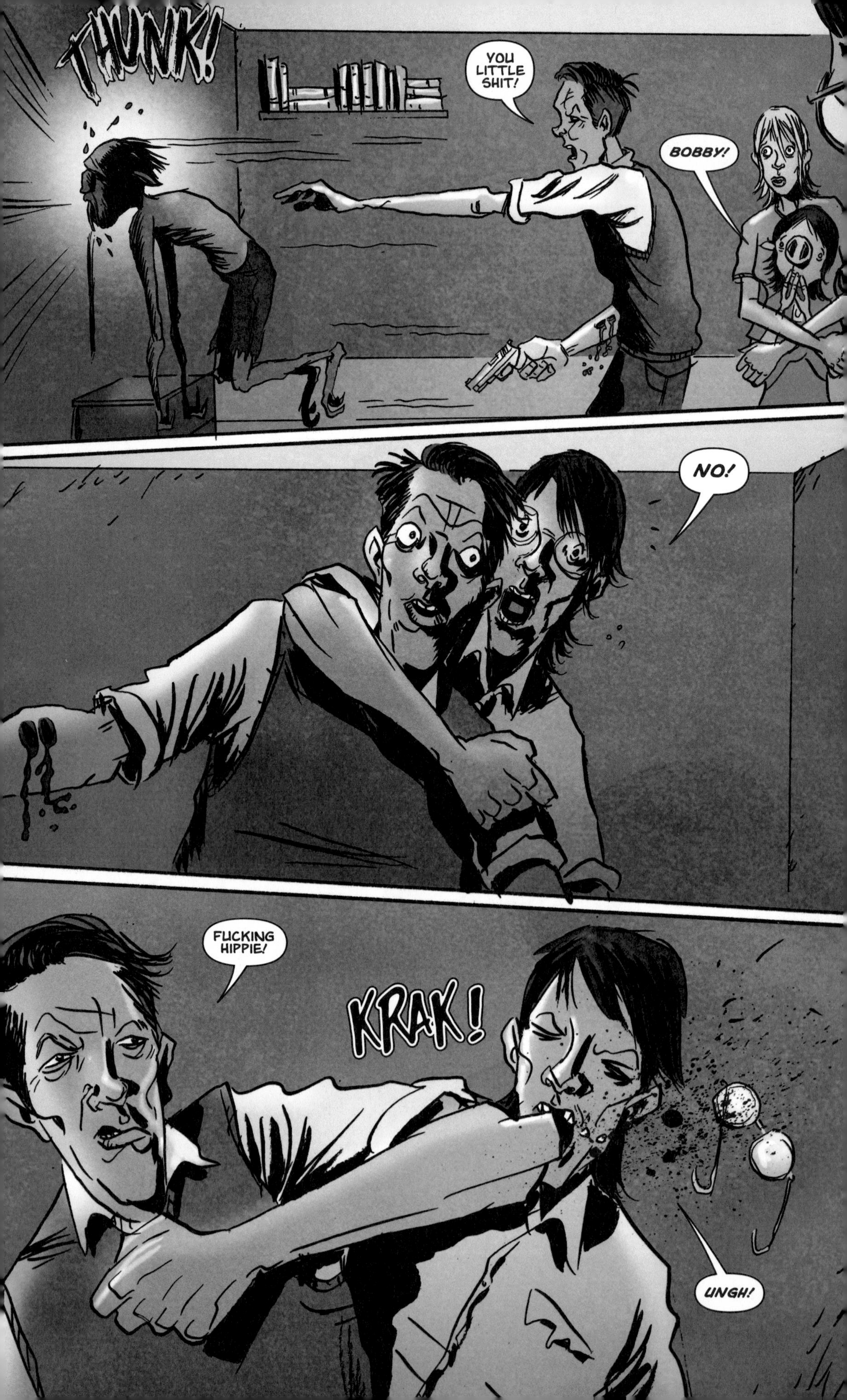
THUNK!
YOU LITTLE SHIT!
BOBBY!
NO!
FUCKING HIPPIE!
KRAK!
UNGH!

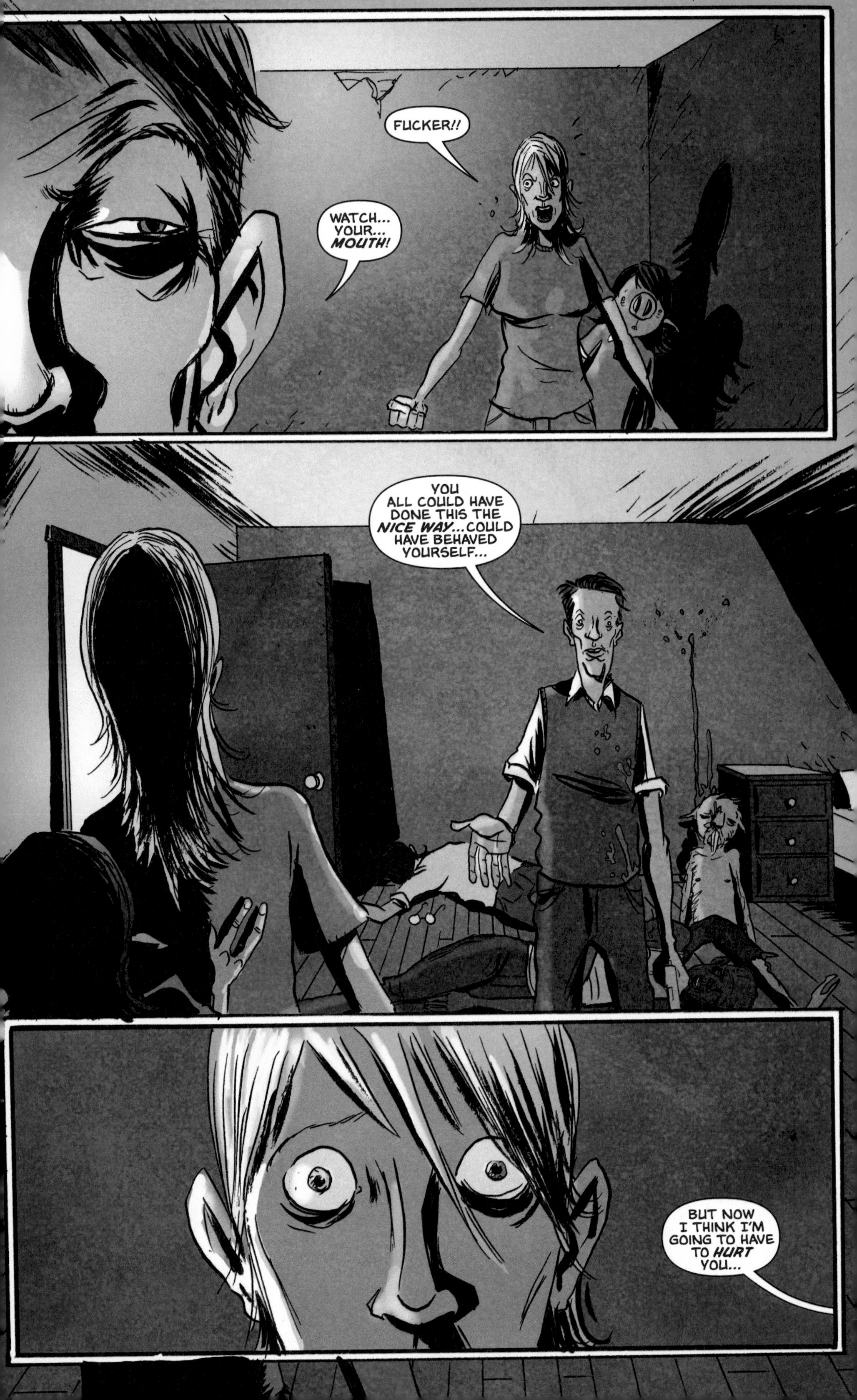
FUCKER!!
WATCH... YOUR... MOUTH!
YOU ALL COULD HAVE DONE THIS THE NICE WAY... COULD HAVE BEHAVED YOURSELF...
BUT NOW I THINK I'M GOING TO HAVE TO HURT YOU...

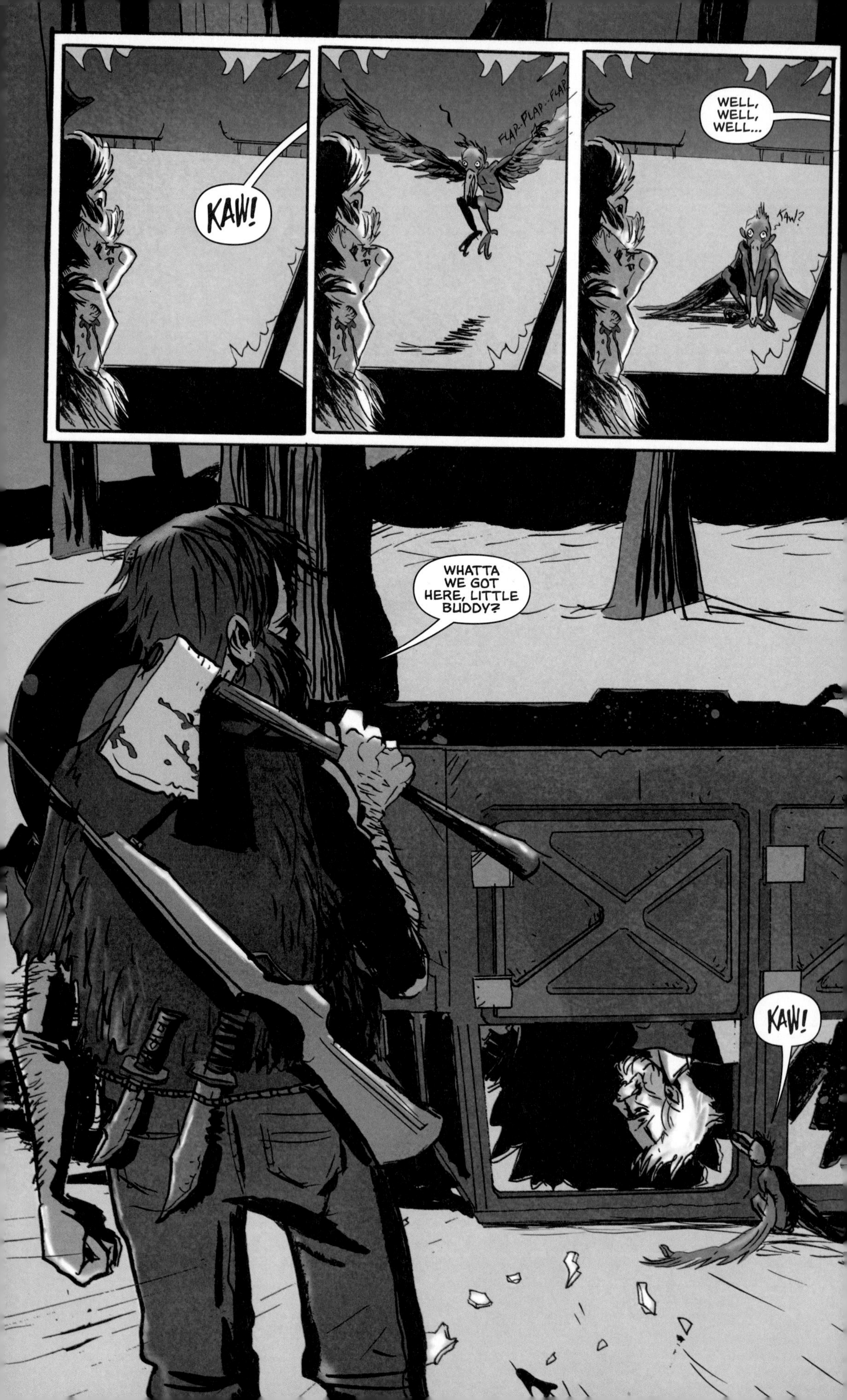
KAW!
FLAP-FLAP-FLAP
WELL, WELL, WELL...
KAW?
WHATTA WE GOT HERE, LITTLE BUDDY?
KAW!

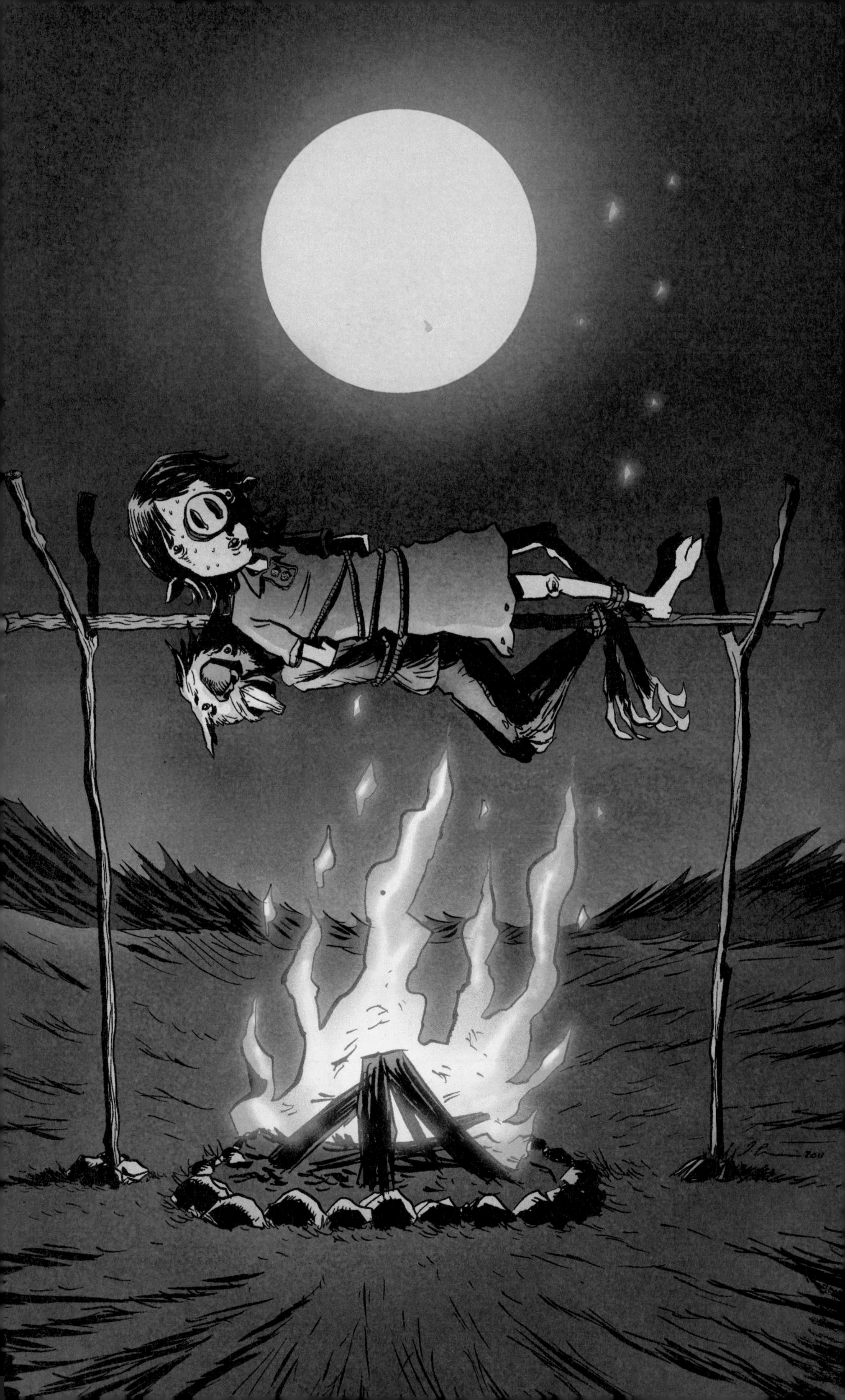
2011

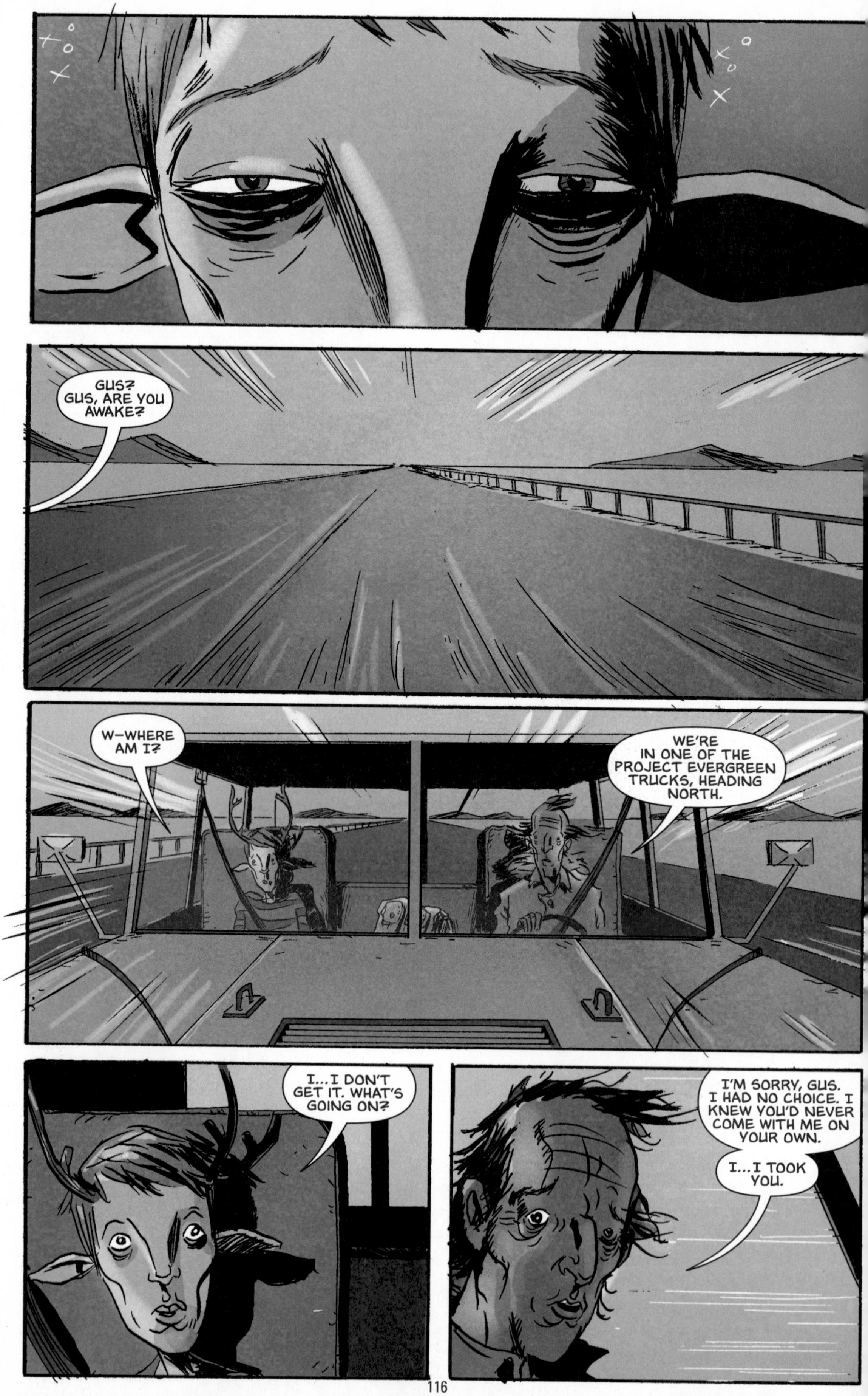
GUS? GUS, ARE YOU AWAKE?
W-WHERE AM I?
WE'RE IN ONE OF THE PROJECT EVERGREEN TRUCKS, HEADING NORTH.
I... I DON'T GET IT. WHAT'S GOING ON?
I'M SORRY, GUS. I HAD NO CHOICE. I KNEW YOU'D NEVER COME WITH ME ON YOUR OWN.
I... I TOOK YOU.

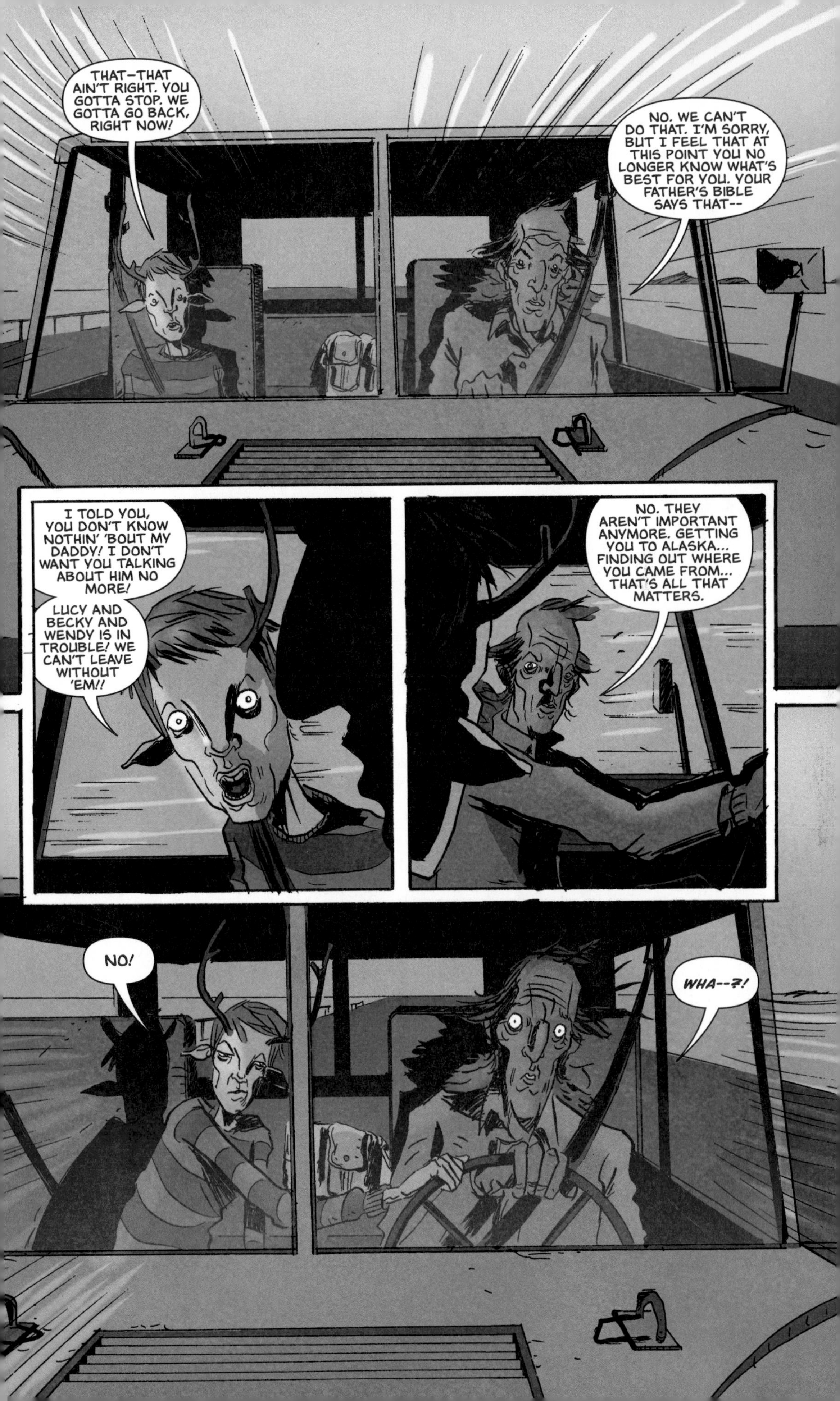
THAT—THAT AIN'T RIGHT. YOU GOTTA STOP. WE GOTTA GO BACK, RIGHT NOW!
NO. WE CAN'T DO THAT. I'M SORRY, BUT I FEEL THAT AT THIS POINT YOU NO LONGER KNOW WHAT'S BEST FOR YOU. YOUR FATHER'S BIBLE SAYS THAT--
I TOLD YOU, YOU DON'T KNOW NOTHIN' 'BOUT MY DADDY! I DON'T WANT YOU TALKING ABOUT HIM NO MORE!
LUCY AND BECKY AND WENDY IS IN TROUBLE! WE CAN'T LEAVE WITHOUT 'EM!!
NO. THEY AREN'T IMPORTANT ANYMORE. GETTING YOU TO ALASKA... FINDING OUT WHERE YOU CAME FROM... THAT'S ALL THAT MATTERS.
NO!
WHA--?!

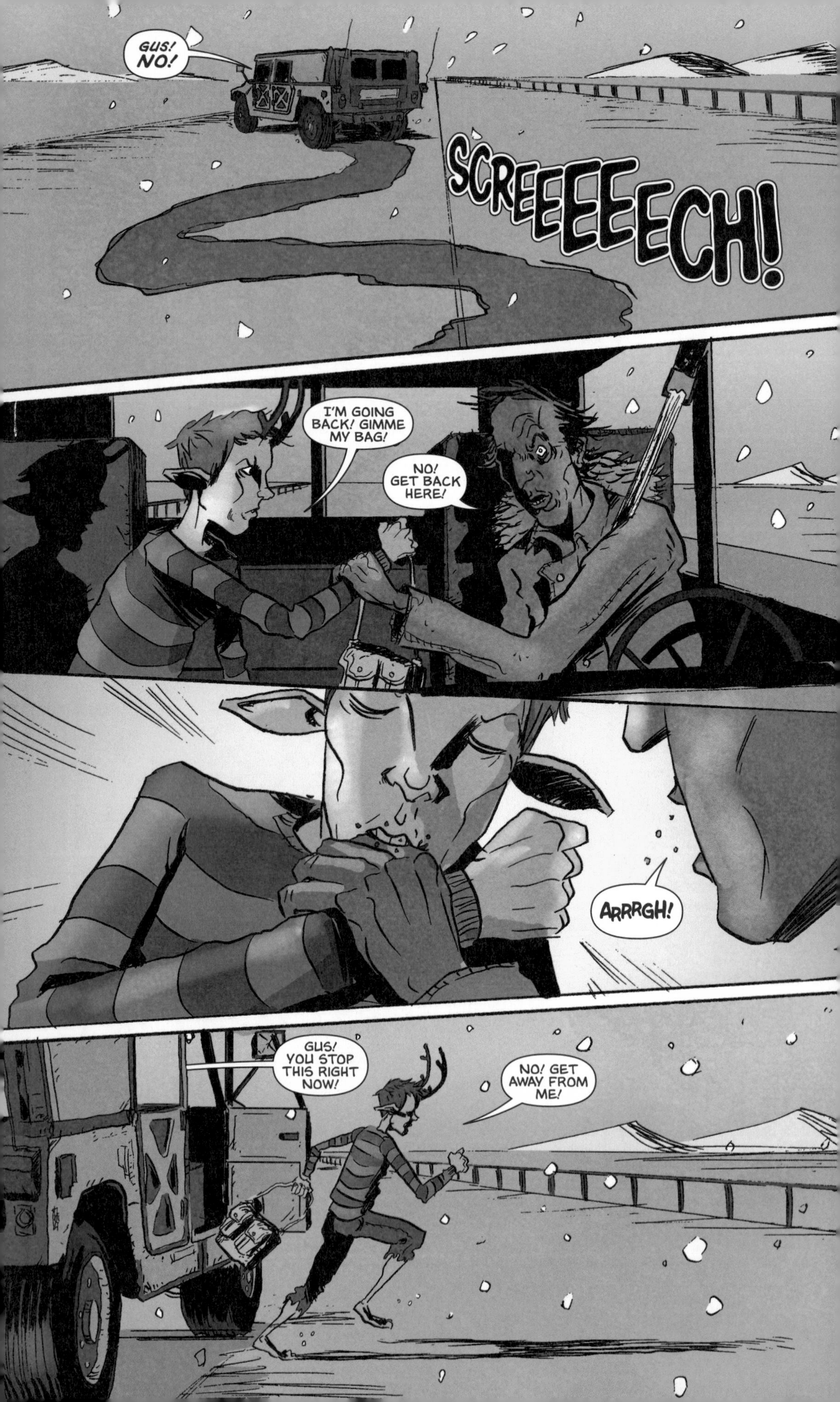
GUS! NO!
SCREEEEEECH!
I'M GOING BACK! GIMME MY BAG!
NO! GET BACK HERE!
ARRRGH!
GUS! YOU STOP THIS RIGHT NOW!
NO! GET AWAY FROM ME!

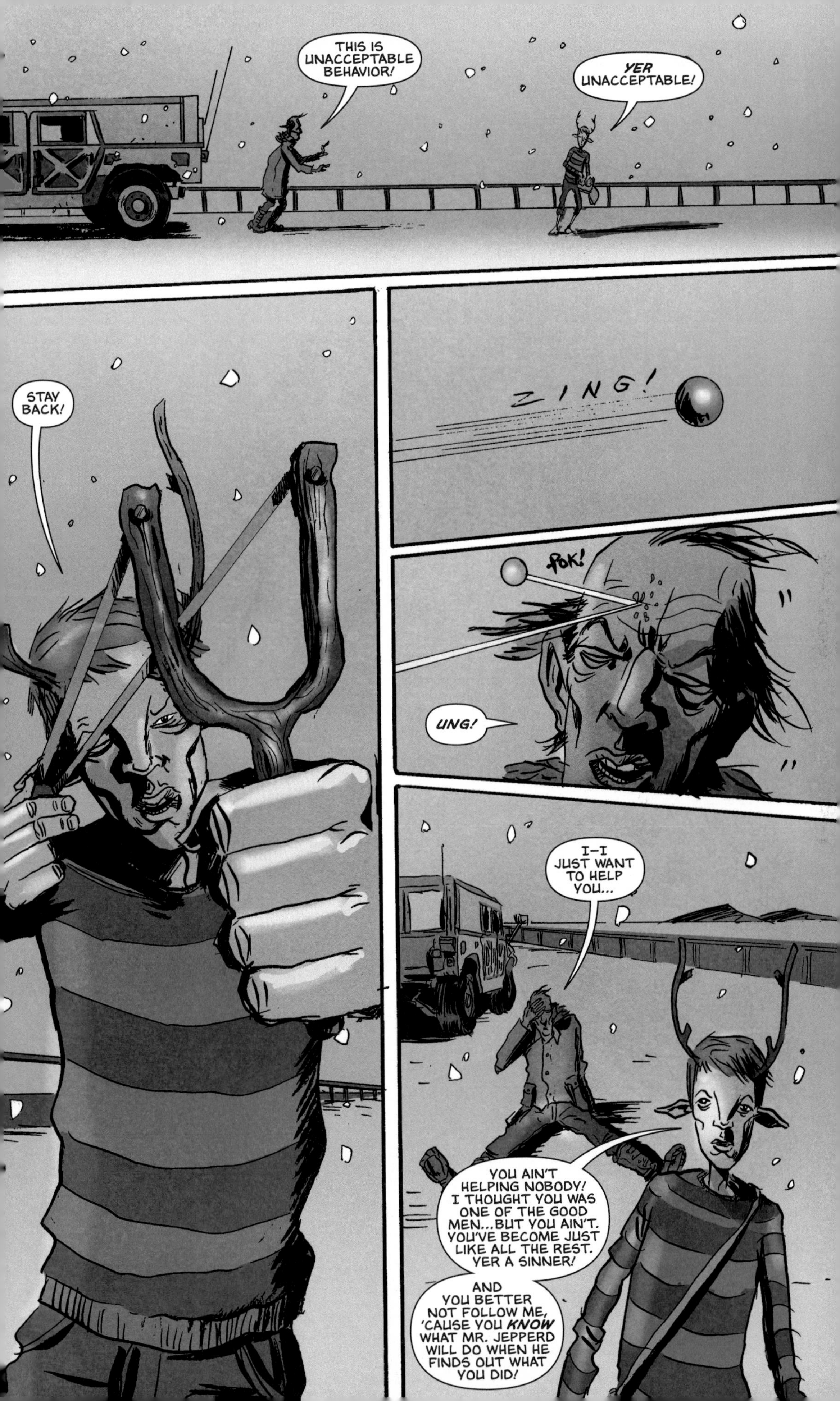

THIS IS UNACCEPTABLE BEHAVIOR!
YER UNACCEPTABLE!
STAY BACK!
ZING!
POK!
UNG!
I--I JUST WANT TO HELP YOU...
YOU AIN'T HELPING NOBODY! I THOUGHT YOU WAS ONE OF THE GOOD MEN...BUT YOU AIN'T. YOU'VE BECOME JUST LIKE ALL THE REST. YER A SINNER!
AND YOU BETTER NOT FOLLOW ME, 'CAUSE YOU *KNOW* WHAT MR. JEPPERD WILL DO WHEN HE FINDS OUT WHAT YOU DID!

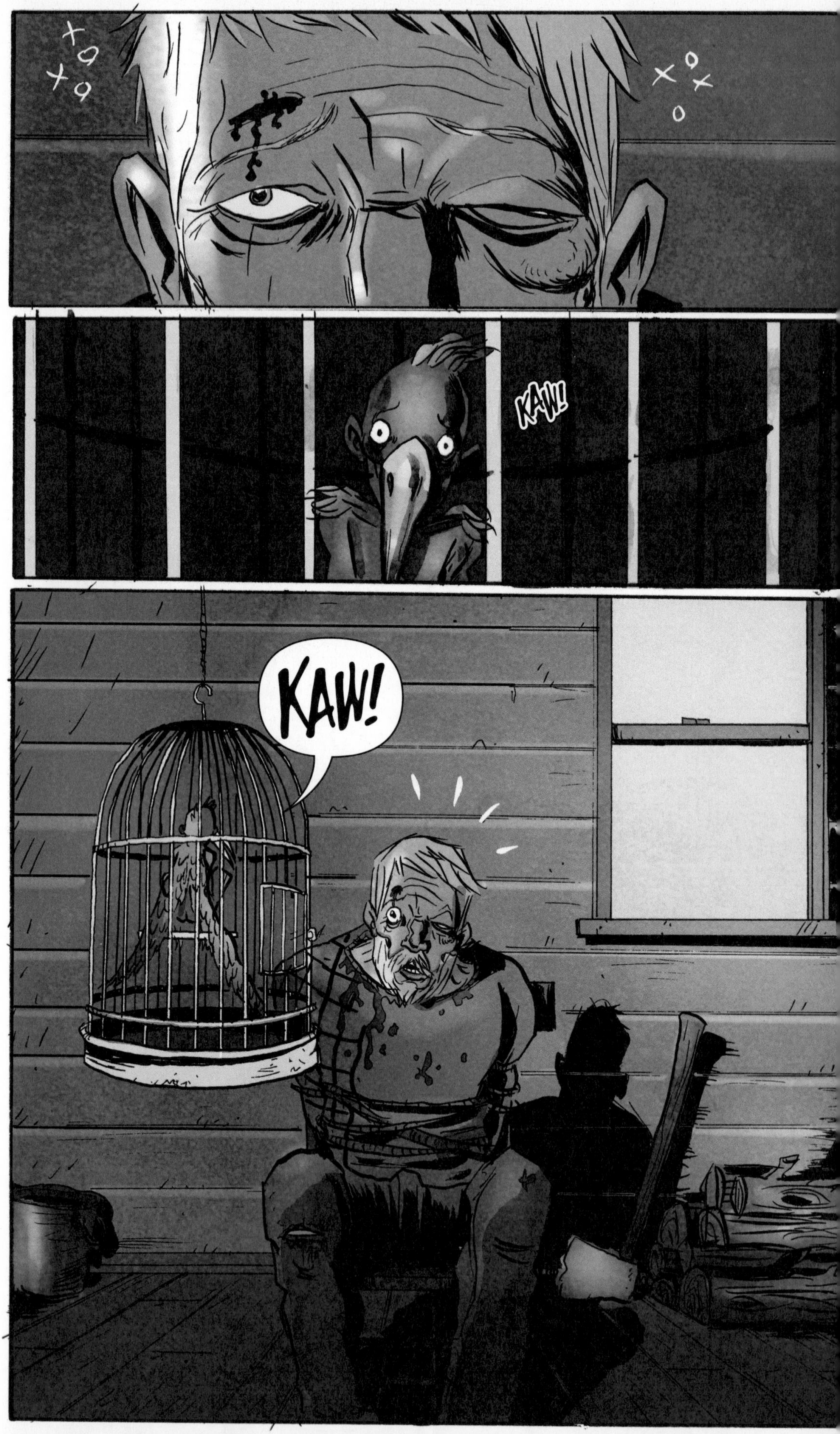

KAW!
KAW!

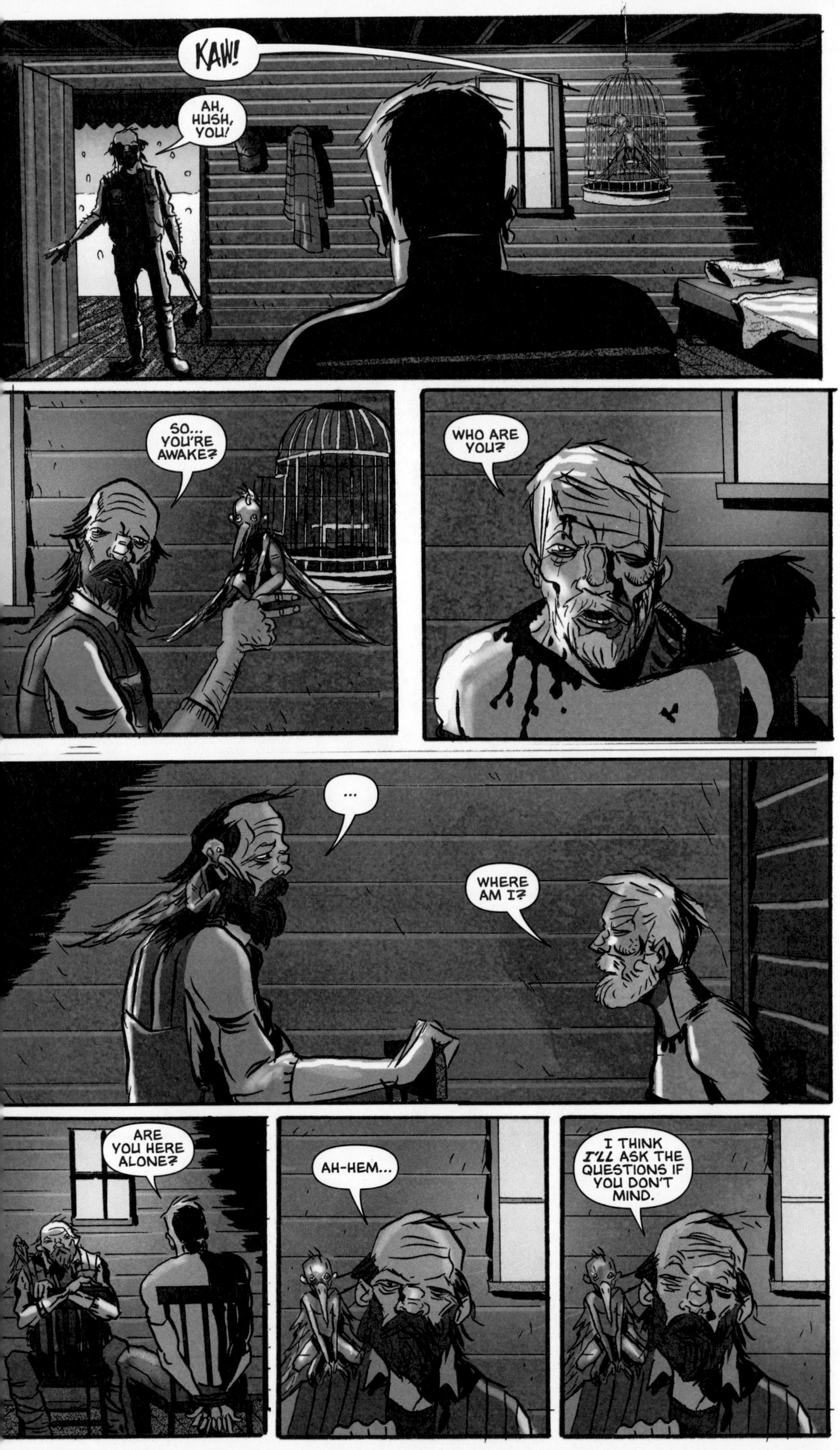
KAW!
AH, HUSH, YOU!
SO... YOU'RE AWAKE?
WHO ARE YOU?
...
WHERE AM I?
ARE YOU HERE ALONE?
AH-HEM...
I THINK I'LL ASK THE QUESTIONS IF YOU DON'T MIND.

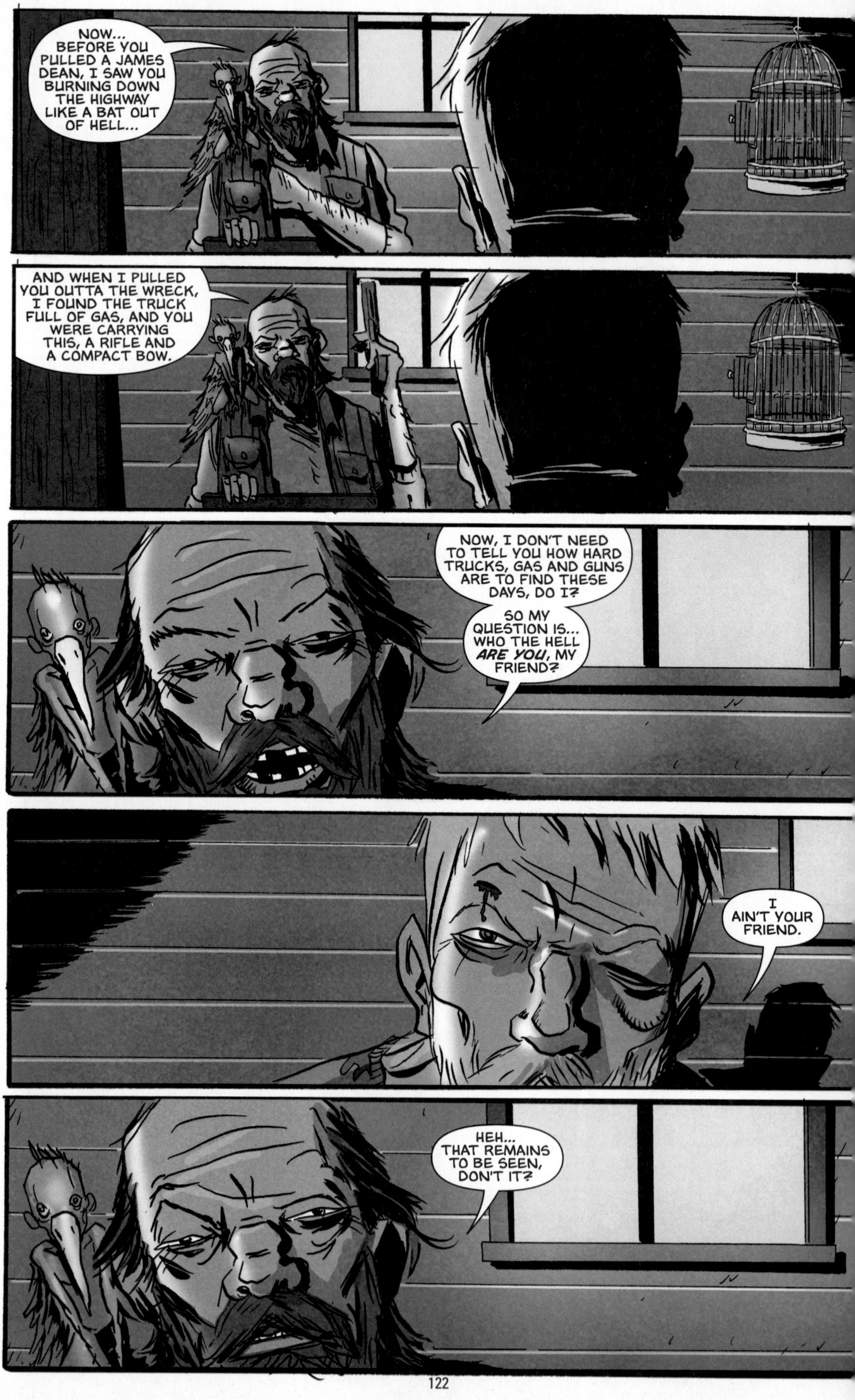
NOW... BEFORE YOU PULLED A JAMES DEAN, I SAW YOU BURNING DOWN THE HIGHWAY LIKE A BAT OUT OF HELL...
AND WHEN I PULLED YOU OUTTA THE WRECK, I FOUND THE TRUCK FULL OF GAS, AND YOU WERE CARRYING THIS, A RIFLE AND A COMPACT BOW.
NOW, I DON'T NEED TO TELL YOU HOW HARD TRUCKS, GAS AND GUNS ARE TO FIND THESE DAYS, DO I?
SO MY QUESTION IS... WHO THE HELL ARE YOU, MY FRIEND?
I AIN'T YOUR FRIEND.
HEH... THAT REMAINS TO BE SEEN, DON'T IT?

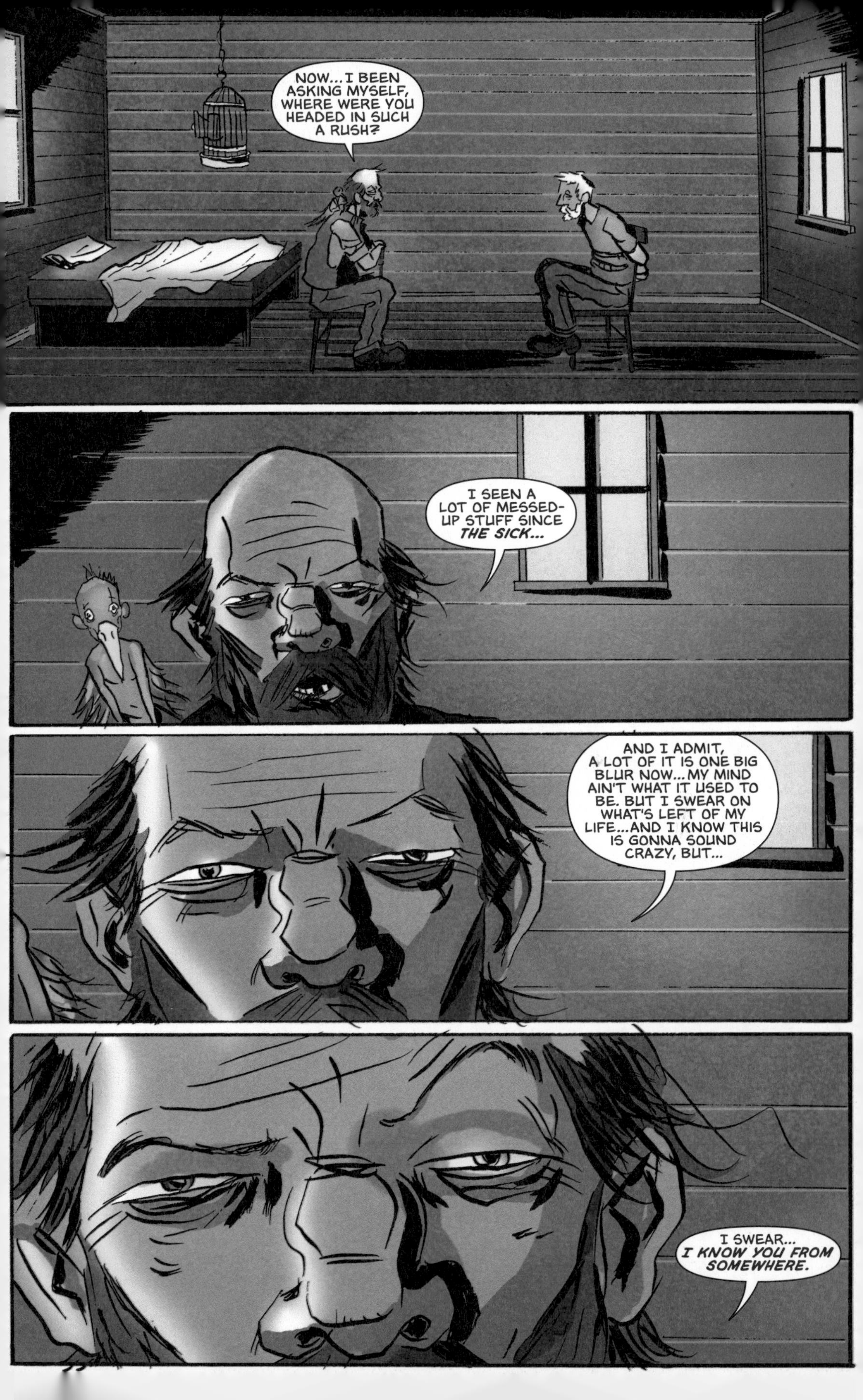
NOW... I BEEN ASKING MYSELF, WHERE WERE YOU HEADED IN SUCH A RUSH?
I SEEN A LOT OF MESSED-UP STUFF SINCE *THE SICK...*
AND I ADMIT, A LOT OF IT IS ONE BIG BLUR NOW... MY MIND AIN'T WHAT IT USED TO BE. BUT I SWEAR ON WHAT'S LEFT OF MY LIFE...AND I KNOW THIS IS GONNA SOUND CRAZY, BUT...
I SWEAR... *I KNOW YOU FROM SOMEWHERE.*

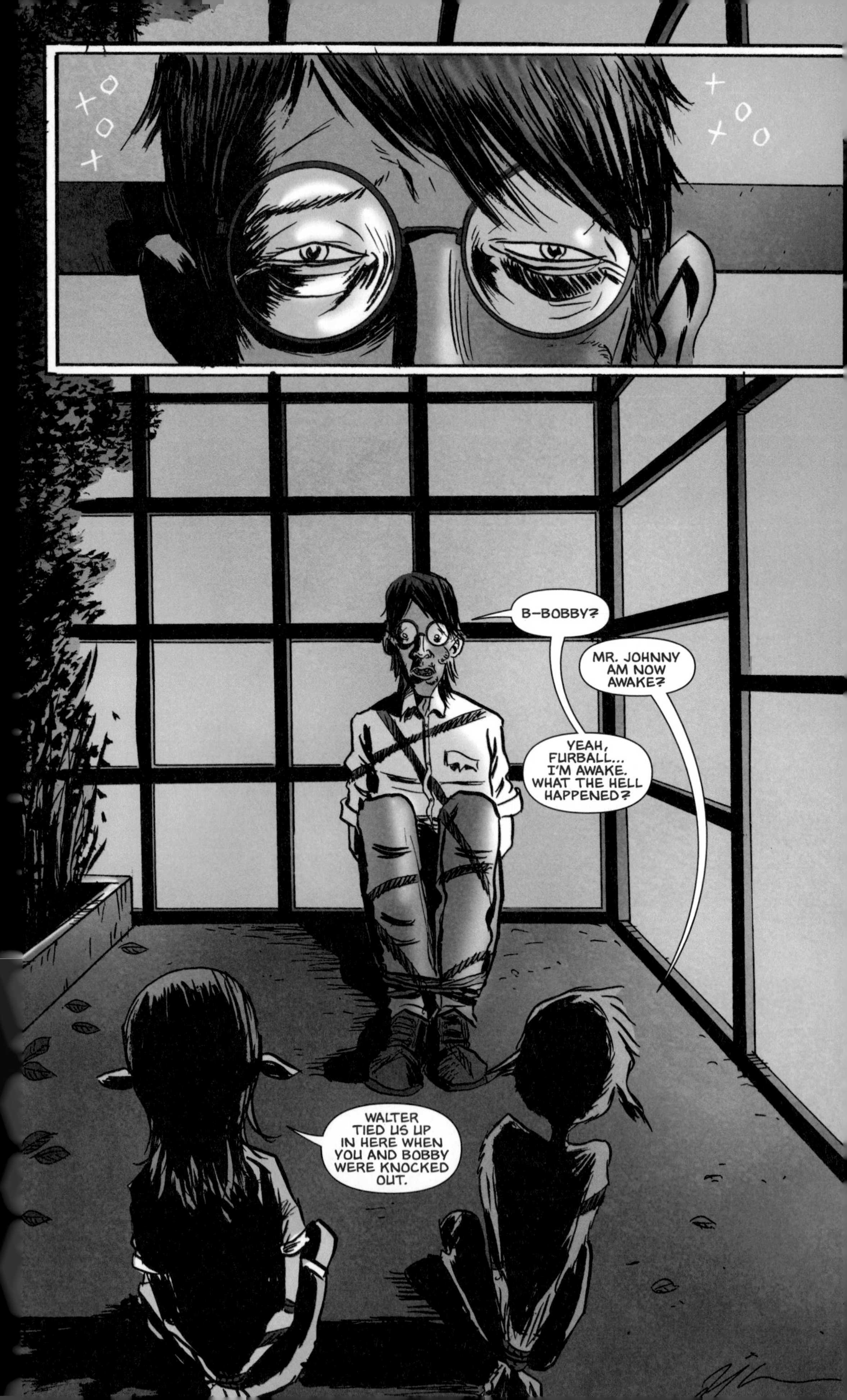
B-BOBBY?
MR. JOHNNY AM NOW AWAKE?
YEAH, FURBALL... I'M AWAKE. WHAT THE HELL HAPPENED?
WALTER TIED US UP IN HERE WHEN YOU AND BOBBY WERE KNOCKED OUT.

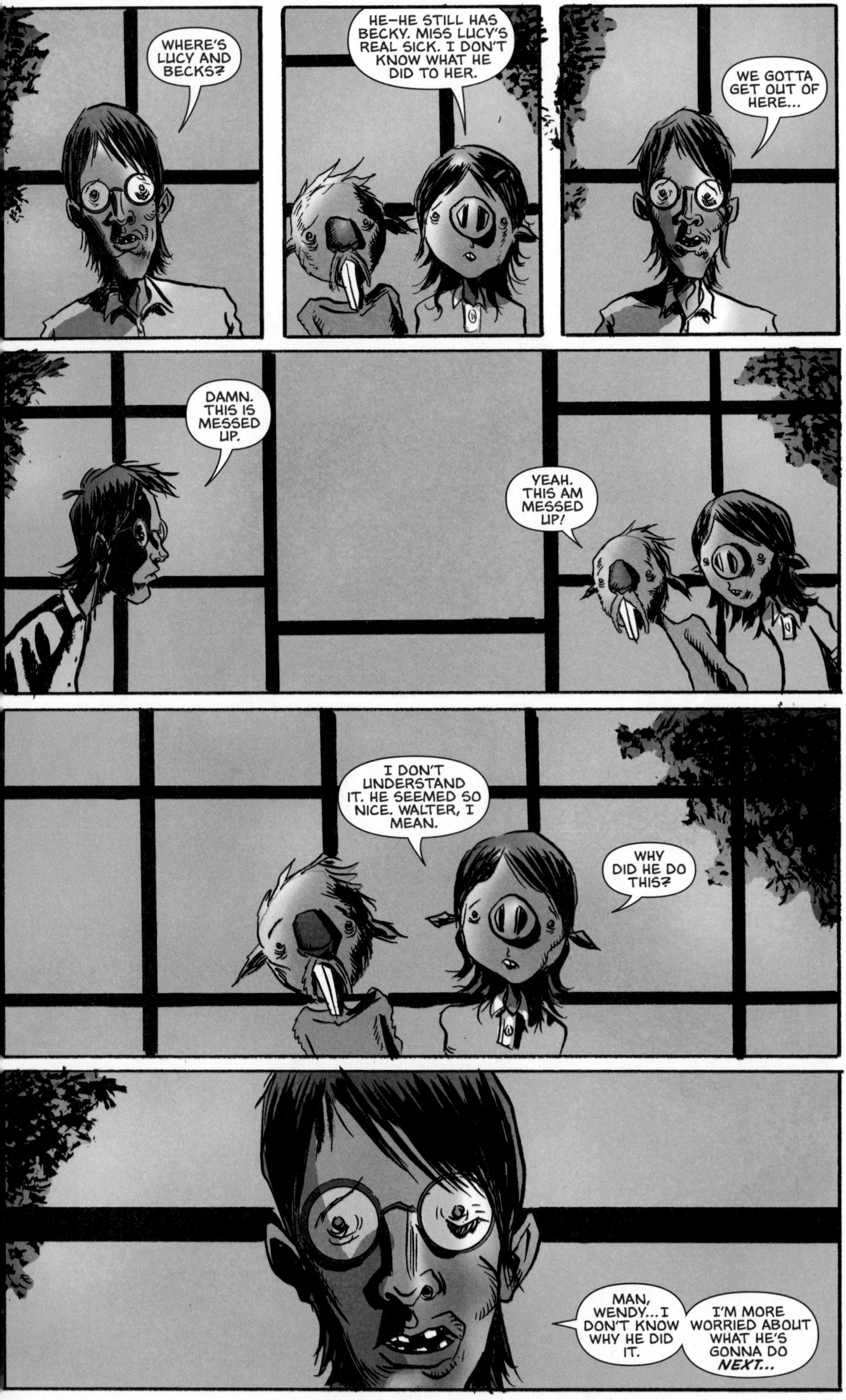
WHERE'S LUCY AND BECKS?
HE—HE STILL HAS BECKY. MISS LUCY'S REAL SICK. I DON'T KNOW WHAT HE DID TO HER.
WE GOTTA GET OUT OF HERE...
DAMN. THIS IS MESSED UP.
YEAH. THIS AM MESSED UP!
I DON'T UNDERSTAND IT. HE SEEMED SO NICE. WALTER, I MEAN.
WHY DID HE DO THIS?
MAN, WENDY... I DON'T KNOW WHY HE DID IT.
I'M MORE WORRIED ABOUT WHAT HE'S GONNA DO *NEXT...*

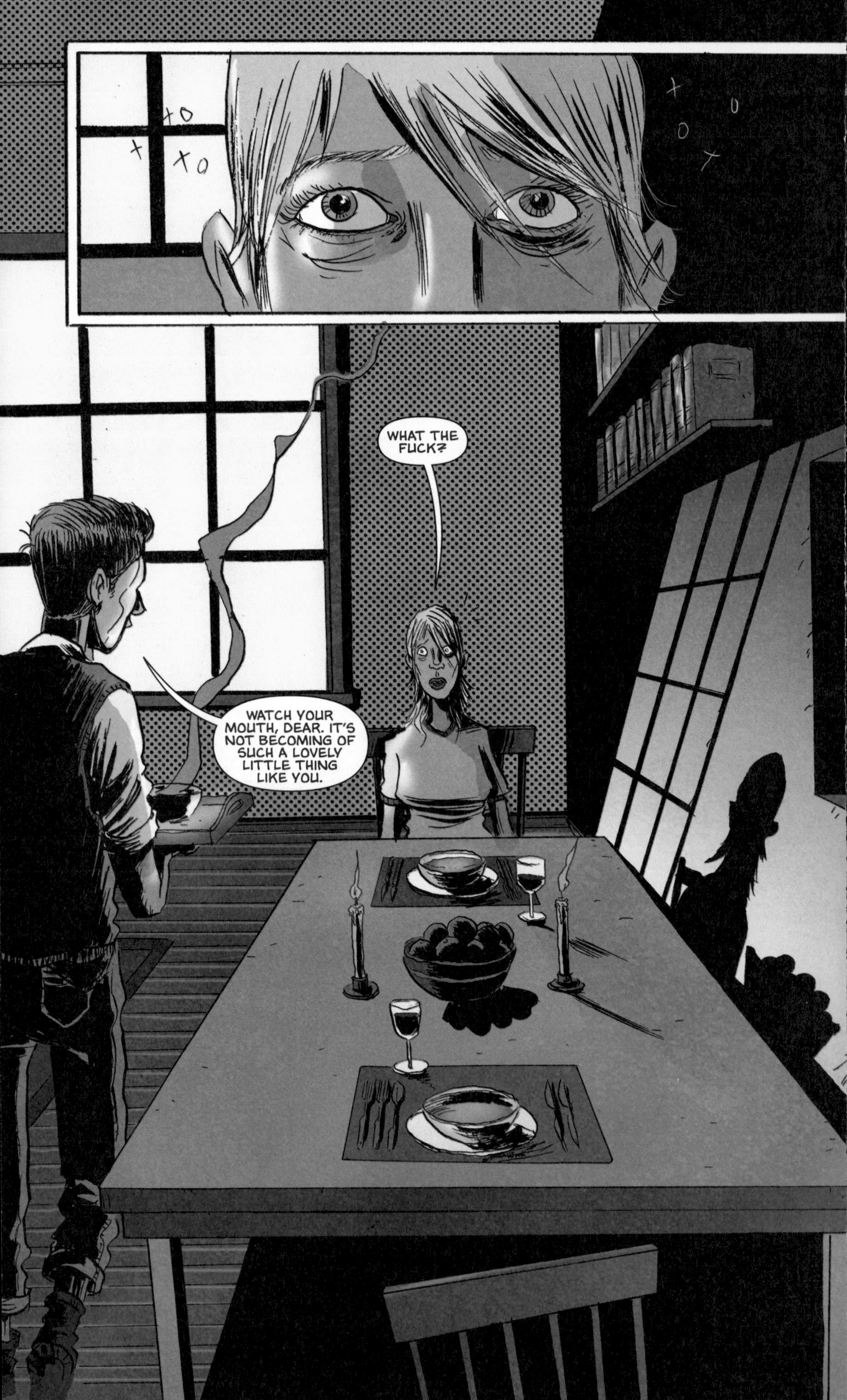
WHAT THE FUCK?
WATCH YOUR MOUTH, DEAR. IT'S NOT BECOMING OF SUCH A LOVELY LITTLE THING LIKE YOU.

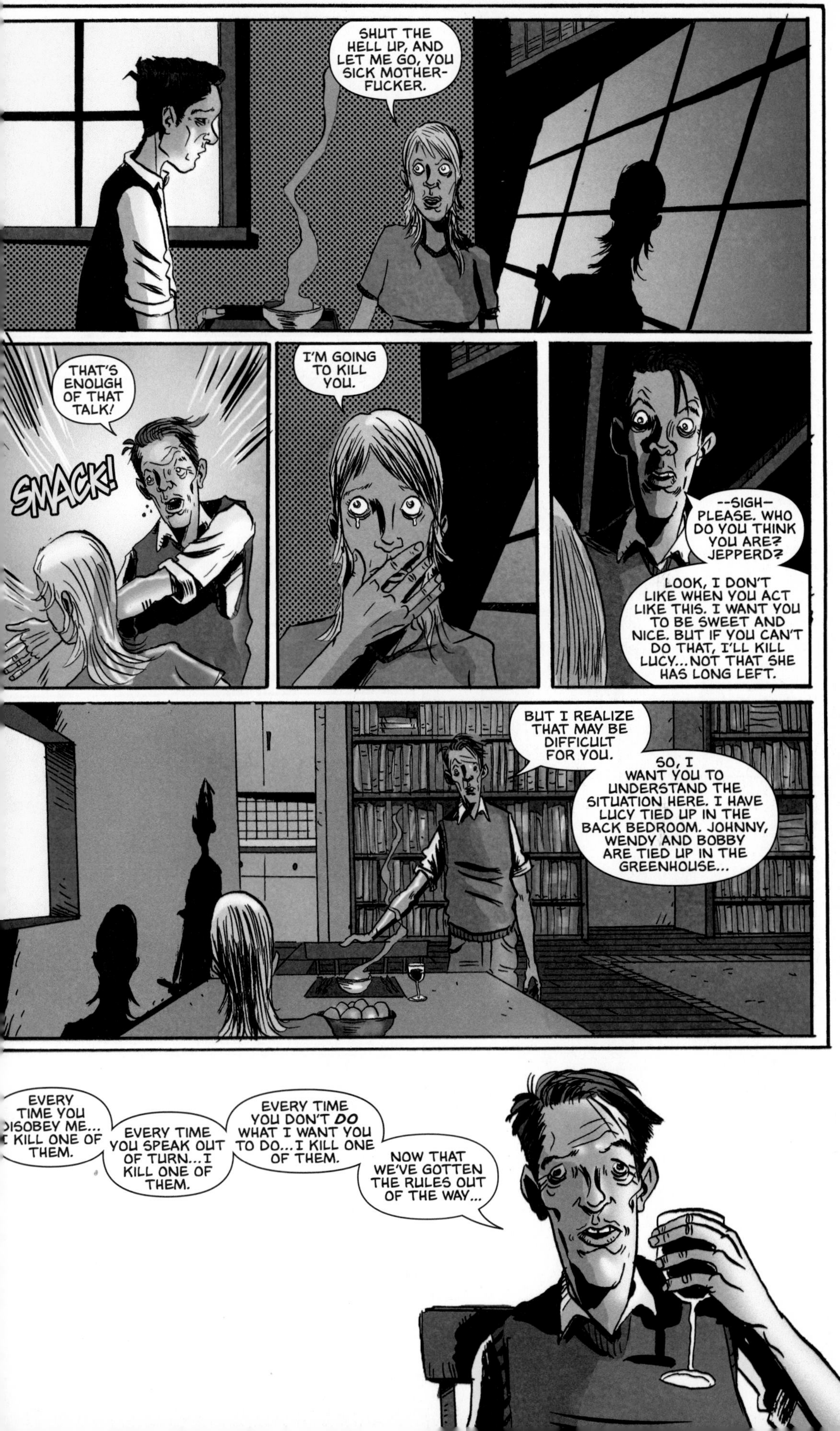
SHUT THE HELL UP, AND LET ME GO, YOU SICK MOTHER-FUCKER.
THAT'S ENOUGH OF THAT TALK!
SMACK!
I'M GOING TO KILL YOU.
--SIGH-- PLEASE. WHO DO YOU THINK YOU ARE? JEPPERD?
LOOK, I DON'T LIKE WHEN YOU ACT LIKE THIS. I WANT YOU TO BE SWEET AND NICE. BUT IF YOU CAN'T DO THAT, I'LL KILL LUCY...NOT THAT SHE HAS LONG LEFT.
BUT I REALIZE THAT MAY BE DIFFICULT FOR YOU.
SO, I WANT YOU TO UNDERSTAND THE SITUATION HERE. I HAVE LUCY TIED UP IN THE BACK BEDROOM. JOHNNY, WENDY AND BOBBY ARE TIED UP IN THE GREENHOUSE...
EVERY TIME YOU DISOBEY ME... I KILL ONE OF THEM.
EVERY TIME YOU SPEAK OUT OF TURN...I KILL ONE OF THEM.
EVERY TIME YOU DON'T DO WHAT I WANT YOU TO DO...I KILL ONE OF THEM.
NOW THAT WE'VE GOTTEN THE RULES OUT OF THE WAY...

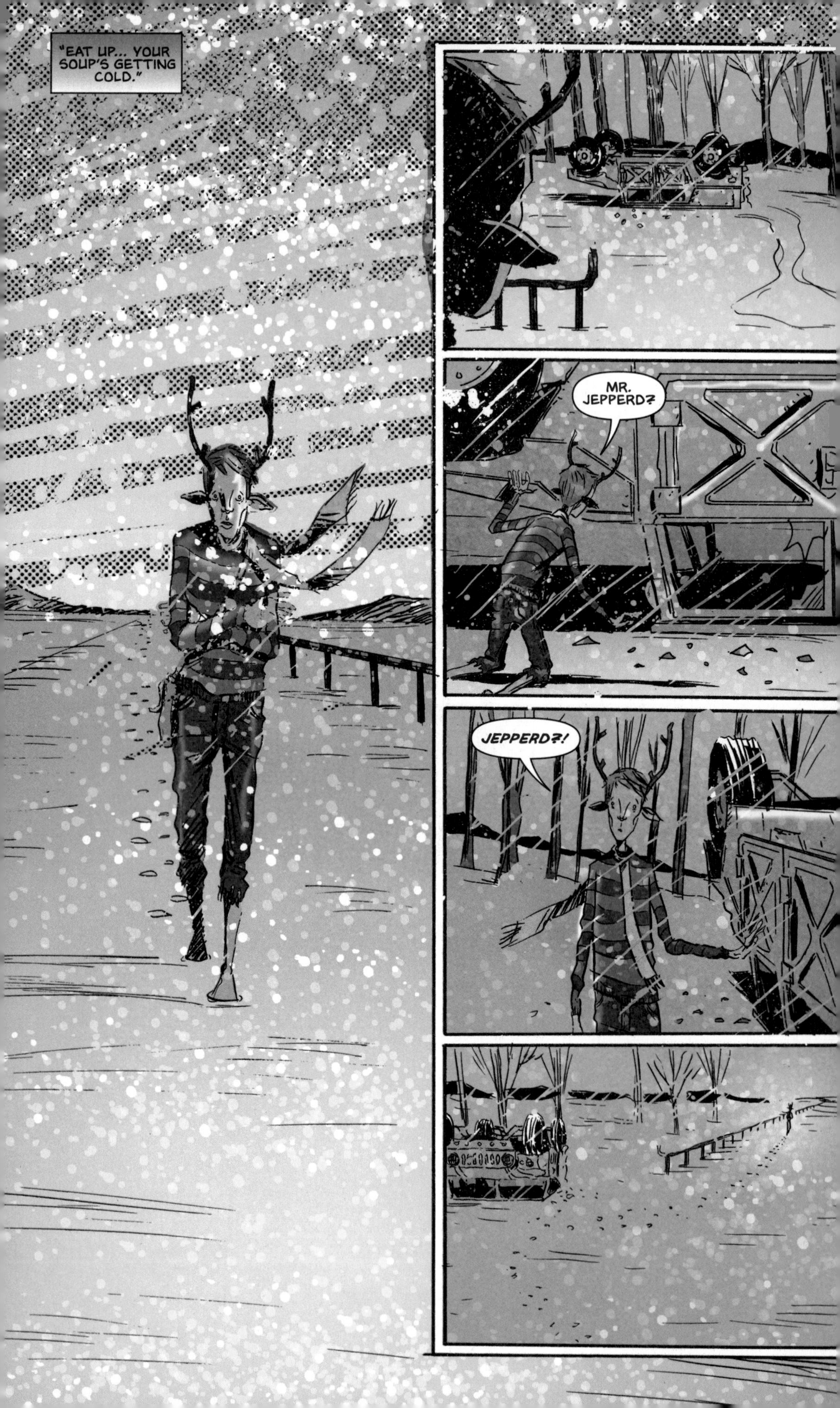
"EAT UP... YOUR SOUP'S GETTING COLD."
MR. JEPPERD?
JEPPERD?!

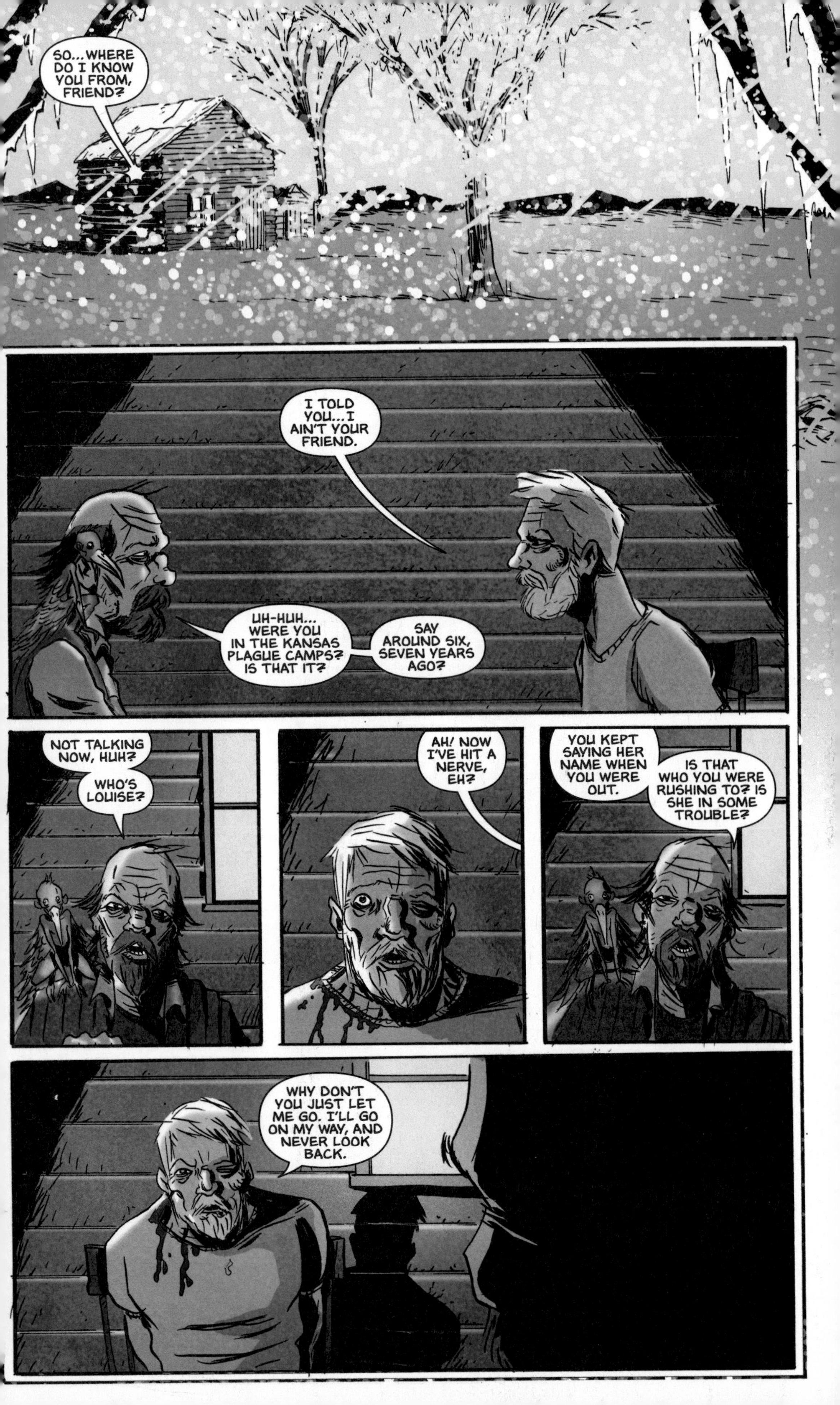
SO...WHERE DO I KNOW YOU FROM, FRIEND?
I TOLD YOU...I AIN'T YOUR FRIEND.
UH-HUH... WERE YOU IN THE KANSAS PLAGUE CAMPS? IS THAT IT?
SAY AROUND SIX, SEVEN YEARS AGO?
NOT TALKING NOW, HUH?
WHO'S LOUISE?
AH! NOW I'VE HIT A NERVE, EH?
YOU KEPT SAYING HER NAME WHEN YOU WERE OUT.
IS THAT WHO YOU WERE RUSHING TO? IS SHE IN SOME TROUBLE?
WHY DON'T YOU JUST LET ME GO. I'LL GO ON MY WAY, AND NEVER LOOK BACK.

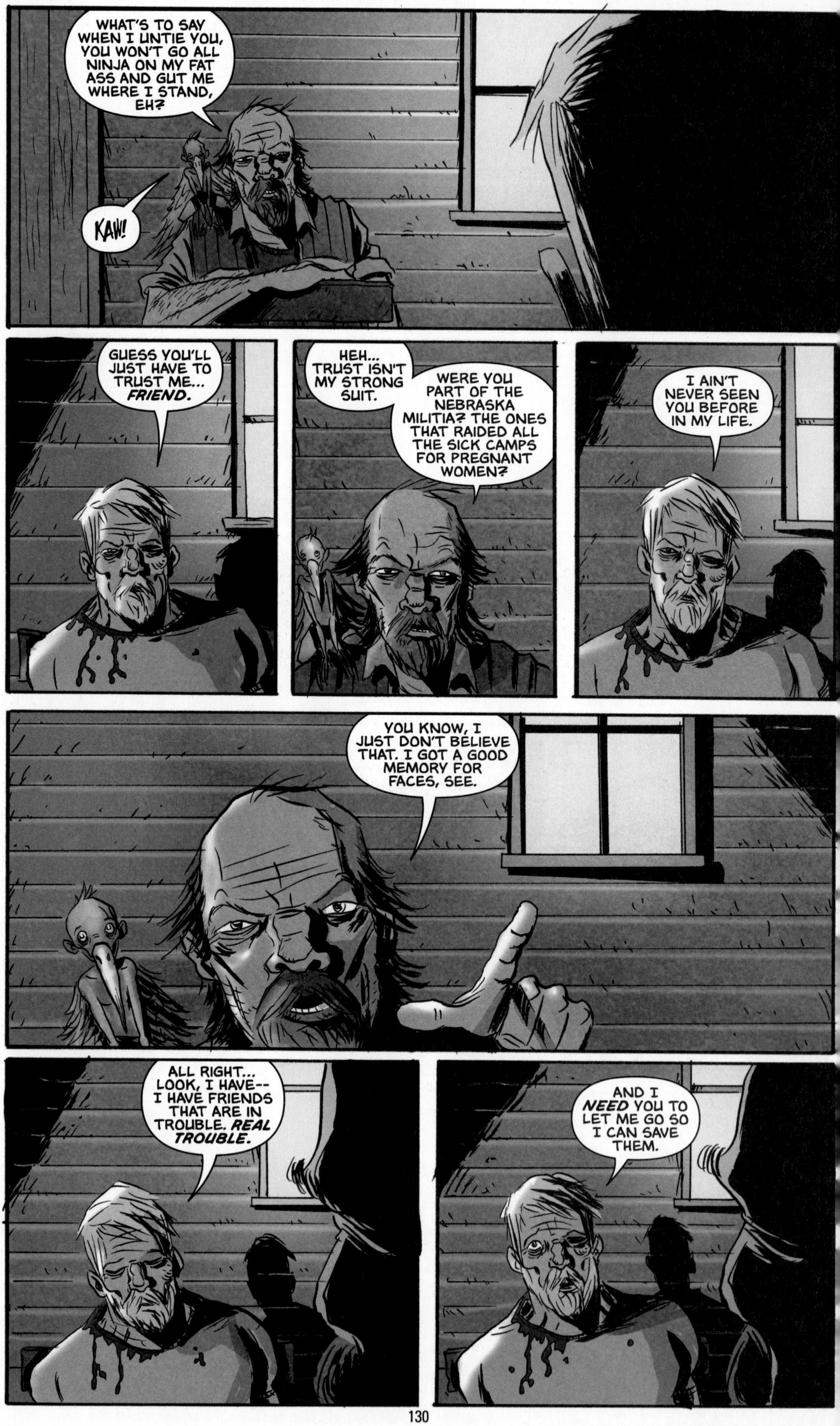
WHAT'S TO SAY WHEN I UNTIE YOU, YOU WON'T GO ALL NINJA ON MY FAT ASS AND GUT ME WHERE I STAND, EH?
KAW!
GUESS YOU'LL JUST HAVE TO TRUST ME... FRIEND.
HEH... TRUST ISN'T MY STRONG SUIT.
WERE YOU PART OF THE NEBRASKA MILITIA? THE ONES THAT RAIDED ALL THE SICK CAMPS FOR PREGNANT WOMEN?
I AIN'T NEVER SEEN YOU BEFORE IN MY LIFE.
YOU KNOW, I JUST DON'T BELIEVE THAT. I GOT A GOOD MEMORY FOR FACES, SEE.
ALL RIGHT... LOOK, I HAVE-- I HAVE FRIENDS THAT ARE IN TROUBLE. REAL TROUBLE.
AND I NEED YOU TO LET ME GO SO I CAN SAVE THEM.

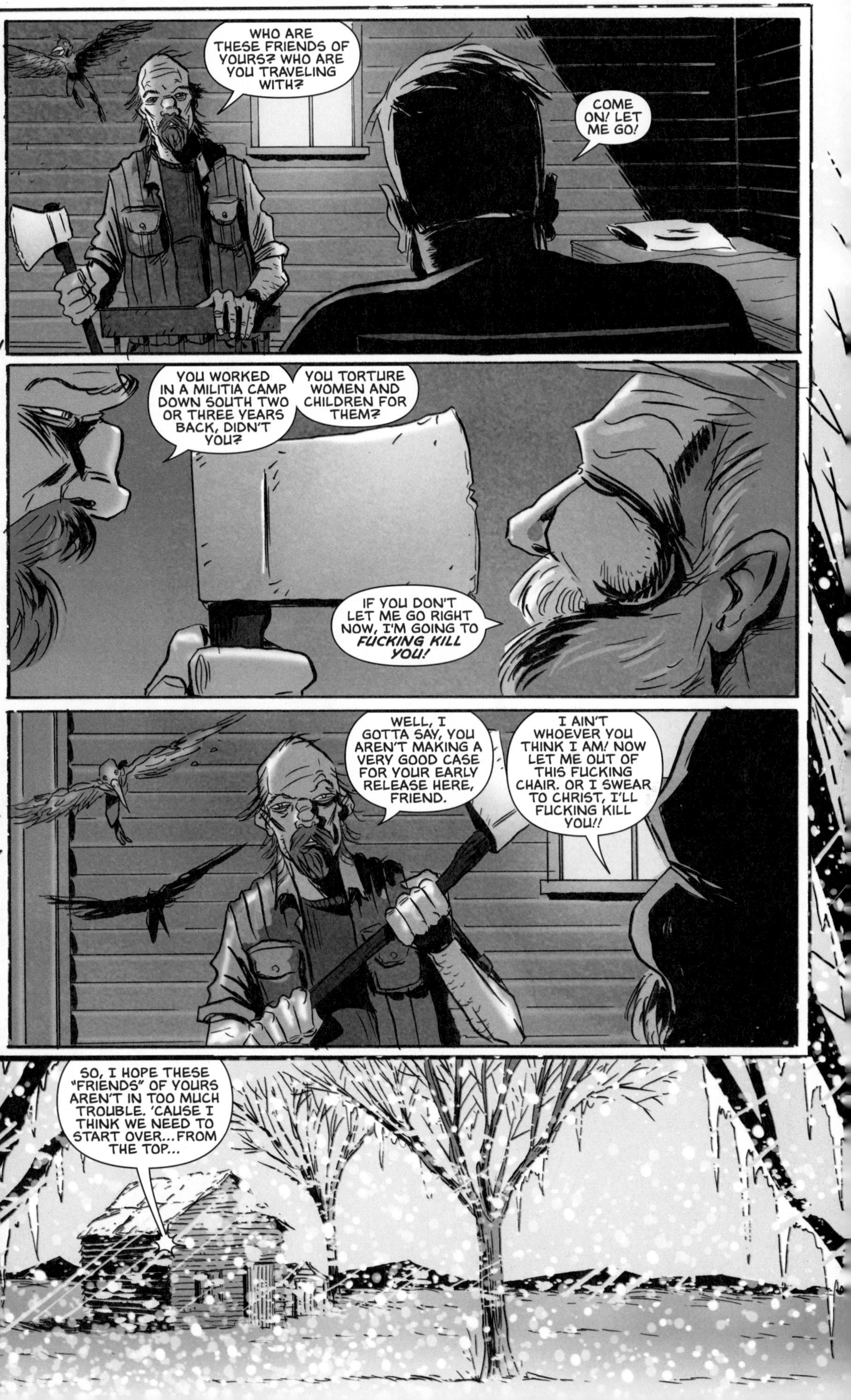
WHO ARE THESE FRIENDS OF YOURS? WHO ARE YOU TRAVELING WITH?
COME ON! LET ME GO!
YOU WORKED IN A MILITIA CAMP DOWN SOUTH TWO OR THREE YEARS BACK, DIDN'T YOU?
YOU TORTURE WOMEN AND CHILDREN FOR THEM?
IF YOU DON'T LET ME GO RIGHT NOW, I'M GOING TO *FUCKING KILL YOU!*
WELL, I GOTTA SAY, YOU AREN'T MAKING A VERY GOOD CASE FOR YOUR EARLY RELEASE HERE, FRIEND.
I AIN'T WHOEVER YOU THINK I AM! NOW LET ME OUT OF THIS FUCKING CHAIR. OR I SWEAR TO CHRIST, I'LL FUCKING KILL YOU!!
SO, I HOPE THESE "FRIENDS" OF YOURS AREN'T IN TOO MUCH TROUBLE. 'CAUSE I THINK WE NEED TO START OVER...FROM THE TOP...

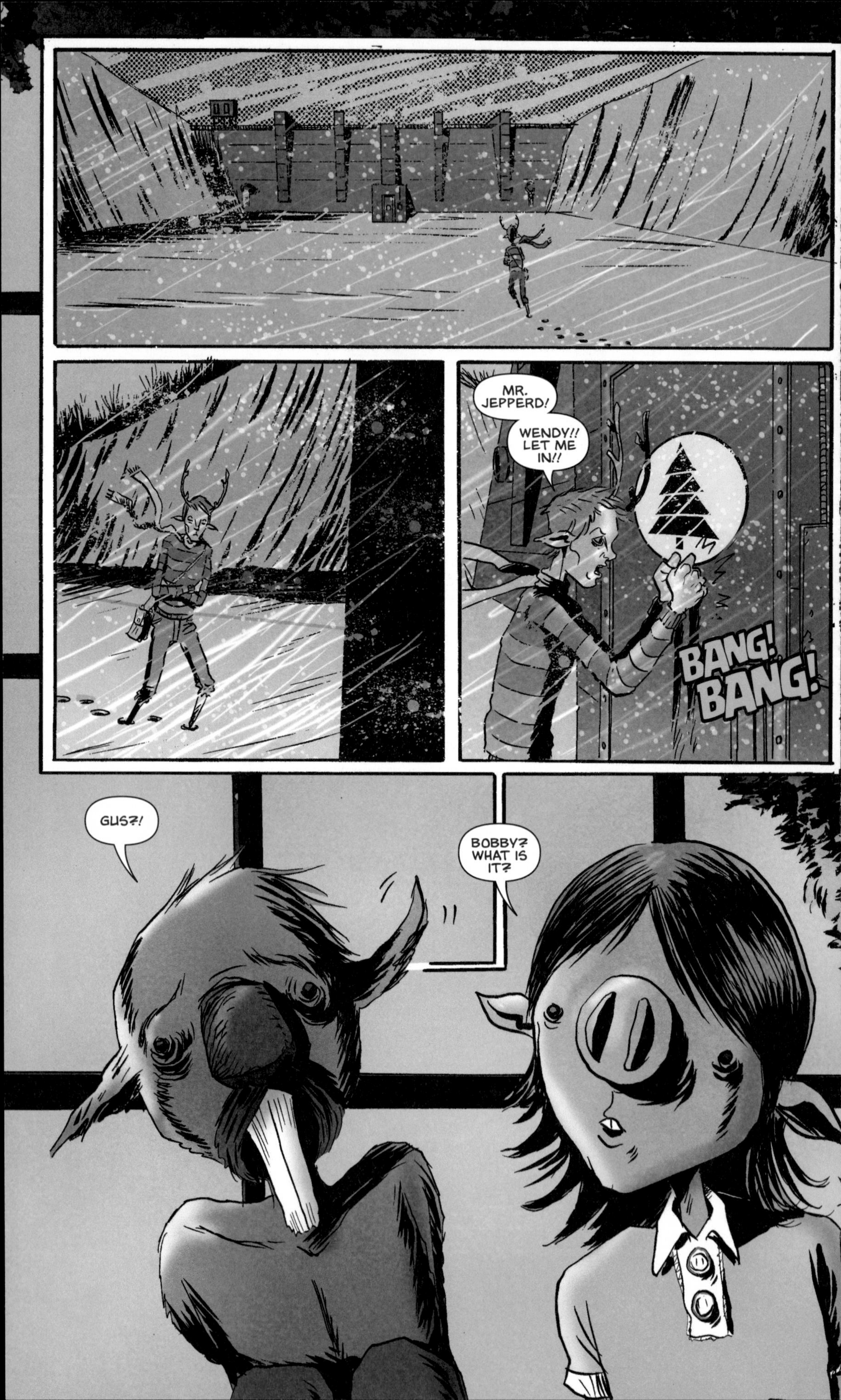
MR. JEPPERD!
WENDY!! LET ME IN!!
BANG! BANG!
GUS?!
BOBBY? WHAT IS IT?

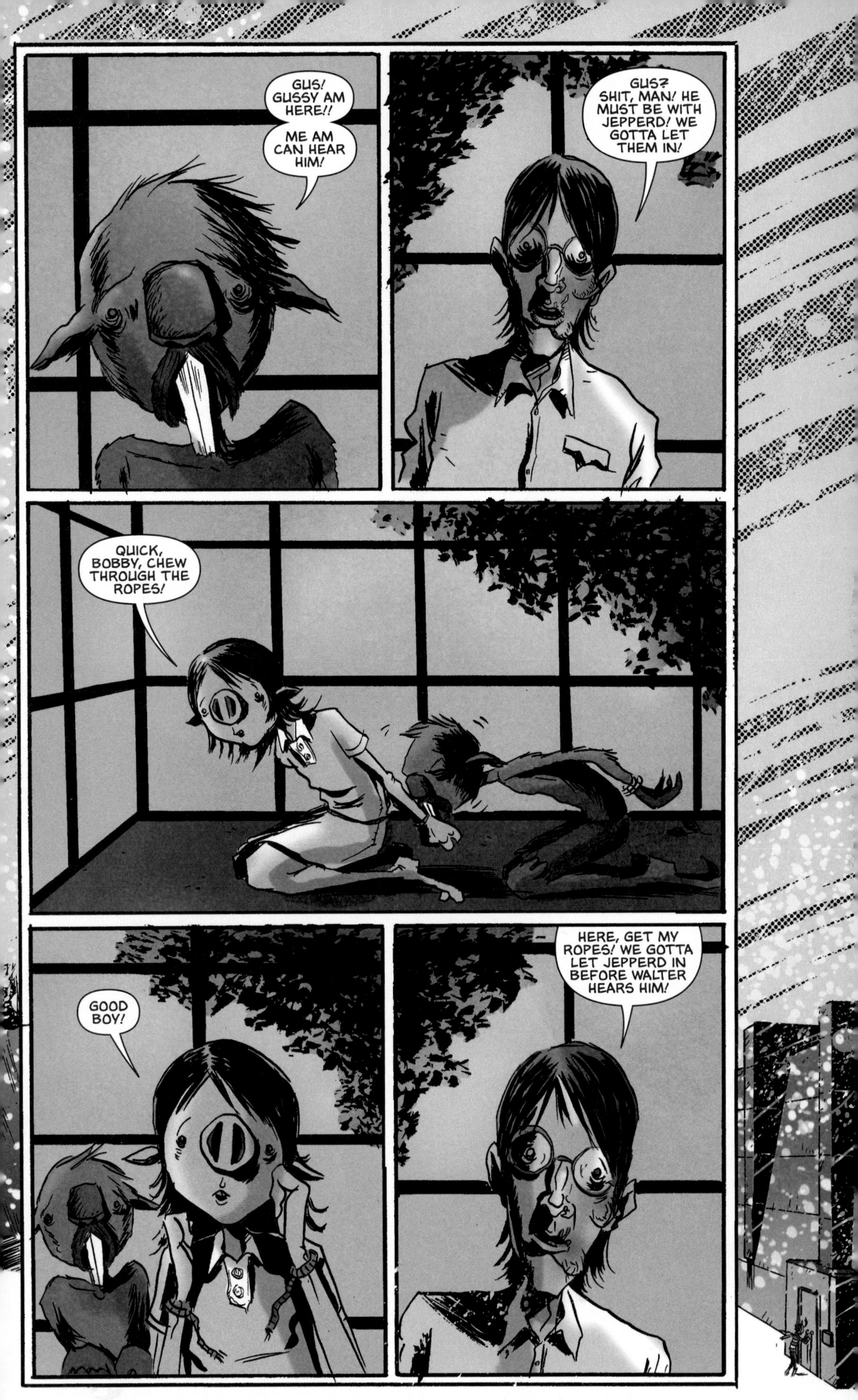
GUS! GUSSY AM HERE!!
ME AM CAN HEAR HIM!
GUS? SHIT, MAN! HE MUST BE WITH JEPPERD! WE GOTTA LET THEM IN!
QUICK, BOBBY, CHEW THROUGH THE ROPES!
GOOD BOY!
HERE, GET MY ROPES! WE GOTTA LET JEPPERD IN BEFORE WALTER HEARS HIM!

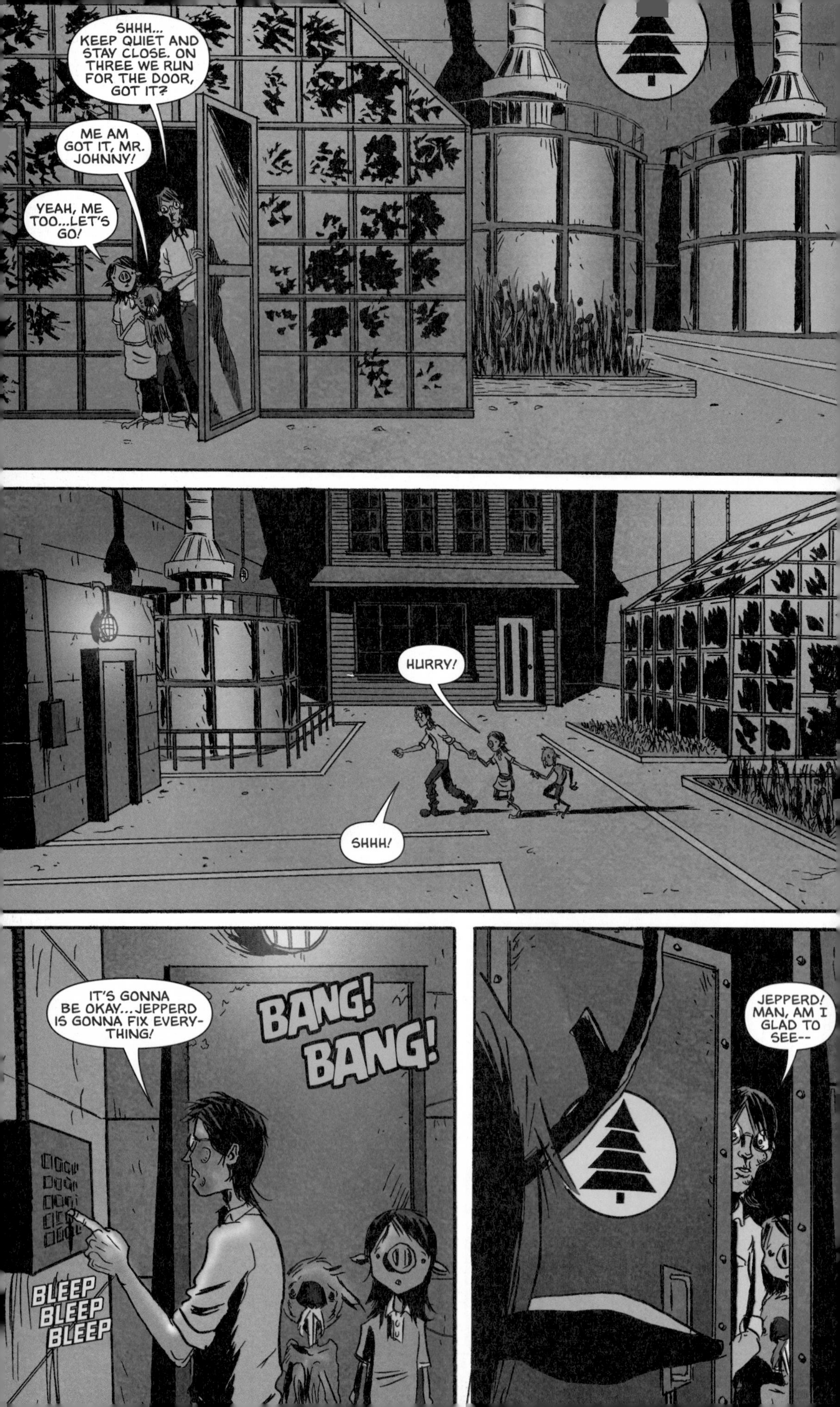
SHHH... KEEP QUIET AND STAY CLOSE. ON THREE WE RUN FOR THE DOOR, GOT IT?
ME AM GOT IT, MR. JOHNNY!
YEAH, ME TOO...LET'S GO!
HURRY!
SHHH!
IT'S GONNA BE OKAY...JEPPERD IS GONNA FIX EVERY-THING!
BANG! BANG!
BLEEP BLEEP BLEEP
JEPPERD! MAN, AM I GLAD TO SEE--

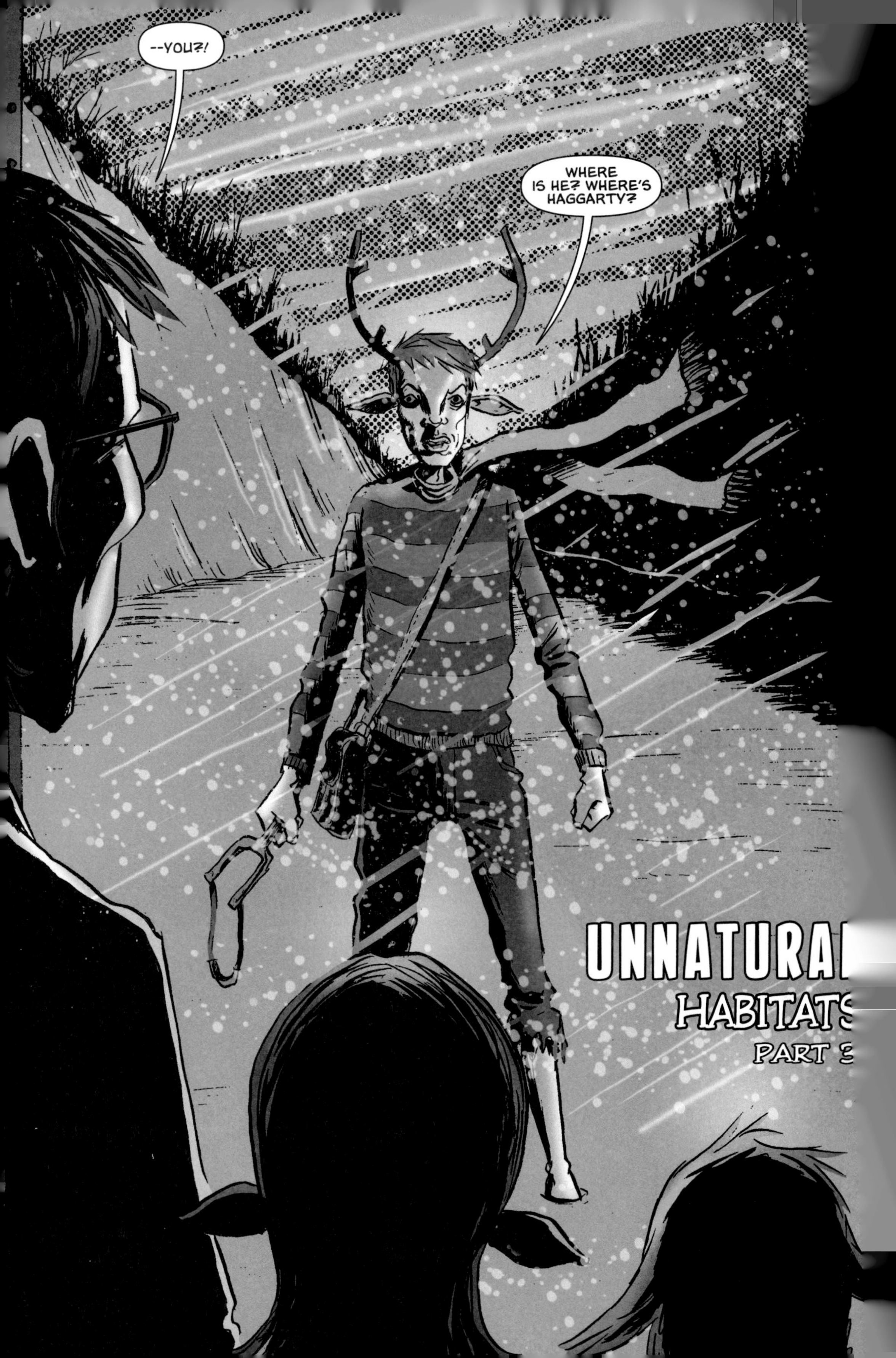
--YOU?!
WHERE IS HE? WHERE'S HAGGARTY?
UNNATURAL
HABITATS
PART 3

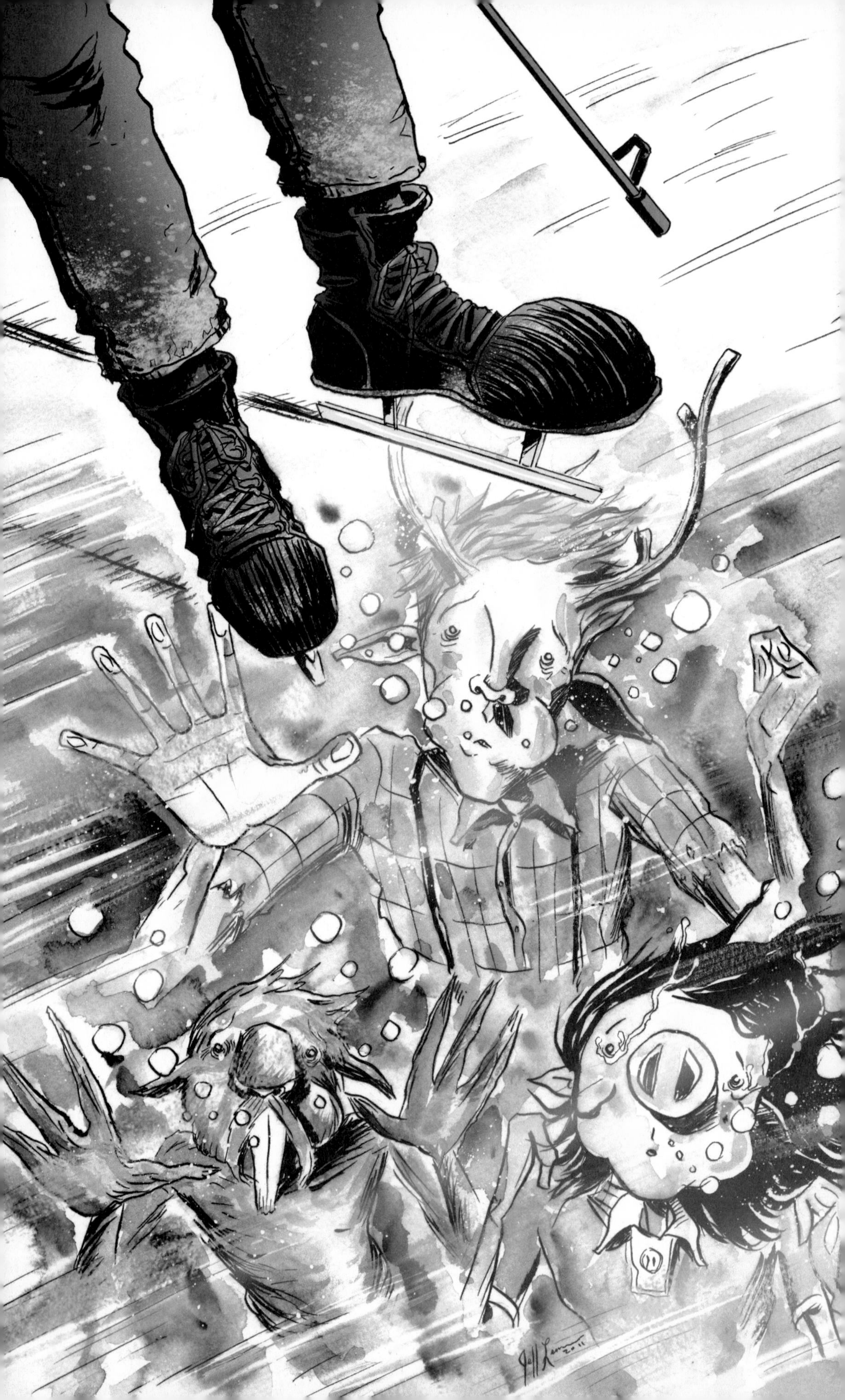

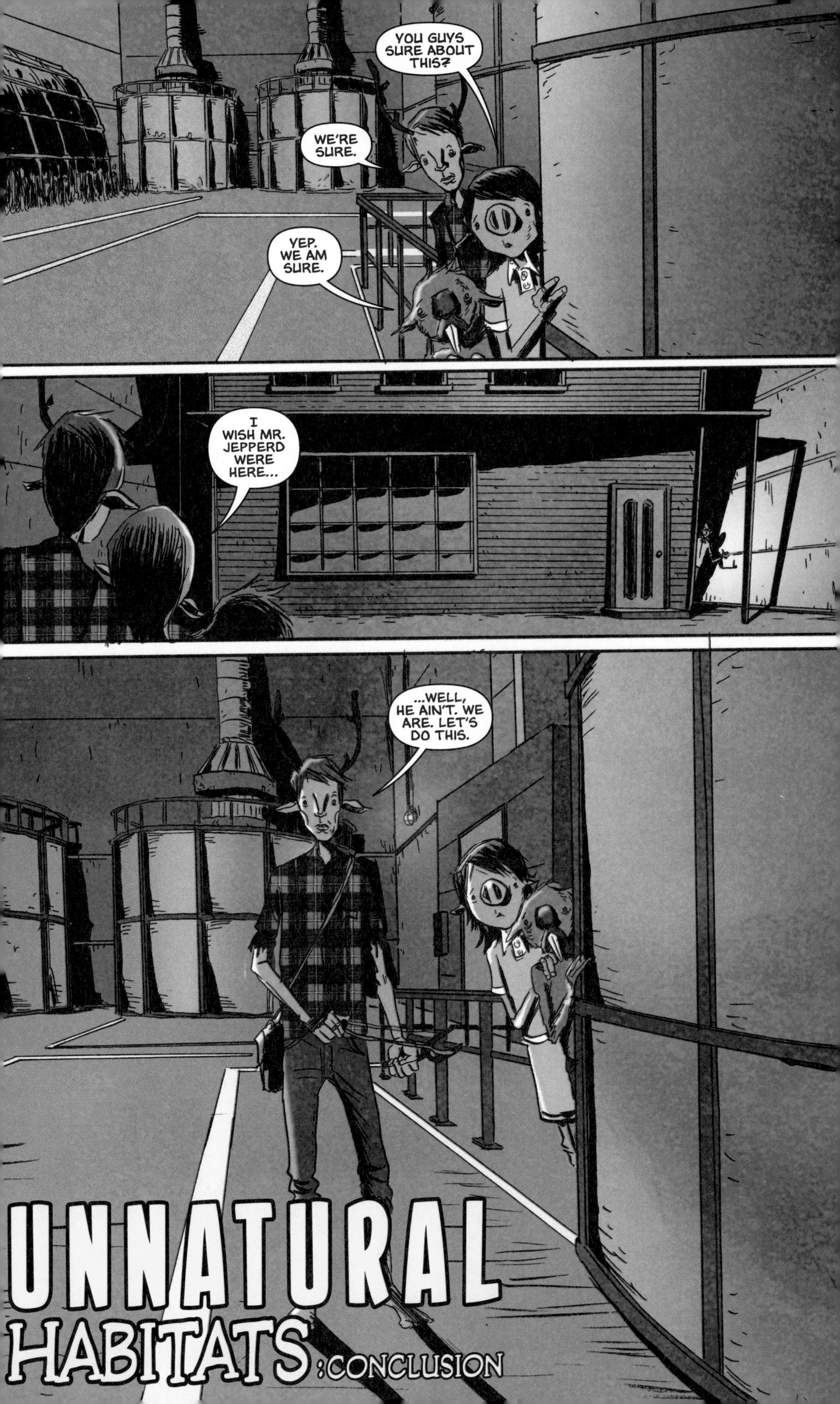
YOU GUYS SURE ABOUT THIS?
WE'RE SURE.
YEP. WE AM SURE.
I WISH MR. JEPPERD WERE HERE...
...WELL, HE AIN'T. WE ARE. LET'S DO THIS.
UNNATURAL HABITATS: CONCLUSION

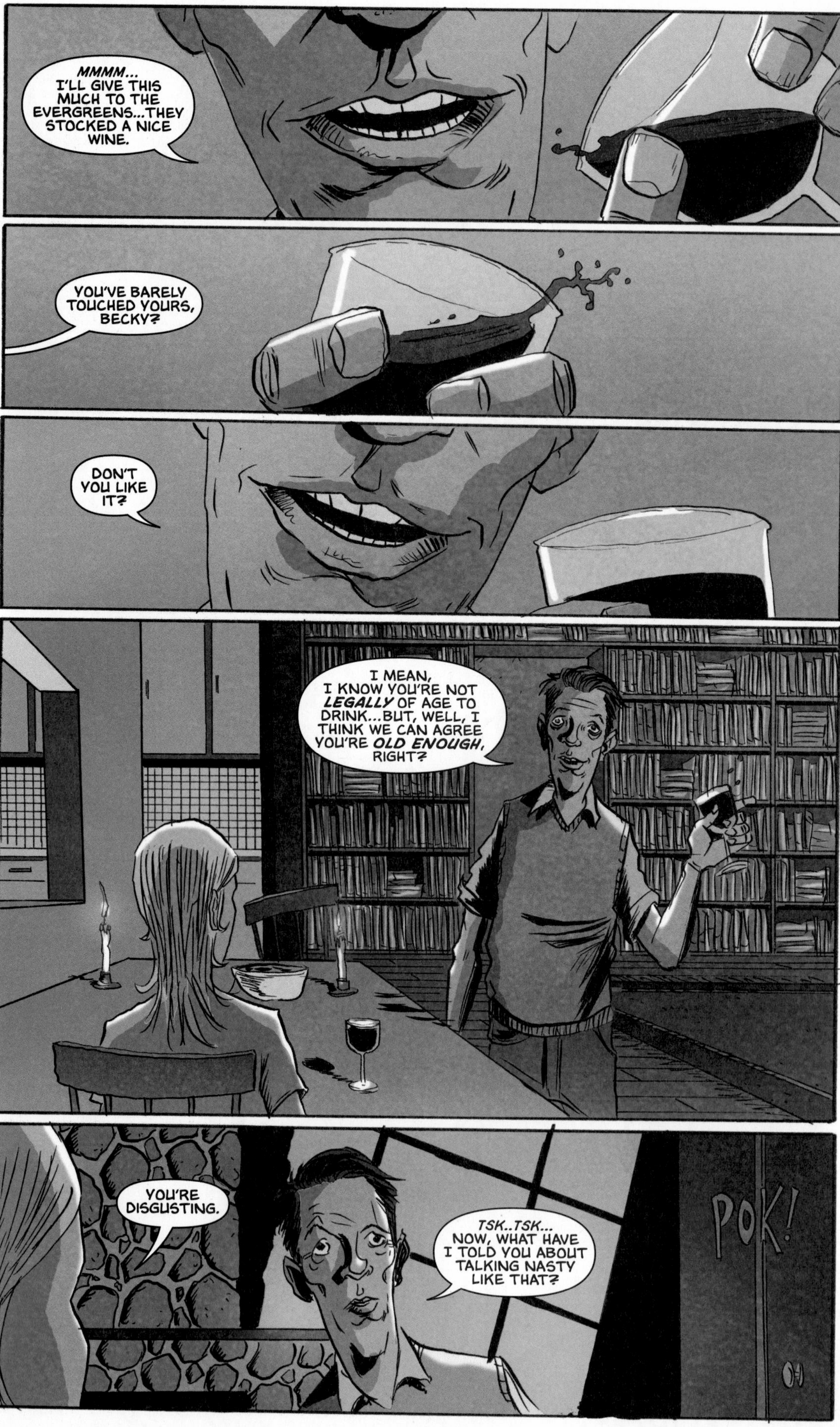

MMMM... I'LL GIVE THIS MUCH TO THE EVERGREENS...THEY STOCKED A NICE WINE.
YOU'VE BARELY TOUCHED YOURS, BECKY?
DON'T YOU LIKE IT?
I MEAN, I KNOW YOU'RE NOT LEGALLY OF AGE TO DRINK...BUT, WELL, I THINK WE CAN AGREE YOU'RE OLD ENOUGH, RIGHT?
YOU'RE DISGUSTING.
TSK..TSK... NOW, WHAT HAVE I TOLD YOU ABOUT TALKING NASTY LIKE THAT?
POK!

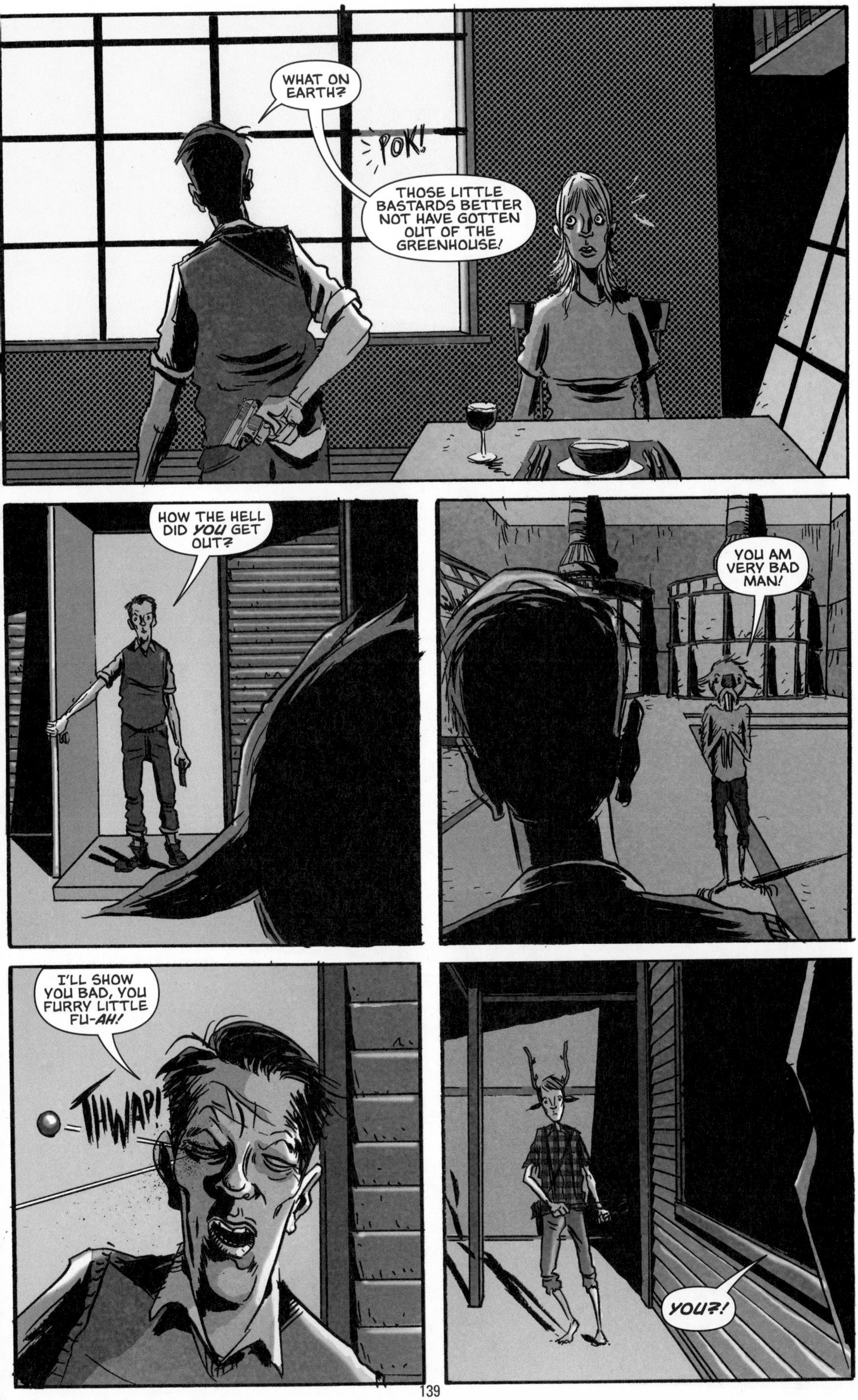
WHAT ON EARTH?
POK!
THOSE LITTLE BASTARDS BETTER NOT HAVE GOTTEN OUT OF THE GREENHOUSE!
HOW THE HELL DID YOU GET OUT?
YOU AM VERY BAD MAN!
I'LL SHOW YOU BAD, YOU FURRY LITTLE FU-AH!
THWAP!
YOU?!

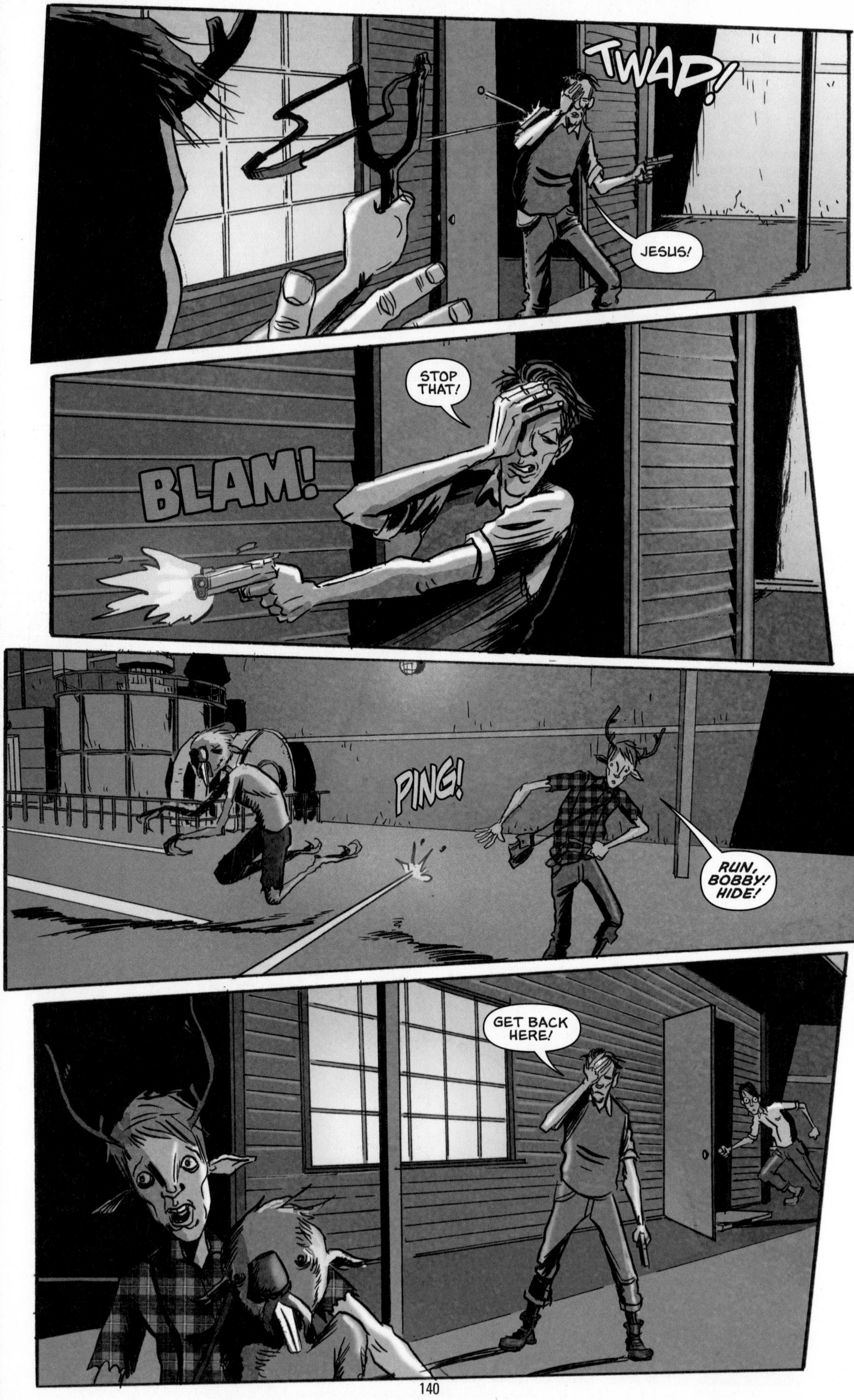

TWAP!
JESUS!
STOP THAT!
BLAM!
PING!
RUN, BOBBY! HIDE!
GET BACK HERE!

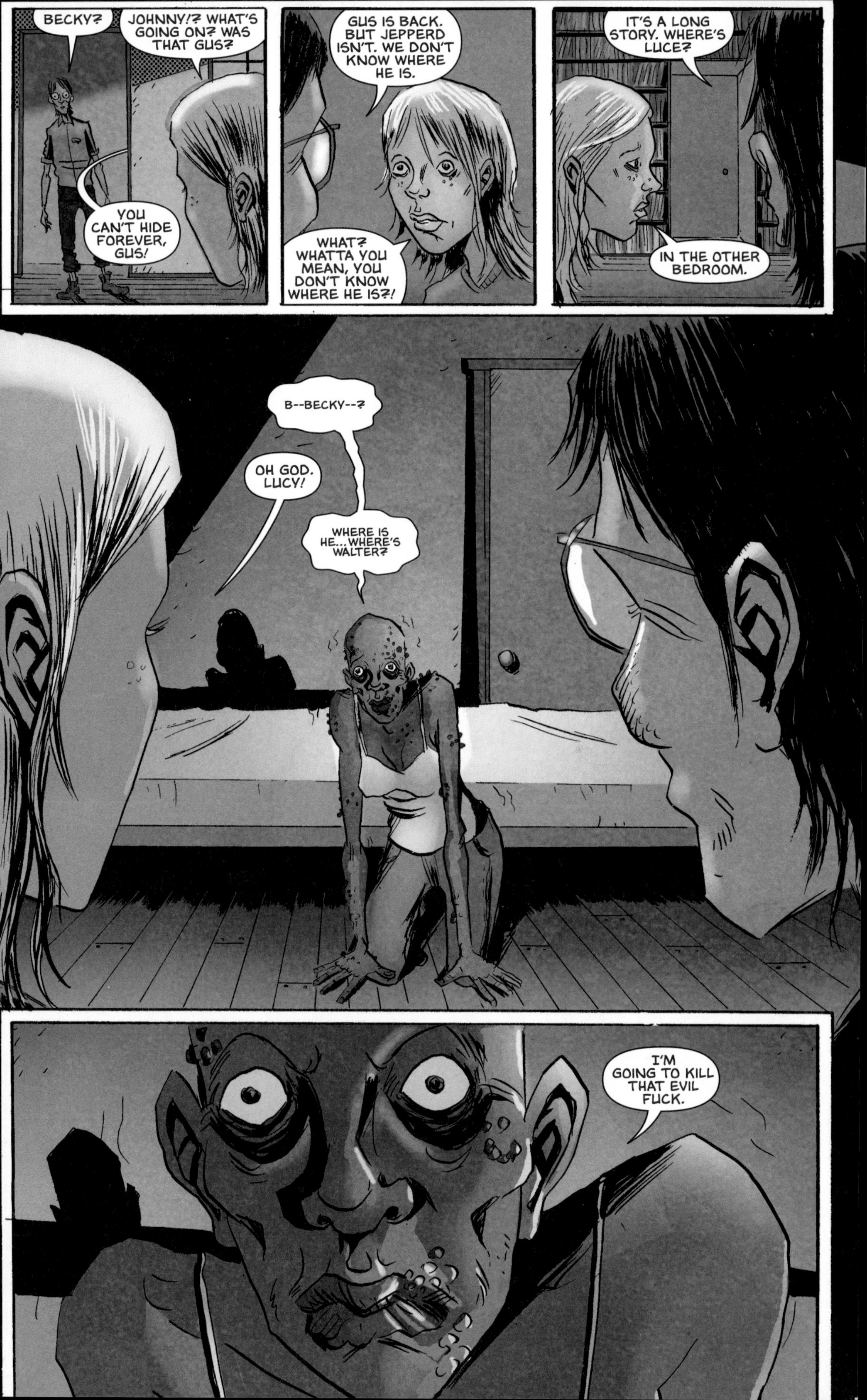
BECKY?
JOHNNY!? WHAT'S GOING ON? WAS THAT GUS?
YOU CAN'T HIDE FOREVER, GUS!
GUS IS BACK. BUT JEPPERD ISN'T. WE DON'T KNOW WHERE HE IS.
WHAT? WHATTA YOU MEAN, YOU DON'T KNOW WHERE HE IS?!
IT'S A LONG STORY. WHERE'S LUCE?
IN THE OTHER BEDROOM.
B--BECKY--?
OH GOD. LUCY!
WHERE IS HE... WHERE'S WALTER?
I'M GOING TO KILL THAT EVIL FUCK.

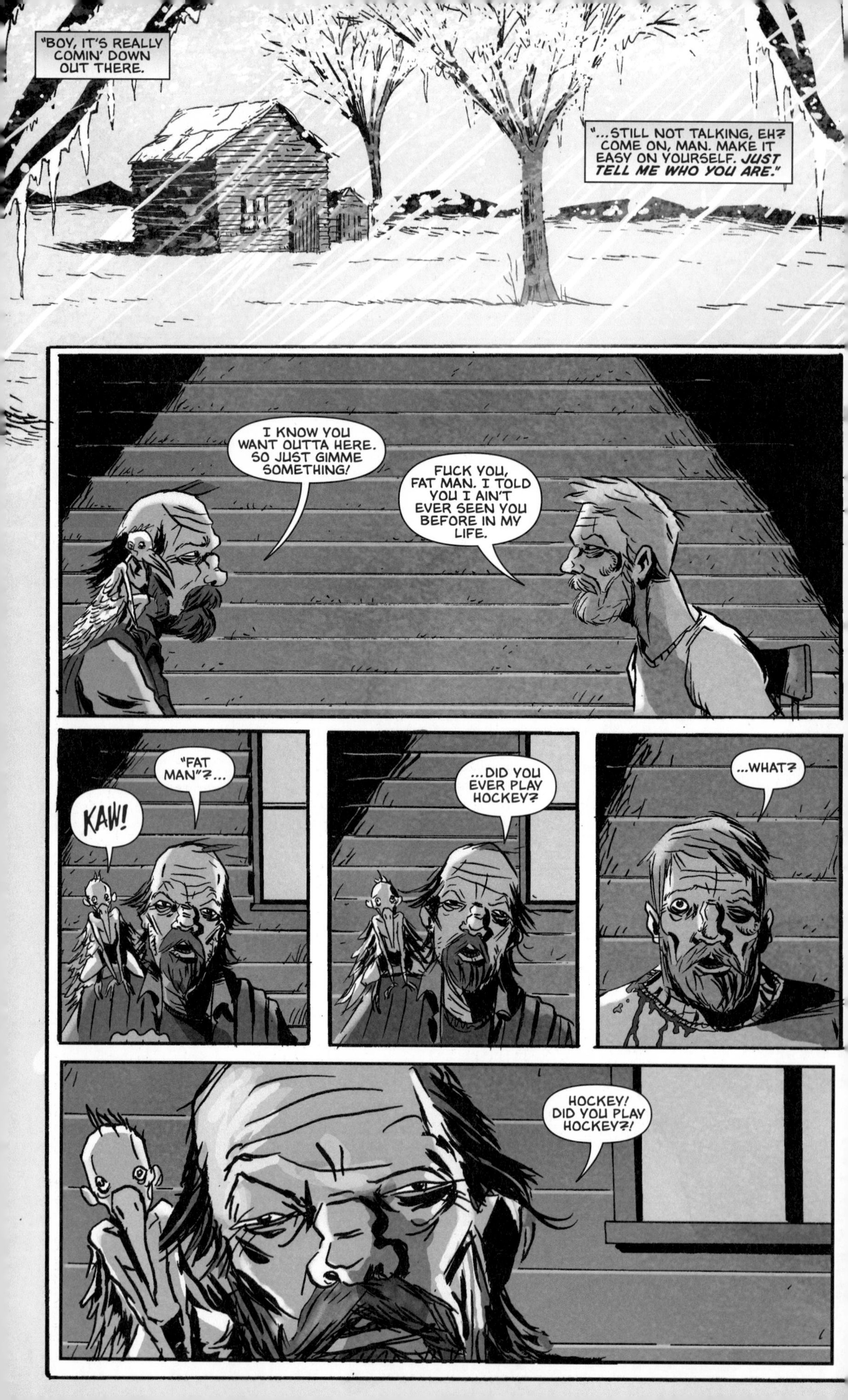
"BOY, IT'S REALLY COMIN' DOWN OUT THERE.
"...STILL NOT TALKING, EH? COME ON, MAN. MAKE IT EASY ON YOURSELF. *JUST TELL ME WHO YOU ARE.*"
I KNOW YOU WANT OUTTA HERE. SO JUST GIMME SOMETHING!
FUCK YOU, FAT MAN. I TOLD YOU I AIN'T EVER SEEN YOU BEFORE IN MY LIFE.
KAW!
"FAT MAN"?...
...DID YOU EVER PLAY HOCKEY?
...WHAT?
HOCKEY! DID YOU PLAY HOCKEY?!

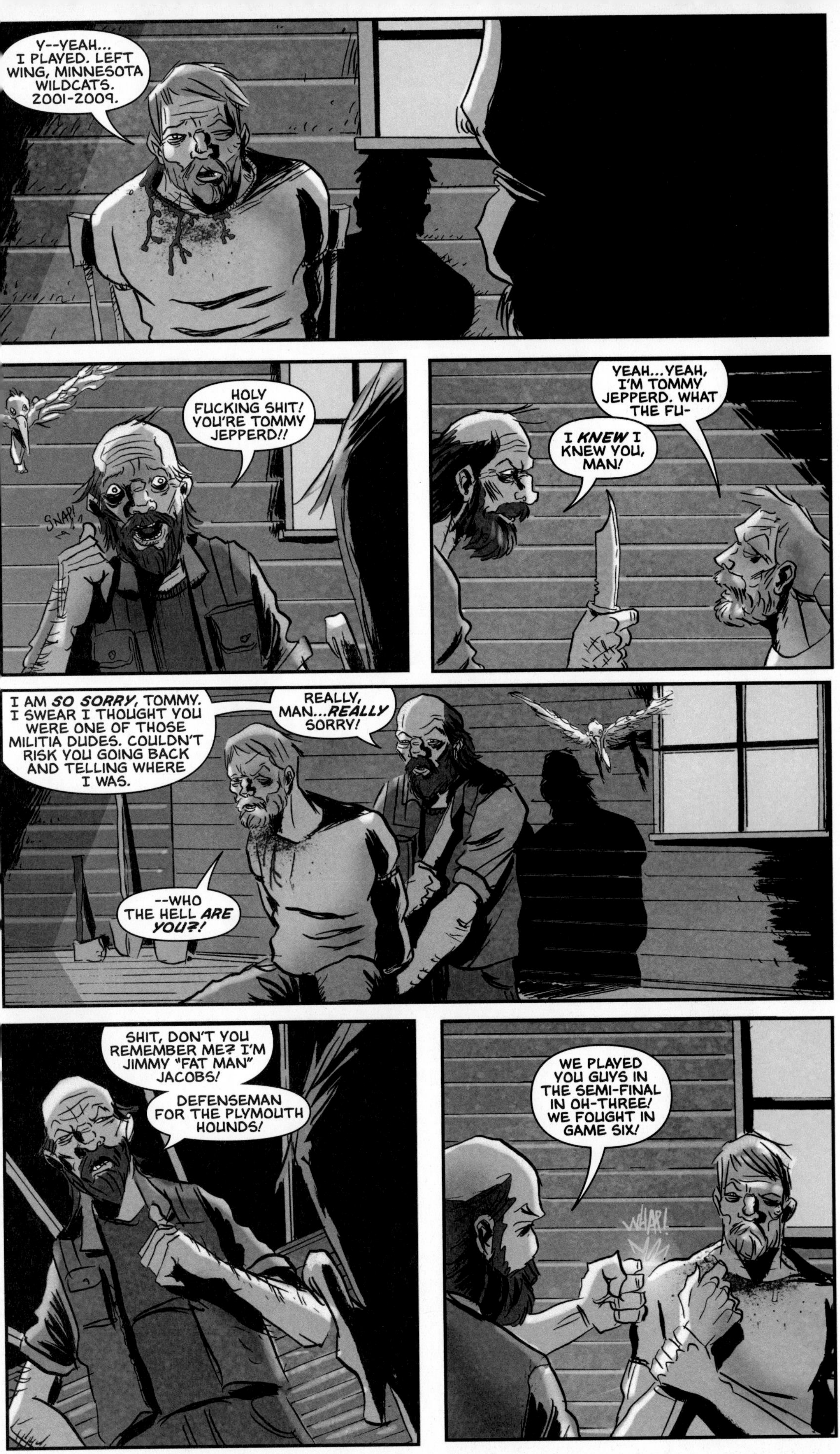
Y--YEAH... I PLAYED. LEFT WING, MINNESOTA WILDCATS. 2001-2009.
HOLY FUCKING SHIT! YOU'RE TOMMY JEPPERD!!
SNAP!
YEAH...YEAH, I'M TOMMY JEPPERD. WHAT THE FU-
I KNEW I KNEW YOU, MAN!
I AM SO SORRY, TOMMY. I SWEAR I THOUGHT YOU WERE ONE OF THOSE MILITIA DUDES. COULDN'T RISK YOU GOING BACK AND TELLING WHERE I WAS.
REALLY, MAN...REALLY SORRY!
--WHO THE HELL ARE YOU?!
SHIT, DON'T YOU REMEMBER ME? I'M JIMMY "FAT MAN" JACOBS!
DEFENSEMAN FOR THE PLYMOUTH HOUNDS!
WE PLAYED YOU GUYS IN THE SEMI-FINAL IN OH-THREE! WE FOUGHT IN GAME SIX!
WHAP!

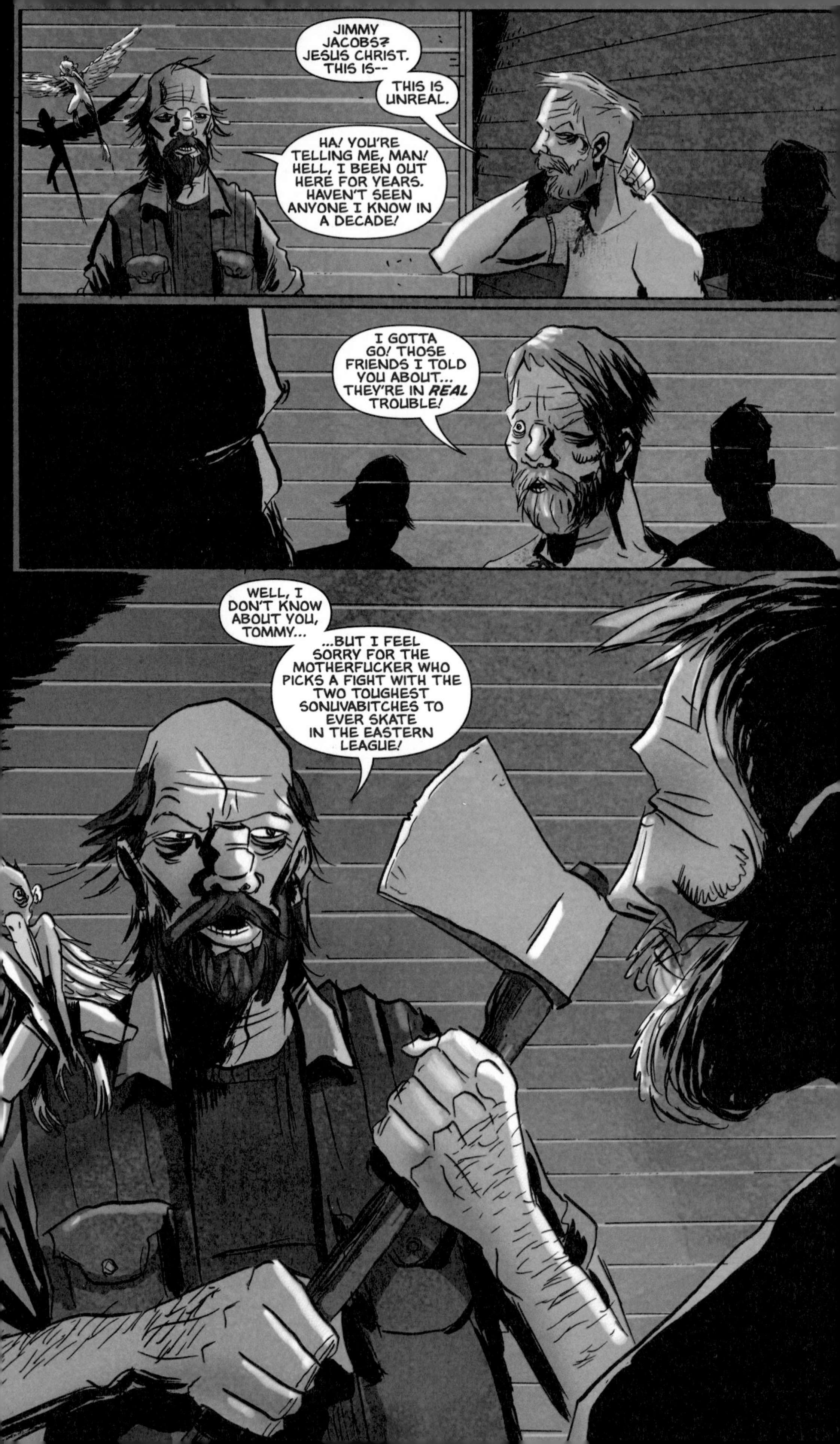
JIMMY JACOBS? JESUS CHRIST. THIS IS--
THIS IS UNREAL.
HA! YOU'RE TELLING ME, MAN! HELL, I BEEN OUT HERE FOR YEARS. HAVEN'T SEEN ANYONE I KNOW IN A DECADE!
I GOTTA GO! THOSE FRIENDS I TOLD YOU ABOUT... THEY'RE IN *REAL* TROUBLE!
WELL, I DON'T KNOW ABOUT YOU, TOMMY...
...BUT I FEEL SORRY FOR THE MOTHERFUCKER WHO PICKS A FIGHT WITH THE TWO TOUGHEST SONUVABITCHES TO EVER SKATE IN THE EASTERN LEAGUE!

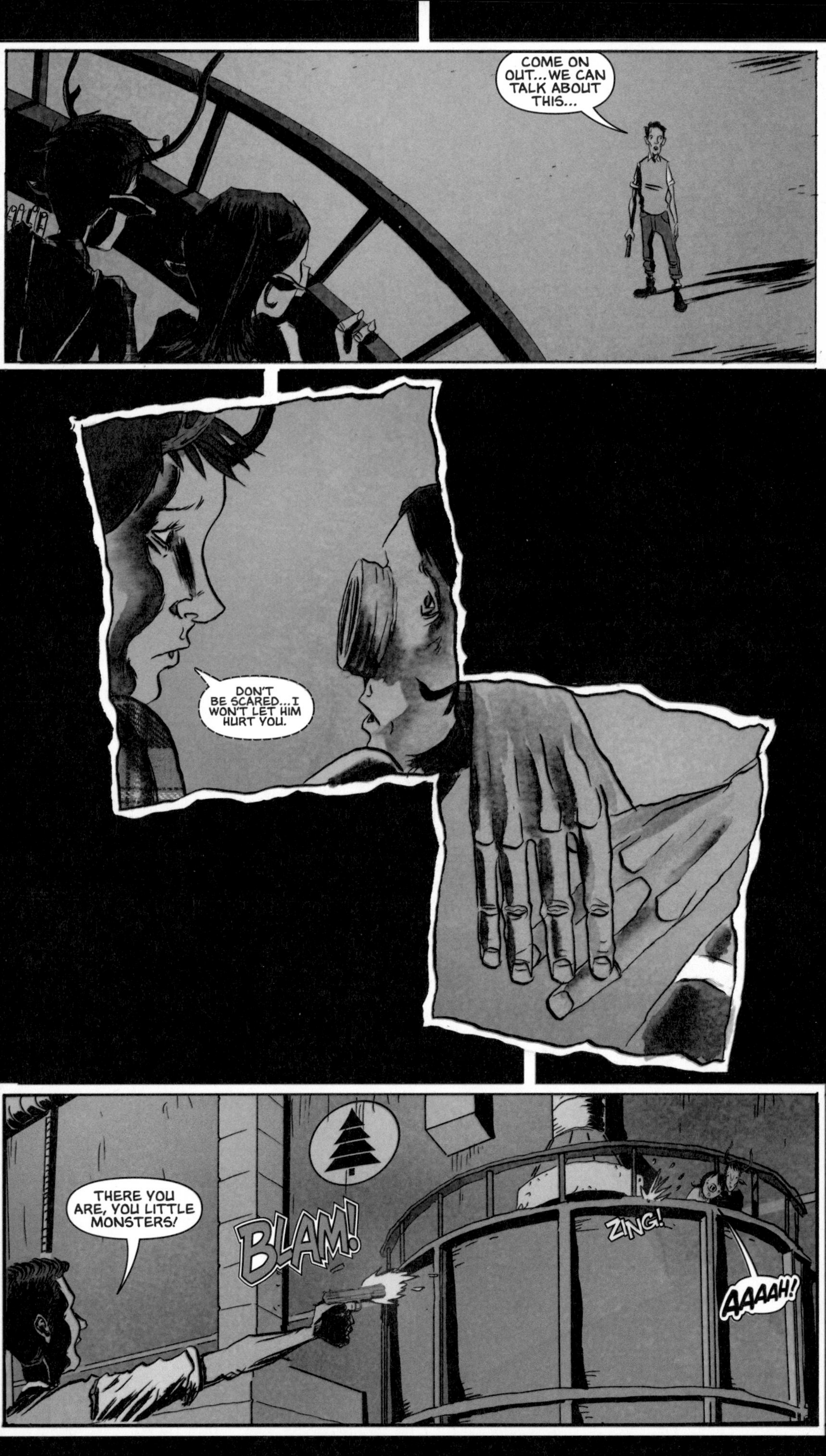
COME ON OUT...WE CAN TALK ABOUT THIS...
DON'T BE SCARED...I WON'T LET HIM HURT YOU.
THERE YOU ARE, YOU LITTLE MONSTERS!
BLAM!
ZING!
AAAAH!

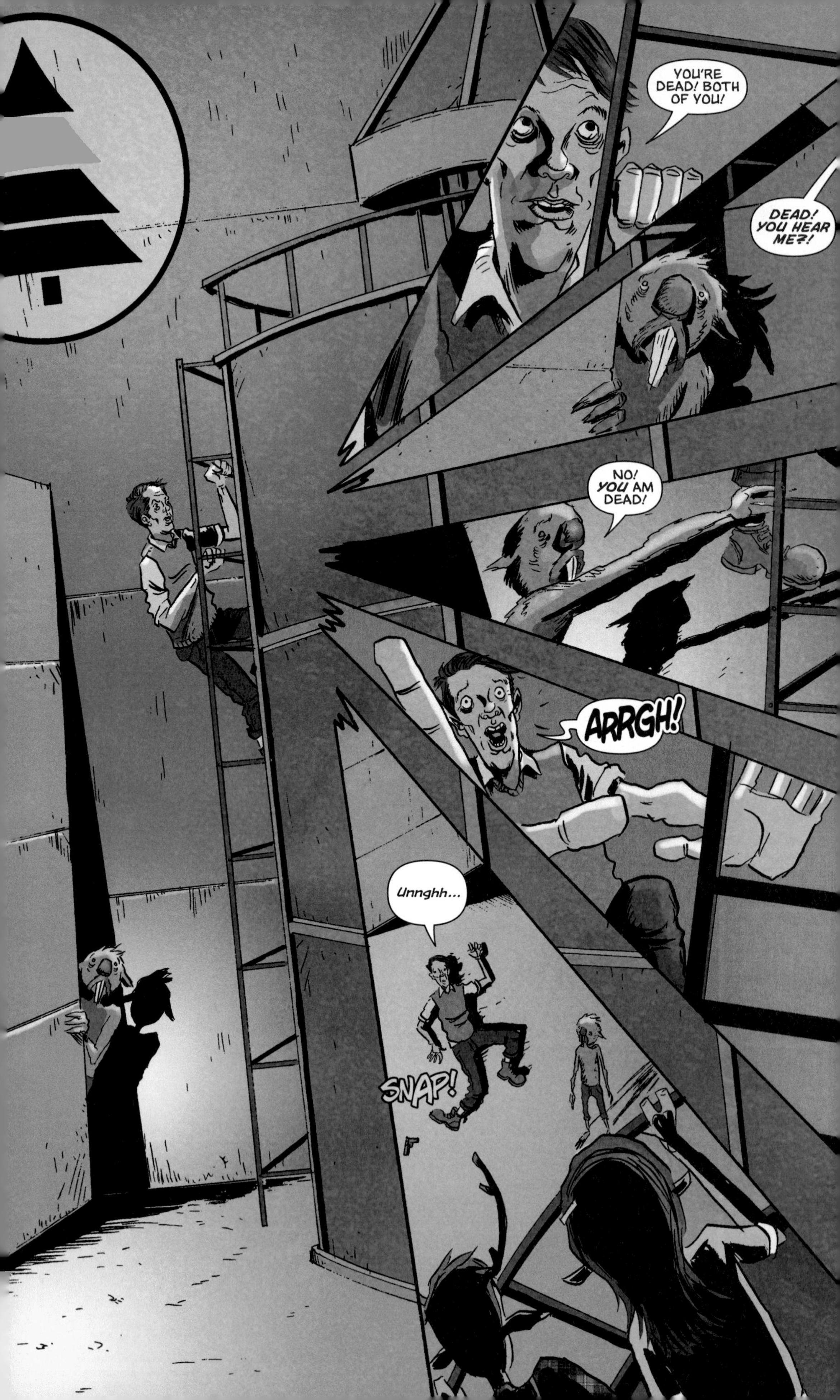

YOU'RE DEAD! BOTH OF YOU!
DEAD! YOU HEAR ME?!
NO! YOU AM DEAD!
ARRGH!
Unnghh...
SNAP!

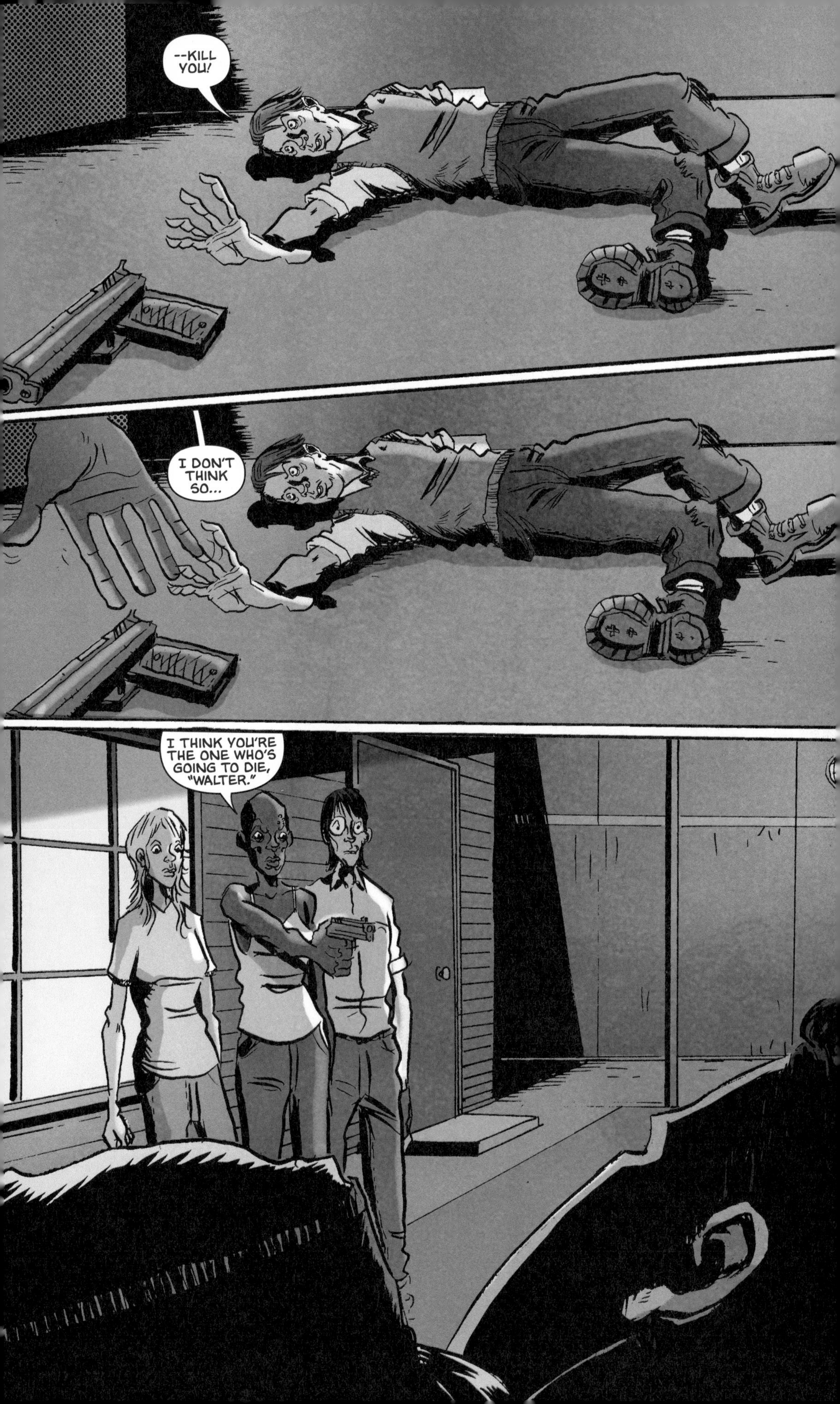
--KILL YOU!
I DON'T THINK SO...
I THINK YOU'RE THE ONE WHO'S GOING TO DIE, "WALTER."

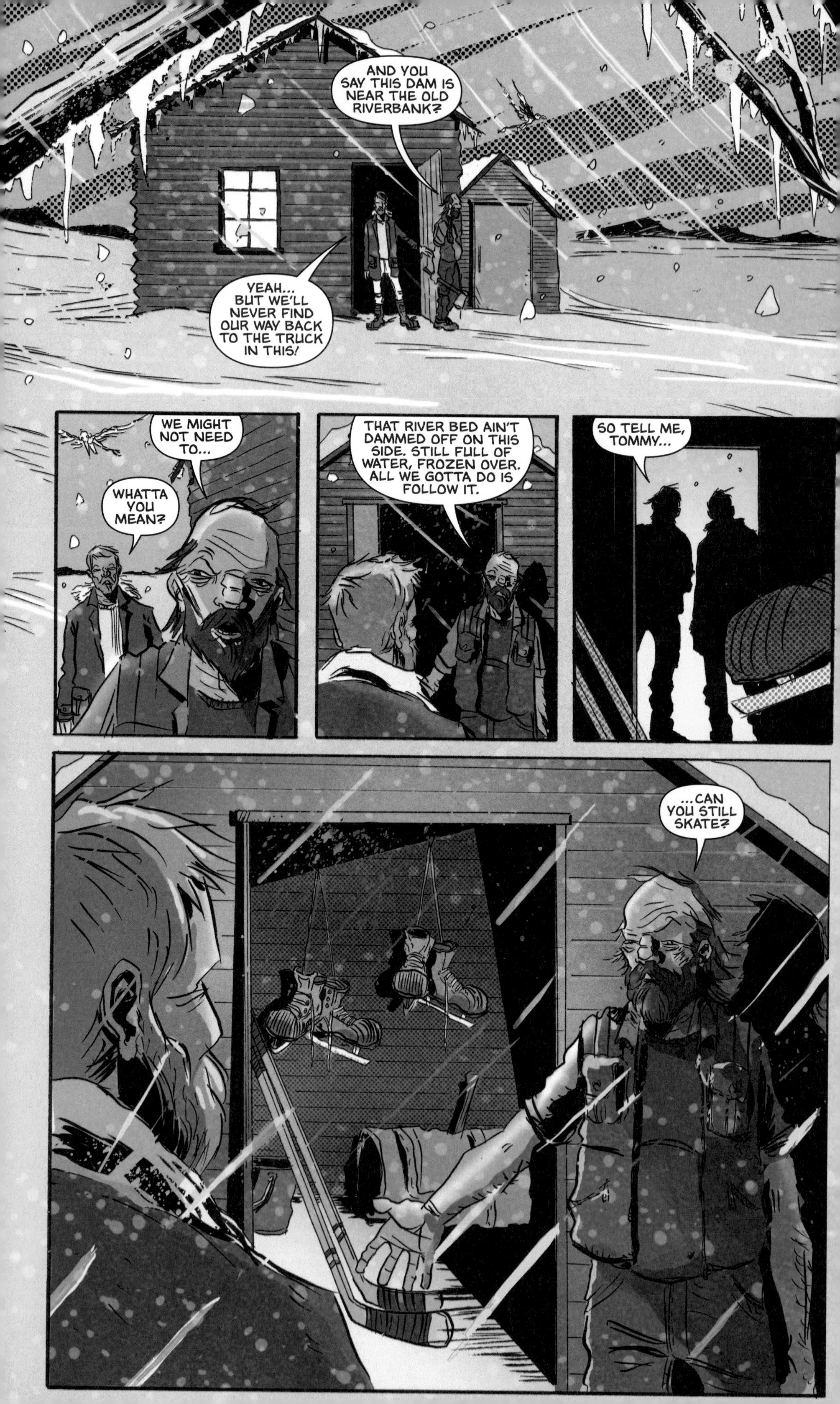
AND YOU SAY THIS DAM IS NEAR THE OLD RIVERBANK?
YEAH... BUT WE'LL NEVER FIND OUR WAY BACK TO THE TRUCK IN THIS!
WE MIGHT NOT NEED TO...
WHATTA YOU MEAN?
THAT RIVER BED AIN'T DAMMED OFF ON THIS SIDE. STILL FULL OF WATER, FROZEN OVER. ALL WE GOTTA DO IS FOLLOW IT.
SO TELL ME, TOMMY...
...CAN YOU STILL SKATE?

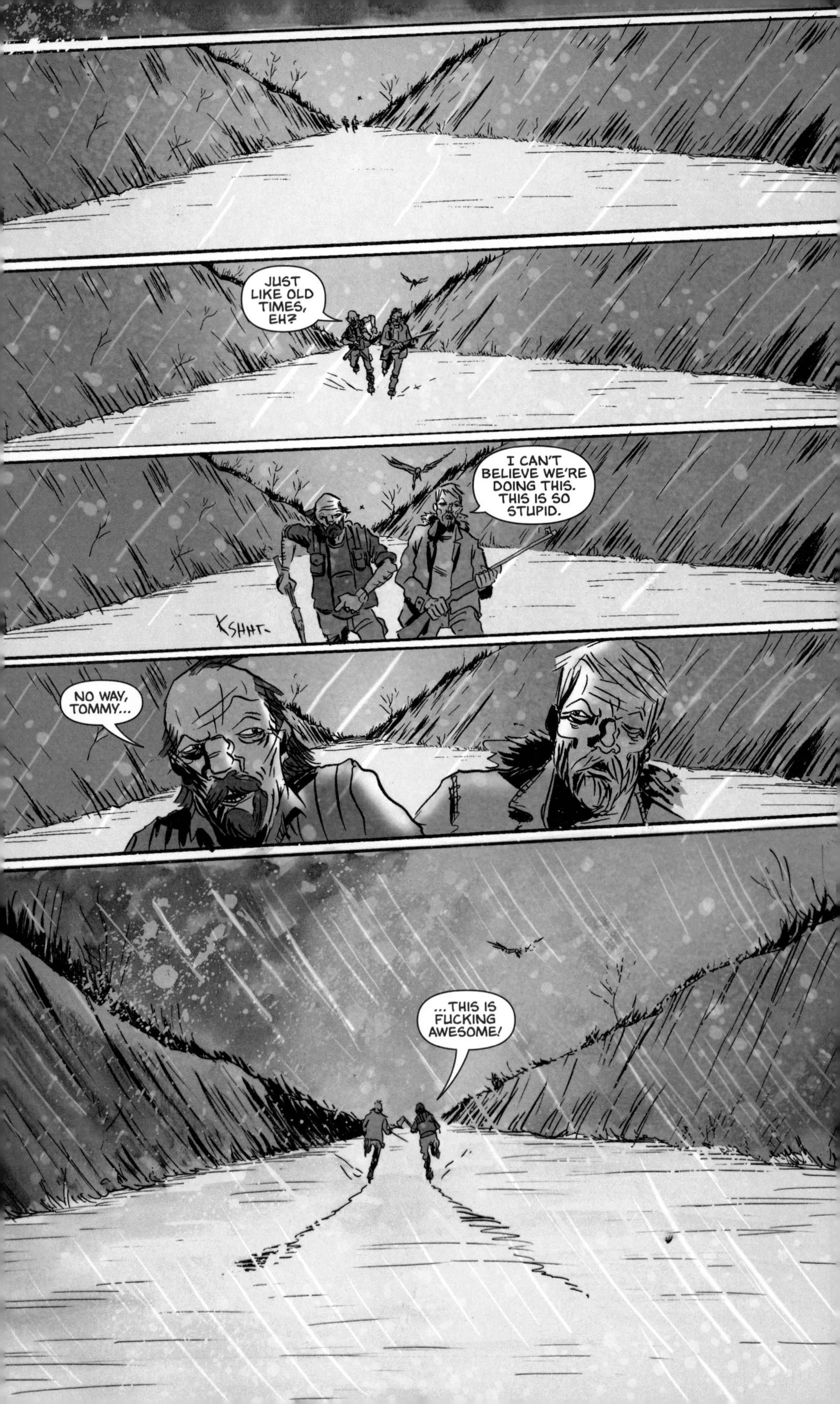
JUST LIKE OLD TIMES, EH?
I CAN'T BELIEVE WE'RE DOING THIS. THIS IS SO STUPID.
KSHHT-
NO WAY, TOMMY...
...THIS IS FUCKING AWESOME!

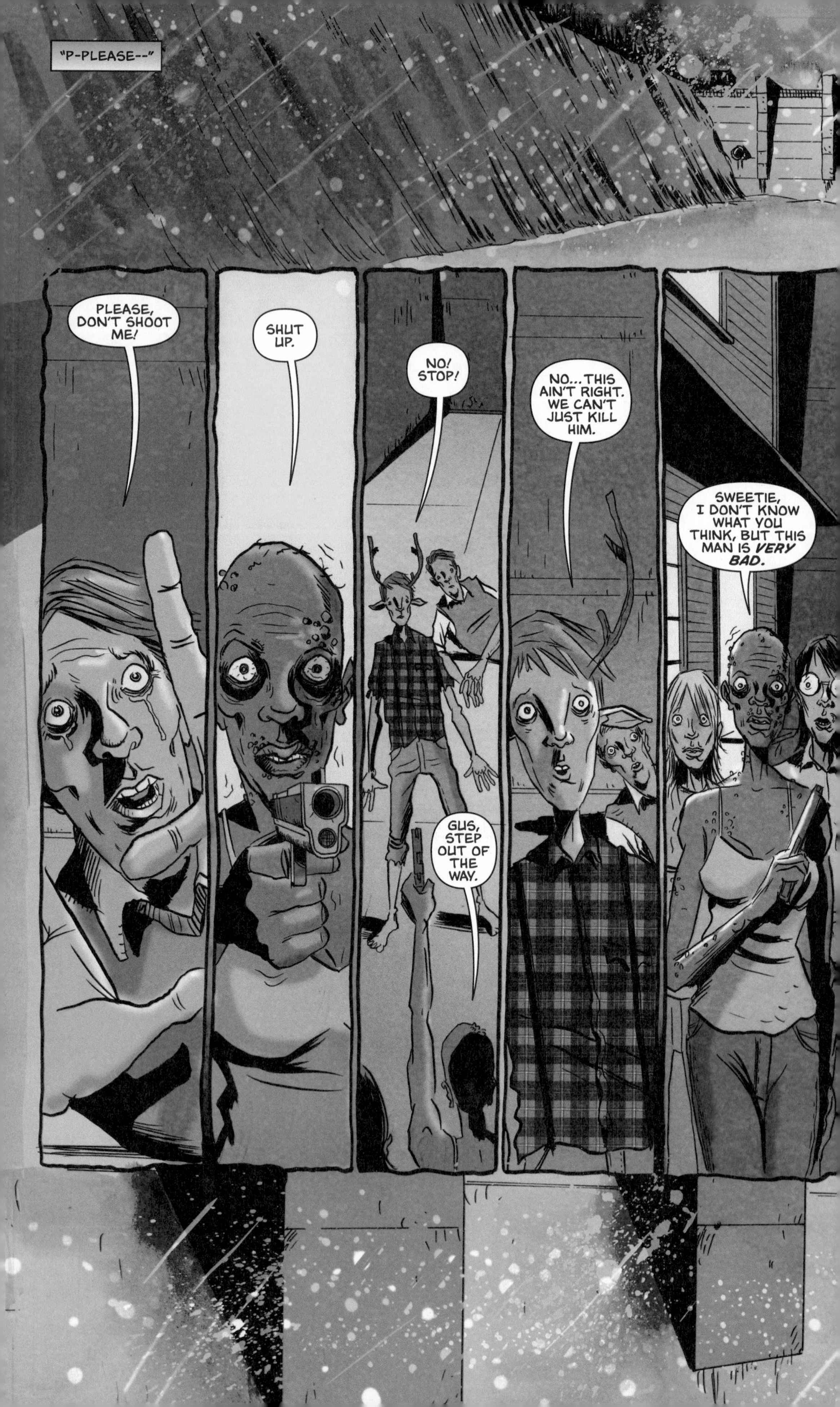
"P-PLEASE--"
PLEASE, DON'T SHOOT ME!
SHUT UP.
NO! STOP!
GUS, STEP OUT OF THE WAY.
NO... THIS AIN'T RIGHT. WE CAN'T JUST KILL HIM.
SWEETIE, I DON'T KNOW WHAT YOU THINK, BUT THIS MAN IS *VERY BAD.*

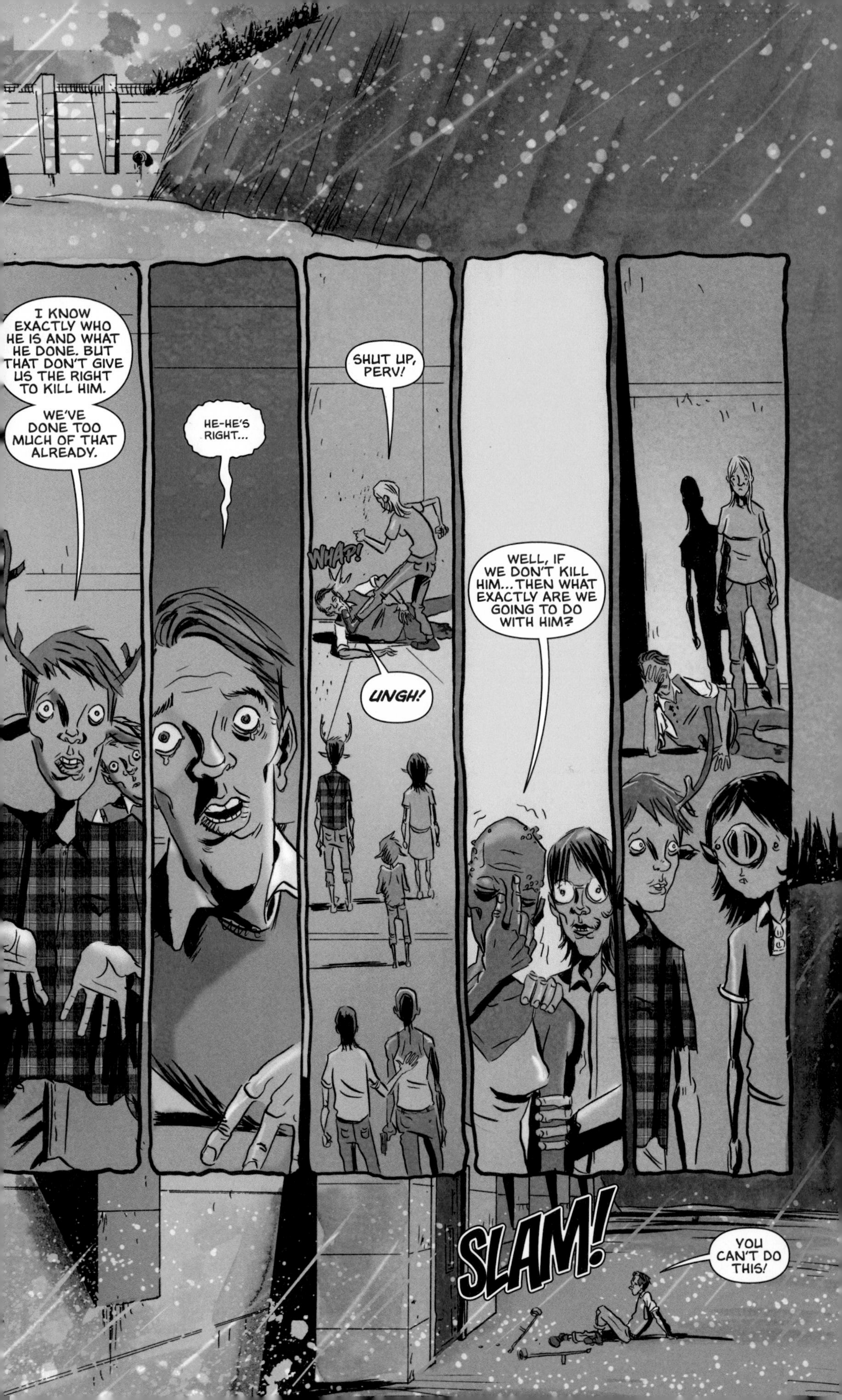

I KNOW EXACTLY WHO HE IS AND WHAT HE DONE. BUT THAT DON'T GIVE US THE RIGHT TO KILL HIM.
WE'VE DONE TOO MUCH OF THAT ALREADY.
HE-HE'S RIGHT...
SHUT UP, PERV!
WHAP!
UNGH!
WELL, IF WE DON'T KILL HIM...THEN WHAT EXACTLY ARE WE GOING TO DO WITH HIM?
SLAM!
YOU CAN'T DO THIS!

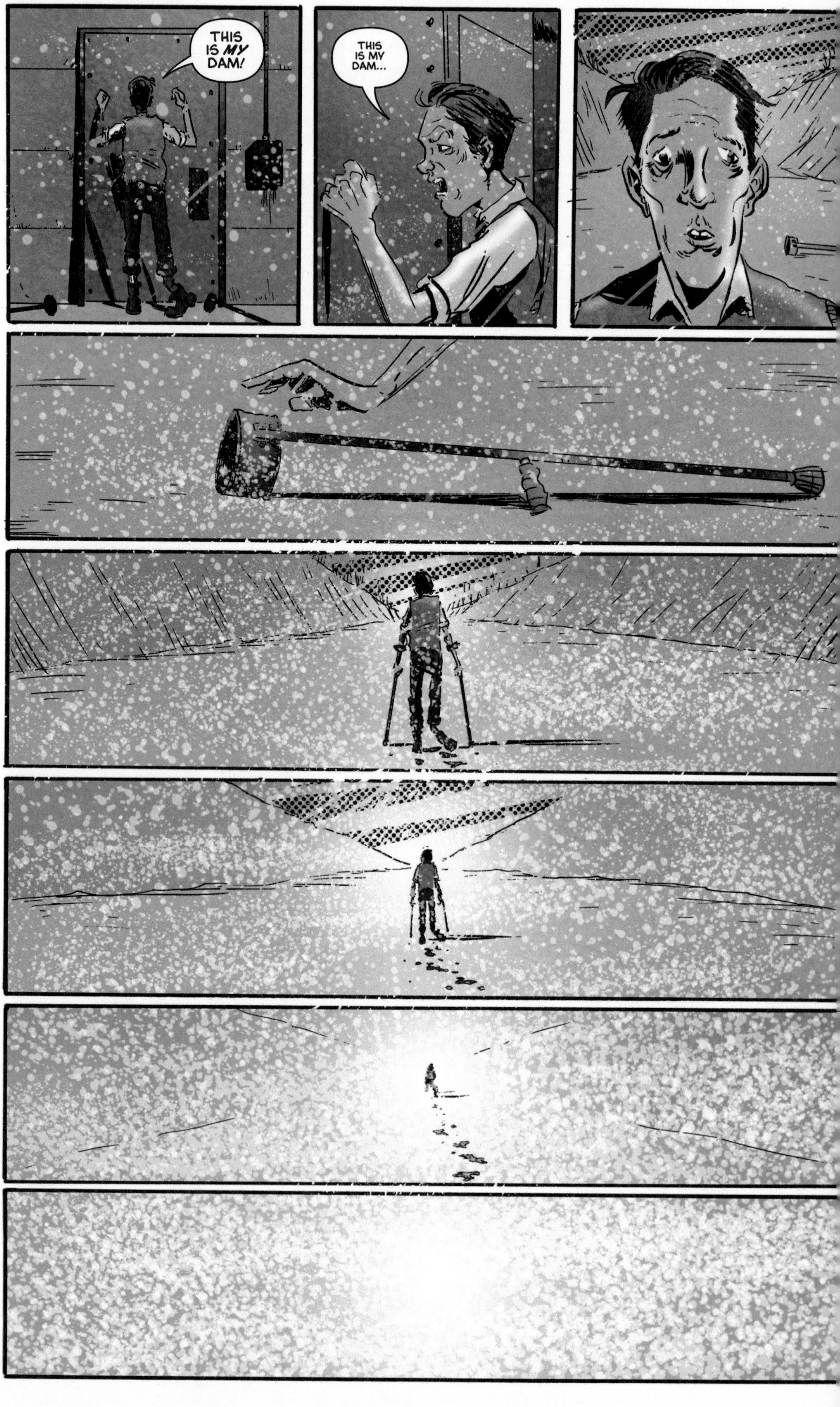
THIS IS *MY* DAM!
THIS IS MY DAM...

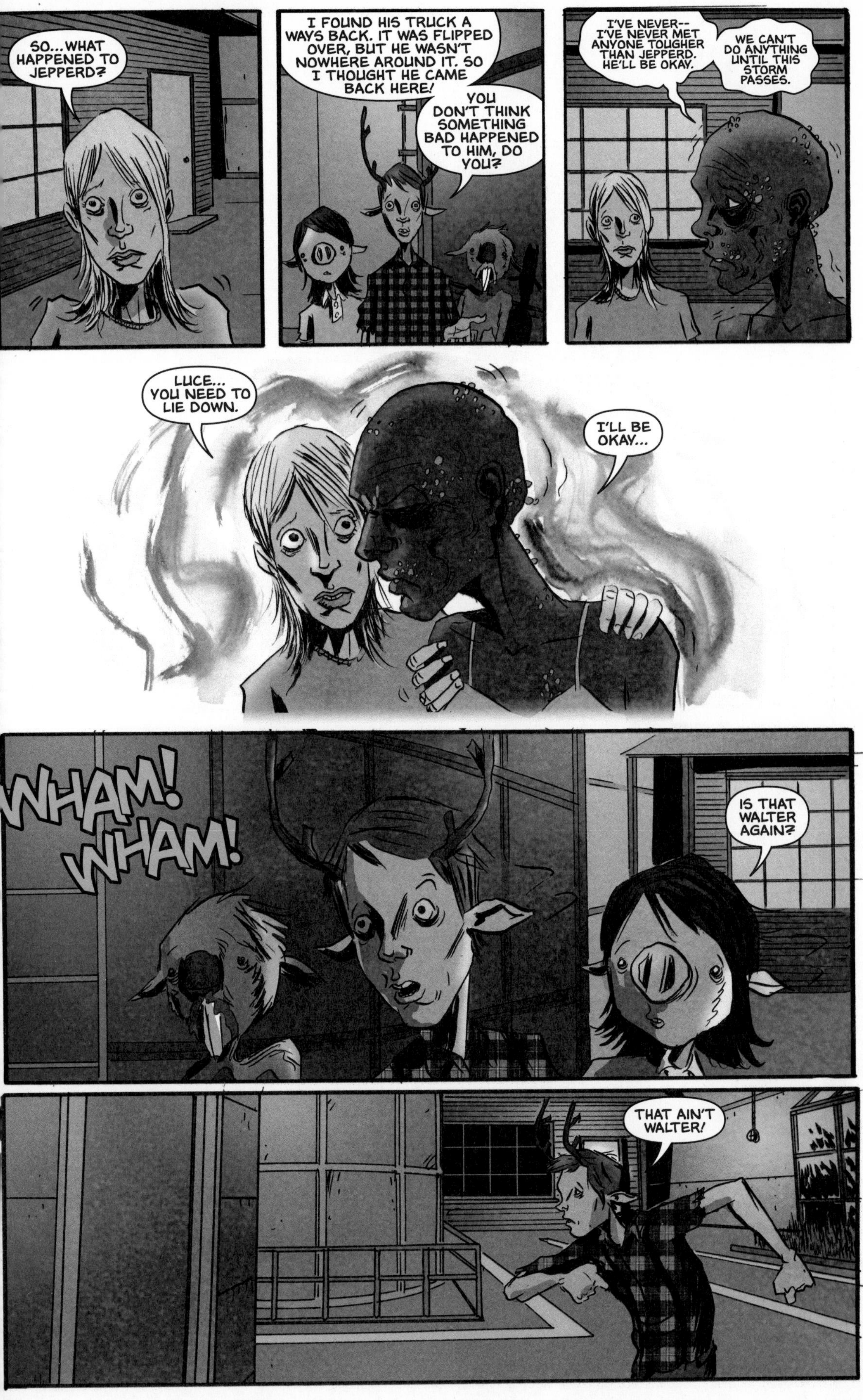
SO...WHAT HAPPENED TO JEPPERD?
I FOUND HIS TRUCK A WAYS BACK. IT WAS FLIPPED OVER, BUT HE WASN'T NOWHERE AROUND IT. SO I THOUGHT HE CAME BACK HERE!
YOU DON'T THINK SOMETHING BAD HAPPENED TO HIM, DO YOU?
I'VE NEVER-- I'VE NEVER MET ANYONE TOUGHER THAN JEPPERD. HE'LL BE OKAY.
WE CAN'T DO ANYTHING UNTIL THIS STORM PASSES.
LUCE... YOU NEED TO LIE DOWN.
I'LL BE OKAY...
WHAM! WHAM!
IS THAT WALTER AGAIN?
THAT AIN'T WALTER!

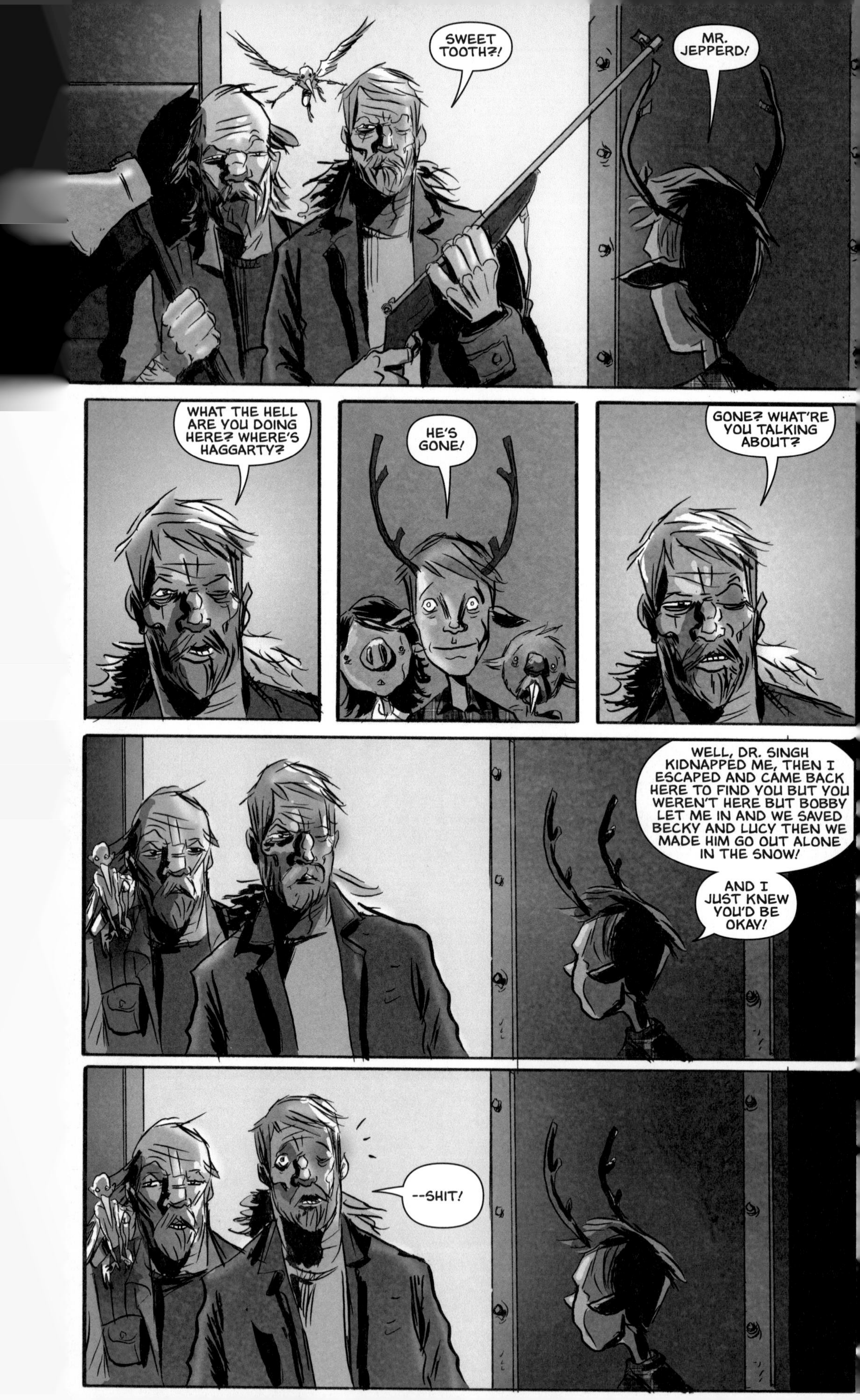
SWEET TOOTH?!
MR. JEPPERD!
WHAT THE HELL ARE YOU DOING HERE? WHERE'S HAGGARTY?
HE'S GONE!
GONE? WHAT'RE YOU TALKING ABOUT?
WELL, DR. SINGH KIDNAPPED ME, THEN I ESCAPED AND CAME BACK HERE TO FIND YOU BUT YOU WEREN'T HERE BUT BOBBY LET ME IN AND WE SAVED BECKY AND LUCY THEN WE MADE HIM GO OUT ALONE IN THE SNOW!
AND I JUST KNEW YOU'D BE OKAY!
--SHIT!

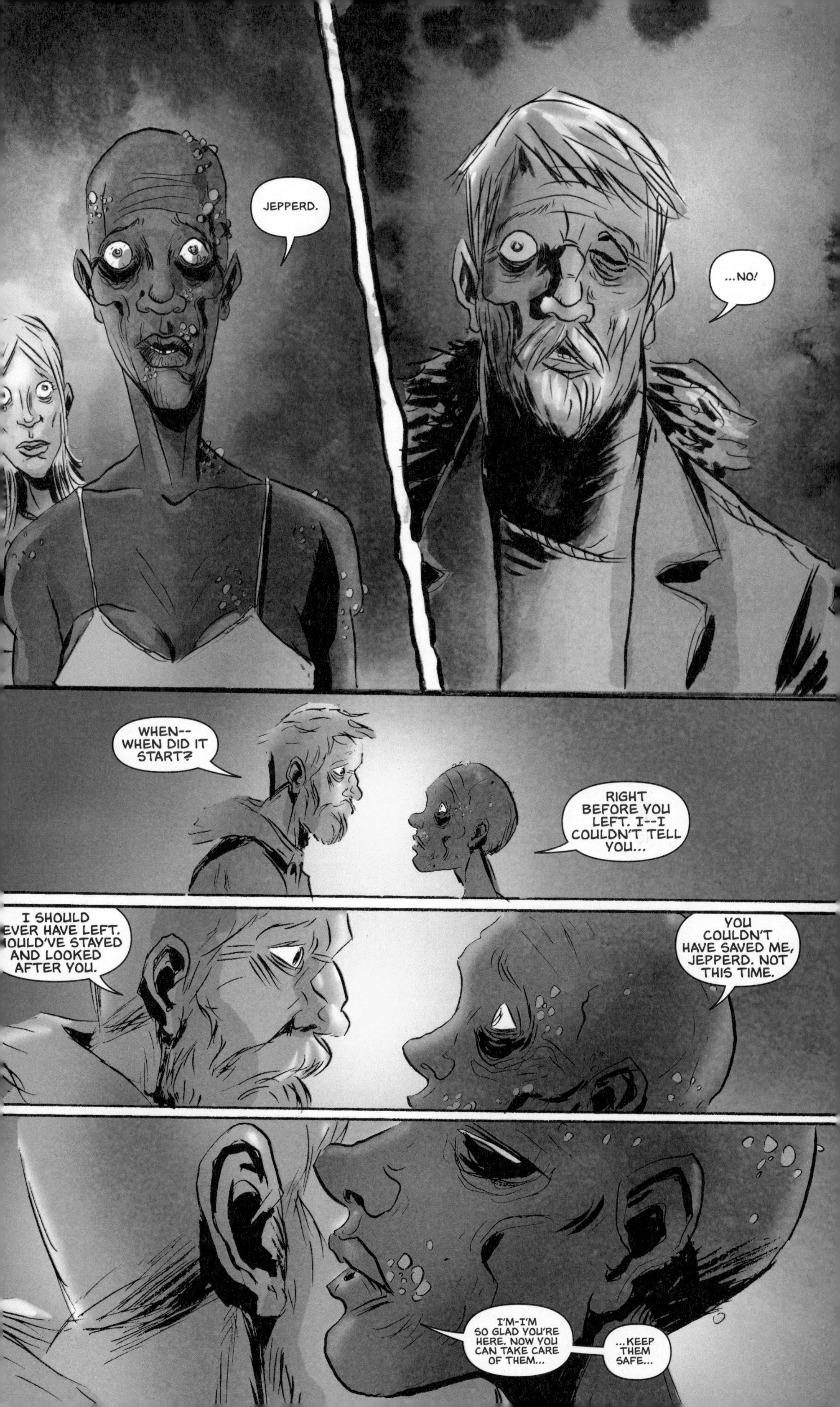
JEPPERD.
...NO!
WHEN-- WHEN DID IT START?
RIGHT BEFORE YOU LEFT. I--I COULDN'T TELL YOU...
I SHOULD EVER HAVE LEFT. OULD'VE STAYED AND LOOKED AFTER YOU.
YOU COULDN'T HAVE SAVED ME, JEPPERD. NOT THIS TIME.
I'M-I'M SO GLAD YOU'RE HERE. NOW YOU CAN TAKE CARE OF THEM...
...KEEP THEM SAFE...

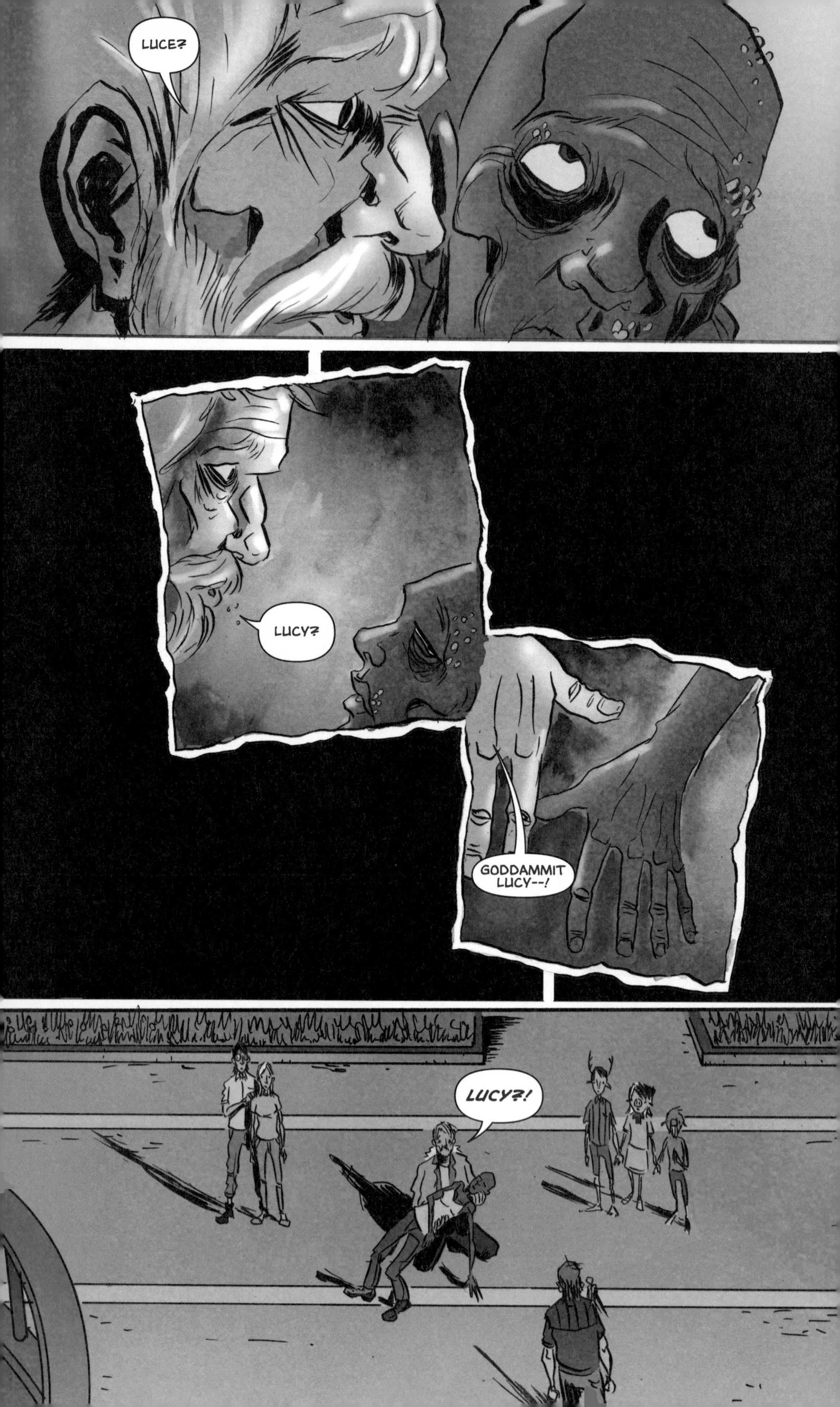
LUCE?
LUCY?
GODDAMMIT LUCY--!
LUCY?!

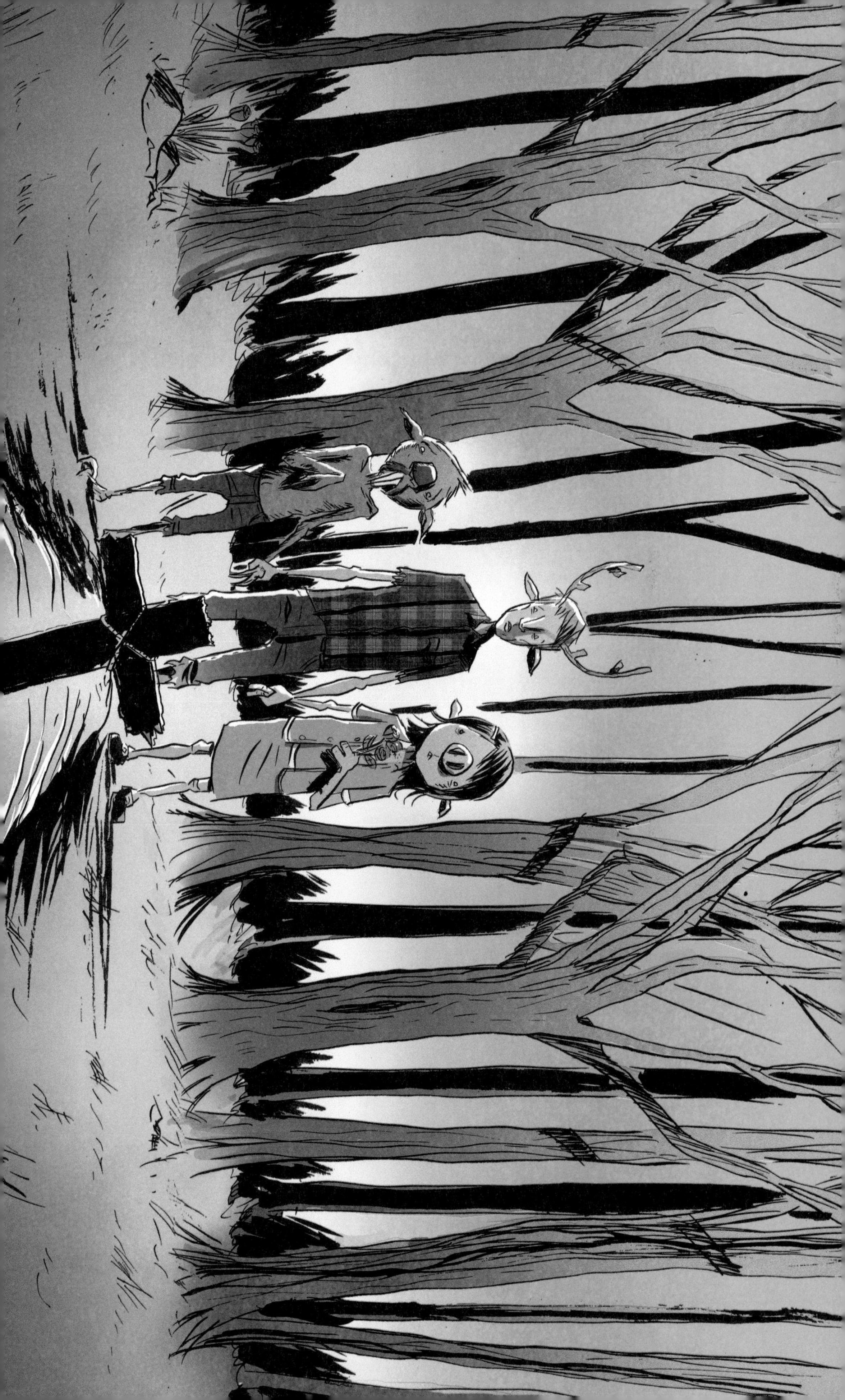

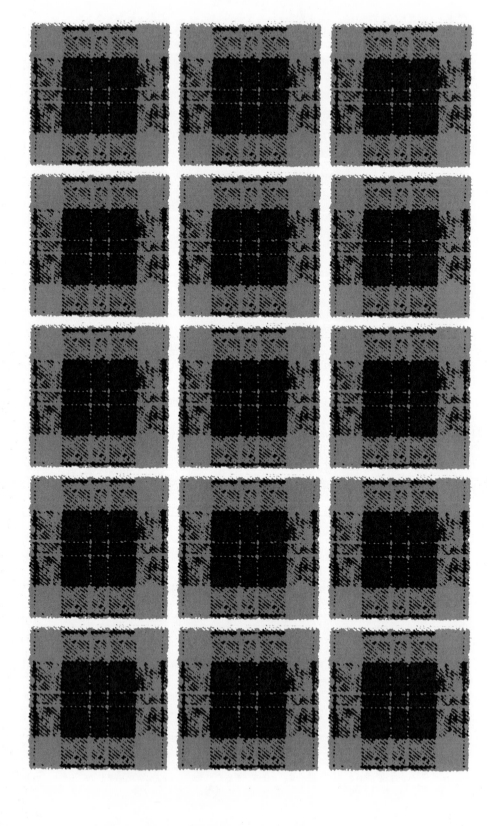

THE CONTINUING ADVENTURES OF THE BIG MAN AND THE BOY

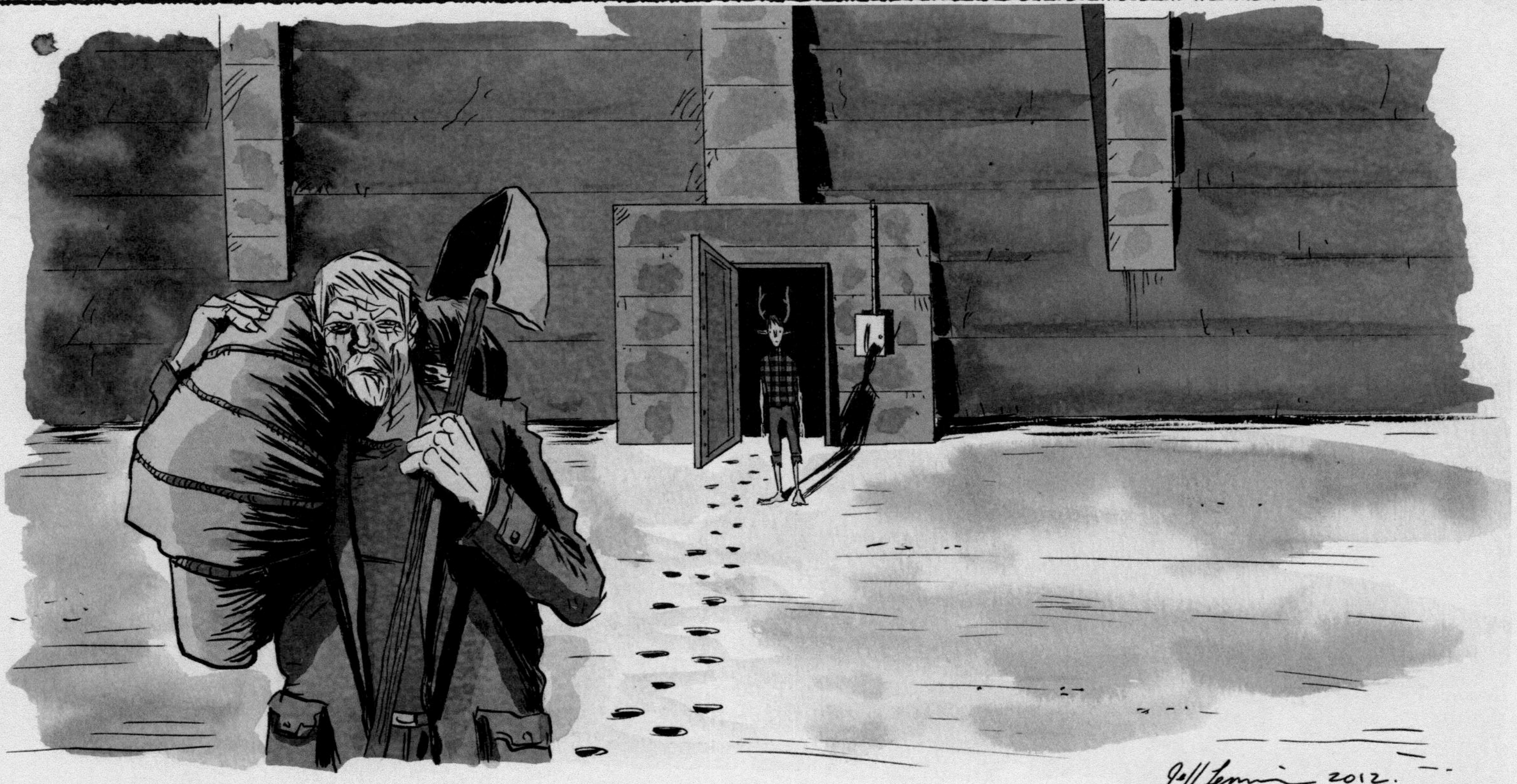
Jeff Lemire 2012.

. . . The Big Man had sat alone in the Dam for nearly three days, barely talking to anyone. Then, on the third day when the blizzard finally passed, he set out with only The Nice Lady's body and a shovel.

The Boy wanted to follow, but he knew that The Big Man needed to do this alone . . .

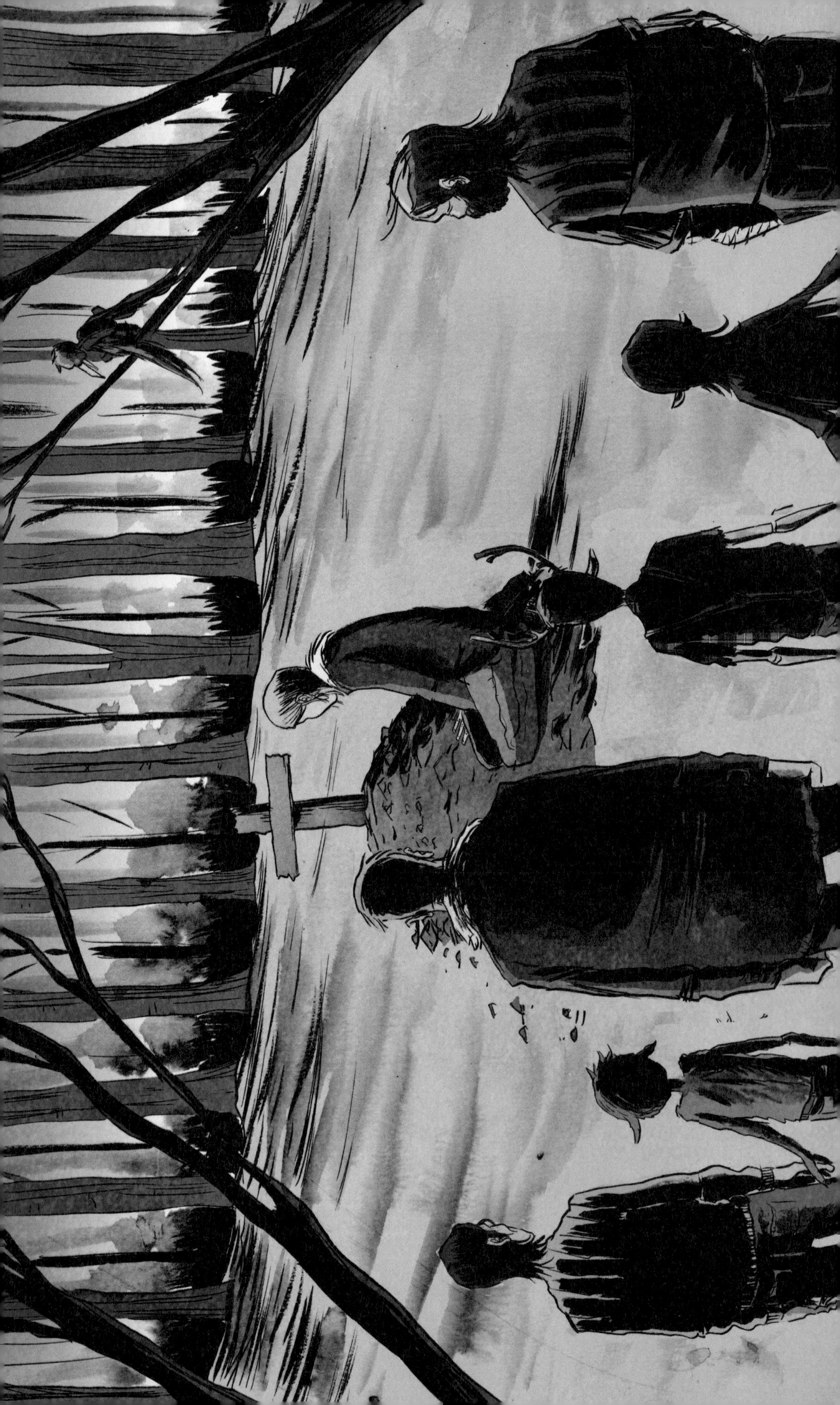

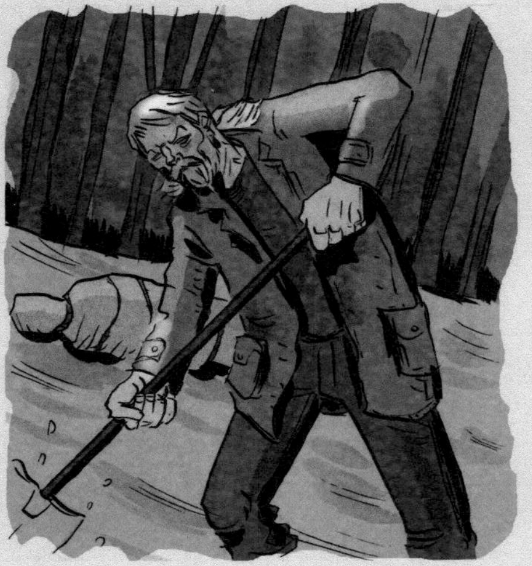

Digging The Nice Lady's grave was hard work. The ground outside was frozen solid. But The Big Man was nothing if not strong and determined. He had chosen a pretty spot to lay her to rest. It was under a nice old Oak tree. The others didn't know it, but this wasn't the first time The Big Man had laid a woman he had loved to rest under such a tree.

That afternoon, they all gathered around and put The Nice Lady back into the earth. No one said much. There wasn't much left to say. She had been their friend, their mother and their sister. She had been strong and brave. And now she was gone.

The Little Boy and The Pig Girl had spent the morning carving a marker (they didn't like the word tombstone) for her grave out of a tabletop from The Dam. The Pretty Girl had helped to spell all the words. It wasn't a fancy thing, but The Nice Lady would have liked it anyway.

It was sturdy and simple, just like her.

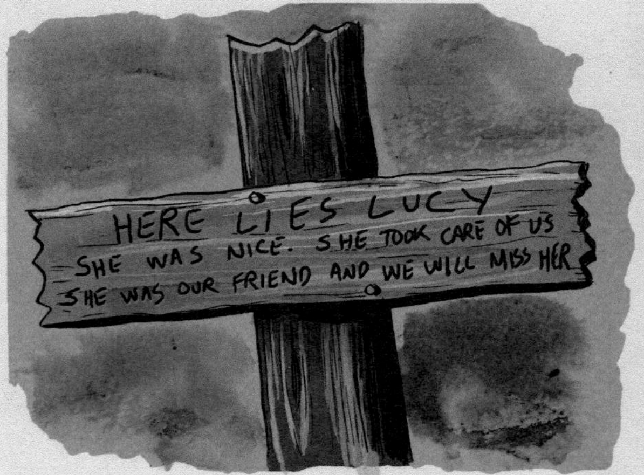
HERE LIES LUCY
SHE WAS NICE. SHE TOOK CARE OF US
SHE WAS OUR FRIEND AND WE WILL MISS HER

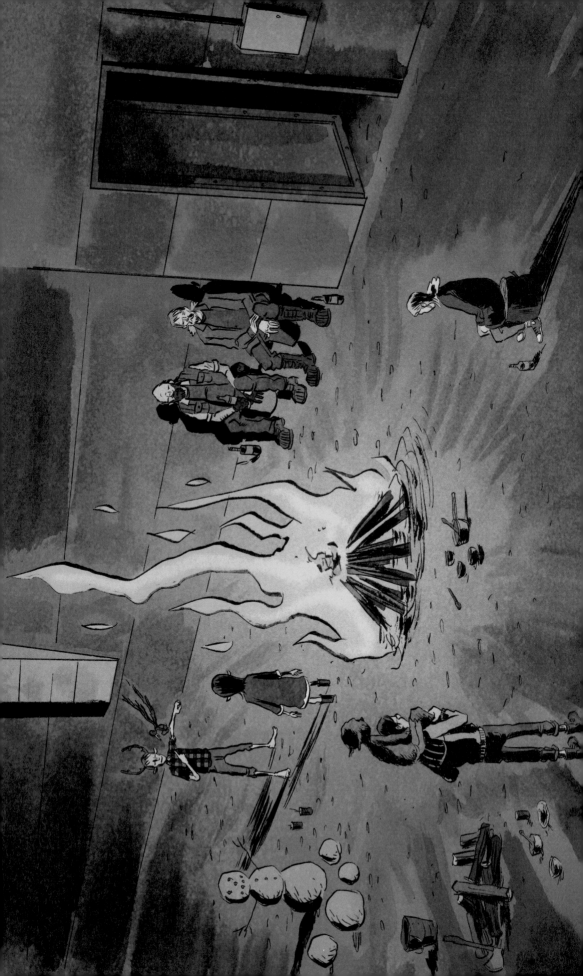

That night they decided not to be sad anymore. The Pretty Girl told them that The Nice Lady wouldn't have wanted them to waste any more time crying.
She said that they all may only have a little time left, and they should be happy.

The funny thing was, even though she had said those very words, The Pretty Girl was the saddest of all of them that night. She had sat off alone, staring into the fire. She had known The Nice Lady the longest, and they had been like sisters. And now she would be alone. As the night went on, the children noticed her head off to the gravesite. They could hear her talking to The Nice Lady.

The Big Man seemed changed though. Something had been lifted from his shoulders. He had brought a new friend to them. And for the first time in a long time, he smiled and laughed. Maybe he didn't feel quite so alone anymore. Maybe he was happy to have someone else to share his load.

They sang and danced and played games well into the night. Eventually, The Pretty Girl came back and joined in.

Then they all slept better than they had in a long, long time.

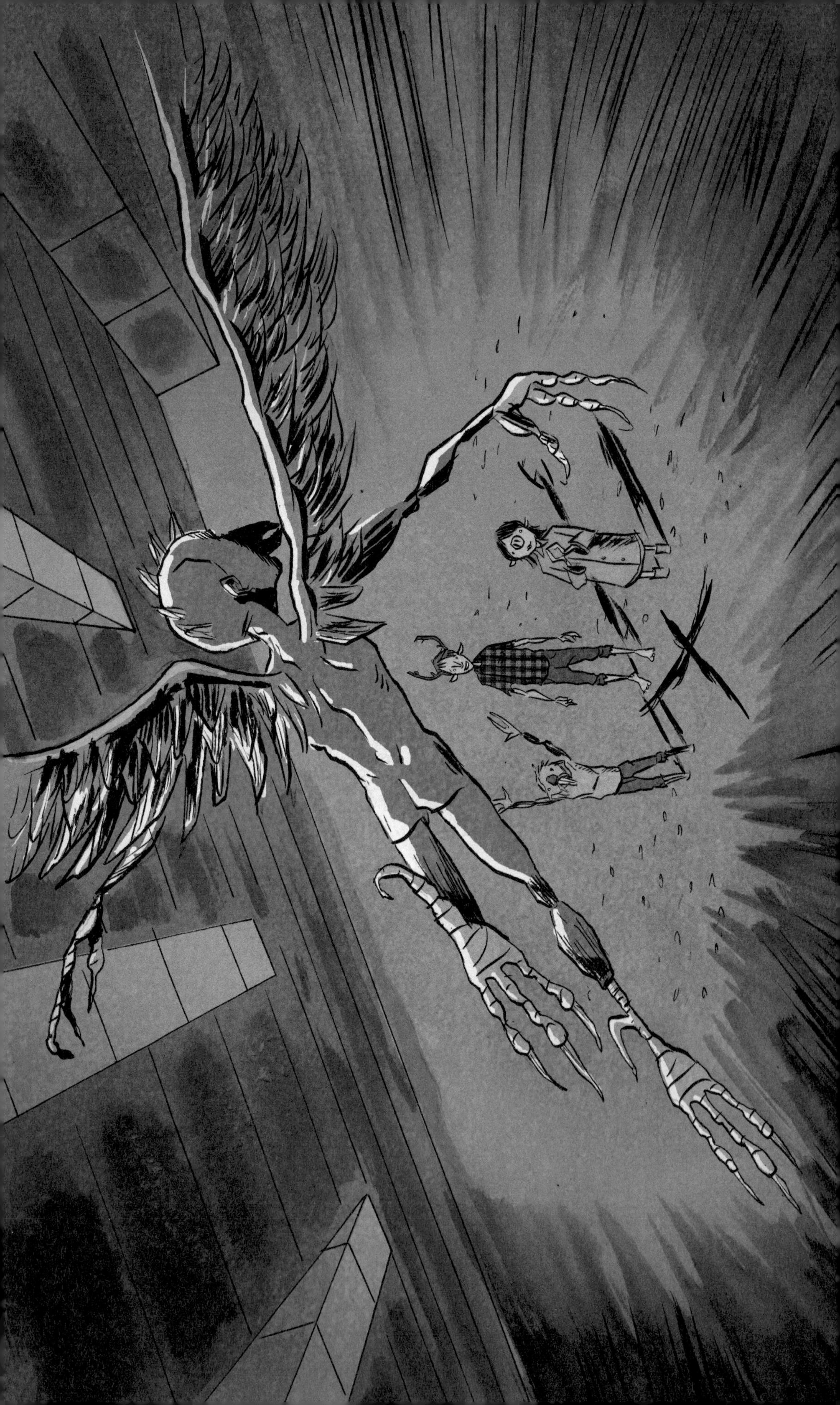

The Big Man wasn't the only one to make a new friend. The Crow-Boy had had come along too, and the other children loved him. He couldn't talk, but he could fly and squawk and he was a lot of fun. They all spent the next few days playing games and being kids.

Later that week, The Big Man and his new friend went to see The Evergreen People. They told them that it was safe to go home. They told them that The Liar was gone and they didn't need to be scared anymore.

The Big Man struck a deal with them. He told The Evergreen People that they could have the Dam back as long as The Big Man could take their last truck. They all agreed and shook on it, just like people used to in the old days before everyone got sick, and people stopped being nice to each other.

But then, on the way back to The Dam, they came across The Liar! But it was clear just by looking at him that he wasn't never gonna lie to no one ever again.

Even though this made The Big Man happy, he was glad the children weren't there to see it.

BUT, BOBBY...DON'T YOU WANNA COME WITH US TO ALASKA?

YEAH. THE DOC EXPLAINED IT ALL TO ME A WHILE BACK. IT'S PART OF HIS NATURAL CYCLE OR SOMETHING.

HE PROBABLY SHOULD HAVE DONE IT EARLIER IN THE WINTER, BUT WITH ALL THE CRAP WE BEEN DOING, HE COULDN'T. ANYWAY, I GUESS IT'S TIME NOW.

WAIT, EXPLAIN THIS TO ME AGAIN... HE'S GOTTA *HIBERNATE?*

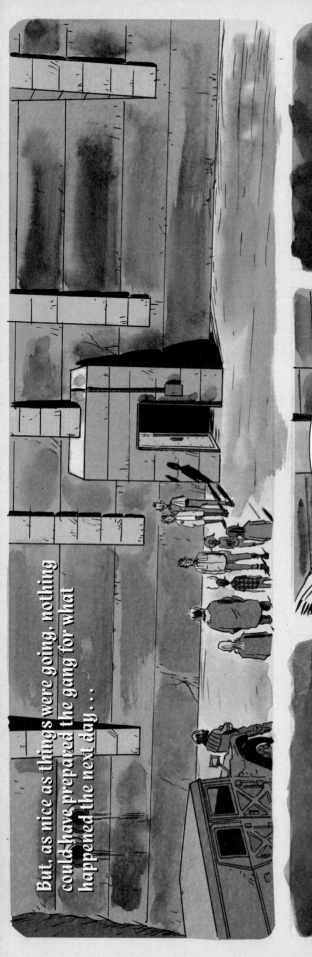

But, as nice as things were going, nothing could have prepared the gang for what happened the next day . . .

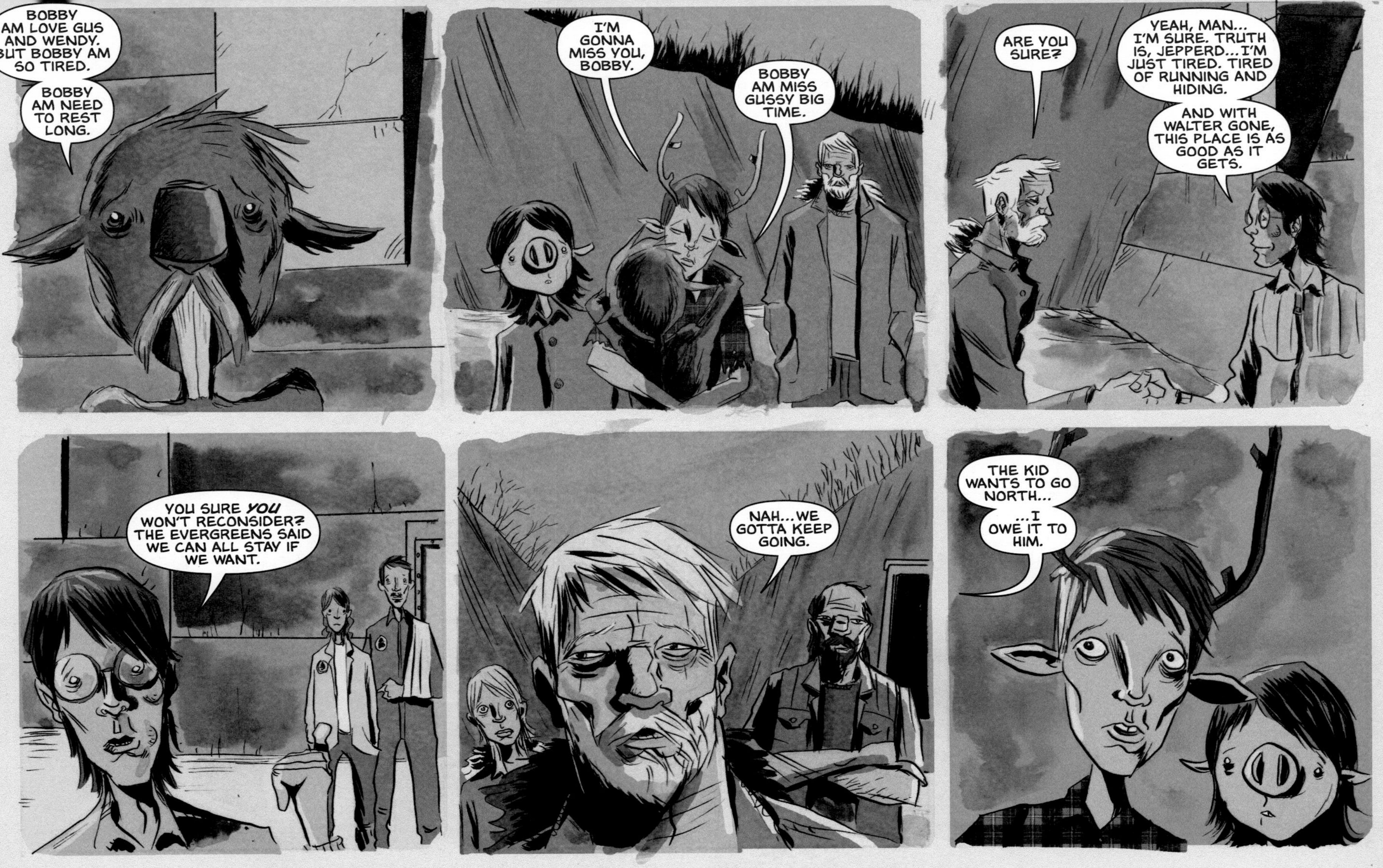
BOBBY AM LOVE GUS AND WENDY. BUT BOBBY AM SO TIRED.
BOBBY AM NEED TO REST LONG.
I'M GONNA MISS YOU, BOBBY.
BOBBY AM MISS GUSSY BIG TIME.
ARE YOU SURE?
YEAH, MAN... I'M SURE. TRUTH IS, JEPPERD... I'M JUST TIRED. TIRED OF RUNNING AND HIDING.
AND WITH WALTER GONE, THIS PLACE IS AS GOOD AS IT GETS.
YOU SURE *YOU* WON'T RECONSIDER? THE EVERGREENS SAID WE CAN ALL STAY IF WE WANT.
NAH... WE GOTTA KEEP GOING.
THE KID WANTS TO GO NORTH...
...I OWE IT TO HIM.

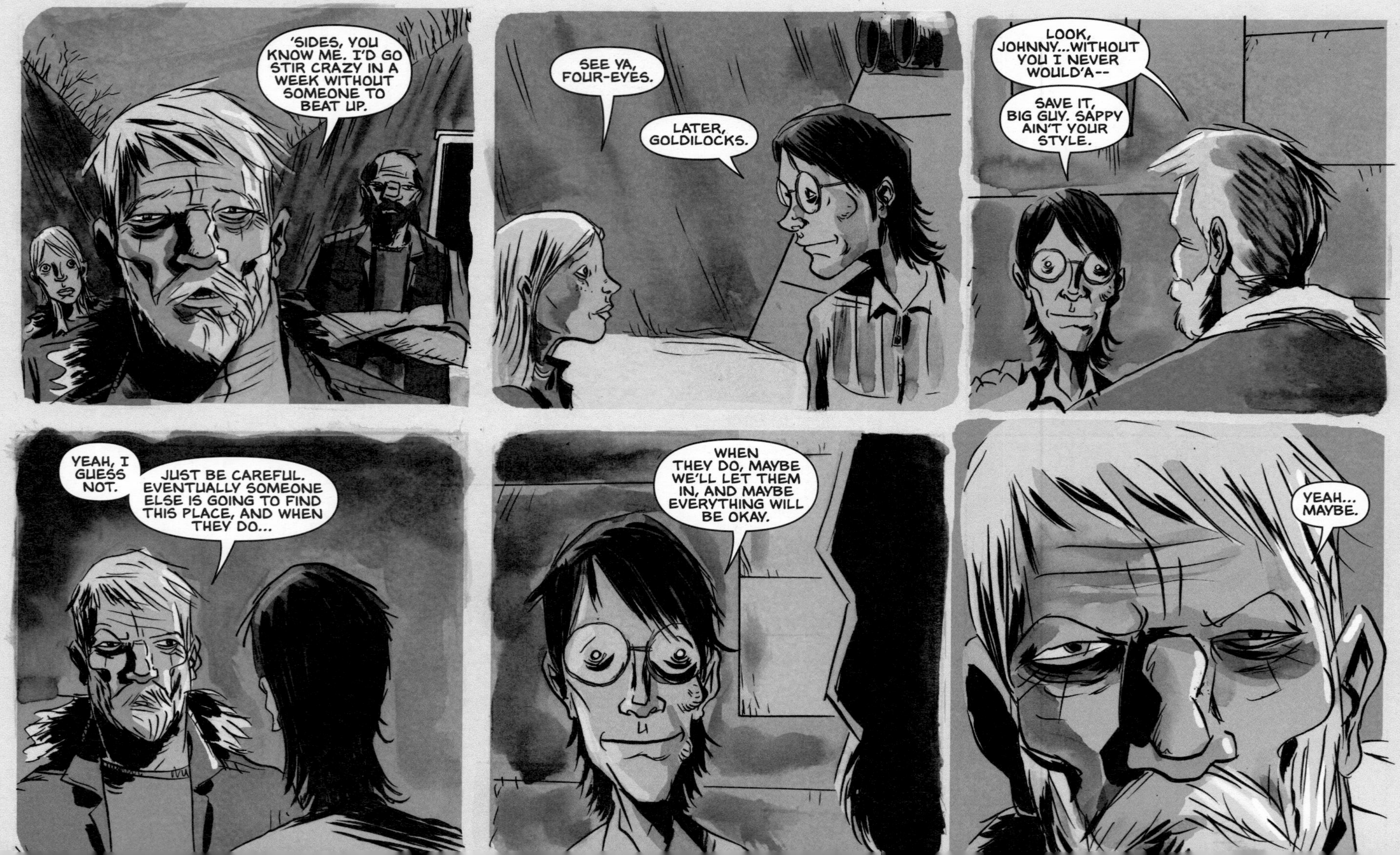
'SIDES, YOU KNOW ME. I'D GO STIR CRAZY IN A WEEK WITHOUT SOMEONE TO BEAT UP.
SEE YA, FOUR-EYES.
LATER, GOLDILOCKS.
LOOK, JOHNNY...WITHOUT YOU I NEVER WOULD'A--
SAVE IT, BIG GUY. SAPPY AIN'T YOUR STYLE.
YEAH, I GUESS NOT.
JUST BE CAREFUL. EVENTUALLY SOMEONE ELSE IS GOING TO FIND THIS PLACE, AND WHEN THEY DO...
WHEN THEY DO, MAYBE WE'LL LET THEM IN, AND MAYBE EVERYTHING WILL BE OKAY.
YEAH... MAYBE.

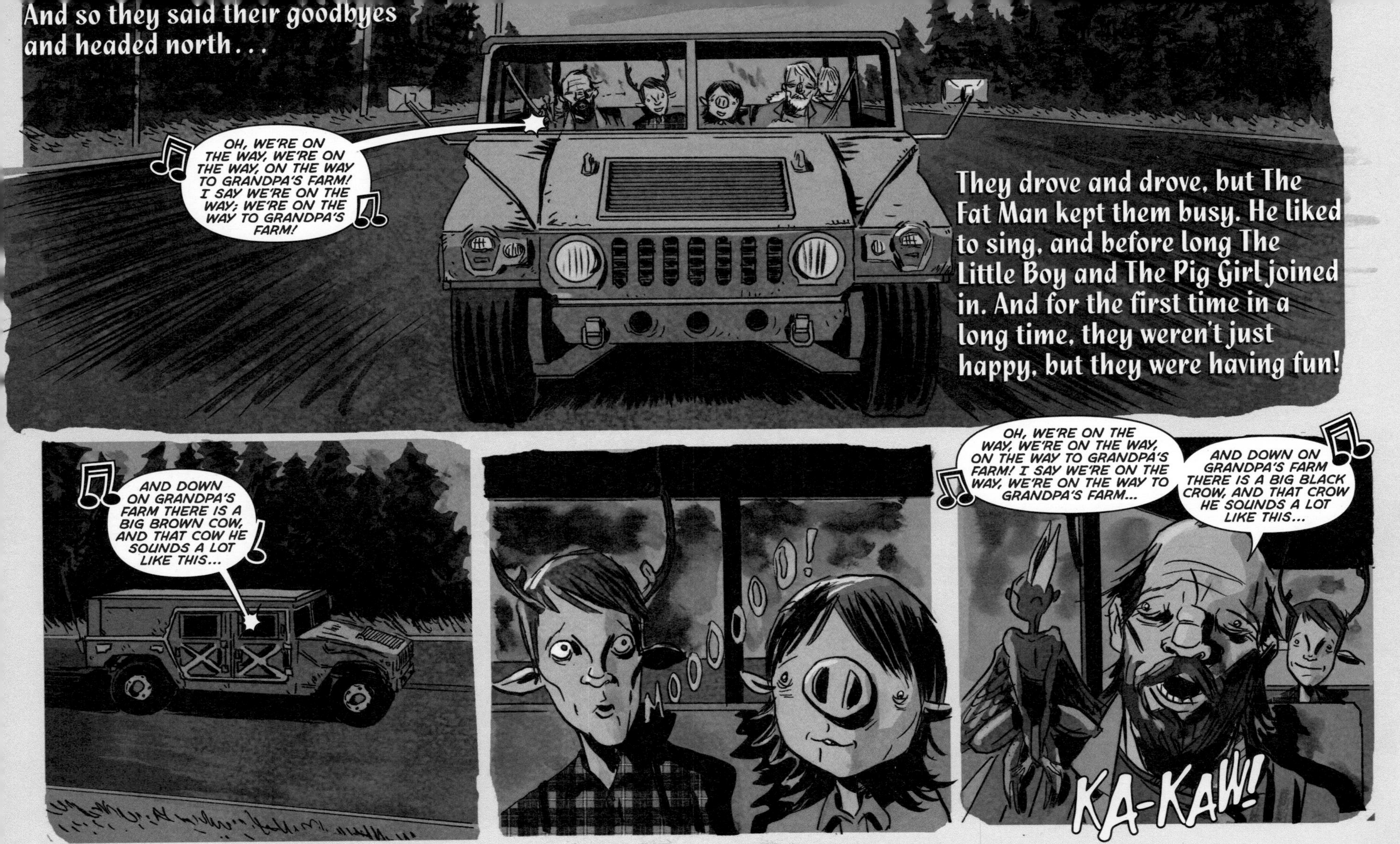
And so they said their goodbyes and headed north...
OH, WE'RE ON THE WAY, WE'RE ON THE WAY, ON THE WAY TO GRANDPA'S FARM! I SAY WE'RE ON THE WAY; WE'RE ON THE WAY TO GRANDPA'S FARM!
They drove and drove, but The Fat Man kept them busy. He liked to sing, and before long The Little Boy and The Pig Girl joined in. And for the first time in a long time, they weren't just happy, but they were having fun!
AND DOWN ON GRANDPA'S FARM THERE IS A BIG BROWN COW, AND THAT COW HE SOUNDS A LOT LIKE THIS...
MOOOOO!
OH, WE'RE ON THE WAY, WE'RE ON THE WAY, ON THE WAY TO GRANDPA'S FARM! I SAY WE'RE ON THE WAY, WE'RE ON THE WAY TO GRANDPA'S FARM...
AND DOWN ON GRANDPA'S FARM THERE IS A BIG BLACK CROW, AND THAT CROW HE SOUNDS A LOT LIKE THIS...
KA-KAW!

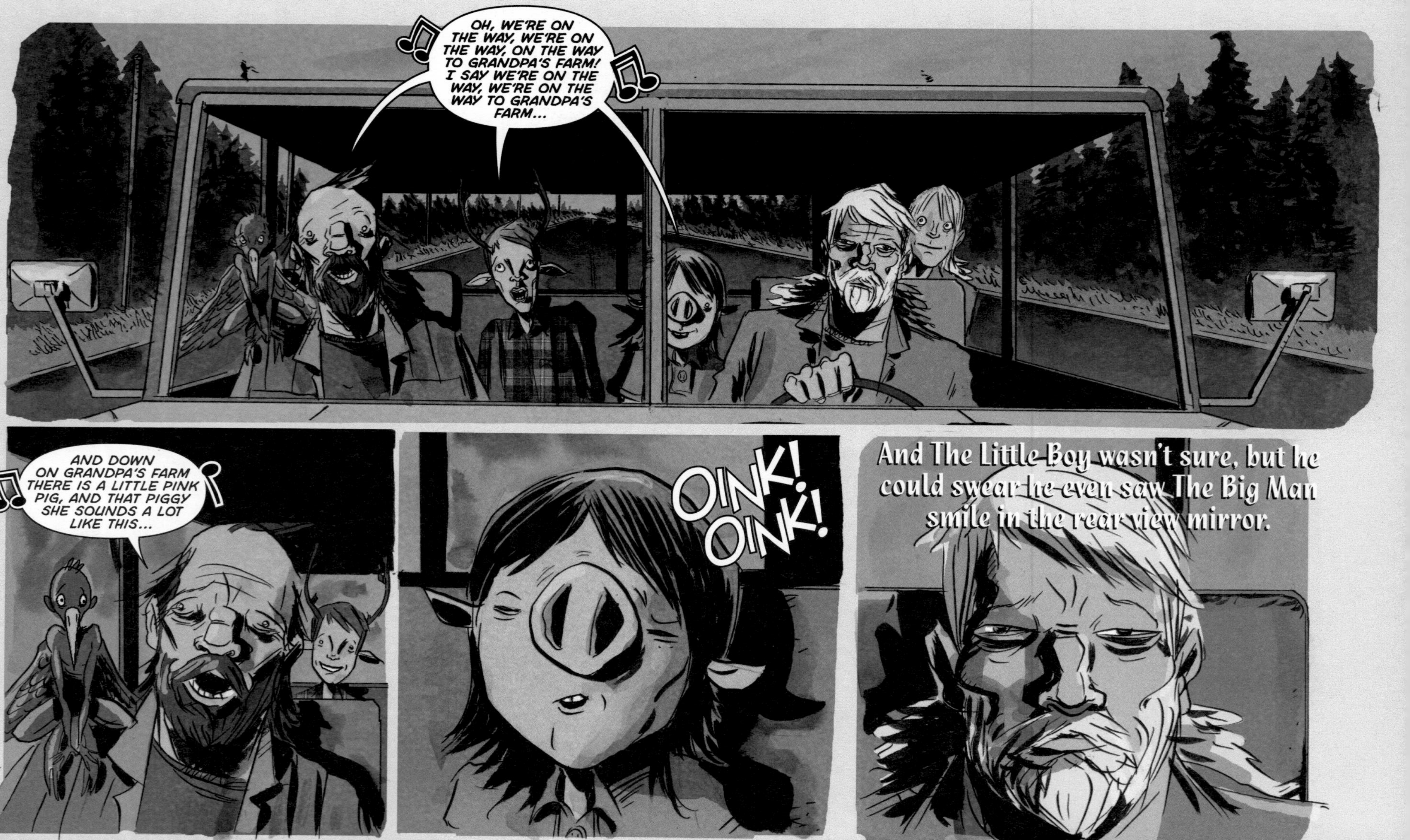
OH, WE'RE ON THE WAY, WE'RE ON THE WAY, ON THE WAY TO GRANDPA'S FARM! I SAY WE'RE ON THE WAY, WE'RE ON THE WAY TO GRANDPA'S FARM...
AND DOWN ON GRANDPA'S FARM THERE IS A LITTLE PINK PIG, AND THAT PIGGY SHE SOUNDS A LOT LIKE THIS...
OINK! OINK!
And The Little Boy wasn't sure, but he could swear he even saw The Big Man smile in the rear view mirror.

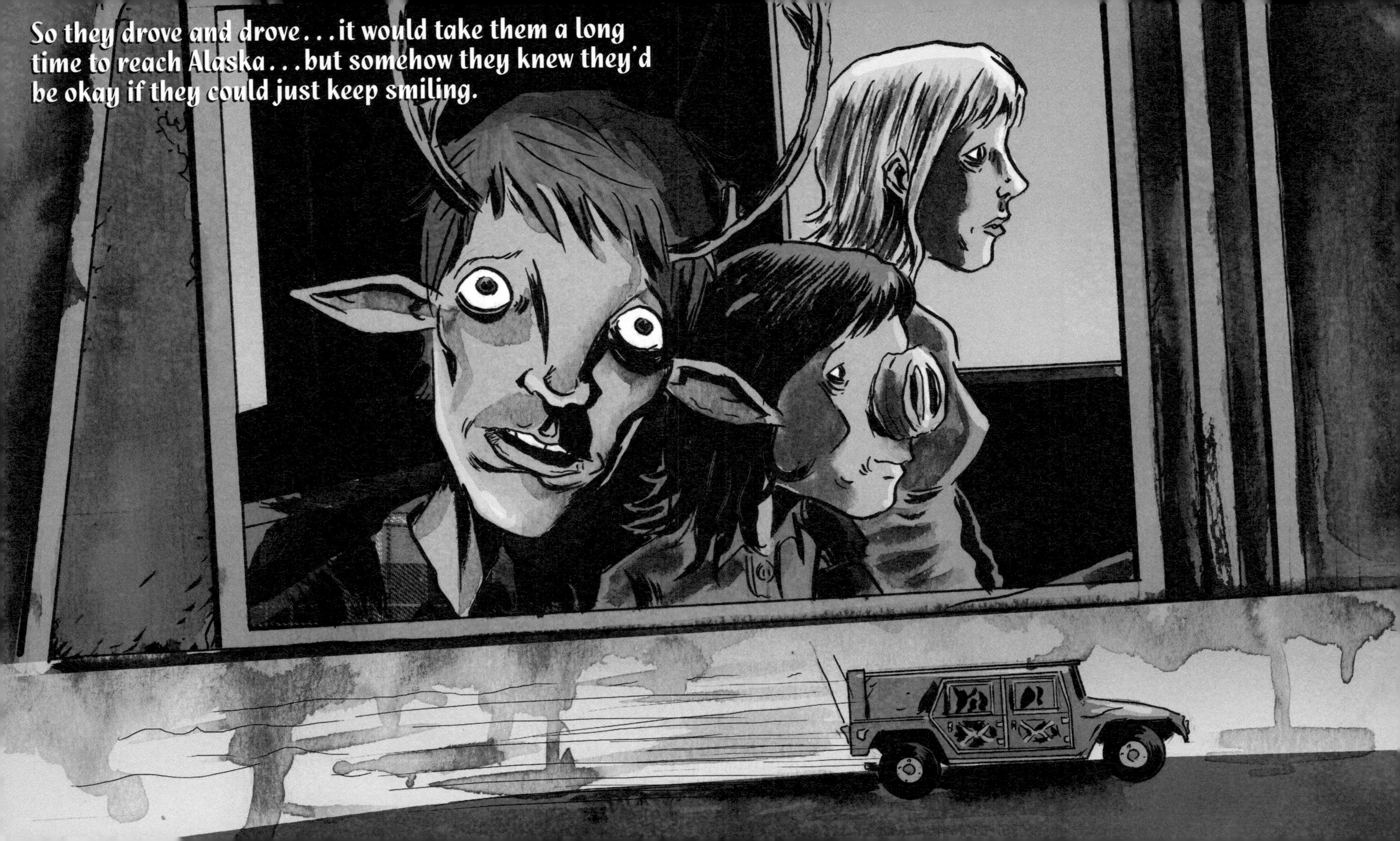
So they drove and drove...it would take them a long time to reach Alaska...but somehow they knew they'd be okay if they could just keep smiling.

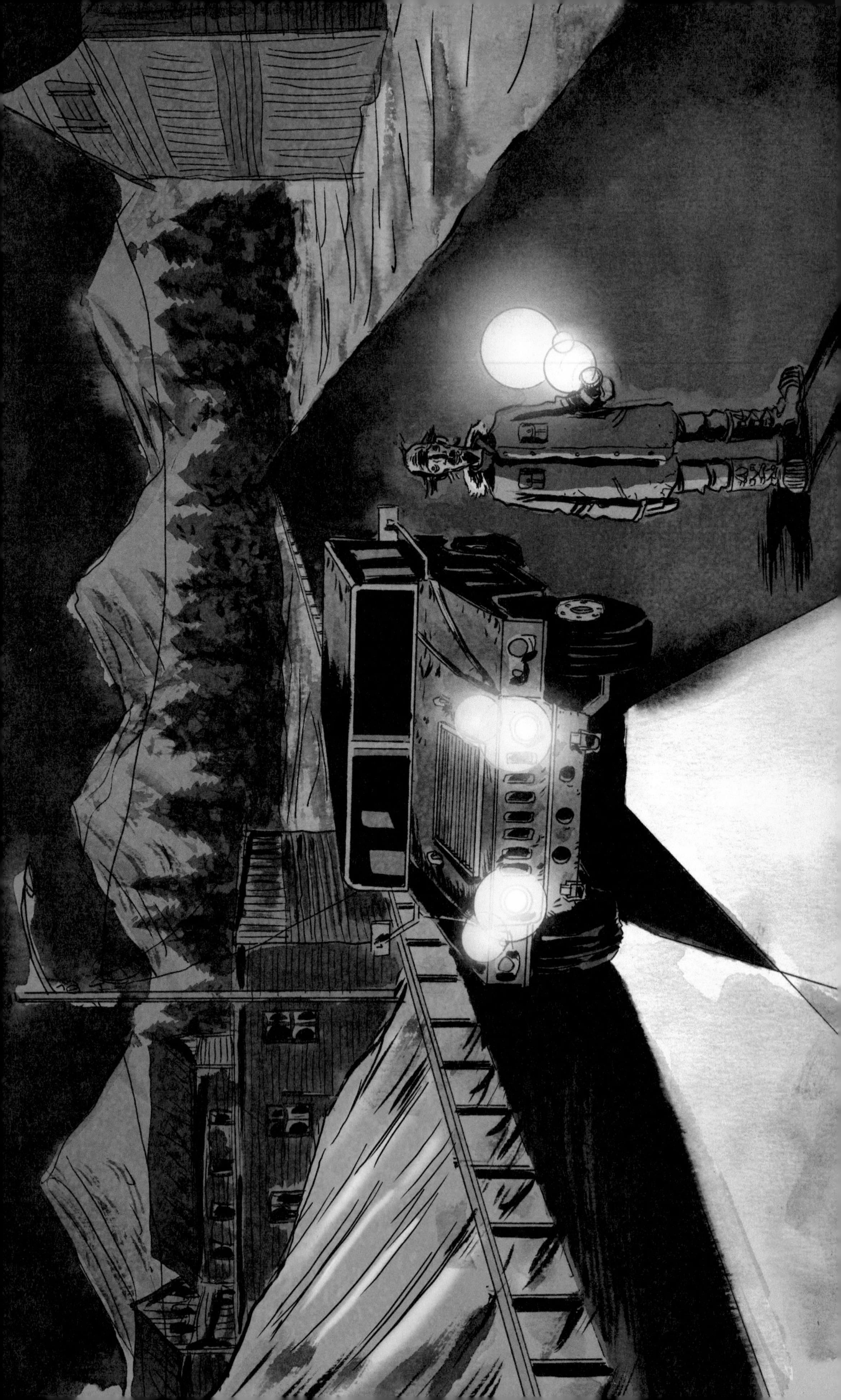

. . . Speaking of Alaska, The Doctor had arrived. After The Little Boy had escaped, he had had no other choice than to keep going on his own. He knew if he went back, The Big Man would surely kill him for what he'd done.

It was a shame that The Little Boy couldn't be here. The Doctor was sure he'd need him to find the secrets he sought, but he also was confident that The Boy would arrive eventually. It was his destiny, after all.

And, The Doctor had managed to get The Bible back from The Boy before he escaped, so everything wasn't lost.

As he searched the dark, cold town a feeling of utter anticipation grew in The Doctor's belly. He knew . . . he just knew that the answers were here, just waiting to be discovered.

Up until now he had thought he was meant to be The Prophet of a new age, but now he started to wonder if he had been wrong. Maybe he was the one destined to become the Messiah himself!

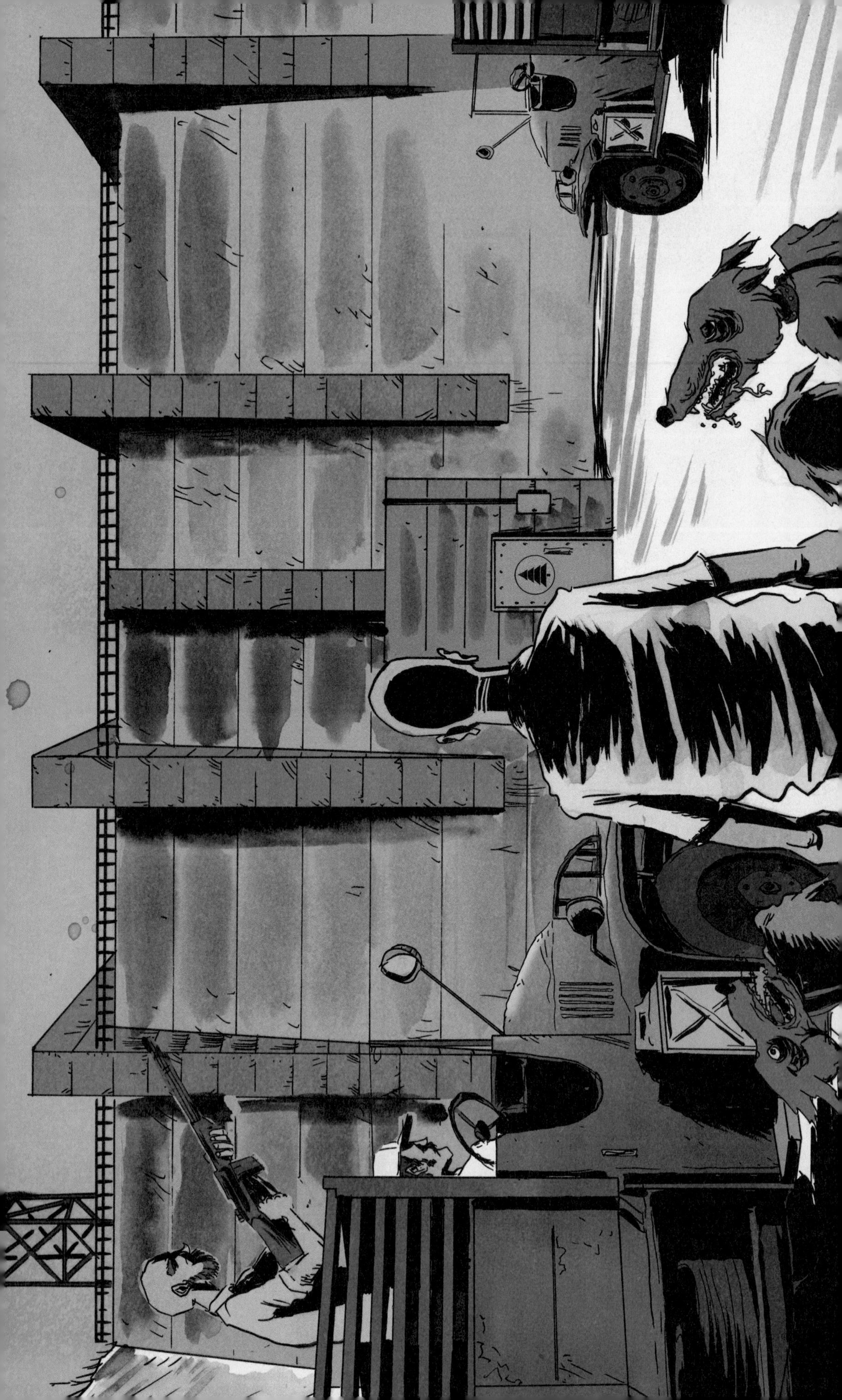

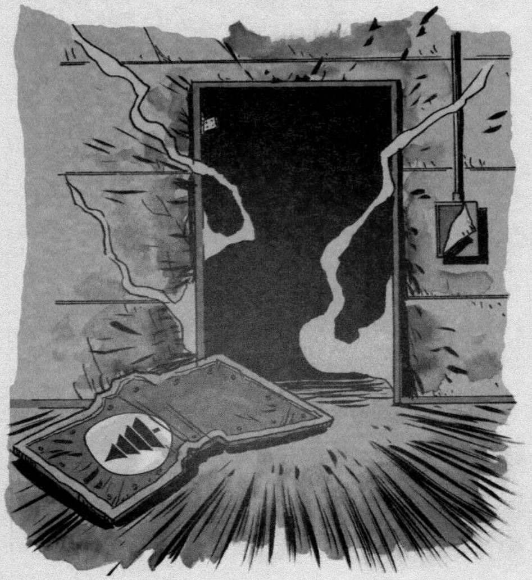

The Doctor's journey was not the only one of note. You see The Bad Man was hot on their trail. In fact he was just arriving at The Dam, only hours behind The Gang. Worst of all, The Bad Man still had The Big Man's son captive. He was sad and confused and just wanted to be free. But that was never going to happen.

The Dog-Boys were there too, and they were excellent trackers. They could smell The Little Boy all over the Dam. The Bad Man wasted no time. He had his army blow the doors in and they stormed The Dam. The Bad Man expected to find The Gang inside, but instead came face to face with his little brother.

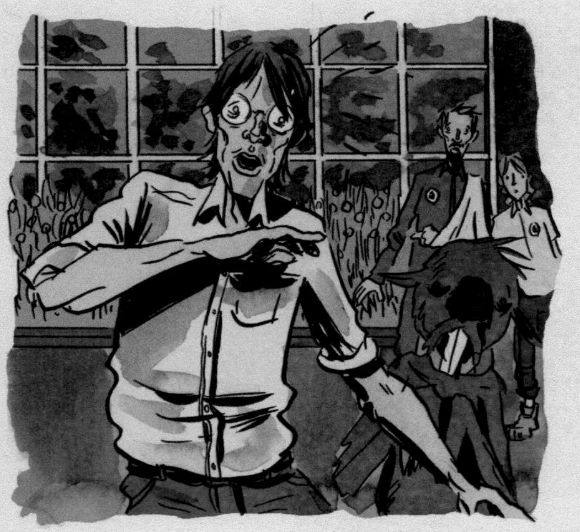

The Bad Man knew it would only be a matter of time before his little brother told him where The Big Man and The Little Boy were headed. He'd make him tell if he had to. . .

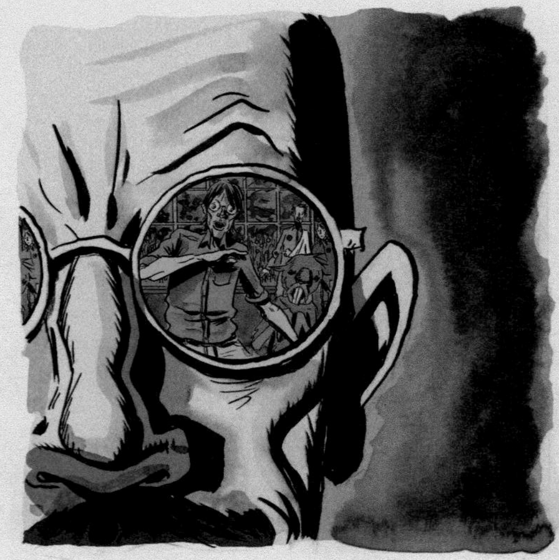

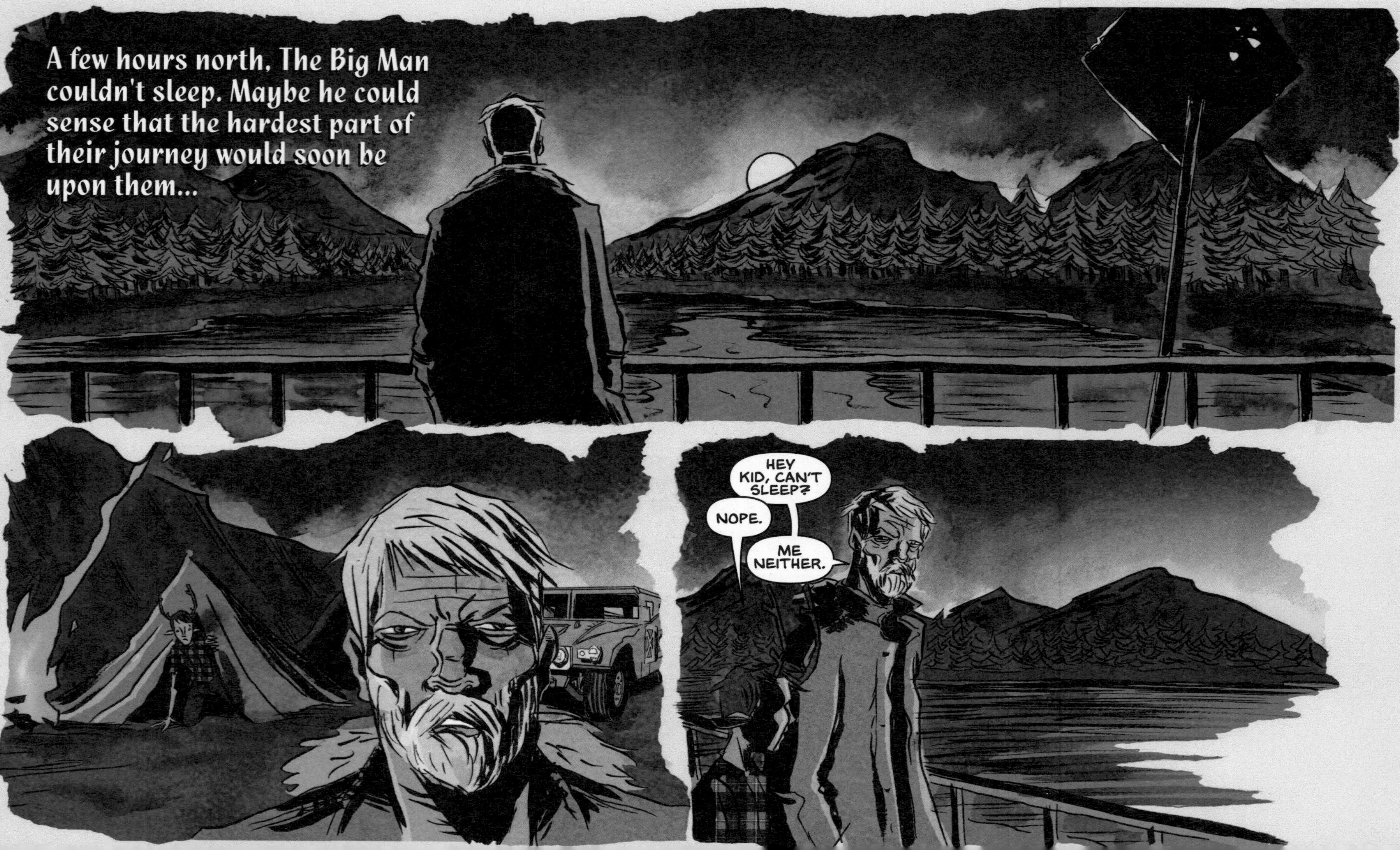
A few hours north, The Big Man couldn't sleep. Maybe he could sense that the hardest part of their journey would soon be upon them...
HEY KID, CAN'T SLEEP?
NOPE.
ME NEITHER.

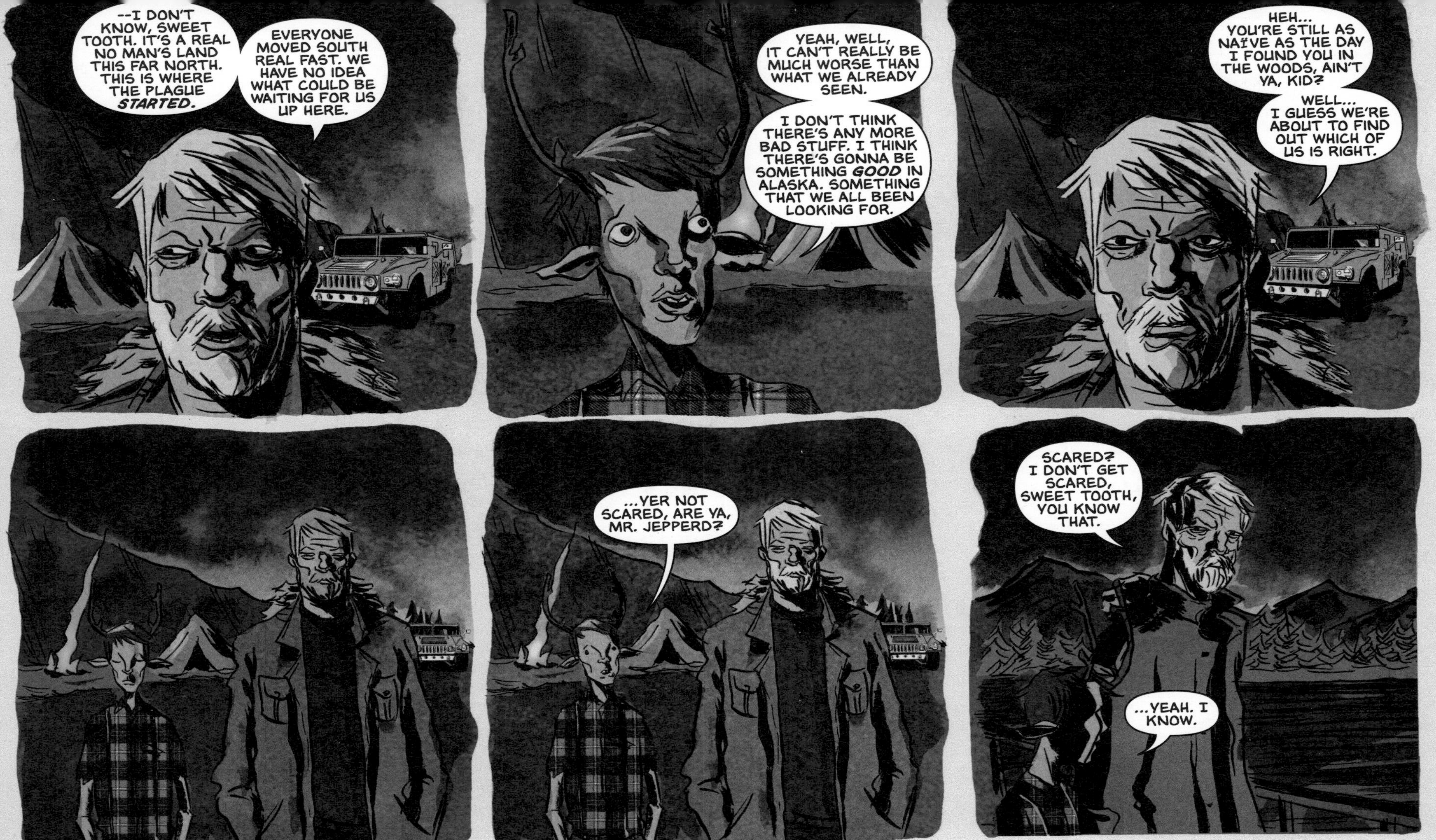
--I DON'T KNOW, SWEET TOOTH. IT'S A REAL NO MAN'S LAND THIS FAR NORTH. THIS IS WHERE THE PLAGUE *STARTED*.
EVERYONE MOVED SOUTH REAL FAST. WE HAVE NO IDEA WHAT COULD BE WAITING FOR US UP HERE.
YEAH, WELL, IT CAN'T REALLY BE MUCH WORSE THAN WHAT WE ALREADY SEEN.
I DON'T THINK THERE'S ANY MORE BAD STUFF. I THINK THERE'S GONNA BE SOMETHING *GOOD* IN ALASKA. SOMETHING THAT WE ALL BEEN LOOKING FOR.
HEH... YOU'RE STILL AS NAÏVE AS THE DAY I FOUND YOU IN THE WOODS, AIN'T YA, KID?
WELL... I GUESS WE'RE ABOUT TO FIND OUT WHICH OF US IS RIGHT.
...YER NOT SCARED, ARE YA, MR. JEPPERD?
SCARED? I DON'T GET SCARED, SWEET TOOTH, YOU KNOW THAT.
...YEAH. I KNOW.

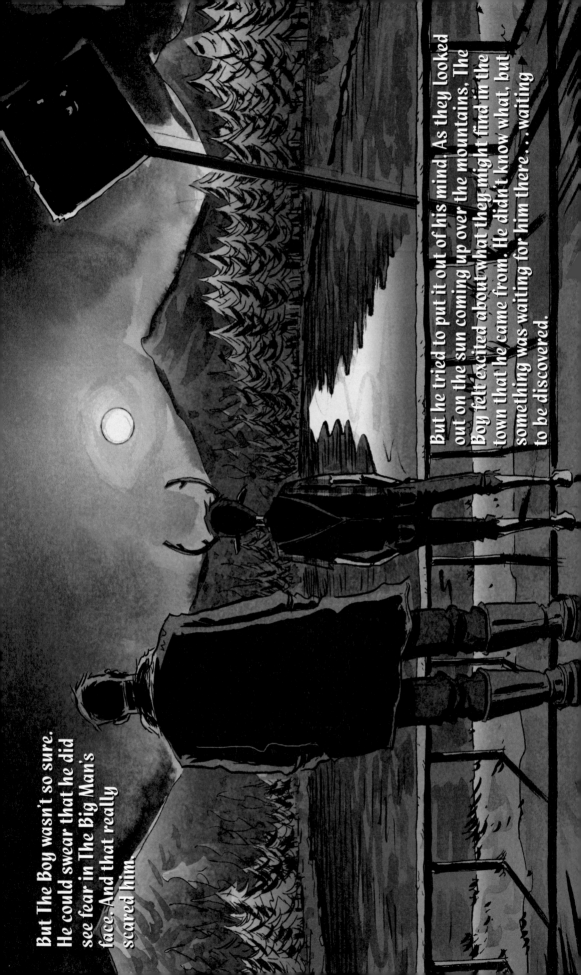

But The Boy wasn't so sure. He could swear that he did see fear in The Big Man's face. And that really scared him.

But he tried to put it out of his mind. As they looked out on the sun coming up over the mountains, The Boy felt excited about what they might find in the town that he came from. He didn't know what, but something was waiting for him there... waiting to be discovered.

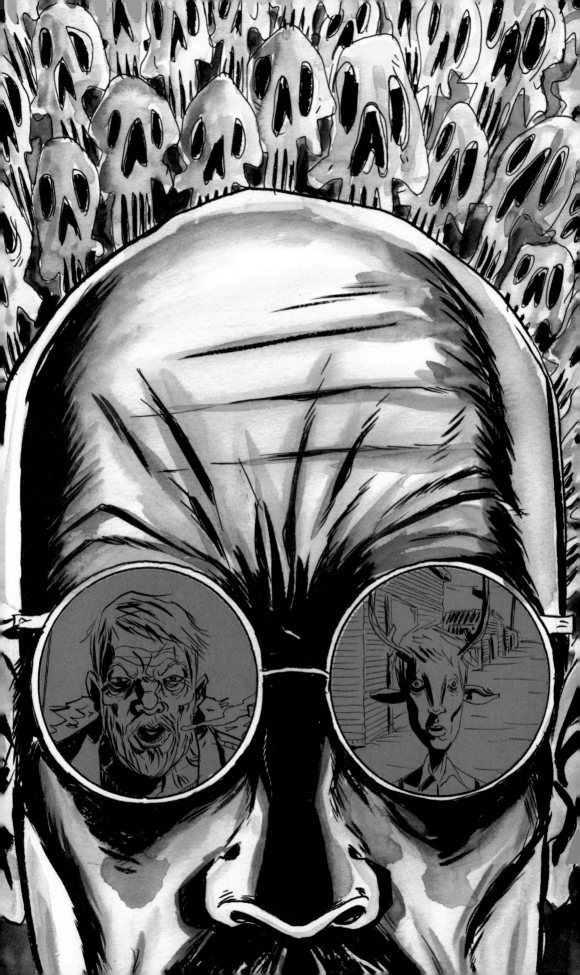

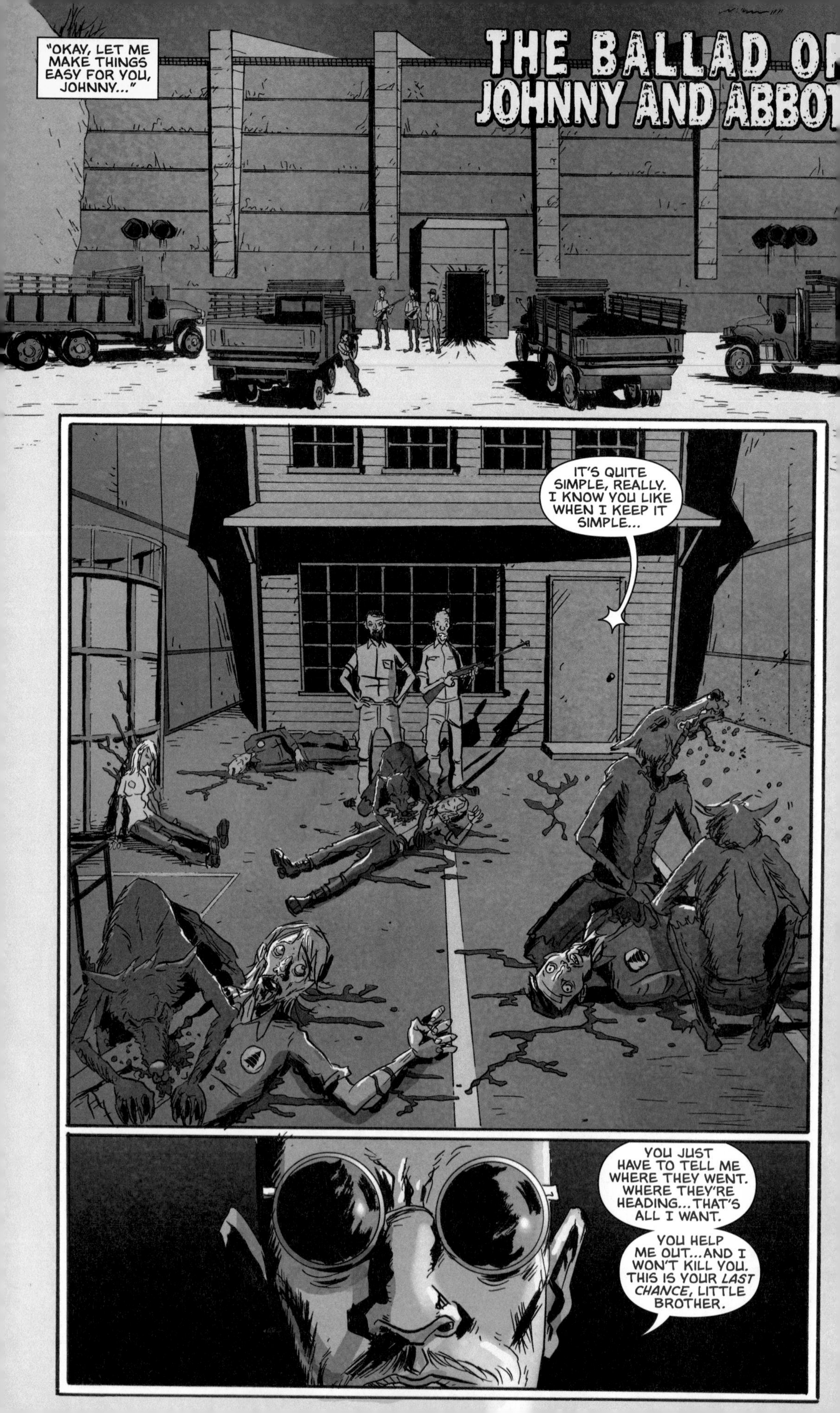

"OKAY, LET ME MAKE THINGS EASY FOR YOU, JOHNNY..."
THE BALLAD OF JOHNNY AND ABBOT
IT'S QUITE SIMPLE, REALLY. I KNOW YOU LIKE WHEN I KEEP IT SIMPLE...
YOU JUST HAVE TO TELL ME WHERE THEY WENT. WHERE THEY'RE HEADING...THAT'S ALL I WANT.
YOU HELP ME OUT...AND I WON'T KILL YOU. THIS IS YOUR *LAST CHANCE*, LITTLE BROTHER.

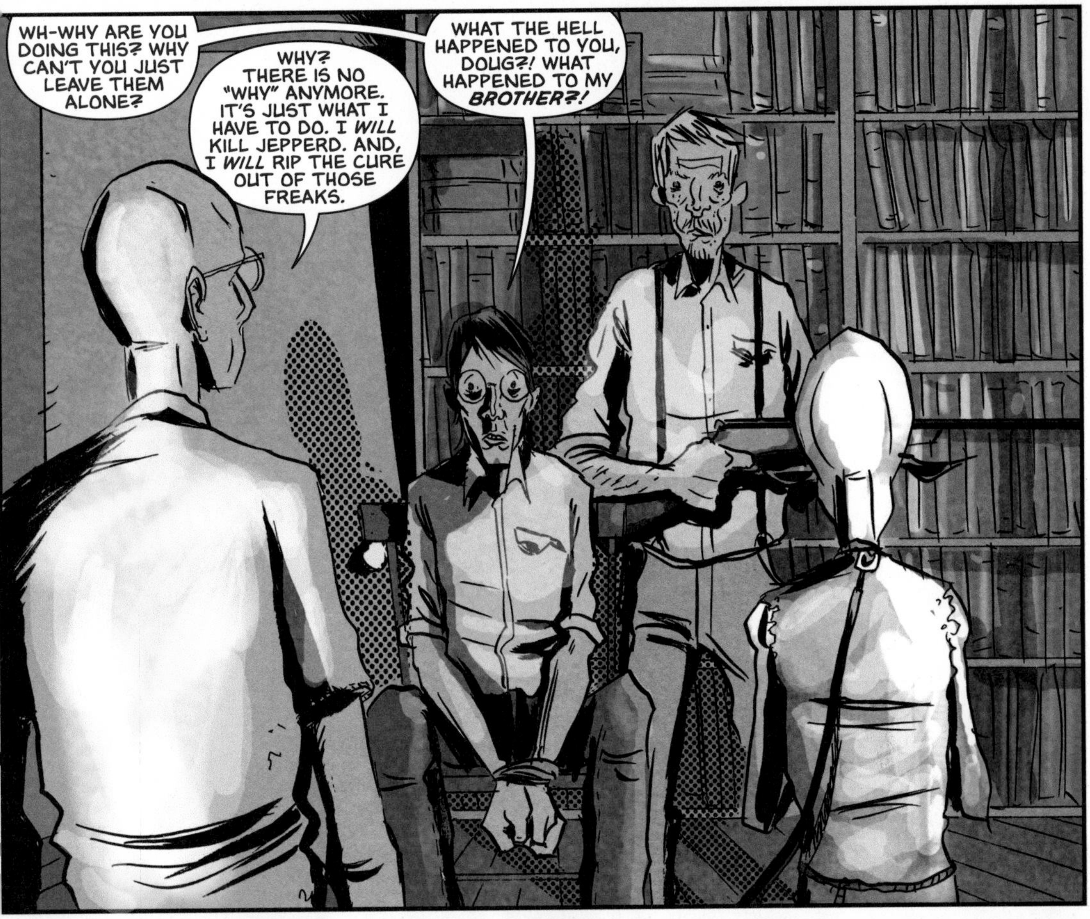
WH-WHY ARE YOU DOING THIS? WHY CAN'T YOU JUST LEAVE THEM ALONE?
WHY? THERE IS NO "WHY" ANYMORE. IT'S JUST WHAT I HAVE TO DO. I *WILL* KILL JEPPERD. AND, I *WILL* RIP THE CURE OUT OF THOSE FREAKS.
WHAT THE HELL HAPPENED TO YOU, DOUG?! WHAT HAPPENED TO MY *BROTHER?!*

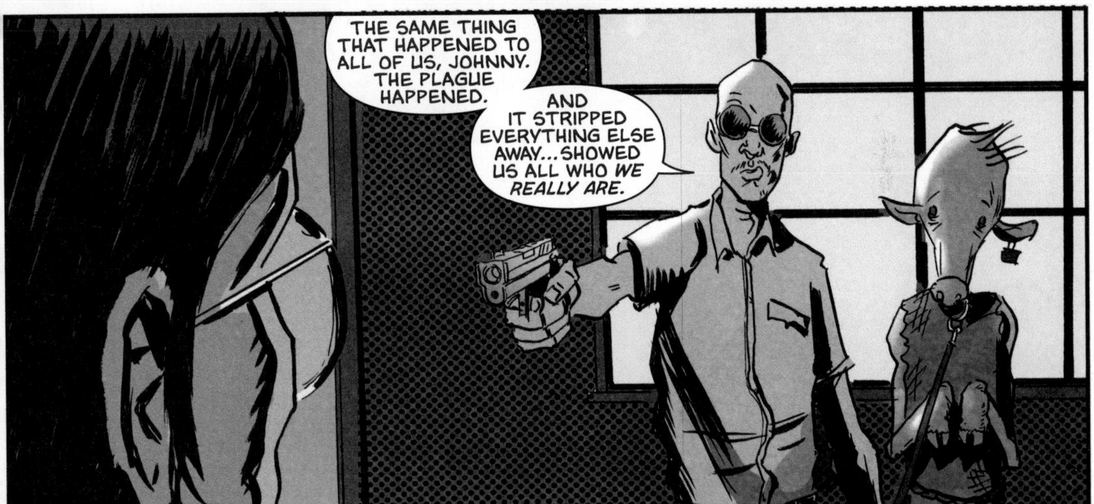
THE SAME THING THAT HAPPENED TO ALL OF US, JOHNNY. THE PLAGUE HAPPENED.
AND IT STRIPPED EVERYTHING ELSE AWAY... SHOWED US ALL WHO *WE REALLY ARE*.

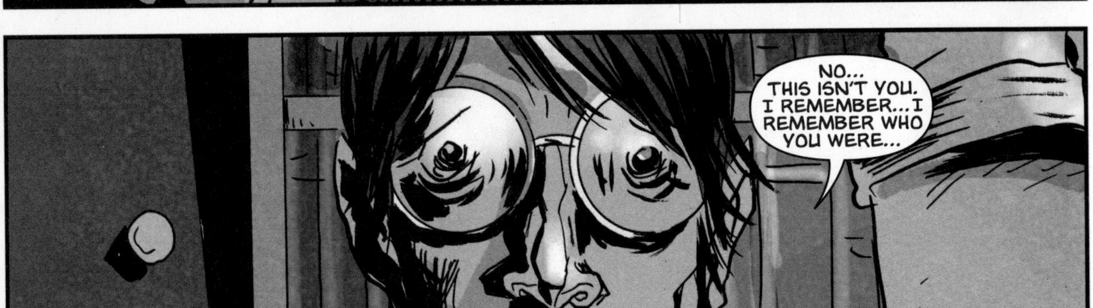
NO... THIS ISN'T YOU. I REMEMBER... I REMEMBER WHO YOU WERE...

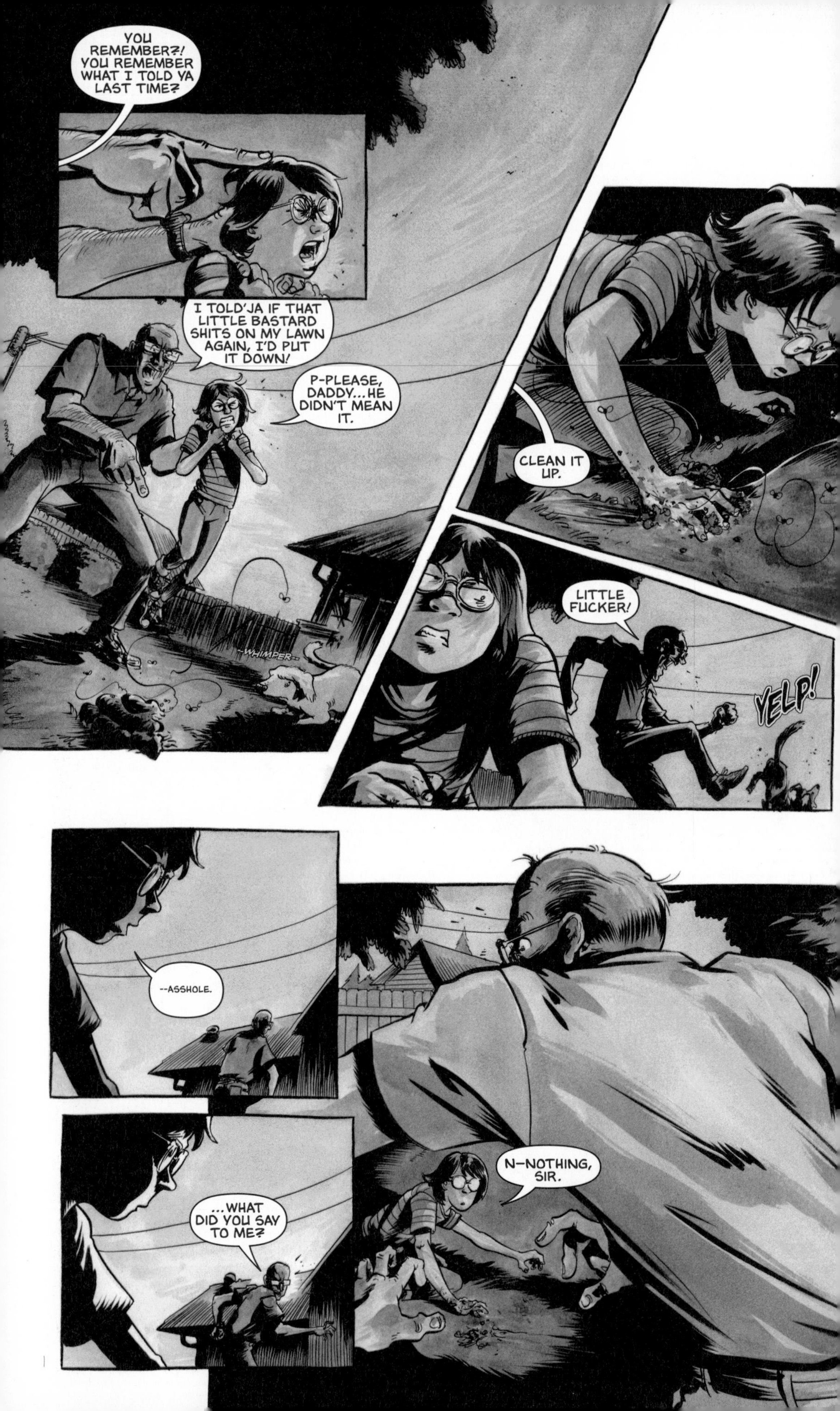

YOU REMEMBER?! YOU REMEMBER WHAT I TOLD YA LAST TIME?
I TOLD'JA IF THAT LITTLE BASTARD SHITS ON MY LAWN AGAIN, I'D PUT IT DOWN!
P-PLEASE, DADDY...HE DIDN'T MEAN IT.
-WHIMPER-
CLEAN IT UP.
LITTLE FUCKER!
YELP!
--ASSHOLE.
...WHAT DID YOU SAY TO ME?
N-NOTHING, SIR.

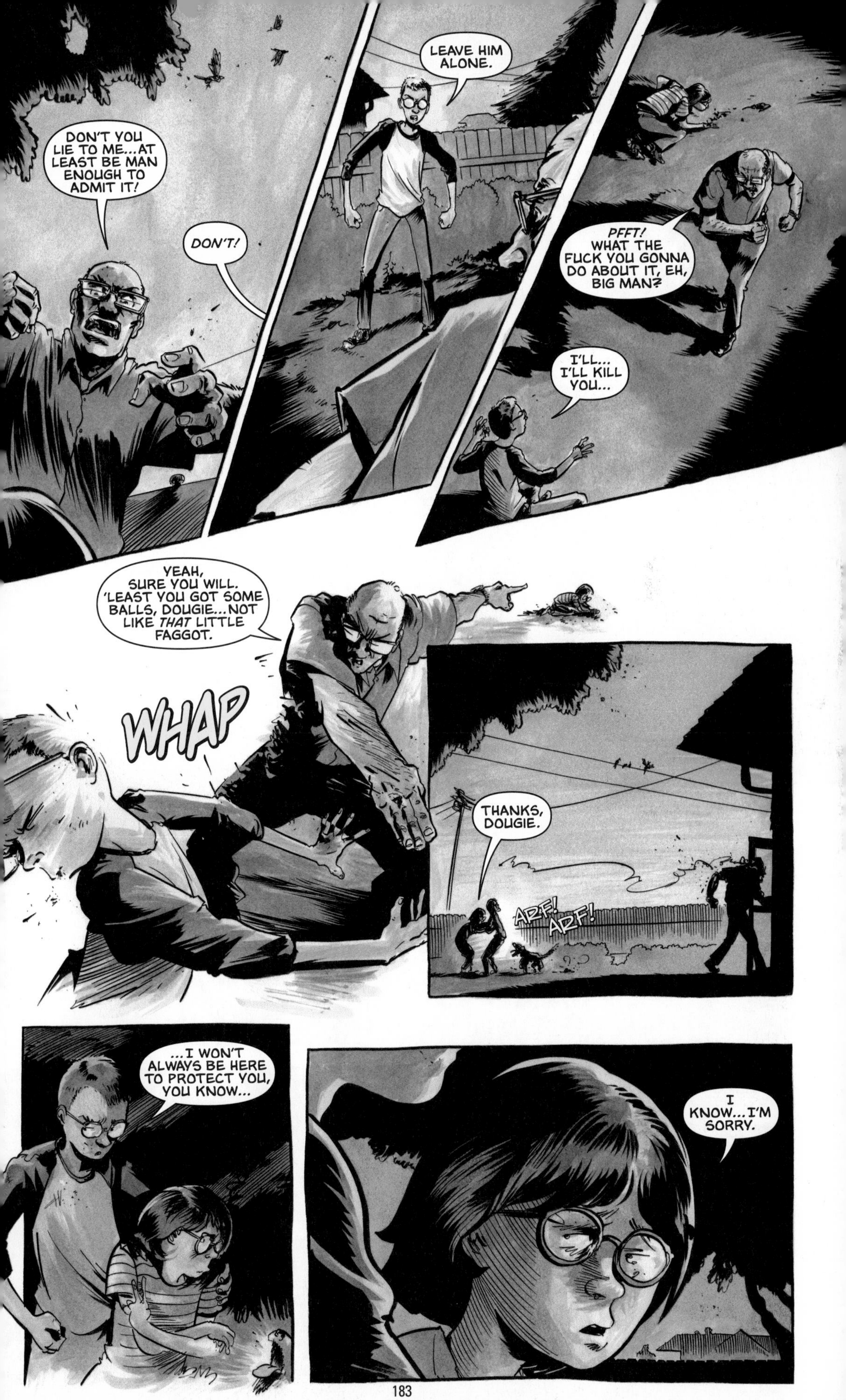
DON'T YOU LIE TO ME...AT LEAST BE MAN ENOUGH TO ADMIT IT!
DON'T!
LEAVE HIM ALONE.
PFFT! WHAT THE FUCK YOU GONNA DO ABOUT IT, EH, BIG MAN?
I'LL... I'LL KILL YOU...
YEAH, SURE YOU WILL. 'LEAST YOU GOT SOME BALLS, DOUGIE...NOT LIKE THAT LITTLE FAGGOT.
WHAP
THANKS, DOUGIE.
ARF! ARF!
...I WON'T ALWAYS BE HERE TO PROTECT YOU, YOU KNOW...
I KNOW...I'M SORRY.

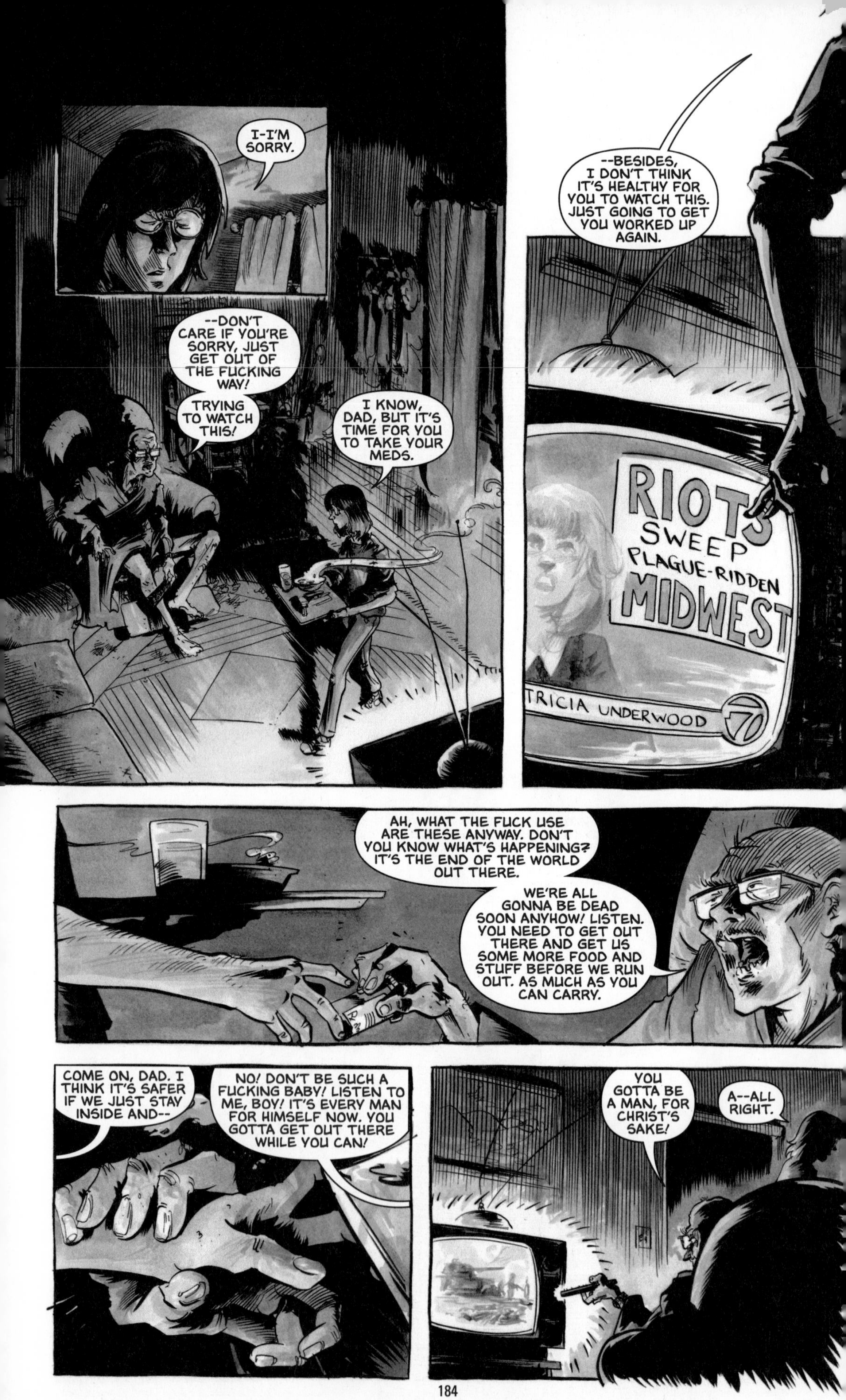
I-I'M SORRY.
--DON'T CARE IF YOU'RE SORRY, JUST GET OUT OF THE FUCKING WAY!
TRYING TO WATCH THIS!
I KNOW, DAD, BUT IT'S TIME FOR YOU TO TAKE YOUR MEDS.
--BESIDES, I DON'T THINK IT'S HEALTHY FOR YOU TO WATCH THIS. JUST GOING TO GET YOU WORKED UP AGAIN.
RIOTS SWEEP PLAGUE-RIDDEN MIDWEST
TRICIA UNDERWOOD
AH, WHAT THE FUCK USE ARE THESE ANYWAY. DON'T YOU KNOW WHAT'S HAPPENING? IT'S THE END OF THE WORLD OUT THERE.
WE'RE ALL GONNA BE DEAD SOON ANYHOW! LISTEN. YOU NEED TO GET OUT THERE AND GET US SOME MORE FOOD AND STUFF BEFORE WE RUN OUT. AS MUCH AS YOU CAN CARRY.
COME ON, DAD. I THINK IT'S SAFER IF WE JUST STAY INSIDE AND--
NO! DON'T BE SUCH A FUCKING BABY! LISTEN TO ME, BOY! IT'S EVERY MAN FOR HIMSELF NOW. YOU GOTTA GET OUT THERE WHILE YOU CAN!
YOU GOTTA BE A MAN, FOR CHRIST'S SAKE!
A--ALL RIGHT.

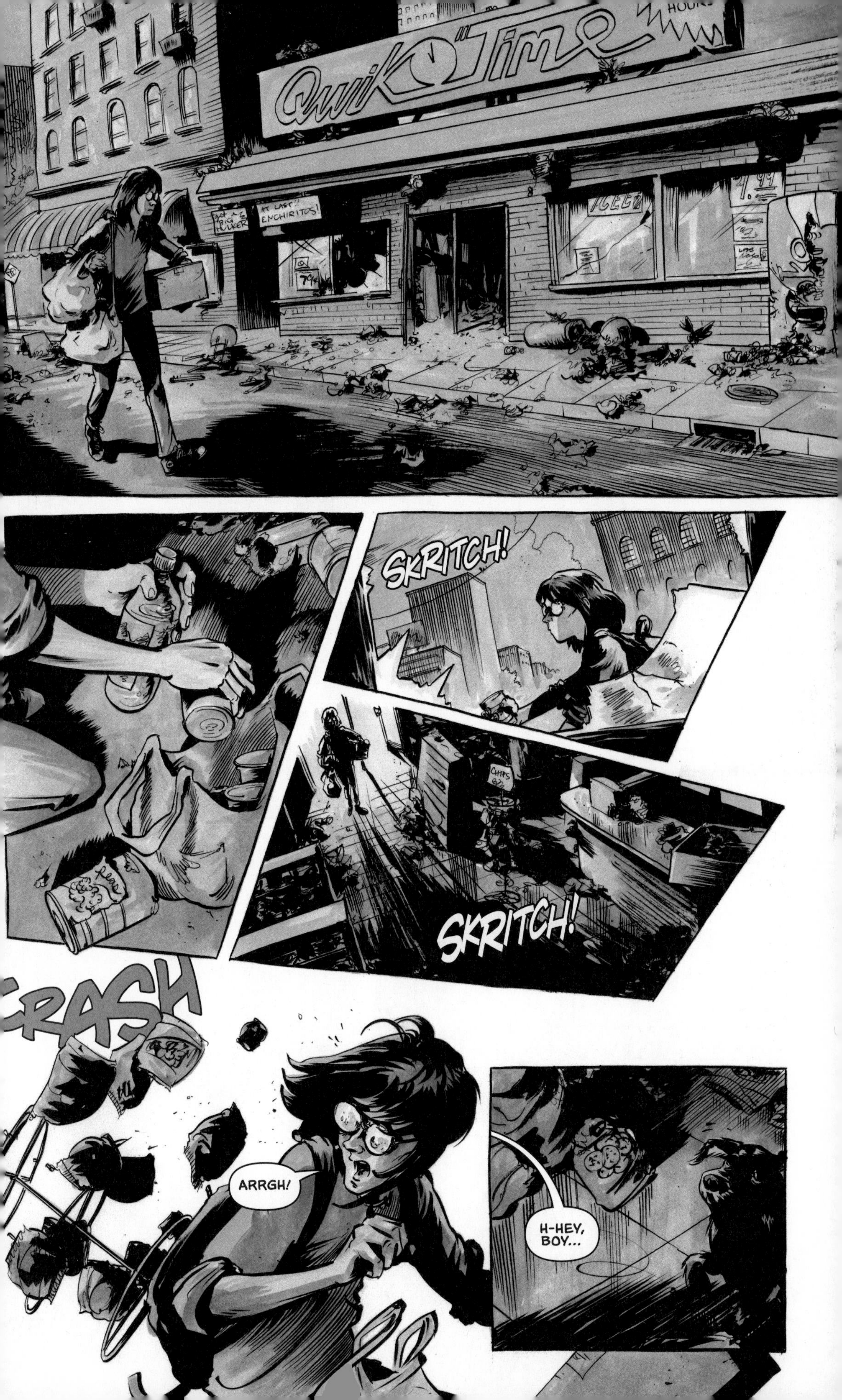

Quik Time
HOURS
AT LAST!! ENCHIRITOS!
ICEE
CHIPS
SKRITCH!
SKRITCH!
CRASH
ARRGH!
H-HEY, BOY...

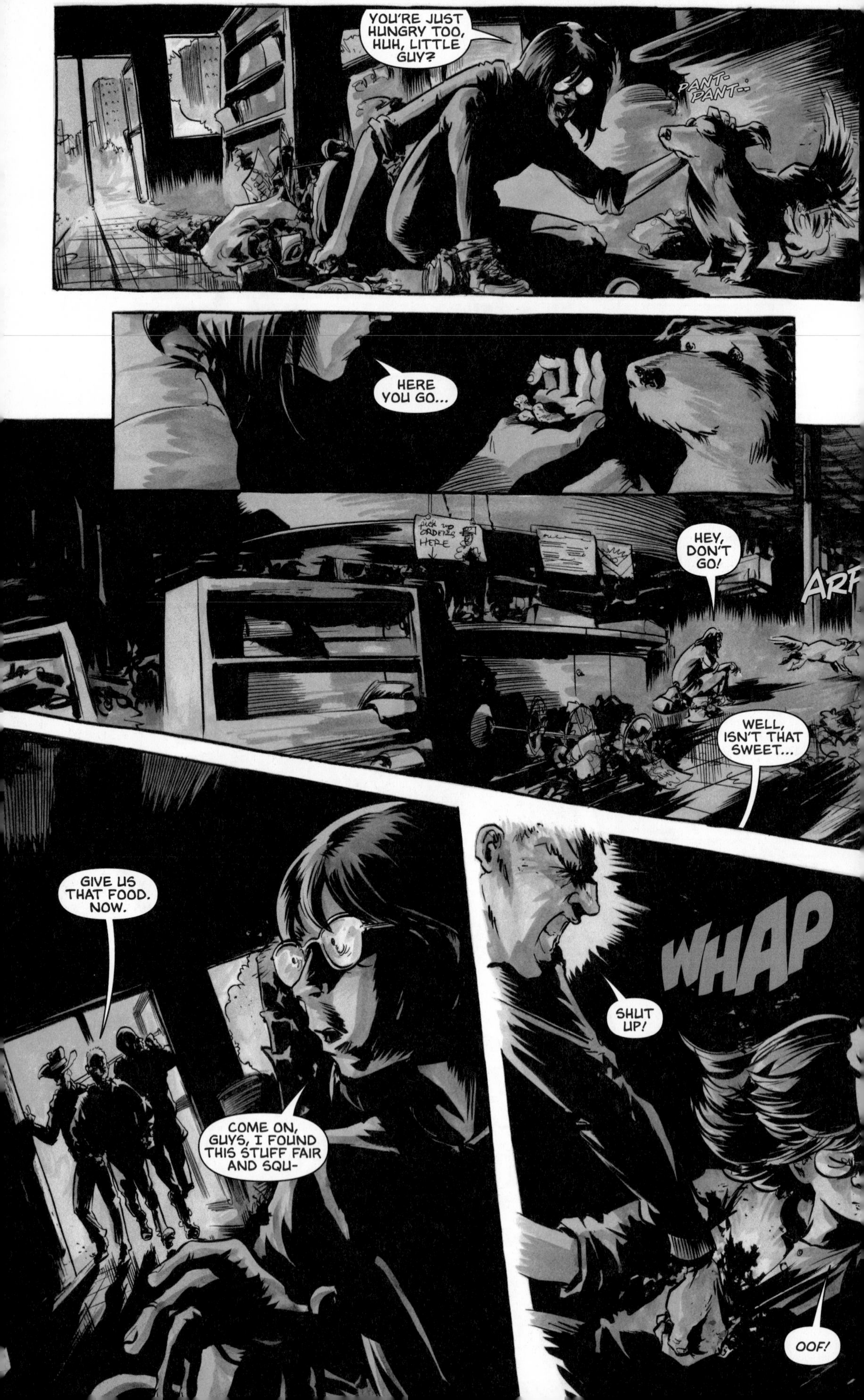
YOU'RE JUST HUNGRY TOO, HUH, LITTLE GUY?
PANT-PANT--
HERE YOU GO...
HEY, DON'T GO!
ARF
WELL, ISN'T THAT SWEET...
GIVE US THAT FOOD. NOW.
COME ON, GUYS, I FOUND THIS STUFF FAIR AND SQU-
WHAP
SHUT UP!
OOF!

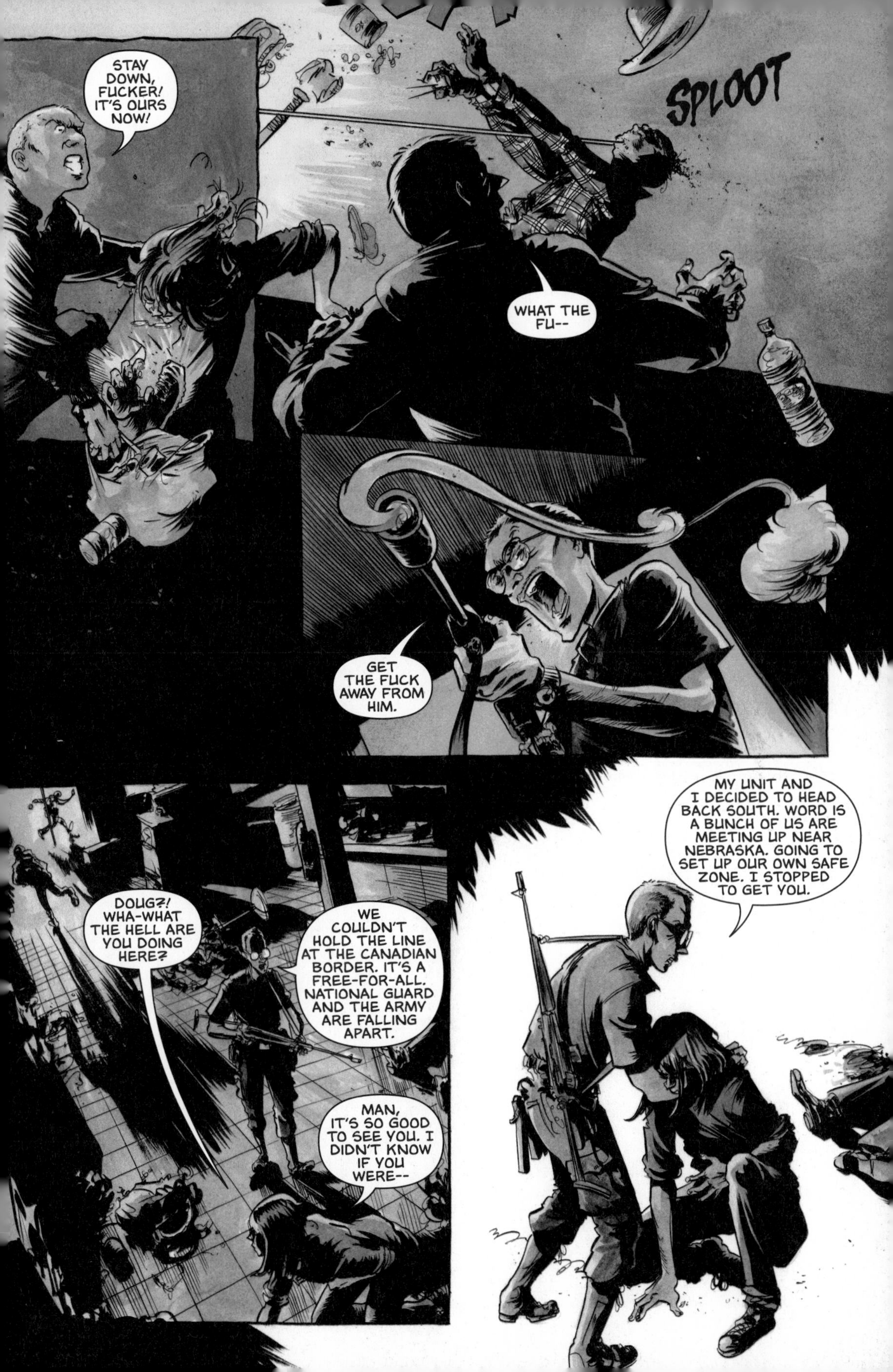

STAY DOWN, FUCKER! IT'S OURS NOW!
SPLOOT
WHAT THE FU--
GET THE FUCK AWAY FROM HIM.
DOUG?! WHA-WHAT THE HELL ARE YOU DOING HERE?
WE COULDN'T HOLD THE LINE AT THE CANADIAN BORDER. IT'S A FREE-FOR-ALL. NATIONAL GUARD AND THE ARMY ARE FALLING APART.
MAN, IT'S SO GOOD TO SEE YOU. I DIDN'T KNOW IF YOU WERE--
MY UNIT AND I DECIDED TO HEAD BACK SOUTH. WORD IS A BUNCH OF US ARE MEETING UP NEAR NEBRASKA. GOING TO SET UP OUR OWN SAFE ZONE. I STOPPED TO GET YOU.

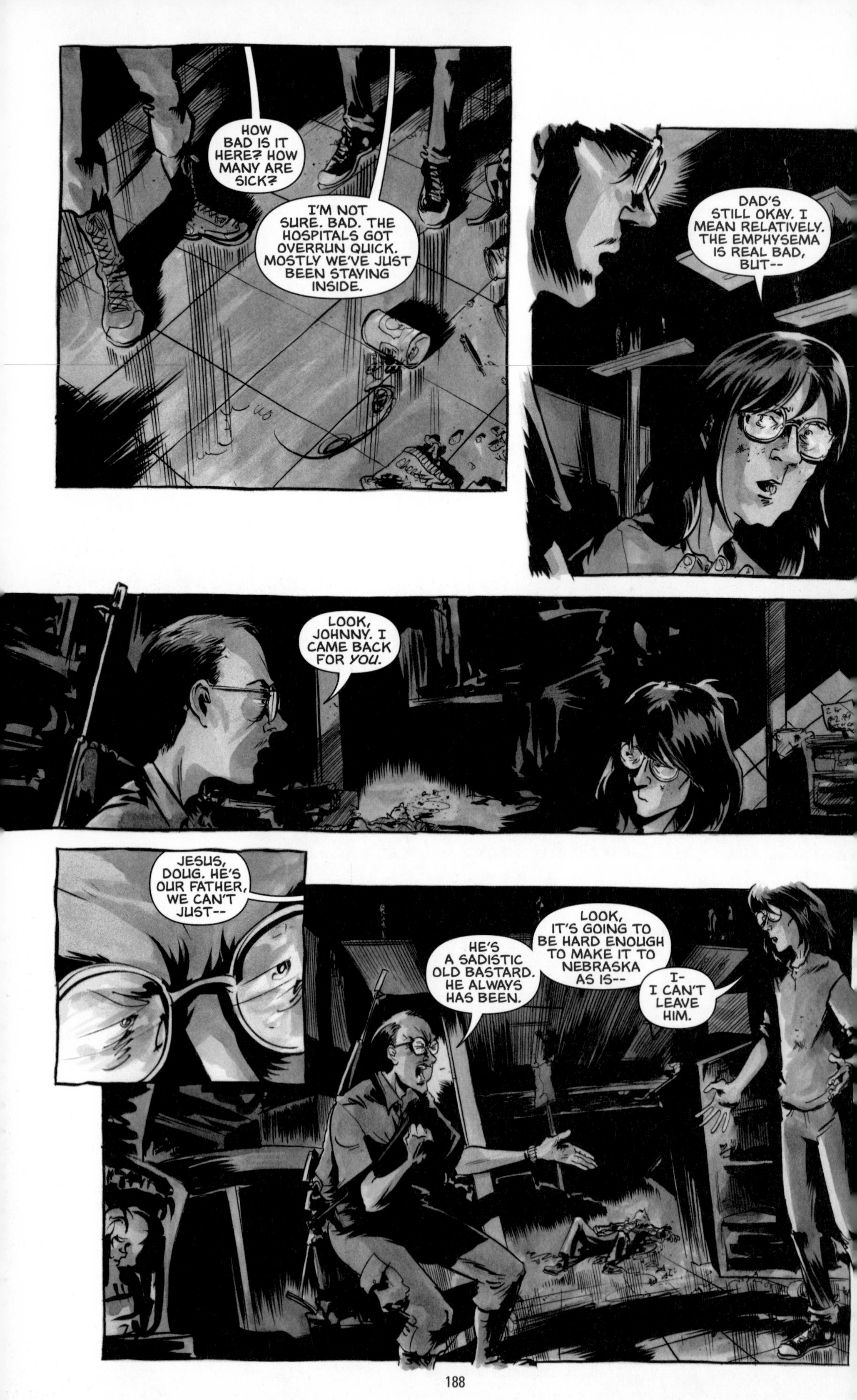
HOW BAD IS IT HERE? HOW MANY ARE SICK?
I'M NOT SURE. BAD. THE HOSPITALS GOT OVERRUN QUICK. MOSTLY WE'VE JUST BEEN STAYING INSIDE.
DAD'S STILL OKAY. I MEAN RELATIVELY. THE EMPHYSEMA IS REAL BAD, BUT--
LOOK, JOHNNY. I CAME BACK FOR *YOU*.
JESUS, DOUG. HE'S OUR FATHER, WE CAN'T JUST--
HE'S A SADISTIC OLD BASTARD. HE ALWAYS HAS BEEN.
LOOK, IT'S GOING TO BE HARD ENOUGH TO MAKE IT TO NEBRASKA AS IS--
I- I CAN'T LEAVE HIM.

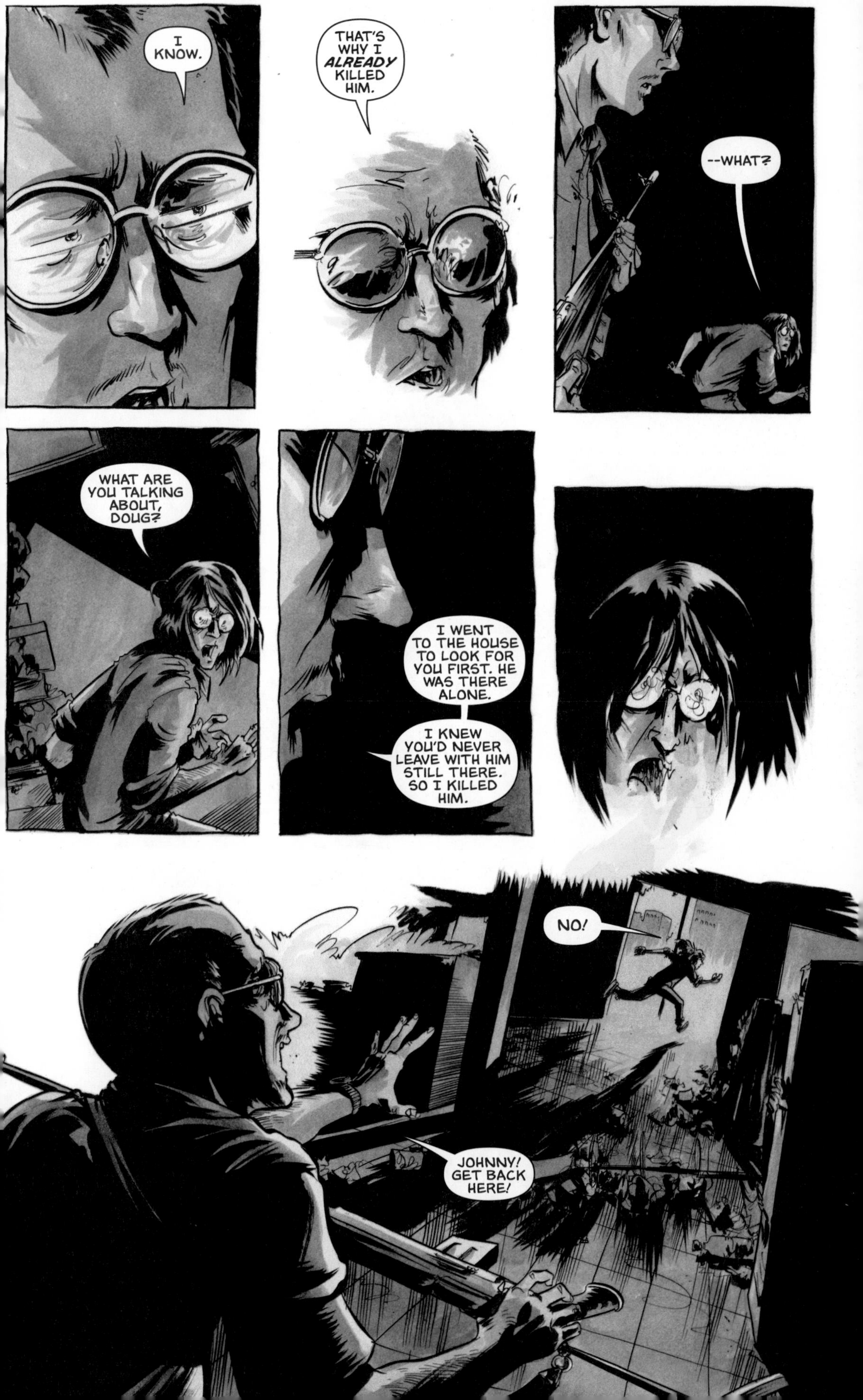

I KNOW.
THAT'S WHY I ALREADY KILLED HIM.
--WHAT?
WHAT ARE YOU TALKING ABOUT, DOUG?
I WENT TO THE HOUSE TO LOOK FOR YOU FIRST. HE WAS THERE ALONE.
I KNEW YOU'D NEVER LEAVE WITH HIM STILL THERE. SO I KILLED HIM.
NO!
JOHNNY! GET BACK HERE!

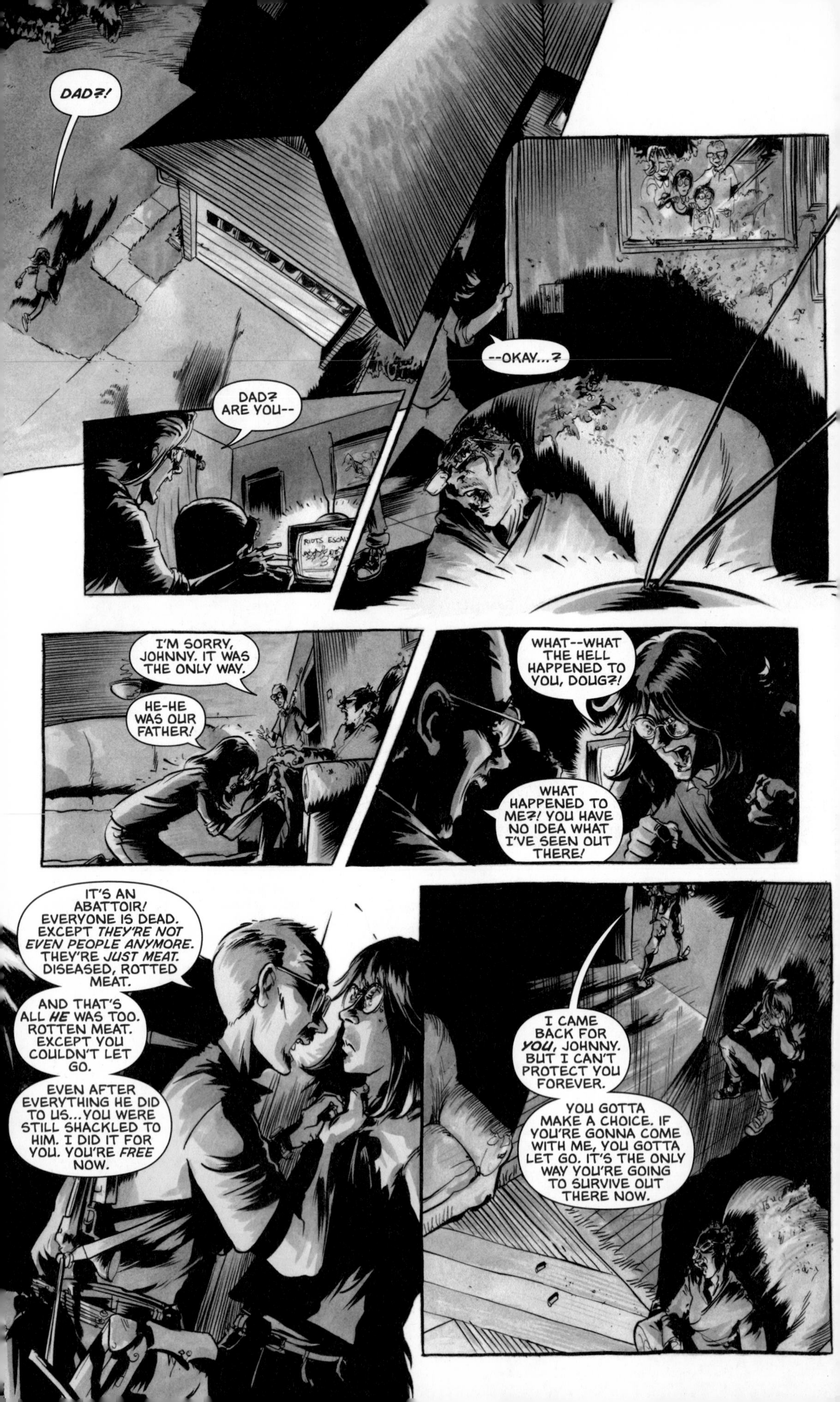
DAD?!
--OKAY...?
DAD? ARE YOU--
RIOTS ESCAL
I'M SORRY, JOHNNY. IT WAS THE ONLY WAY.
HE-HE WAS OUR FATHER!
WHAT--WHAT THE HELL HAPPENED TO YOU, DOUG?!
WHAT HAPPENED TO ME?! YOU HAVE NO IDEA WHAT I'VE SEEN OUT THERE!
IT'S AN ABATTOIR! EVERYONE IS DEAD. EXCEPT THEY'RE NOT EVEN PEOPLE ANYMORE. THEY'RE JUST MEAT. DISEASED, ROTTED MEAT.
AND THAT'S ALL HE WAS TOO. ROTTEN MEAT. EXCEPT YOU COULDN'T LET GO.
EVEN AFTER EVERYTHING HE DID TO US...YOU WERE STILL SHACKLED TO HIM. I DID IT FOR YOU. YOU'RE FREE NOW.
I CAME BACK FOR YOU, JOHNNY. BUT I CAN'T PROTECT YOU FOREVER.
YOU GOTTA MAKE A CHOICE. IF YOU'RE GONNA COME WITH ME, YOU GOTTA LET GO. IT'S THE ONLY WAY YOU'RE GOING TO SURVIVE OUT THERE NOW.

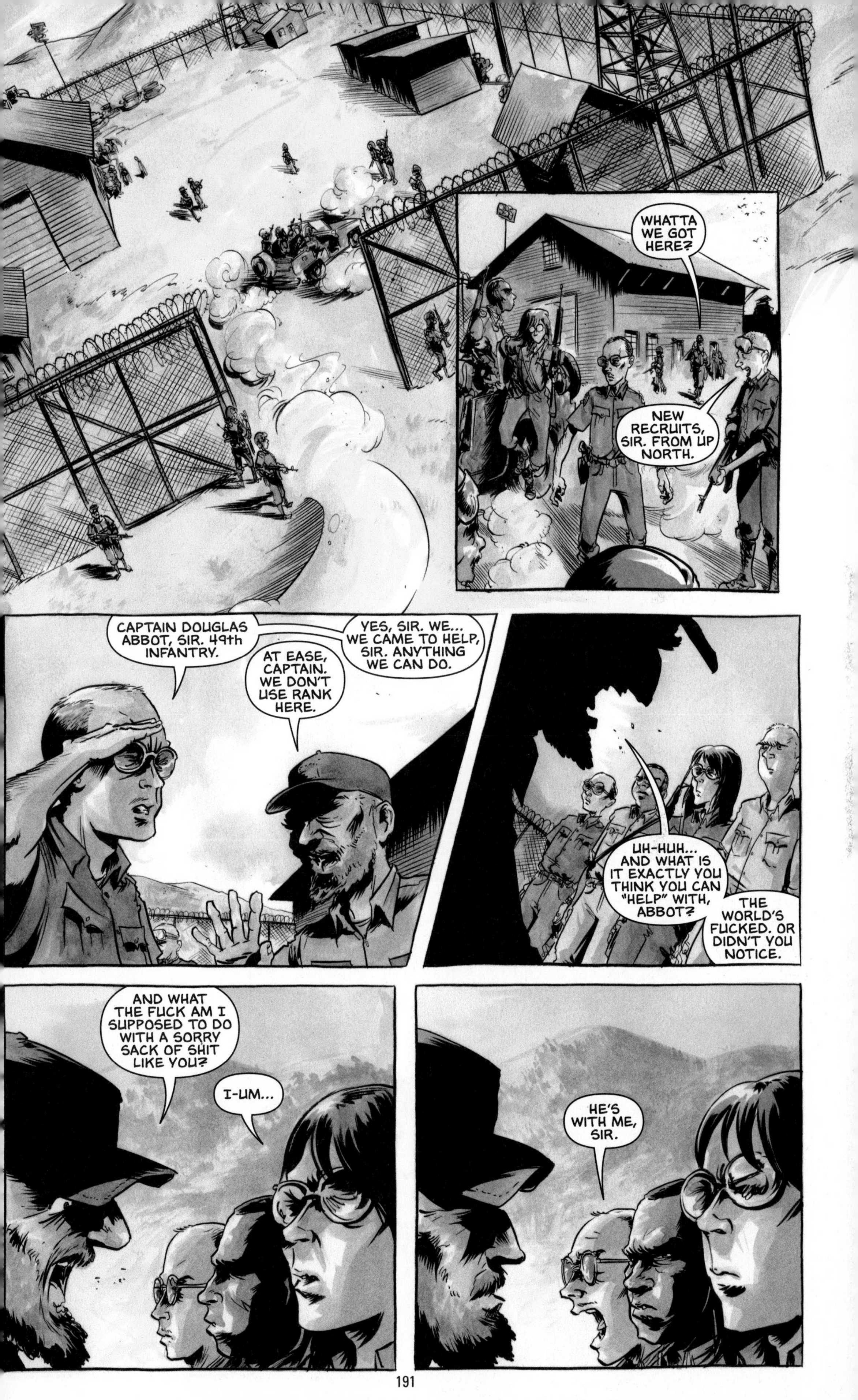
WHATTA WE GOT HERE?
NEW RECRUITS, SIR. FROM UP NORTH.
CAPTAIN DOUGLAS ABBOT, SIR. 49th INFANTRY.
AT EASE, CAPTAIN. WE DON'T USE RANK HERE.
YES, SIR. WE... WE CAME TO HELP, SIR. ANYTHING WE CAN DO.
UH-HUH... AND WHAT IS IT EXACTLY YOU THINK YOU CAN "HELP" WITH, ABBOT?
THE WORLD'S FUCKED. OR DIDN'T YOU NOTICE.
AND WHAT THE FUCK AM I SUPPOSED TO DO WITH A SORRY SACK OF SHIT LIKE YOU?
I-UM...
HE'S WITH ME, SIR.

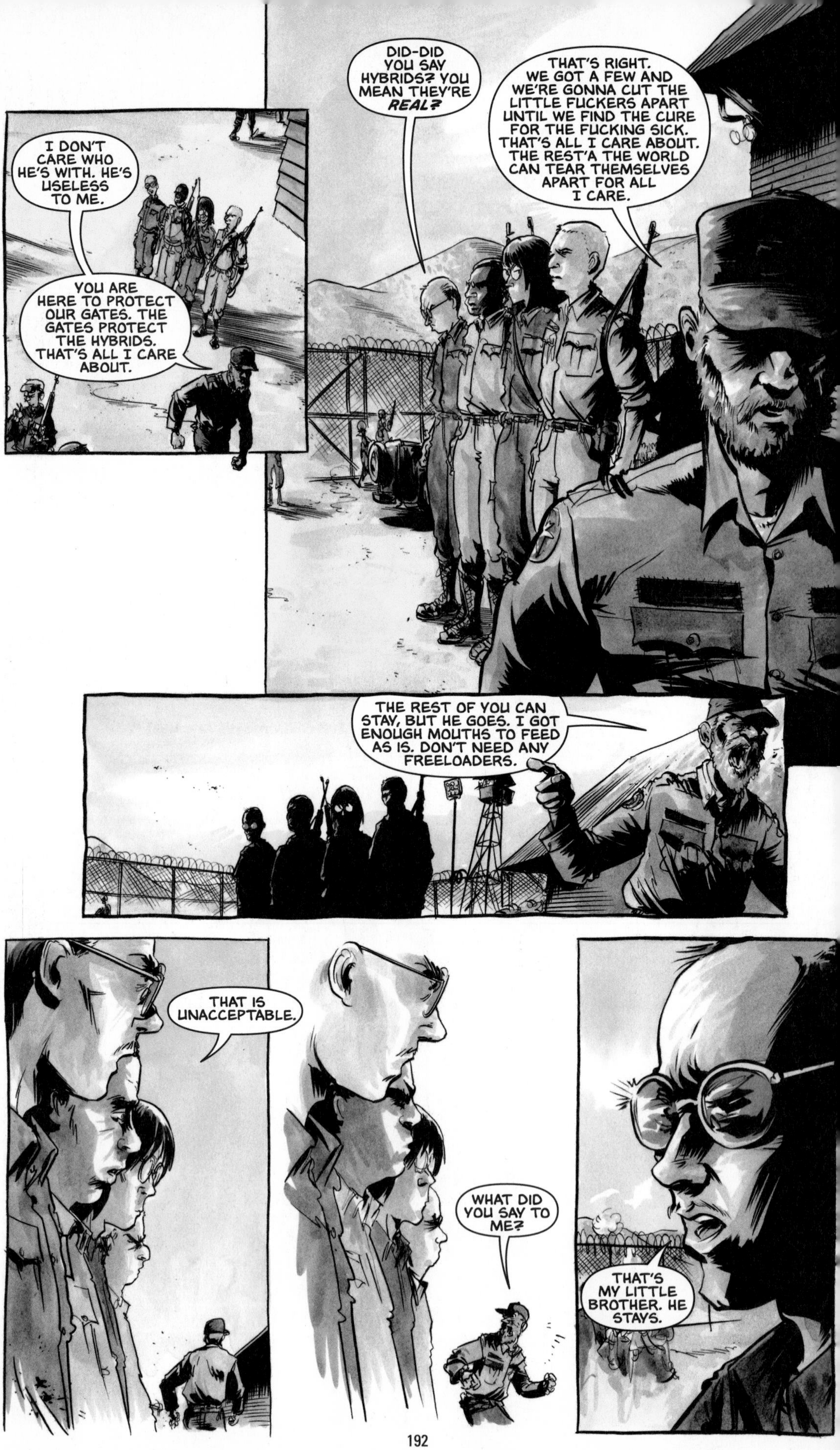
I DON'T CARE WHO HE'S WITH. HE'S USELESS TO ME.
YOU ARE HERE TO PROTECT OUR GATES. THE GATES PROTECT THE HYBRIDS. THAT'S ALL I CARE ABOUT.
DID-DID YOU SAY HYBRIDS? YOU MEAN THEY'RE REAL?
THAT'S RIGHT. WE GOT A FEW AND WE'RE GONNA CUT THE LITTLE FUCKERS APART UNTIL WE FIND THE CURE FOR THE FUCKING SICK. THAT'S ALL I CARE ABOUT. THE REST'A THE WORLD CAN TEAR THEMSELVES APART FOR ALL I CARE.
THE REST OF YOU CAN STAY, BUT HE GOES. I GOT ENOUGH MOUTHS TO FEED AS IS. DON'T NEED ANY FREELOADERS.
THAT IS UNACCEPTABLE.
WHAT DID YOU SAY TO ME?
THAT'S MY LITTLE BROTHER. HE STAYS.

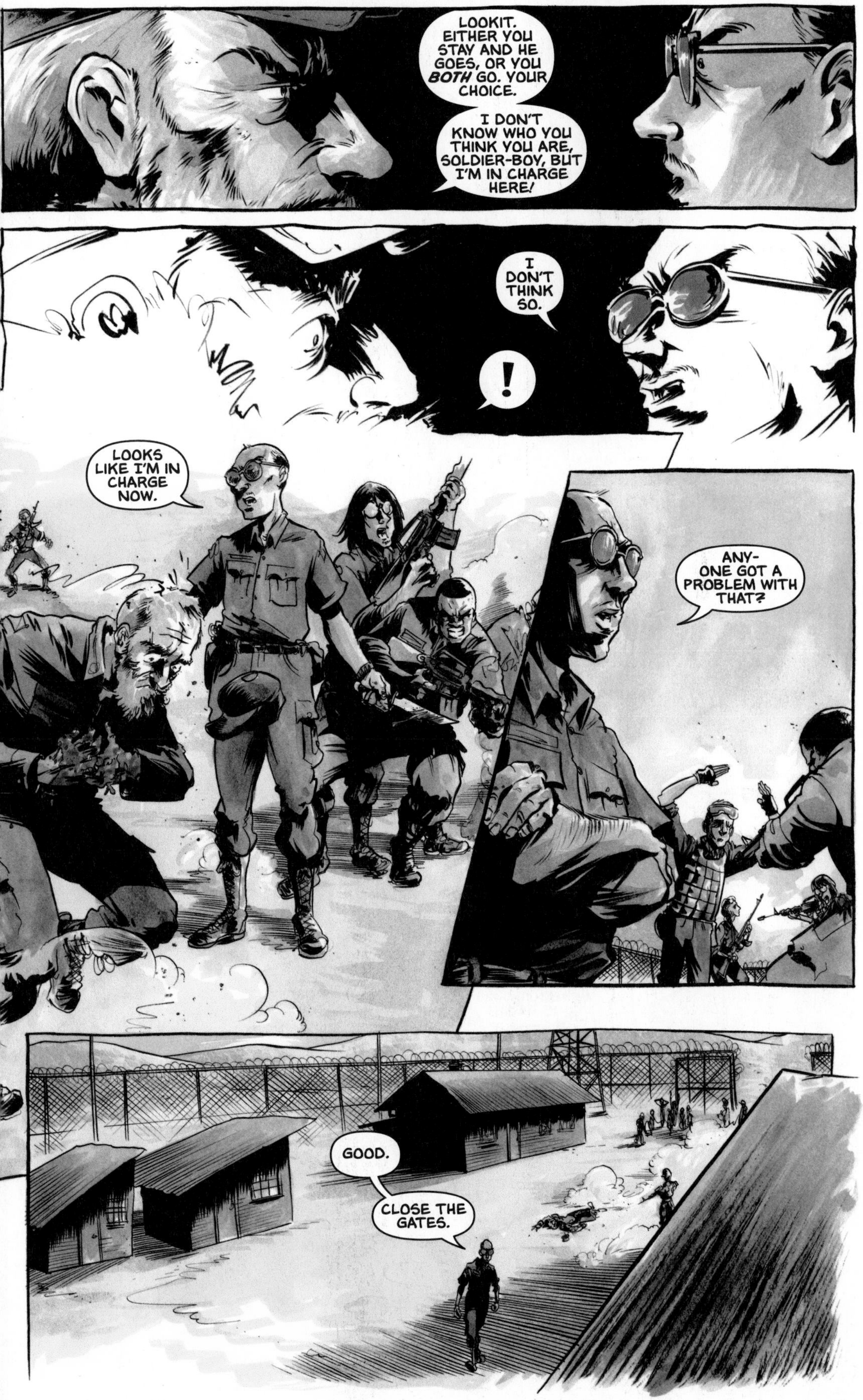
LOOKIT. EITHER YOU STAY AND HE GOES, OR YOU *BOTH* GO. YOUR CHOICE.
I DON'T KNOW WHO YOU THINK YOU ARE, SOLDIER-BOY, BUT I'M IN CHARGE HERE!
I DON'T THINK SO.
!
LOOKS LIKE I'M IN CHARGE NOW.
ANY-ONE GOT A PROBLEM WITH THAT?
GOOD.
CLOSE THE GATES.

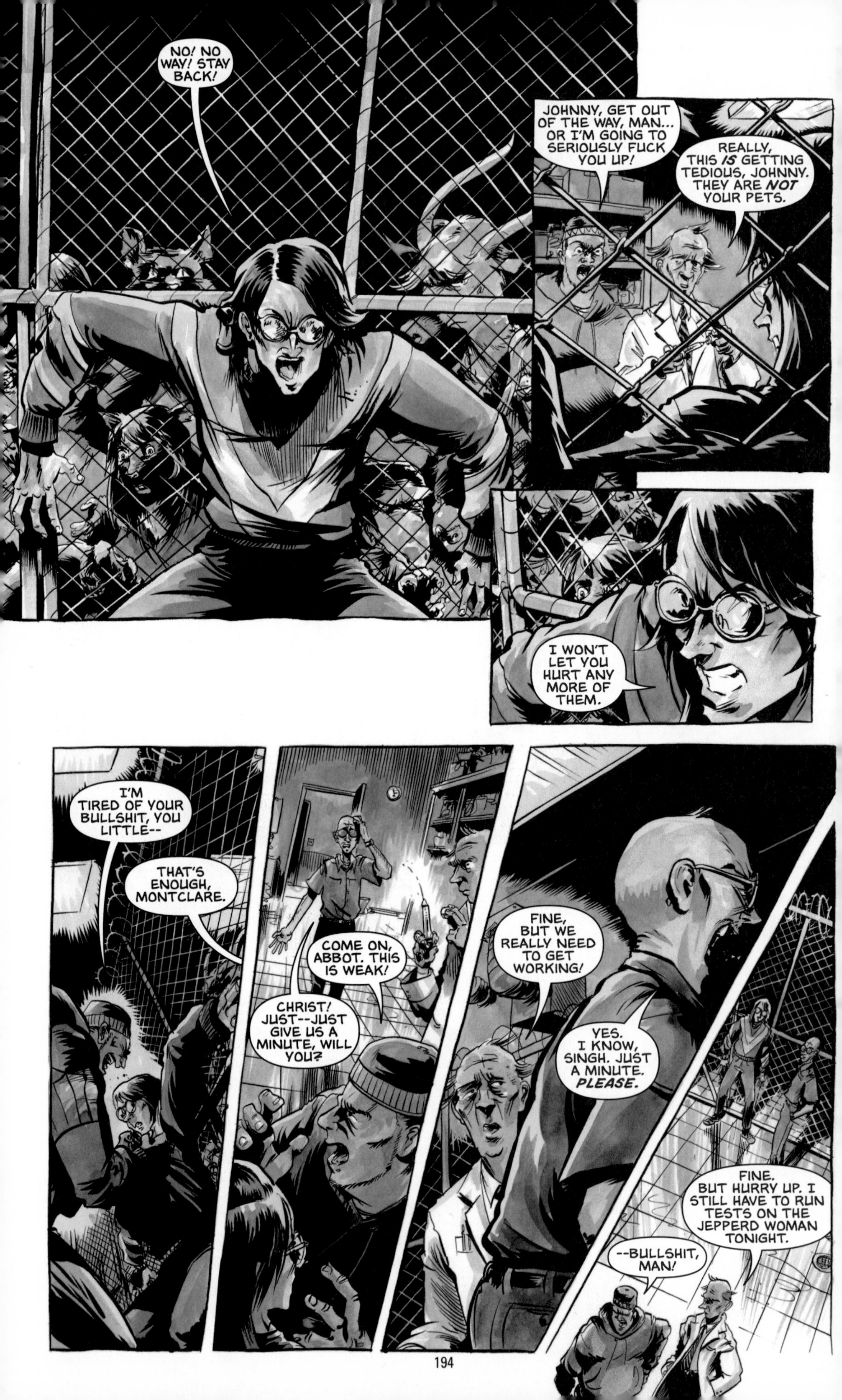

NO! NO WAY! STAY BACK!
JOHNNY, GET OUT OF THE WAY, MAN... OR I'M GOING TO SERIOUSLY FUCK YOU UP!
REALLY, THIS *IS* GETTING TEDIOUS, JOHNNY. THEY ARE *NOT* YOUR PETS.
I WON'T LET YOU HURT ANY MORE OF THEM.
I'M TIRED OF YOUR BULLSHIT, YOU LITTLE--
THAT'S ENOUGH, MONTCLARE.
COME ON, ABBOT. THIS IS WEAK!
CHRIST! JUST--JUST GIVE US A MINUTE, WILL YOU?
FINE, BUT WE REALLY NEED TO GET WORKING!
YES. I KNOW, SINGH. JUST A MINUTE. ***PLEASE.***
FINE. BUT HURRY UP. I STILL HAVE TO RUN TESTS ON THE JEPPERD WOMAN TONIGHT.
--BULLSHIT, MAN!

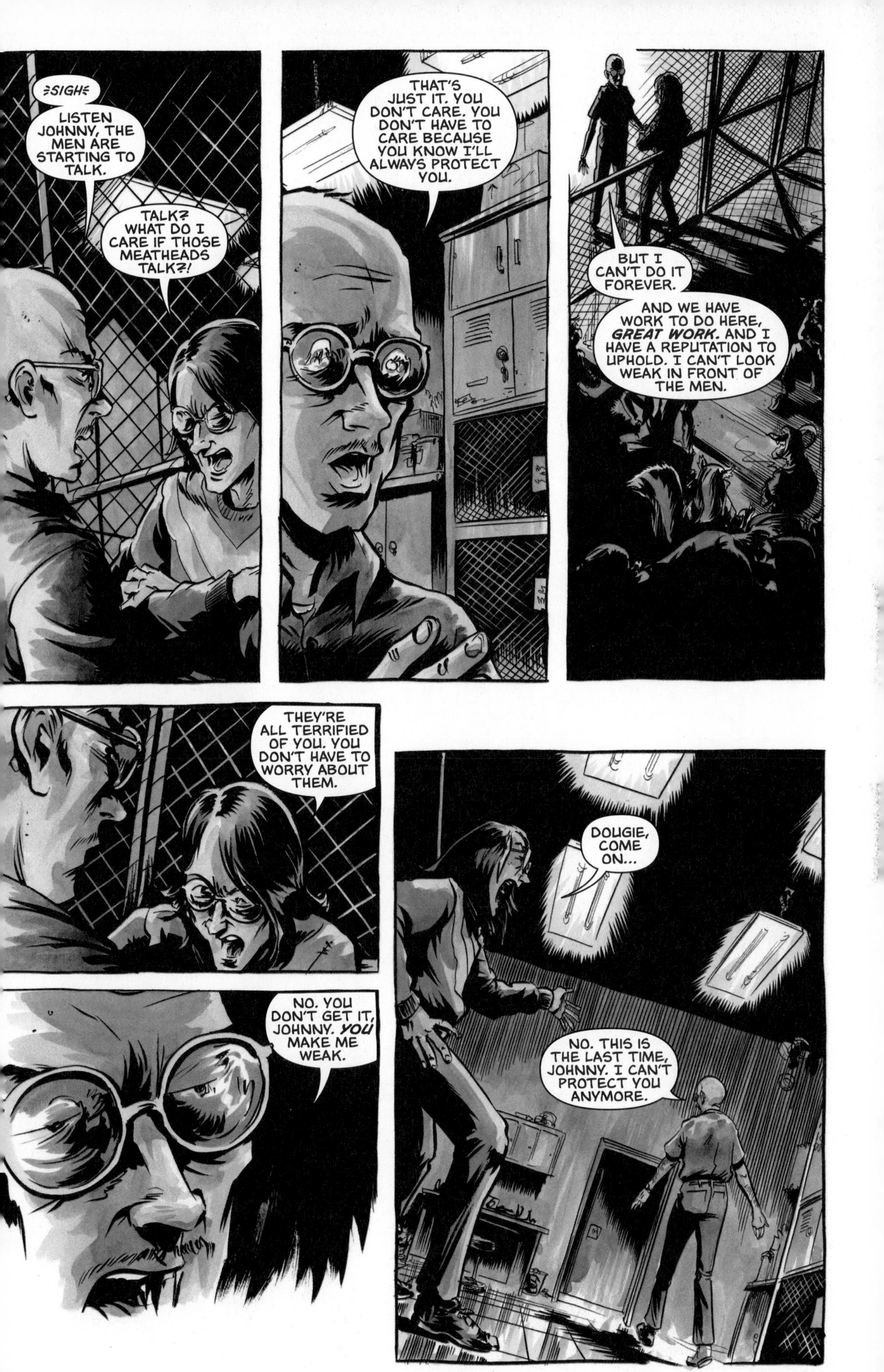

SIGH
LISTEN JOHNNY, THE MEN ARE STARTING TO TALK.
TALK? WHAT DO I CARE IF THOSE MEATHEADS TALK?!
THAT'S JUST IT. YOU DON'T CARE. YOU DON'T HAVE TO CARE BECAUSE YOU KNOW I'LL ALWAYS PROTECT YOU.
BUT I CAN'T DO IT FOREVER.
AND WE HAVE WORK TO DO HERE, ***GREAT WORK.*** AND I HAVE A REPUTATION TO UPHOLD. I CAN'T LOOK WEAK IN FRONT OF THE MEN.
THEY'RE ALL TERRIFIED OF YOU. YOU DON'T HAVE TO WORRY ABOUT THEM.
NO. YOU DON'T GET IT, JOHNNY. ***YOU*** MAKE ME WEAK.
DOUGIE, COME ON...
NO. THIS IS THE LAST TIME, JOHNNY. I CAN'T PROTECT YOU ANYMORE.

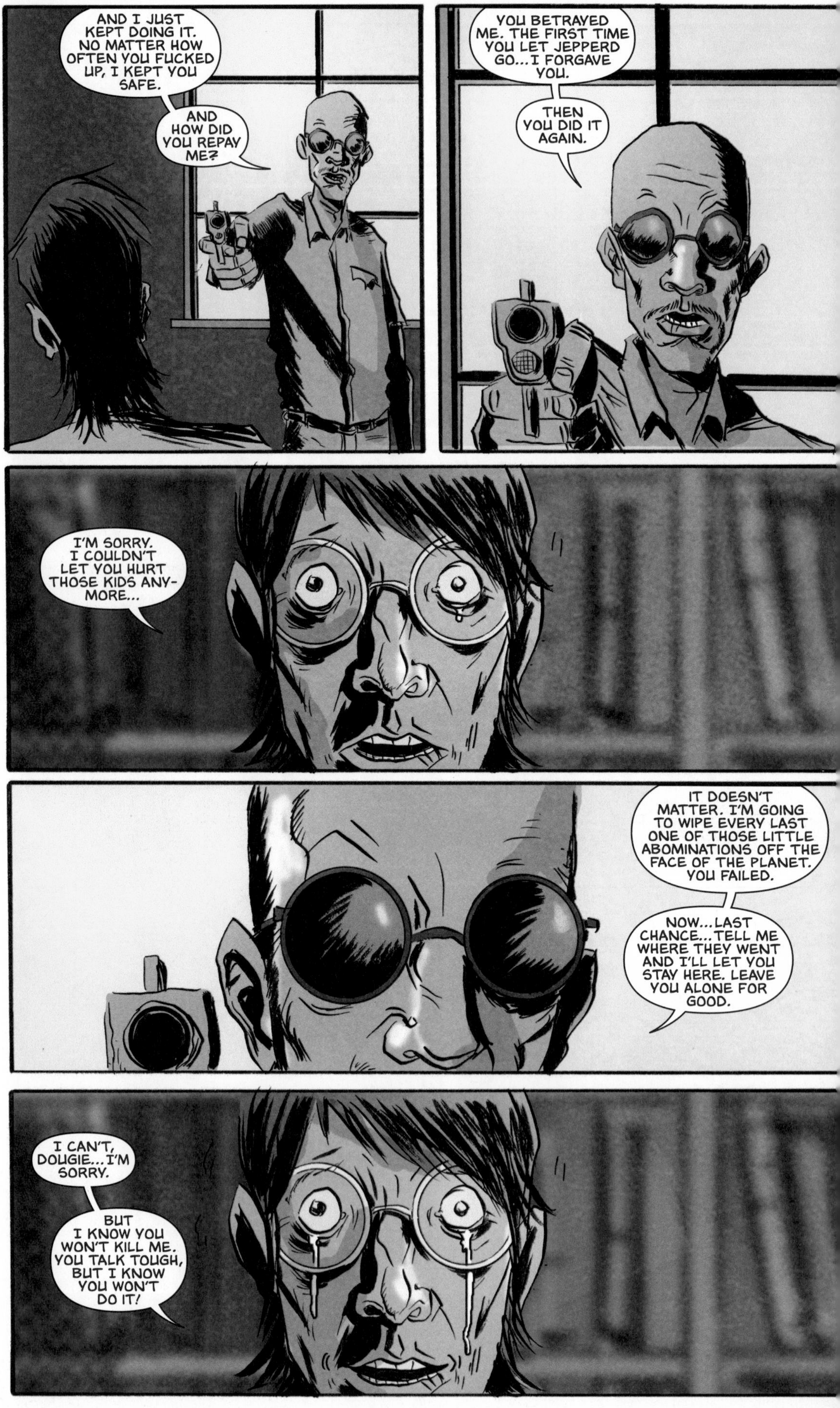
AND I JUST KEPT DOING IT. NO MATTER HOW OFTEN YOU FUCKED UP, I KEPT YOU SAFE.
AND HOW DID YOU REPAY ME?
YOU BETRAYED ME. THE FIRST TIME YOU LET JEPPERD GO... I FORGAVE YOU.
THEN YOU DID IT AGAIN.
I'M SORRY. I COULDN'T LET YOU HURT THOSE KIDS ANY-MORE...
IT DOESN'T MATTER. I'M GOING TO WIPE EVERY LAST ONE OF THOSE LITTLE ABOMINATIONS OFF THE FACE OF THE PLANET. YOU FAILED.
NOW... LAST CHANCE... TELL ME WHERE THEY WENT AND I'LL LET YOU STAY HERE. LEAVE YOU ALONE FOR GOOD.
I CAN'T, DOUGIE... I'M SORRY.
BUT I KNOW YOU WON'T KILL ME. YOU TALK TOUGH, BUT I KNOW YOU WON'T DO IT!

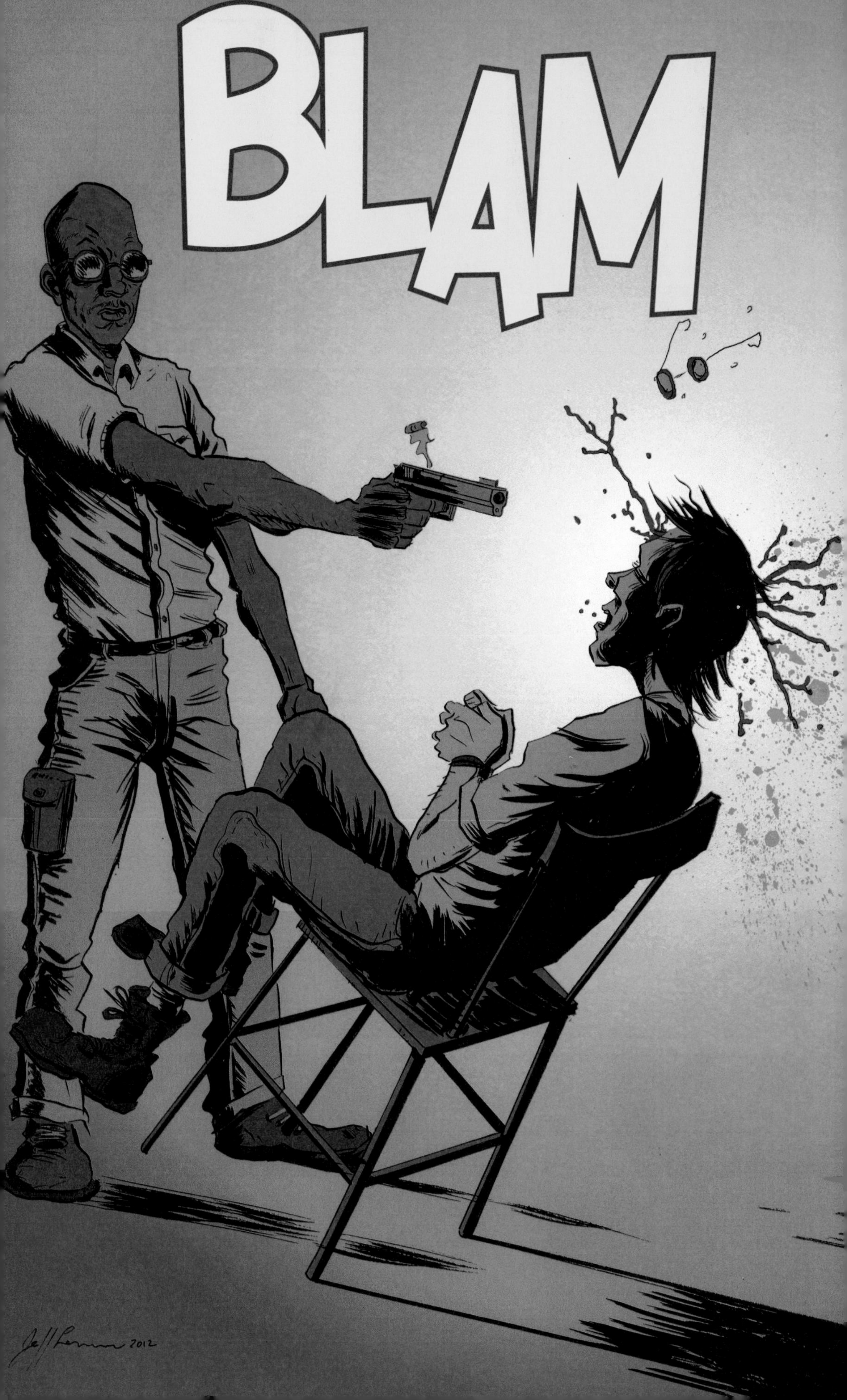
BLAM

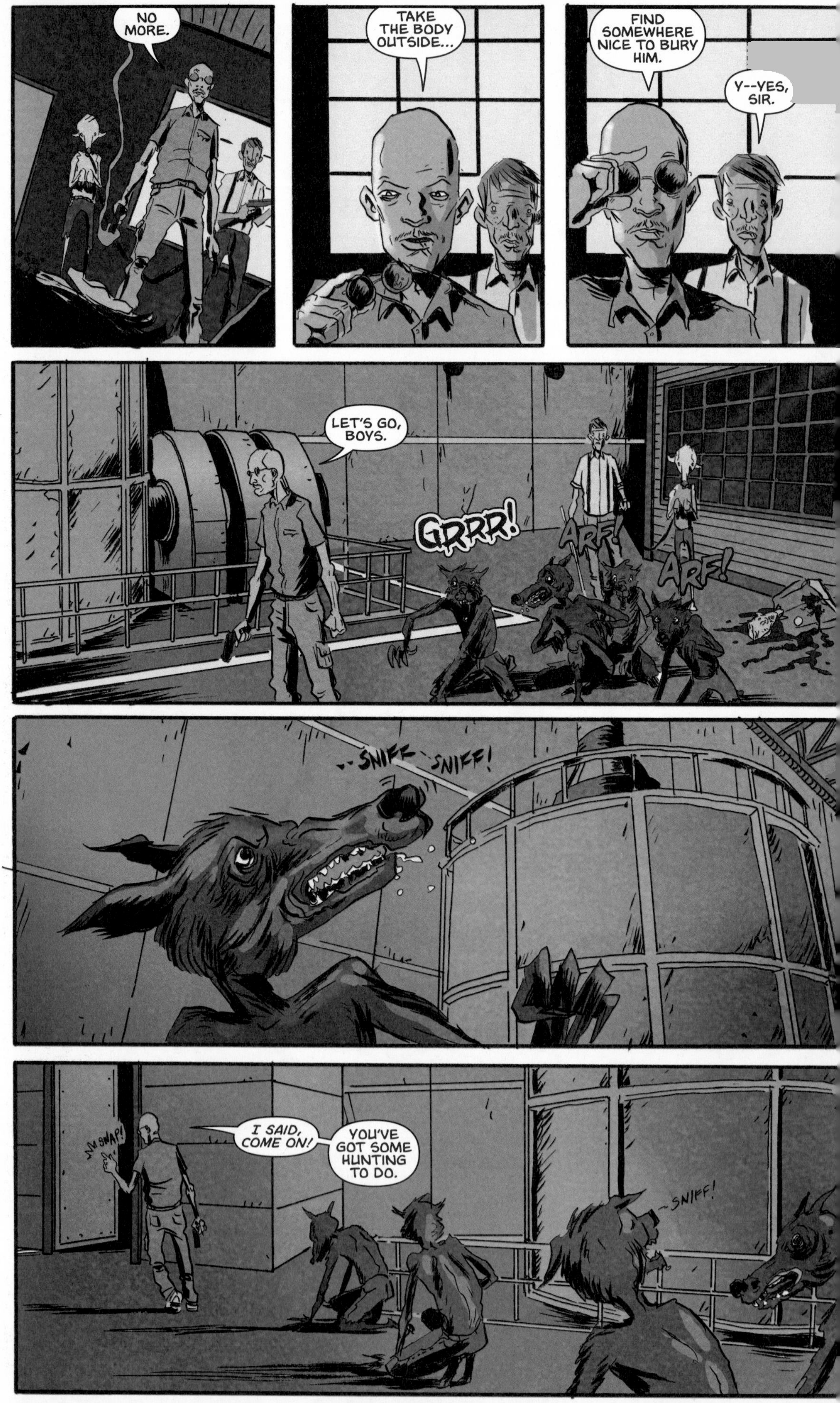
NO MORE.
TAKE THE BODY OUTSIDE...
FIND SOMEWHERE NICE TO BURY HIM.
Y--YES, SIR.
LET'S GO, BOYS.
GRRR!
ARF!
ARF!
SNIFF SNIFF!
SNAP!
I SAID, COME ON!
YOU'VE GOT SOME HUNTING TO DO.
SNIFF!

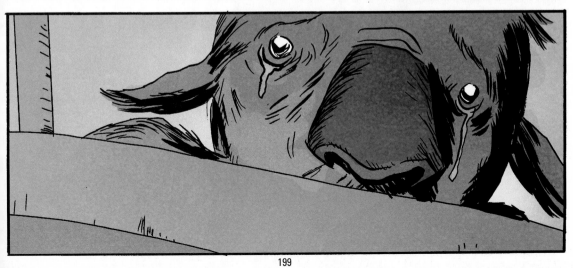

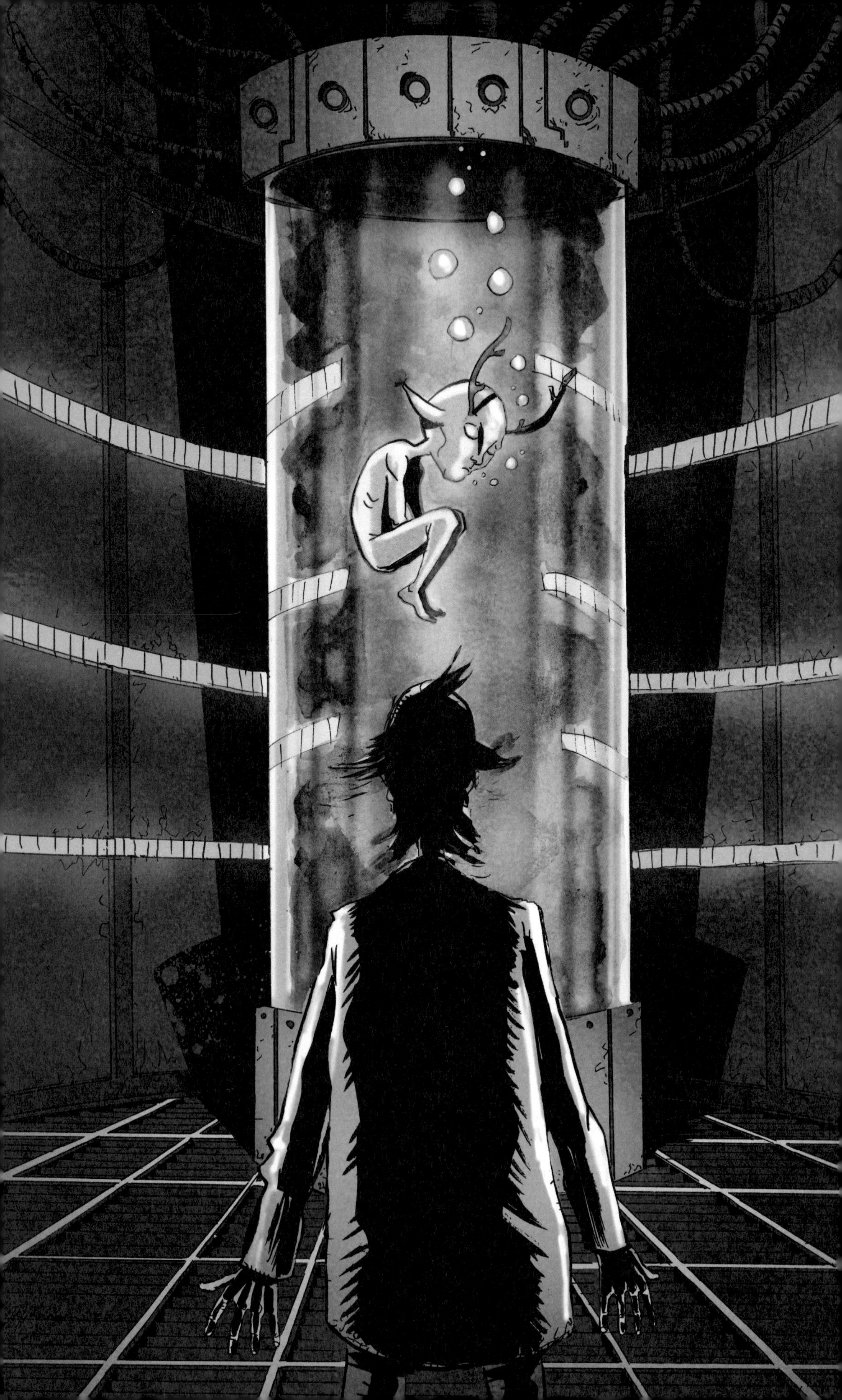

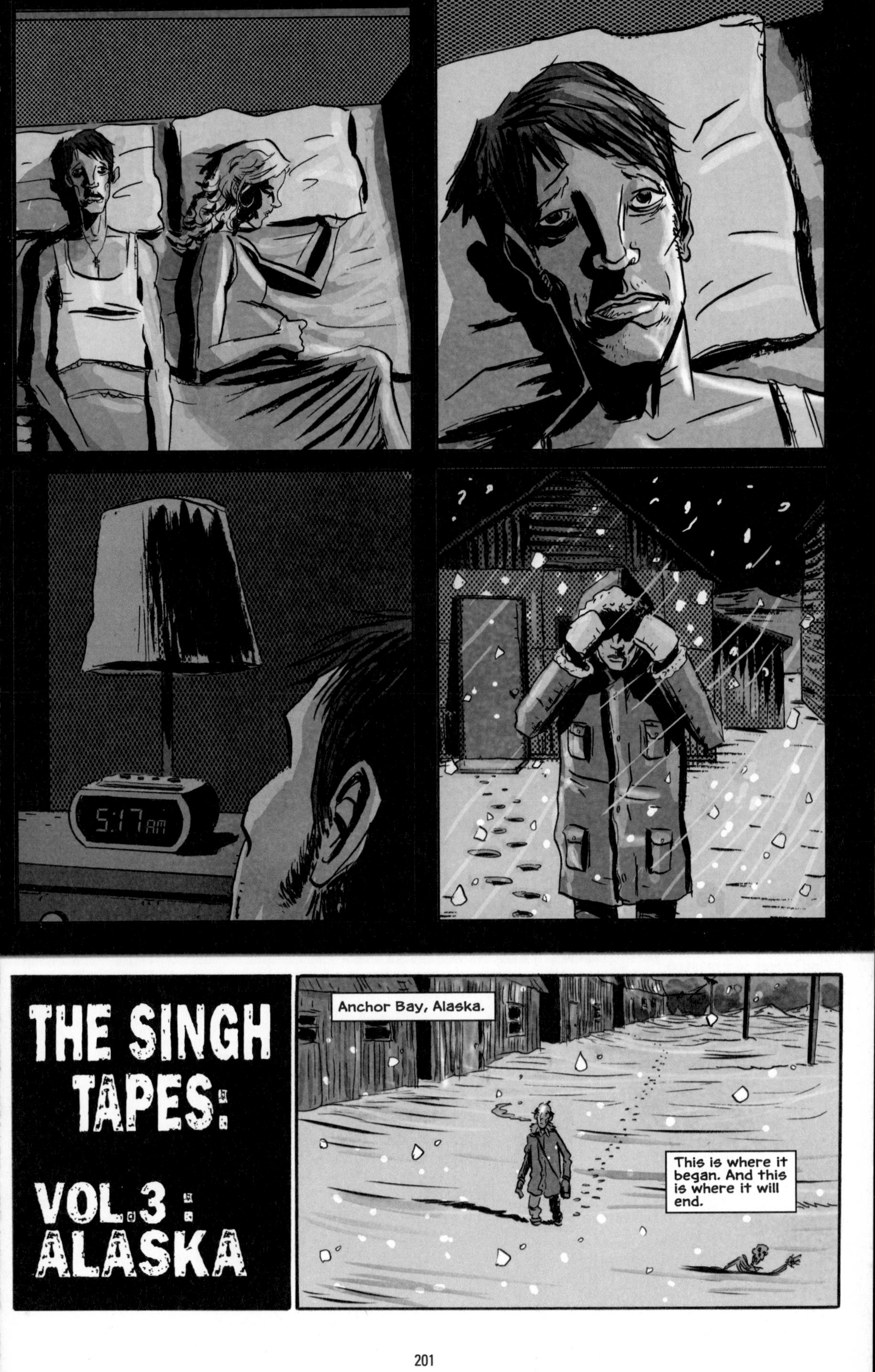
5:17 AM
THE SINGH TAPES:
VOL.3 : ALASKA
Anchor Bay, Alaska.
This is where it began. And this is where it will end.

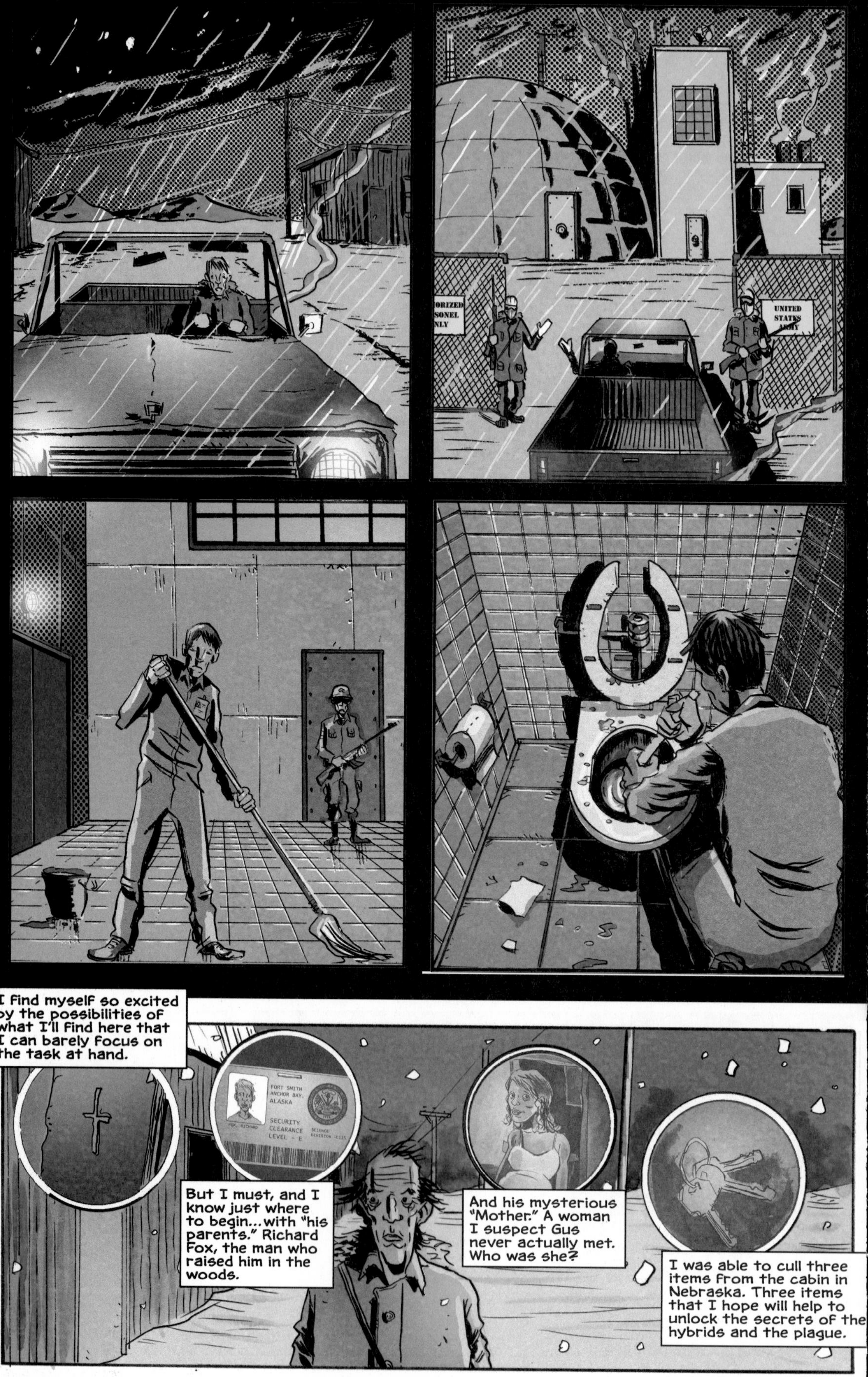
UNITED STATES ARMY
I find myself so excited by the possibilities of what I'll find here that I can barely focus on the task at hand.
FORT SMITH
ANCHOR BAY, ALASKA
SECURITY CLEARANCE LEVEL - E
But I must, and I know just where to begin...with "his parents." Richard Fox, the man who raised him in the woods.
And his mysterious "Mother." A woman I suspect Gus never actually met. Who was she?
I was able to cull three items from the cabin in Nebraska. Three items that I hope will help to unlock the secrets of the hybrids and the plague.

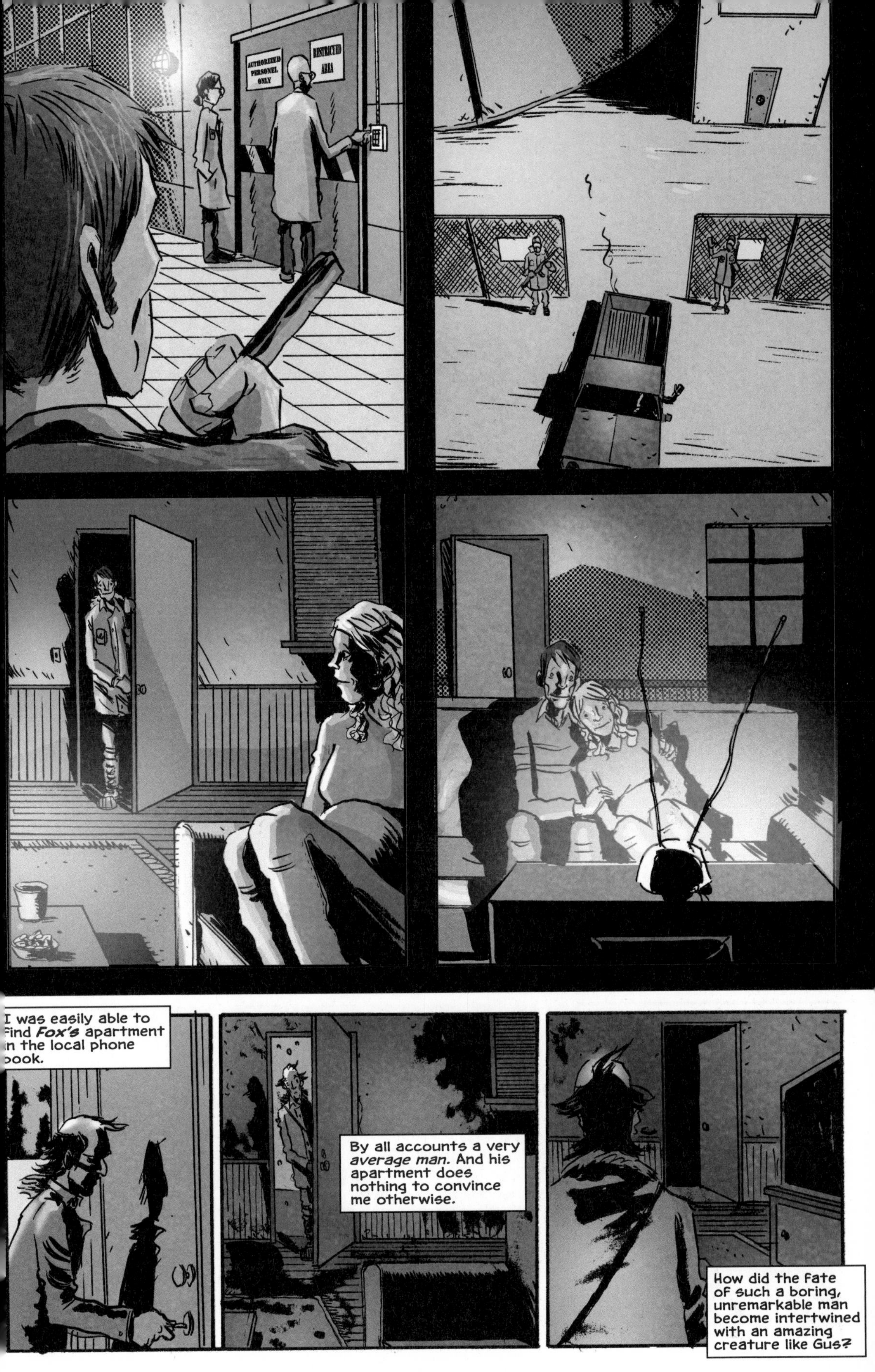
AUTHORIZED PERSONEL ONLY
RESTRICTED AREA
I was easily able to Find *Fox's* apartment n the local phone ook.
By all accounts a very *average man.* And his apartment does nothing to convince me otherwise.
How did the Fate of such a boring, unremarkable man become intertwined with an amazing creature like Gus?

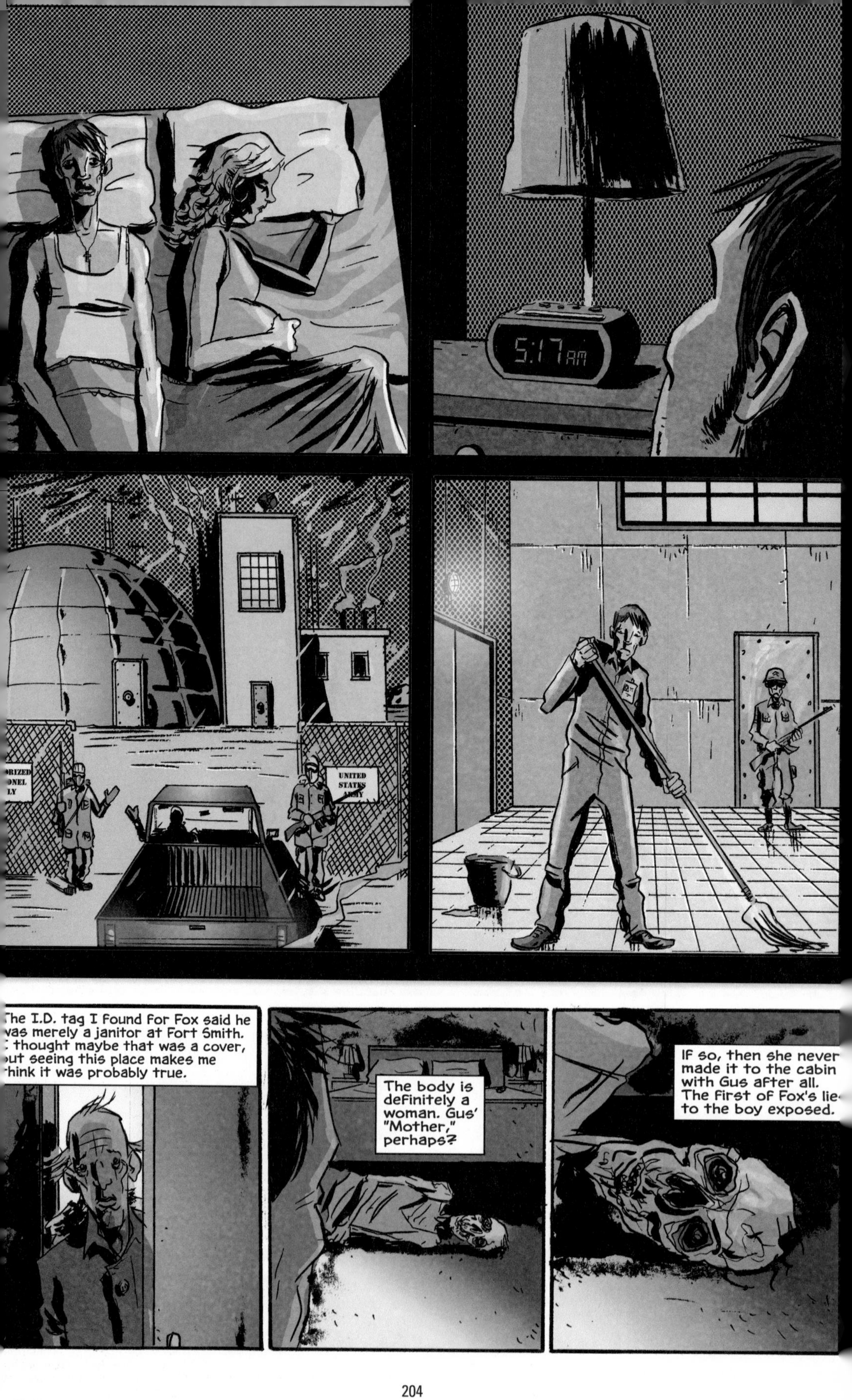
5:17 AM
UNITED STATES ARMY
RIZED
ONEL
LY
The I.D. tag I found for Fox said he was merely a janitor at Fort Smith. I thought maybe that was a cover, but seeing this place makes me think it was probably true.
The body is definitely a woman. Gus' "Mother," perhaps?
If so, then she never made it to the cabin with Gus after all. The first of Fox's lies to the boy exposed.

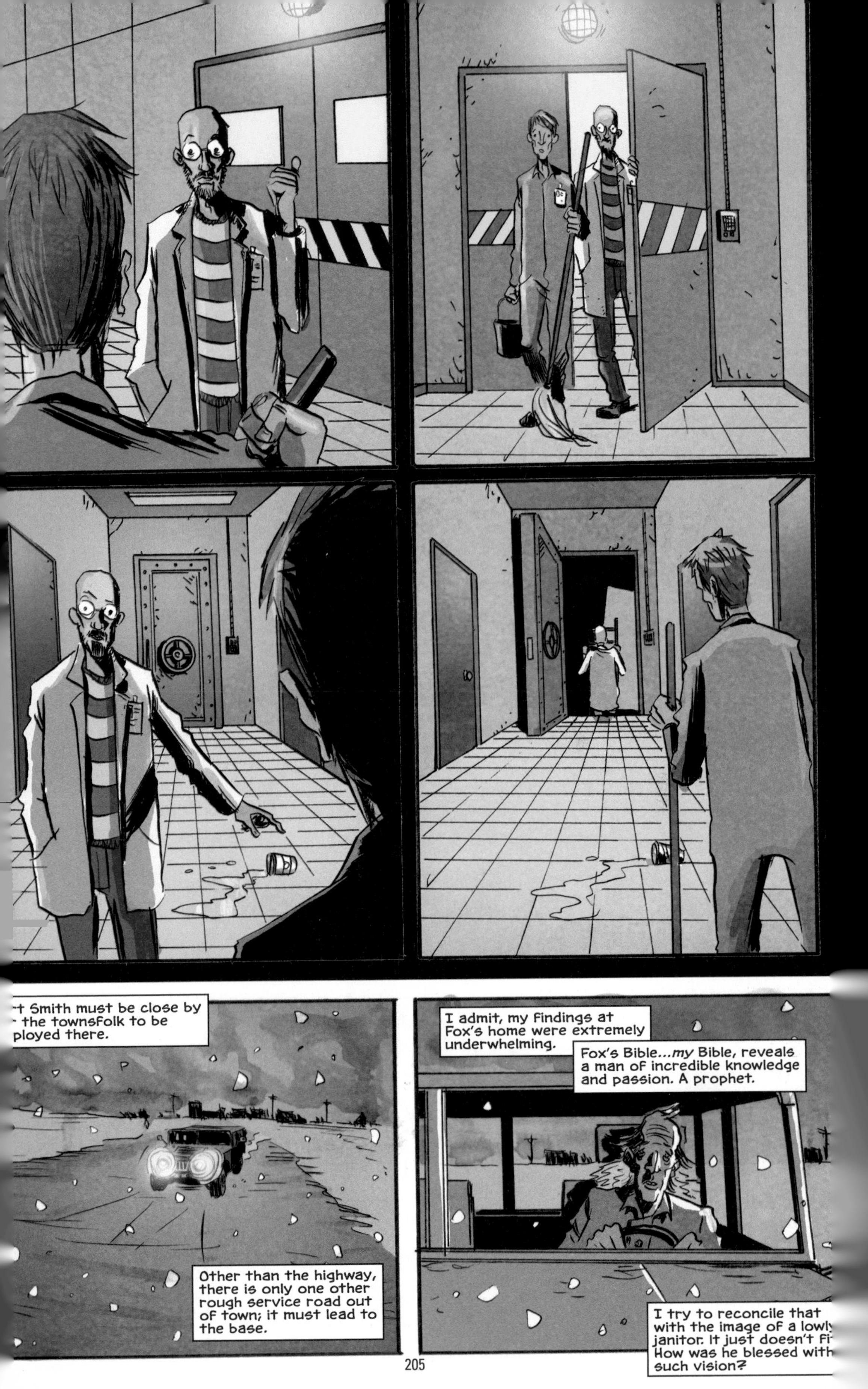
-t Smith must be close by
- the townsfolk to be
ployed there.
Other than the highway, there is only one other rough service road out of town; it must lead to the base.
I admit, my findings at Fox's home were extremely underwhelming.
Fox's Bible...*my* Bible, reveals a man of incredible knowledge and passion. A prophet.
I try to reconcile that with the image of a lowly janitor. It just doesn't fi
How was he blessed with such vision?

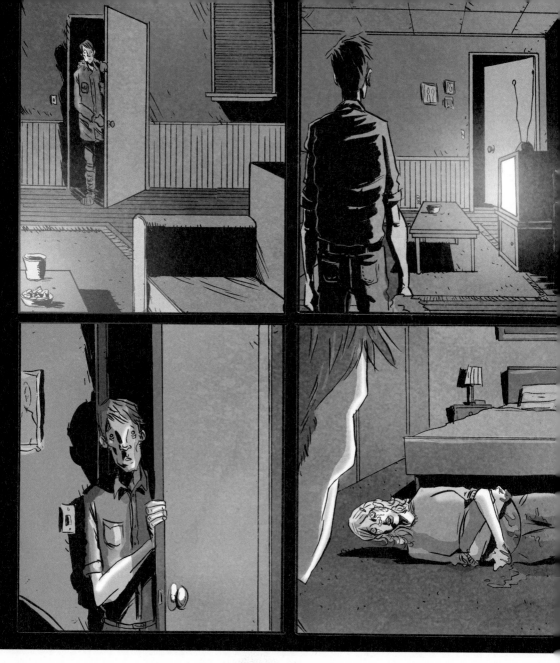

Any questions I have about Fox will have to be answered here.

I'm not surprised to find it abandoned. Yet I can't shake the feeling that I'm being watched.

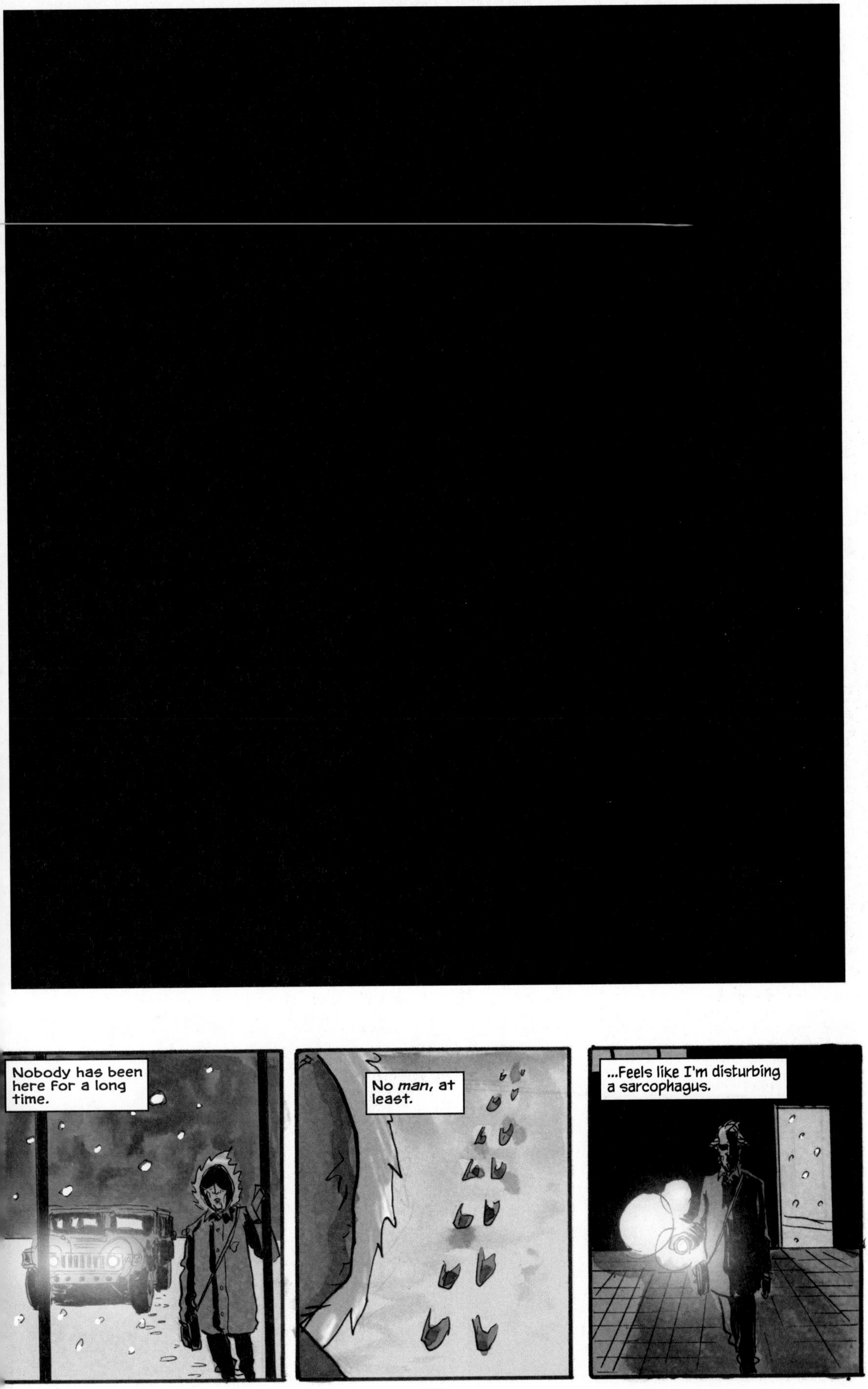
Nobody has been here for a long time.
No *man*, at least.
...Feels like I'm disturbing a sarcophagus.

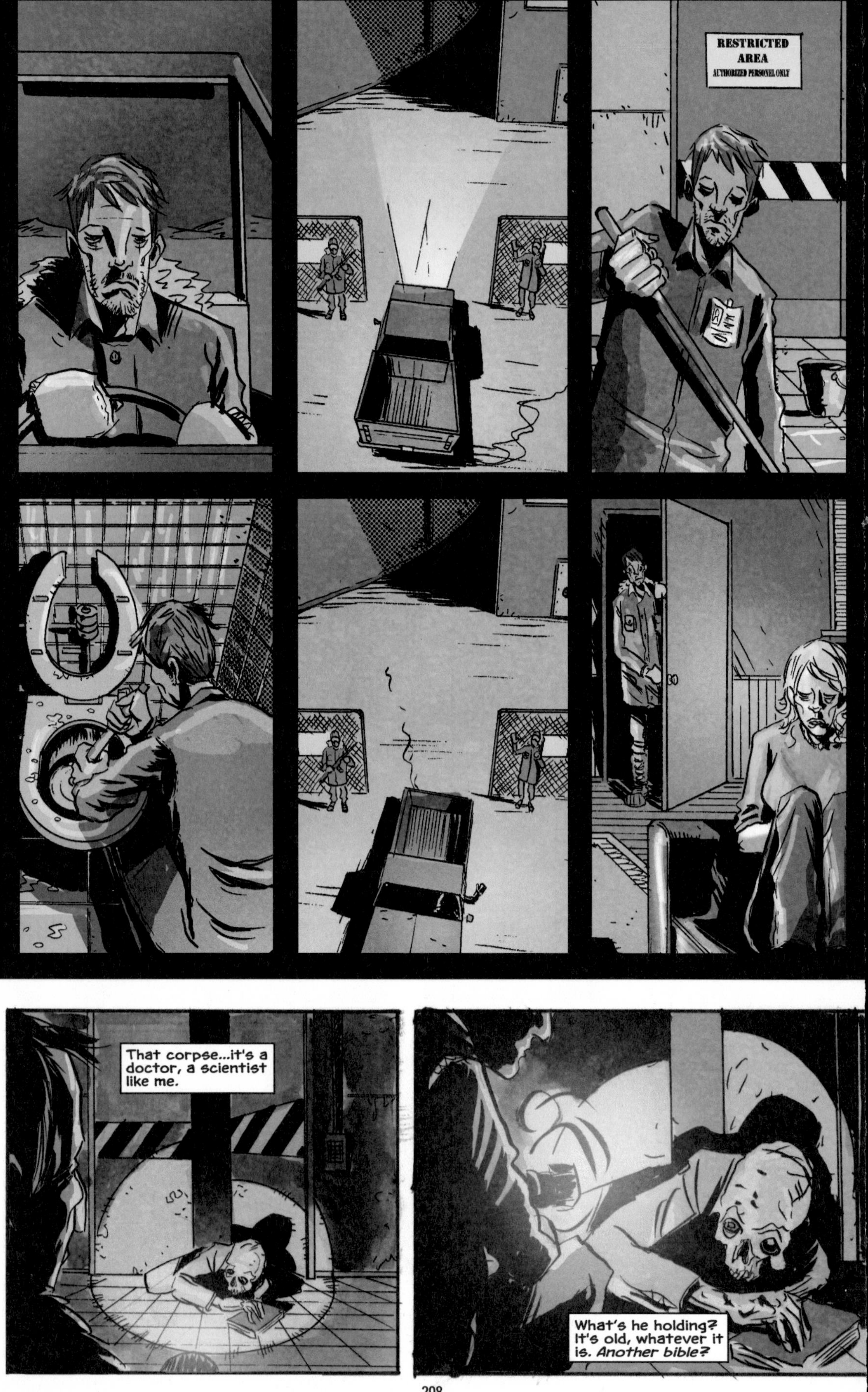
RESTRICTED
AREA
AUTHORIZED PERSONEL ONLY
That corpse...it's a doctor, a scientist like me.
What's he holding? It's old, whatever it is. *Another bible?*

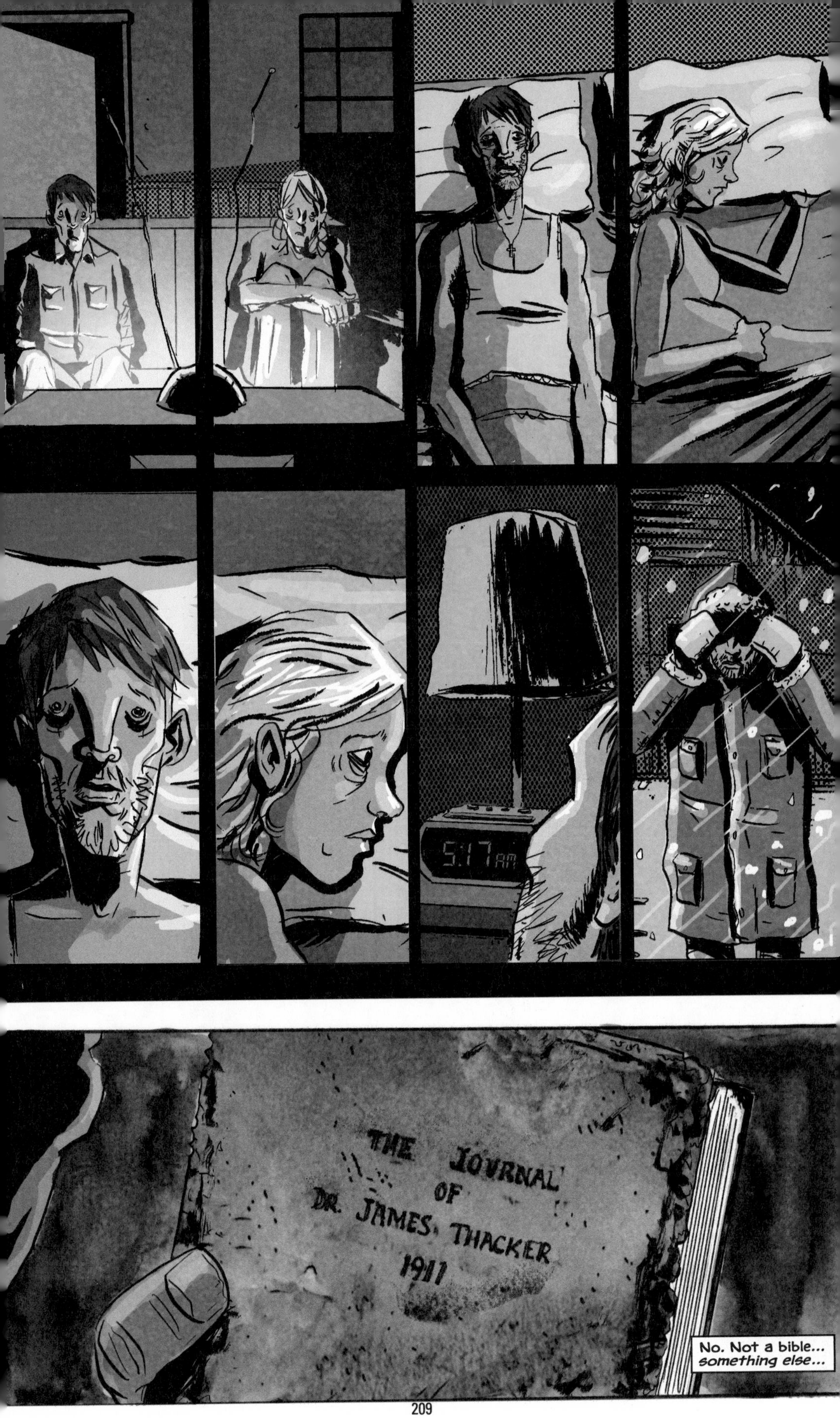
5:17 AM
THE JOURNAL OF DR. JAMES THACKER 1911
No. Not a bible... something else...

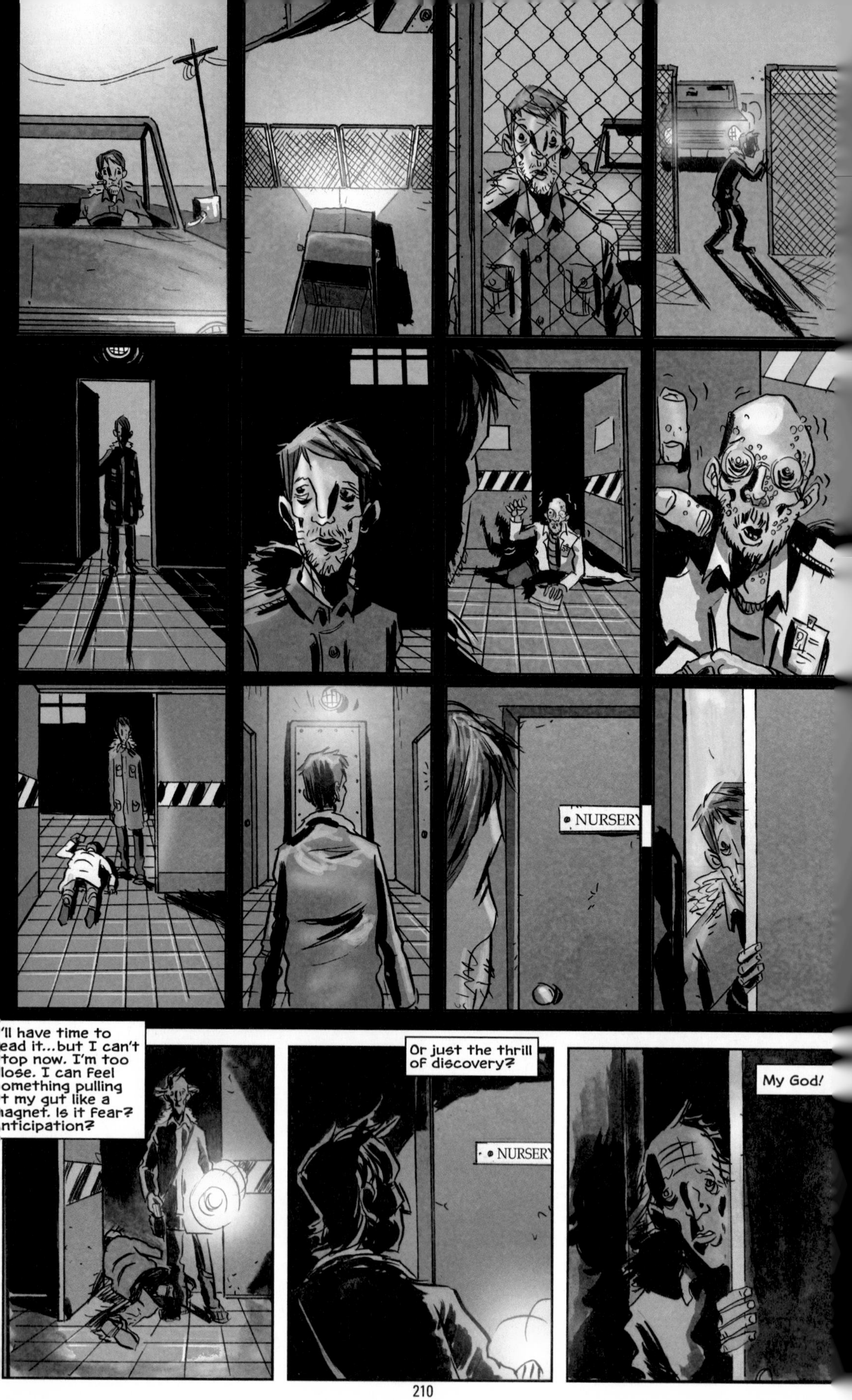

NURSERY
'll have time to
ead it...but I can't
top now. I'm too
lose. I can feel
omething pulling
t my gut like a
agnet. Is it fear?
nticipation?
Or just the thrill
of discovery?
NURSERY
My God!

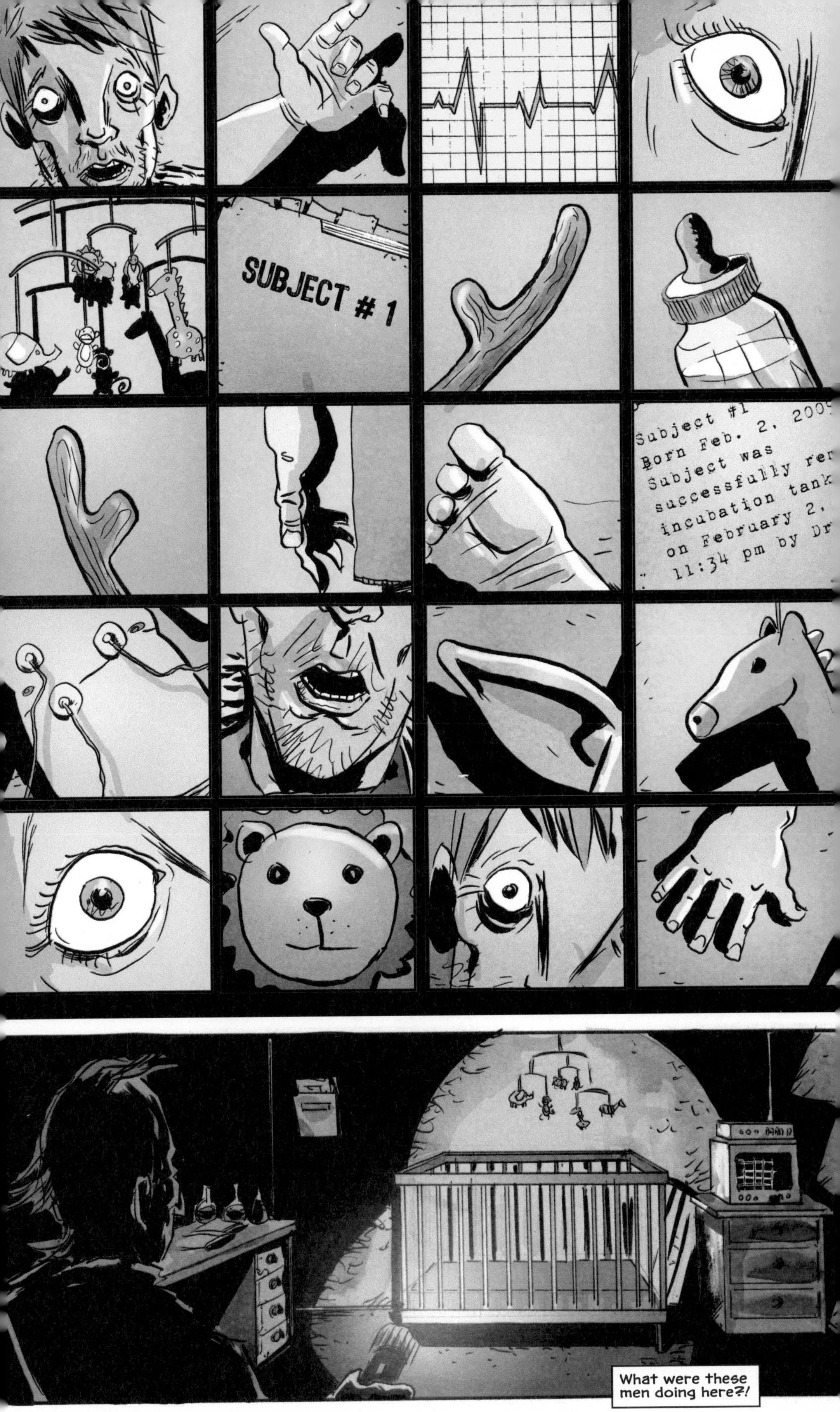
SUBJECT # 1
Subject #1
Born Feb. 2, 2009
Subject was
successfully re
incubation tank
on February 2,
11:34 pm by Dr
What were these men doing here?!

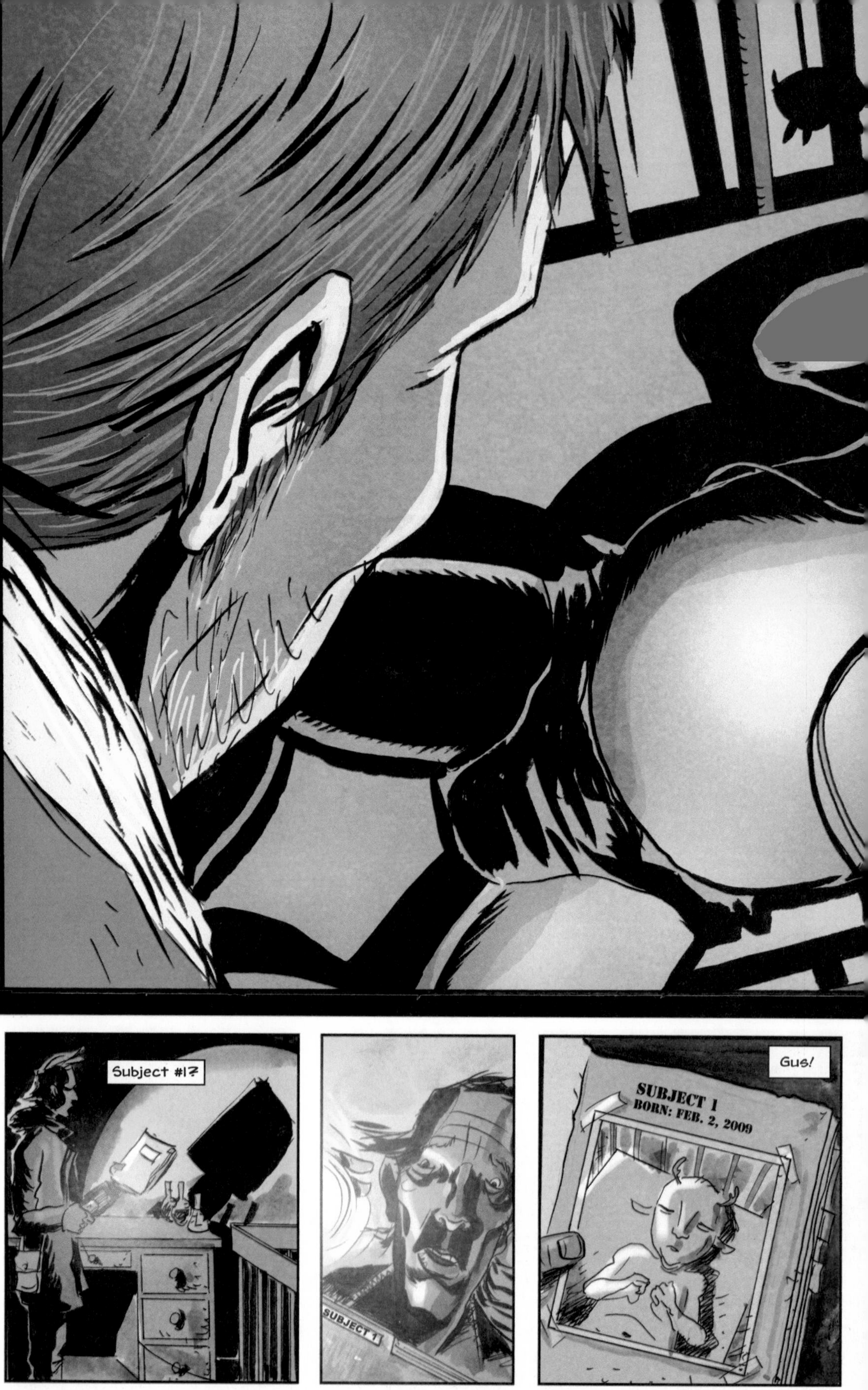
Subject #1?
SUBJECT 1
SUBJECT 1
BORN: FEB. 2, 2009
Gus!

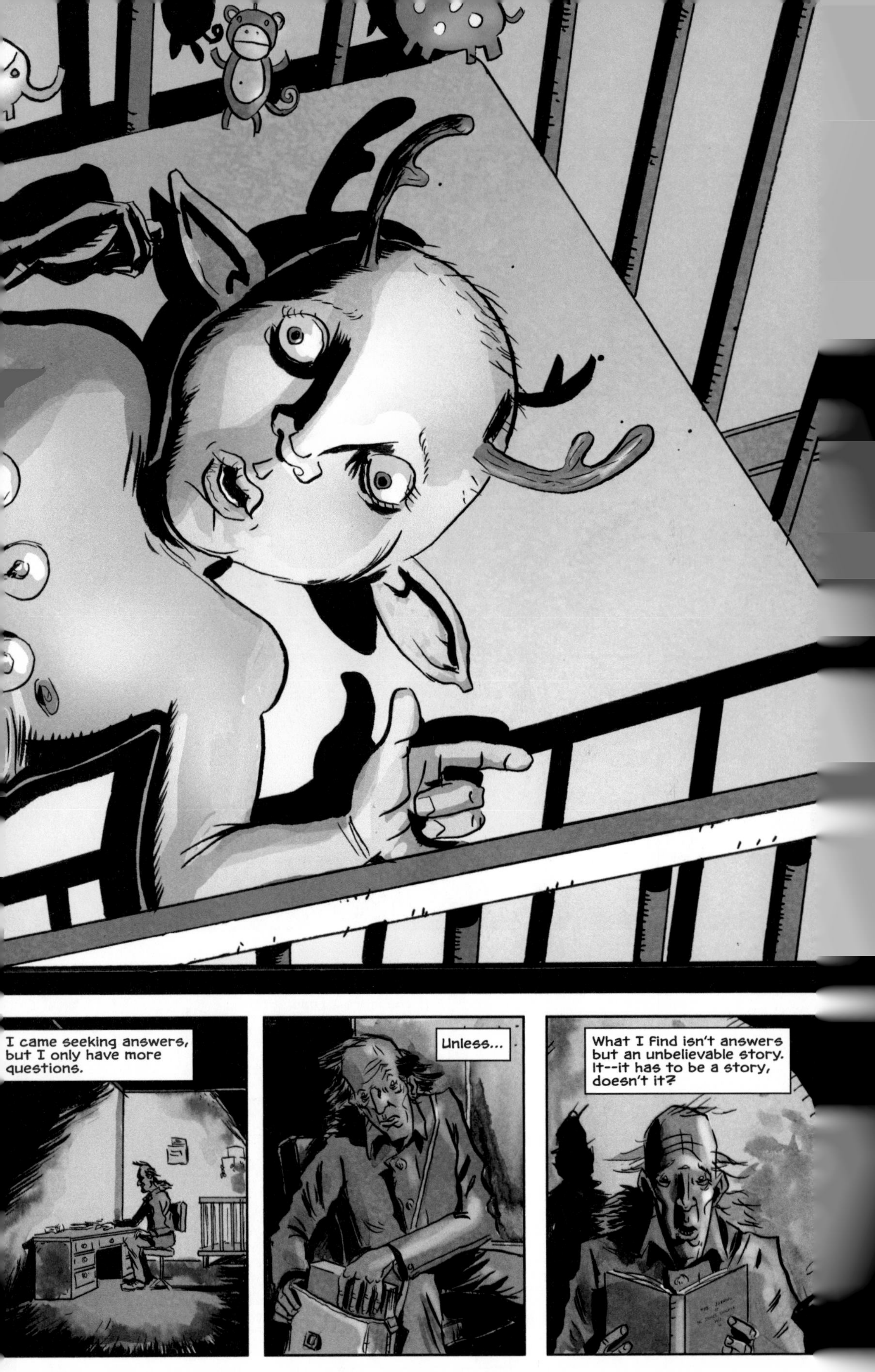
I came seeking answers, but I only have more questions.
Unless...
What I find isn't answers but an unbelievable story. It--it has to be a story, doesn't it?

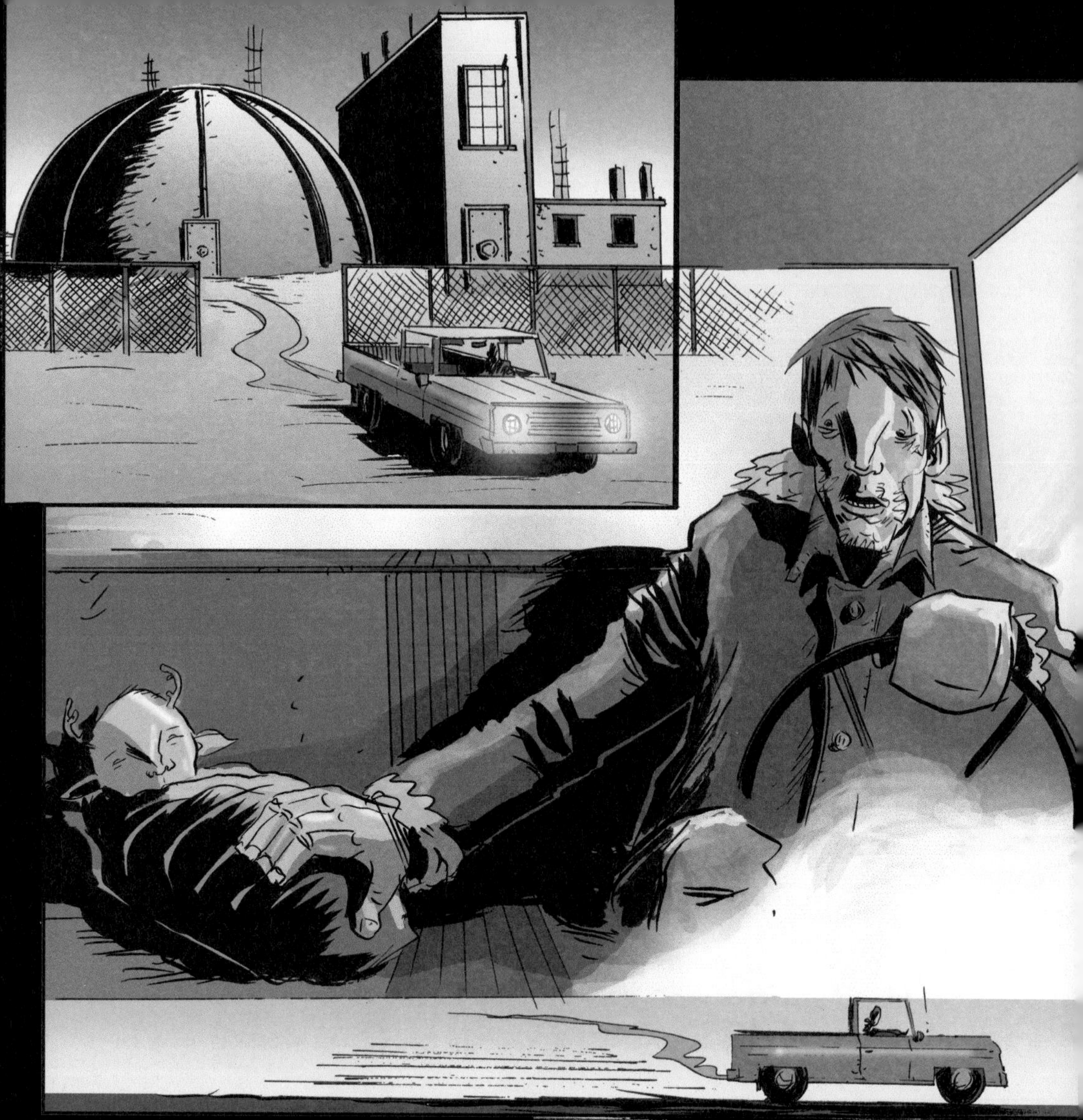

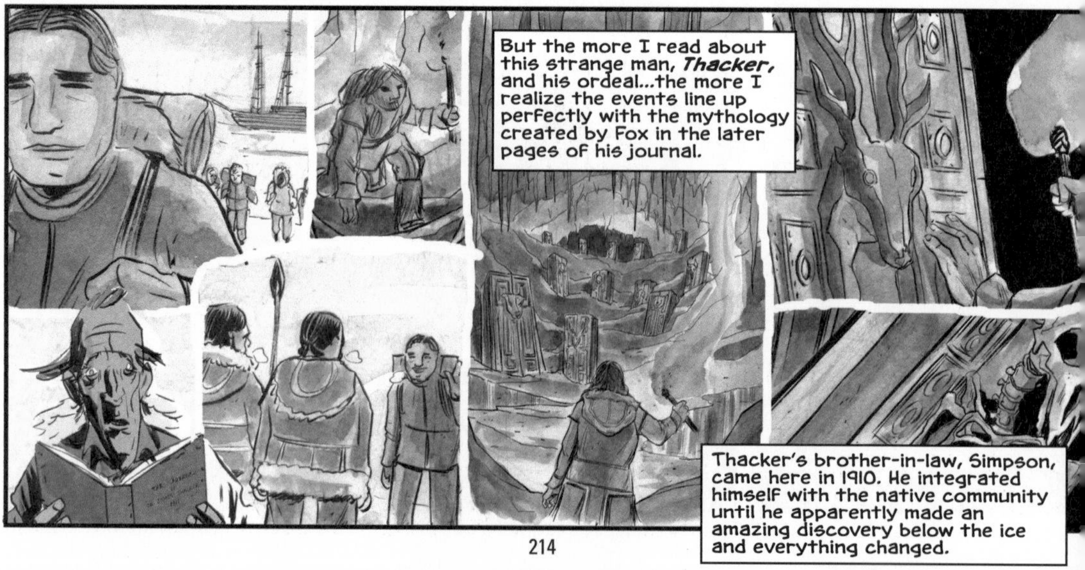
But the more I read about this strange man, *Thacker,* and his ordeal...the more I realize the events line up perfectly with the mythology created by Fox in the later pages of his journal.
Thacker's brother-in-law, Simpson, came here in 1910. He integrated himself with the native community until he apparently made an amazing discovery below the ice and everything changed.

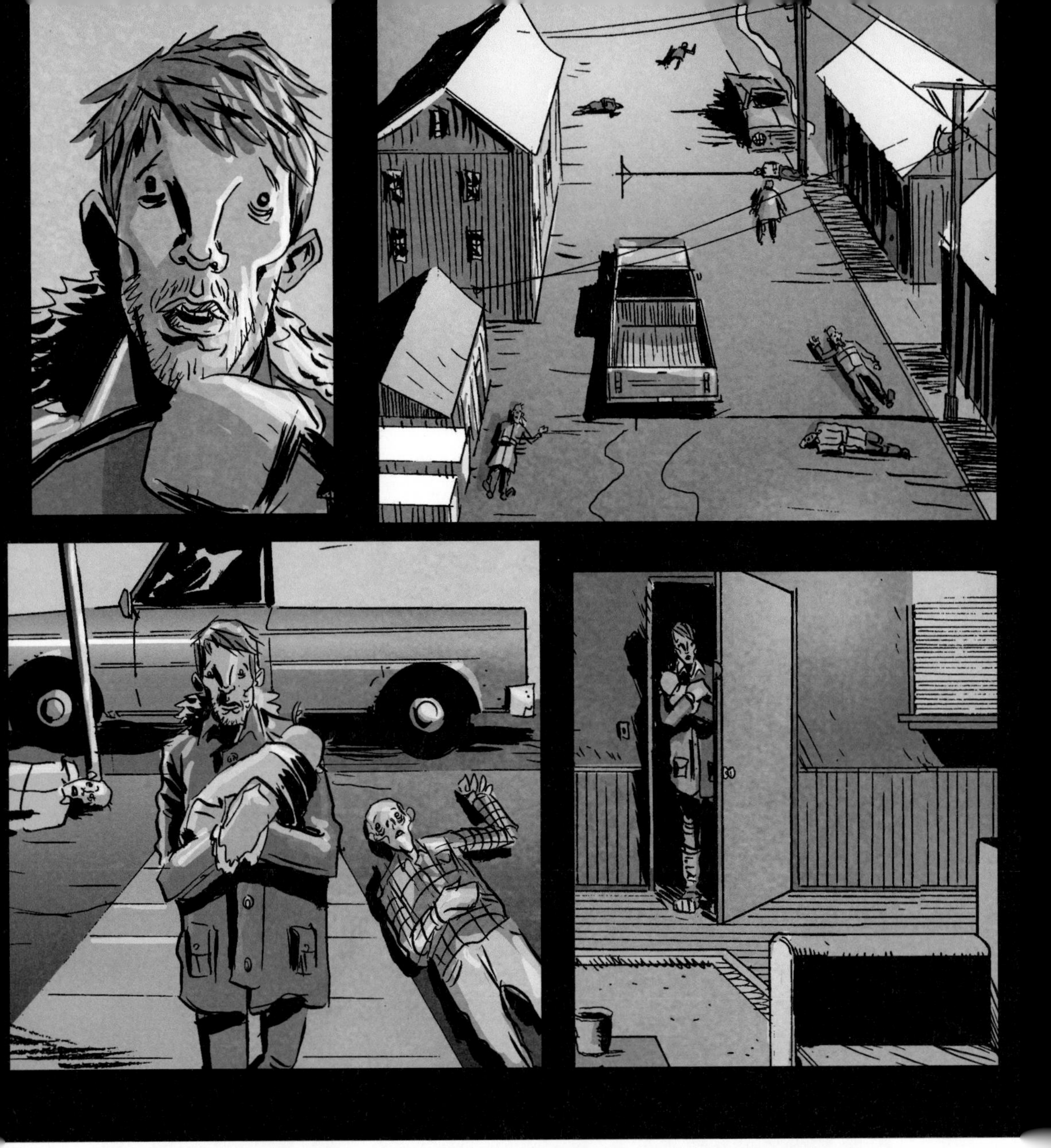

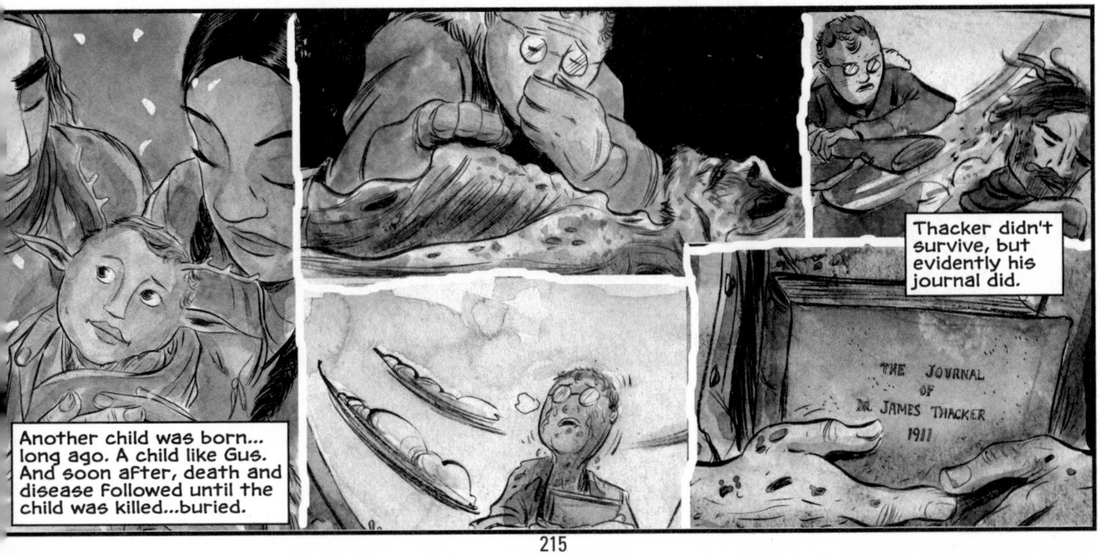
Another child was born... long ago. A child like Gus. And soon after, death and disease followed until the child was killed...buried.
Thacker didn't survive, but evidently his journal did.
THE JOURNAL OF DR. JAMES THACKER 1911

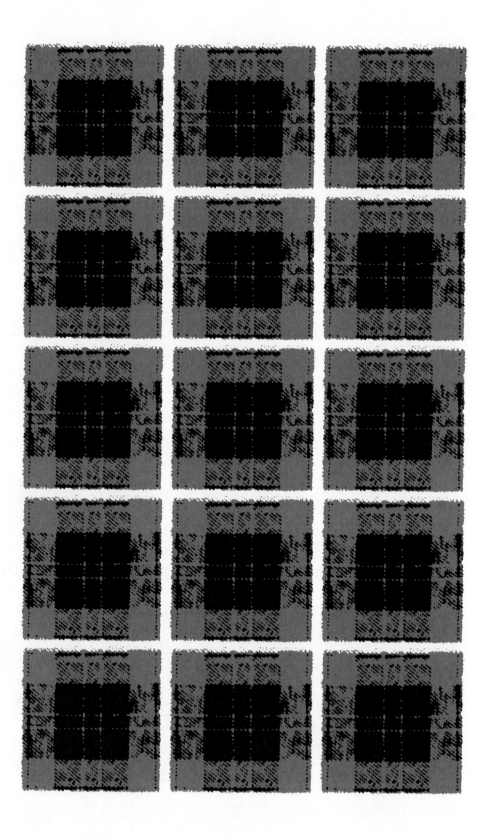

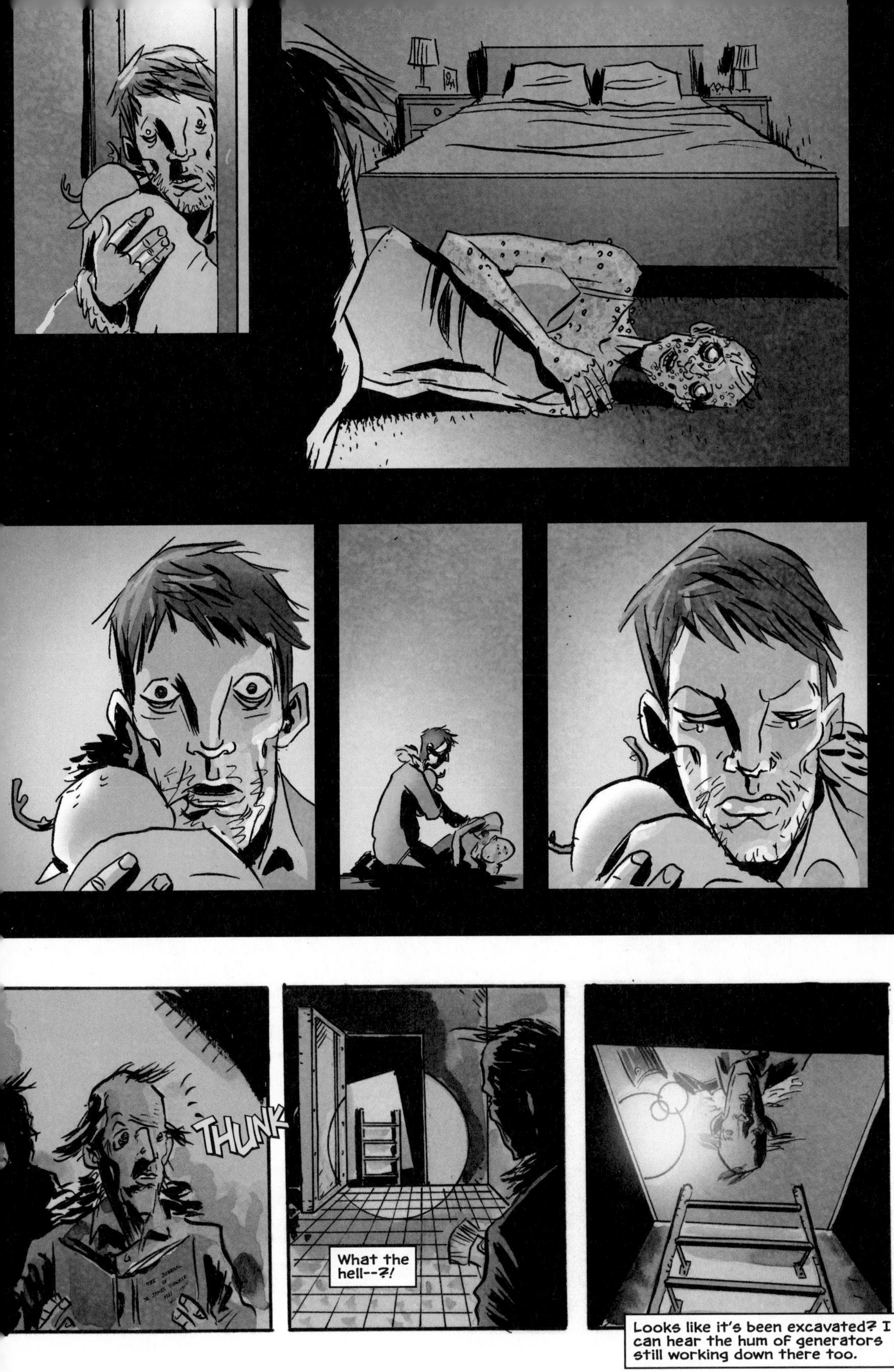
THUNK
What the hell--?!
Looks like it's been excavated? I can hear the hum of generators still working down there too.

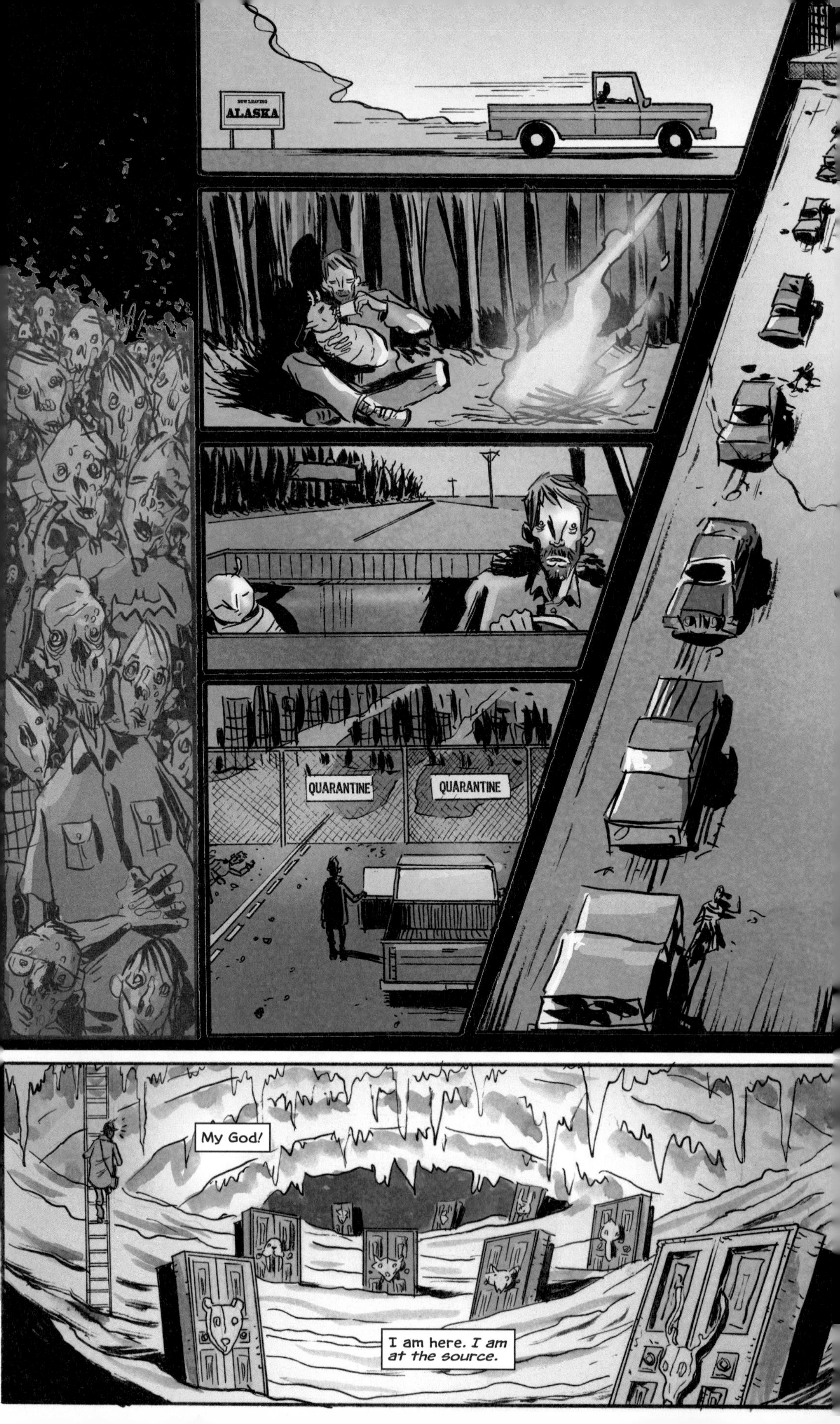

NOW LEAVING
ALASKA
QUARANTINE
QUARANTINE
My God!
I am here. *I am at the source.*

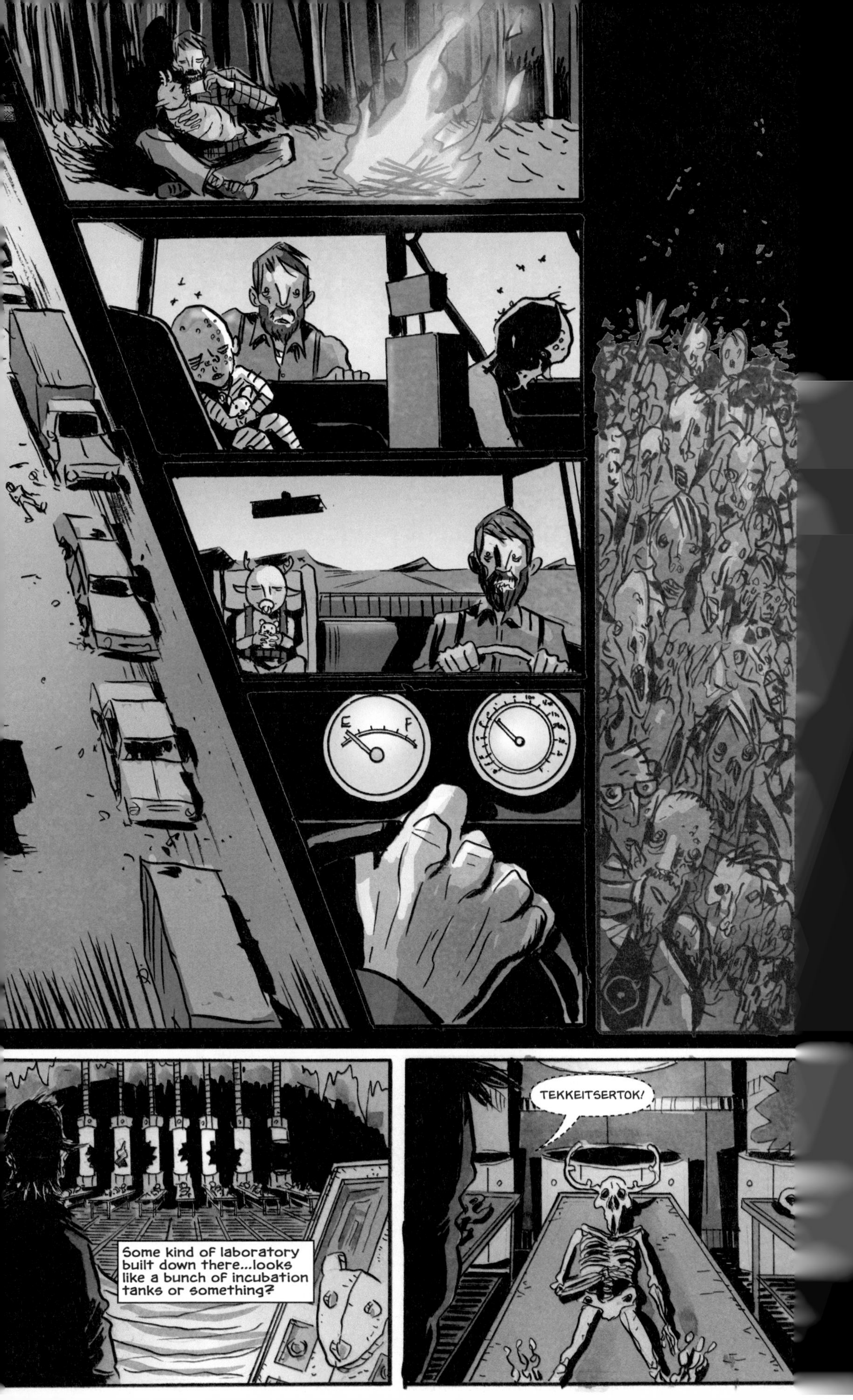
Some kind of laboratory built down there...looks like a bunch of incubation tanks or something?
TEKKEITSERTOK!

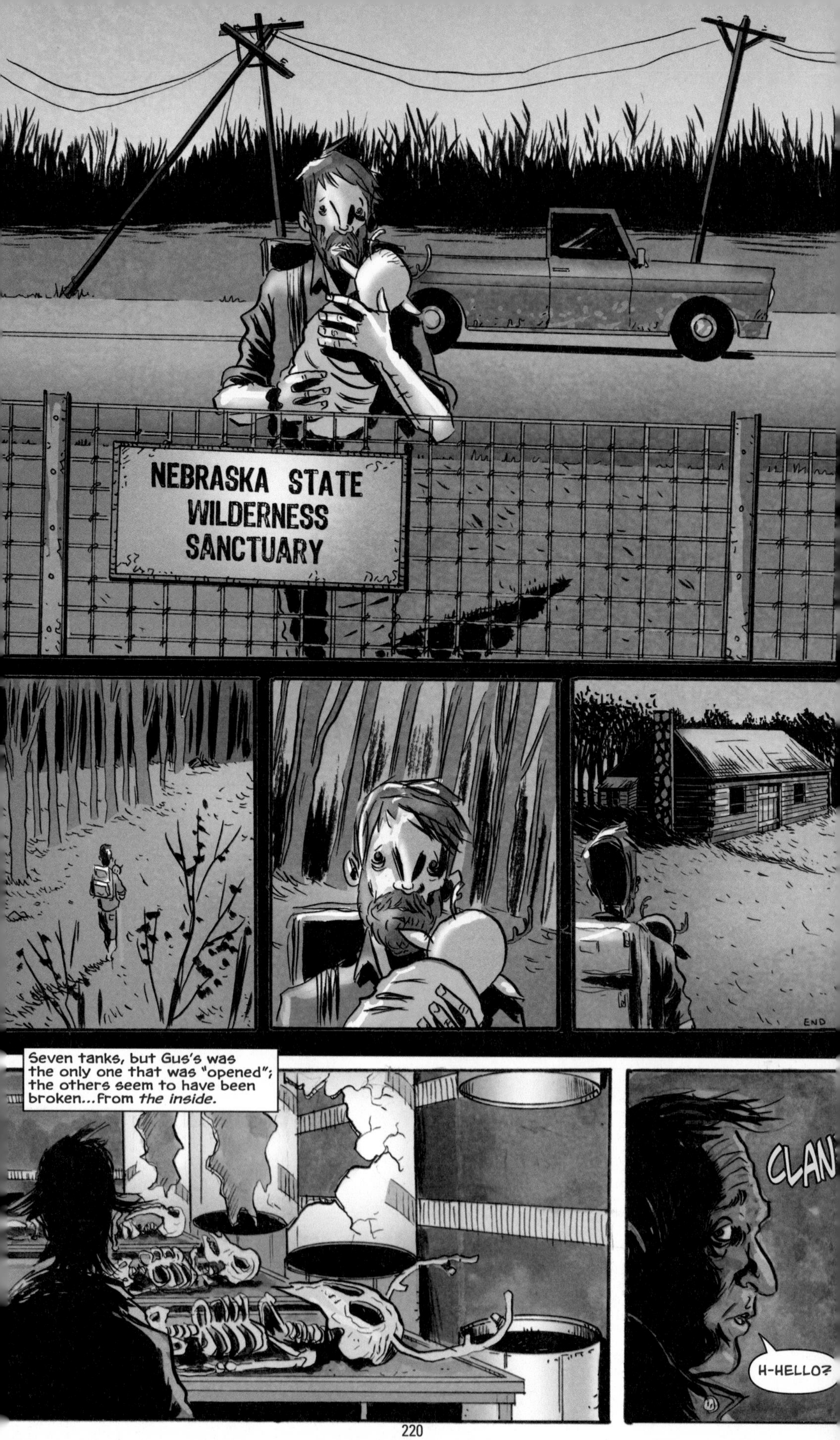
NEBRASKA STATE
WILDERNESS
SANCTUARY
END
Seven tanks, but Gus's was the only one that was "opened"; the others seem to have been broken...from *the inside*.
CLAN
H-HELLO?

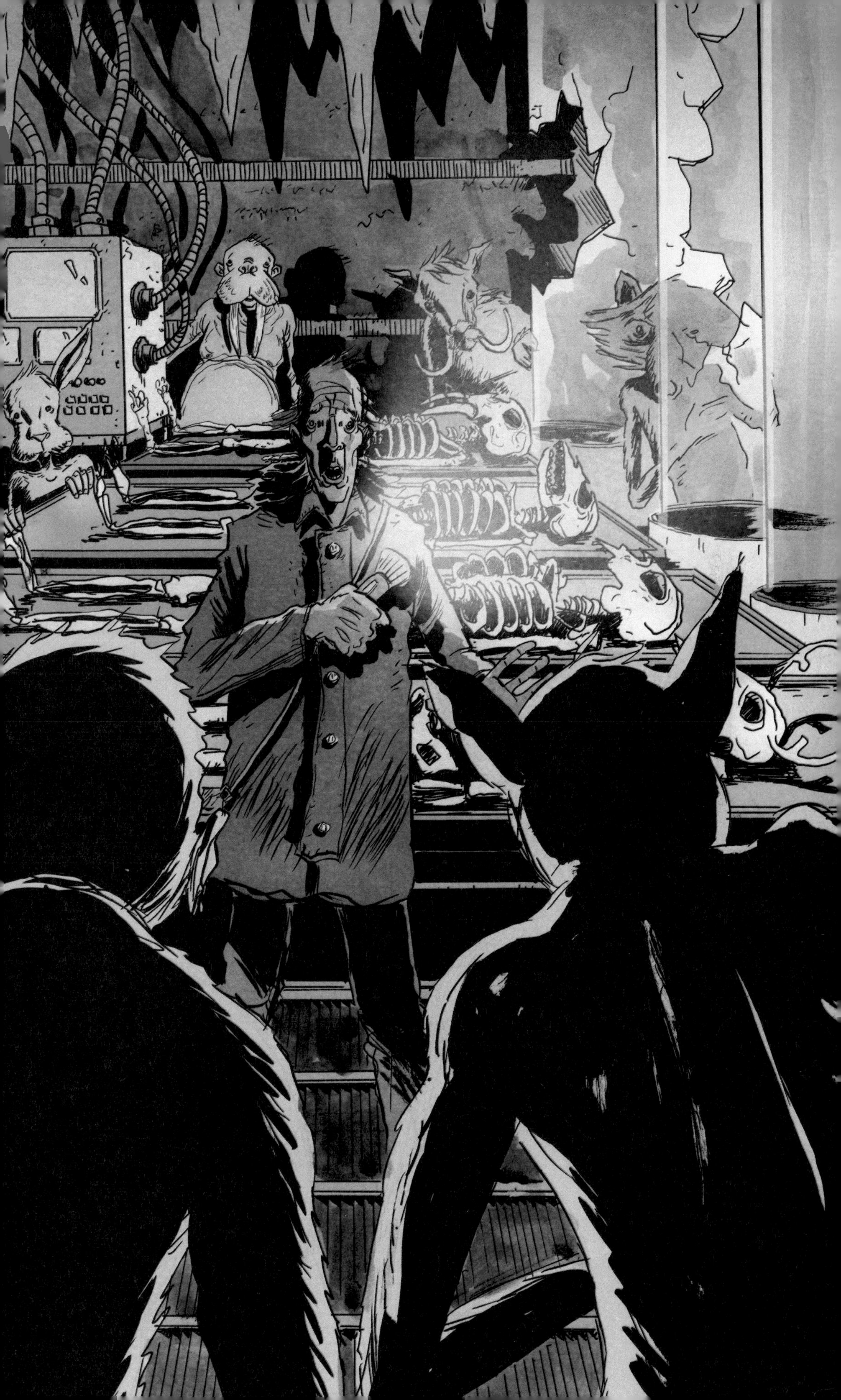

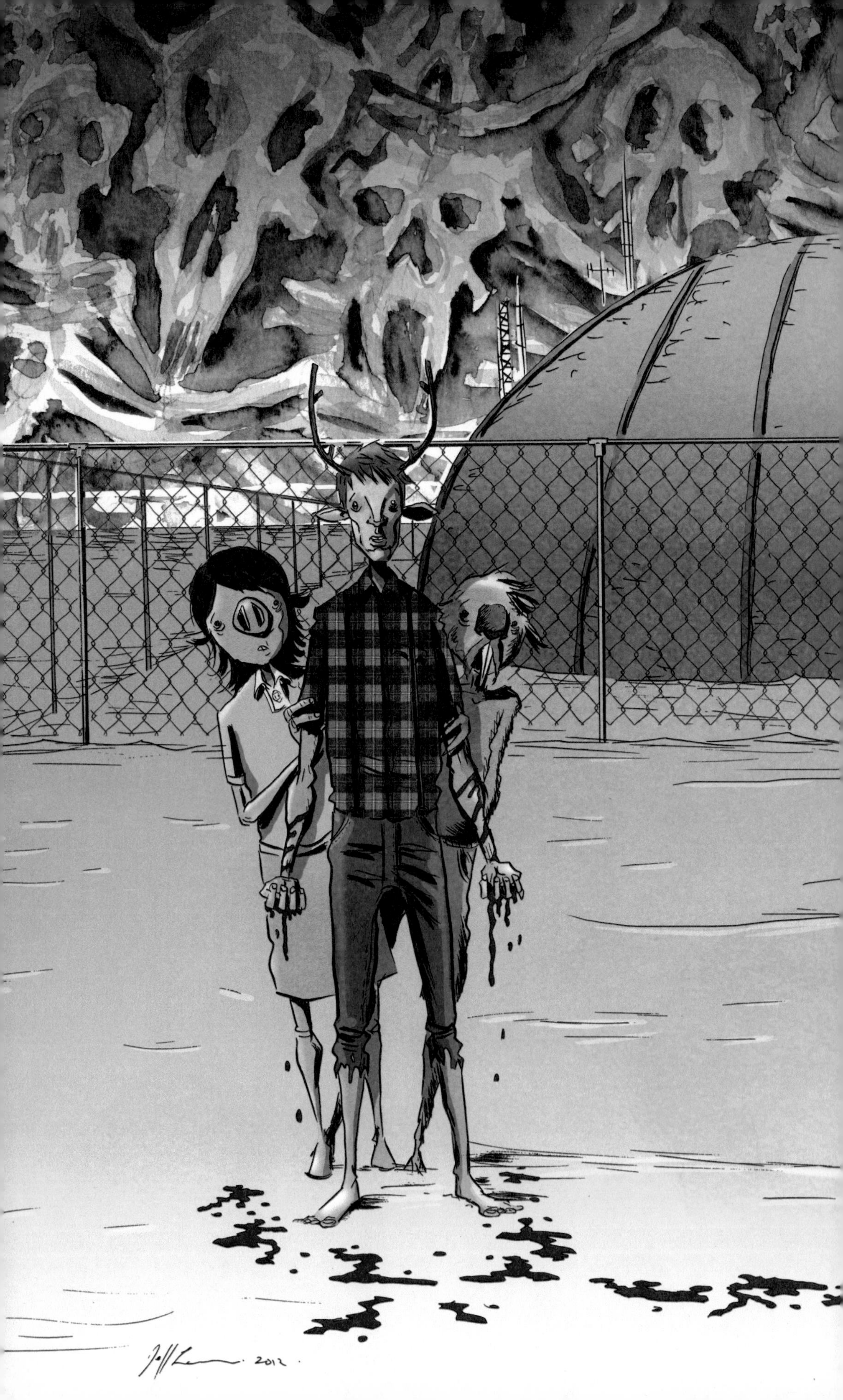

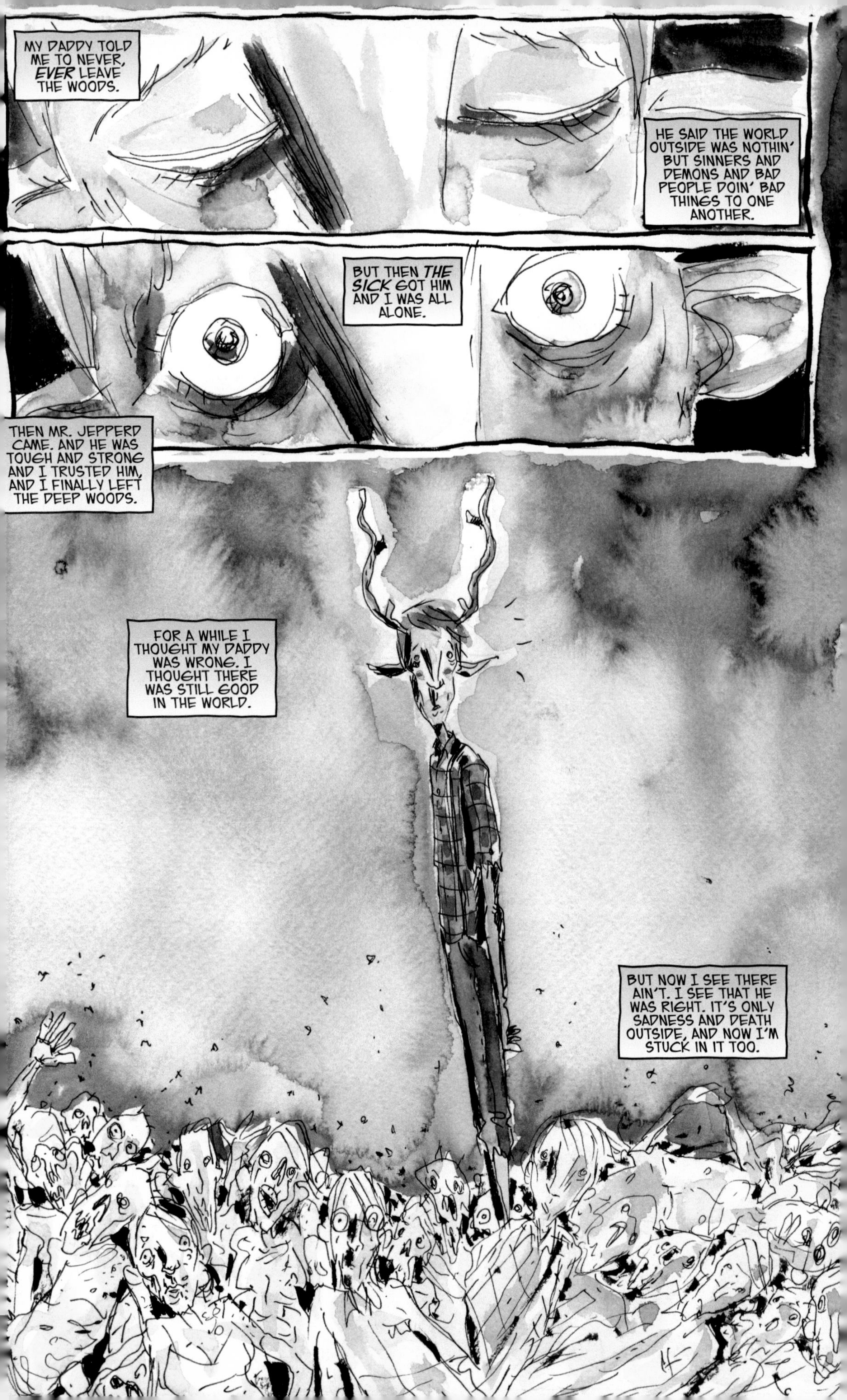

MY DADDY TOLD ME TO NEVER, EVER LEAVE THE WOODS.
HE SAID THE WORLD OUTSIDE WAS NOTHIN' BUT SINNERS AND DEMONS AND BAD PEOPLE DOIN' BAD THINGS TO ONE ANOTHER.
BUT THEN THE SICK GOT HIM AND I WAS ALL ALONE.
THEN MR. JEPPERD CAME. AND HE WAS TOUGH AND STRONG AND I TRUSTED HIM, AND I FINALLY LEFT THE DEEP WOODS.
FOR A WHILE I THOUGHT MY DADDY WAS WRONG. I THOUGHT THERE WAS STILL GOOD IN THE WORLD.
BUT NOW I SEE THERE AIN'T. I SEE THAT HE WAS RIGHT. IT'S ONLY SADNESS AND DEATH OUTSIDE, AND NOW I'M STUCK IN IT TOO.

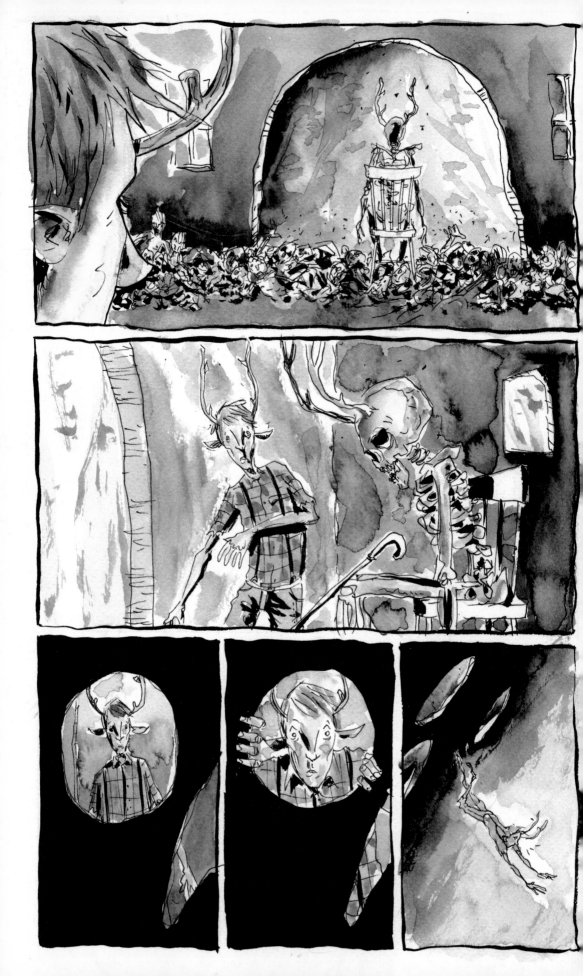

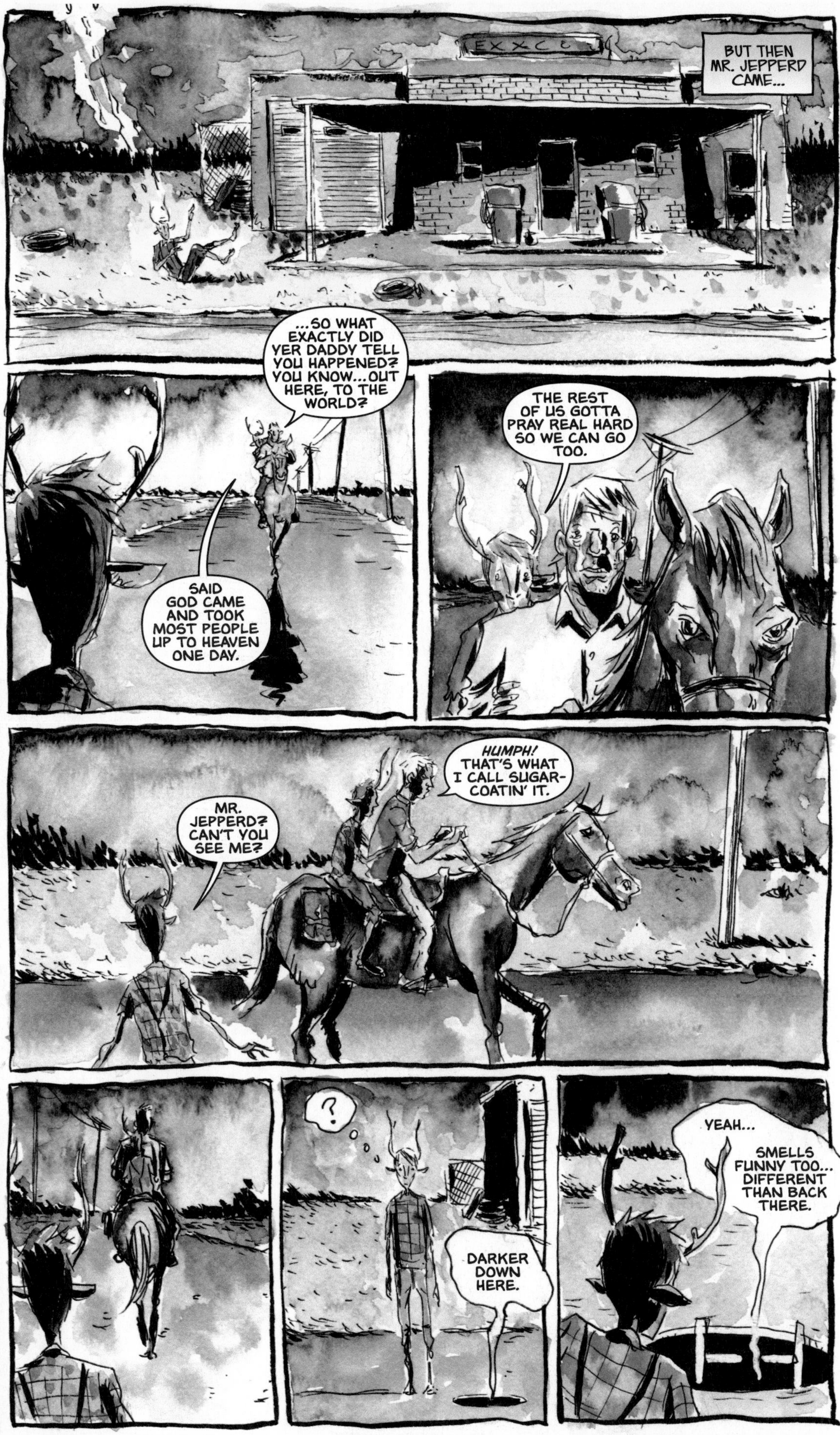

EXXCO
BUT THEN MR. JEPPERD CAME...
...SO WHAT EXACTLY DID YER DADDY TELL YOU HAPPENED? YOU KNOW...OUT HERE, TO THE WORLD?
SAID GOD CAME AND TOOK MOST PEOPLE UP TO HEAVEN ONE DAY.
THE REST OF US GOTTA PRAY REAL HARD SO WE CAN GO TOO.
HUMPH! THAT'S WHAT I CALL SUGAR-COATIN' IT.
MR. JEPPERD? CAN'T YOU SEE ME?
?
DARKER DOWN HERE.
YEAH...
SMELLS FUNNY TOO... DIFFERENT THAN BACK THERE.

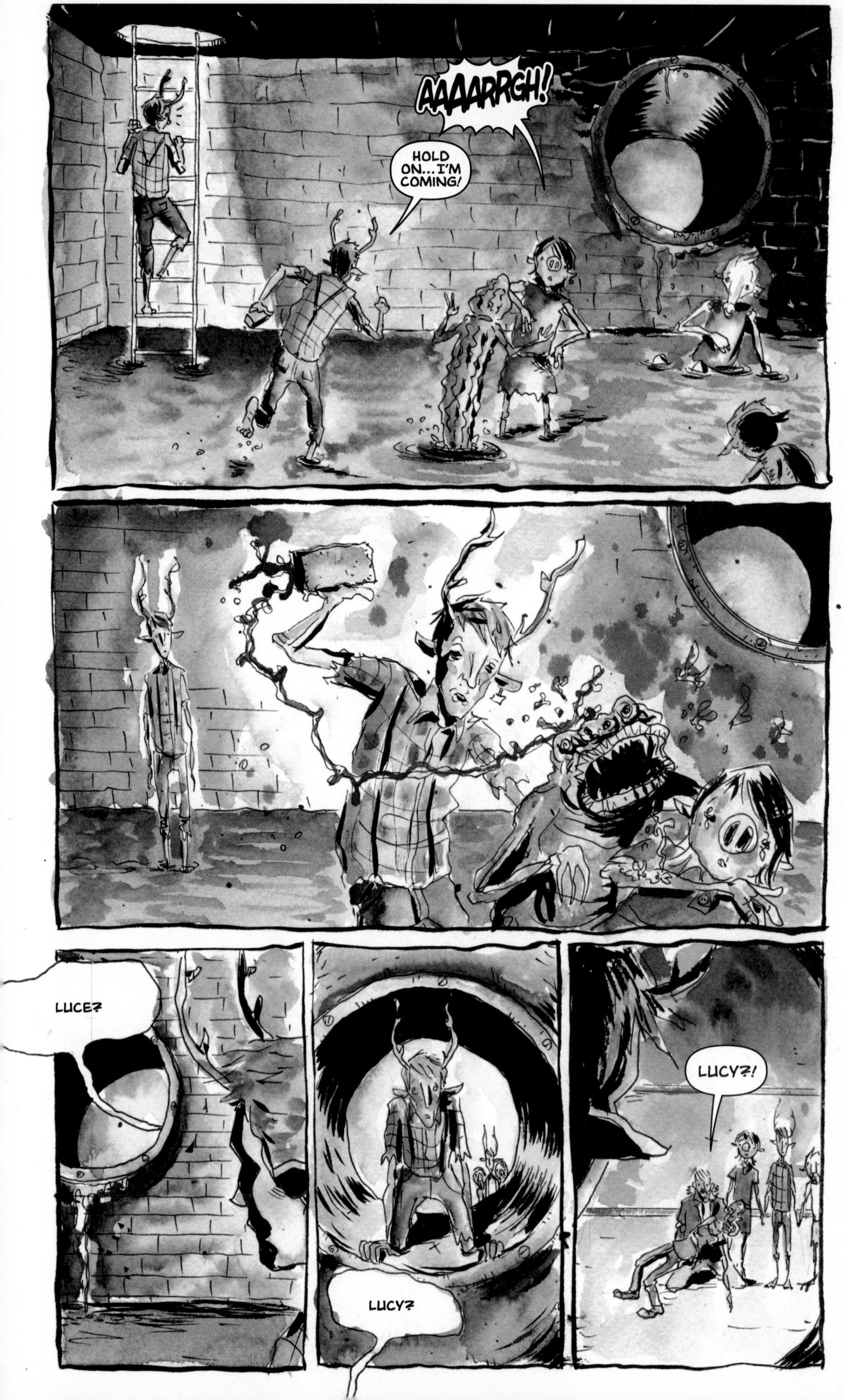
AAAARRGH!
HOLD ON...I'M COMING!
LUCE?
LUCY?
LUCY?!

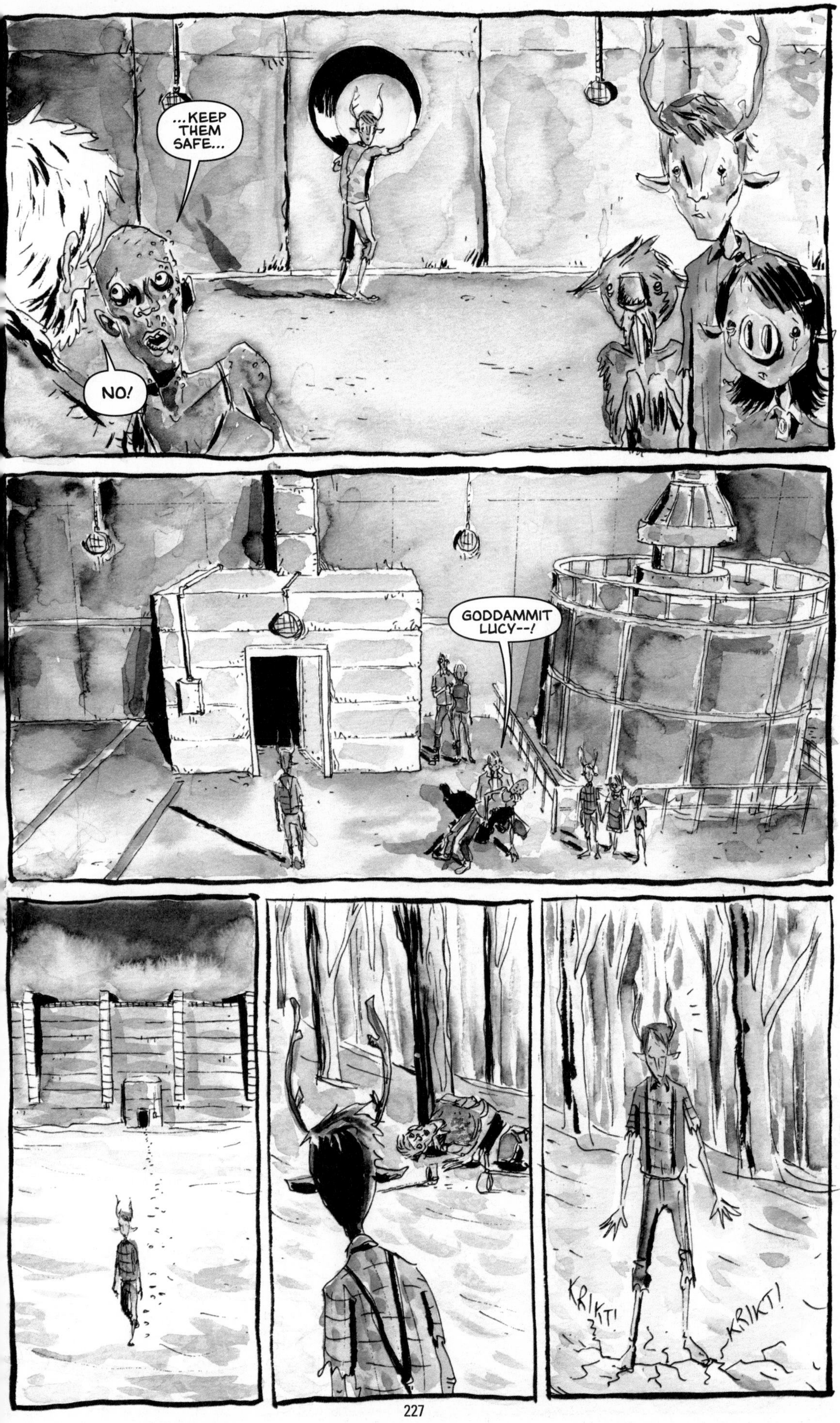
...KEEP THEM SAFE...
NO!
GODDAMMIT LUCY--!
KRIKT!
KRIKT!

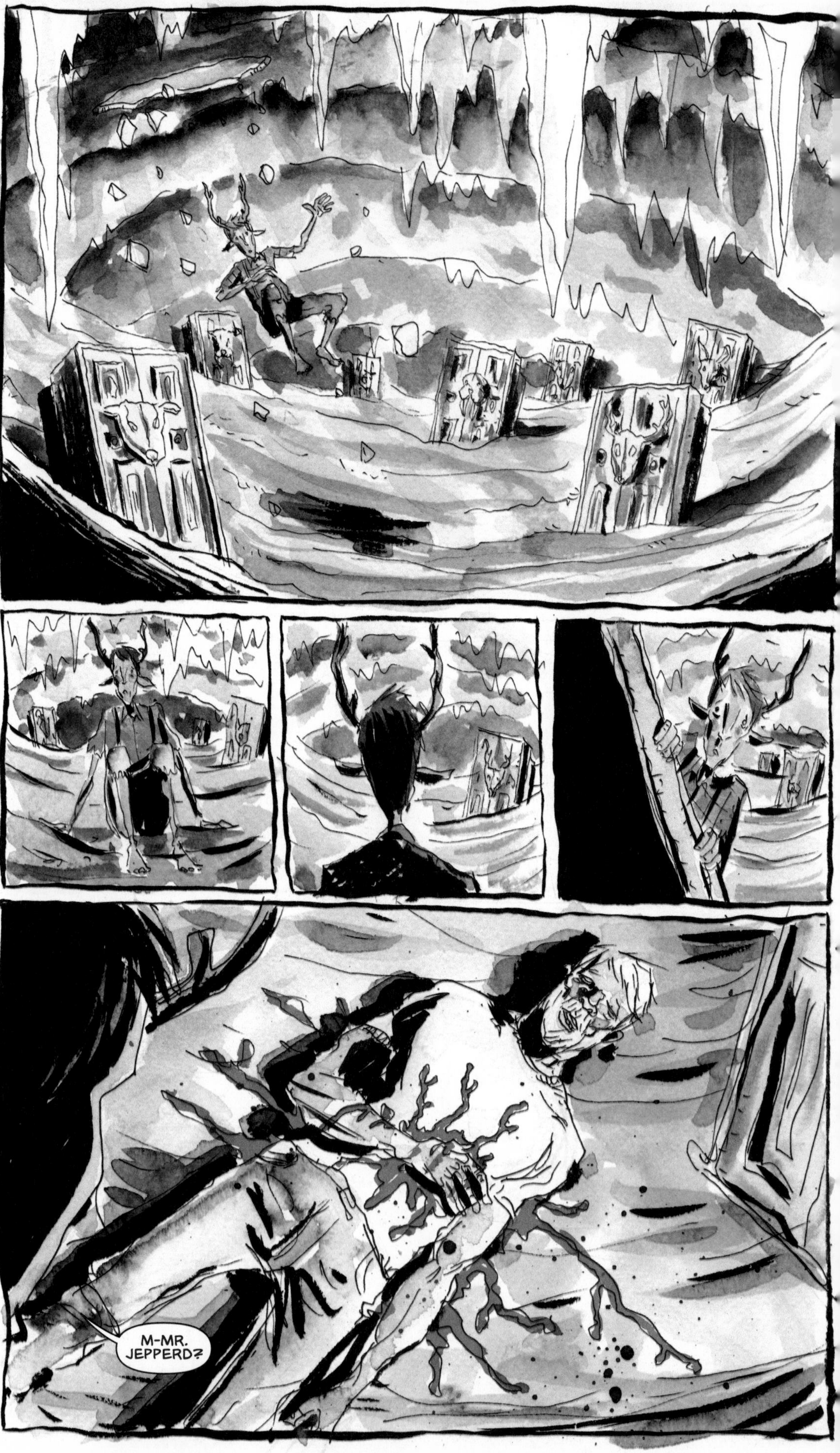
M-MR. JEPPERD?

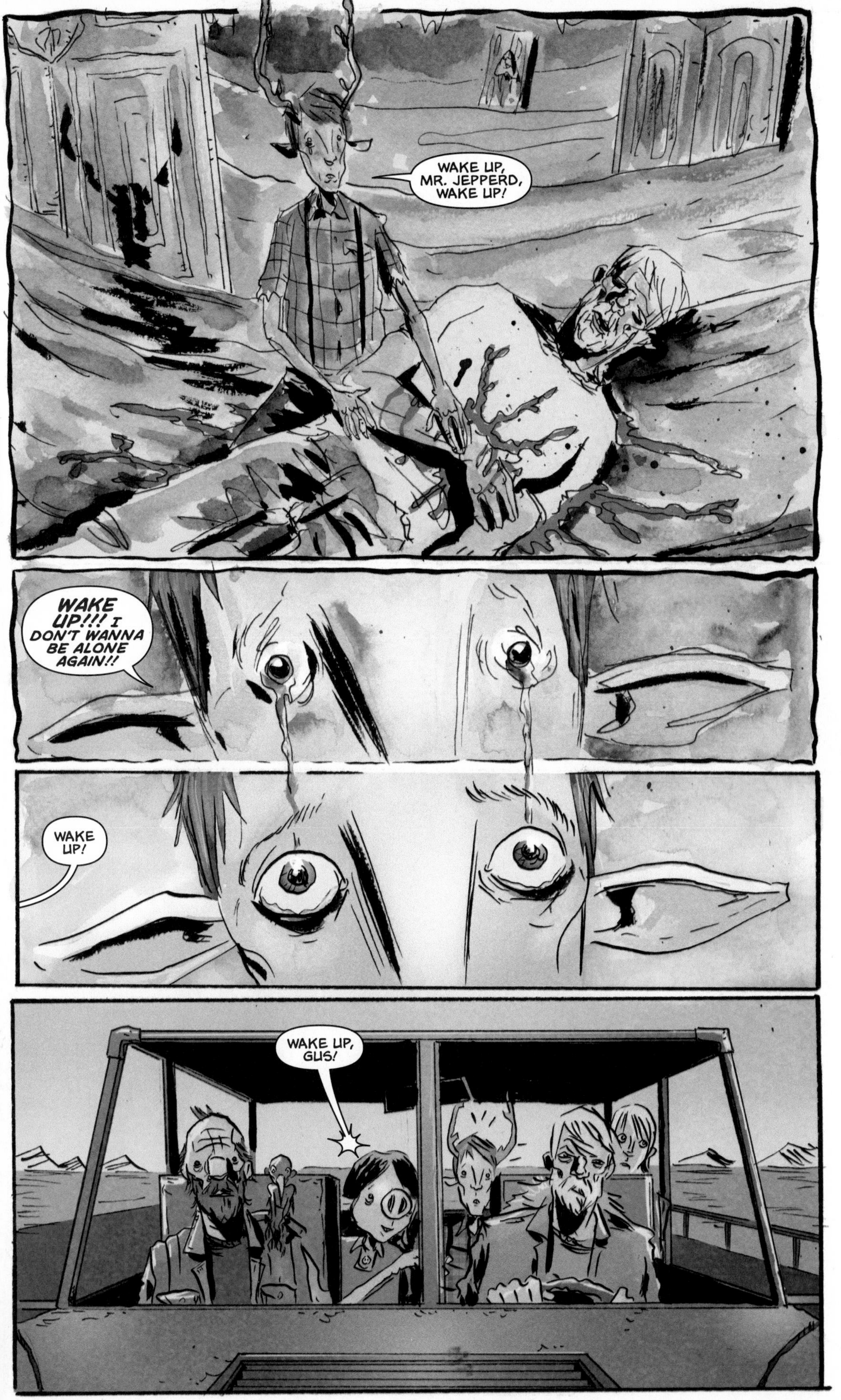
WAKE UP, MR. JEPPERD, WAKE UP!
WAKE UP!!! I DON'T WANNA BE ALONE AGAIN!!
WAKE UP!
WAKE UP, GUS!

WILD GAME
PART 1 of 4

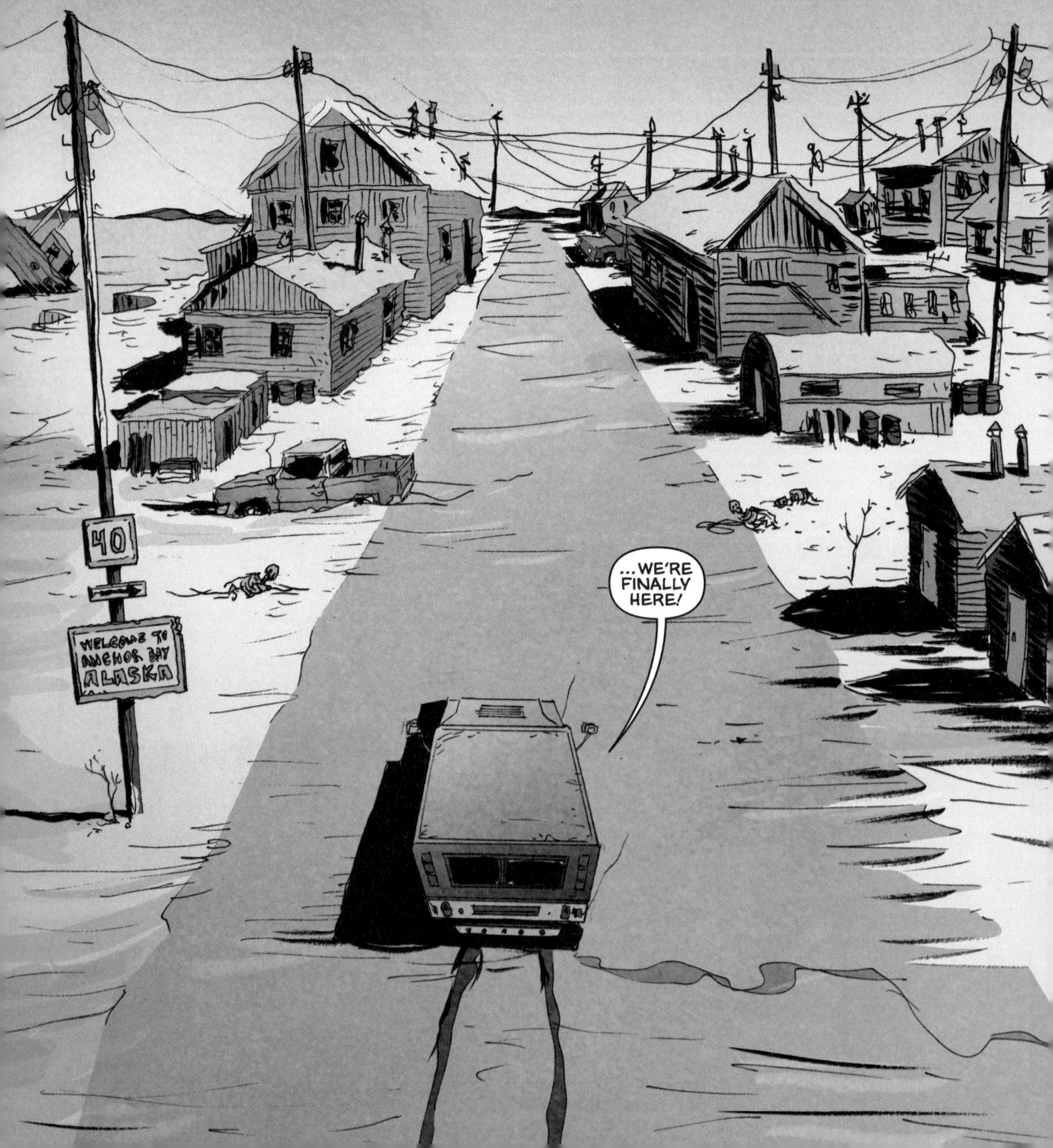
40
WELCOME TO ANCHOR BAY ALASKA
...WE'RE FINALLY HERE!

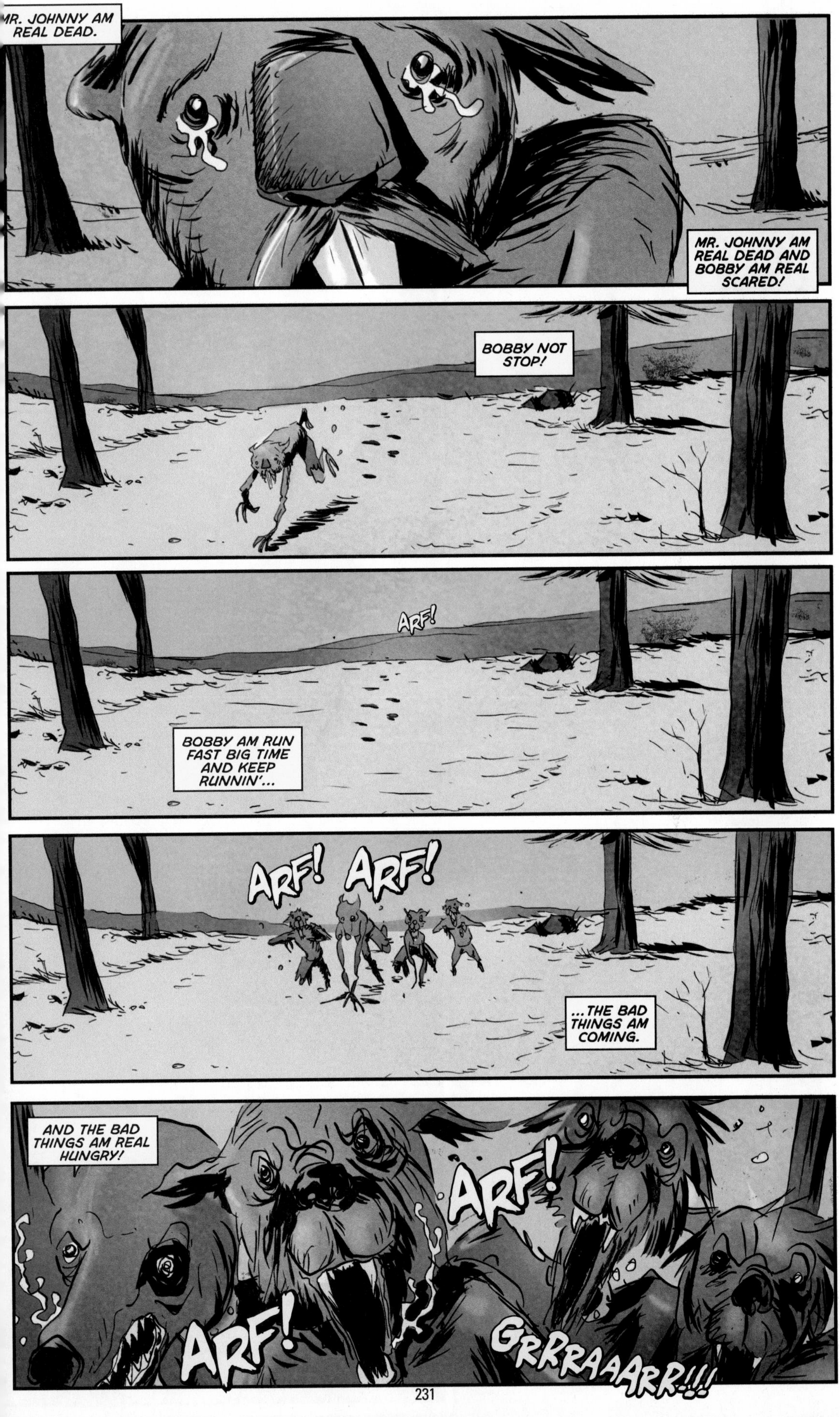
MR. JOHNNY AM REAL DEAD.
MR. JOHNNY AM REAL DEAD AND BOBBY AM REAL SCARED!
BOBBY NOT STOP!
ARF!
BOBBY AM RUN FAST BIG TIME AND KEEP RUNNIN'...
ARF! ARF!
...THE BAD THINGS AM COMING.
AND THE BAD THINGS AM REAL HUNGRY!
ARF!
ARF!
GRRRAAARR!!!

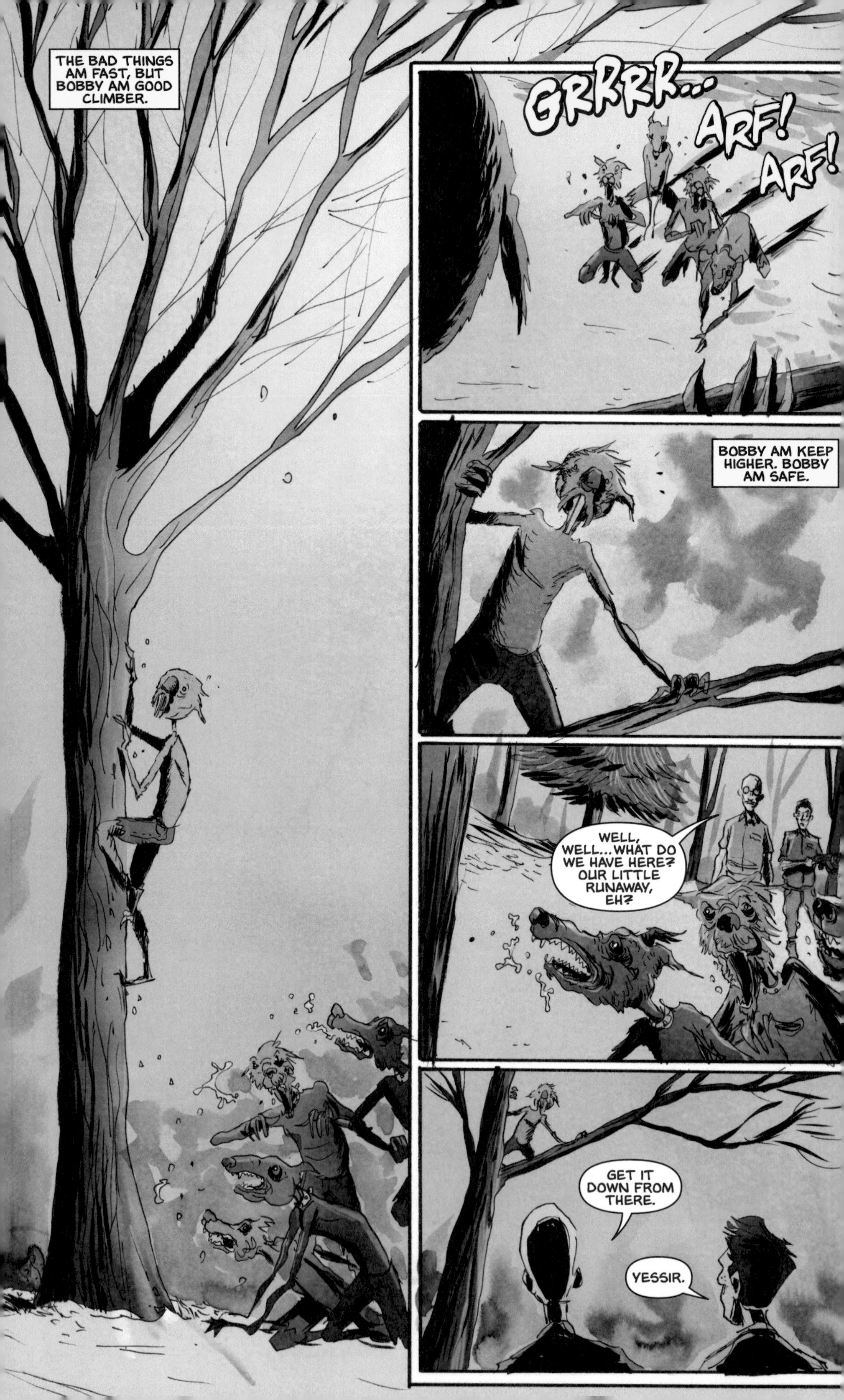
THE BAD THINGS AM FAST, BUT BOBBY AM GOOD CLIMBER.
GRRRR...
ARF!
ARF!
BOBBY AM KEEP HIGHER. BOBBY AM SAFE.
WELL, WELL...WHAT DO WE HAVE HERE? OUR LITTLE RUNAWAY, EH?
GET IT DOWN FROM THERE.
YESSIR.

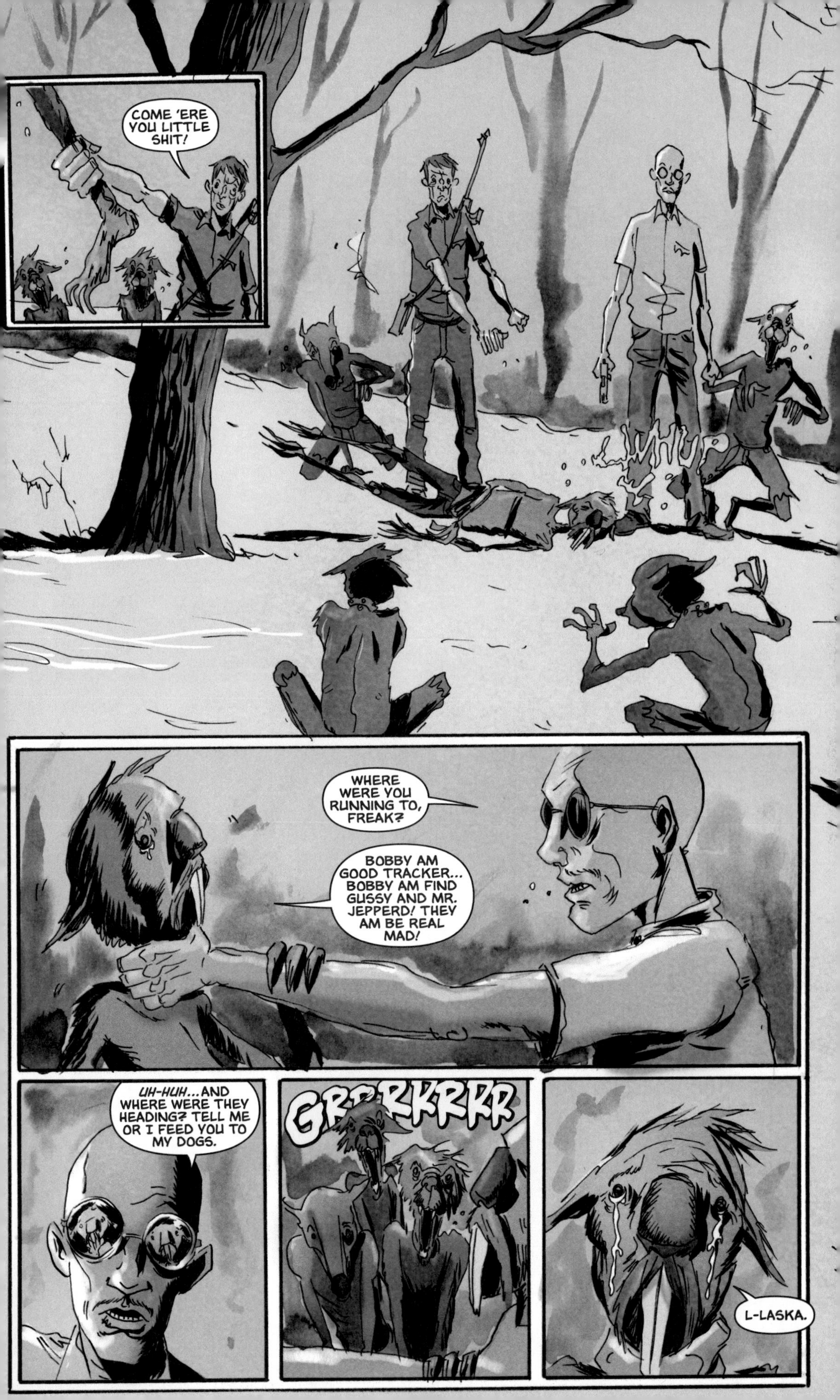
COME 'ERE YOU LITTLE SHIT!
WHUP
WHERE WERE YOU RUNNING TO, FREAK?
BOBBY AM GOOD TRACKER... BOBBY AM FIND GUSSY AND MR. JEPPERD! THEY AM BE REAL MAD!
UH-HUH...AND WHERE WERE THEY HEADING? TELL ME OR I FEED YOU TO MY DOGS.
GRRRKRRR
L-LASKA.

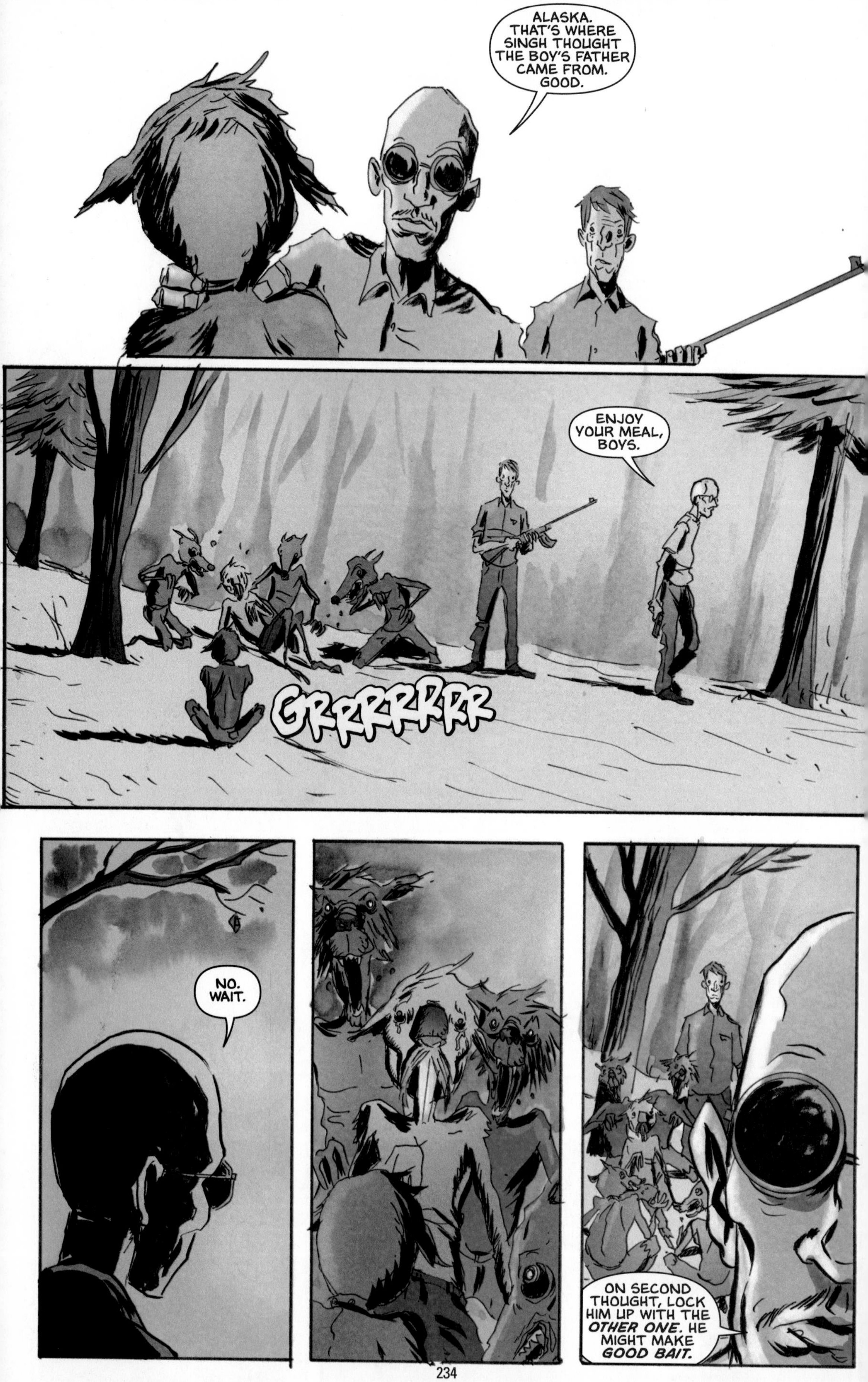

ALASKA. THAT'S WHERE SINGH THOUGHT THE BOY'S FATHER CAME FROM. GOOD.
ENJOY YOUR MEAL, BOYS.
GRRRRRRR
NO. WAIT.
ON SECOND THOUGHT, LOCK HIM UP WITH THE *OTHER ONE*. HE MIGHT MAKE *GOOD BAIT*.

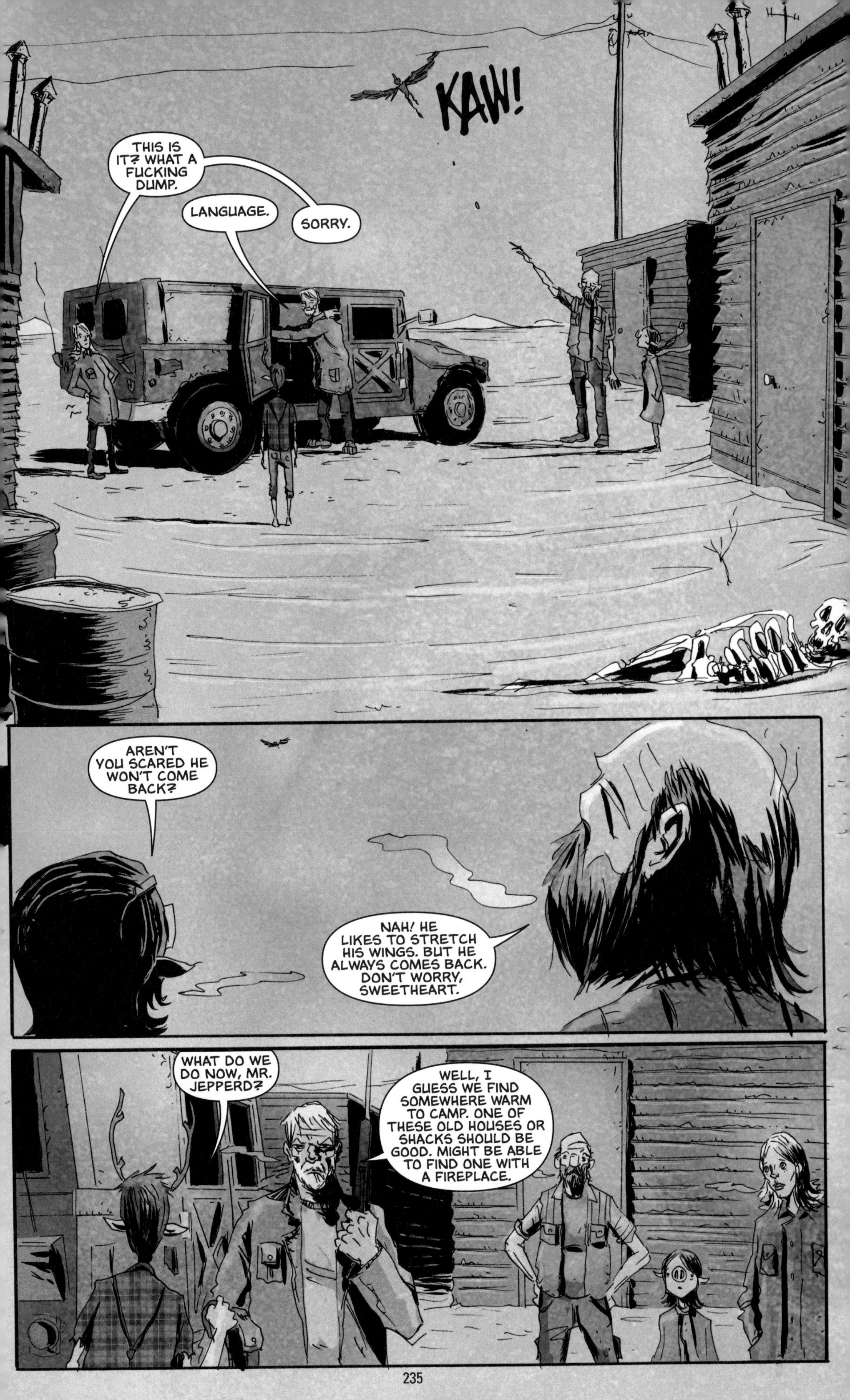
KAW!
THIS IS IT? WHAT A FUCKING DUMP.
LANGUAGE.
SORRY.
AREN'T YOU SCARED HE WON'T COME BACK?
NAH! HE LIKES TO STRETCH HIS WINGS. BUT HE ALWAYS COMES BACK. DON'T WORRY, SWEETHEART.
WHAT DO WE DO NOW, MR. JEPPERD?
WELL, I GUESS WE FIND SOMEWHERE WARM TO CAMP. ONE OF THESE OLD HOUSES OR SHACKS SHOULD BE GOOD. MIGHT BE ABLE TO FIND ONE WITH A FIREPLACE.

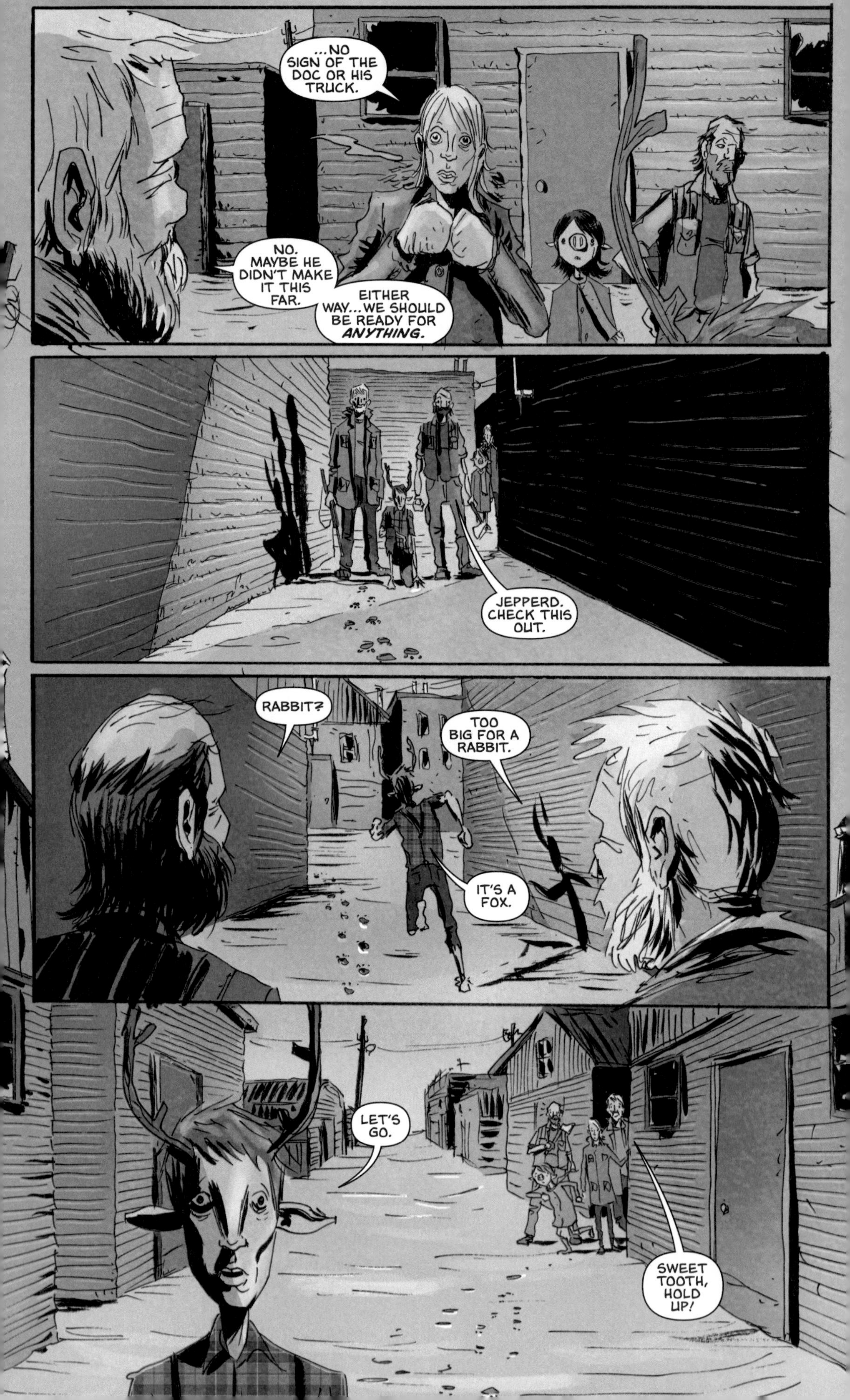
...NO SIGN OF THE DOC OR HIS TRUCK.
NO. MAYBE HE DIDN'T MAKE IT THIS FAR.
EITHER WAY...WE SHOULD BE READY FOR *ANYTHING.*
JEPPERD. CHECK THIS OUT.
RABBIT?
TOO BIG FOR A RABBIT.
IT'S A FOX.
LET'S GO.
SWEET TOOTH, HOLD UP!

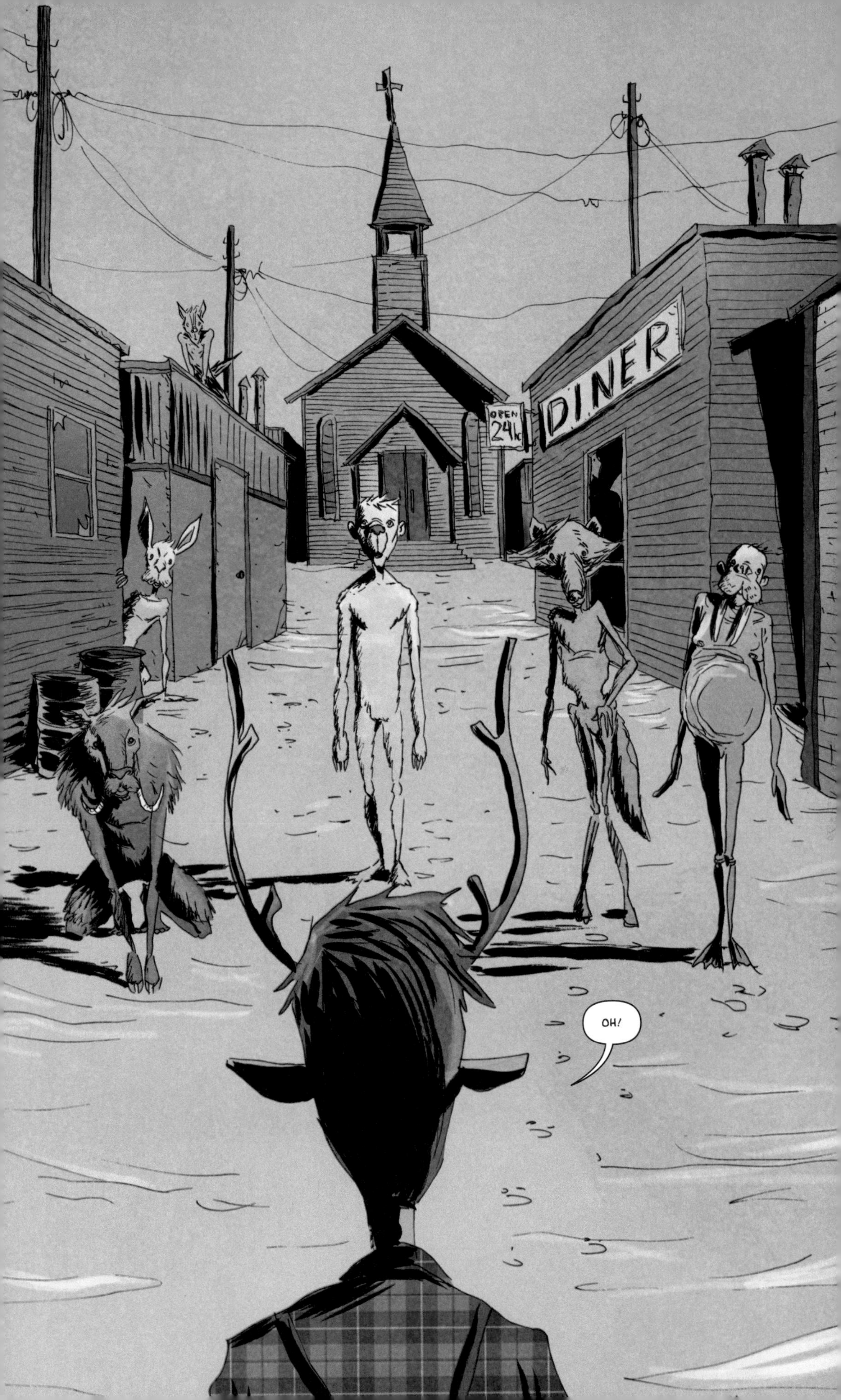
OPEN 24h
DINER
OH!

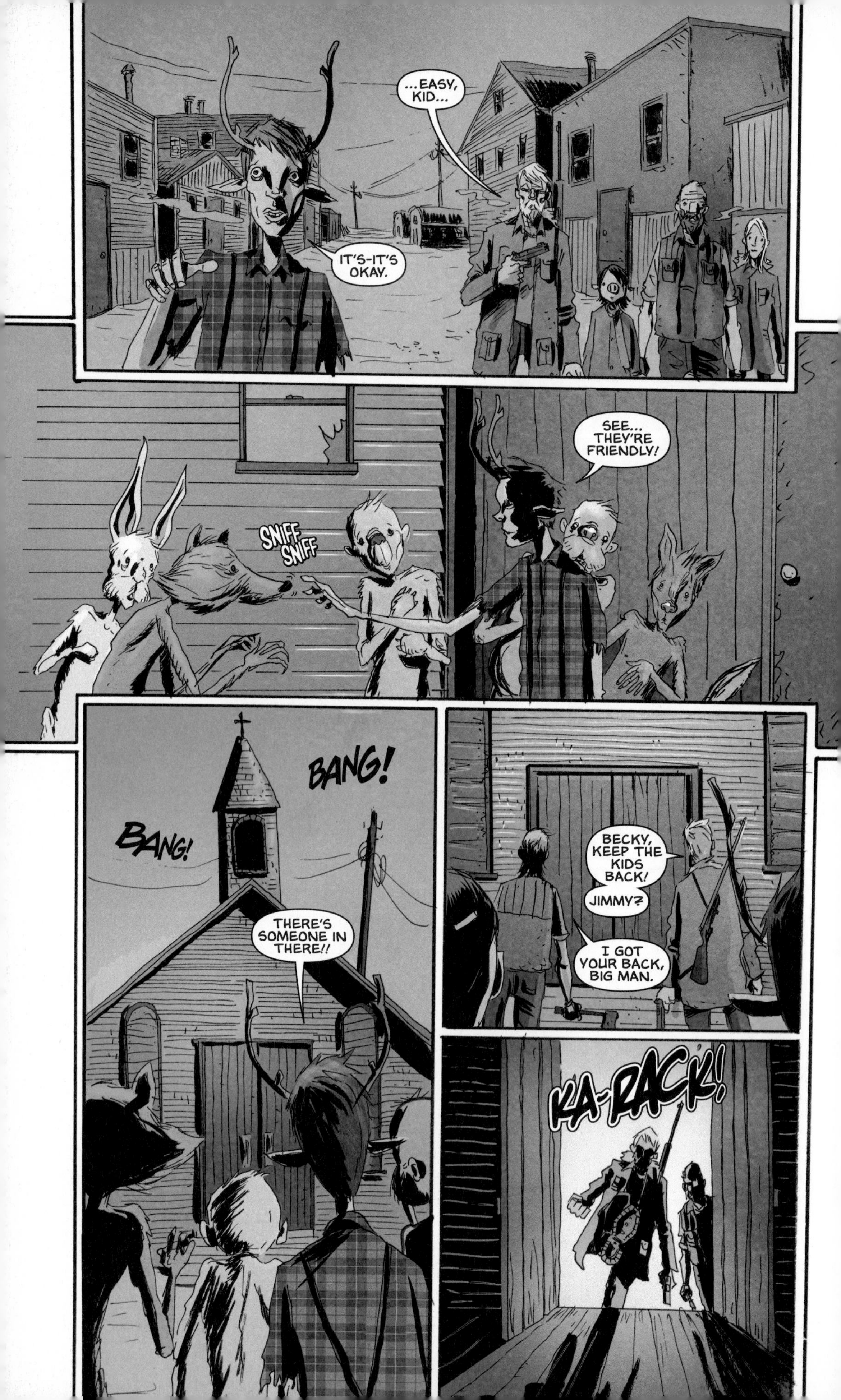

...EASY, KID...
IT'S-IT'S OKAY.
SNIFF SNIFF
SEE... THEY'RE FRIENDLY!
BANG!
BANG!
THERE'S SOMEONE IN THERE!!
BECKY, KEEP THE KIDS BACK!
JIMMY?
I GOT YOUR BACK, BIG MAN.
KA-RACK!

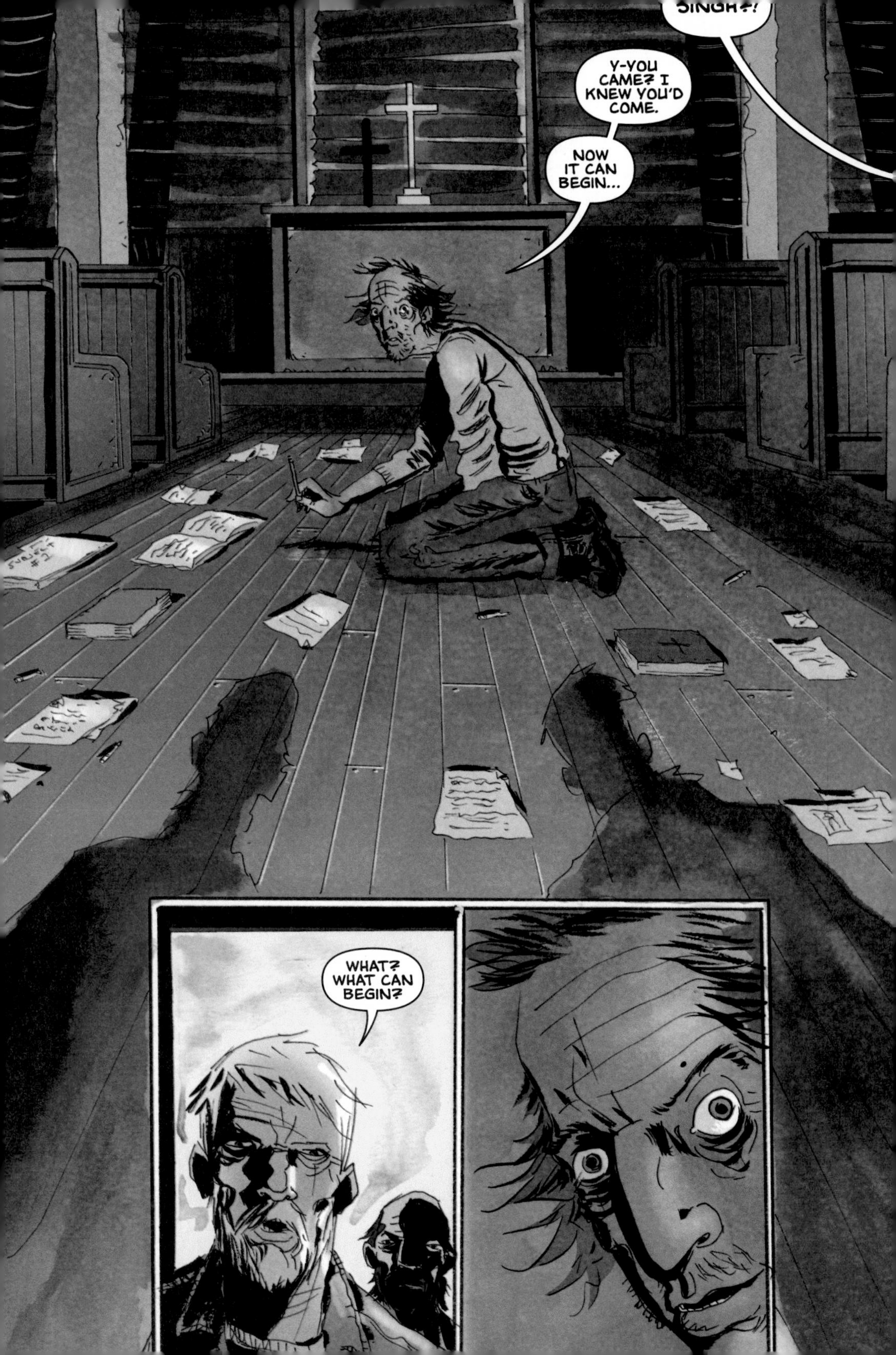
SINGH?!
Y-YOU CAME? I KNEW YOU'D COME.
NOW IT CAN BEGIN...
SUBJECT #2
WHAT? WHAT CAN BEGIN?

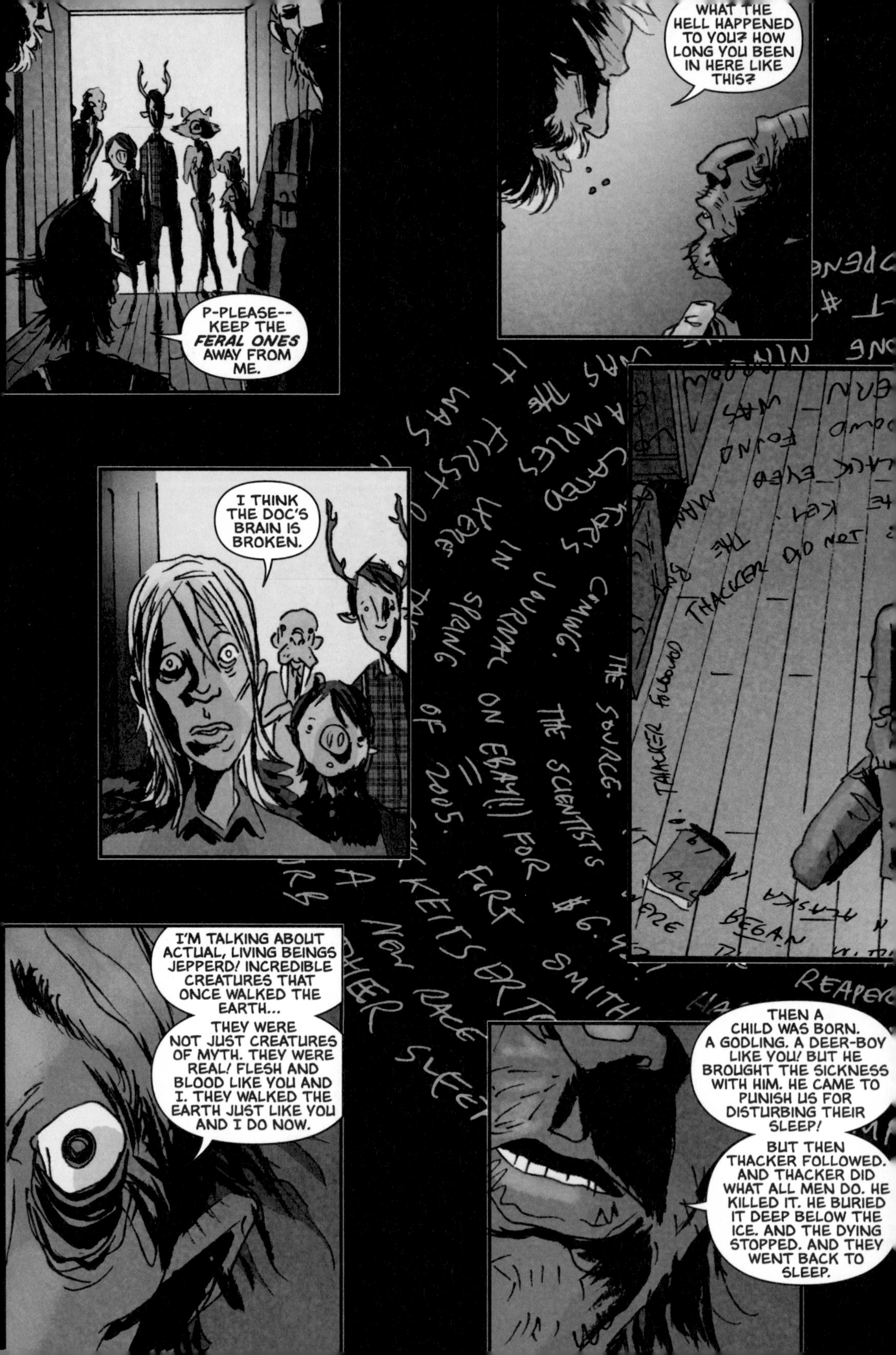

P-PLEASE-- KEEP THE FERAL ONES AWAY FROM ME.
WHAT THE HELL HAPPENED TO YOU? HOW LONG YOU BEEN IN HERE LIKE THIS?
I THINK THE DOC'S BRAIN IS BROKEN.
I'M TALKING ABOUT ACTUAL, LIVING BEINGS JEPPERD! INCREDIBLE CREATURES THAT ONCE WALKED THE EARTH...
THEY WERE NOT JUST CREATURES OF MYTH. THEY WERE REAL! FLESH AND BLOOD LIKE YOU AND I. THEY WALKED THE EARTH JUST LIKE YOU AND I DO NOW.
THEN A CHILD WAS BORN. A GODLING. A DEER-BOY LIKE YOU! BUT HE BROUGHT THE SICKNESS WITH HIM. HE CAME TO PUNISH US FOR DISTURBING THEIR SLEEP!
BUT THEN THACKER FOLLOWED. AND THACKER DID WHAT ALL MEN DO. HE KILLED IT. HE BURIED IT DEEP BELOW THE ICE. AND THE DYING STOPPED. AND THEY WENT BACK TO SLEEP.

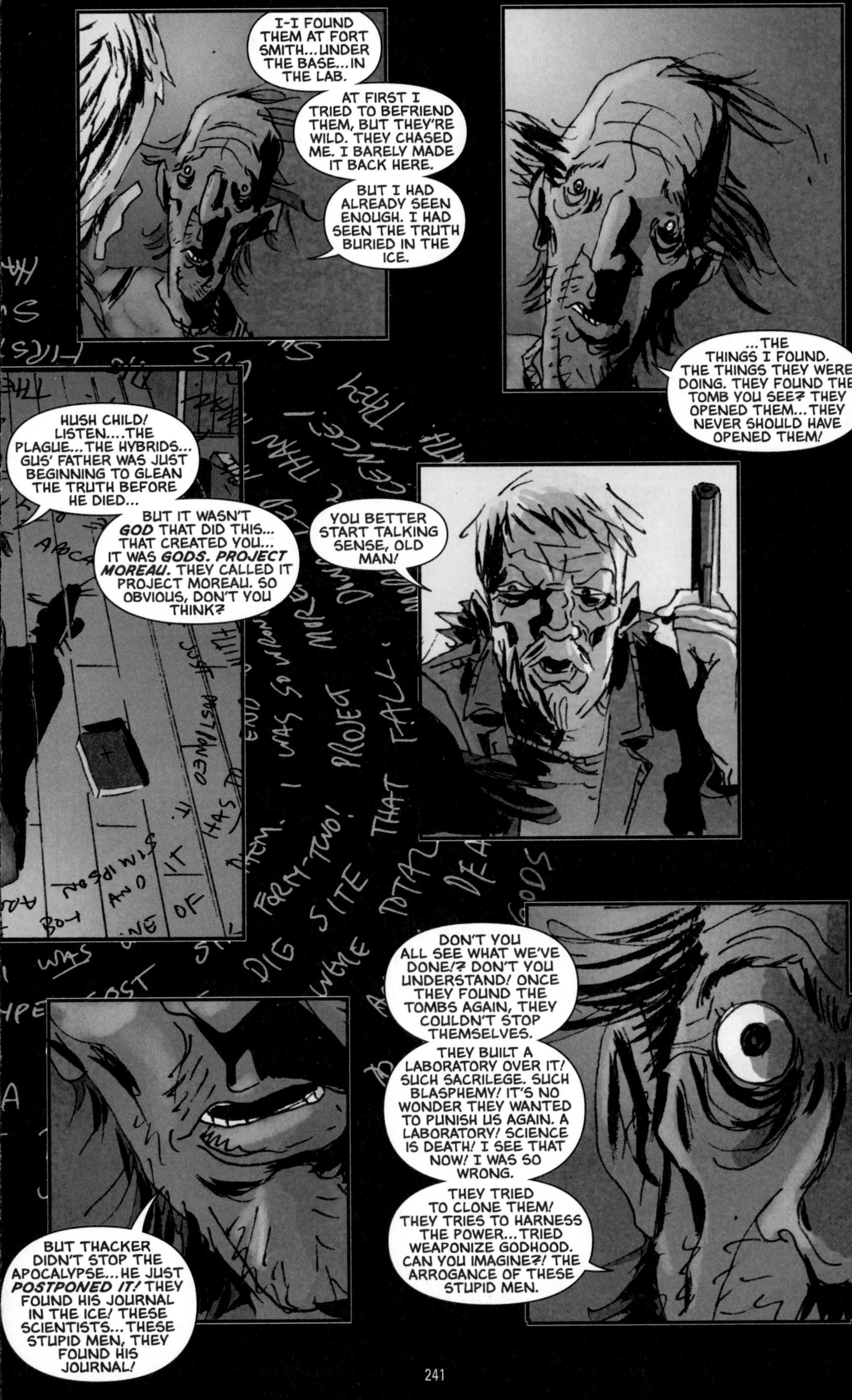

I-I FOUND THEM AT FORT SMITH...UNDER THE BASE...IN THE LAB.
AT FIRST I TRIED TO BEFRIEND THEM, BUT THEY'RE WILD. THEY CHASED ME. I BARELY MADE IT BACK HERE.
BUT I HAD ALREADY SEEN ENOUGH. I HAD SEEN THE TRUTH BURIED IN THE ICE.
...THE THINGS I FOUND. THE THINGS THEY WERE DOING. THEY FOUND THE TOMB YOU SEE? THEY OPENED THEM...THEY NEVER SHOULD HAVE OPENED THEM!
HUSH CHILD! LISTEN....THE PLAGUE...THE HYBRIDS... GUS' FATHER WAS JUST BEGINNING TO GLEAN THE TRUTH BEFORE HE DIED...
BUT IT WASN'T ***GOD*** THAT DID THIS... THAT CREATED YOU... IT WAS ***GODS. PROJECT MOREAU.*** THEY CALLED IT PROJECT MOREAU. SO OBVIOUS, DON'T YOU THINK?
YOU BETTER START TALKING SENSE, OLD MAN!
BUT THACKER DIDN'T STOP THE APOCALYPSE...HE JUST ***POSTPONED IT!*** THEY FOUND HIS JOURNAL IN THE ICE! THESE SCIENTISTS...THESE STUPID MEN, THEY FOUND HIS JOURNAL!
DON'T YOU ALL SEE WHAT WE'VE DONE!? DON'T YOU UNDERSTAND! ONCE THEY FOUND THE TOMBS AGAIN, THEY COULDN'T STOP THEMSELVES.
THEY BUILT A LABORATORY OVER IT! SUCH SACRILEGE. SUCH BLASPHEMY! IT'S NO WONDER THEY WANTED TO PUNISH US AGAIN. A LABORATORY! SCIENCE IS DEATH! I SEE THAT NOW! I WAS SO WRONG.
THEY TRIED TO CLONE THEM! THEY TRIES TO HARNESS THE POWER...TRIED WEAPONIZE GODHOOD. CAN YOU IMAGINE?! THE ARROGANCE OF THESE STUPID MEN.

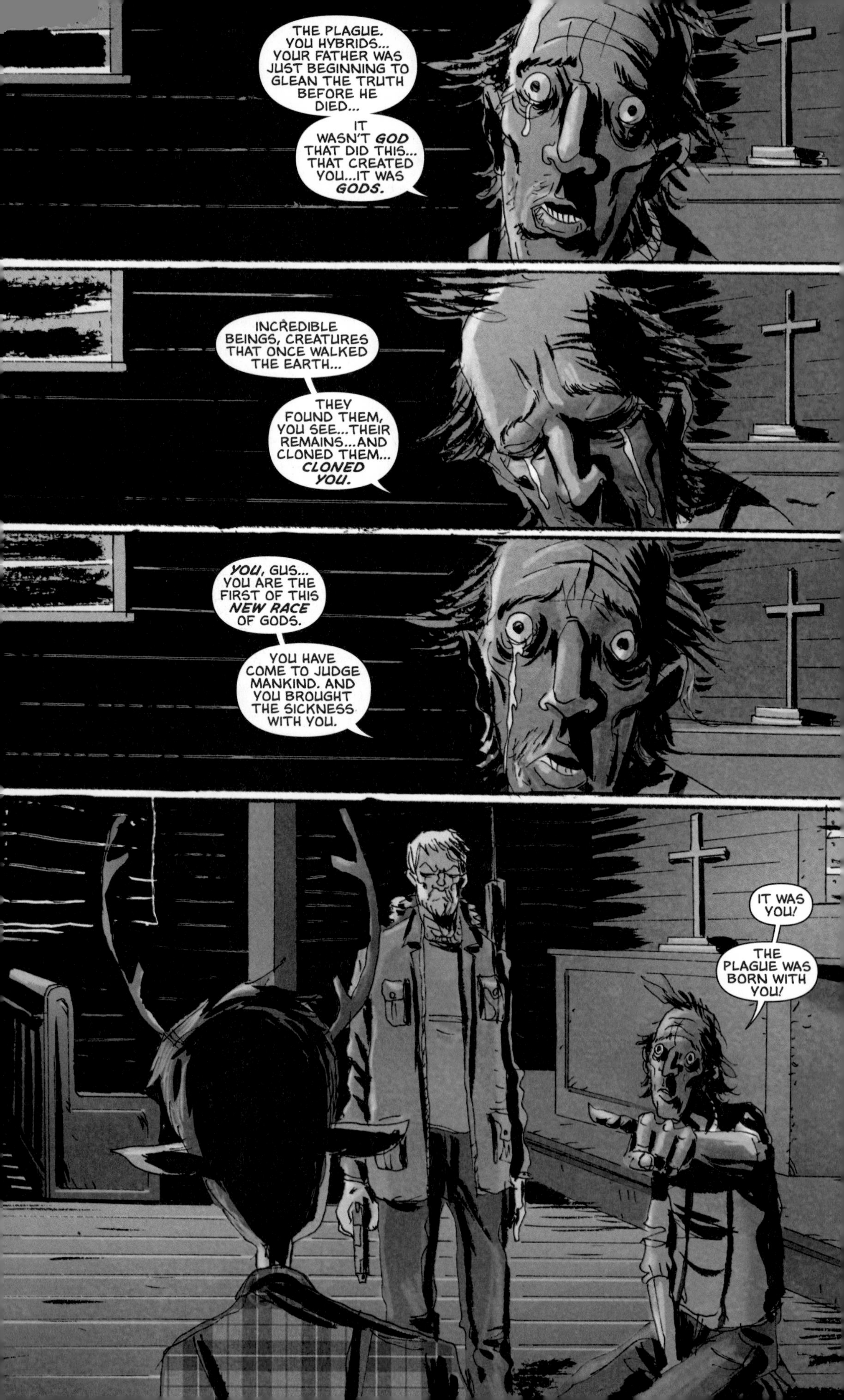
THE PLAGUE. YOU HYBRIDS... YOUR FATHER WAS JUST BEGINNING TO GLEAN THE TRUTH BEFORE HE DIED...
IT WASN'T GOD THAT DID THIS... THAT CREATED YOU...IT WAS GODS.
INCREDIBLE BEINGS, CREATURES THAT ONCE WALKED THE EARTH...
THEY FOUND THEM, YOU SEE...THEIR REMAINS...AND CLONED THEM... CLONED YOU.
YOU, GUS... YOU ARE THE FIRST OF THIS NEW RACE OF GODS.
YOU HAVE COME TO JUDGE MANKIND. AND YOU BROUGHT THE SICKNESS WITH YOU.
IT WAS YOU!
THE PLAGUE WAS BORN WITH YOU!

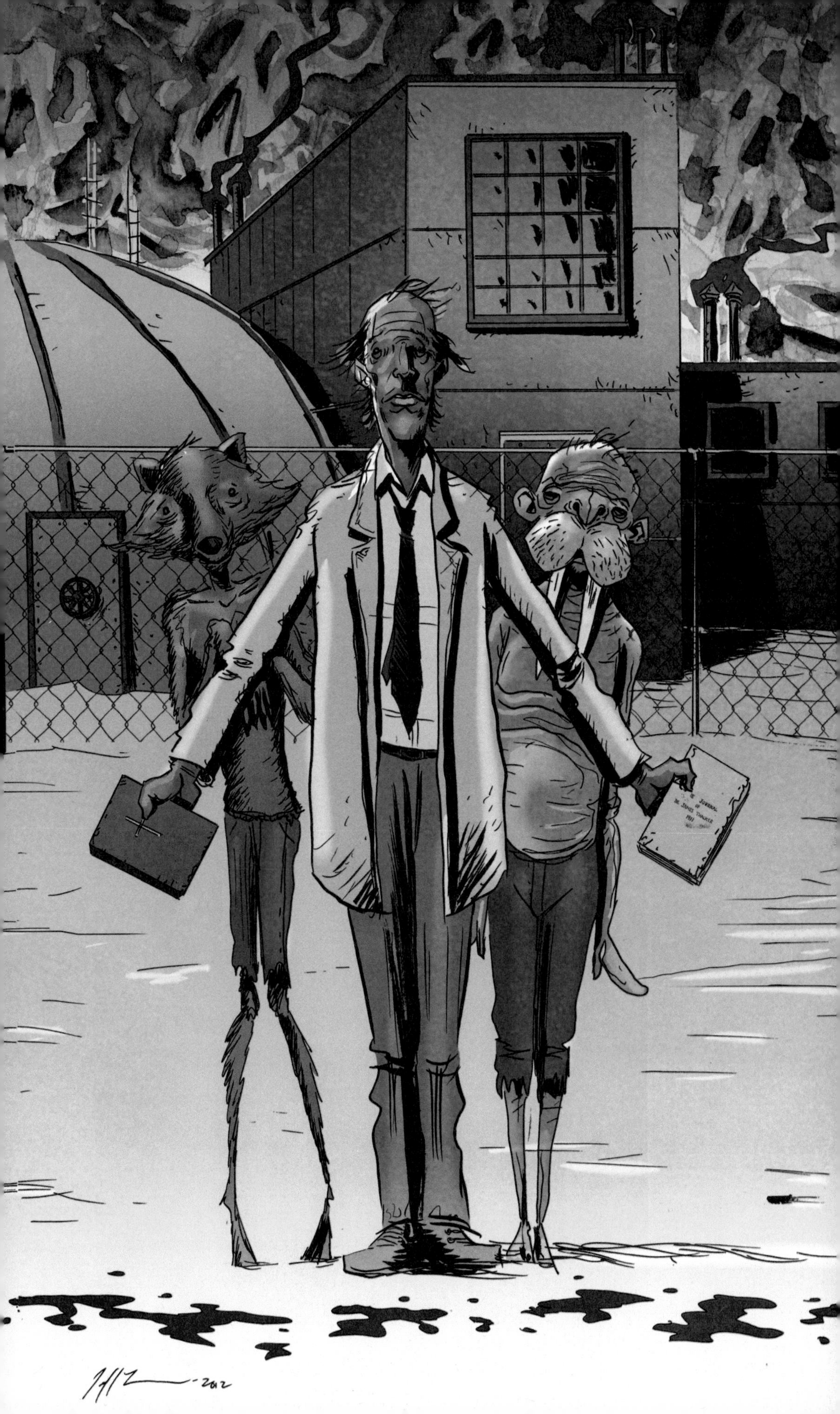
JOURNAL
OF
DR. JAMES THACKER

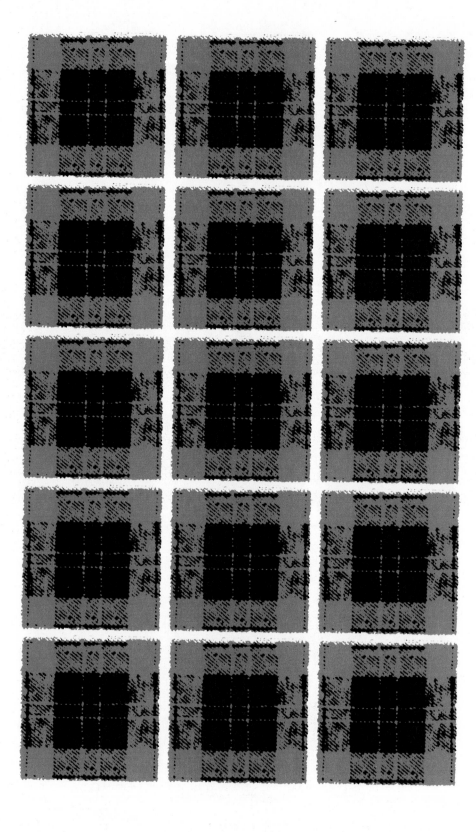

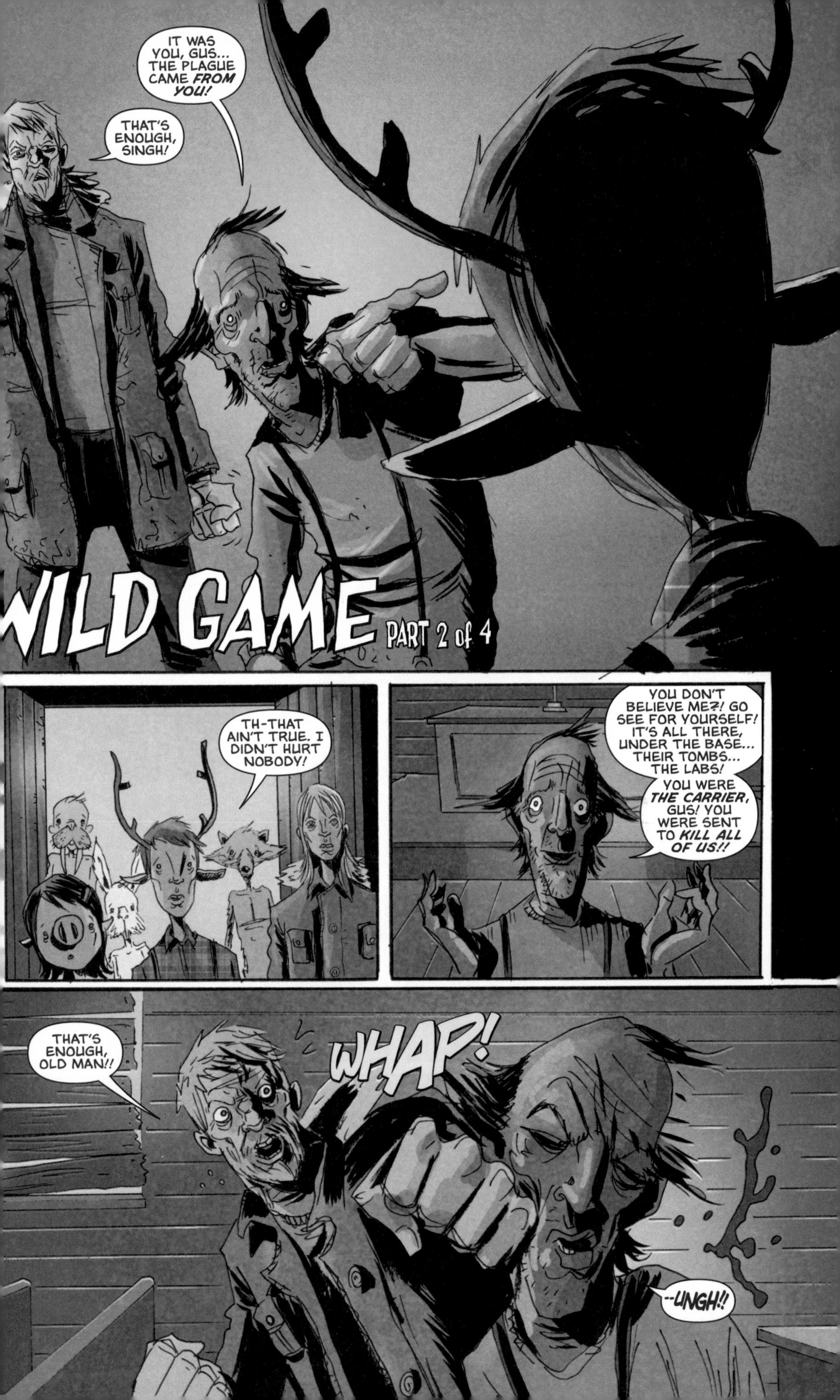
IT WAS YOU, GUS... THE PLAGUE CAME FROM YOU!
THAT'S ENOUGH, SINGH!
WILD GAME PART 2 of 4
TH-THAT AIN'T TRUE. I DIDN'T HURT NOBODY!
YOU DON'T BELIEVE ME?! GO SEE FOR YOURSELF! IT'S ALL THERE, UNDER THE BASE... THEIR TOMBS... THE LABS!
YOU WERE THE CARRIER, GUS! YOU WERE SENT TO KILL ALL OF US!!
THAT'S ENOUGH, OLD MAN!!
WHAP!
--UNGH!!

YOU'RE LUCKY I DON'T KILL YOU.

--WOULDN'T MATTER.

GUS?

WE'RE TOO LATE!! TOO LATE!!

DON'T TO LISTEN TO HIM, GUS.

SHE'S RIGHT, KID. HE'S LOST IT.

NO. I WANT TO SEE IT. I WANT TO SEE WHERE I CAME FROM.

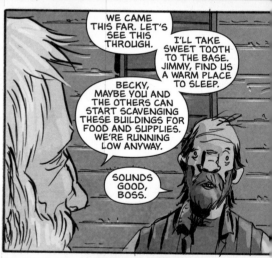

WE CAME THIS FAR. LET'S SEE THIS THROUGH.

I'LL TAKE SWEET TOOTH TO THE BASE. JIMMY, FIND US A WARM PLACE TO SLEEP.

BECKY, MAYBE YOU AND THE OTHERS CAN START SCAVENGING THESE BUILDINGS FOR FOOD AND SUPPLIES. WE'RE RUNNING LOW ANYWAY.

SOUNDS GOOD, BOSS.

UM... WHAT ABOUT THESE GUYS?

THEY SEEM TO HAVE TAKEN A LIKING TO YA, DARLIN'.

THEY THINK YER THEIR MOMMA!

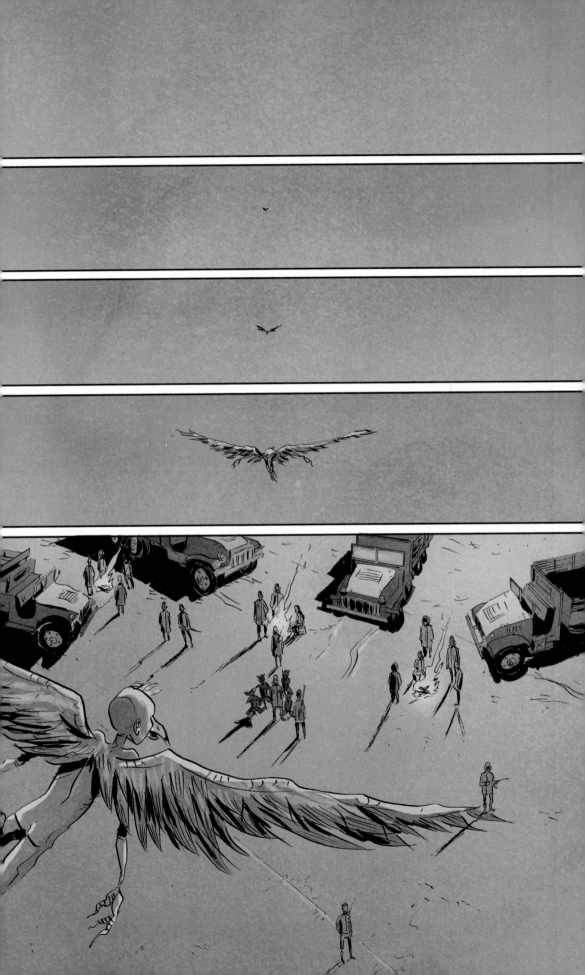

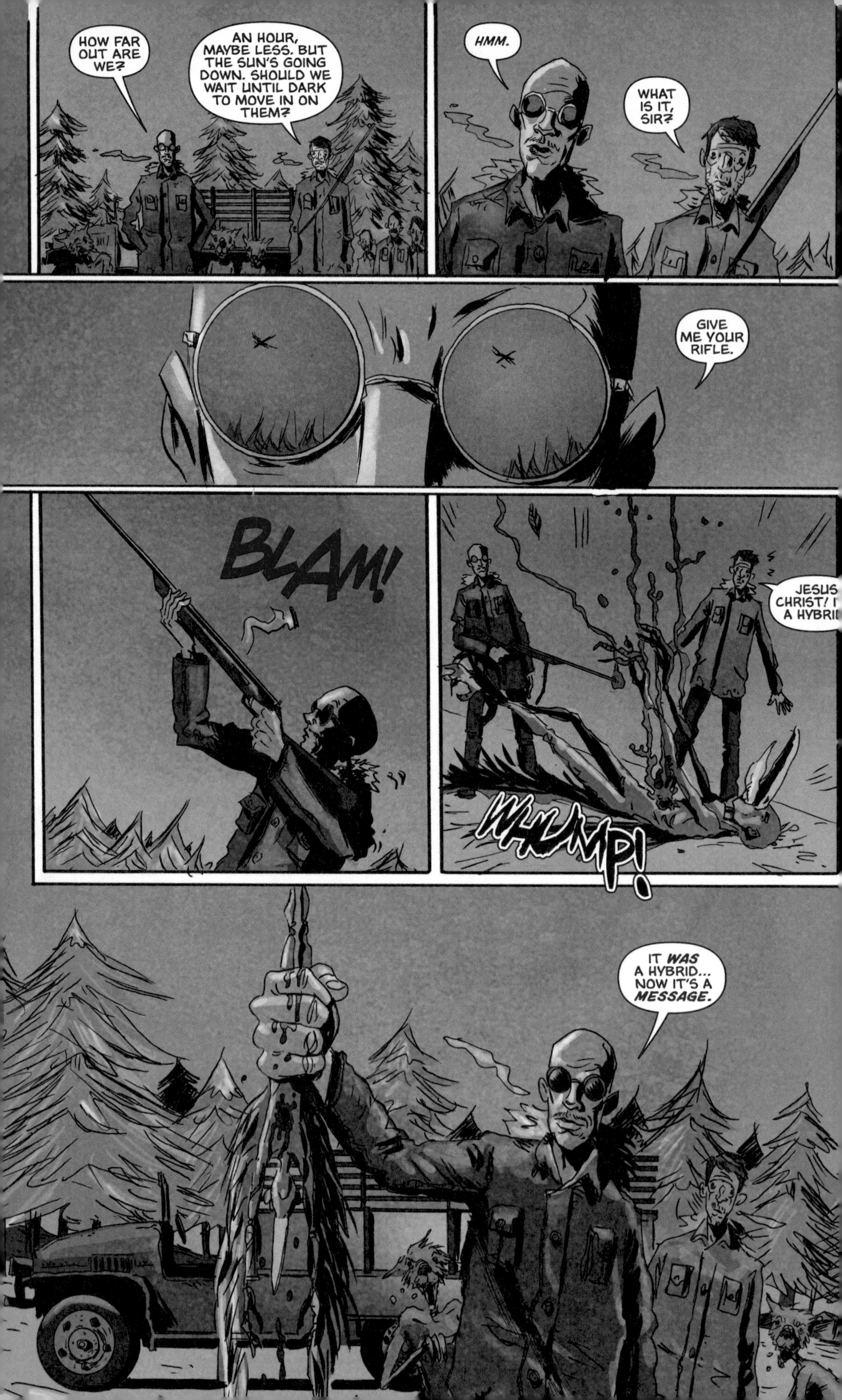
HOW FAR OUT ARE WE?
AN HOUR, MAYBE LESS. BUT THE SUN'S GOING DOWN. SHOULD WE WAIT UNTIL DARK TO MOVE IN ON THEM?
HMM.
WHAT IS IT, SIR?
GIVE ME YOUR RIFLE.
BLAM!
JESUS CHRIST! I A HYBRI
WHUMP!
IT WAS A HYBRID... NOW IT'S A MESSAGE.

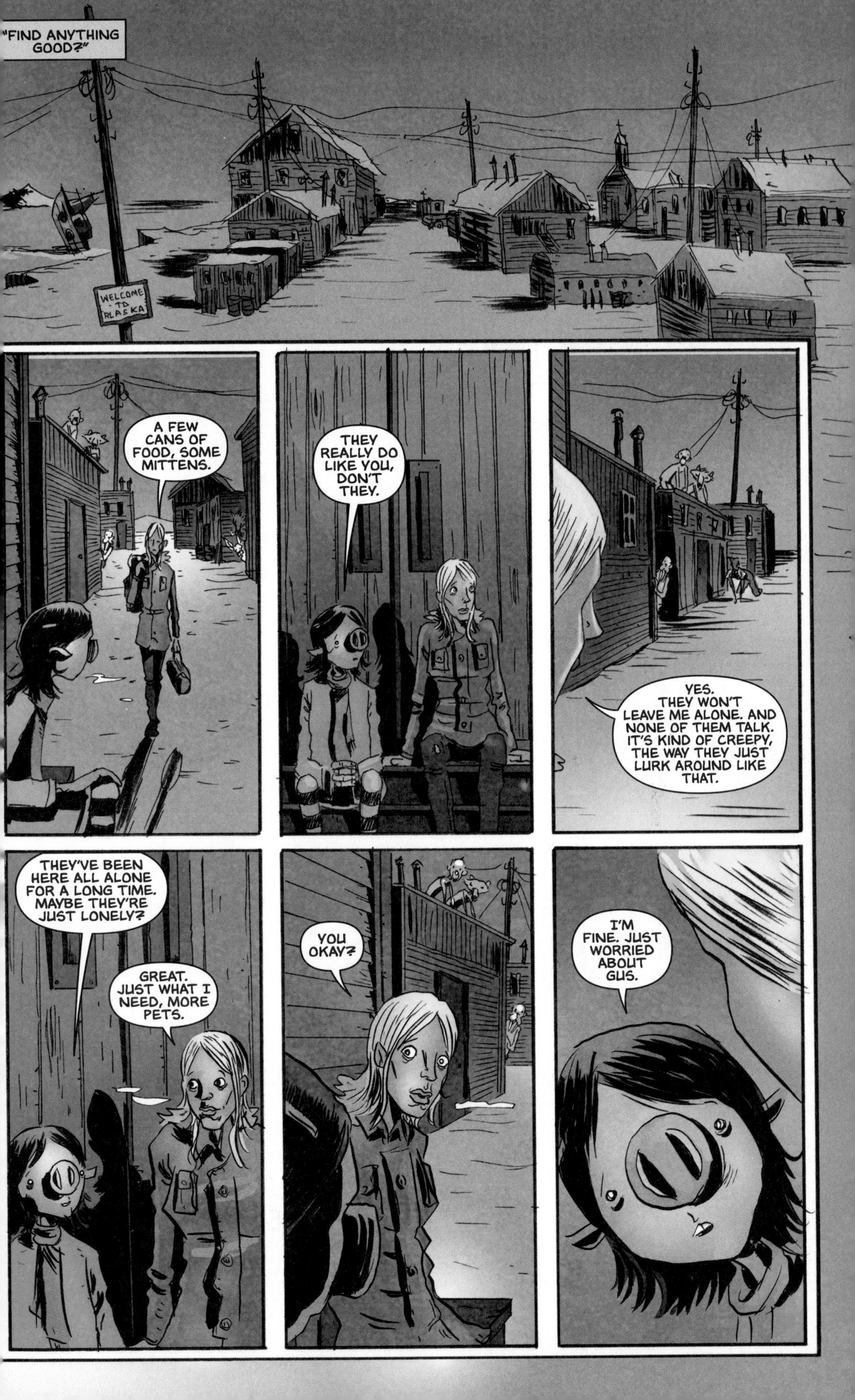
"FIND ANYTHING GOOD?"
WELCOME TO ALASKA
A FEW CANS OF FOOD, SOME MITTENS.
THEY REALLY DO LIKE YOU, DON'T THEY.
YES. THEY WON'T LEAVE ME ALONE. AND NONE OF THEM TALK. IT'S KIND OF CREEPY, THE WAY THEY JUST LURK AROUND LIKE THAT.
THEY'VE BEEN HERE ALL ALONE FOR A LONG TIME. MAYBE THEY'RE JUST LONELY?
GREAT. JUST WHAT I NEED, MORE PETS.
YOU OKAY?
I'M FINE. JUST WORRIED ABOUT GUS.

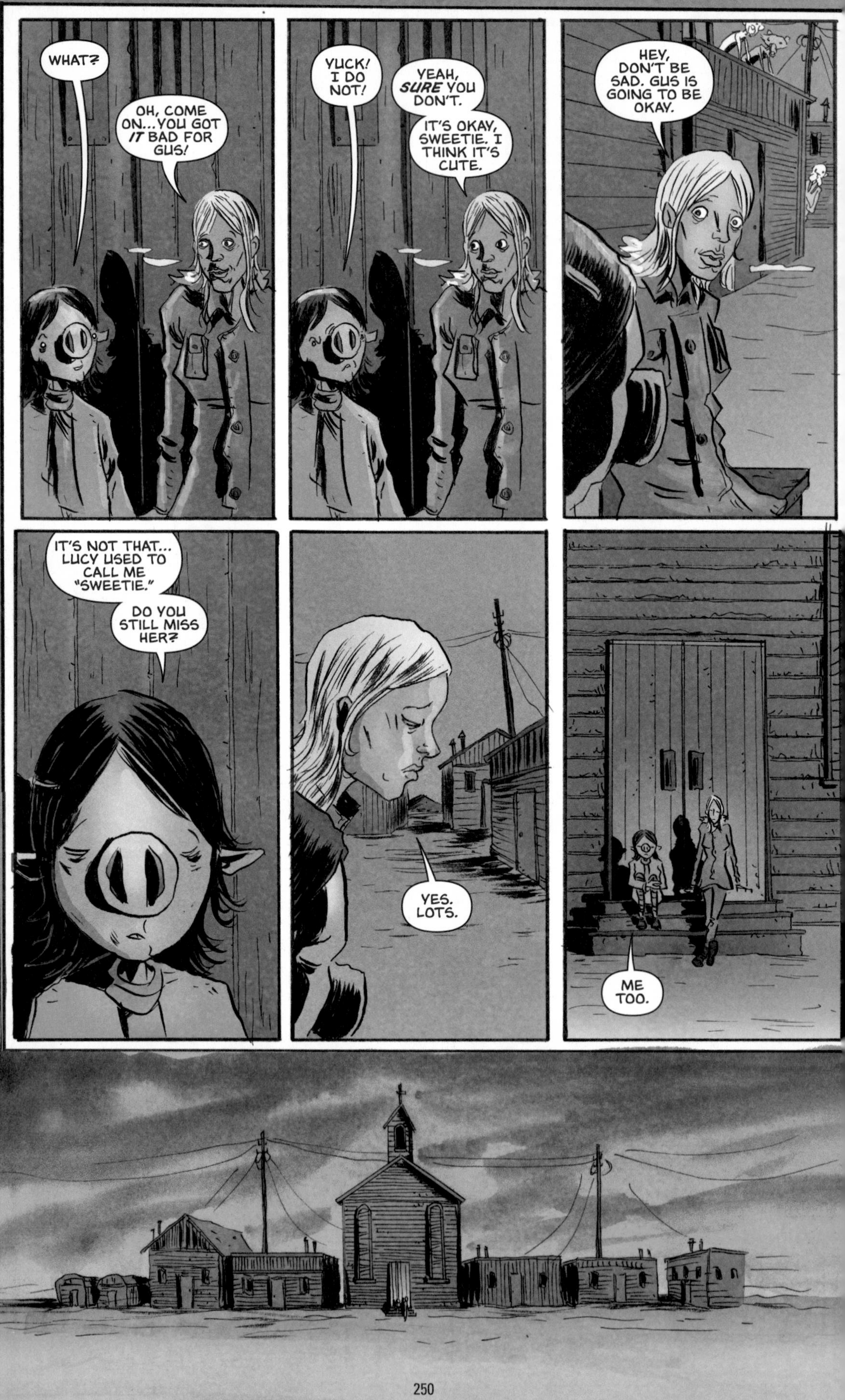
WHAT?
OH, COME ON...YOU GOT IT BAD FOR GUS!
YUCK! I DO NOT!
YEAH, SURE YOU DON'T.
IT'S OKAY, SWEETIE. I THINK IT'S CUTE.
HEY, DON'T BE SAD. GUS IS GOING TO BE OKAY.
IT'S NOT THAT... LUCY USED TO CALL ME "SWEETIE."
DO YOU STILL MISS HER?
YES. LOTS.
ME TOO.

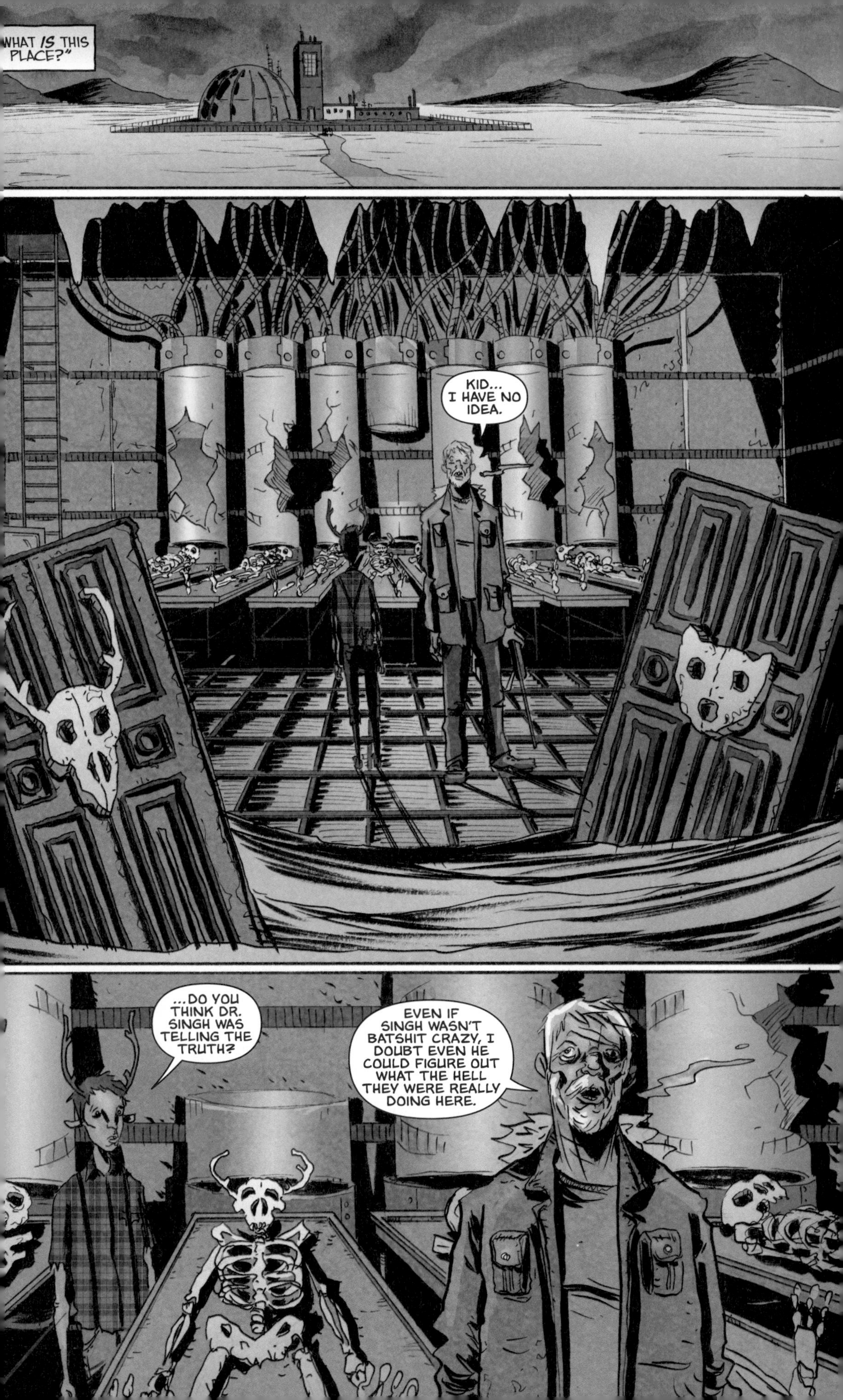
"WHAT IS THIS PLACE?"
KID... I HAVE NO IDEA.
...DO YOU THINK DR. SINGH WAS TELLING THE TRUTH?
EVEN IF SINGH WASN'T BATSHIT CRAZY, I DOUBT EVEN HE COULD FIGURE OUT WHAT THE HELL THEY WERE REALLY DOING HERE.

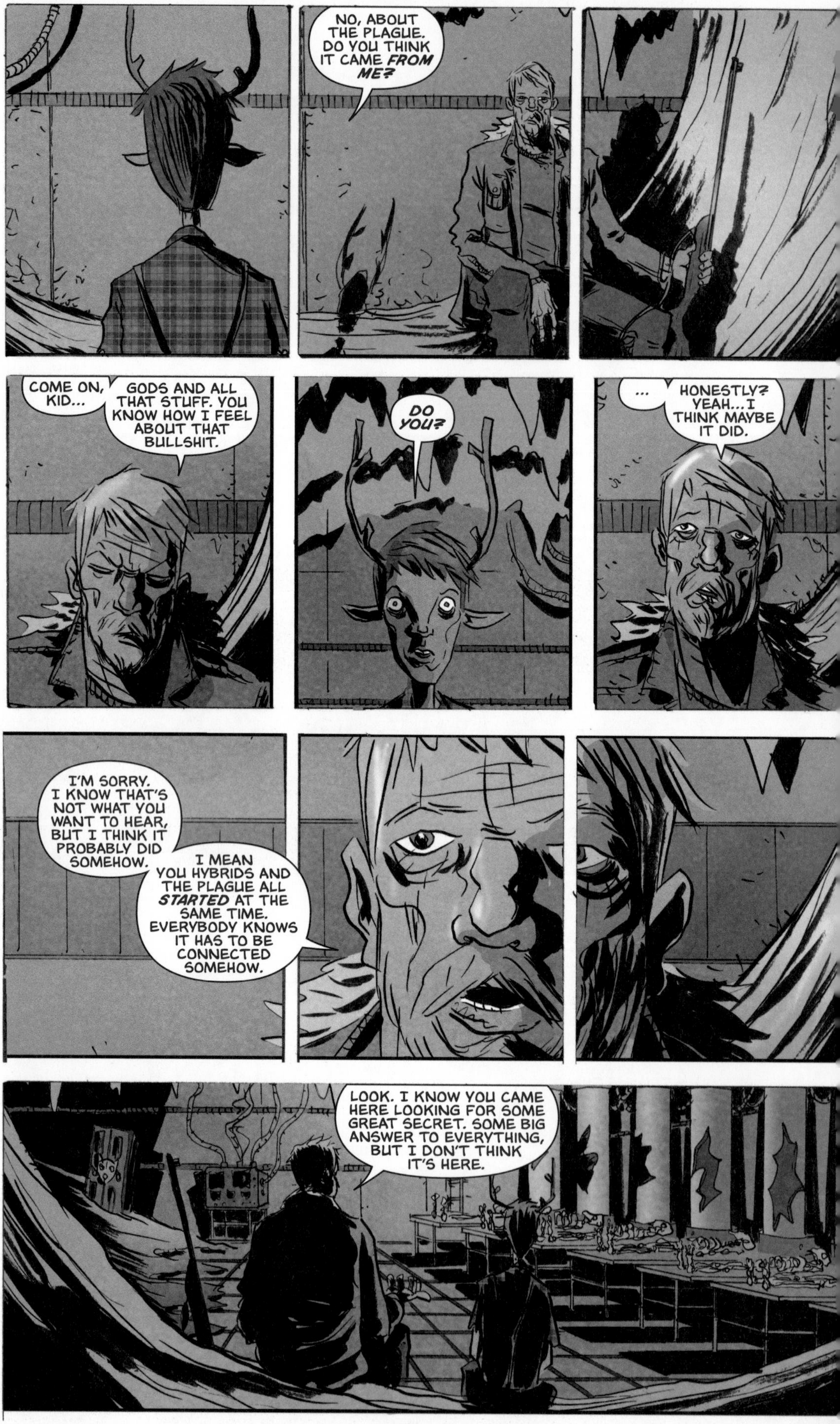
NO, ABOUT THE PLAGUE. DO YOU THINK IT CAME *FROM ME?*
COME ON, KID...
GODS AND ALL THAT STUFF. YOU KNOW HOW I FEEL ABOUT THAT BULLSHIT.
DO YOU?
...
HONESTLY? YEAH...I THINK MAYBE IT DID.
I'M SORRY. I KNOW THAT'S NOT WHAT YOU WANT TO HEAR, BUT I THINK IT PROBABLY DID SOMEHOW.
I MEAN YOU HYBRIDS AND THE PLAGUE ALL *STARTED* AT THE SAME TIME. EVERYBODY KNOWS IT HAS TO BE CONNECTED SOMEHOW.
LOOK. I KNOW YOU CAME HERE LOOKING FOR SOME GREAT SECRET. SOME BIG ANSWER TO EVERYTHING, BUT I DON'T THINK IT'S HERE.

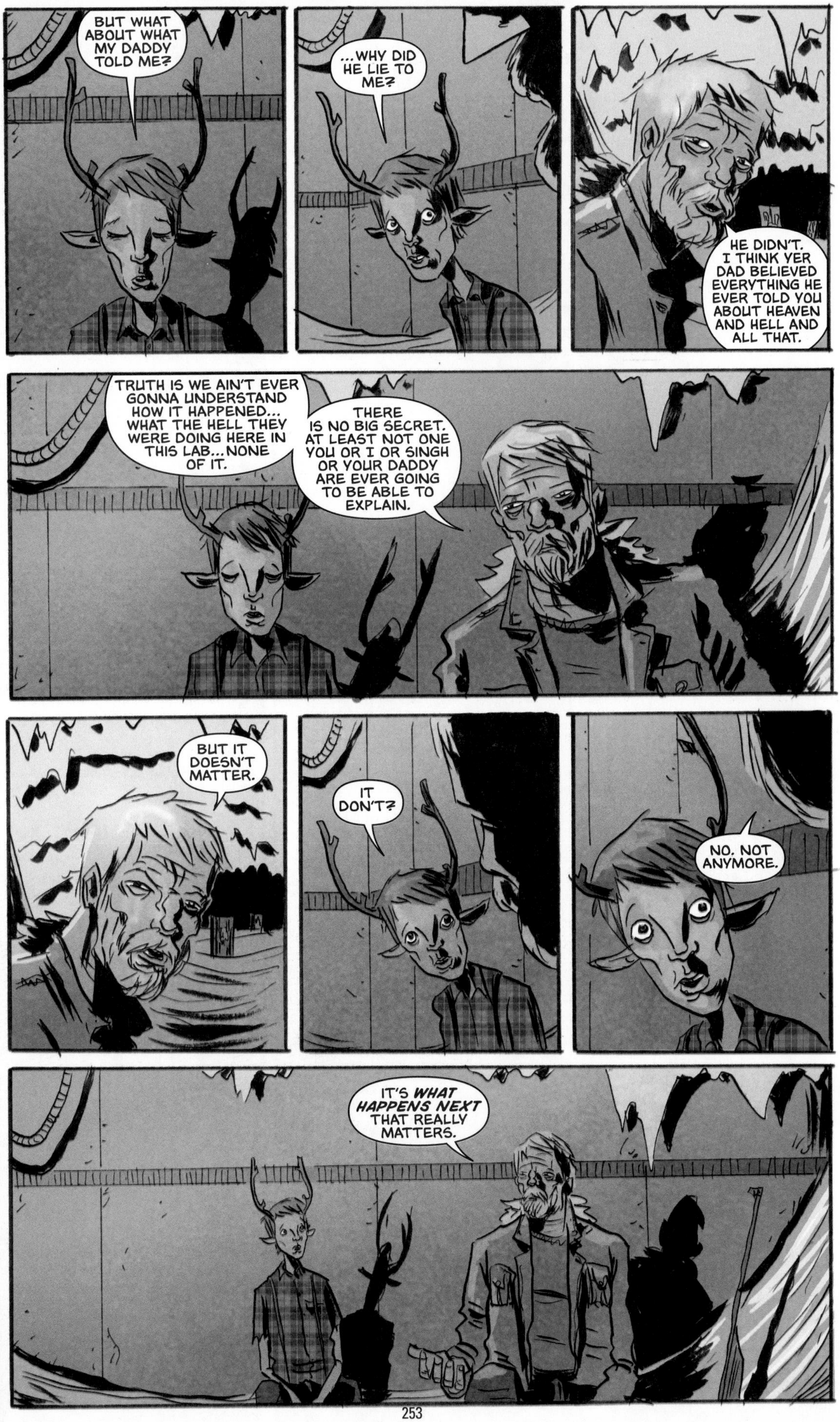
BUT WHAT ABOUT WHAT MY DADDY TOLD ME?
...WHY DID HE LIE TO ME?
HE DIDN'T. I THINK YER DAD BELIEVED EVERYTHING HE EVER TOLD YOU ABOUT HEAVEN AND HELL AND ALL THAT.
TRUTH IS WE AIN'T EVER GONNA UNDERSTAND HOW IT HAPPENED... WHAT THE HELL THEY WERE DOING HERE IN THIS LAB...NONE OF IT.
THERE IS NO BIG SECRET. AT LEAST NOT ONE YOU OR I OR SINGH OR YOUR DADDY ARE EVER GOING TO BE ABLE TO EXPLAIN.
BUT IT DOESN'T MATTER.
IT DON'T?
NO. NOT ANYMORE.
IT'S *WHAT HAPPENS NEXT* THAT REALLY MATTERS.

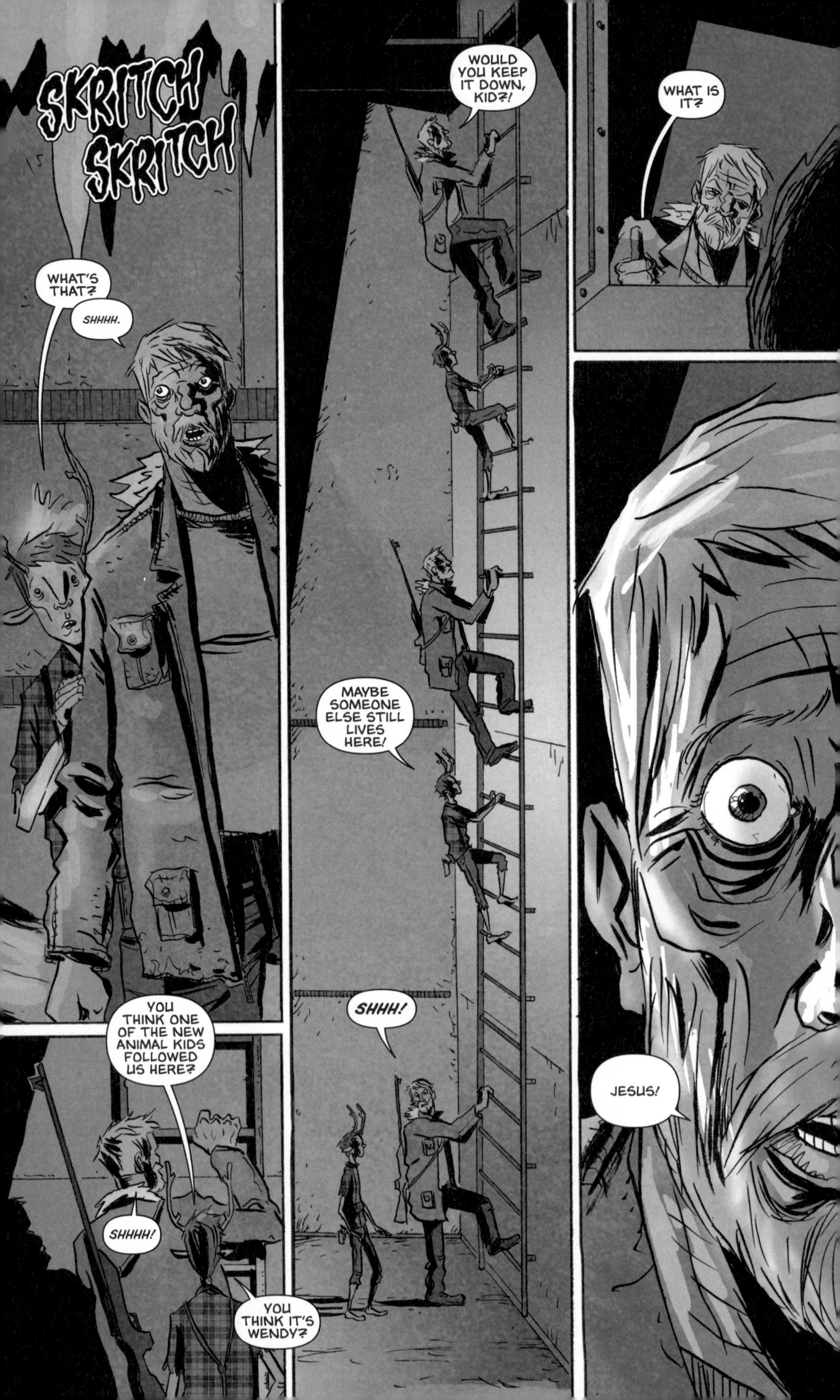

SKRITCH SKRITCH
WHAT'S THAT?
SHHHH.
YOU THINK ONE OF THE NEW ANIMAL KIDS FOLLOWED US HERE?
SHHHH!
YOU THINK IT'S WENDY?
WOULD YOU KEEP IT DOWN, KID?!
MAYBE SOMEONE ELSE STILL LIVES HERE!
SHHH!
WHAT IS IT?
JESUS!

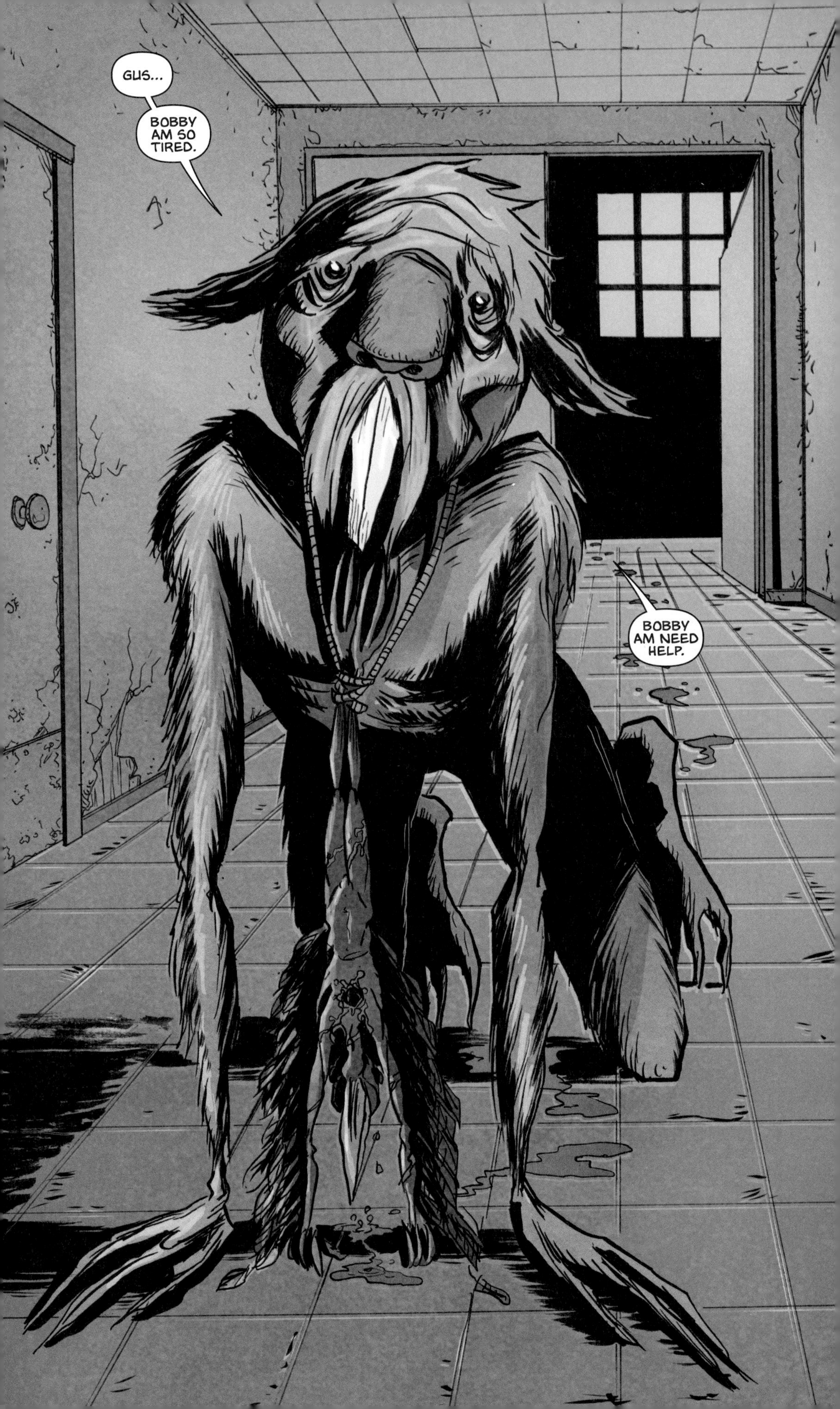
GUS...
BOBBY AM SO TIRED.
BOBBY AM NEED HELP.

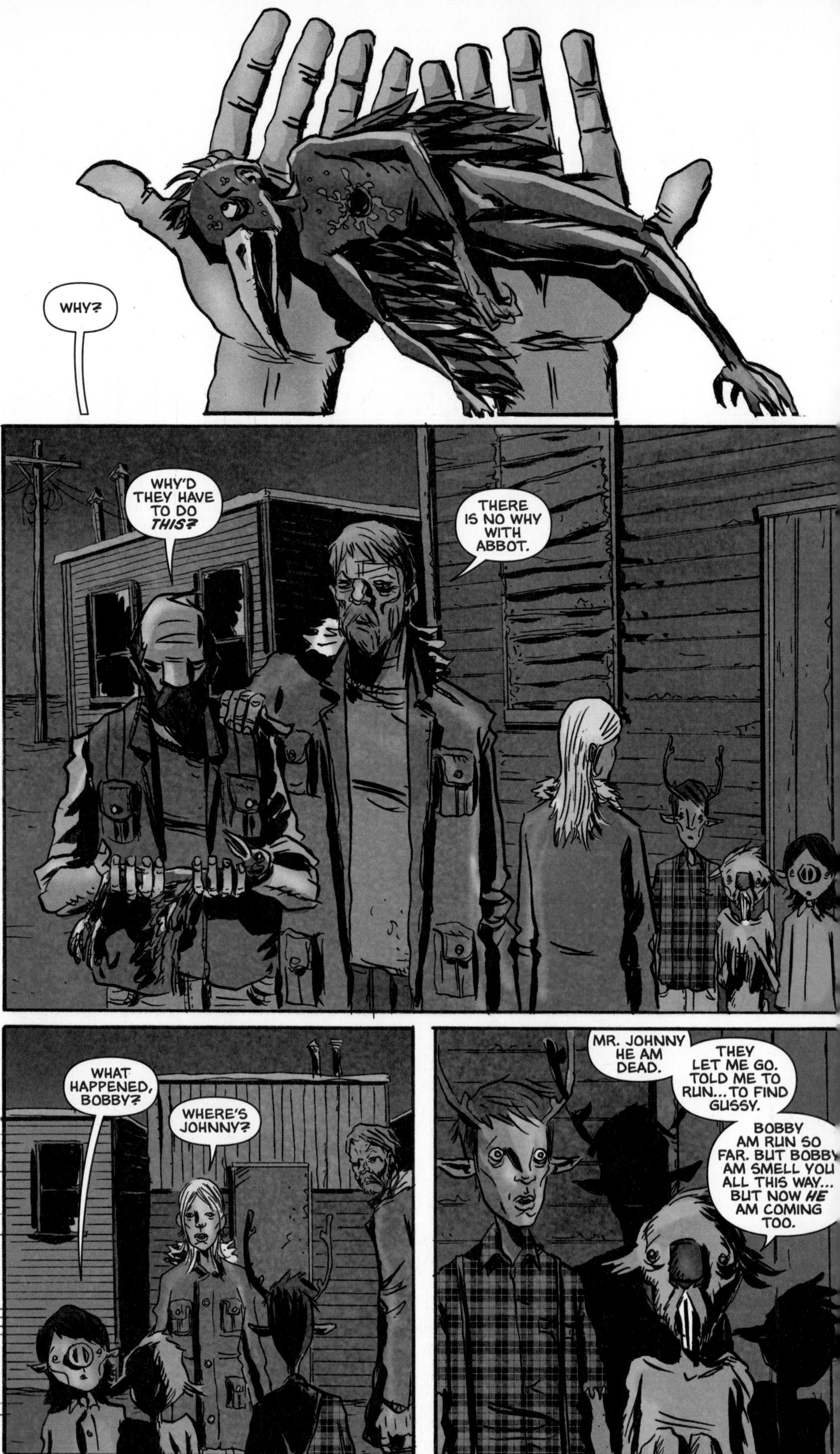
WHY?
WHY'D THEY HAVE TO DO *THIS?*
THERE IS NO WHY WITH ABBOT.
WHAT HAPPENED, BOBBY?
WHERE'S JOHNNY?
MR. JOHNNY HE AM DEAD.
THEY LET ME GO. TOLD ME TO RUN...TO FIND GUSSY.
BOBBY AM RUN SO FAR. BUT BOBBY AM SMELL YOU ALL THIS WAY... BUT NOW *HE* AM COMING TOO.

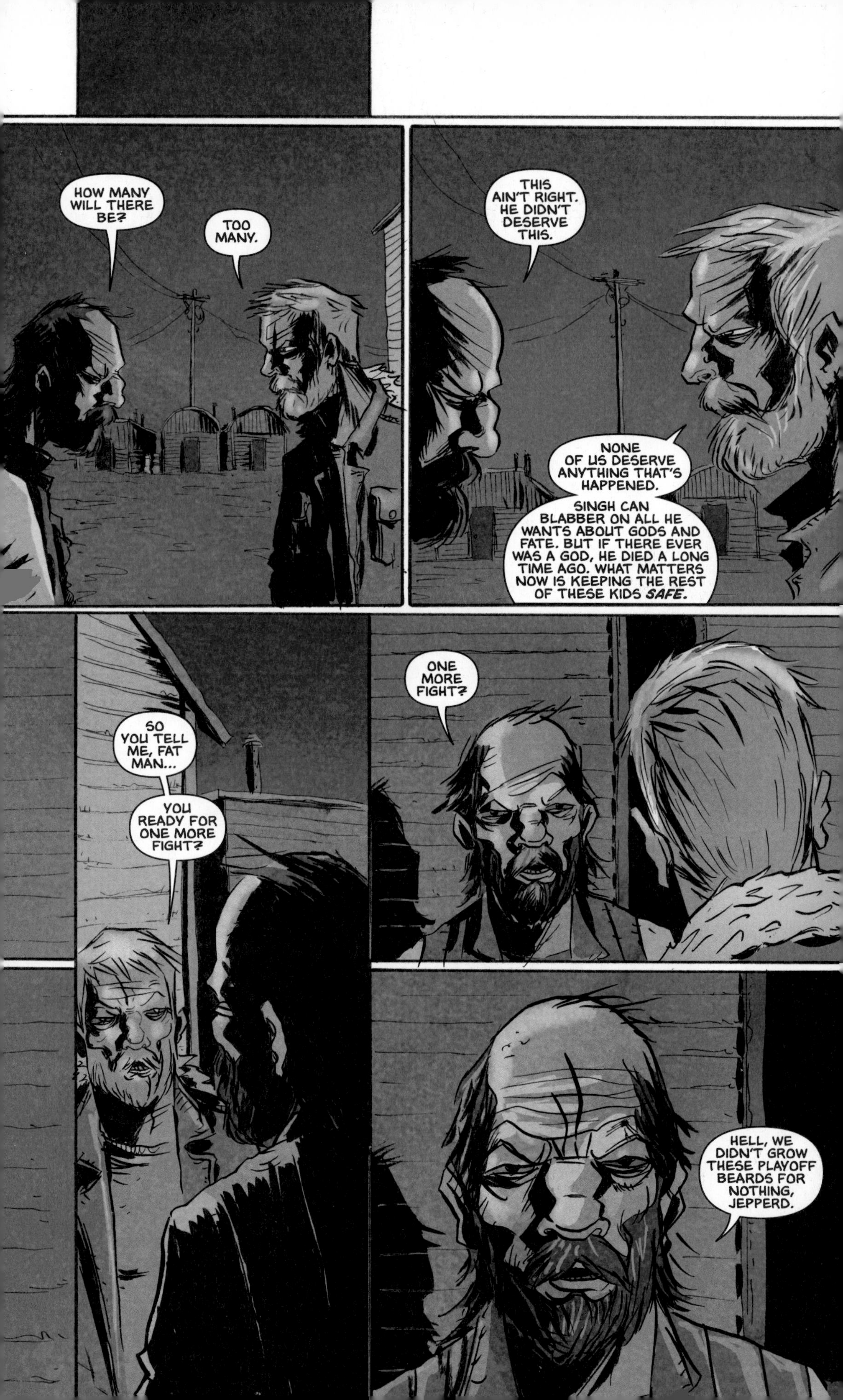
HOW MANY WILL THERE BE?
TOO MANY.
THIS AIN'T RIGHT. HE DIDN'T DESERVE THIS.
NONE OF US DESERVE ANYTHING THAT'S HAPPENED.
SINGH CAN BLABBER ON ALL HE WANTS ABOUT GODS AND FATE. BUT IF THERE EVER WAS A GOD, HE DIED A LONG TIME AGO. WHAT MATTERS NOW IS KEEPING THE REST OF THESE KIDS *SAFE.*
SO YOU TELL ME, FAT MAN...
YOU READY FOR ONE MORE FIGHT?
ONE MORE FIGHT?
HELL, WE DIDN'T GROW THESE PLAYOFF BEARDS FOR NOTHING, JEPPERD.

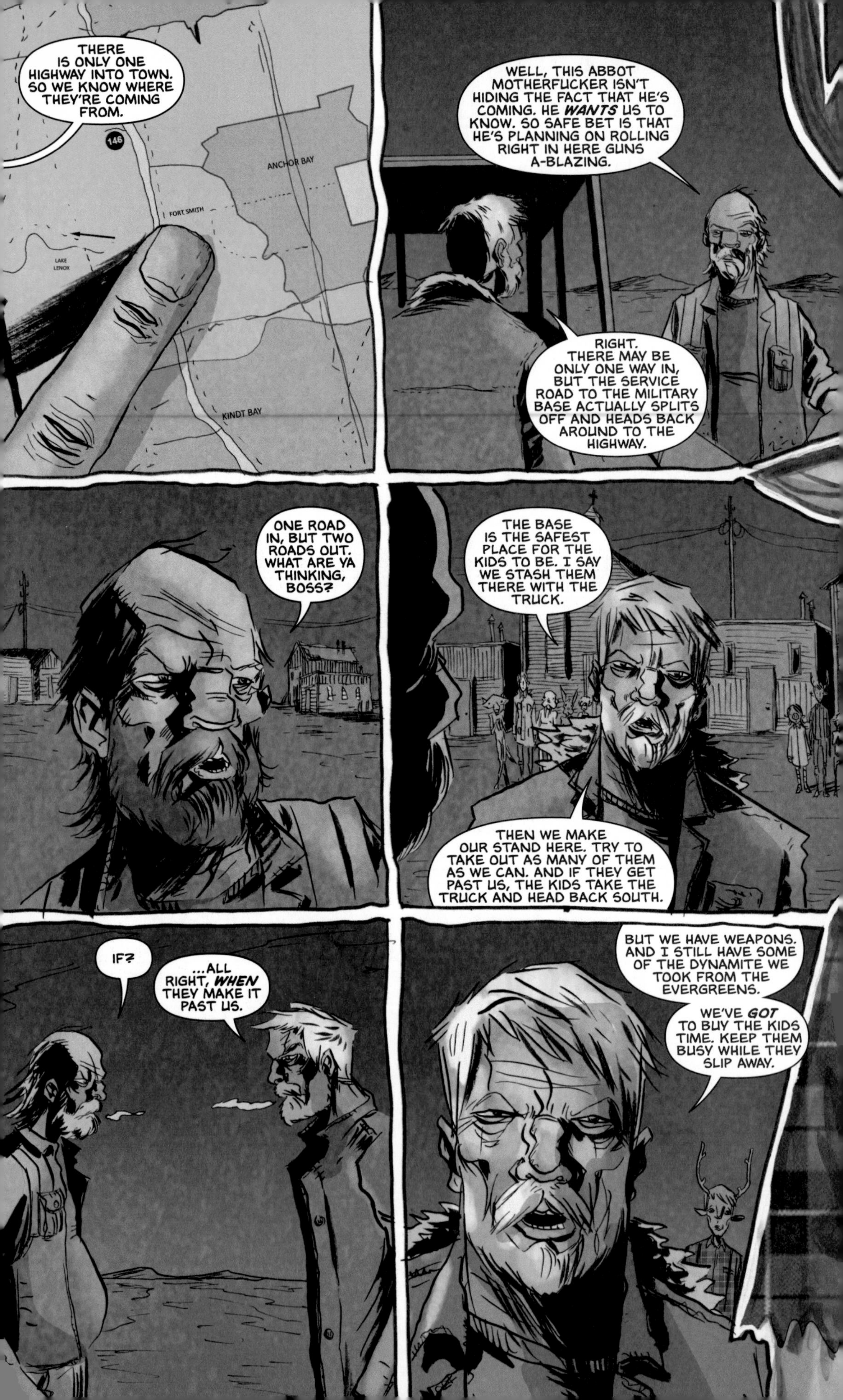
THERE IS ONLY ONE HIGHWAY INTO TOWN. SO WE KNOW WHERE THEY'RE COMING FROM.
146
ANCHOR BAY
FORT SMITH
LAKE LENOX
KINDT BAY
WELL, THIS ABBOT MOTHERFUCKER ISN'T HIDING THE FACT THAT HE'S COMING. HE *WANTS* US TO KNOW. SO SAFE BET IS THAT HE'S PLANNING ON ROLLING RIGHT IN HERE GUNS A-BLAZING.
RIGHT. THERE MAY BE ONLY ONE WAY IN, BUT THE SERVICE ROAD TO THE MILITARY BASE ACTUALLY SPLITS OFF AND HEADS BACK AROUND TO THE HIGHWAY.
ONE ROAD IN, BUT TWO ROADS OUT. WHAT ARE YA THINKING, BOSS?
THE BASE IS THE SAFEST PLACE FOR THE KIDS TO BE. I SAY WE STASH THEM THERE WITH THE TRUCK.
THEN WE MAKE OUR STAND HERE. TRY TO TAKE OUT AS MANY OF THEM AS WE CAN. AND IF THEY GET PAST US, THE KIDS TAKE THE TRUCK AND HEAD BACK SOUTH.
IF?
...ALL RIGHT, *WHEN* THEY MAKE IT PAST US.
BUT WE HAVE WEAPONS. AND I STILL HAVE SOME OF THE DYNAMITE WE TOOK FROM THE EVERGREENS.
WE'VE *GOT* TO BUY THE KIDS TIME. KEEP THEM BUSY WHILE THEY SLIP AWAY.

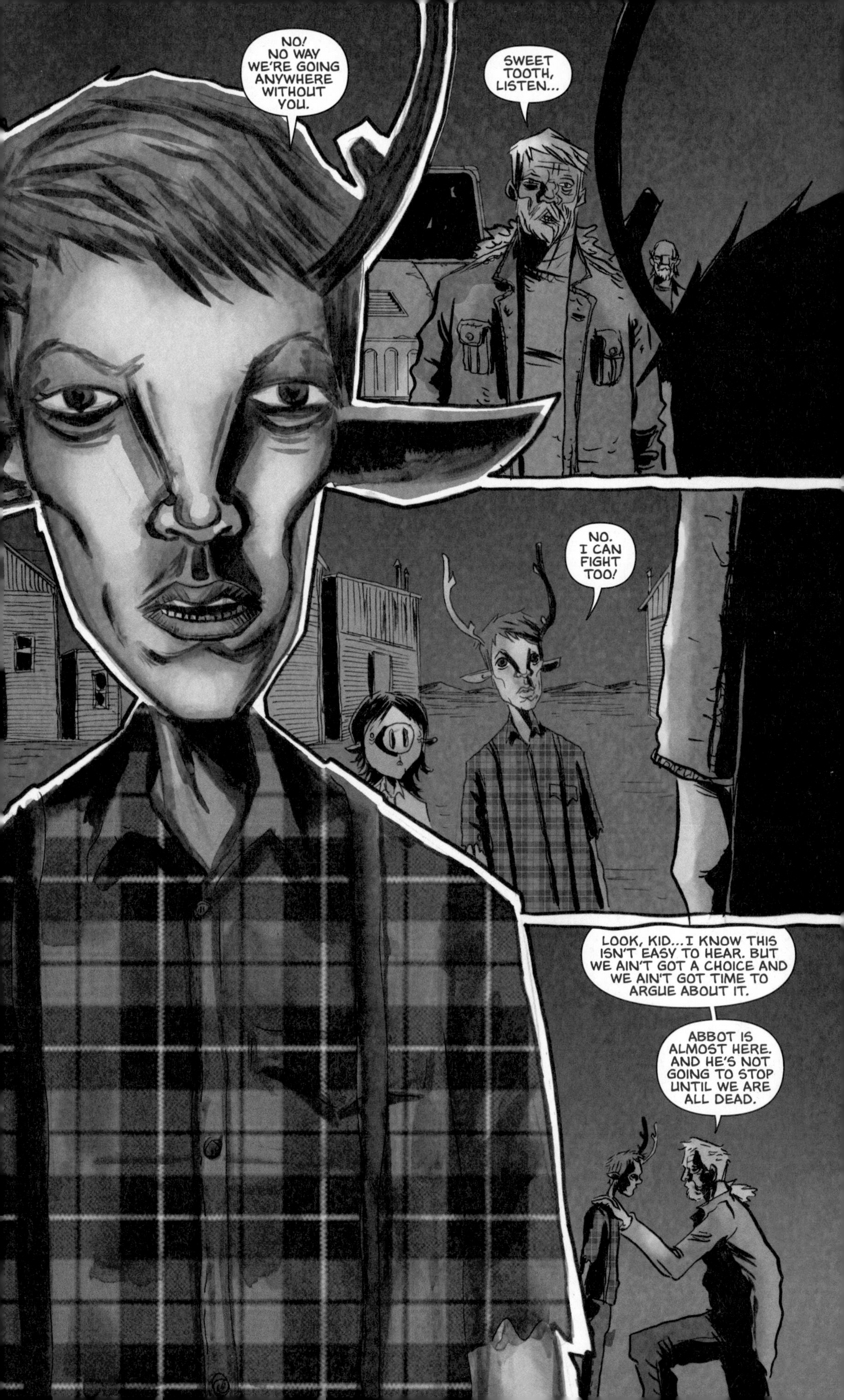
NO! NO WAY WE'RE GOING ANYWHERE WITHOUT YOU.
SWEET TOOTH, LISTEN...
NO. I CAN FIGHT TOO!
LOOK, KID... I KNOW THIS ISN'T EASY TO HEAR. BUT WE AIN'T GOT A CHOICE AND WE AIN'T GOT TIME TO ARGUE ABOUT IT.
ABBOT IS ALMOST HERE. AND HE'S NOT GOING TO STOP UNTIL WE ARE ALL DEAD.

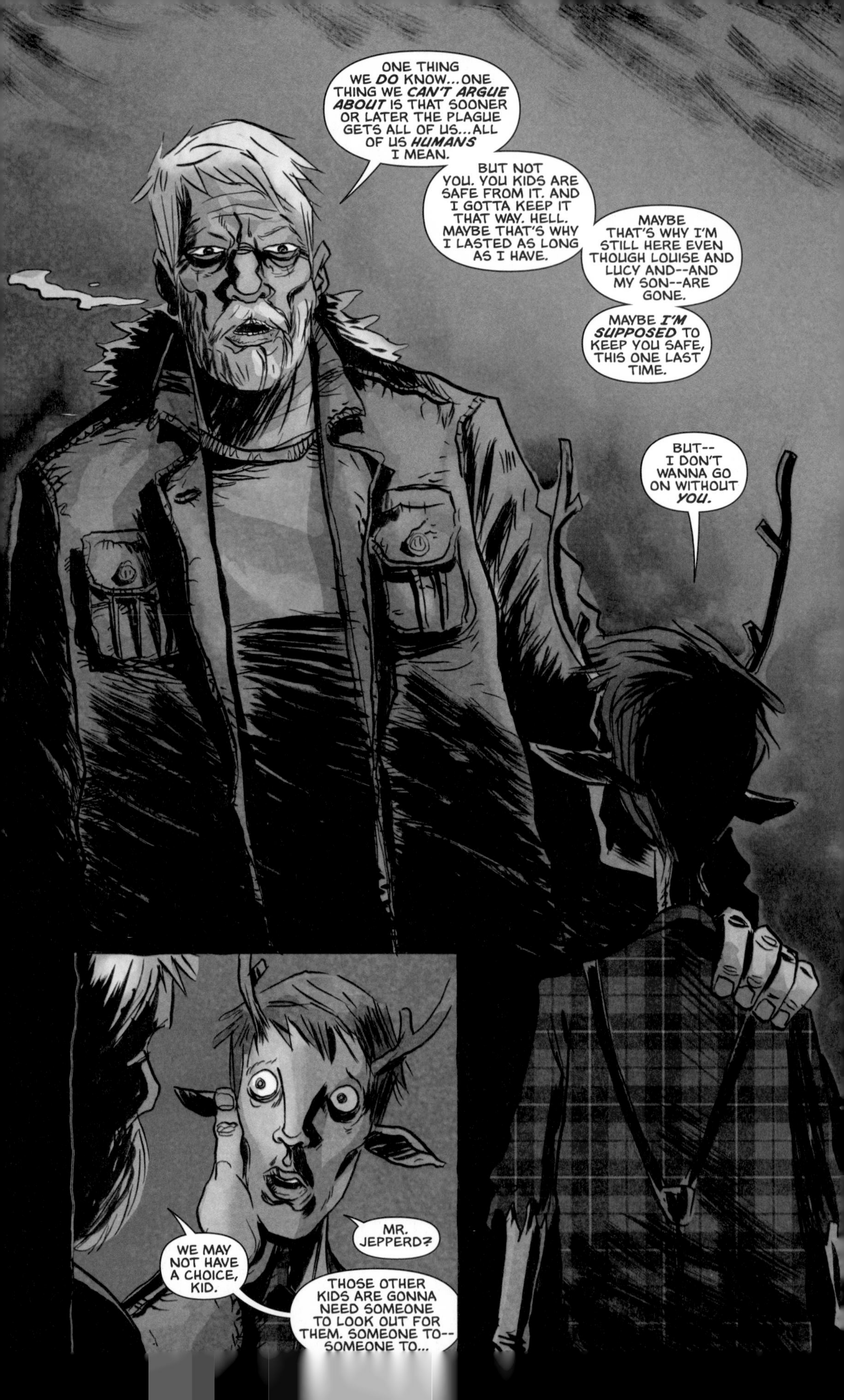
ONE THING WE DO KNOW...ONE THING WE CAN'T ARGUE ABOUT IS THAT SOONER OR LATER THE PLAGUE GETS ALL OF US...ALL OF US HUMANS I MEAN.
BUT NOT YOU. YOU KIDS ARE SAFE FROM IT. AND I GOTTA KEEP IT THAT WAY. HELL. MAYBE THAT'S WHY I LASTED AS LONG AS I HAVE.
MAYBE THAT'S WHY I'M STILL HERE EVEN THOUGH LOUISE AND LUCY AND--AND MY SON--ARE GONE.
MAYBE I'M SUPPOSED TO KEEP YOU SAFE, THIS ONE LAST TIME.
BUT-- I DON'T WANNA GO ON WITHOUT YOU.
MR. JEPPERD?
WE MAY NOT HAVE A CHOICE, KID.
THOSE OTHER KIDS ARE GONNA NEED SOMEONE TO LOOK OUT FOR THEM. SOMEONE TO-- SOMEONE TO...

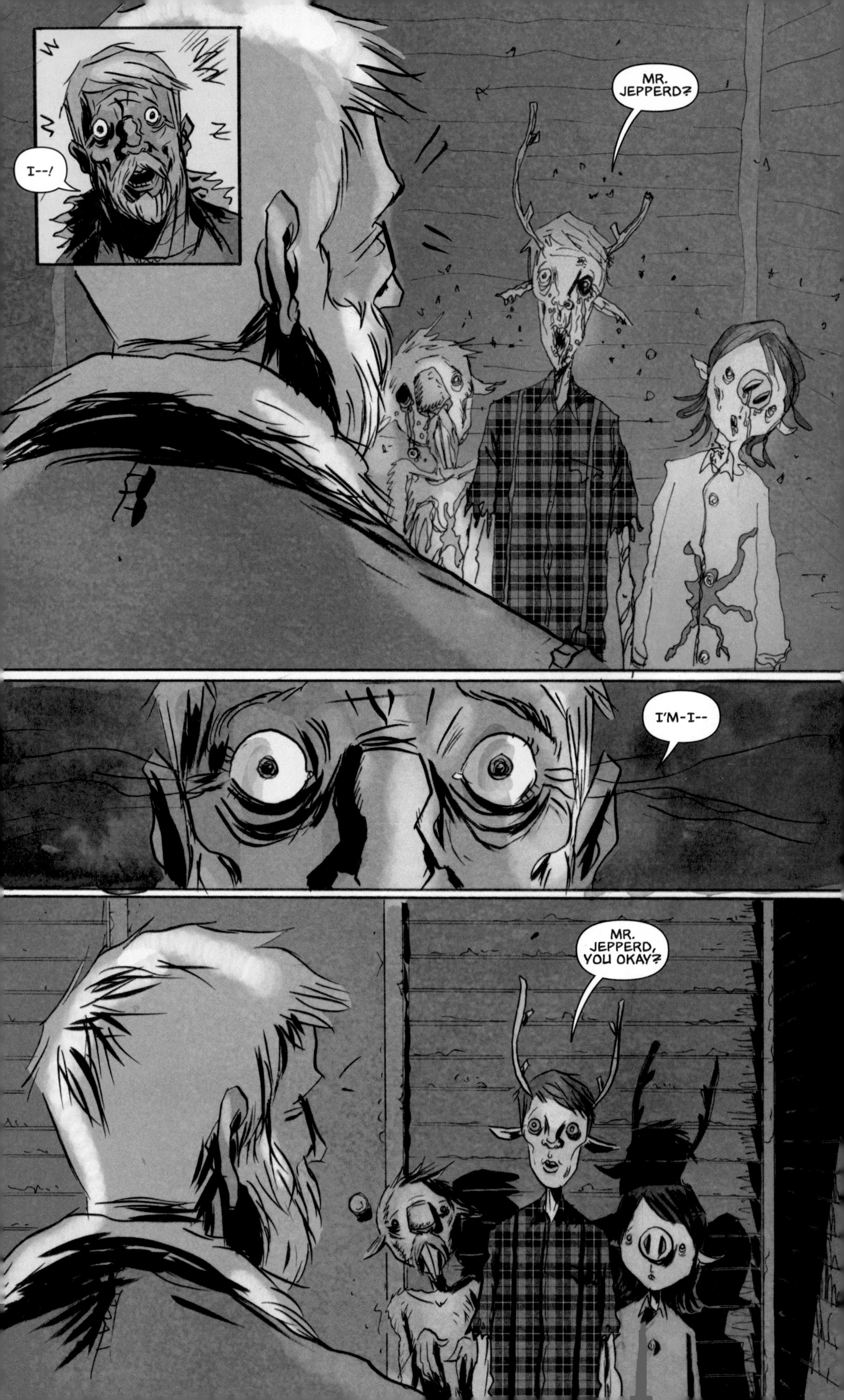
I--!
MR. JEPPERD?
I'M-I--
MR. JEPPERD, YOU OKAY?

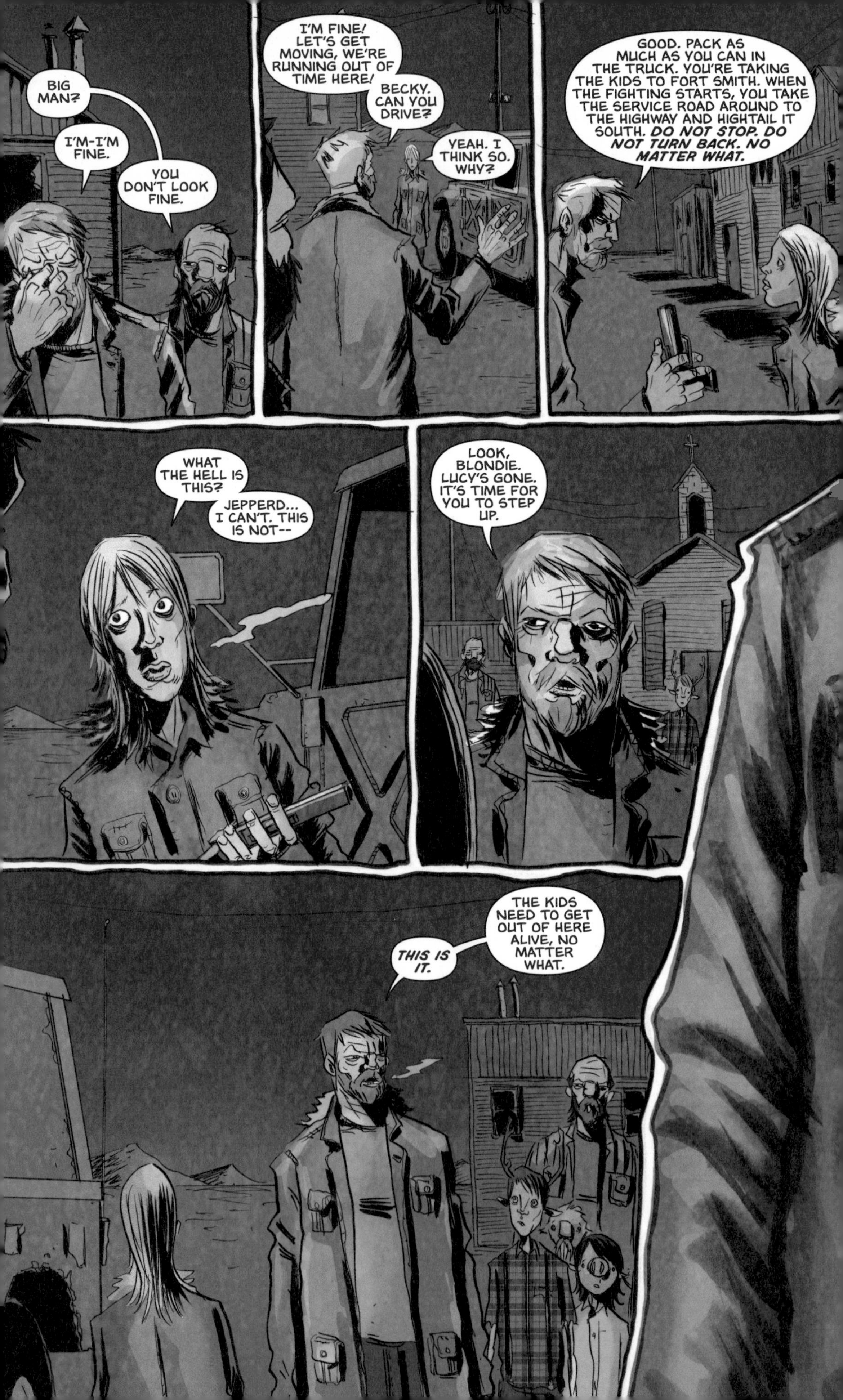
BIG MAN?
I'M-I'M FINE.
YOU DON'T LOOK FINE.
I'M FINE! LET'S GET MOVING, WE'RE RUNNING OUT OF TIME HERE!
BECKY. CAN YOU DRIVE?
YEAH. I THINK SO. WHY?
GOOD. PACK AS MUCH AS YOU CAN IN THE TRUCK. YOU'RE TAKING THE KIDS TO FORT SMITH. WHEN THE FIGHTING STARTS, YOU TAKE THE SERVICE ROAD AROUND TO THE HIGHWAY AND HIGHTAIL IT SOUTH. *DO NOT STOP. DO NOT TURN BACK. NO MATTER WHAT.*
WHAT THE HELL IS THIS?
JEPPERD... I CAN'T. THIS IS NOT--
LOOK, BLONDIE. LUCY'S GONE. IT'S TIME FOR YOU TO STEP UP.
THIS IS IT.
THE KIDS NEED TO GET OUT OF HERE ALIVE, NO MATTER WHAT.

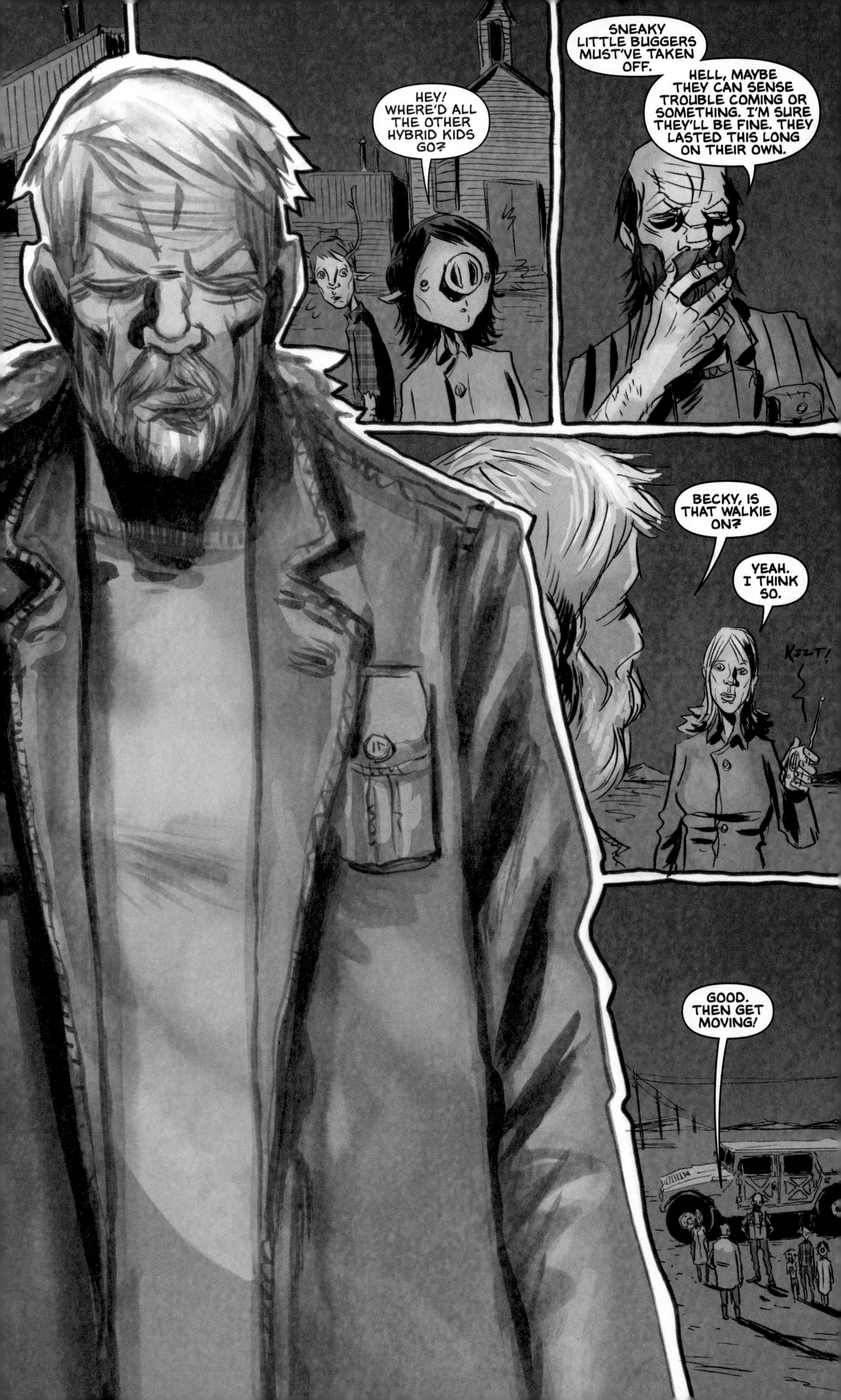
HEY! WHERE'D ALL THE OTHER HYBRID KIDS GO?
SNEAKY LITTLE BUGGERS MUST'VE TAKEN OFF.
HELL, MAYBE THEY CAN SENSE TROUBLE COMING OR SOMETHING. I'M SURE THEY'LL BE FINE. THEY LASTED THIS LONG ON THEIR OWN.
BECKY, IS THAT WALKIE ON?
YEAH. I THINK SO.
KZZT!
GOOD. THEN GET MOVING!

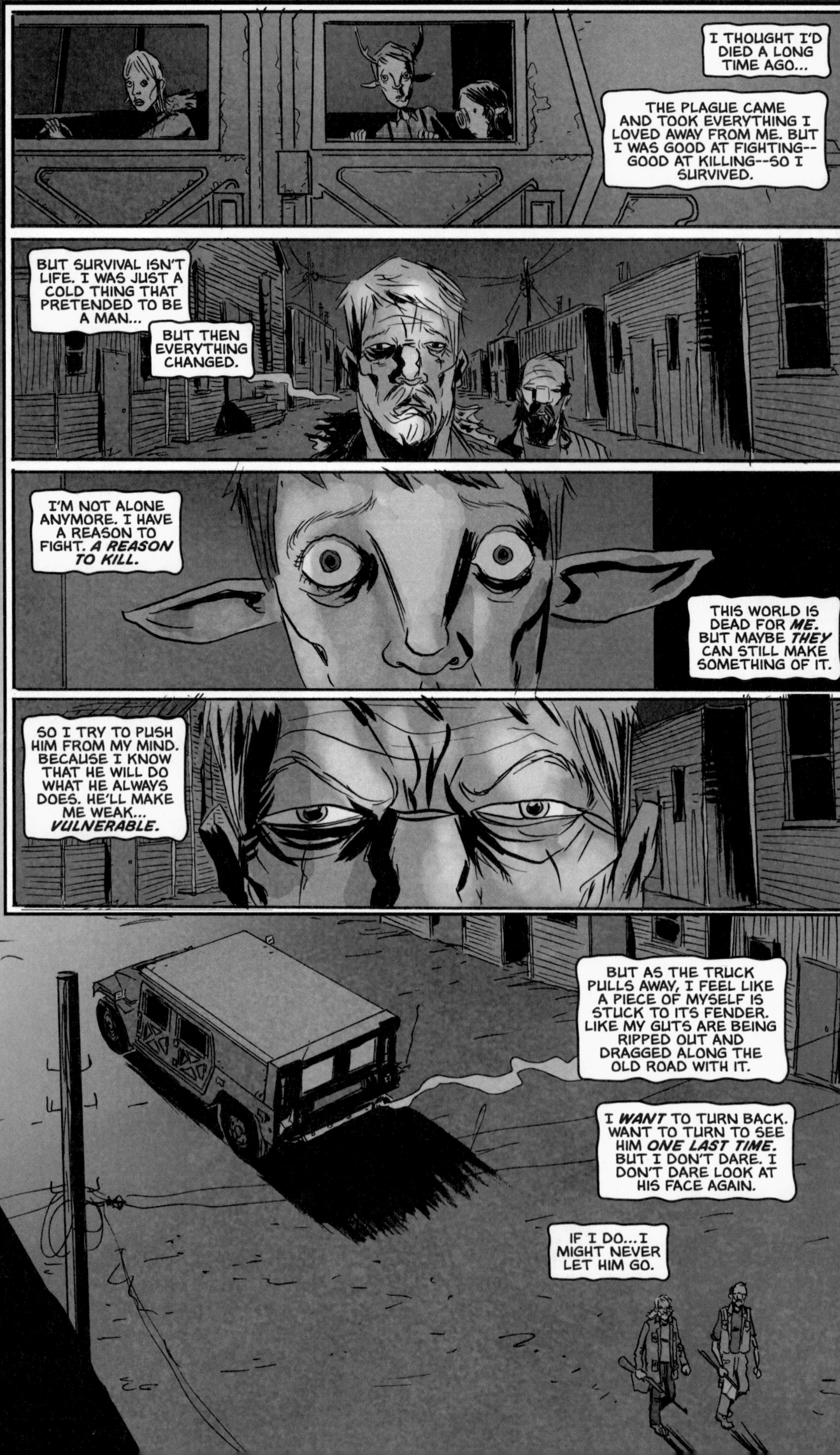
I THOUGHT I'D DIED A LONG TIME AGO...
THE PLAGUE CAME AND TOOK EVERYTHING I LOVED AWAY FROM ME. BUT I WAS GOOD AT FIGHTING--GOOD AT KILLING--SO I SURVIVED.
BUT SURVIVAL ISN'T LIFE. I WAS JUST A COLD THING THAT PRETENDED TO BE A MAN...
BUT THEN EVERYTHING CHANGED.
I'M NOT ALONE ANYMORE. I HAVE A REASON TO FIGHT. *A REASON TO KILL.*
THIS WORLD IS DEAD FOR *ME.* BUT MAYBE *THEY* CAN STILL MAKE SOMETHING OF IT.
SO I TRY TO PUSH HIM FROM MY MIND. BECAUSE I KNOW THAT HE WILL DO WHAT HE ALWAYS DOES. HE'LL MAKE ME WEAK... ***VULNERABLE.***
BUT AS THE TRUCK PULLS AWAY, I FEEL LIKE A PIECE OF MYSELF IS STUCK TO ITS FENDER. LIKE MY GUTS ARE BEING RIPPED OUT AND DRAGGED ALONG THE OLD ROAD WITH IT.
I *WANT* TO TURN BACK. WANT TO TURN TO SEE HIM *ONE LAST TIME.* BUT I DON'T DARE. I DON'T DARE LOOK AT HIS FACE AGAIN.
IF I DO...I MIGHT NEVER LET HIM GO.

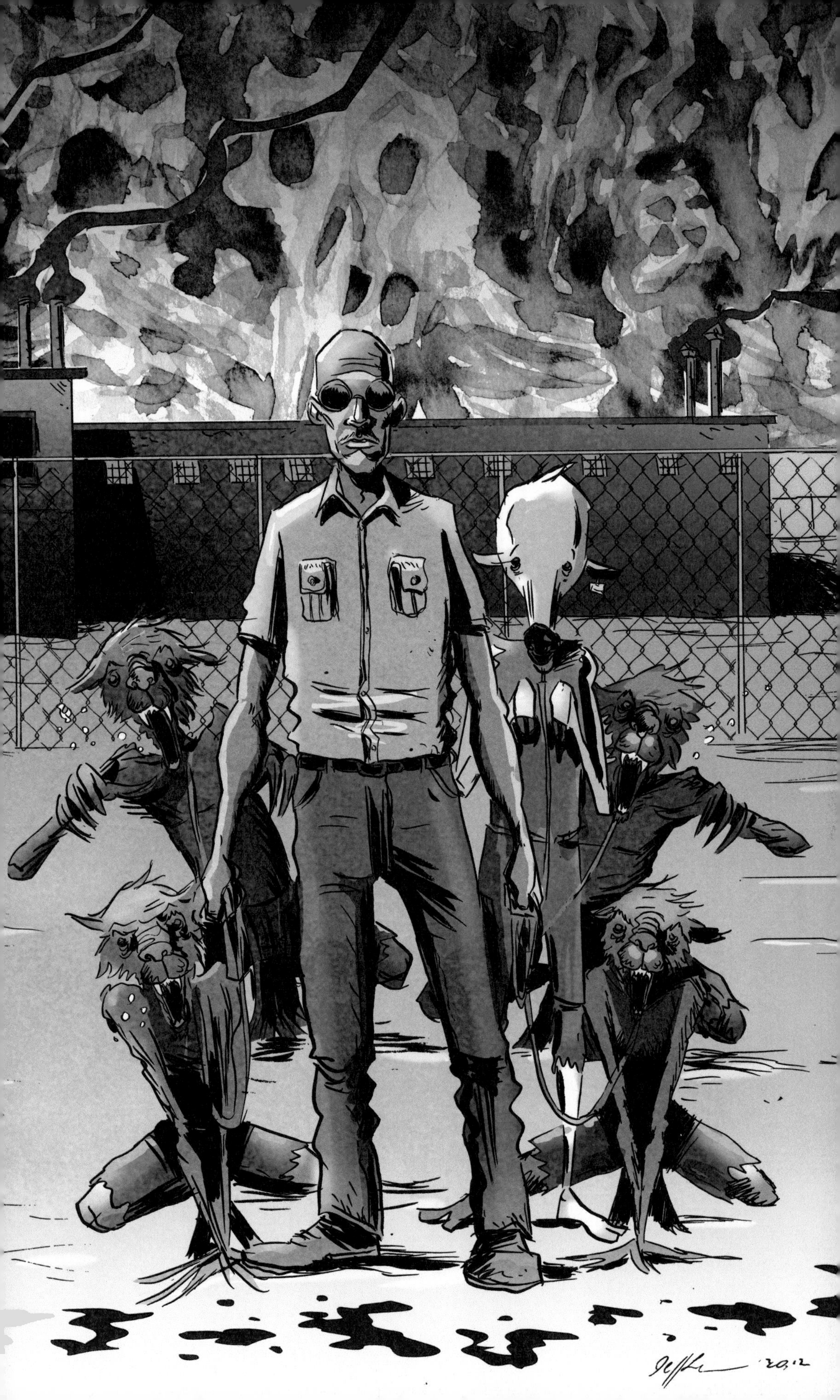

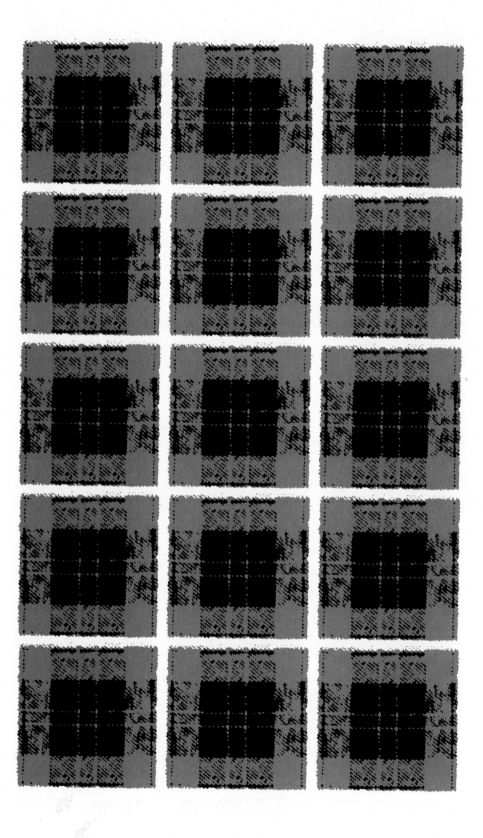

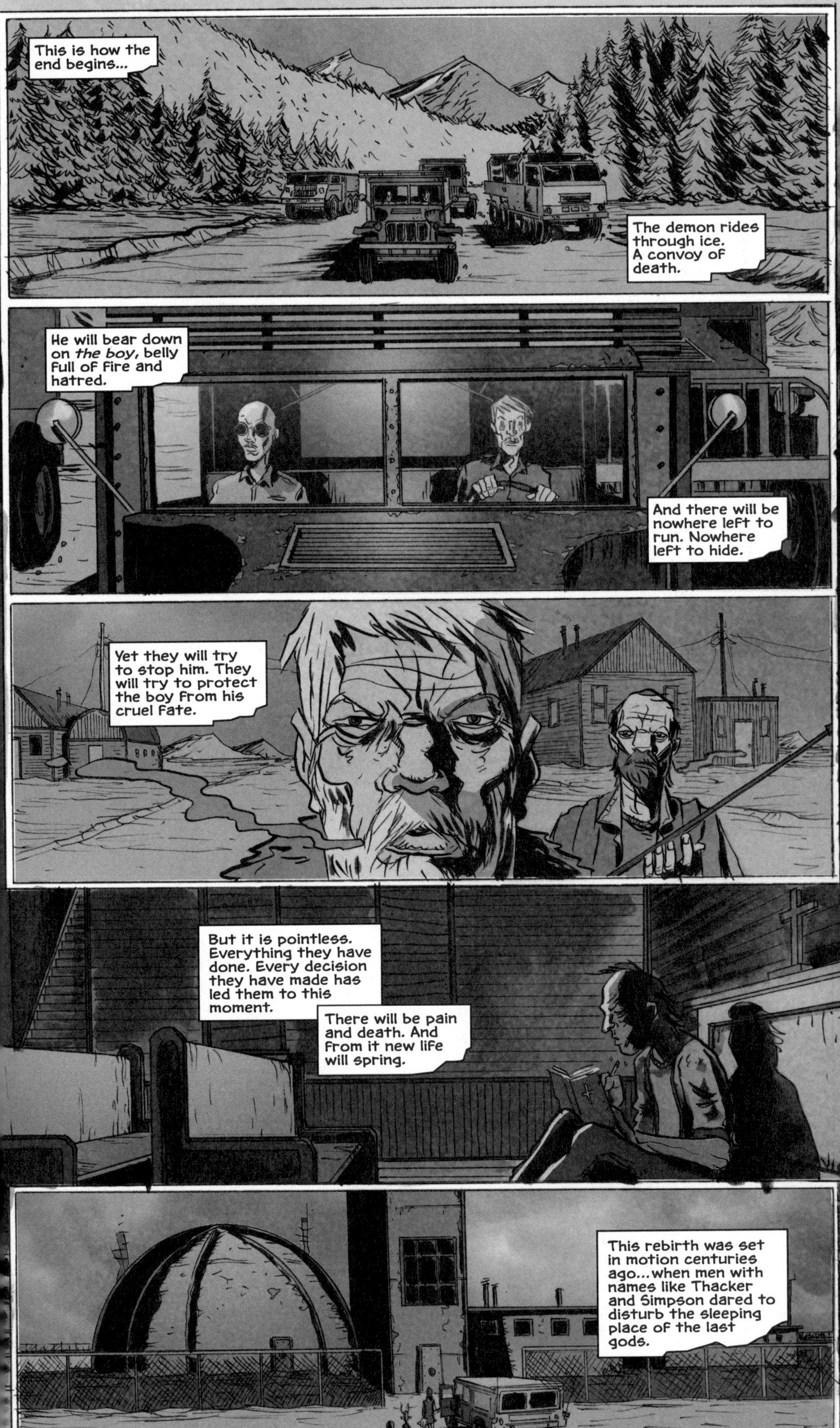
This is how the end begins...
The demon rides through ice. A convoy of death.
He will bear down on *the boy,* belly full of fire and hatred.
And there will be nowhere left to run. Nowhere left to hide.
Yet they will try to stop him. They will try to protect the boy from his cruel fate.
But it is pointless. Everything they have done. Every decision they have made has led them to this moment.
There will be pain and death. And from it new life will spring.
This rebirth was set in motion centuries ago...when men with names like Thacker and Simpson dared to disturb the sleeping place of the last gods.

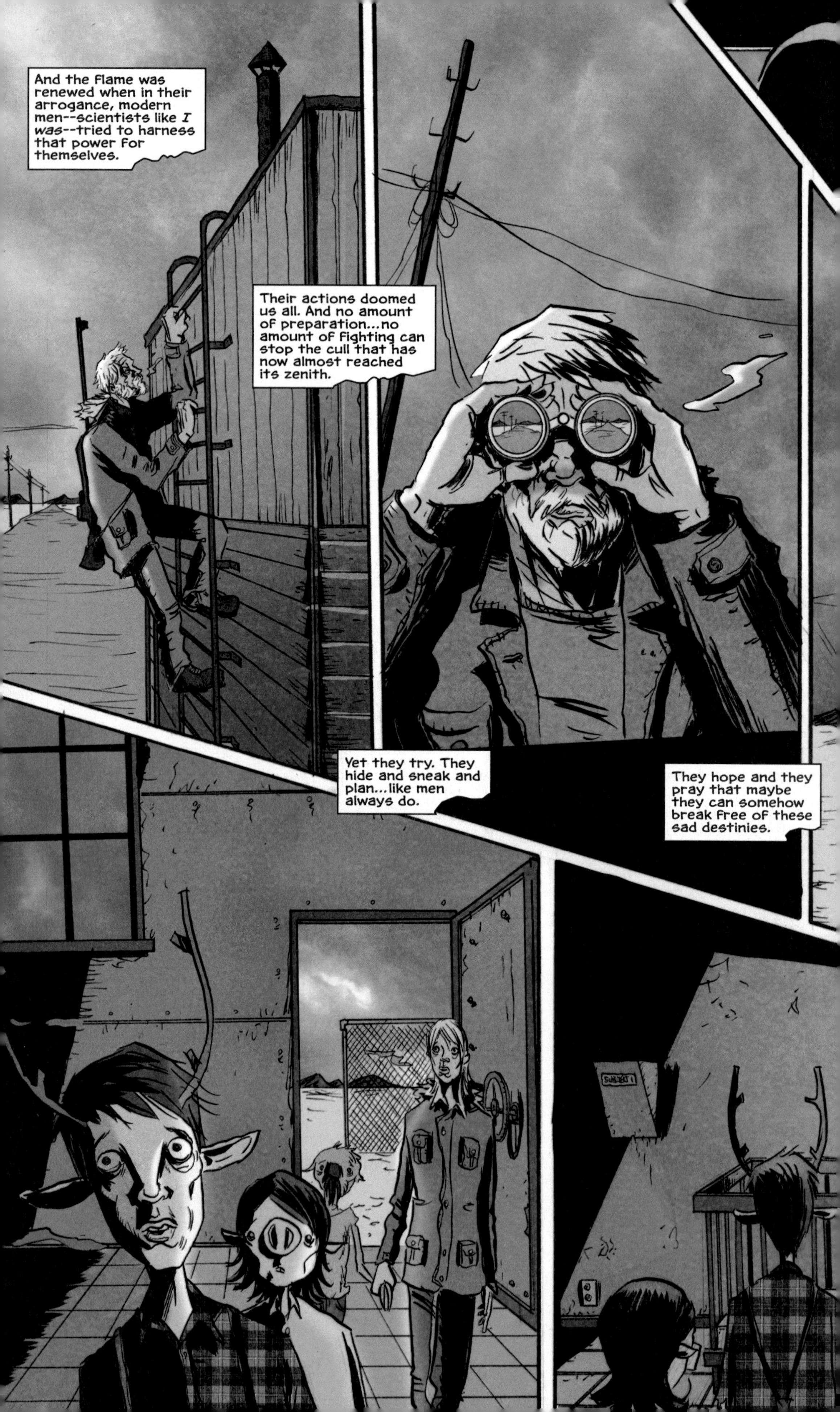
And the Flame was renewed when in their arrogance, modern men--scientists like *I was*--tried to harness that power for themselves.
Their actions doomed us all. And no amount of preparation...no amount of fighting can stop the cull that has now almost reached its zenith.
Yet they try. They hide and sneak and plan...like men always do.
They hope and they pray that maybe they can somehow break free of these sad destinies.

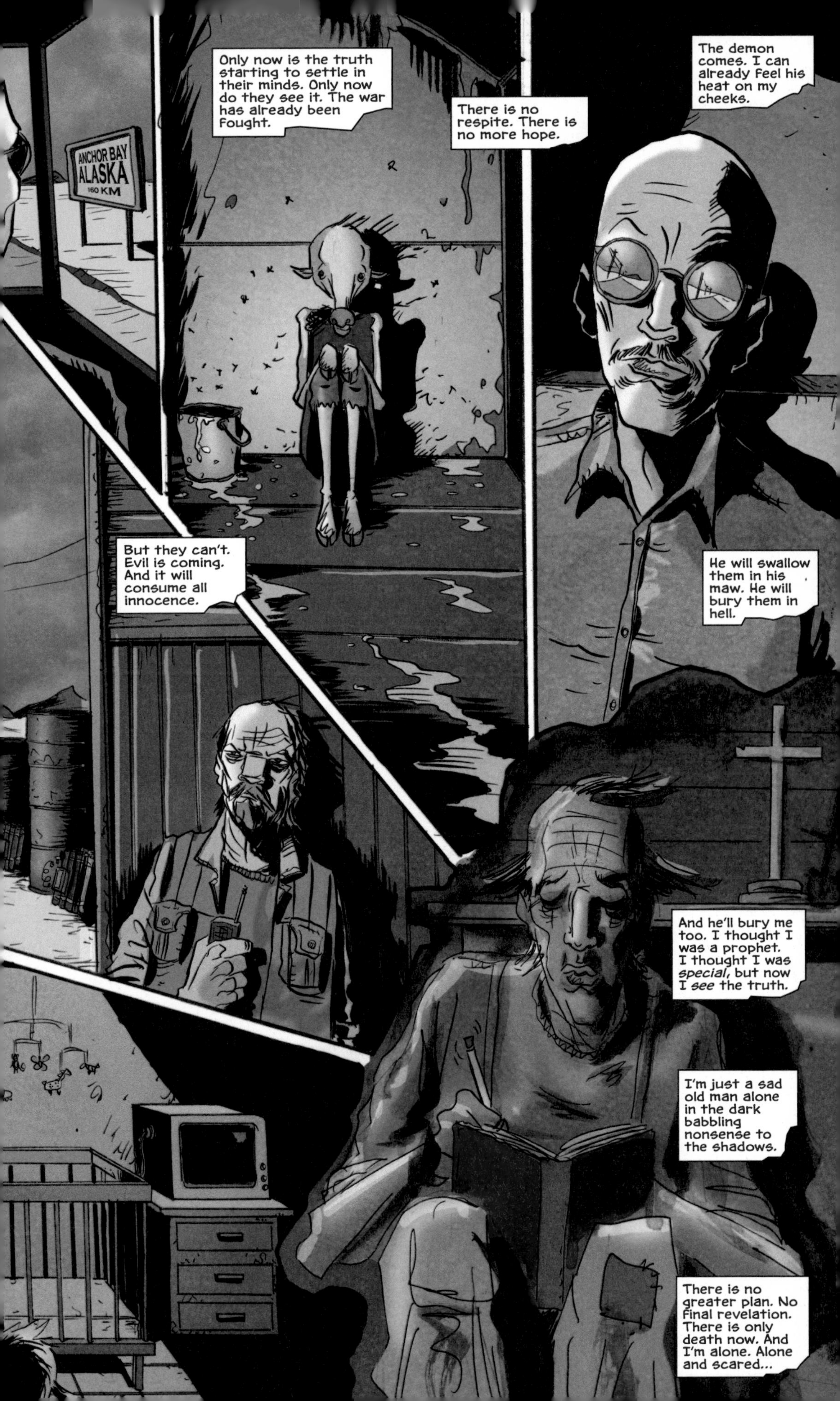
ANCHOR BAY
ALASKA
160 KM
Only now is the truth starting to settle in their minds. Only now do they see it. The war has already been fought.
There is no respite. There is no more hope.
The demon comes. I can already feel his heat on my cheeks.
But they can't. Evil is coming. And it will consume all innocence.
He will swallow them in his maw. He will bury them in hell.
And he'll bury me too. I thought I was a prophet. I thought I was *special*, but now I *see* the truth.
I'm just a sad old man alone in the dark babbling nonsense to the shadows.
There is no greater plan. No final revelation. There is only death now. And I'm alone. Alone and scared...

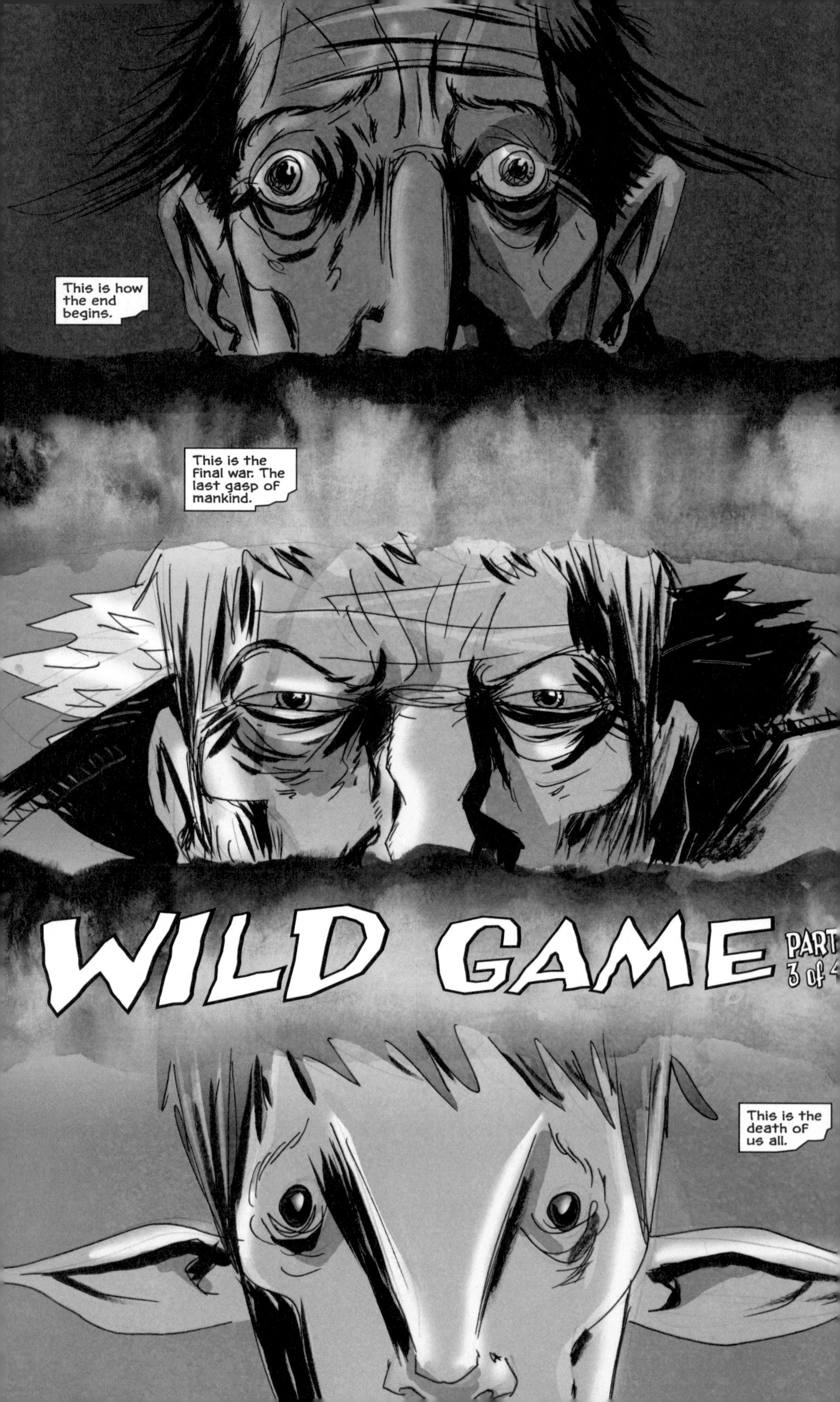
This is how the end begins.
This is the final war. The last gasp of mankind.
WILD GAME PART 3 of 4
This is the death of us all.

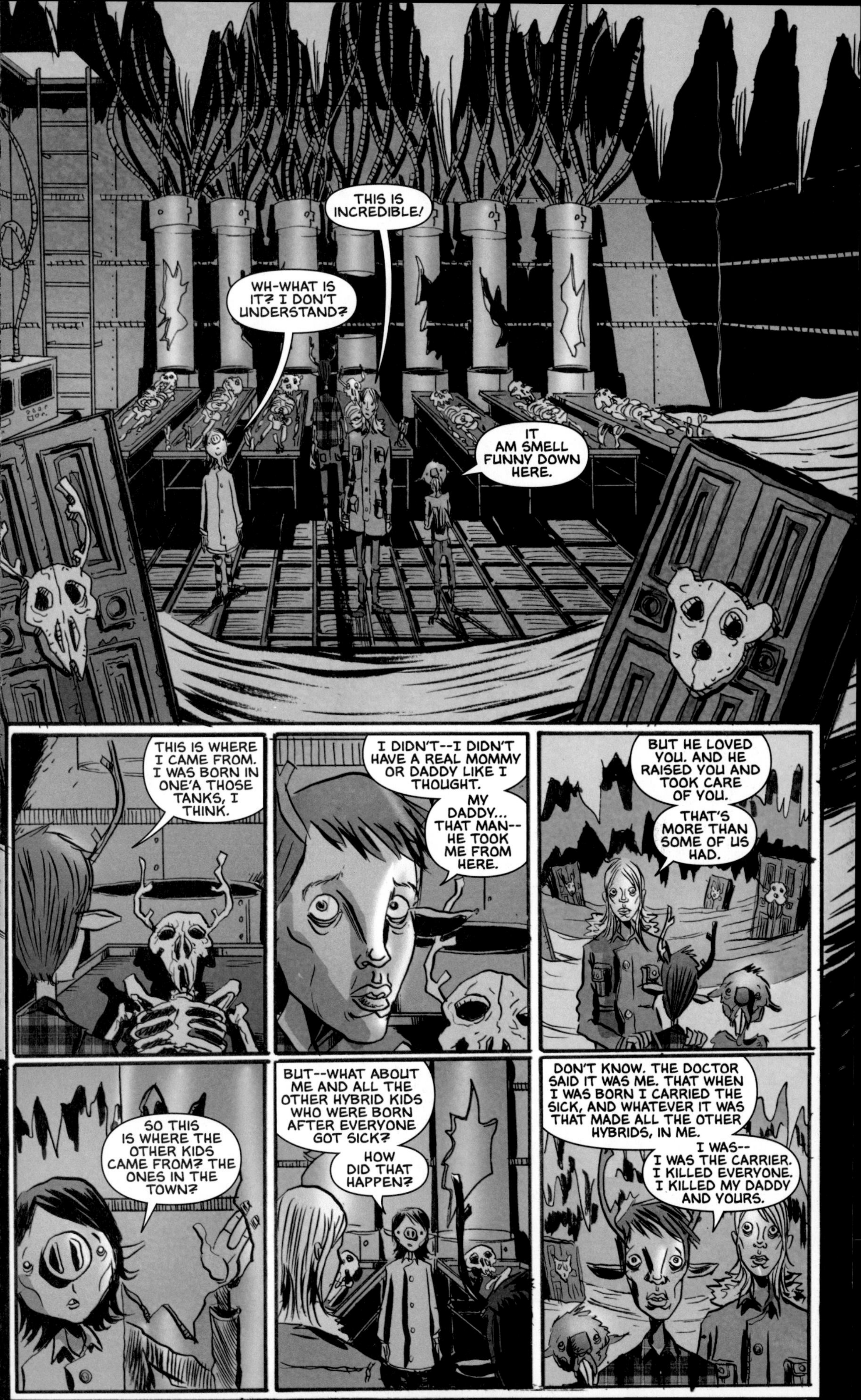
THIS IS INCREDIBLE!
WH-WHAT IS IT? I DON'T UNDERSTAND?
IT AM SMELL FUNNY DOWN HERE.
THIS IS WHERE I CAME FROM. I WAS BORN IN ONE'A THOSE TANKS, I THINK.
I DIDN'T--I DIDN'T HAVE A REAL MOMMY OR DADDY LIKE I THOUGHT.
MY DADDY... THAT MAN-- HE TOOK ME FROM HERE.
BUT HE LOVED YOU. AND HE RAISED YOU AND TOOK CARE OF YOU.
THAT'S MORE THAN SOME OF US HAD.
SO THIS IS WHERE THE OTHER KIDS CAME FROM? THE ONES IN THE TOWN?
BUT--WHAT ABOUT ME AND ALL THE OTHER HYBRID KIDS WHO WERE BORN AFTER EVERYONE GOT SICK?
HOW DID THAT HAPPEN?
DON'T KNOW. THE DOCTOR SAID IT WAS ME. THAT WHEN I WAS BORN I CARRIED THE SICK, AND WHATEVER IT WAS THAT MADE ALL THE OTHER HYBRIDS, IN ME.
I WAS-- I WAS THE CARRIER. I KILLED EVERYONE. I KILLED MY DADDY AND YOURS.

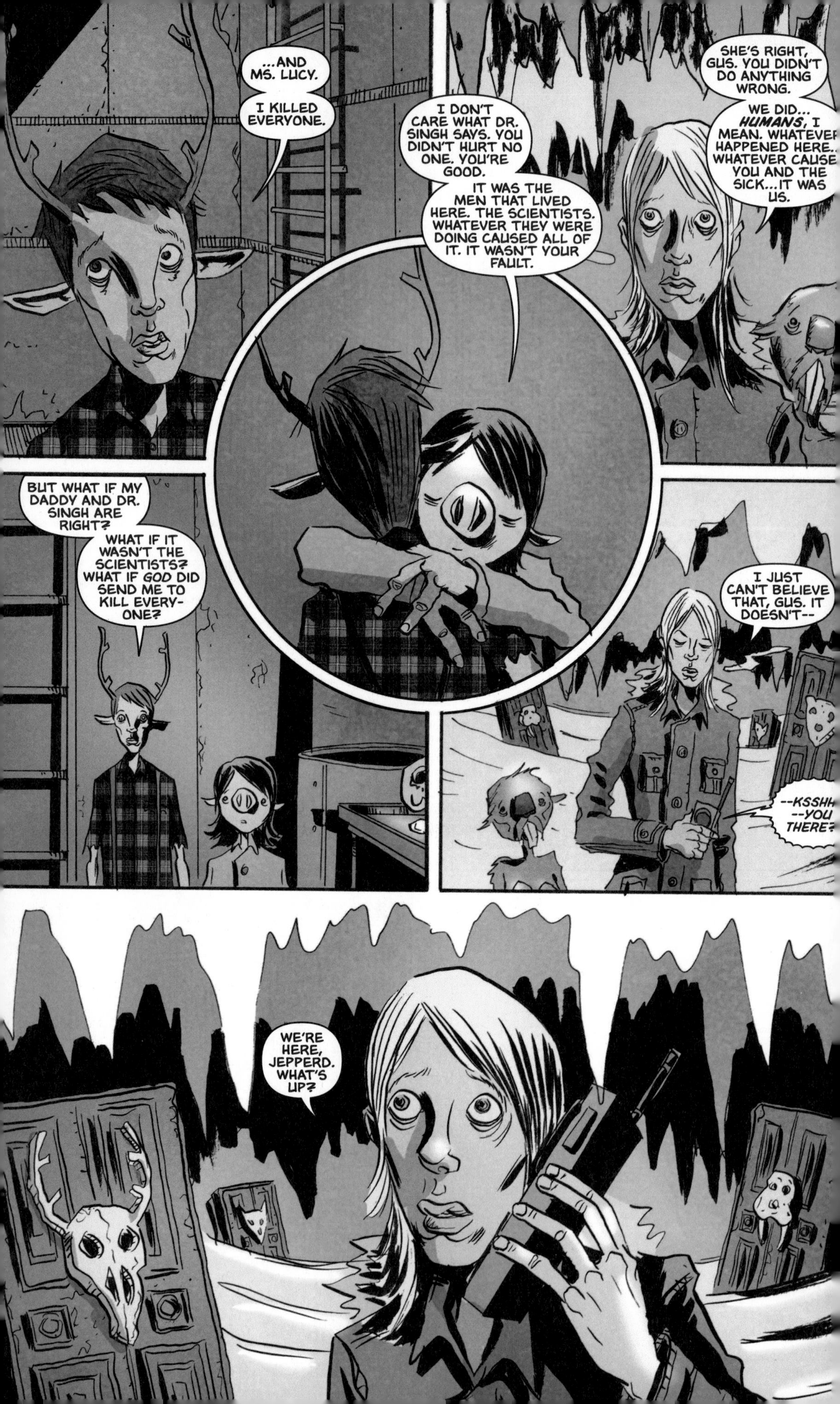

...AND MS. LUCY.
I KILLED EVERYONE.
I DON'T CARE WHAT DR. SINGH SAYS. YOU DIDN'T HURT NO ONE. YOU'RE GOOD.
IT WAS THE MEN THAT LIVED HERE. THE SCIENTISTS. WHATEVER THEY WERE DOING CAUSED ALL OF IT. IT WASN'T YOUR FAULT.
SHE'S RIGHT, GUS. YOU DIDN'T DO ANYTHING WRONG.
WE DID... *HUMANS*, I MEAN. WHATEVER HAPPENED HERE. WHATEVER CAUSED YOU AND THE SICK...IT WAS US.
BUT WHAT IF MY DADDY AND DR. SINGH ARE RIGHT?
WHAT IF IT WASN'T THE SCIENTISTS? WHAT IF *GOD* DID SEND ME TO KILL EVERY-ONE?
I JUST CAN'T BELIEVE THAT, GUS. IT DOESN'T--
--KSSHH --YOU THERE?
WE'RE HERE, JEPPERD. WHAT'S UP?

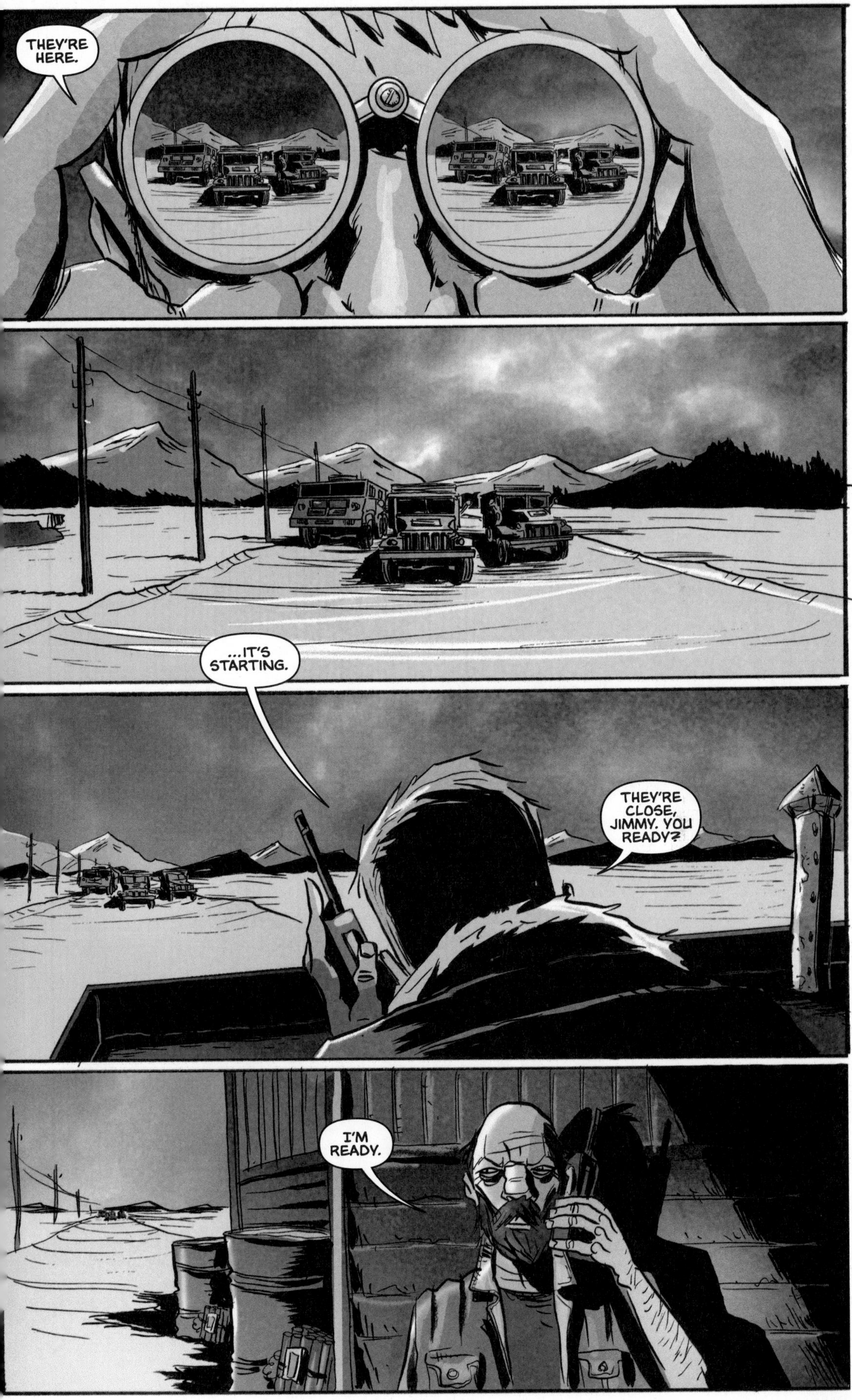
THEY'RE HERE.
...IT'S STARTING.
THEY'RE CLOSE, JIMMY. YOU READY?
I'M READY.

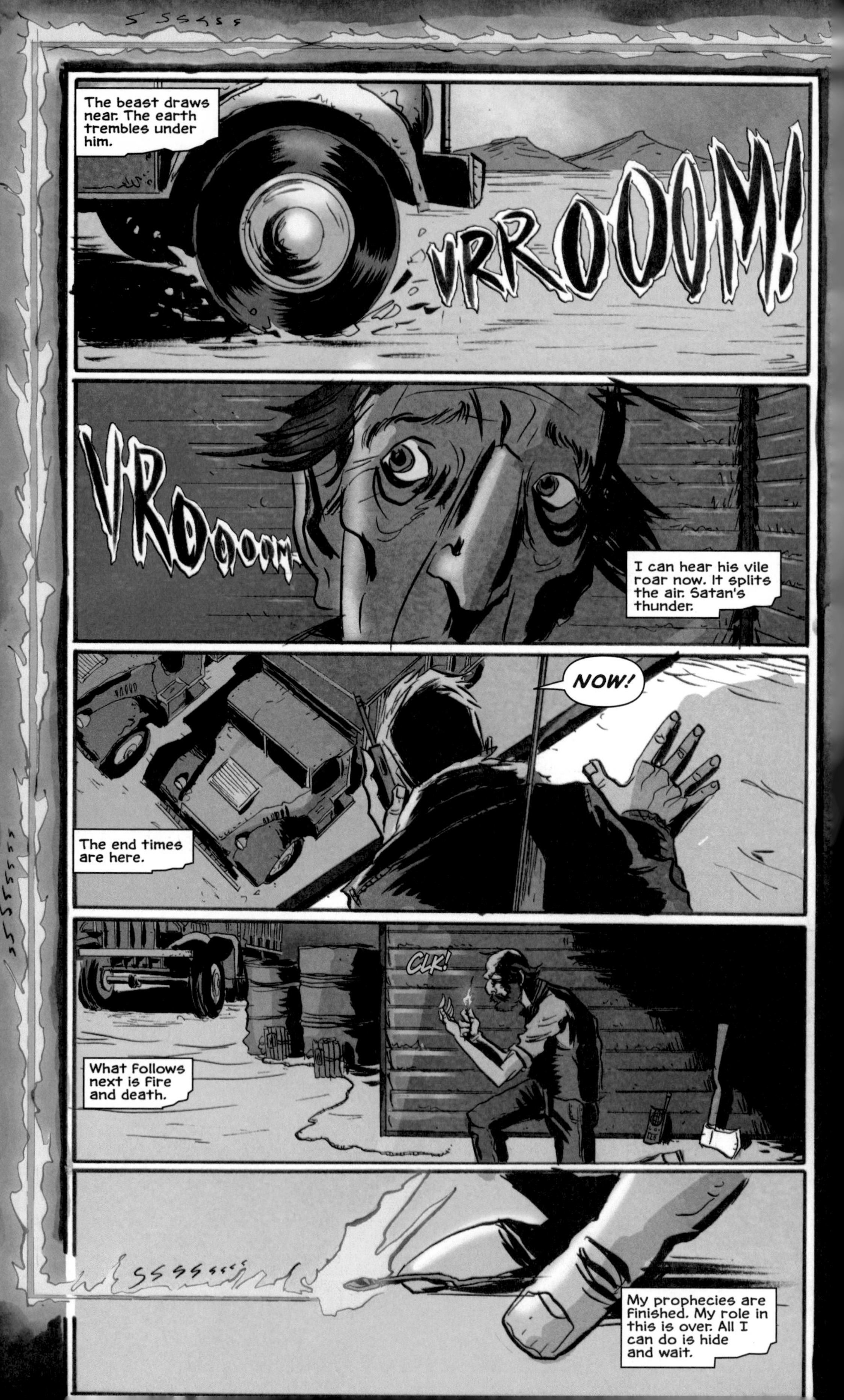
S SSSSS
The beast draws near. The earth trembles under him.
VRROOOM!
VROoooom
I can hear his vile roar now. It splits the air. Satan's thunder.
NOW!
The end times are here.
CLK!
What follows next is fire and death.
SSSSSSS
My prophecies are finished. My role in this is over. All I can do is hide and wait.

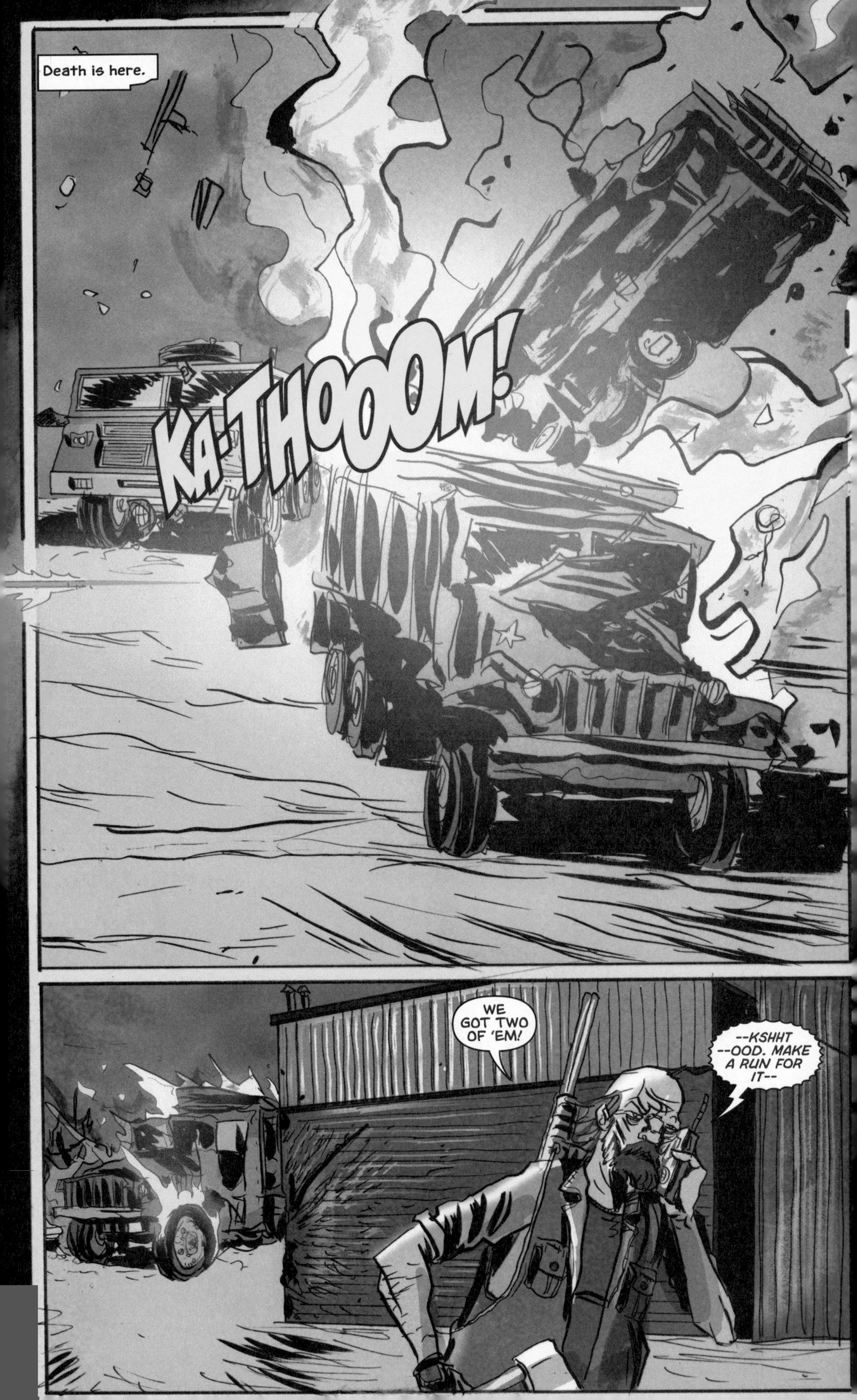
Death is here.
KA-THOOOM!
WE GOT TWO OF 'EM!
--KSHHT --OOD. MAKE A RUN FOR IT--

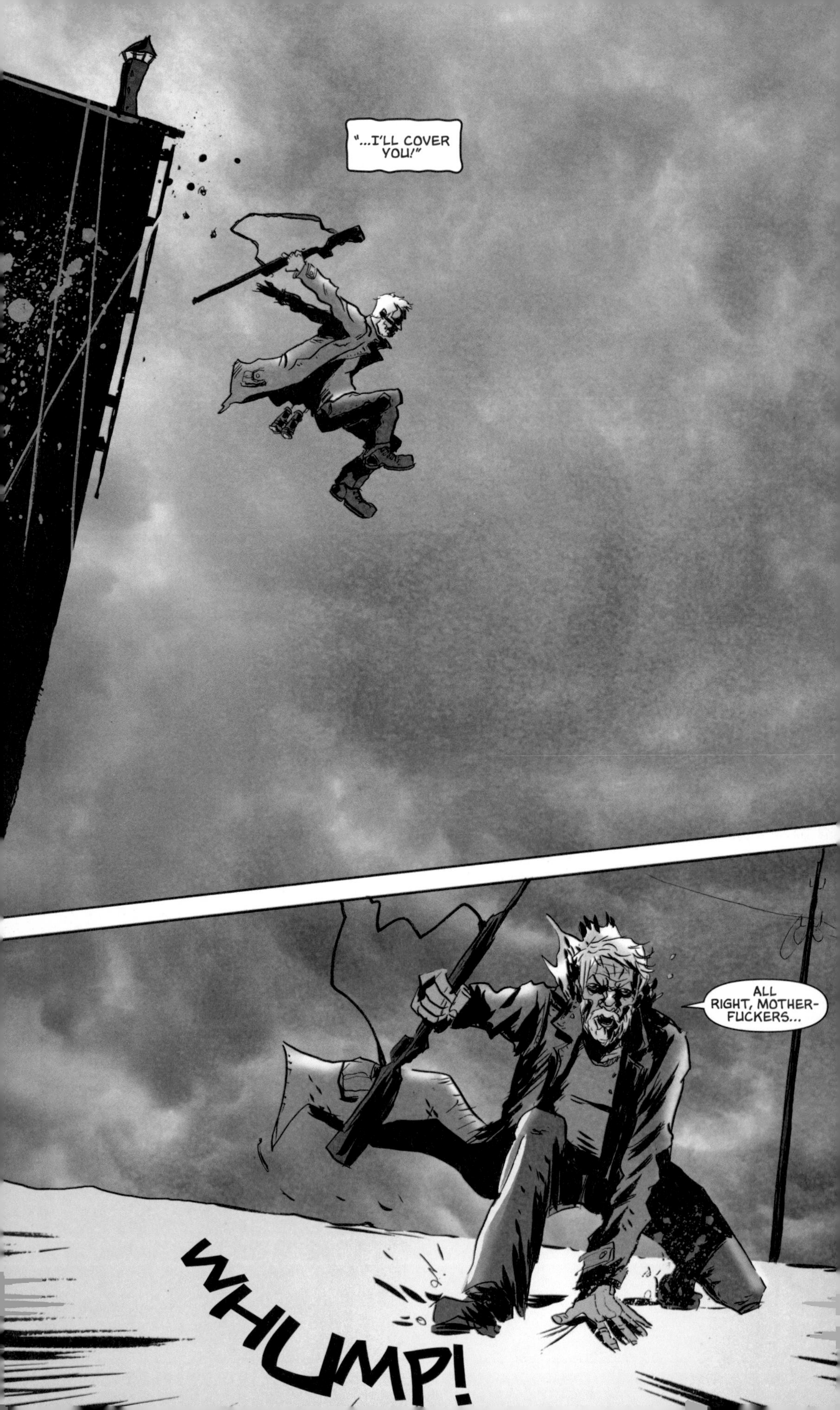
"...I'LL COVER YOU!"
ALL RIGHT, MOTHER-FUCKERS...
WHUMP!

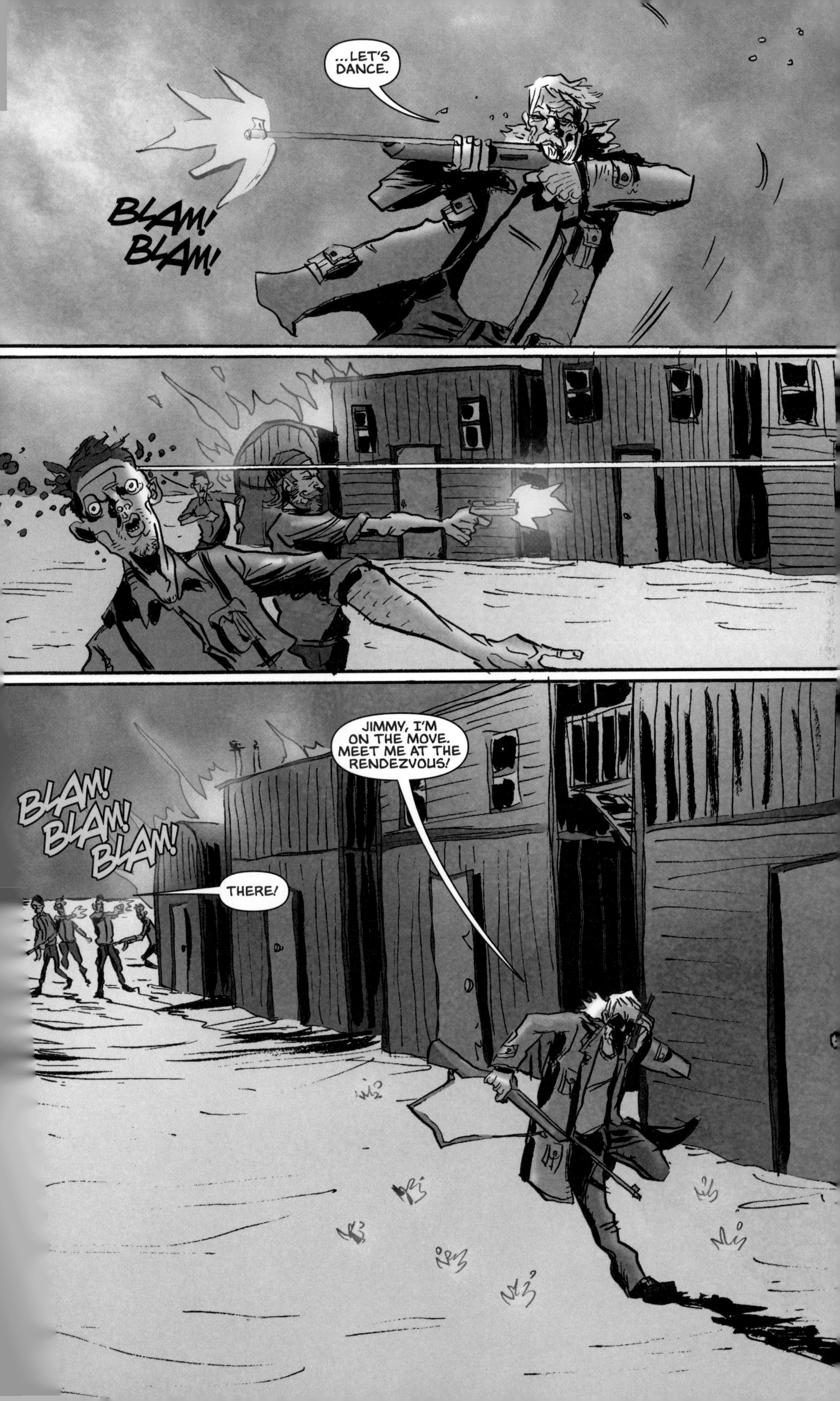
...LET'S DANCE.
BLAM! BLAM!
JIMMY, I'M ON THE MOVE. MEET ME AT THE RENDEZVOUS!
BLAM! BLAM! BLAM!
THERE!

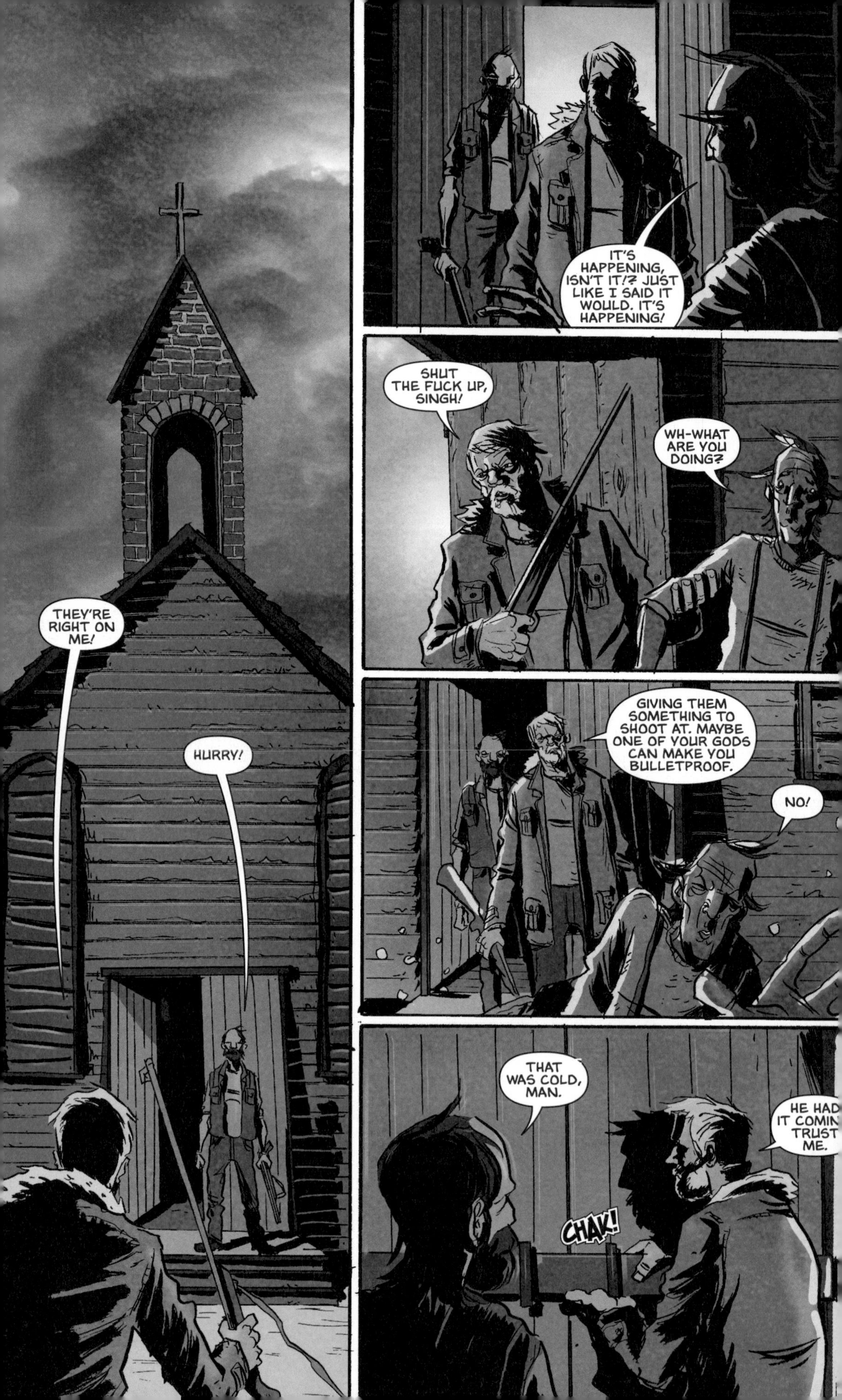
THEY'RE RIGHT ON ME!
HURRY!
IT'S HAPPENING, ISN'T IT!? JUST LIKE I SAID IT WOULD. IT'S HAPPENING!
SHUT THE FUCK UP, SINGH!
WH-WHAT ARE YOU DOING?
GIVING THEM SOMETHING TO SHOOT AT. MAYBE ONE OF YOUR GODS CAN MAKE YOU BULLETPROOF.
NO!
THAT WAS COLD, MAN.
HE HAD IT COMIN TRUST ME.
CHAK!

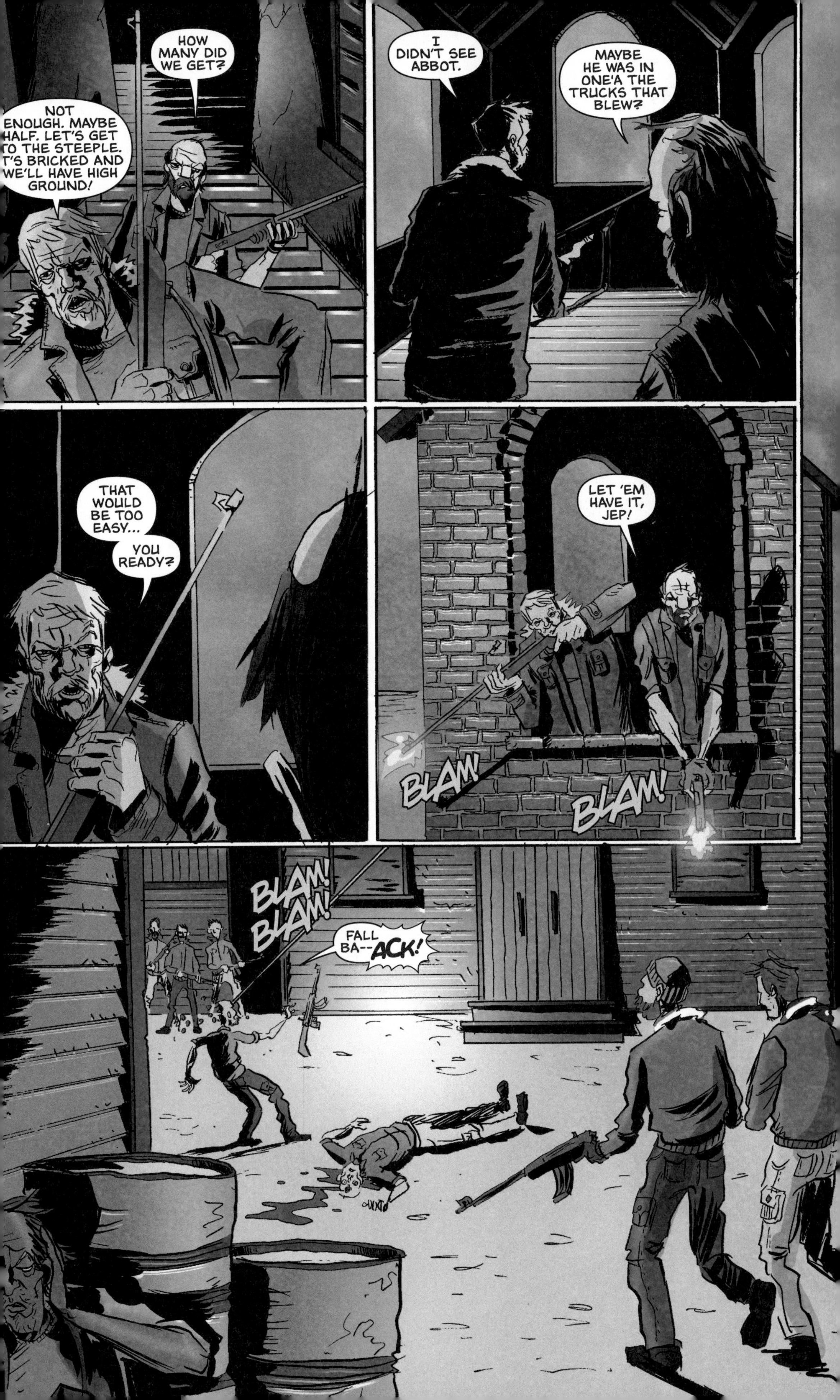
NOT ENOUGH. MAYBE HALF. LET'S GET TO THE STEEPLE. IT'S BRICKED AND WE'LL HAVE HIGH GROUND!
HOW MANY DID WE GET?
I DIDN'T SEE ABBOT.
MAYBE HE WAS IN ONE'A THE TRUCKS THAT BLEW?
THAT WOULD BE TOO EASY...
YOU READY?
LET 'EM HAVE IT, JEP!
BLAM!
BLAM!
BLAM!
BLAM!
FALL BA--ACK!

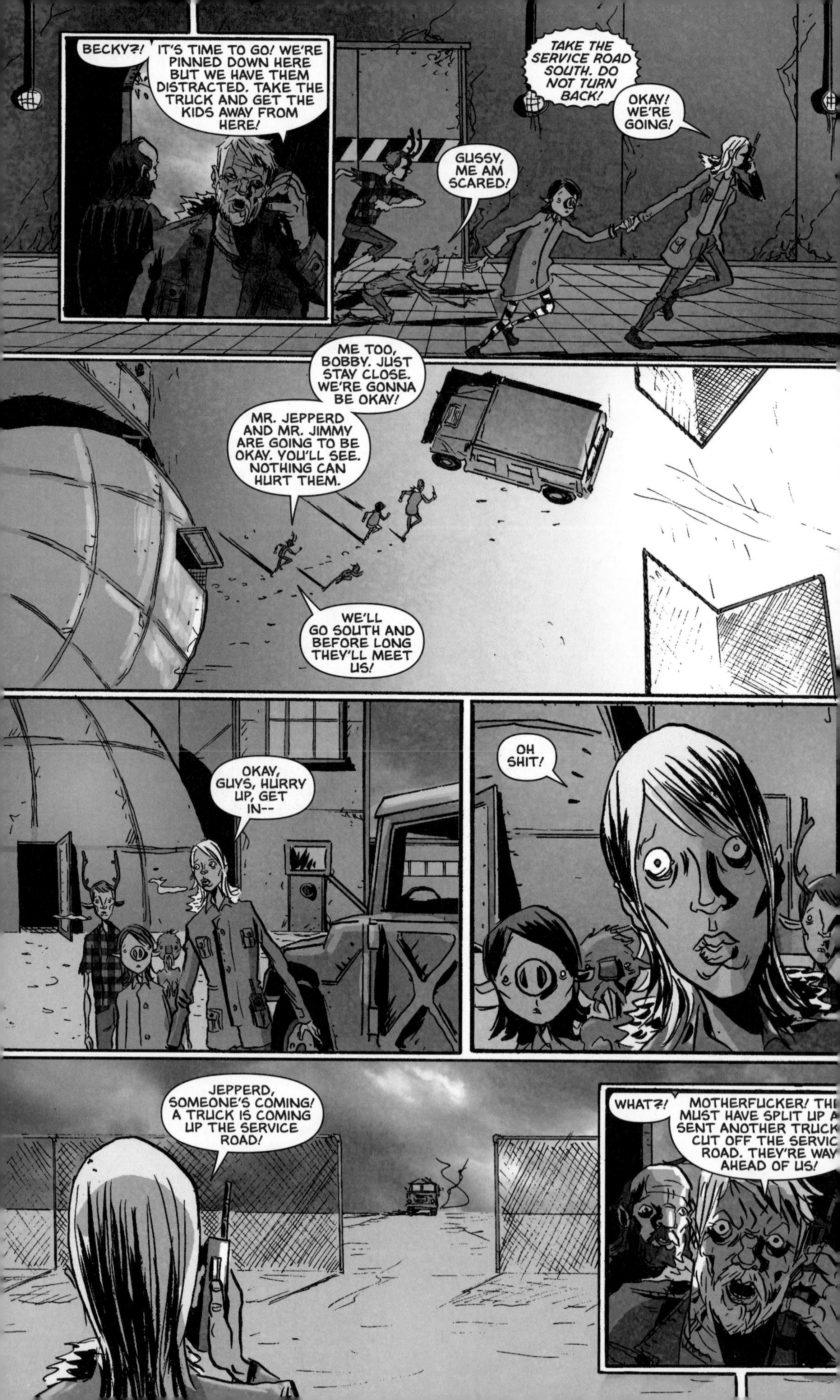
BECKY?!
IT'S TIME TO GO! WE'RE PINNED DOWN HERE BUT WE HAVE THEM DISTRACTED. TAKE THE TRUCK AND GET THE KIDS AWAY FROM HERE!
TAKE THE SERVICE ROAD SOUTH. DO NOT TURN BACK!
OKAY! WE'RE GOING!
GUSSY, ME AM SCARED!
ME TOO, BOBBY. JUST STAY CLOSE. WE'RE GONNA BE OKAY!
MR. JEPPERD AND MR. JIMMY ARE GOING TO BE OKAY. YOU'LL SEE. NOTHING CAN HURT THEM.
WE'LL GO SOUTH AND BEFORE LONG THEY'LL MEET US!
OKAY, GUYS, HURRY UP, GET IN--
OH SHIT!
JEPPERD, SOMEONE'S COMING! A TRUCK IS COMING UP THE SERVICE ROAD!
WHAT?!
MOTHERFUCKER! THE MUST HAVE SPLIT UP A SENT ANOTHER TRUCK CUT OFF THE SERVIC ROAD. THEY'RE WAY AHEAD OF US!

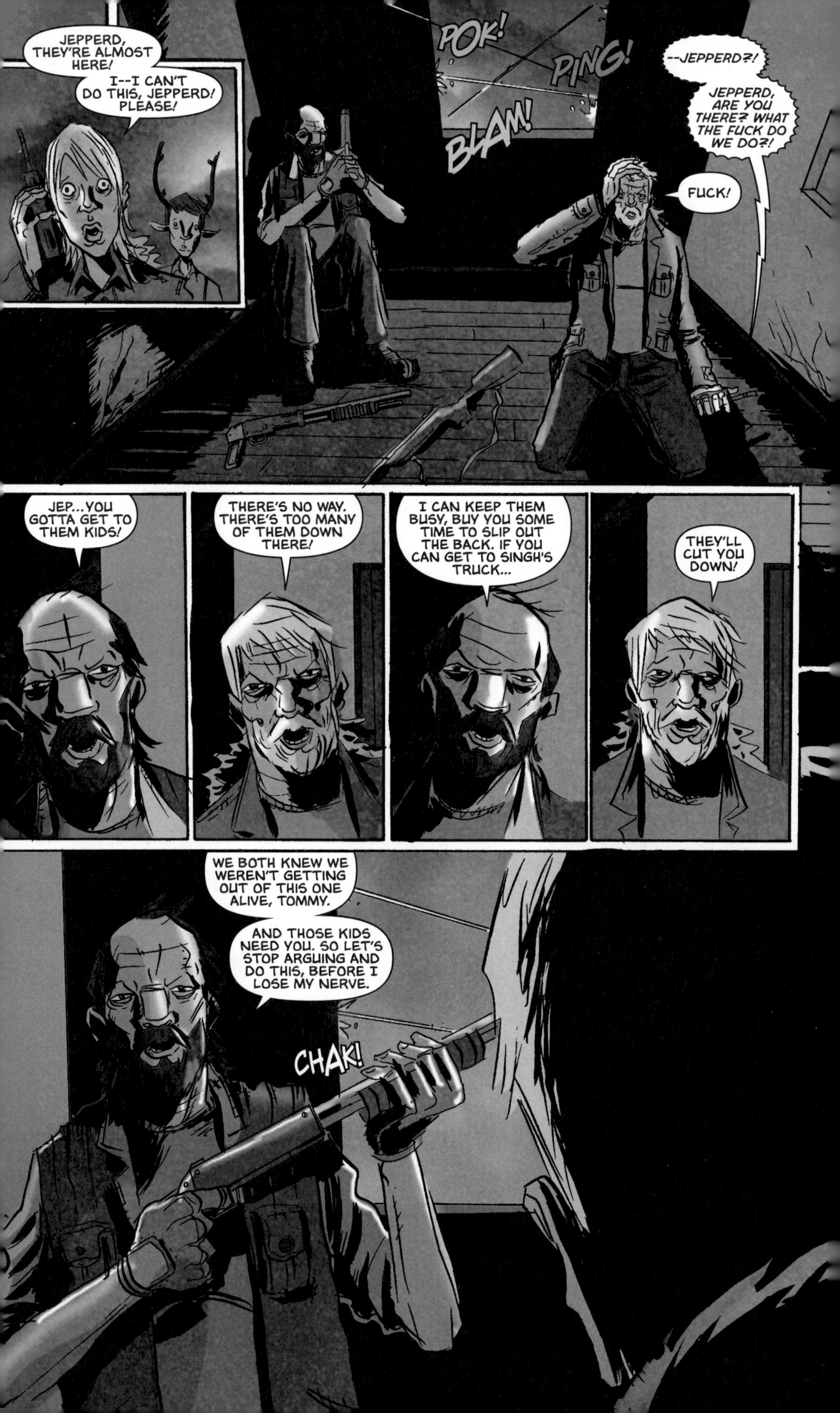

JEPPERD, THEY'RE ALMOST HERE!
I--I CAN'T DO THIS, JEPPERD! PLEASE!
POK!
PING!
BLAM!
--JEPPERD?!
JEPPERD, ARE YOU THERE? WHAT THE FUCK DO WE DO?!
FUCK!
JEP...YOU GOTTA GET TO THEM KIDS!
THERE'S NO WAY. THERE'S TOO MANY OF THEM DOWN THERE!
I CAN KEEP THEM BUSY, BUY YOU SOME TIME TO SLIP OUT THE BACK. IF YOU CAN GET TO SINGH'S TRUCK...
THEY'LL CUT YOU DOWN!
WE BOTH KNEW WE WEREN'T GETTING OUT OF THIS ONE ALIVE, TOMMY.
AND THOSE KIDS NEED YOU. SO LET'S STOP ARGUING AND DO THIS, BEFORE I LOSE MY NERVE.
CHAK!

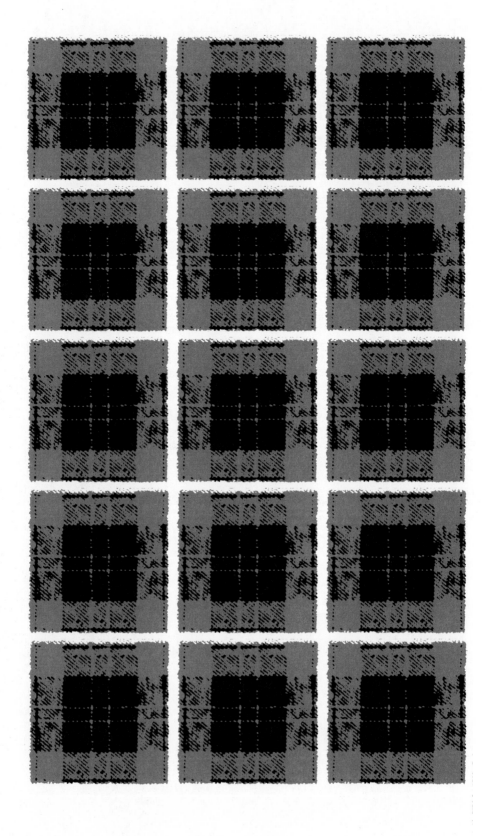

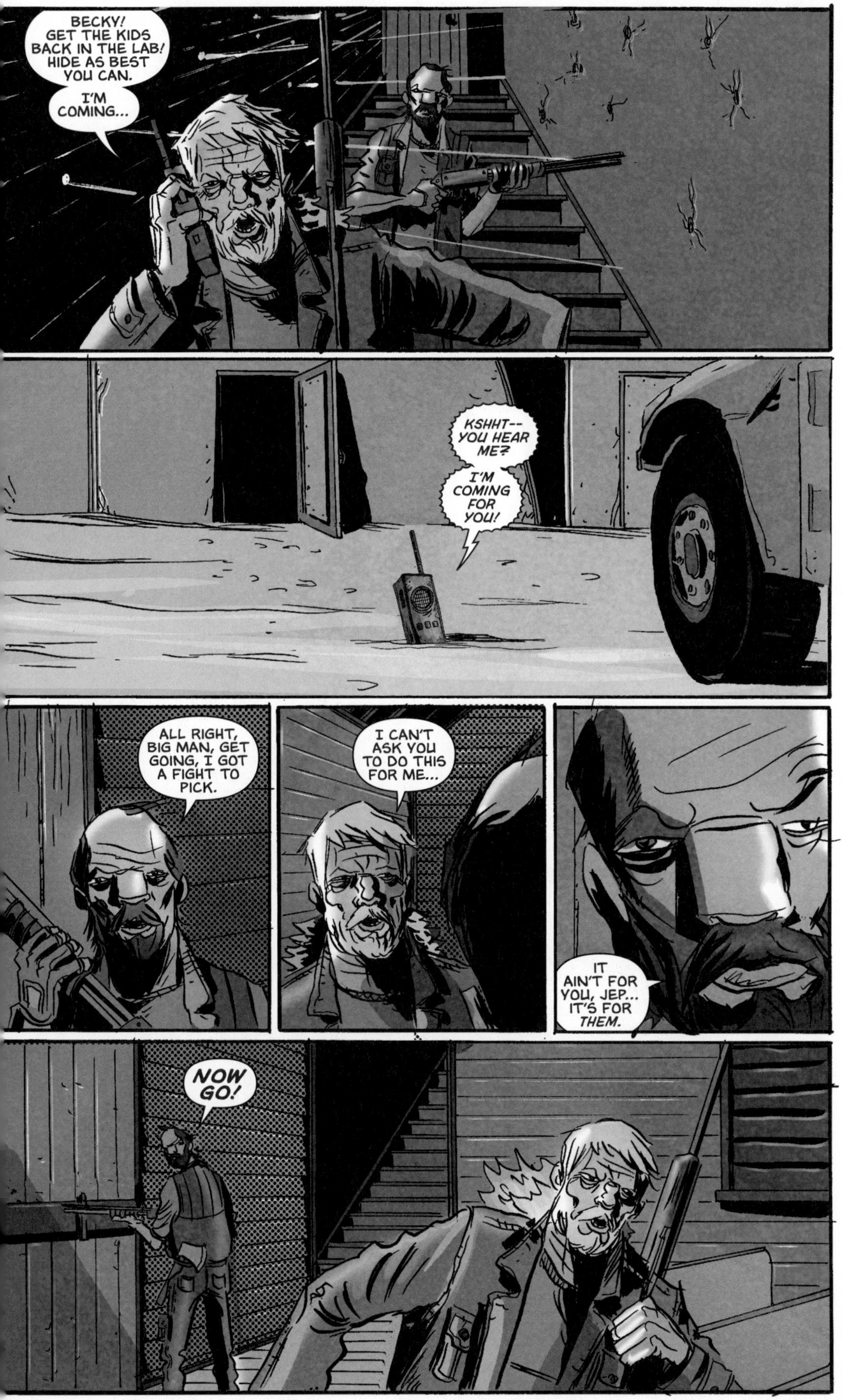
BECKY! GET THE KIDS BACK IN THE LAB! HIDE AS BEST YOU CAN.
I'M COMING...
KSHHT-- YOU HEAR ME?
I'M COMING FOR YOU!
ALL RIGHT, BIG MAN, GET GOING, I GOT A FIGHT TO PICK.
I CAN'T ASK YOU TO DO THIS FOR ME...
IT AIN'T FOR YOU, JEP... IT'S FOR *THEM*.
NOW GO!

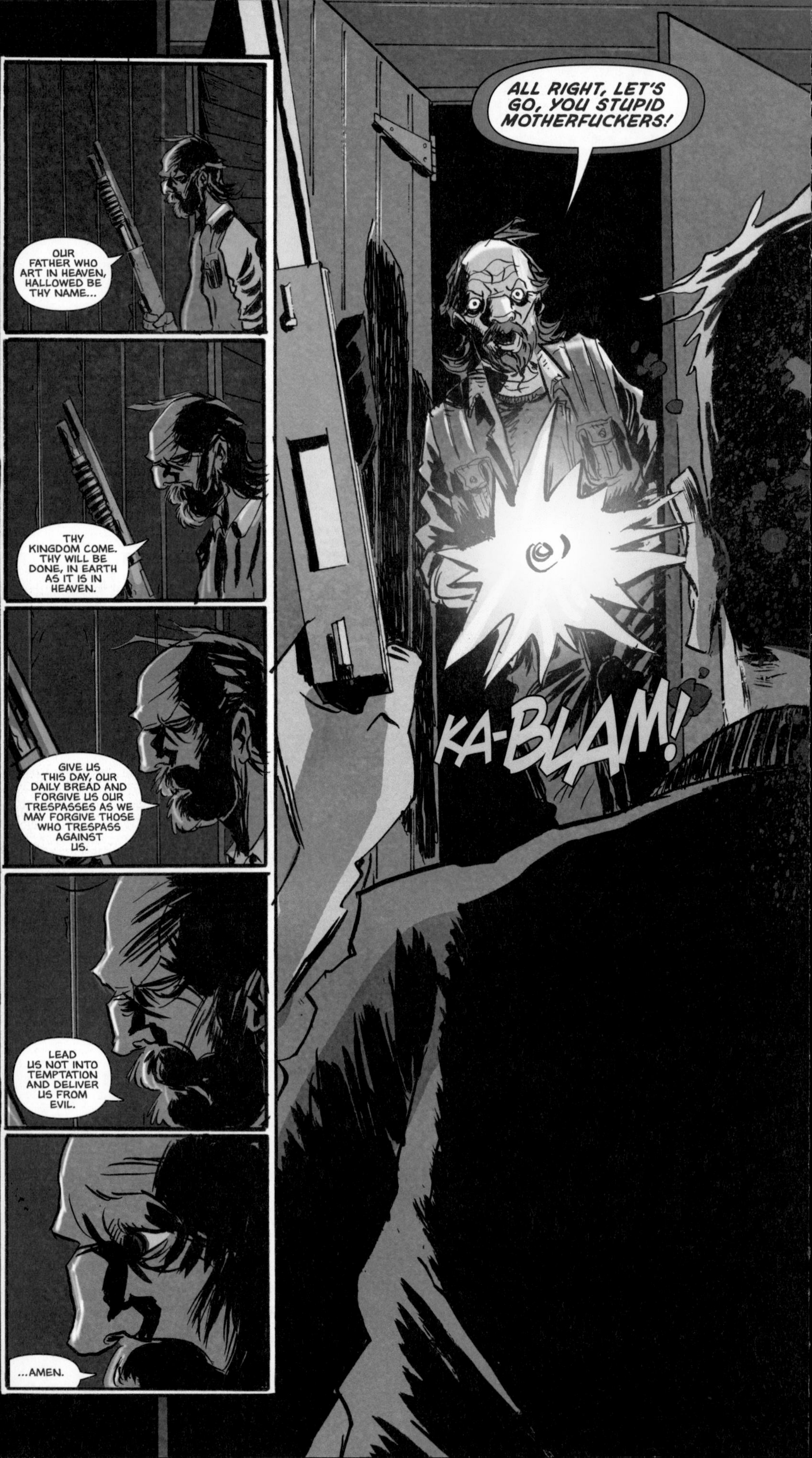
OUR FATHER WHO ART IN HEAVEN, HALLOWED BE THY NAME...
THY KINGDOM COME. THY WILL BE DONE, IN EARTH AS IT IS IN HEAVEN.
GIVE US THIS DAY, OUR DAILY BREAD AND FORGIVE US OUR TRESPASSES AS WE MAY FORGIVE THOSE WHO TRESPASS AGAINST US.
LEAD US NOT INTO TEMPTATION AND DELIVER US FROM EVIL.
...AMEN.
ALL RIGHT, LET'S GO, YOU STUPID MOTHERFUCKERS!
KA-BLAM!

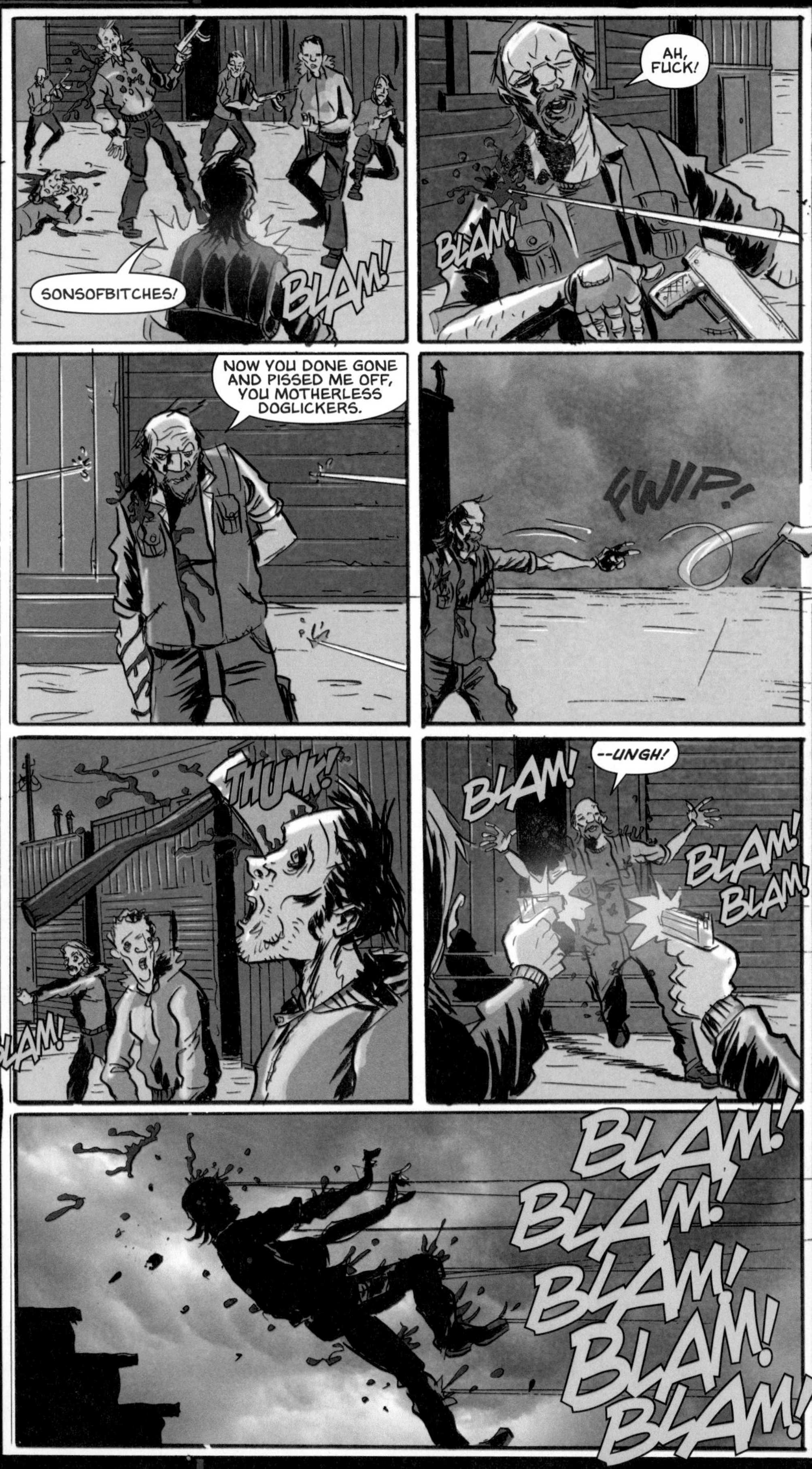
SONSOFBITCHES!
BLAM!
AH, FUCK!
BLAM!
NOW YOU DONE GONE AND PISSED ME OFF, YOU MOTHERLESS DOGLICKERS.
FWIP!
THUNK!
BLAM!
BLAM!
--UNGH!
BLAM!
BLAM!
BLAM!
BLAM!
BLAM!
BLAM!
BLAM!

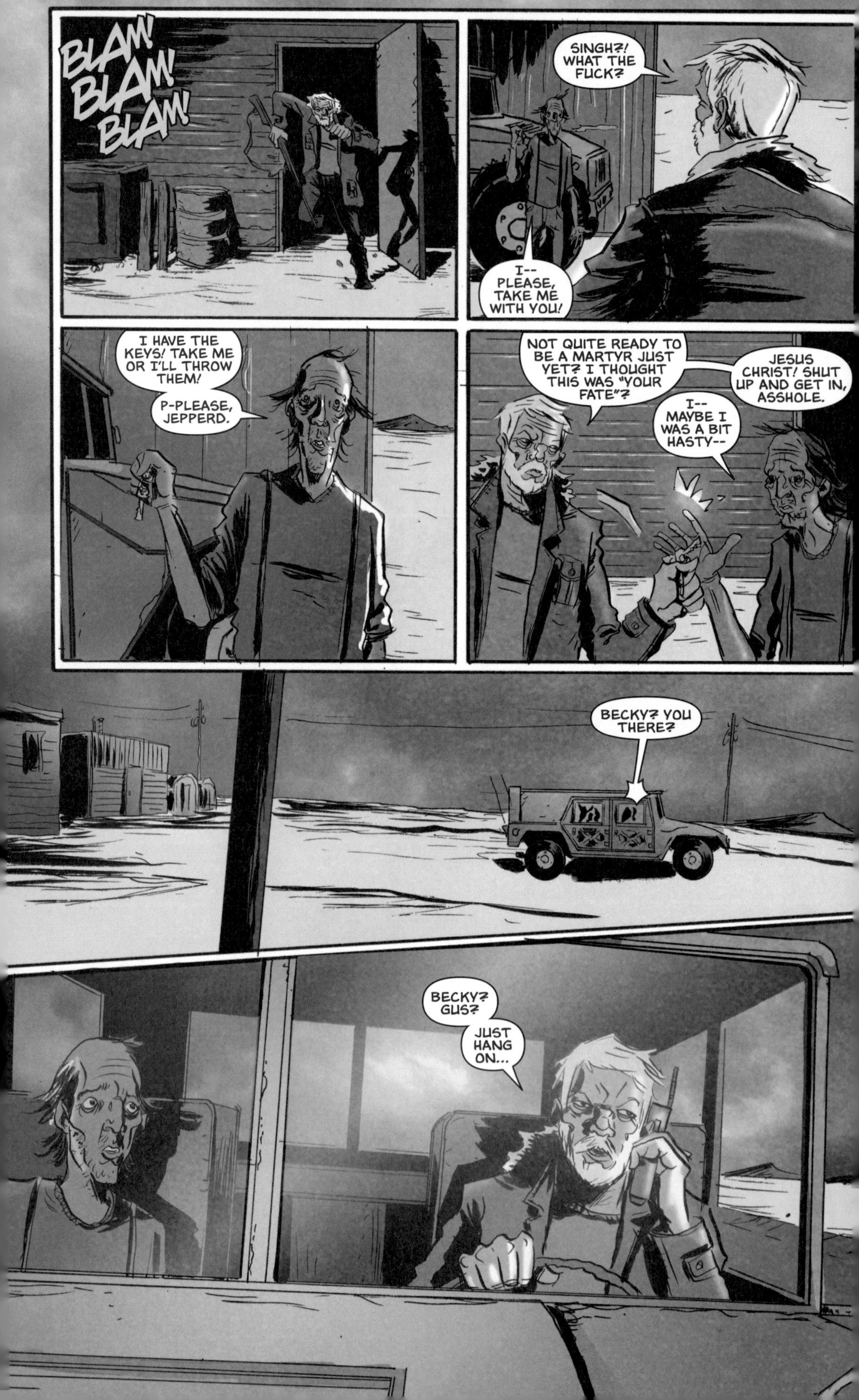
BLAM! BLAM! BLAM!
SINGH?! WHAT THE FUCK?
I-- PLEASE, TAKE ME WITH YOU!
I HAVE THE KEYS! TAKE ME OR I'LL THROW THEM!
P-PLEASE, JEPPERD.
NOT QUITE READY TO BE A MARTYR JUST YET? I THOUGHT THIS WAS "YOUR FATE"?
I-- MAYBE I WAS A BIT HASTY--
JESUS CHRIST! SHUT UP AND GET IN, ASSHOLE.
BECKY? YOU THERE?
BECKY? GUS?
JUST HANG ON...

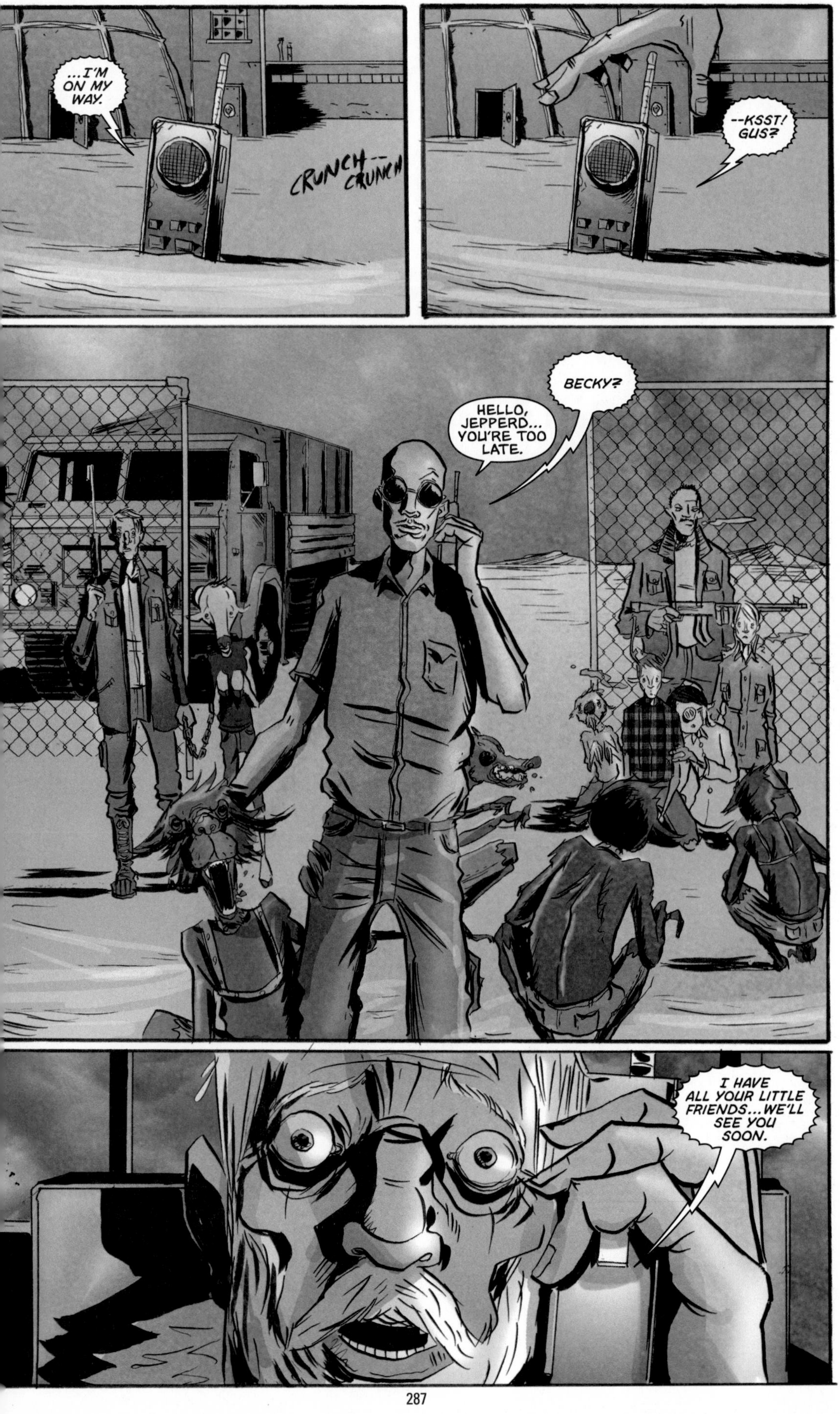
...I'M ON MY WAY.
CRUNCH--CRUNCH
--KSST! GUS?
HELLO, JEPPERD... YOU'RE TOO LATE.
BECKY?
I HAVE ALL YOUR LITTLE FRIENDS...WE'LL SEE YOU SOON.

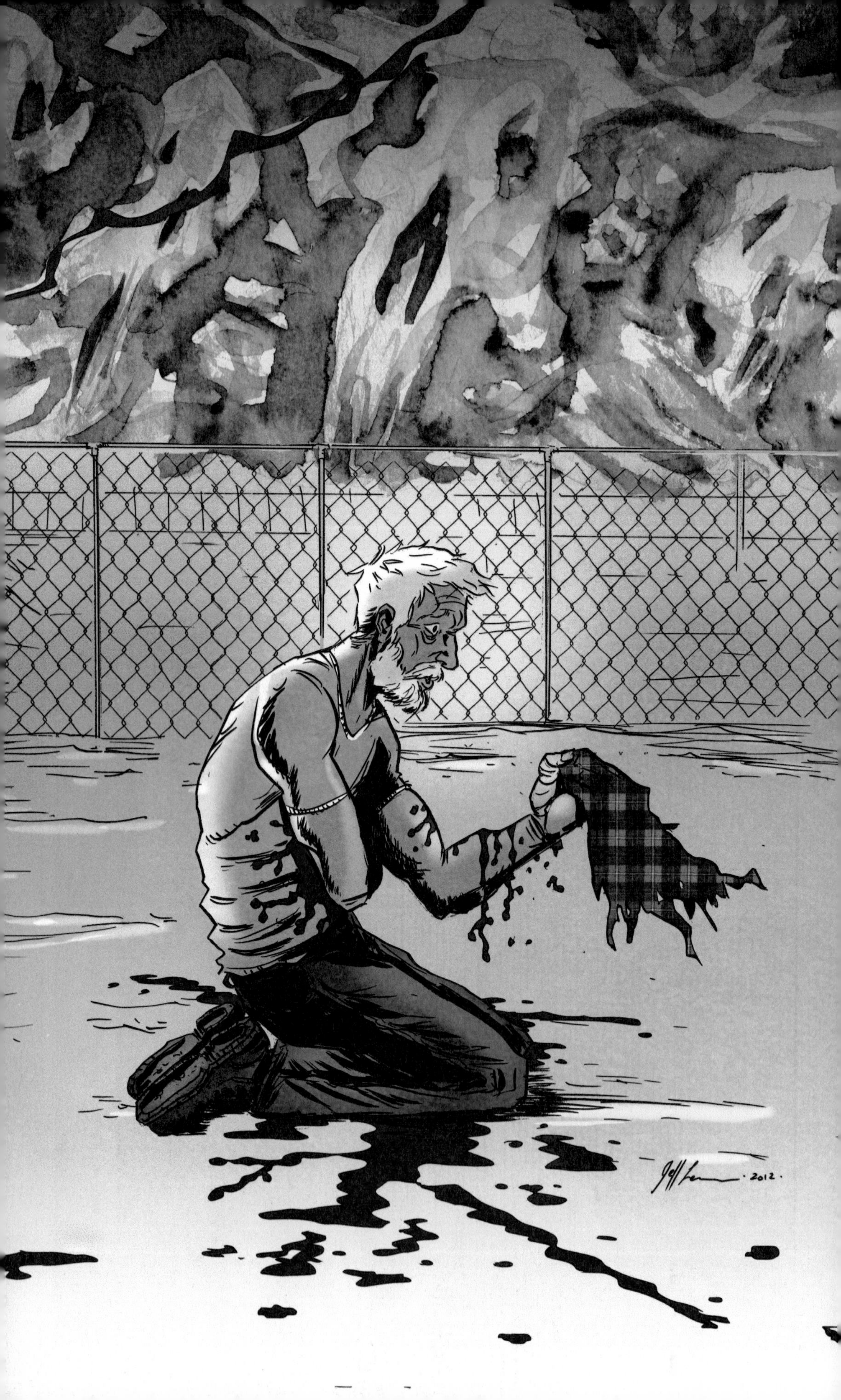

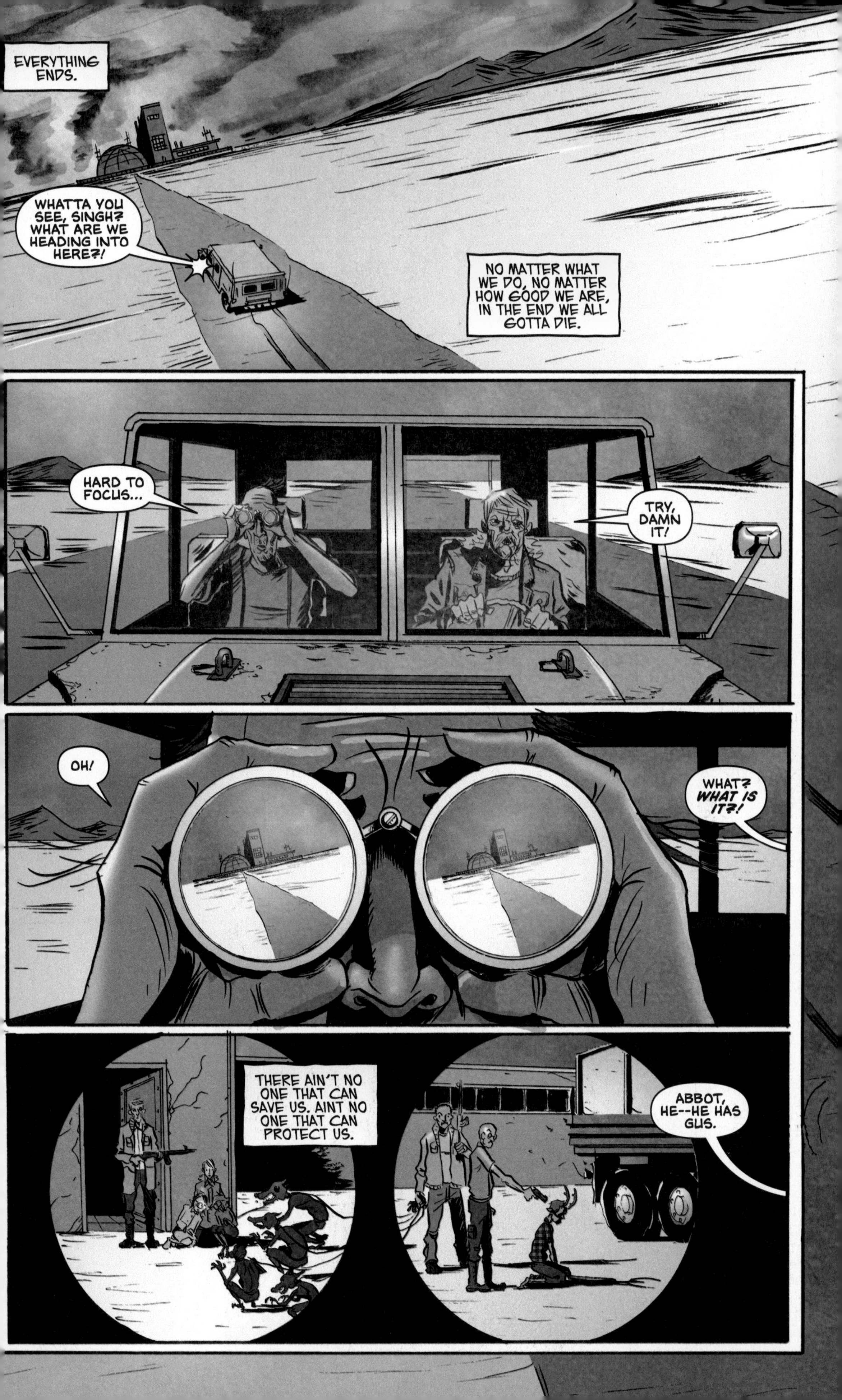
EVERYTHING ENDS.
WHATTA YOU SEE, SINGH? WHAT ARE WE HEADING INTO HERE?!
NO MATTER WHAT WE DO, NO MATTER HOW GOOD WE ARE, IN THE END WE ALL GOTTA DIE.
HARD TO FOCUS...
TRY, DAMN IT!
OH!
WHAT? WHAT IS IT?!
THERE AIN'T NO ONE THAT CAN SAVE US. AINT NO ONE THAT CAN PROTECT US.
ABBOT, HE--HE HAS GUS.

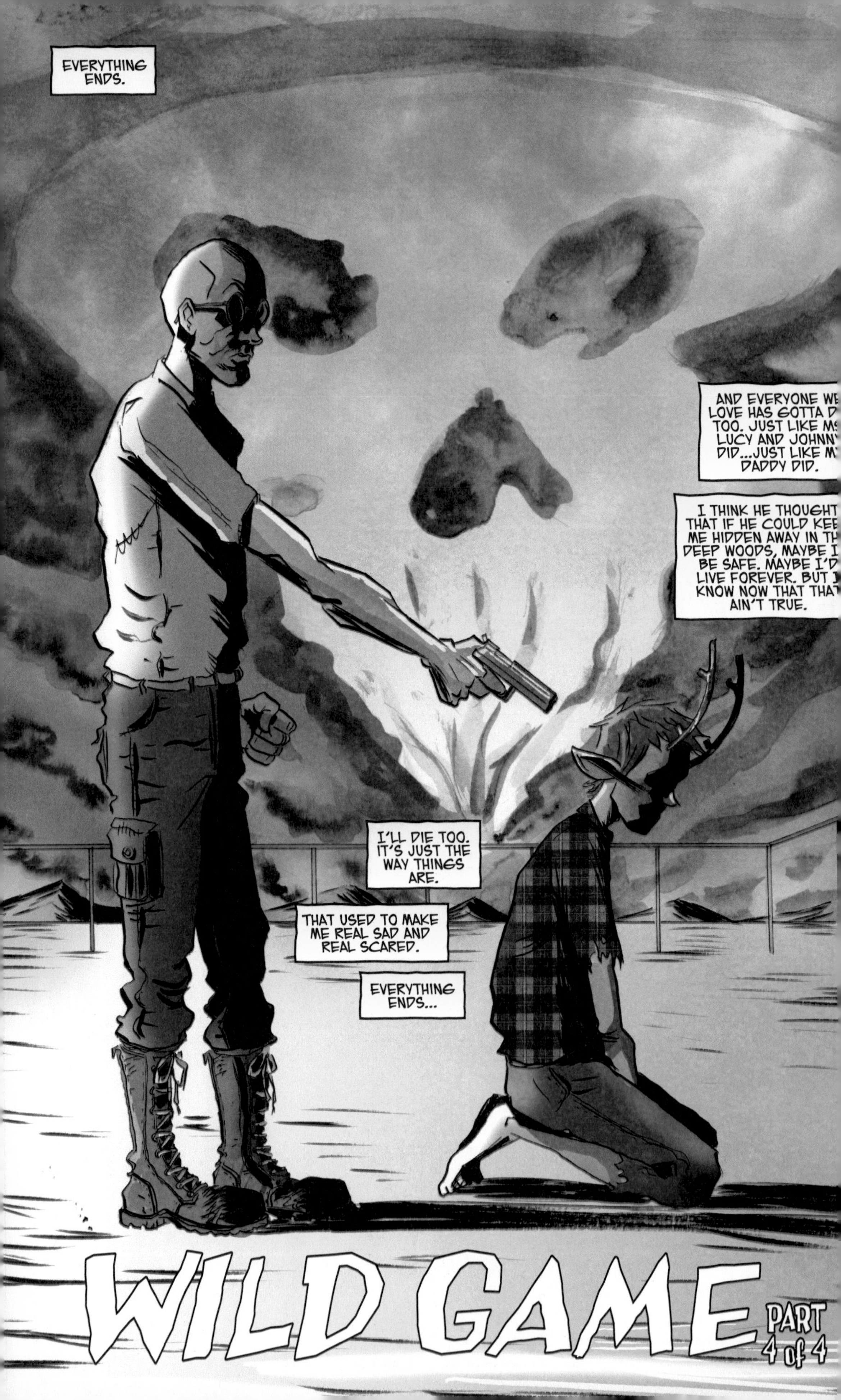
EVERYTHING ENDS.
AND EVERYONE WE LOVE HAS GOTTA D TOO. JUST LIKE MS LUCY AND JOHNNY DID...JUST LIKE MY DADDY DID.
I THINK HE THOUGHT THAT IF HE COULD KEE ME HIDDEN AWAY IN TH DEEP WOODS, MAYBE I BE SAFE. MAYBE I'D LIVE FOREVER. BUT I KNOW NOW THAT THAT AIN'T TRUE.
I'LL DIE TOO. IT'S JUST THE WAY THINGS ARE.
THAT USED TO MAKE ME REAL SAD AND REAL SCARED.
EVERYTHING ENDS...
WILD GAME
PART 4 of 4

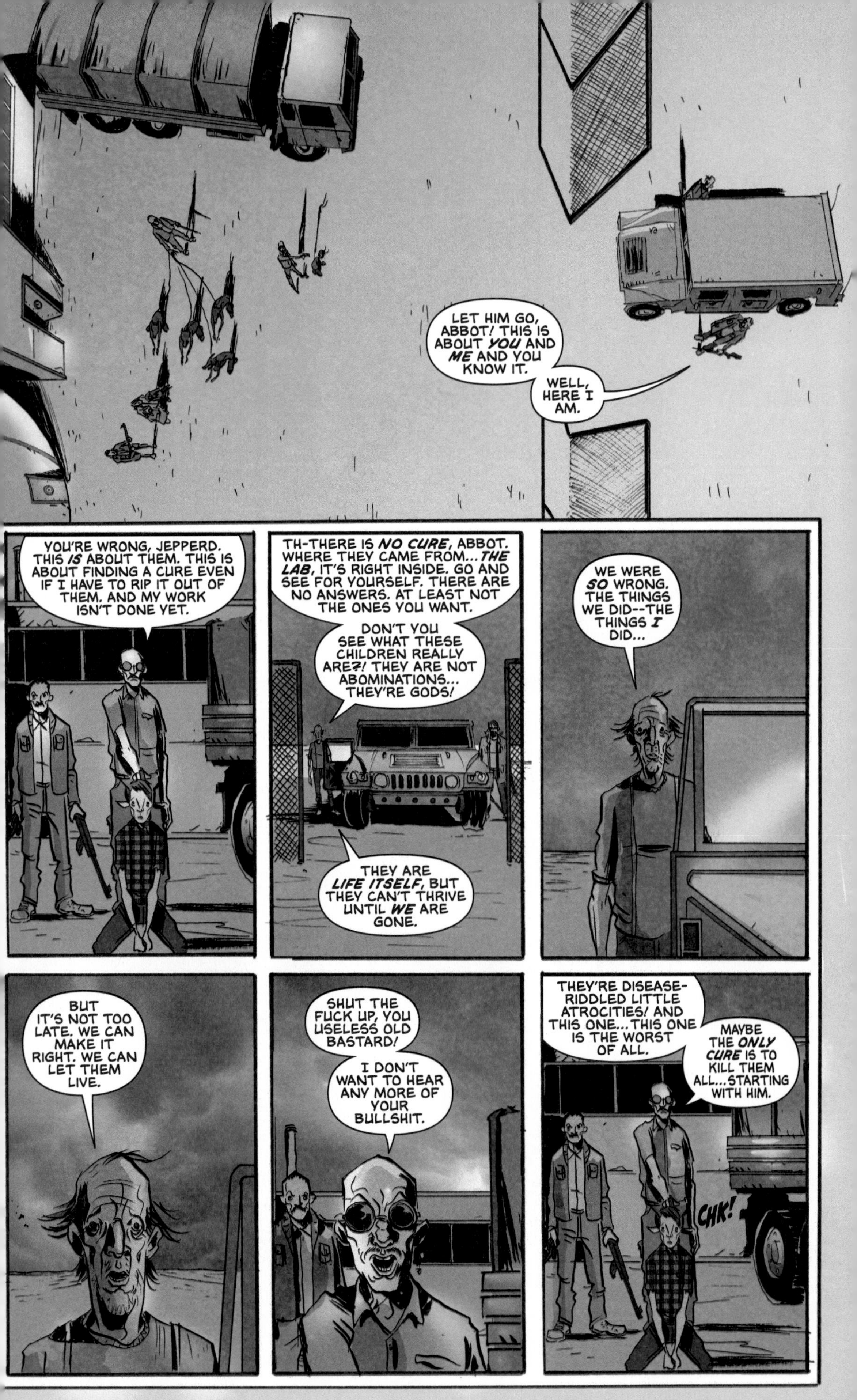
LET HIM GO, ABBOT! THIS IS ABOUT *YOU* AND *ME* AND YOU KNOW IT.
WELL, HERE I AM.
YOU'RE WRONG, JEPPERD. THIS *IS* ABOUT THEM. THIS IS ABOUT FINDING A CURE EVEN IF I HAVE TO RIP IT OUT OF THEM. AND MY WORK ISN'T DONE YET.
TH-THERE IS *NO CURE*, ABBOT. WHERE THEY CAME FROM... *THE LAB*, IT'S RIGHT INSIDE. GO AND SEE FOR YOURSELF. THERE ARE NO ANSWERS. AT LEAST NOT THE ONES YOU WANT.
DON'T YOU SEE WHAT THESE CHILDREN REALLY ARE?! THEY ARE NOT ABOMINATIONS... THEY'RE GODS!
THEY ARE *LIFE ITSELF*, BUT THEY CAN'T THRIVE UNTIL *WE* ARE GONE.
WE WERE *SO* WRONG. THE THINGS WE DID--THE THINGS *I* DID...
BUT IT'S NOT TOO LATE. WE CAN MAKE IT RIGHT. WE CAN LET THEM LIVE.
SHUT THE FUCK UP, YOU USELESS OLD BASTARD!
I DON'T WANT TO HEAR ANY MORE OF YOUR BULLSHIT.
THEY'RE DISEASE-RIDDLED LITTLE ATROCITIES! AND THIS ONE...THIS ONE IS THE WORST OF ALL.
MAYBE THE *ONLY CURE* IS TO KILL THEM ALL...STARTING WITH HIM.
CHK!

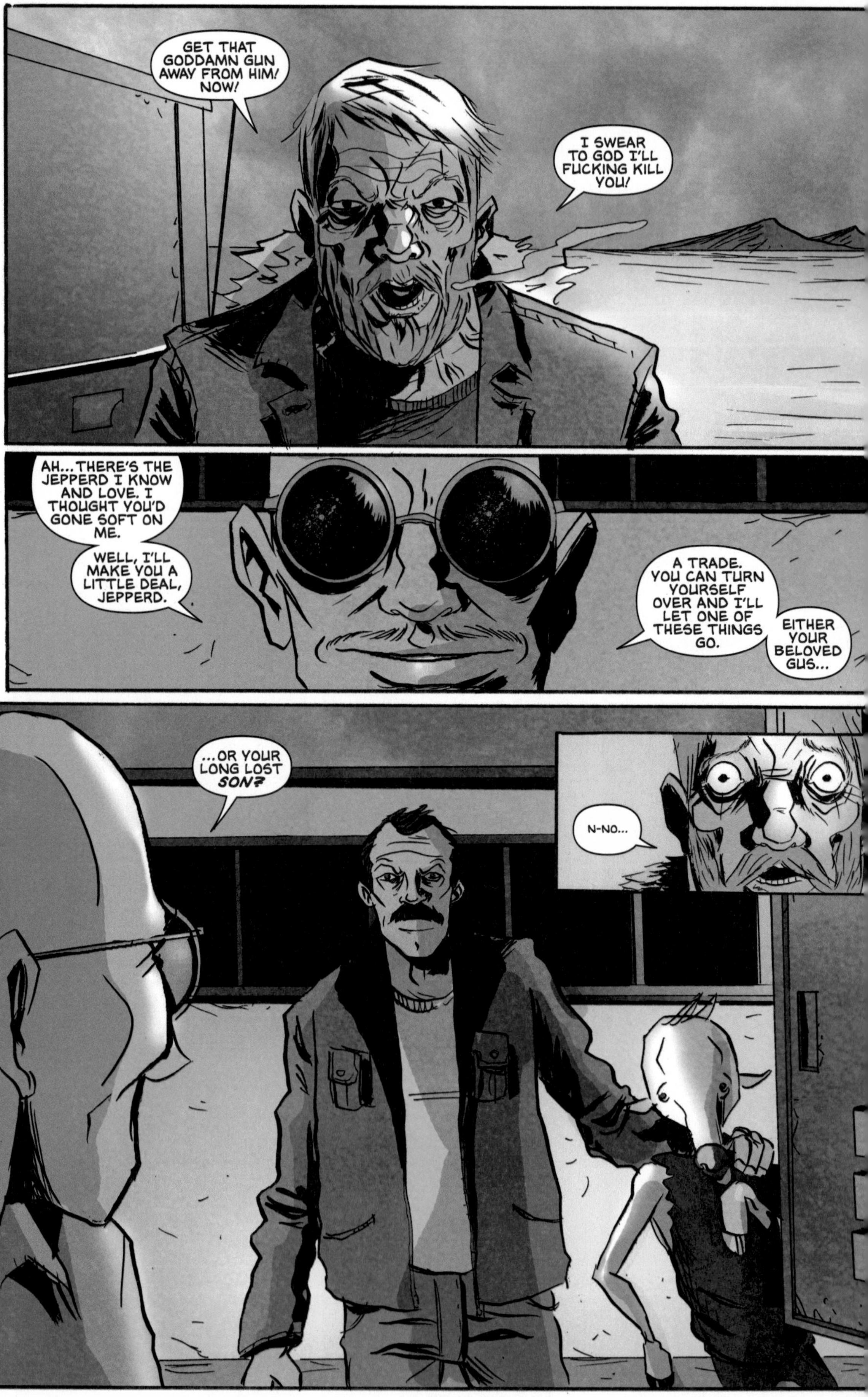
GET THAT GODDAMN GUN AWAY FROM HIM! NOW!
I SWEAR TO GOD I'LL FUCKING KILL YOU!
AH...THERE'S THE JEPPERD I KNOW AND LOVE. I THOUGHT YOU'D GONE SOFT ON ME.
WELL, I'LL MAKE YOU A LITTLE DEAL, JEPPERD.
A TRADE. YOU CAN TURN YOURSELF OVER AND I'LL LET ONE OF THESE THINGS GO.
EITHER YOUR BELOVED GUS...
...OR YOUR LONG LOST SON?
N-NO...

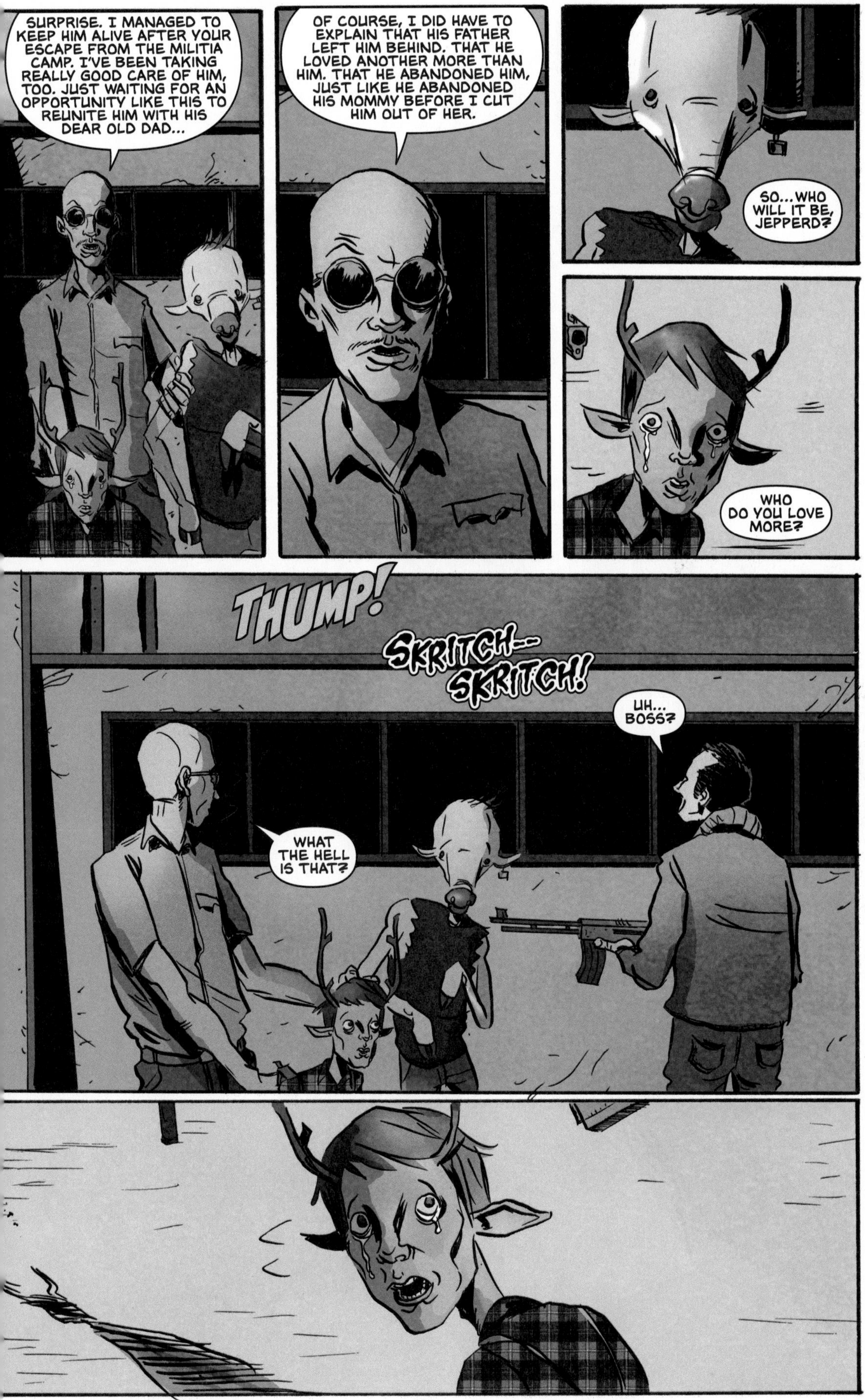

SURPRISE. I MANAGED TO KEEP HIM ALIVE AFTER YOUR ESCAPE FROM THE MILITIA CAMP. I'VE BEEN TAKING REALLY GOOD CARE OF HIM, TOO. JUST WAITING FOR AN OPPORTUNITY LIKE THIS TO REUNITE HIM WITH HIS DEAR OLD DAD...
OF COURSE, I DID HAVE TO EXPLAIN THAT HIS FATHER LEFT HIM BEHIND. THAT HE LOVED ANOTHER MORE THAN HIM. THAT HE ABANDONED HIM, JUST LIKE HE ABANDONED HIS MOMMY BEFORE I CUT HIM OUT OF HER.
SO... WHO WILL IT BE, JEPPERD?
WHO DO YOU LOVE MORE?
THUMP!
SKRITCH-- SKRITCH!
UH... BOSS?
WHAT THE HELL IS THAT?

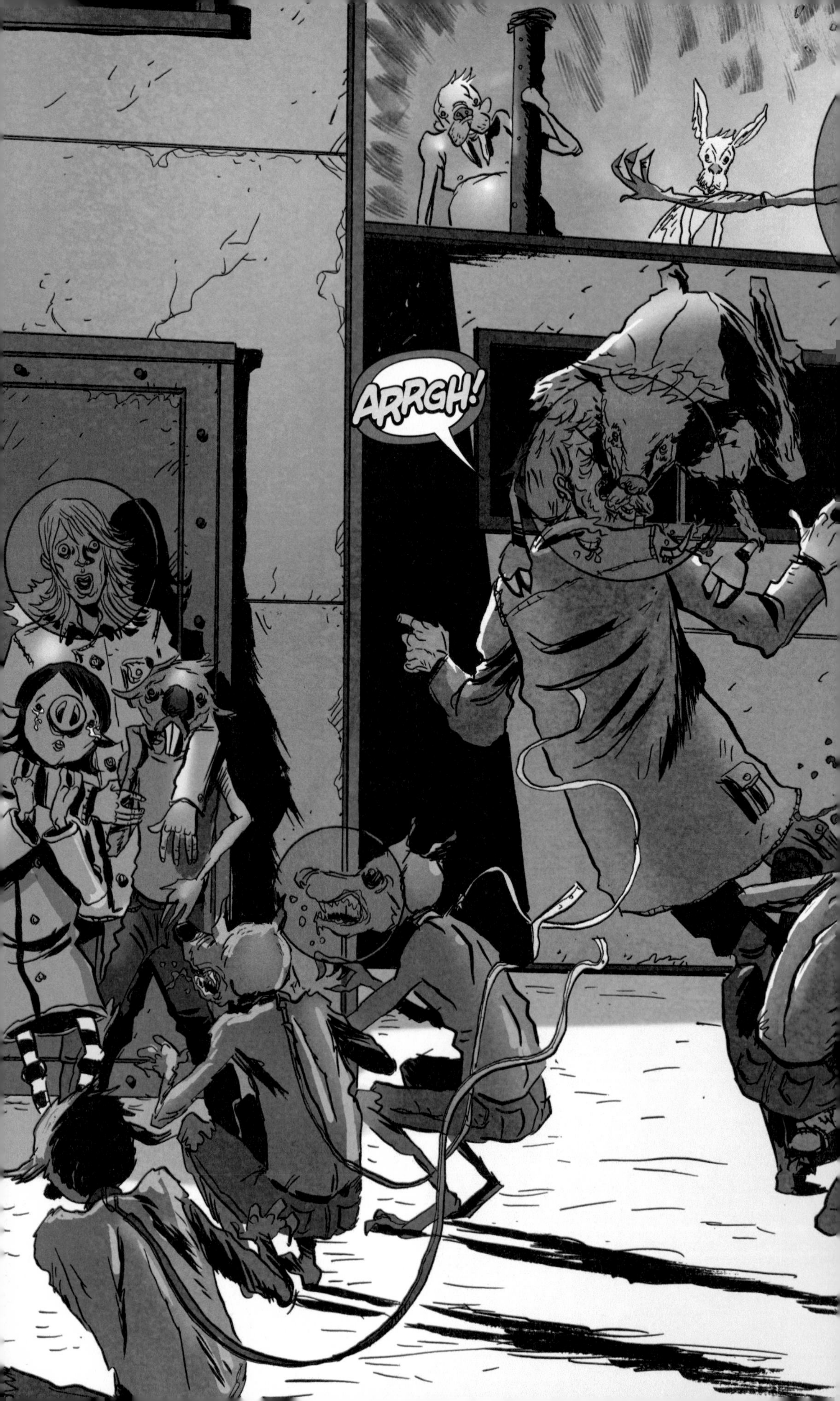
ARRGH!

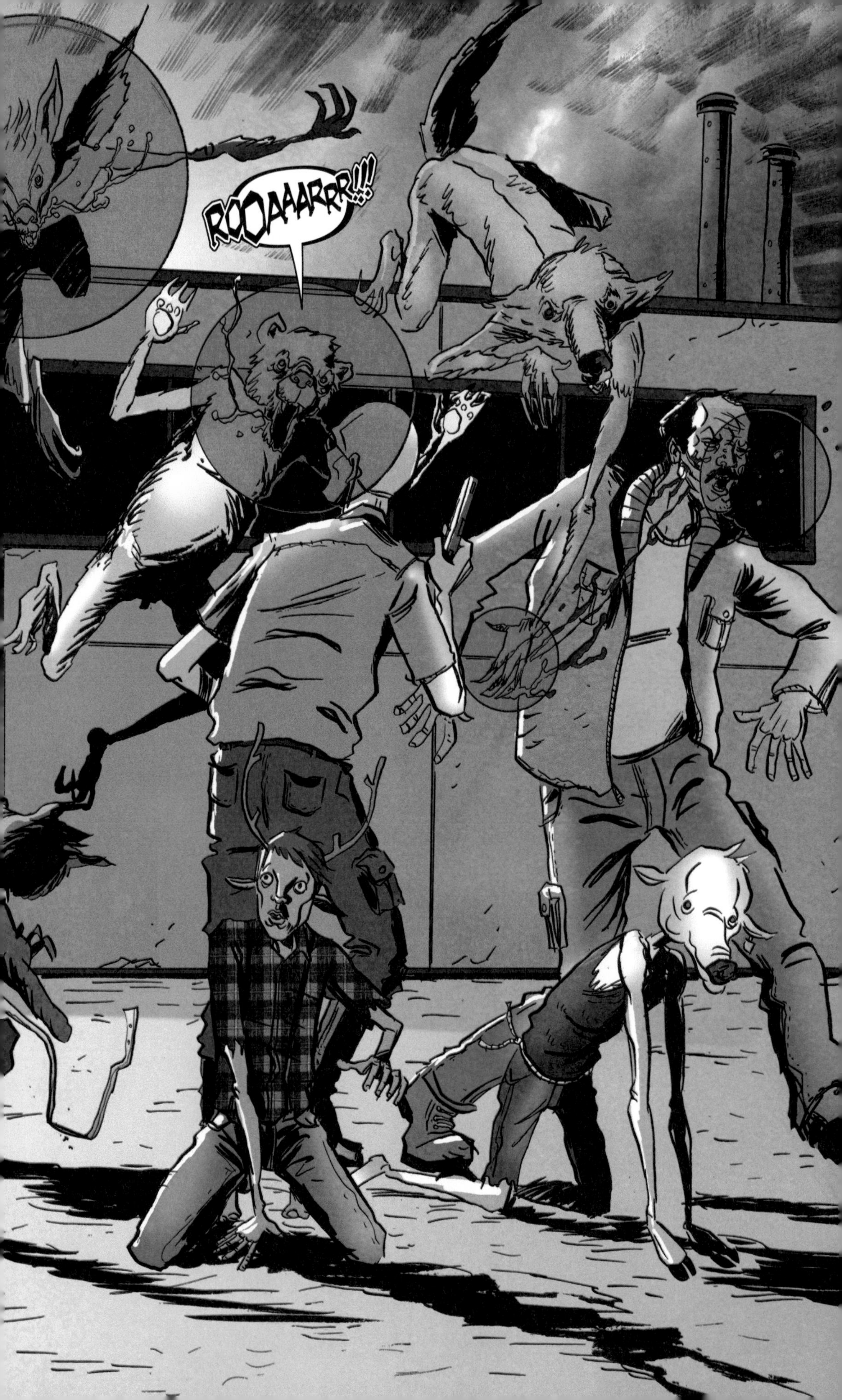
ROOAAARRR!!!

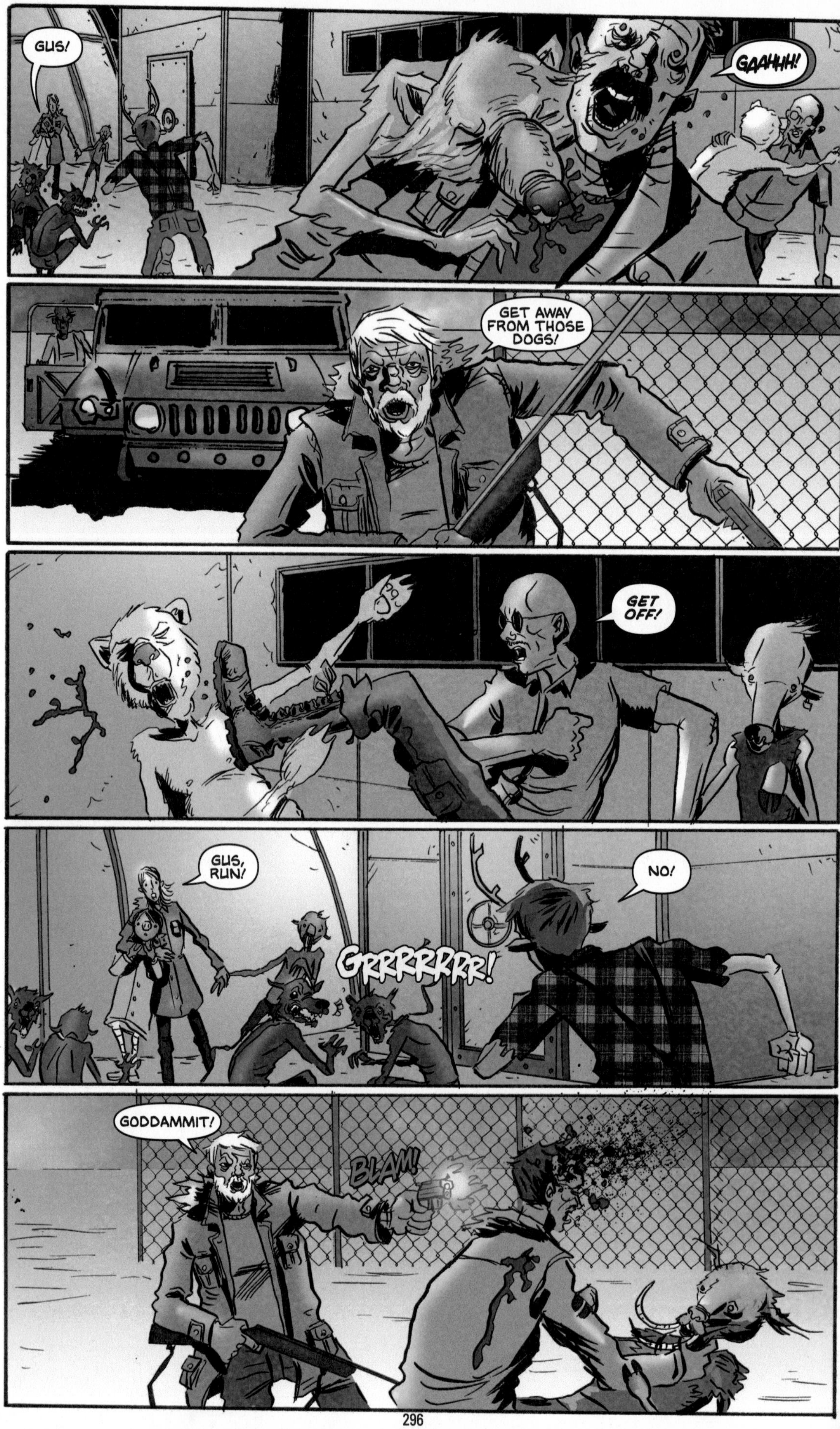
GUS!
GAAHHH!
GET AWAY FROM THOSE DOGS!
GET OFF!
GUS, RUN!
NO!
GRRRRRRR!
GODDAMMIT!
BLAM!

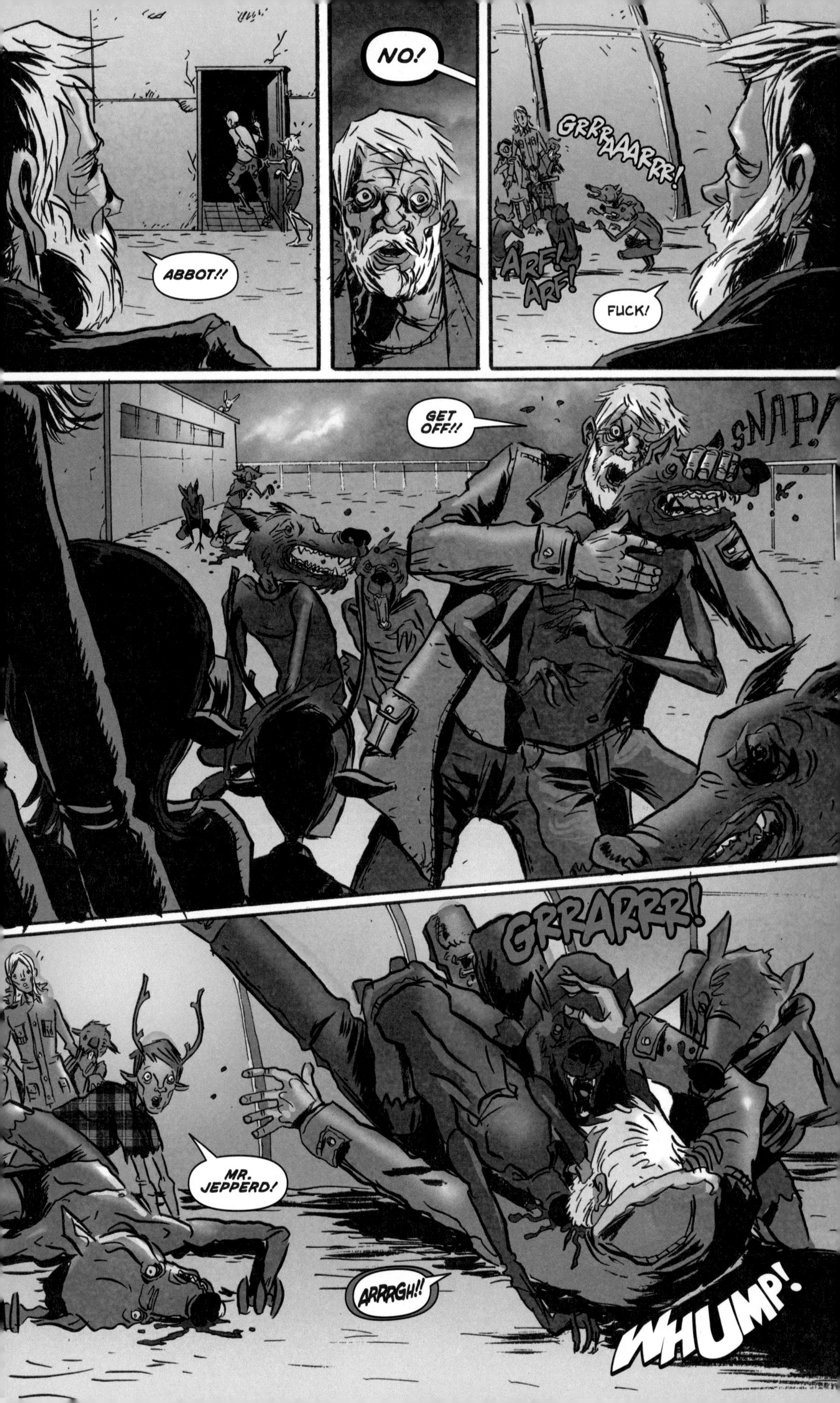
ABBOT!!
NO!
GRRRAAARRR!
ARF! ARF!
FUCK!
GET OFF!!
SNAP!
GRRARRR!
MR. JEPPERD!
ARRRGH!!
WHUMP!

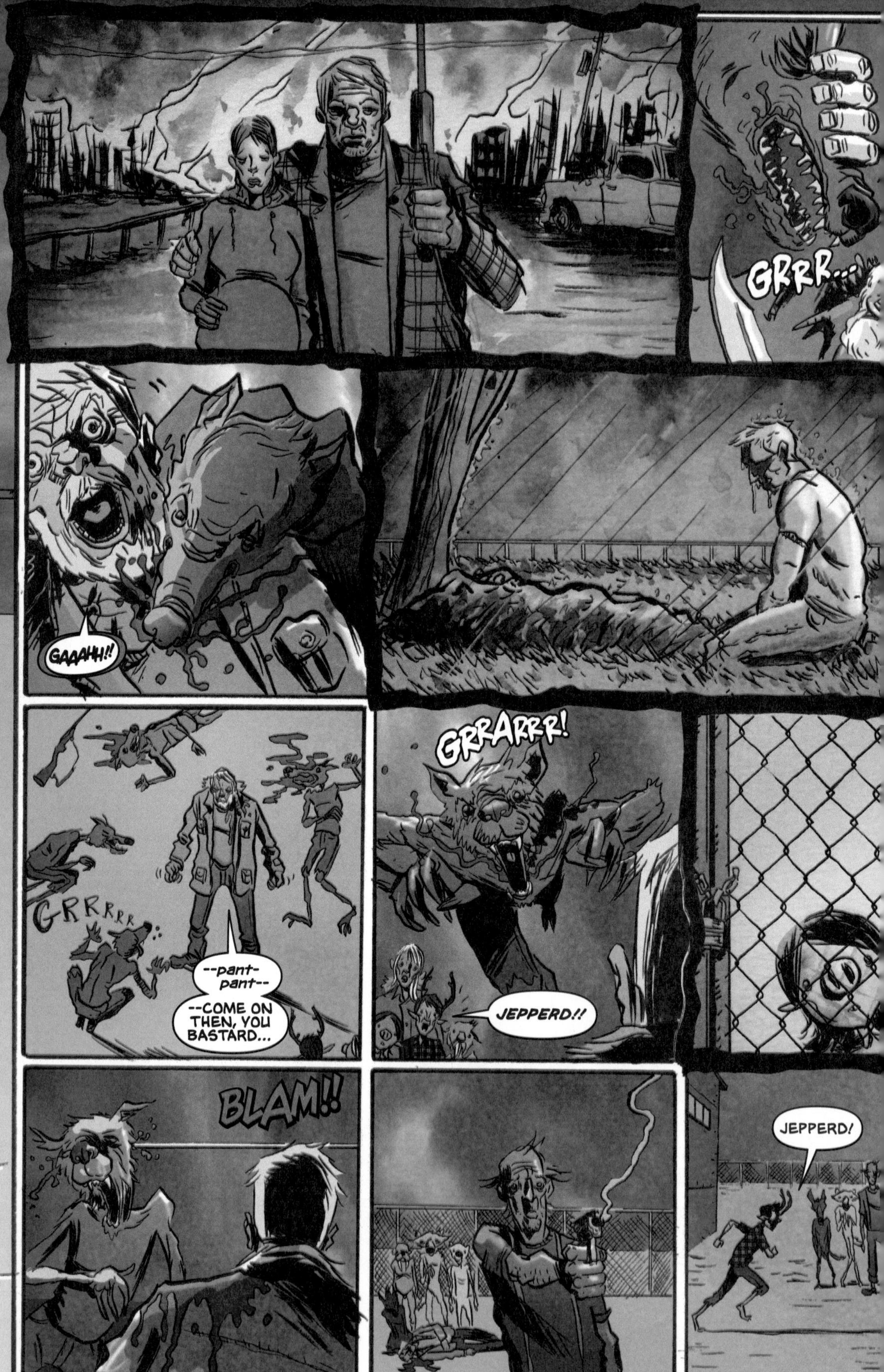
GRRR...
GAAAHH!!
GRRRRR
--pant-
pant--
--COME ON
THEN, YOU
BASTARD...
GRRARRR!
JEPPERD!!
BLAM!!
JEPPERD!

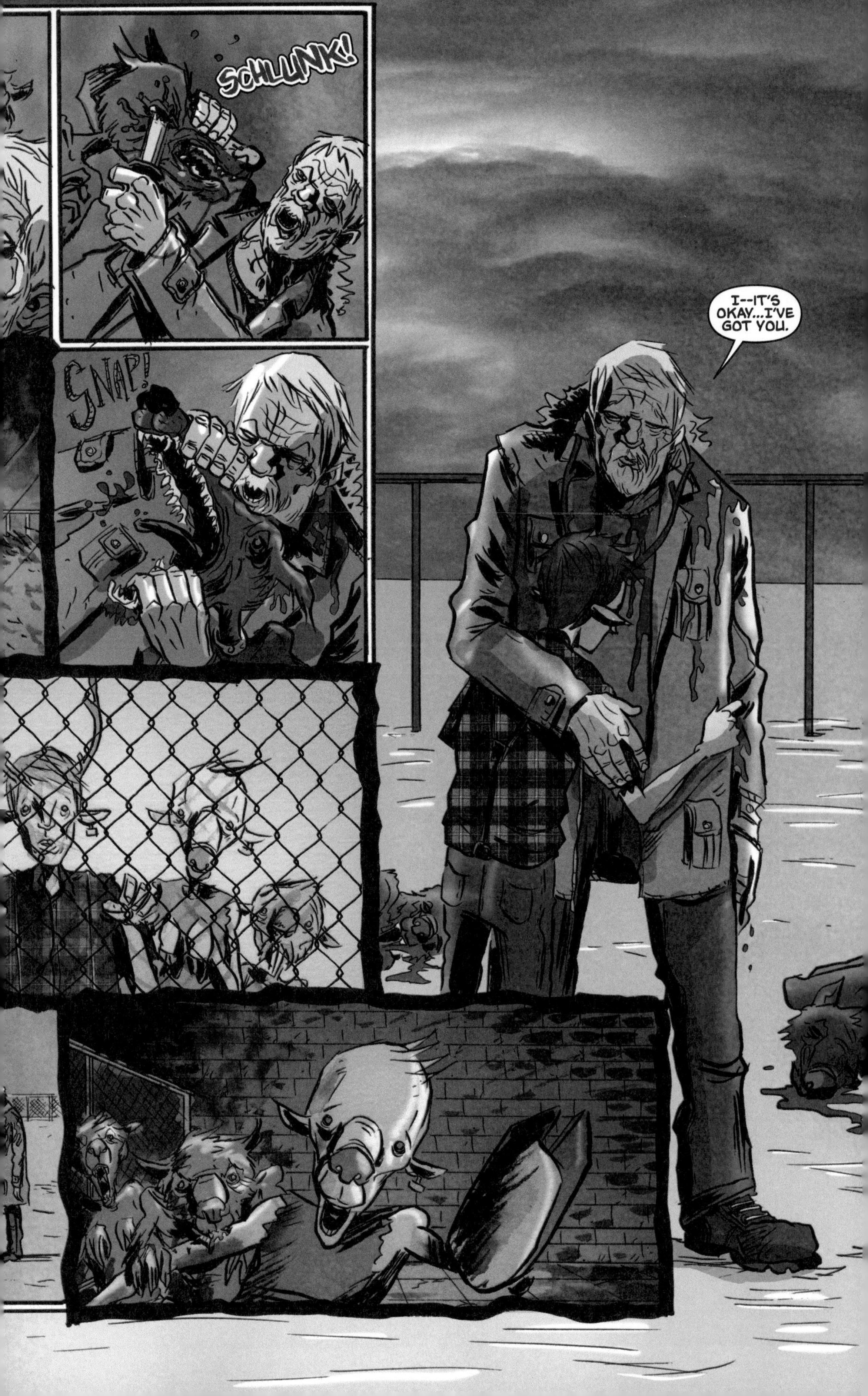
SCHLUNK!
SNAP!
I--IT'S OKAY...I'VE GOT YOU.

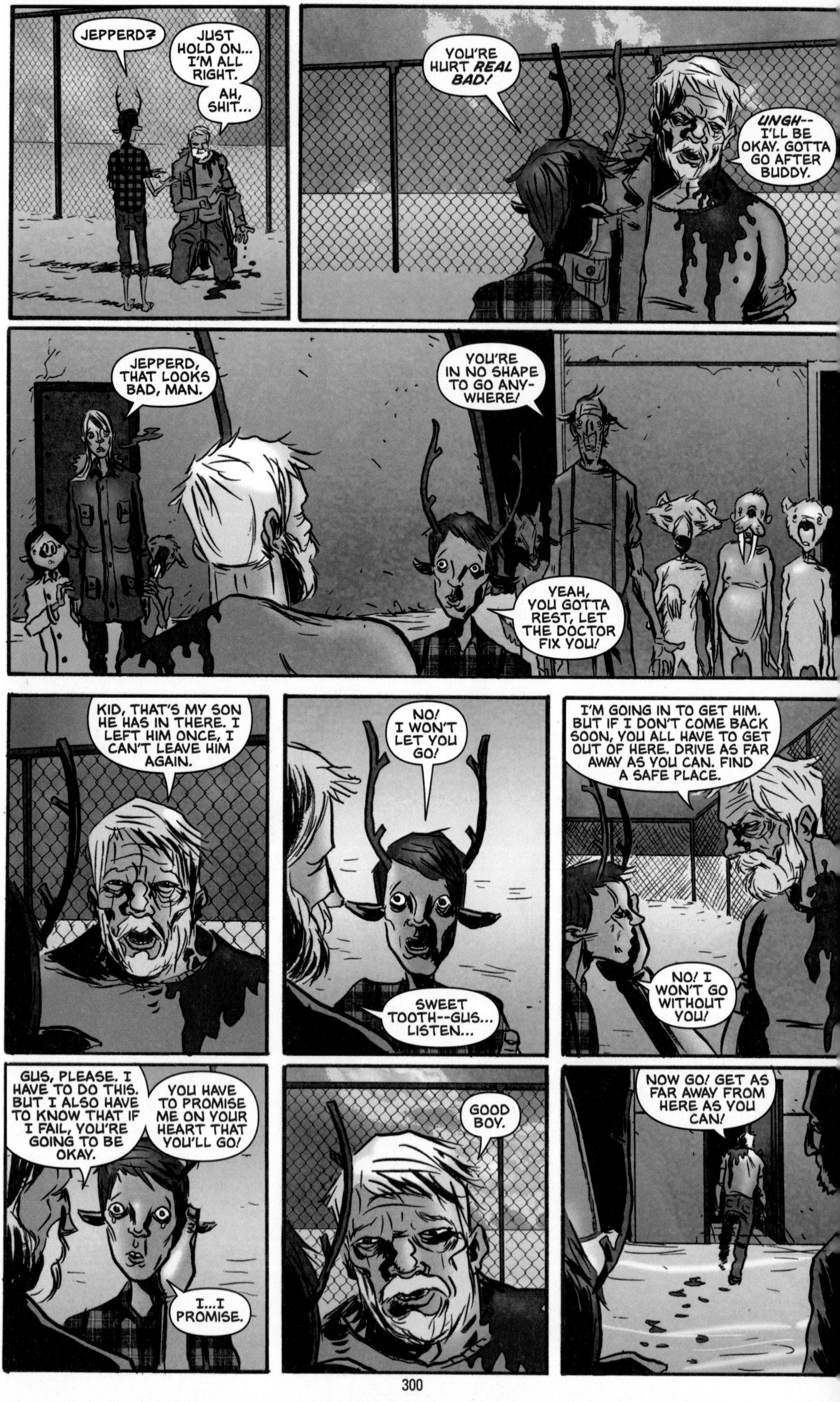
JEPPERD?
JUST HOLD ON... I'M ALL RIGHT.
AH, SHIT...
YOU'RE HURT REAL BAD!
UNGH-- I'LL BE OKAY. GOTTA GO AFTER BUDDY.
JEPPERD, THAT LOOKS BAD, MAN.
YOU'RE IN NO SHAPE TO GO ANY-WHERE!
YEAH, YOU GOTTA REST, LET THE DOCTOR FIX YOU!
KID, THAT'S MY SON HE HAS IN THERE. I LEFT HIM ONCE, I CAN'T LEAVE HIM AGAIN.
NO! I WON'T LET YOU GO!
SWEET TOOTH--GUS... LISTEN...
I'M GOING IN TO GET HIM. BUT IF I DON'T COME BACK SOON, YOU ALL HAVE TO GET OUT OF HERE. DRIVE AS FAR AWAY AS YOU CAN. FIND A SAFE PLACE.
NO! I WON'T GO WITHOUT YOU!
GUS, PLEASE. I HAVE TO DO THIS. BUT I ALSO HAVE TO KNOW THAT IF I FAIL, YOU'RE GOING TO BE OKAY.
YOU HAVE TO PROMISE ME ON YOUR HEART THAT YOU'LL GO!
I...I PROMISE.
GOOD BOY.
NOW GO! GET AS FAR AWAY FROM HERE AS YOU CAN!

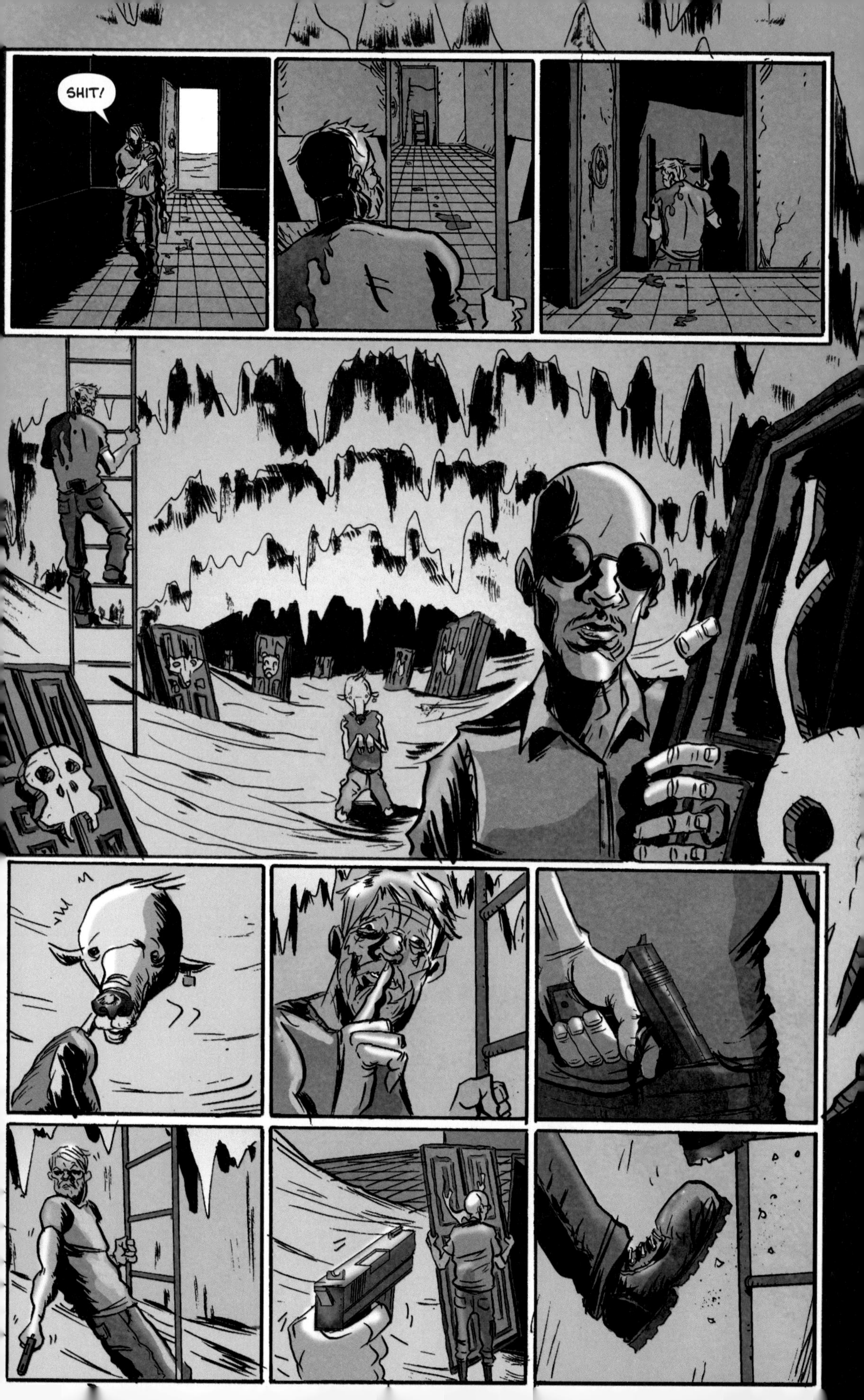
SHIT!

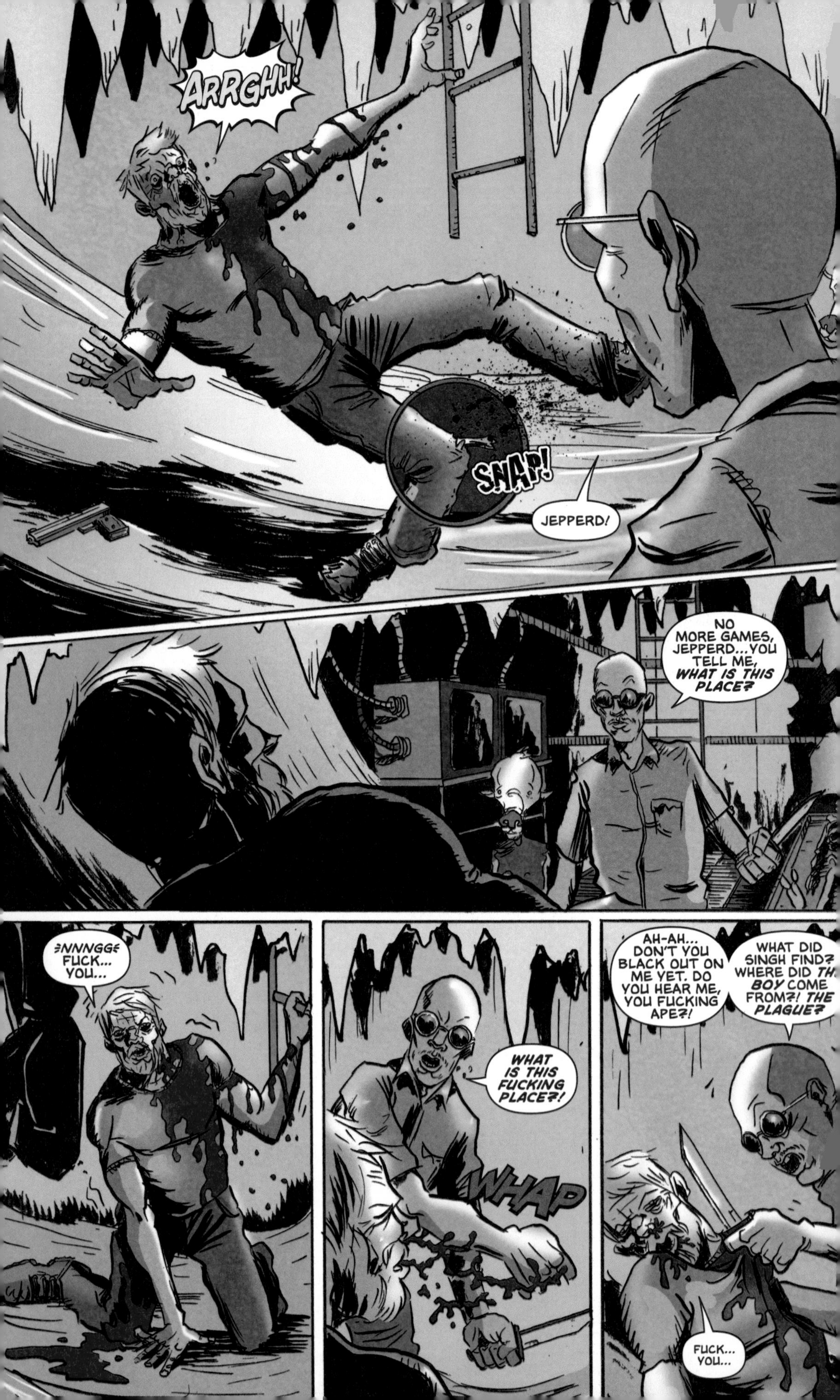
ARRGHH!
SNAP!
JEPPERD!
NO MORE GAMES, JEPPERD...YOU TELL ME, WHAT IS THIS PLACE?
NNNGG FUCK... YOU...
WHAT IS THIS FUCKING PLACE?!
WHAP
AH-AH... DON'T YOU BLACK OUT ON ME YET. DO YOU HEAR ME, YOU FUCKING APE?!
WHAT DID SINGH FIND? WHERE DID THE BOY COME FROM?! THE PLAGUE?
FUCK... YOU...

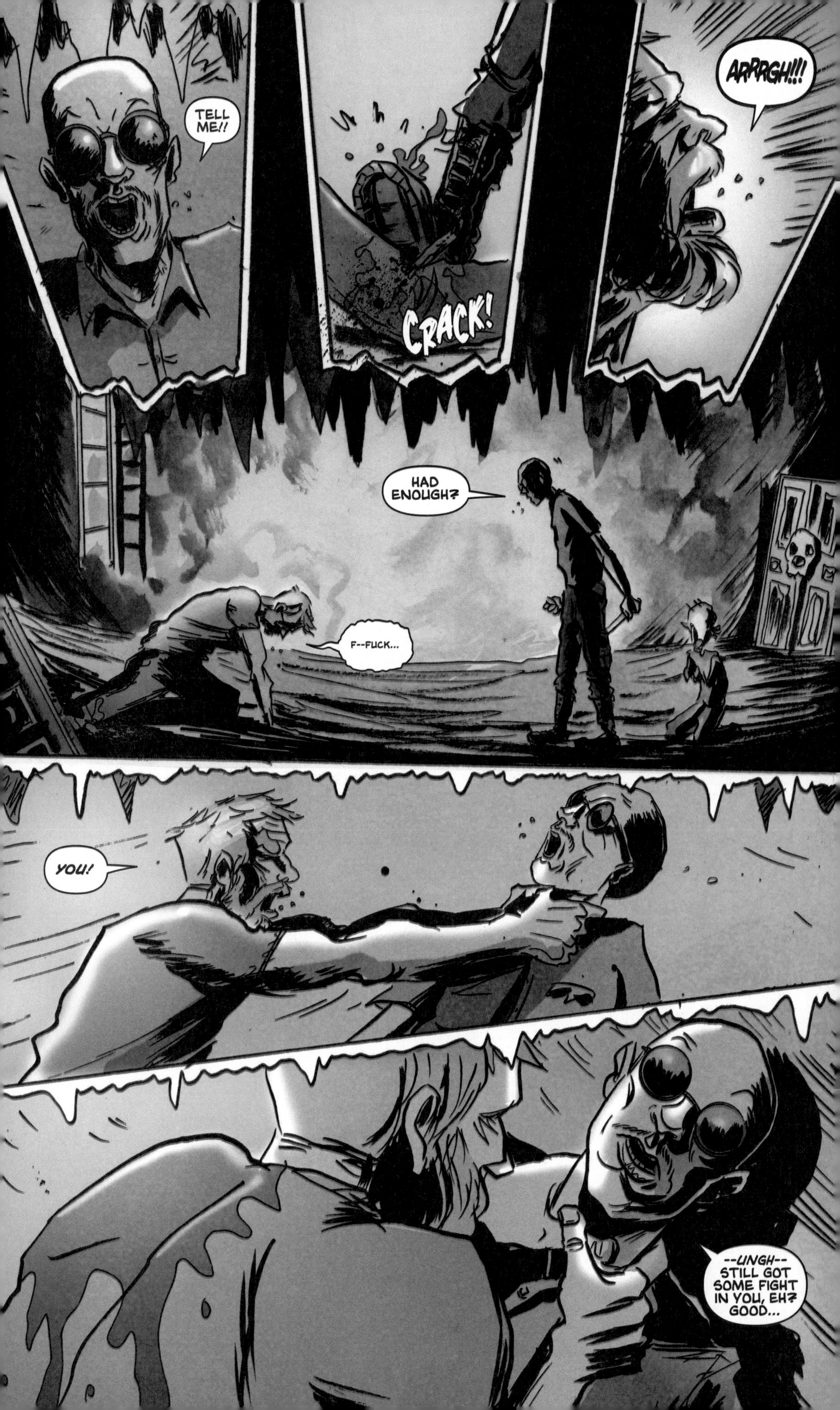
TELL ME!!
CRACK!
ARRRGH!!!
HAD ENOUGH?
F--FUCK...
YOU!
--UNGH--
STILL GOT SOME FIGHT IN YOU, EH? GOOD...

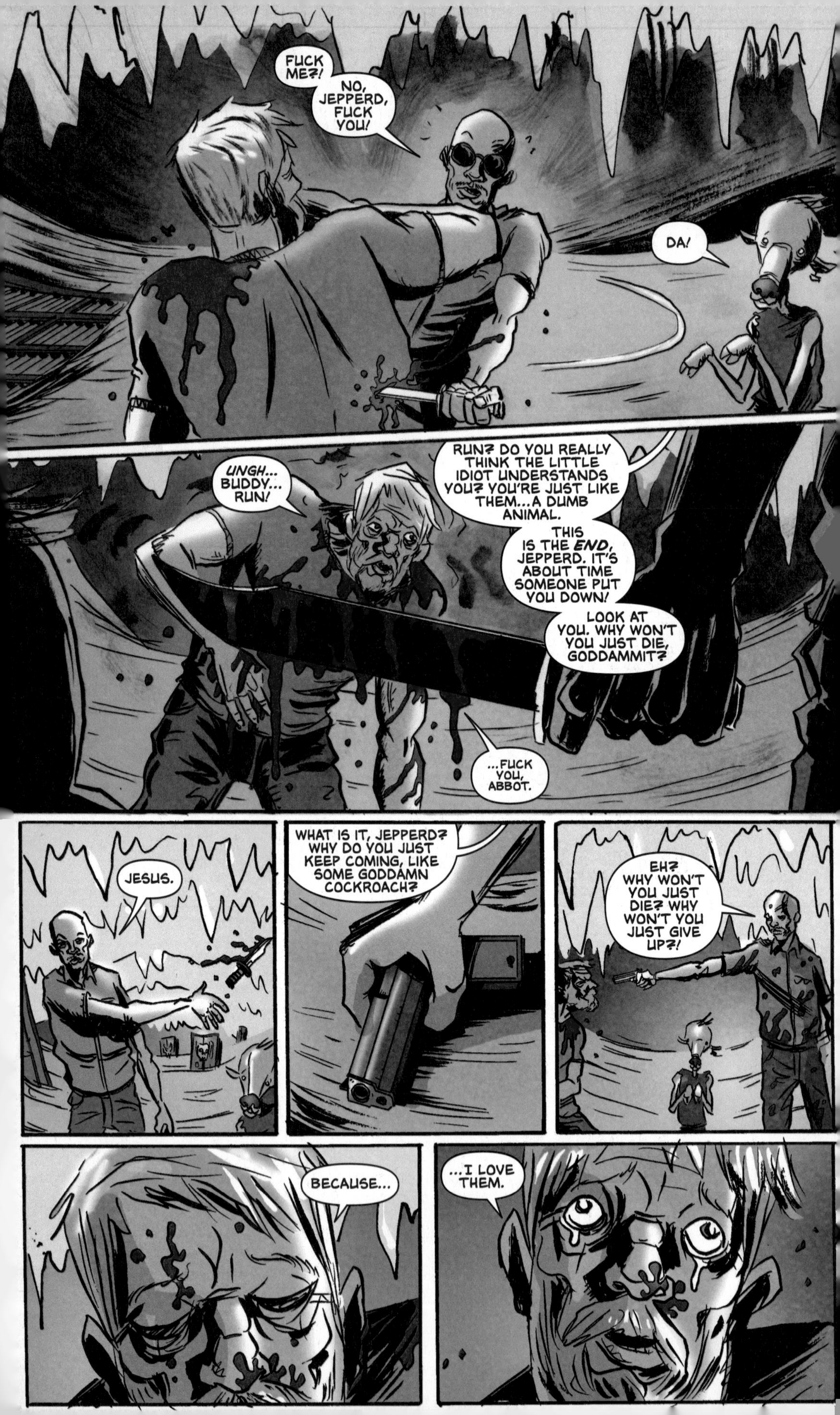
FUCK ME?!
NO, JEPPERD, FUCK YOU!
DA!
UNGH... BUDDY... RUN!
RUN? DO YOU REALLY THINK THE LITTLE IDIOT UNDERSTANDS YOU? YOU'RE JUST LIKE THEM...A DUMB ANIMAL.
THIS IS THE *END*, JEPPERD. IT'S ABOUT TIME SOMEONE PUT YOU DOWN!
LOOK AT YOU. WHY WON'T YOU JUST DIE, GODDAMMIT?
...FUCK YOU, ABBOT.
JESUS.
WHAT IS IT, JEPPERD? WHY DO YOU JUST KEEP COMING, LIKE SOME GODDAMN COCKROACH?
EH? WHY WON'T YOU JUST DIE? WHY WON'T YOU JUST GIVE UP?!
BECAUSE...
...I LOVE THEM.

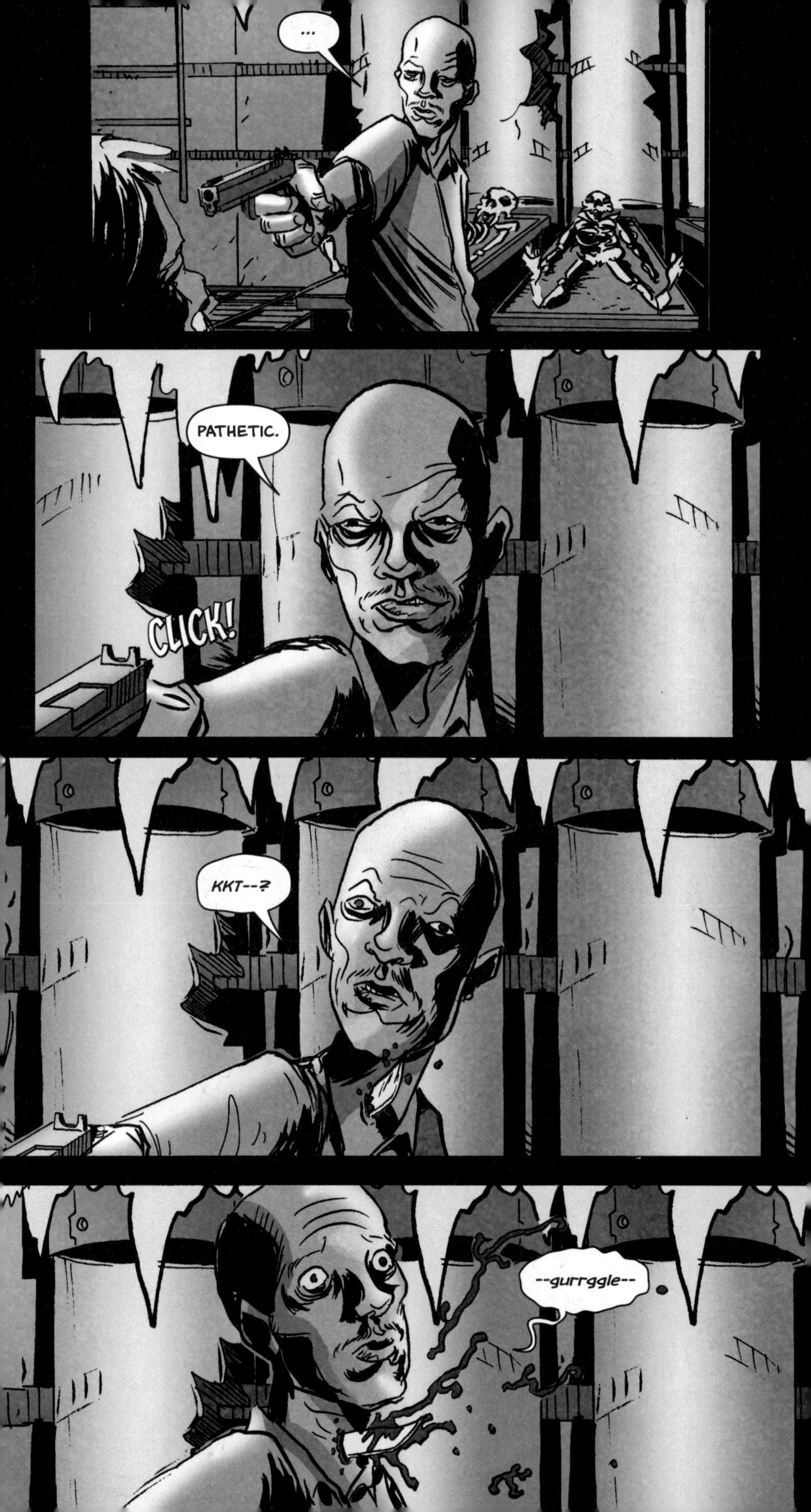
...
PATHETIC.
CLICK!
KKT--?
--gurrggle--

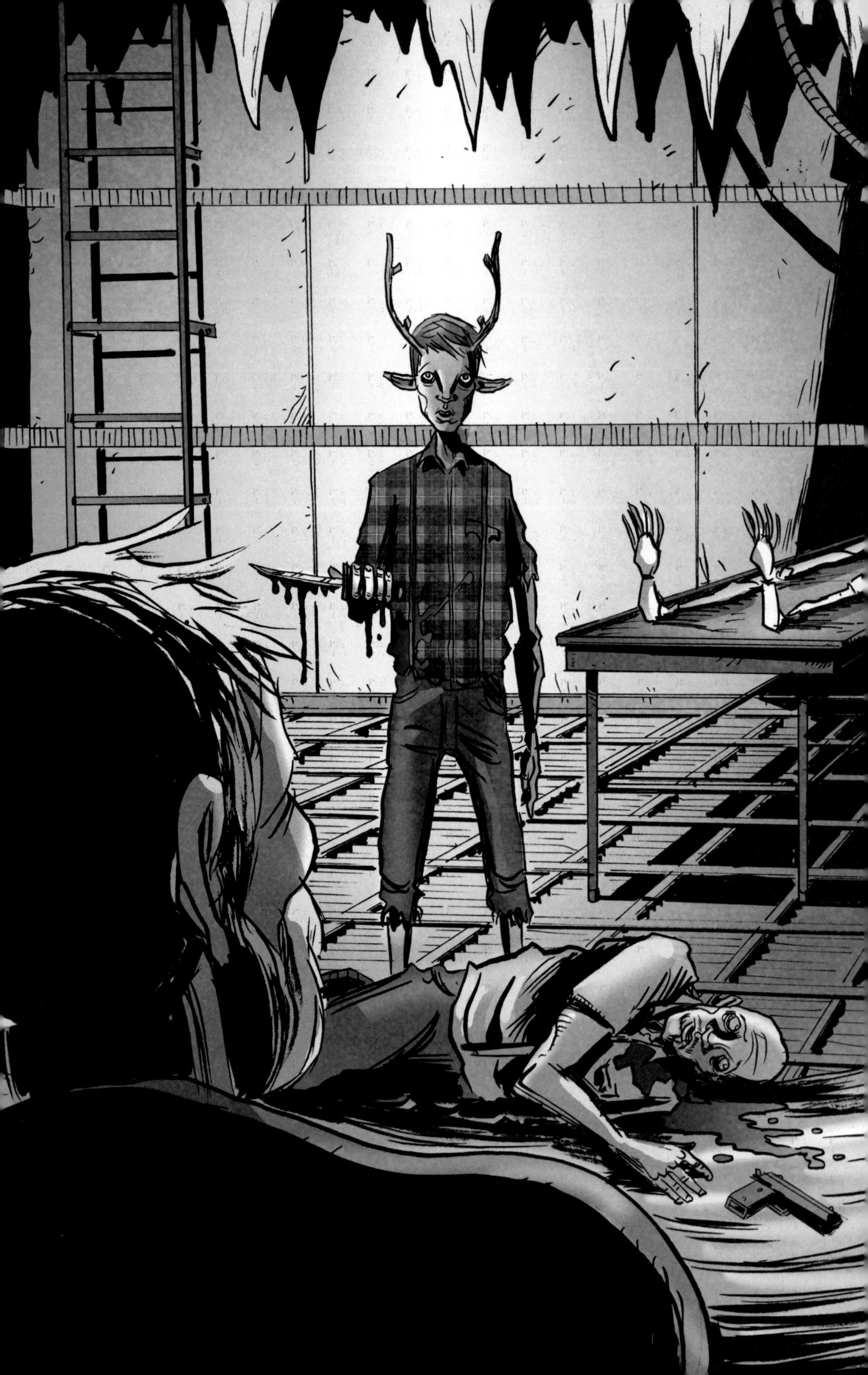

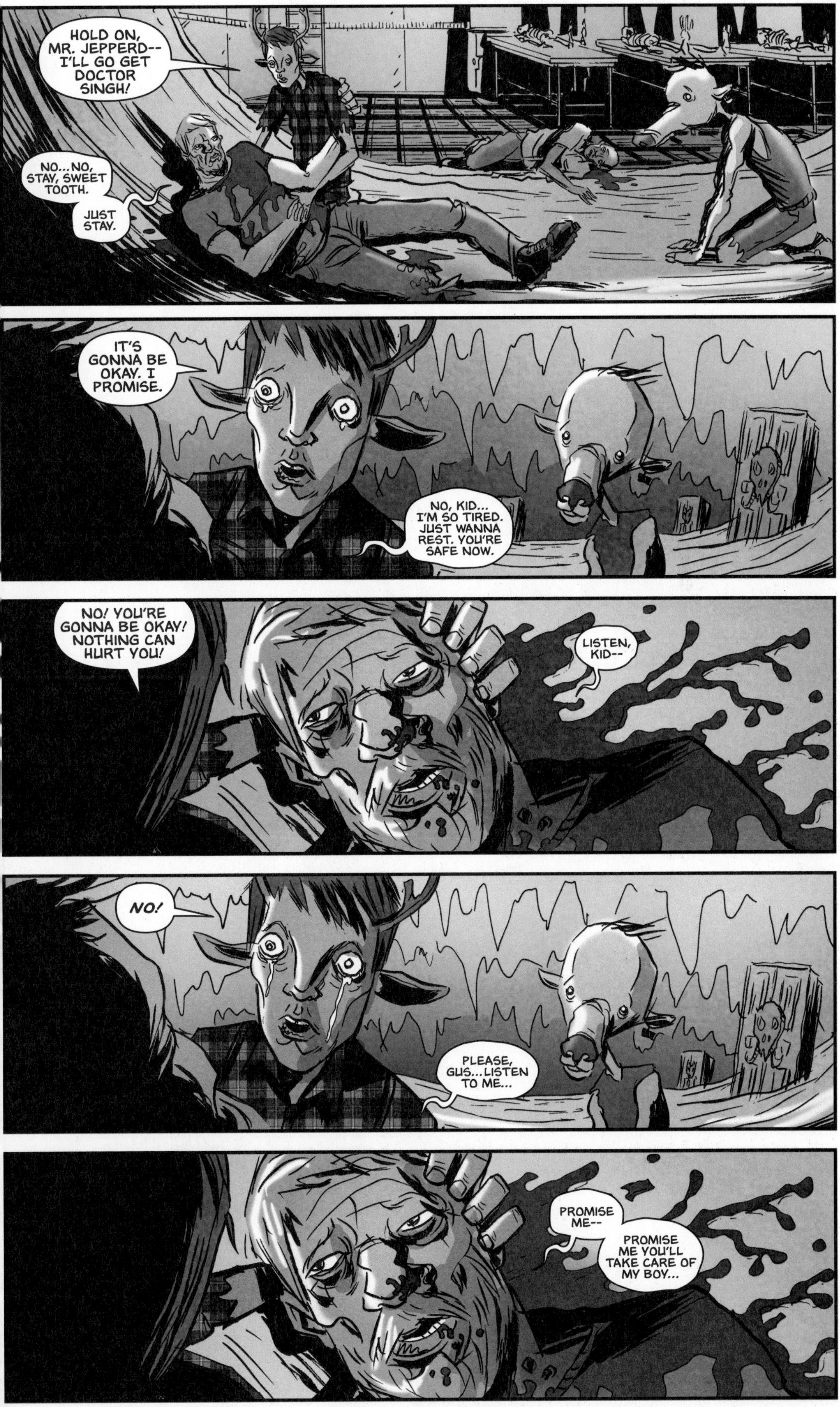
HOLD ON, MR. JEPPERD-- I'LL GO GET DOCTOR SINGH!
NO...NO, STAY, SWEET TOOTH.
JUST STAY.
IT'S GONNA BE OKAY. I PROMISE.
NO, KID... I'M SO TIRED. JUST WANNA REST. YOU'RE SAFE NOW.
NO! YOU'RE GONNA BE OKAY! NOTHING CAN HURT YOU!
LISTEN, KID--
NO!
PLEASE, GUS...LISTEN TO ME...
PROMISE ME--
PROMISE ME YOU'LL TAKE CARE OF MY BOY...

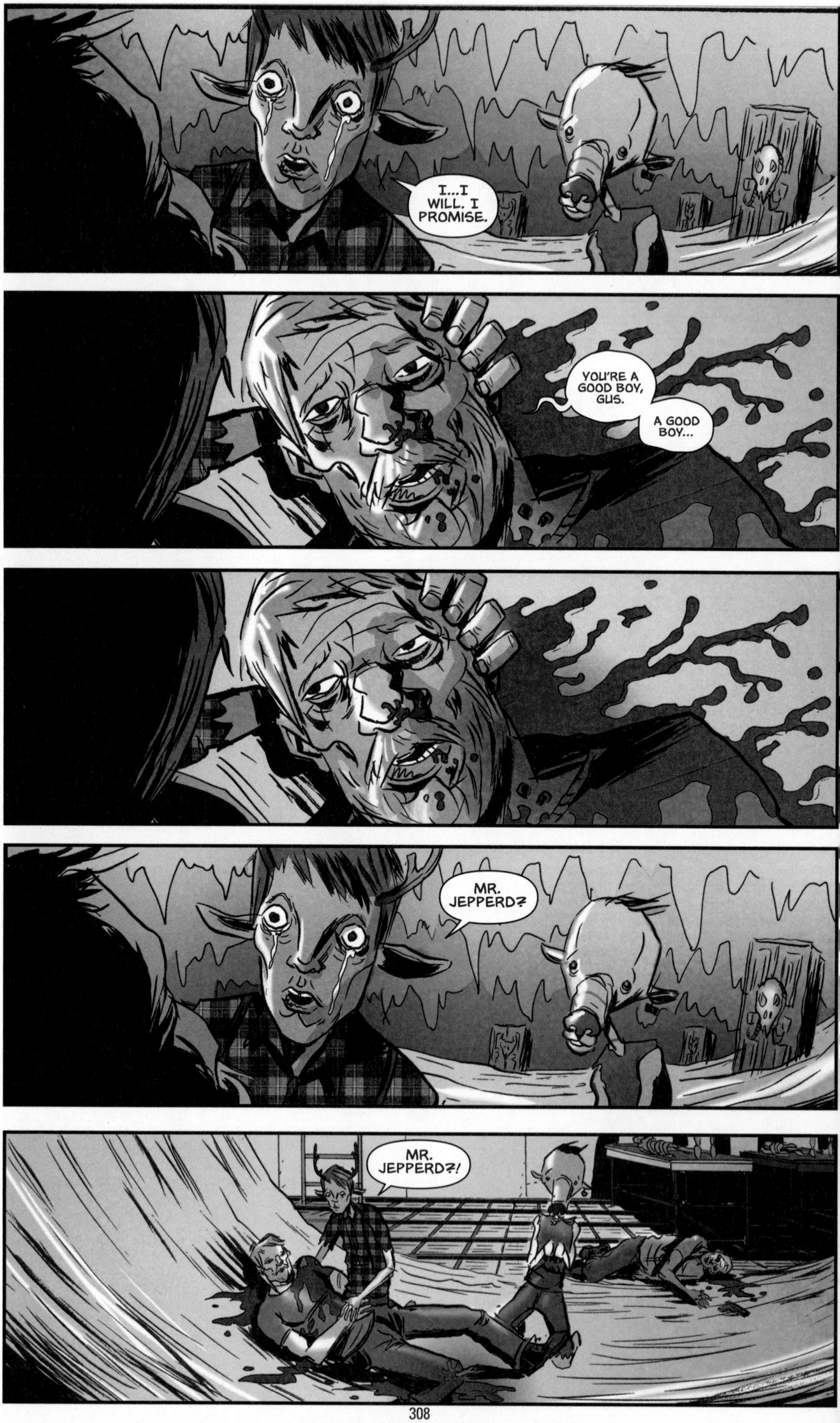
I...I WILL. I PROMISE.
YOU'RE A GOOD BOY, GUS.
A GOOD BOY...
MR. JEPPERD?
MR. JEPPERD?!

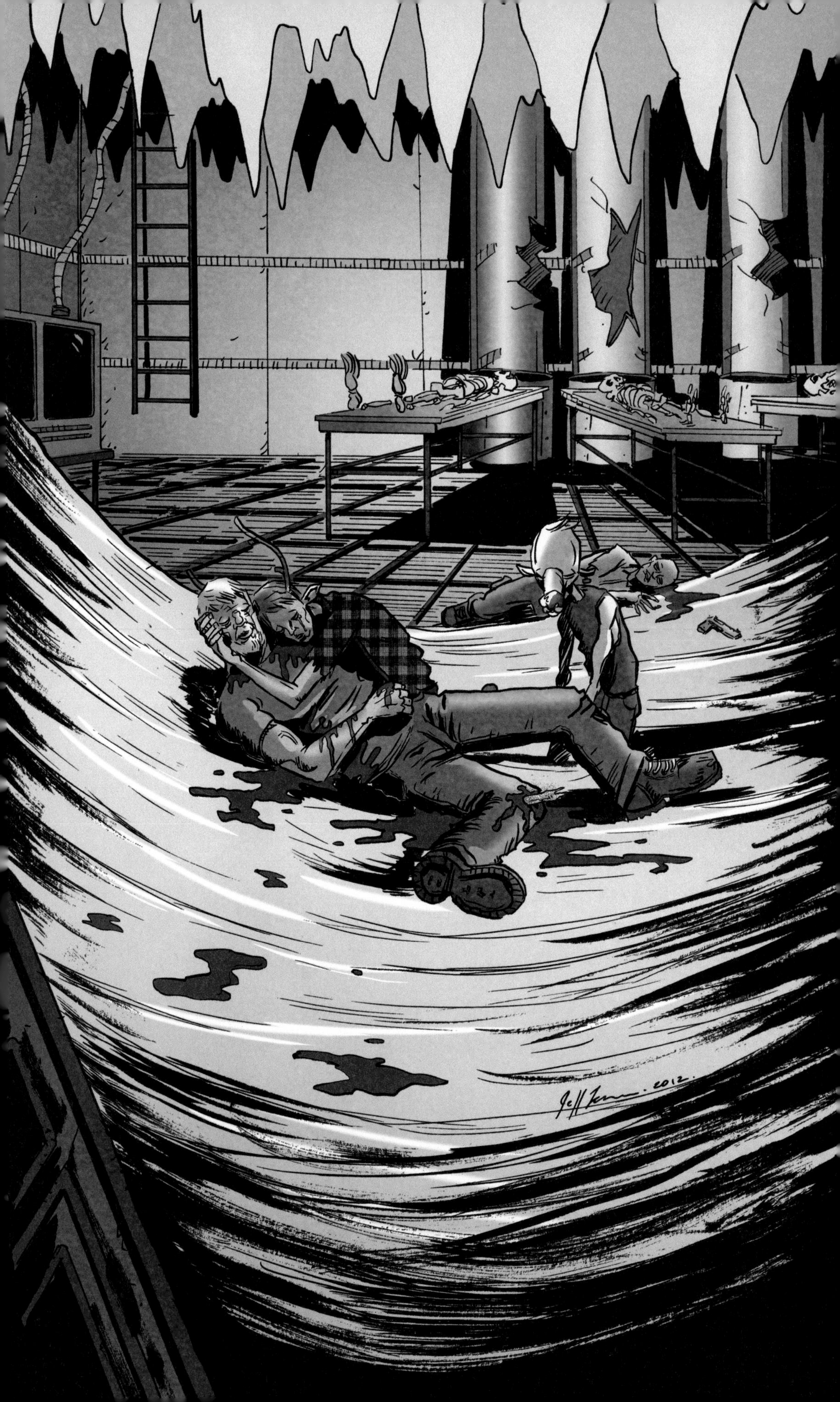

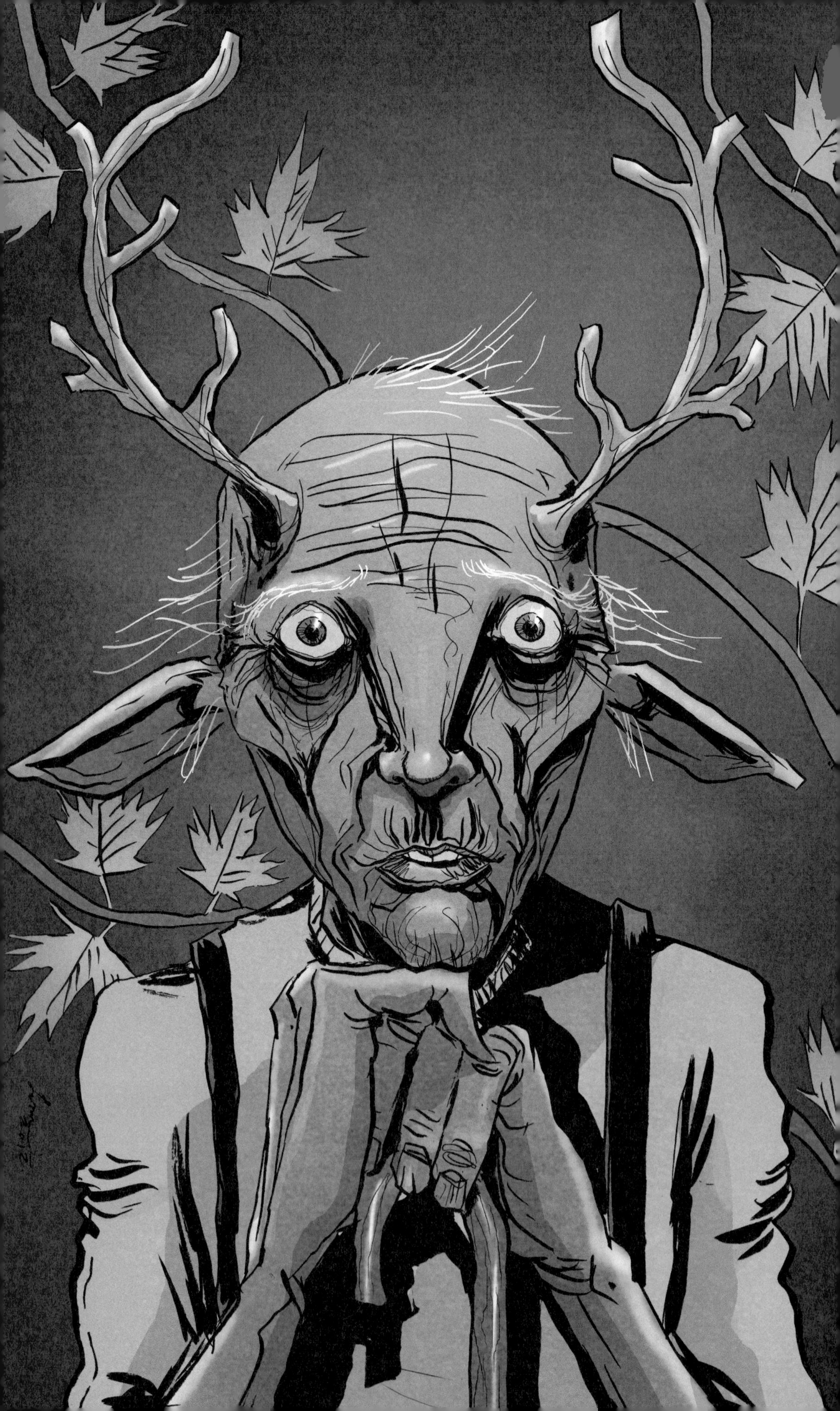

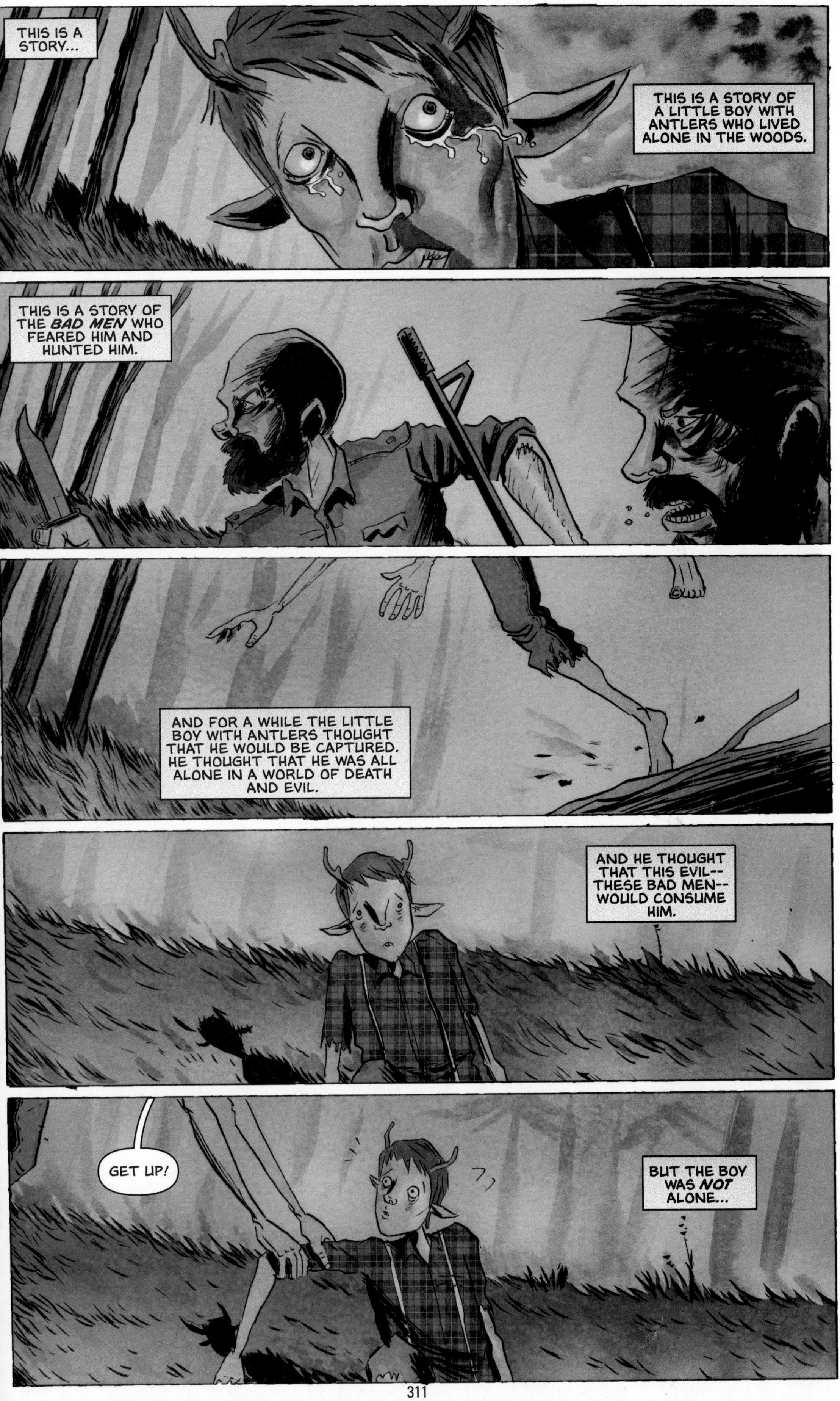
THIS IS A STORY...
THIS IS A STORY OF A LITTLE BOY WITH ANTLERS WHO LIVED ALONE IN THE WOODS.
THIS IS A STORY OF THE *BAD MEN* WHO FEARED HIM AND HUNTED HIM.
AND FOR A WHILE THE LITTLE BOY WITH ANTLERS THOUGHT THAT HE WOULD BE CAPTURED. HE THOUGHT THAT HE WAS ALL ALONE IN A WORLD OF DEATH AND EVIL.
AND HE THOUGHT THAT THIS EVIL-- THESE BAD MEN-- WOULD CONSUME HIM.
GET UP!
BUT THE BOY WAS *NOT* ALONE...

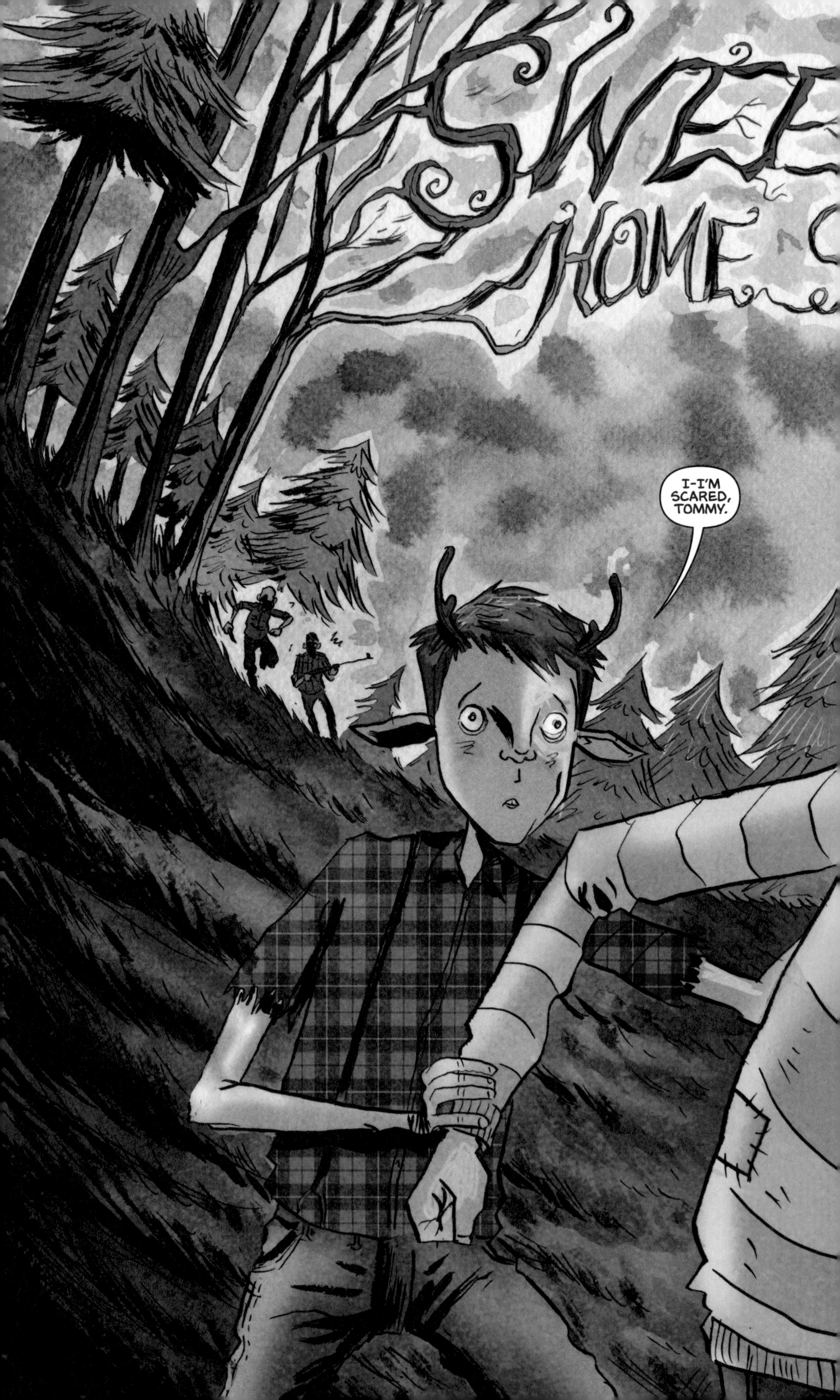
SWEET
HOME
I-I'M SCARED, TOMMY.

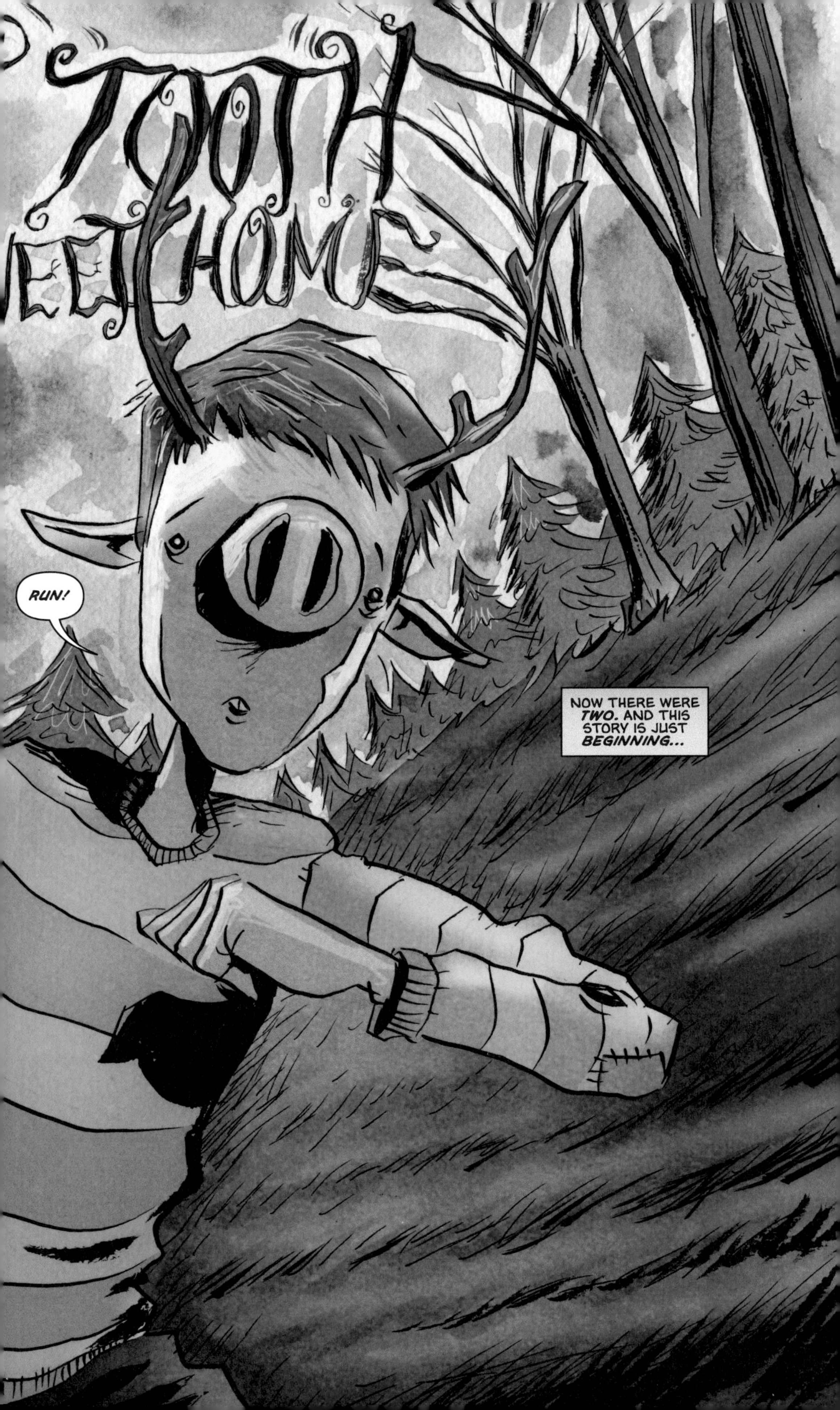
RUN!
NOW THERE WERE TWO. AND THIS STORY IS JUST BEGINNING...

WENT IN HERE.

MIGHT BE A TRAP. THEY'S SNEAKY LITTLE FUCKERS.

JUST A COUPLE OF KIDS. AIN'T NO TRAP.

SHIT, MAN... I DON'T LIKE THIS. WE'RE TOO CLOSE TO *THE ZOO* FOR THIS.

THIS WAY!

ZOO'S AT LEAST A DAY NORTH. SO, STOP YER PISSING AND MOANING AND KEEP YOUR HEAD UP.

SHIT, DON'T HAVE TO GET MAD. JUST SAYIN' IS ALL.

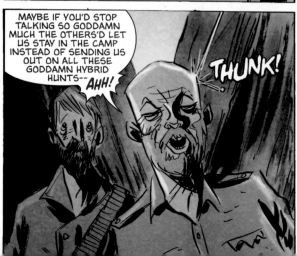

MAYBE IF YOU'D STOP TALKING SO GODDAMN MUCH THE OTHERS'D LET US STAY IN THE CAMP INSTEAD OF SENDING US OUT ON ALL THESE GODDAMN HYBRID HUNTS--*AHH!*

THUNK!

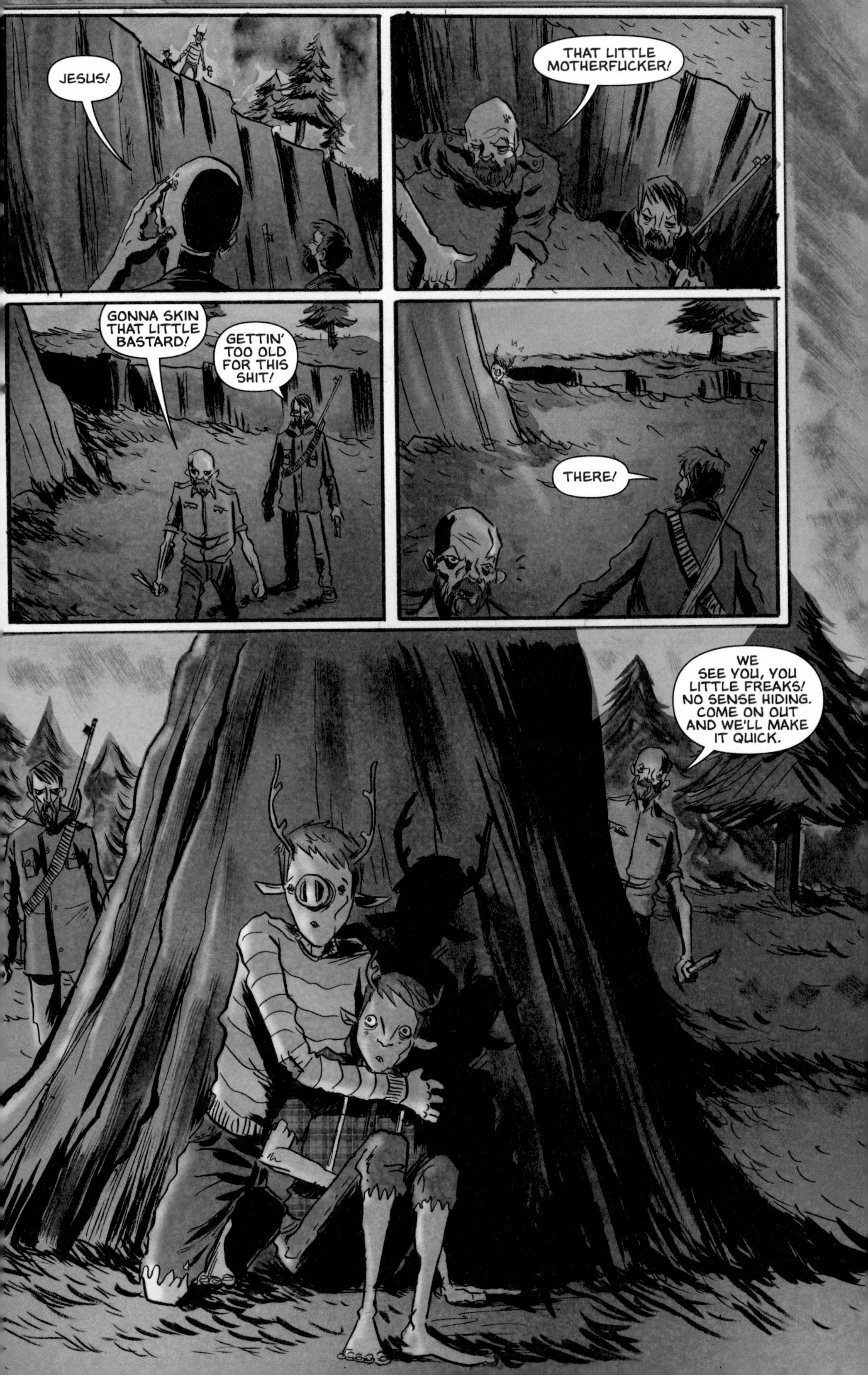
JESUS!
THAT LITTLE MOTHERFUCKER!
GONNA SKIN THAT LITTLE BASTARD!
GETTIN' TOO OLD FOR THIS SHIT!
THERE!
WE SEE YOU, YOU LITTLE FREAKS! NO SENSE HIDING. COME ON OUT AND WE'LL MAKE IT QUICK.

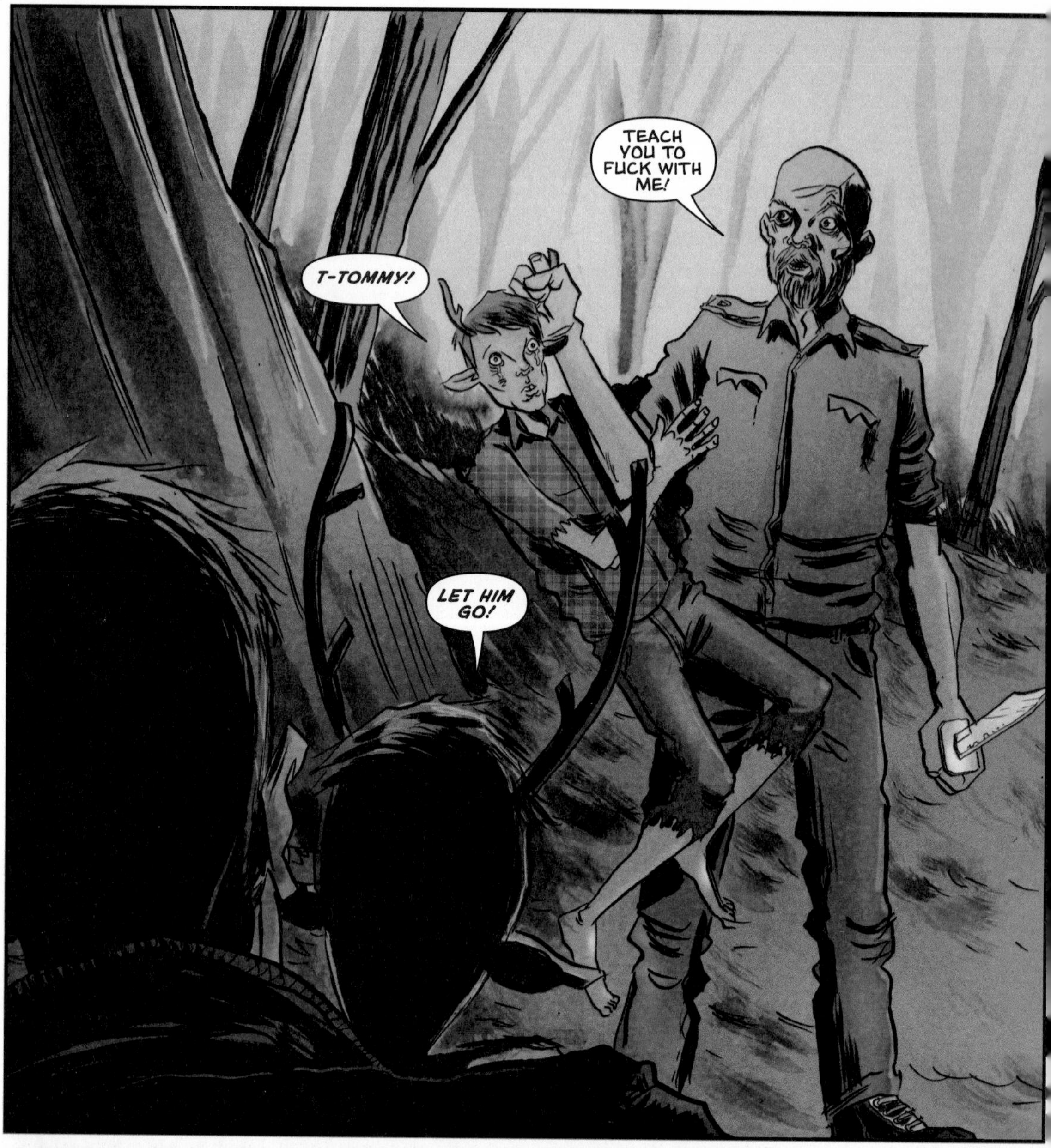
TEACH YOU TO FUCK WITH ME!
T-TOMMY!
LET HIM GO!

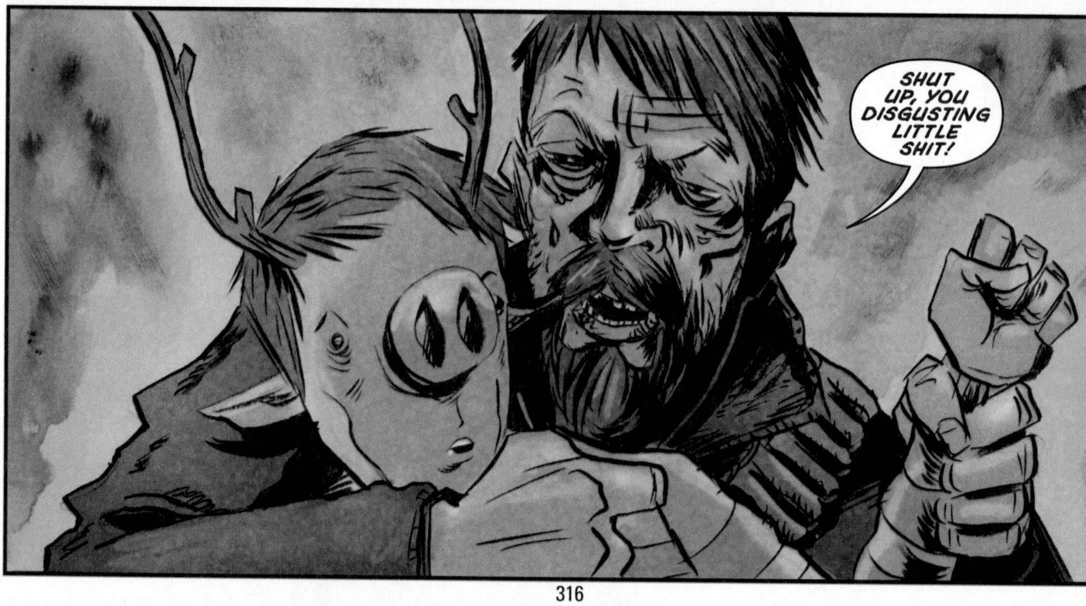
SHUT UP, YOU DISGUSTING LITTLE SHIT!

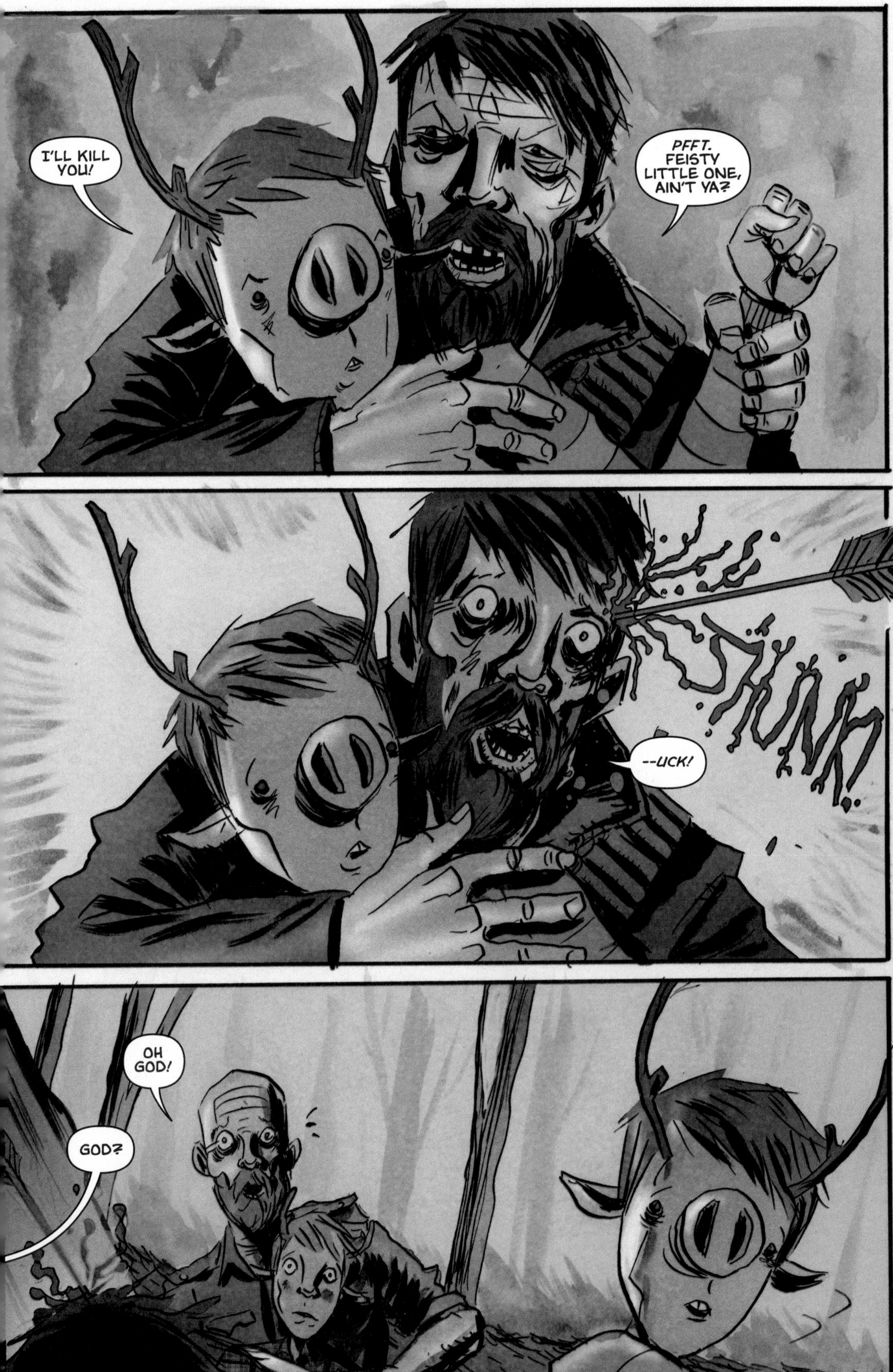
I'LL KILL YOU!
PFFT. FEISTY LITTLE ONE, AIN'T YA?
SHUNK!
--UCK!
OH GOD!
GOD?

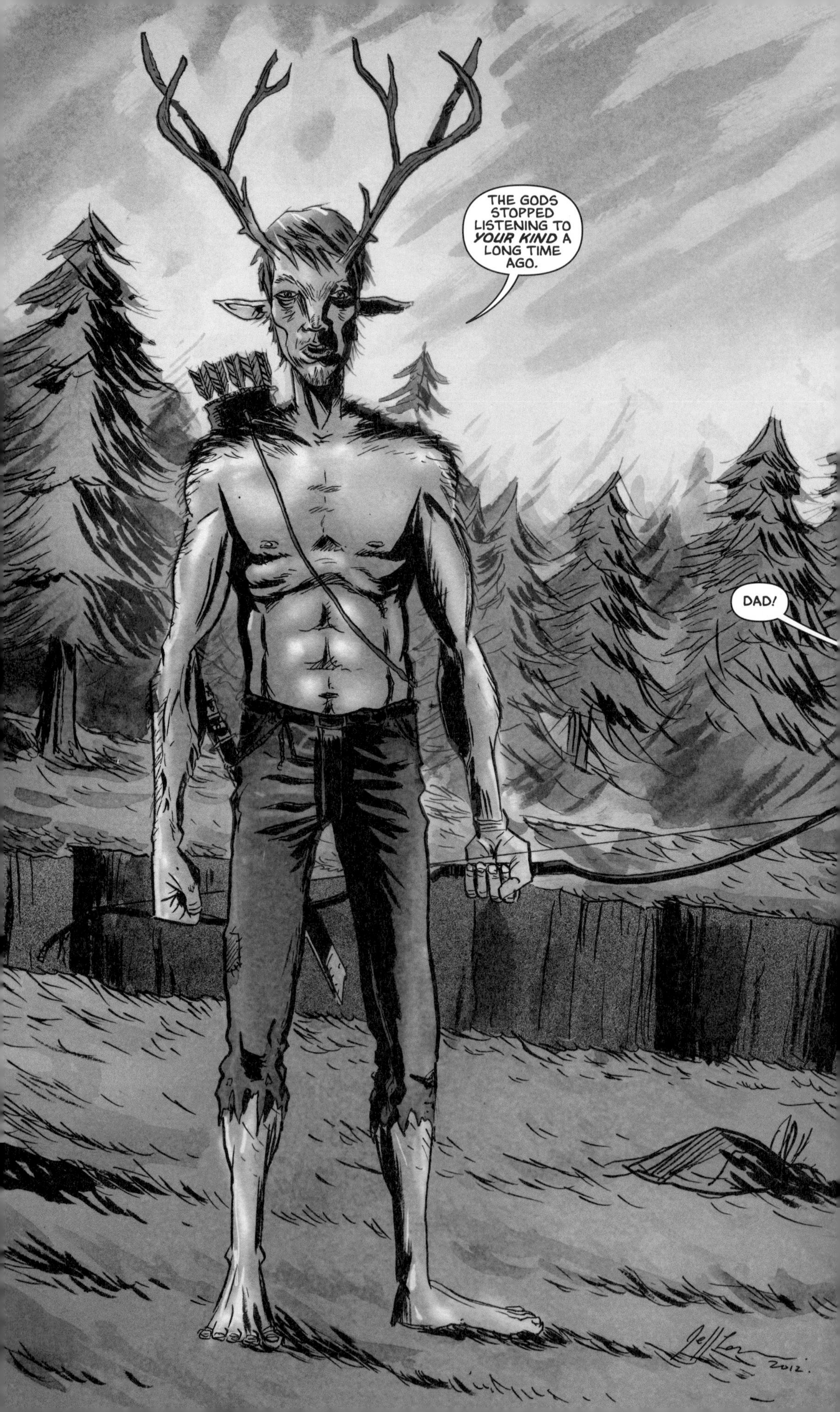
THE GODS STOPPED LISTENING TO *YOUR KIND* A LONG TIME AGO.
DAD!

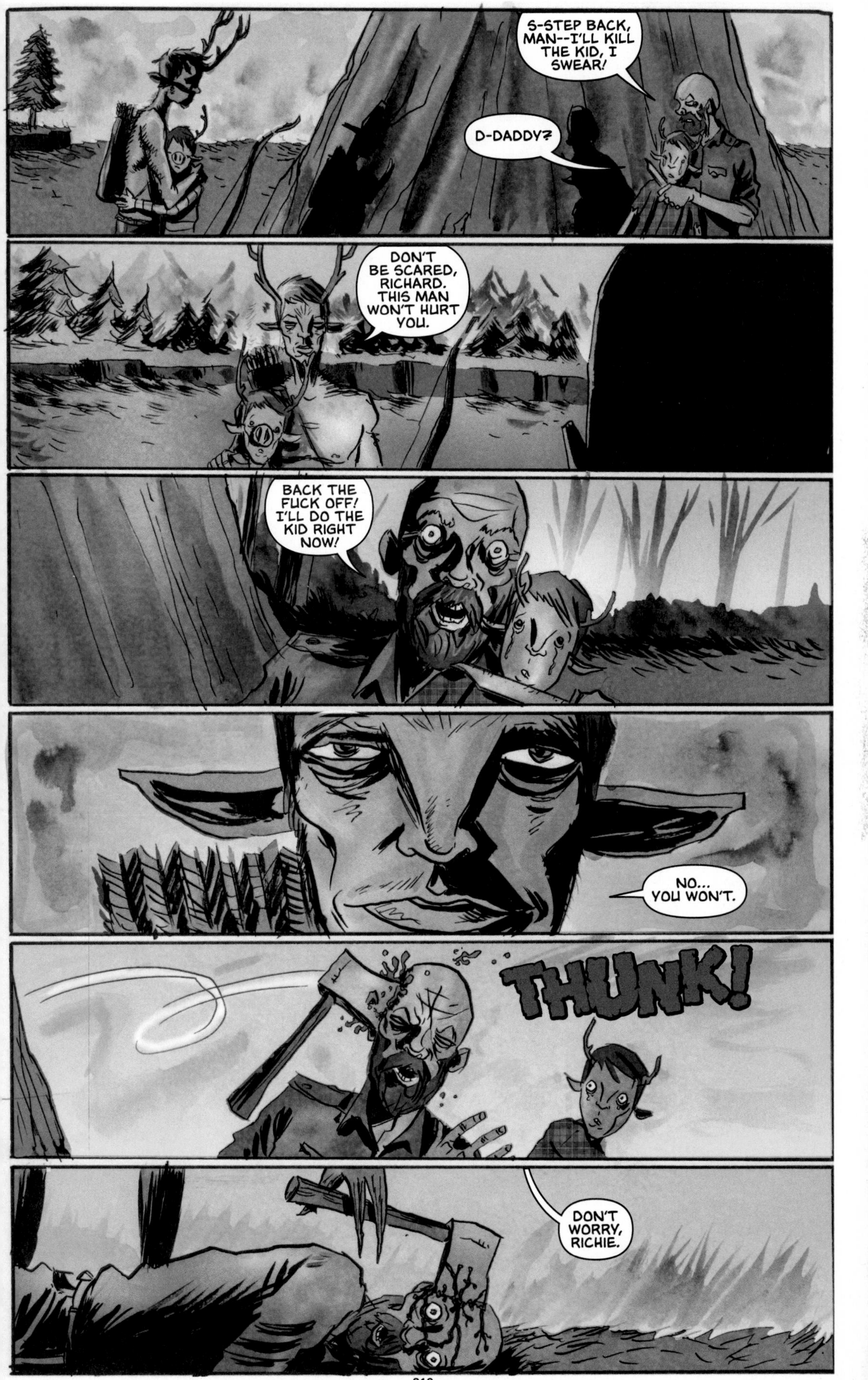
S-STEP BACK, MAN--I'LL KILL THE KID, I SWEAR!
D-DADDY?
DON'T BE SCARED, RICHARD. THIS MAN WON'T HURT YOU.
BACK THE FUCK OFF! I'LL DO THE KID RIGHT NOW!
NO... YOU WON'T.
THUNK!
DON'T WORRY, RICHIE.

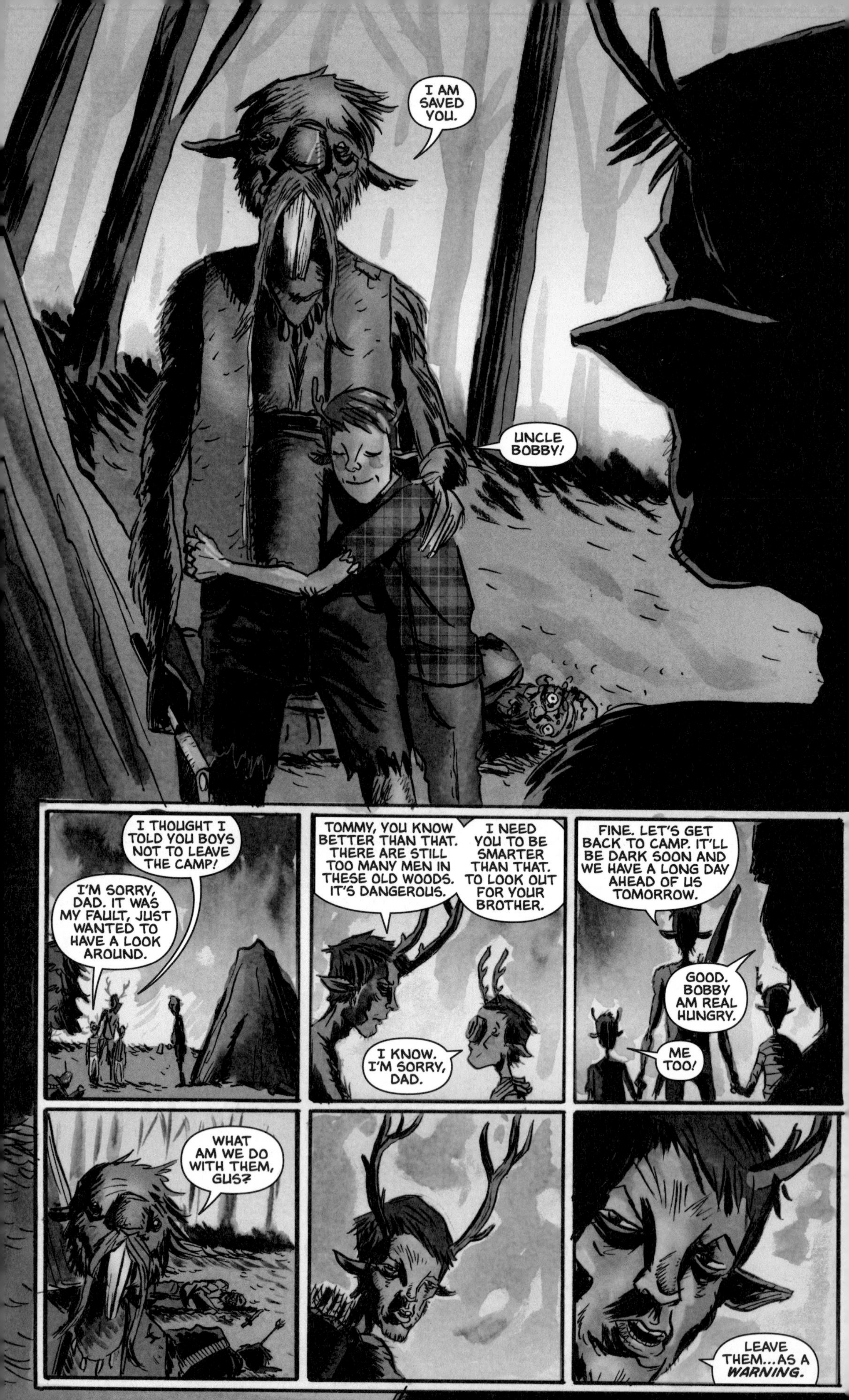
I AM SAVED YOU.
UNCLE BOBBY!
I THOUGHT I TOLD YOU BOYS NOT TO LEAVE THE CAMP!
I'M SORRY, DAD. IT WAS MY FAULT, JUST WANTED TO HAVE A LOOK AROUND.
TOMMY, YOU KNOW BETTER THAN THAT. THERE ARE STILL TOO MANY MEN IN THESE OLD WOODS. IT'S DANGEROUS.
I NEED YOU TO BE SMARTER THAN THAT. TO LOOK OUT FOR YOUR BROTHER.
I KNOW. I'M SORRY, DAD.
FINE. LET'S GET BACK TO CAMP. IT'LL BE DARK SOON AND WE HAVE A LONG DAY AHEAD OF US TOMORROW.
GOOD. BOBBY AM REAL HUNGRY.
ME TOO!
WHAT AM WE DO WITH THEM, GUS?
LEAVE THEM...AS A *WARNING.*

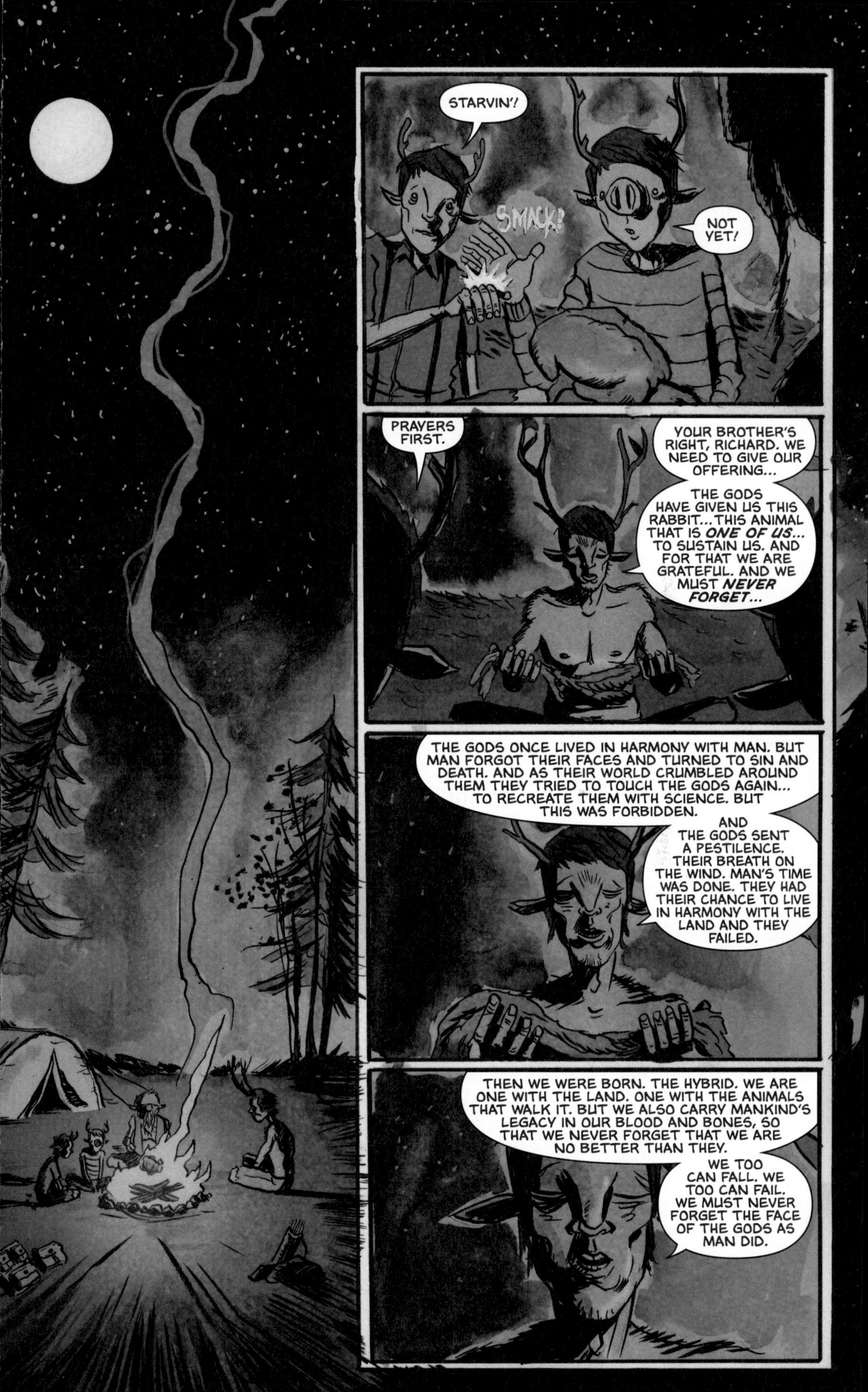
STARVIN'!
SMACK!
NOT YET!
PRAYERS FIRST.
YOUR BROTHER'S RIGHT, RICHARD. WE NEED TO GIVE OUR OFFERING...
THE GODS HAVE GIVEN US THIS RABBIT...THIS ANIMAL THAT IS ONE OF US... TO SUSTAIN US. AND FOR THAT WE ARE GRATEFUL. AND WE MUST NEVER FORGET...
THE GODS ONCE LIVED IN HARMONY WITH MAN. BUT MAN FORGOT THEIR FACES AND TURNED TO SIN AND DEATH. AND AS THEIR WORLD CRUMBLED AROUND THEM THEY TRIED TO TOUCH THE GODS AGAIN... TO RECREATE THEM WITH SCIENCE. BUT THIS WAS FORBIDDEN.
AND THE GODS SENT A PESTILENCE. THEIR BREATH ON THE WIND. MAN'S TIME WAS DONE. THEY HAD THEIR CHANCE TO LIVE IN HARMONY WITH THE LAND AND THEY FAILED.
THEN WE WERE BORN. THE HYBRID. WE ARE ONE WITH THE LAND. ONE WITH THE ANIMALS THAT WALK IT. BUT WE ALSO CARRY MANKIND'S LEGACY IN OUR BLOOD AND BONES, SO THAT WE NEVER FORGET THAT WE ARE NO BETTER THAN THEY.
WE TOO CAN FALL. WE TOO CAN FAIL. WE MUST NEVER FORGET THE FACE OF THE GODS AS MAN DID.

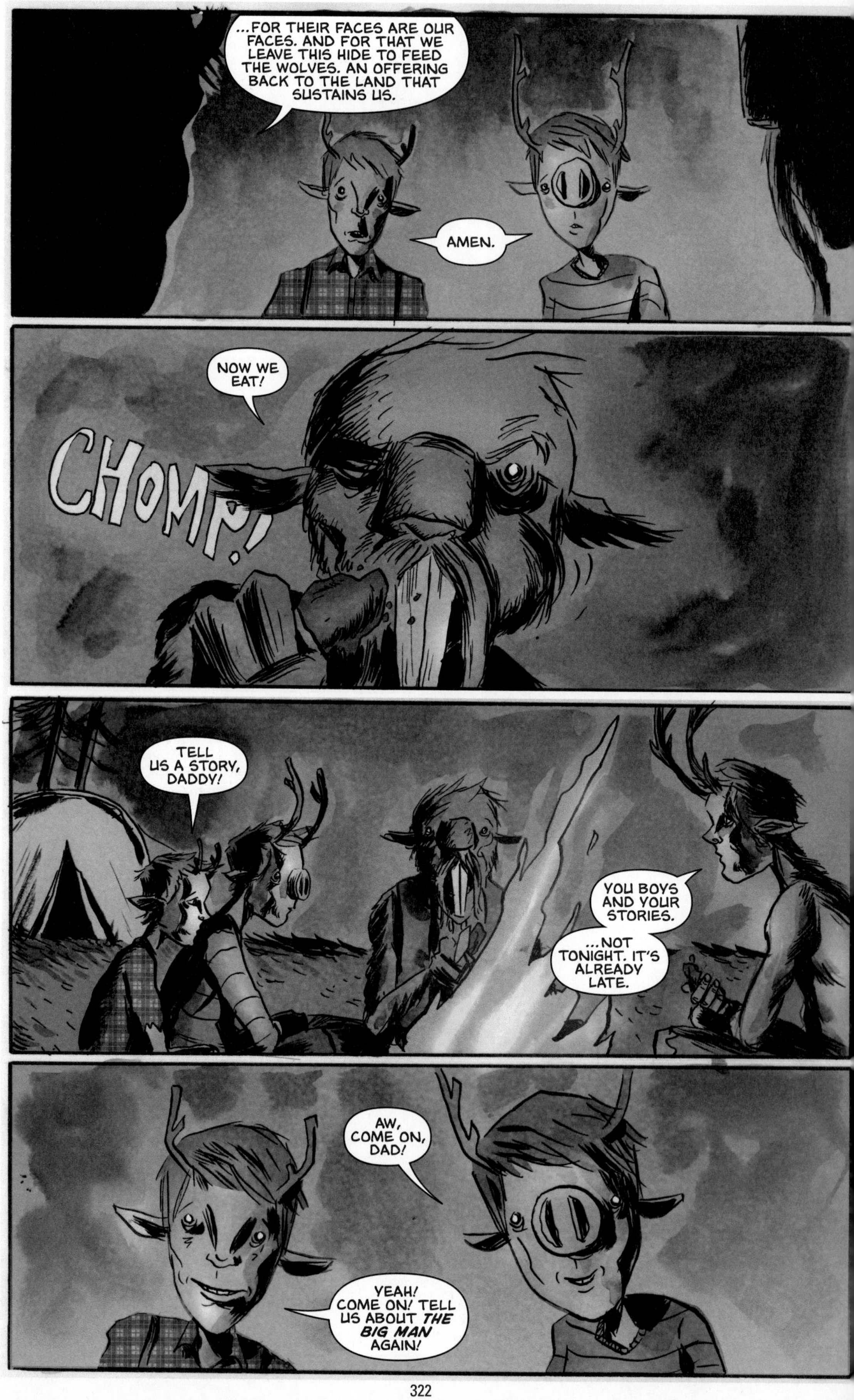
...FOR THEIR FACES ARE OUR FACES. AND FOR THAT WE LEAVE THIS HIDE TO FEED THE WOLVES. AN OFFERING BACK TO THE LAND THAT SUSTAINS US.
AMEN.
NOW WE EAT!
CHOMP!
TELL US A STORY, DADDY!
YOU BOYS AND YOUR STORIES.
...NOT TONIGHT. IT'S ALREADY LATE.
AW, COME ON, DAD!
YEAH! COME ON! TELL US ABOUT *THE BIG MAN* AGAIN!

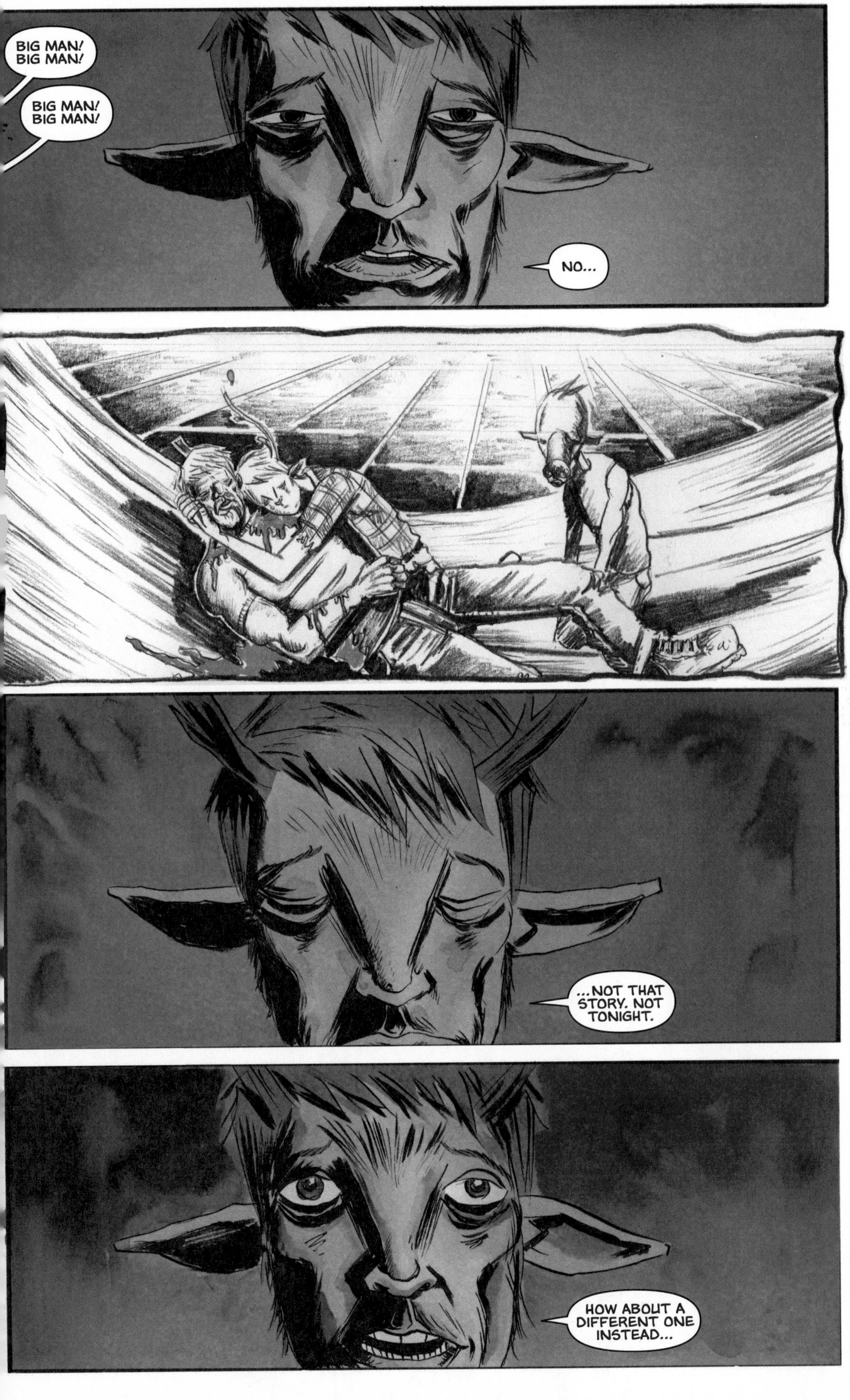
BIG MAN! BIG MAN!
BIG MAN! BIG MAN!
NO...
...NOT THAT STORY. NOT TONIGHT.
HOW ABOUT A DIFFERENT ONE INSTEAD...

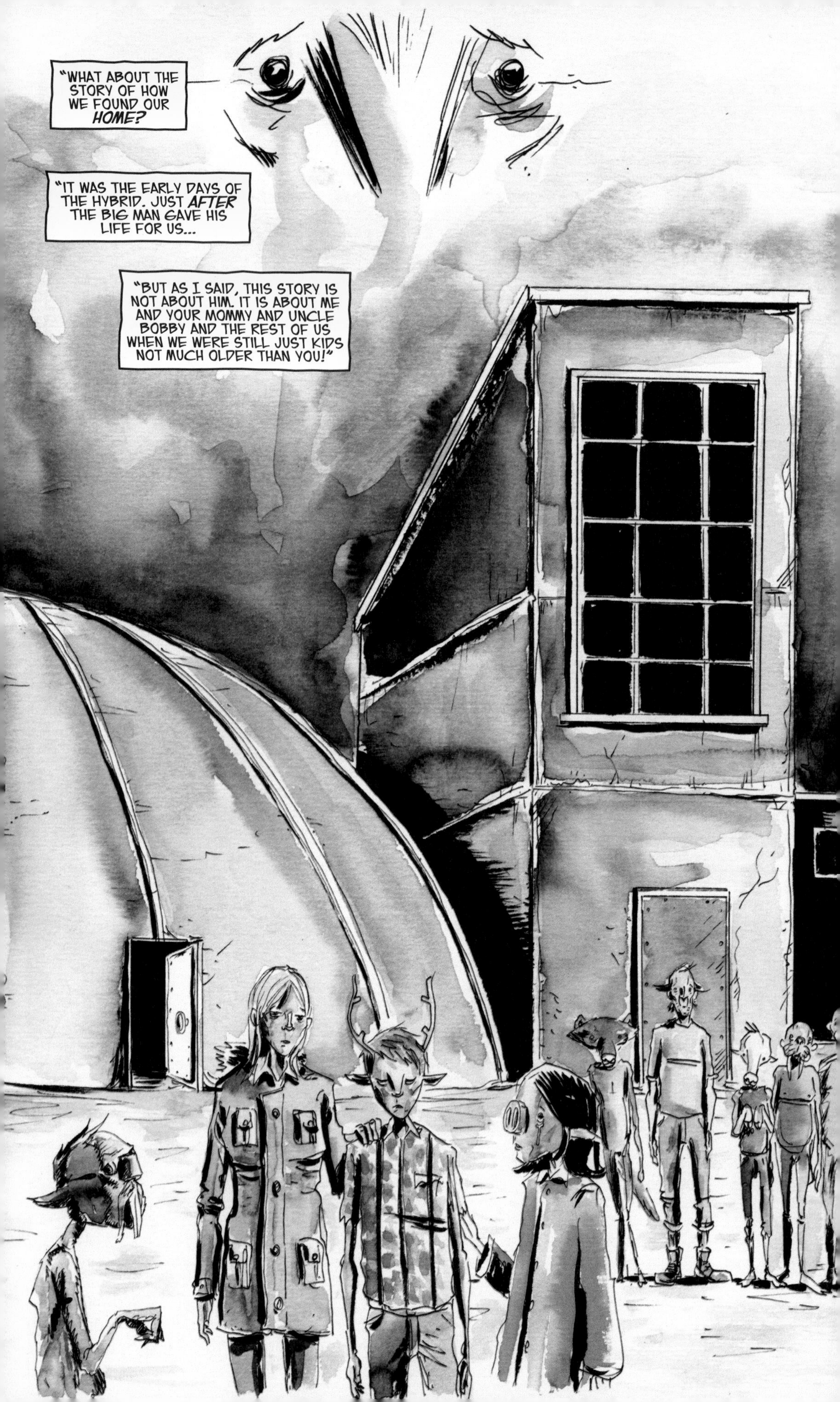
"WHAT ABOUT THE STORY OF HOW WE FOUND OUR HOME?
"IT WAS THE EARLY DAYS OF THE HYBRID. JUST AFTER THE BIG MAN GAVE HIS LIFE FOR US...
"BUT AS I SAID, THIS STORY IS NOT ABOUT HIM. IT IS ABOUT ME AND YOUR MOMMY AND UNCLE BOBBY AND THE REST OF US WHEN WE WERE STILL JUST KIDS NOT MUCH OLDER THAN YOU!"

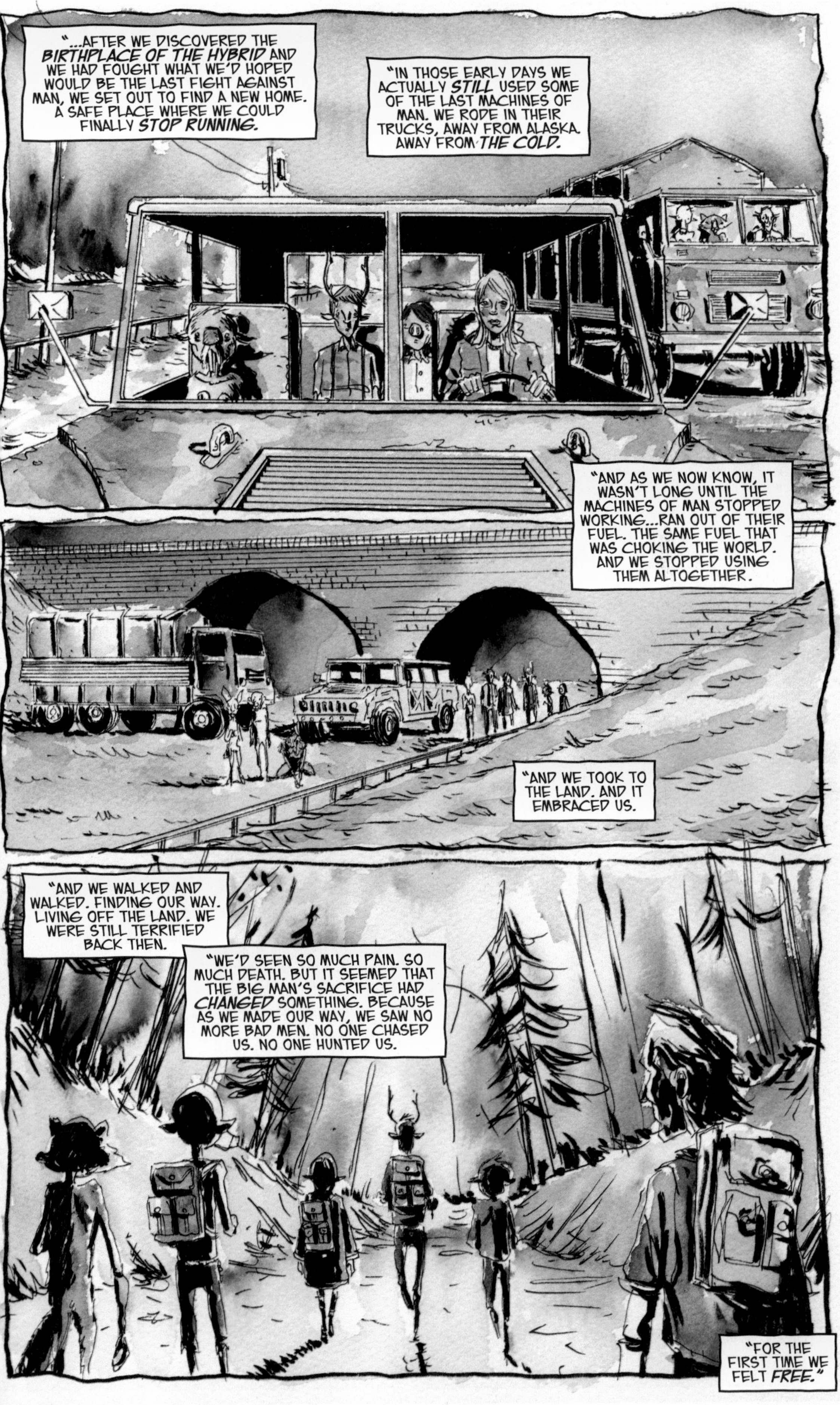
"...AFTER WE DISCOVERED THE BIRTHPLACE OF THE HYBRID AND WE HAD FOUGHT WHAT WE'D HOPED WOULD BE THE LAST FIGHT AGAINST MAN, WE SET OUT TO FIND A NEW HOME. A SAFE PLACE WHERE WE COULD FINALLY STOP RUNNING.
"IN THOSE EARLY DAYS WE ACTUALLY STILL USED SOME OF THE LAST MACHINES OF MAN. WE RODE IN THEIR TRUCKS, AWAY FROM ALASKA. AWAY FROM THE COLD.
"AND AS WE NOW KNOW, IT WASN'T LONG UNTIL THE MACHINES OF MAN STOPPED WORKING...RAN OUT OF THEIR FUEL. THE SAME FUEL THAT WAS CHOKING THE WORLD. AND WE STOPPED USING THEM ALTOGETHER.
"AND WE TOOK TO THE LAND. AND IT EMBRACED US.
"AND WE WALKED AND WALKED. FINDING OUR WAY. LIVING OFF THE LAND. WE WERE STILL TERRIFIED BACK THEN.
"WE'D SEEN SO MUCH PAIN. SO MUCH DEATH. BUT IT SEEMED THAT THE BIG MAN'S SACRIFICE HAD CHANGED SOMETHING. BECAUSE AS WE MADE OUR WAY, WE SAW NO MORE BAD MEN. NO ONE CHASED US. NO ONE HUNTED US.
"FOR THE FIRST TIME WE FELT FREE."

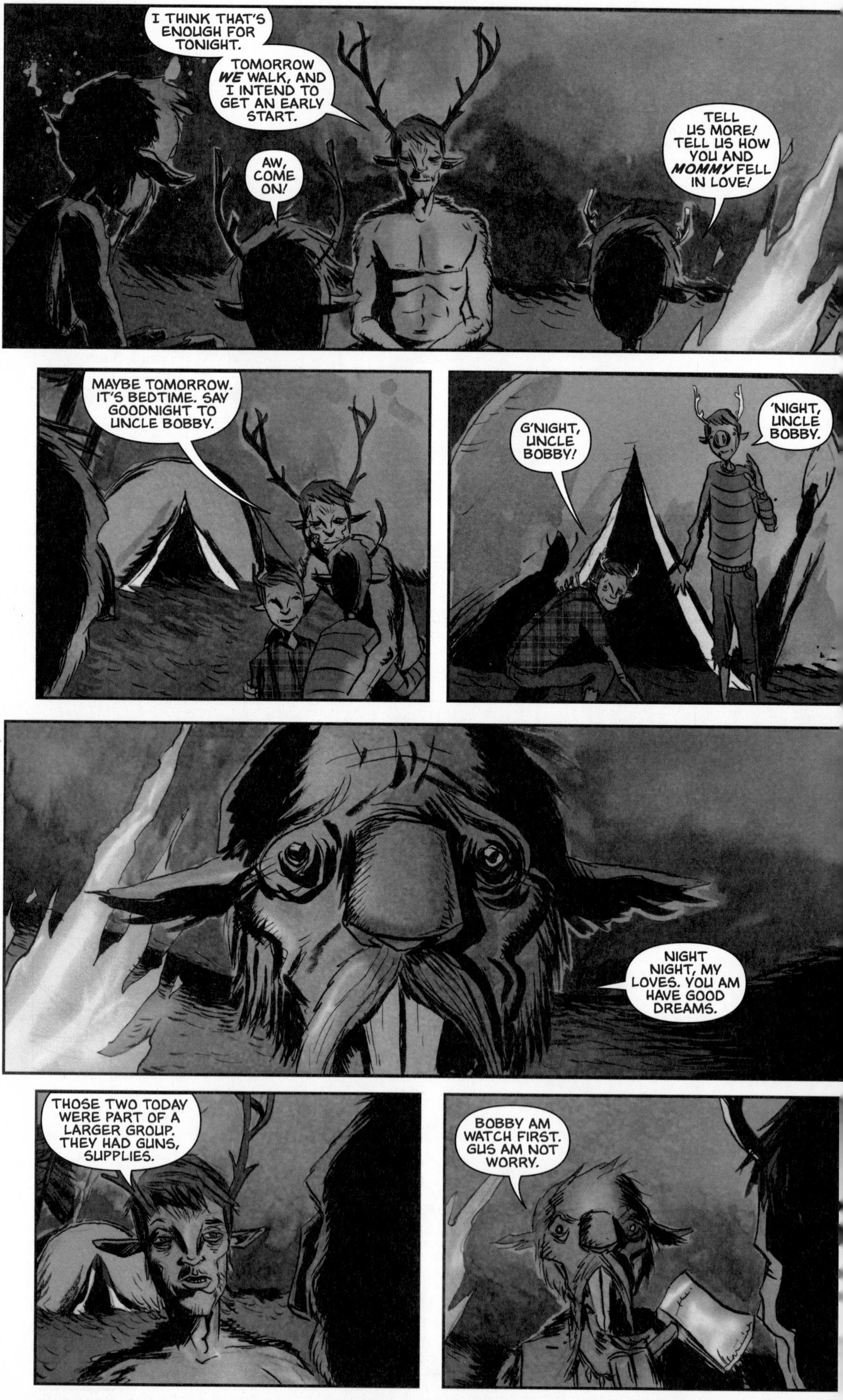
I THINK THAT'S ENOUGH FOR TONIGHT.
TOMORROW *WE* WALK, AND I INTEND TO GET AN EARLY START.
AW, COME ON!
TELL US MORE! TELL US HOW YOU AND *MOMMY* FELL IN LOVE!
MAYBE TOMORROW. IT'S BEDTIME. SAY GOODNIGHT TO UNCLE BOBBY.
G'NIGHT, UNCLE BOBBY!
'NIGHT, UNCLE BOBBY.
NIGHT NIGHT, MY LOVES. YOU AM HAVE GOOD DREAMS.
THOSE TWO TODAY WERE PART OF A LARGER GROUP. THEY HAD GUNS, SUPPLIES.
BOBBY AM WATCH FIRST. GUS AM NOT WORRY.

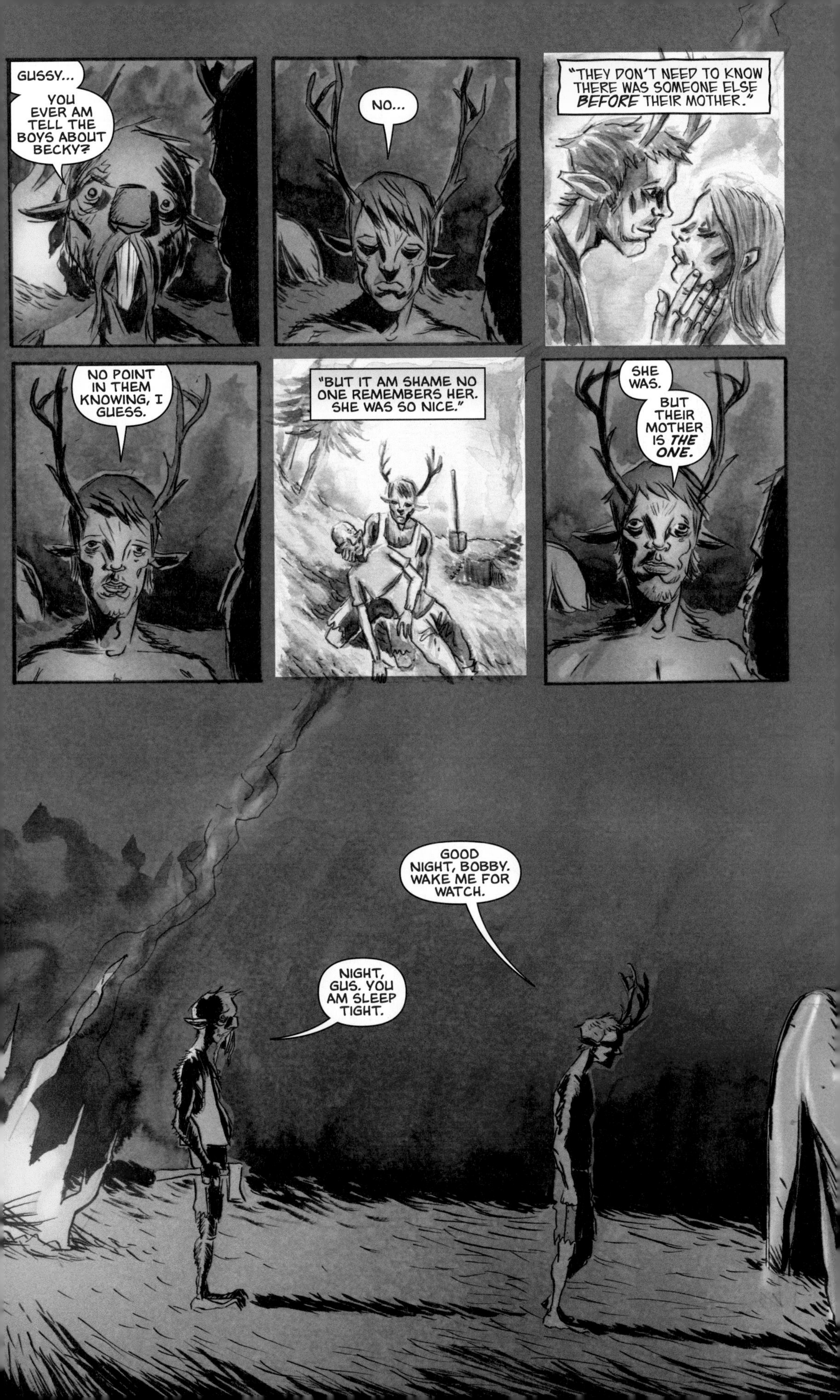
GUSSY...
YOU EVER AM TELL THE BOYS ABOUT BECKY?
NO...
"THEY DON'T NEED TO KNOW THERE WAS SOMEONE ELSE BEFORE THEIR MOTHER."
NO POINT IN THEM KNOWING, I GUESS.
"BUT IT AM SHAME NO ONE REMEMBERS HER. SHE WAS SO NICE."
SHE WAS.
BUT THEIR MOTHER IS THE ONE.
GOOD NIGHT, BOBBY. WAKE ME FOR WATCH.
NIGHT, GUS. YOU AM SLEEP TIGHT.

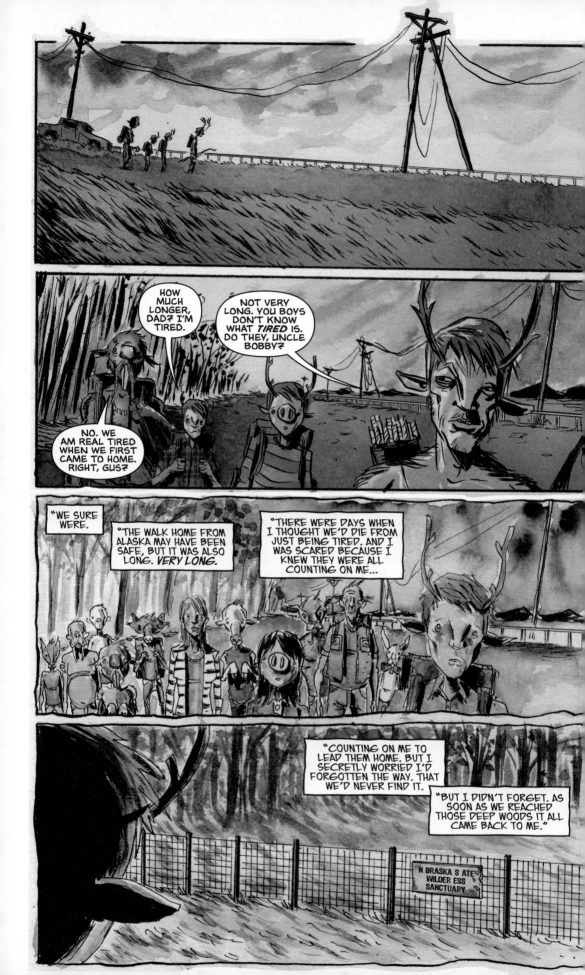

HOW MUCH LONGER, DAD? I'M TIRED.

NOT VERY LONG. YOU BOYS DON'T KNOW WHAT *TIRED* IS. DO THEY, UNCLE BOBBY?

NO. WE AM REAL TIRED WHEN WE FIRST CAME TO HOME. RIGHT, GUS?

"WE SURE WERE.

"THE WALK HOME FROM ALASKA MAY HAVE BEEN SAFE, BUT IT WAS ALSO LONG. *VERY LONG.*

"THERE WERE DAYS WHEN I THOUGHT WE'D DIE FROM JUST BEING TIRED. AND I WAS SCARED BECAUSE I KNEW THEY WERE ALL COUNTING ON ME...

"COUNTING ON ME TO LEAD THEM HOME. BUT I SECRETLY WORRIED I'D FORGOTTEN THE WAY. THAT WE'D NEVER FIND IT.

"BUT I DIDN'T FORGET. AS SOON AS WE REACHED THOSE DEEP WOODS IT ALL CAME BACK TO ME."

N BRASKA S ATE WILDER ESS SANCTUARY

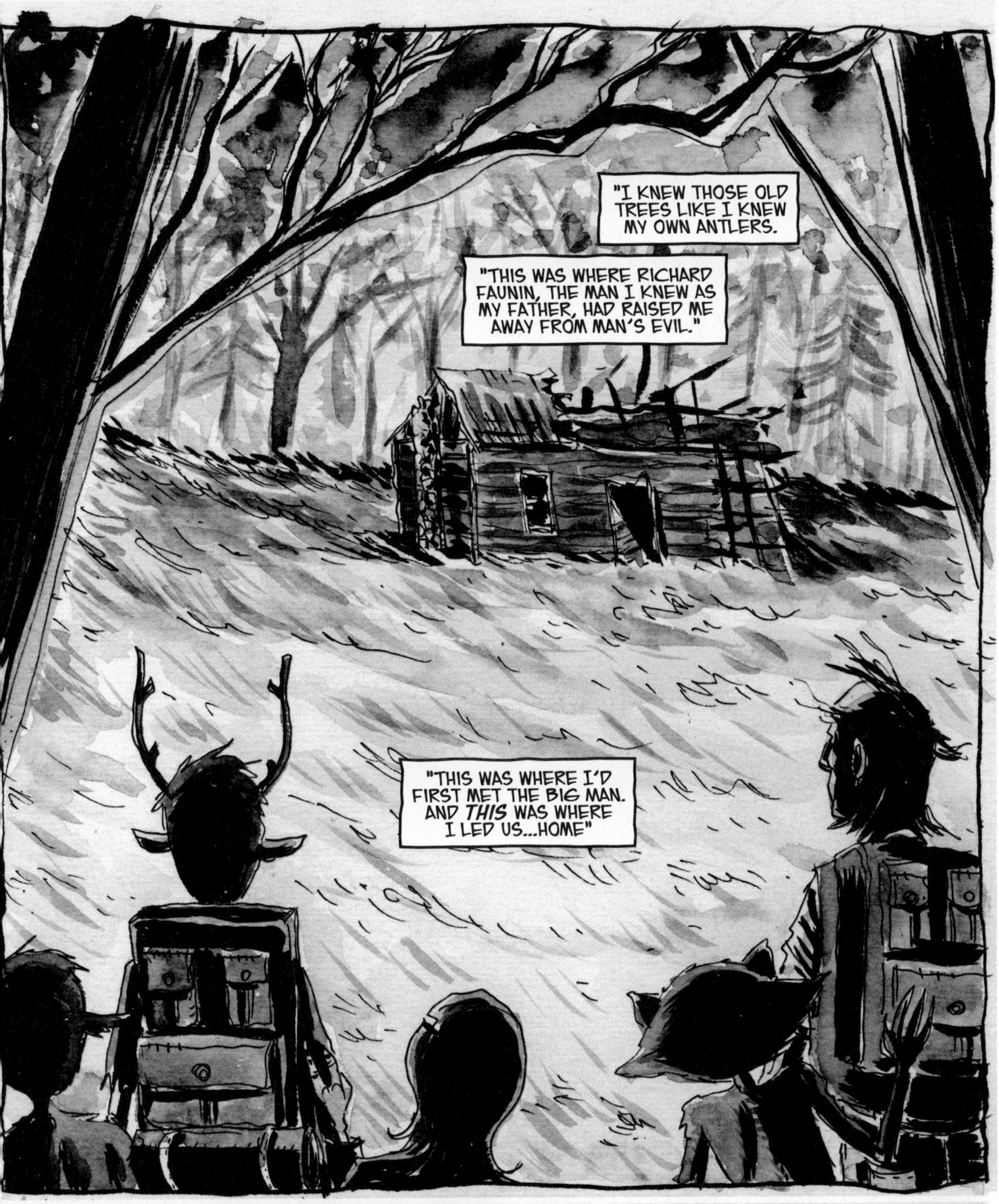
"I KNEW THOSE OLD TREES LIKE I KNEW MY OWN ANTLERS.
"THIS WAS WHERE RICHARD FAUNIN, THE MAN I KNEW AS MY FATHER, HAD RAISED ME AWAY FROM MAN'S EVIL."
"THIS WAS WHERE I'D FIRST MET THE BIG MAN. AND *THIS* WAS WHERE I LED US...HOME"

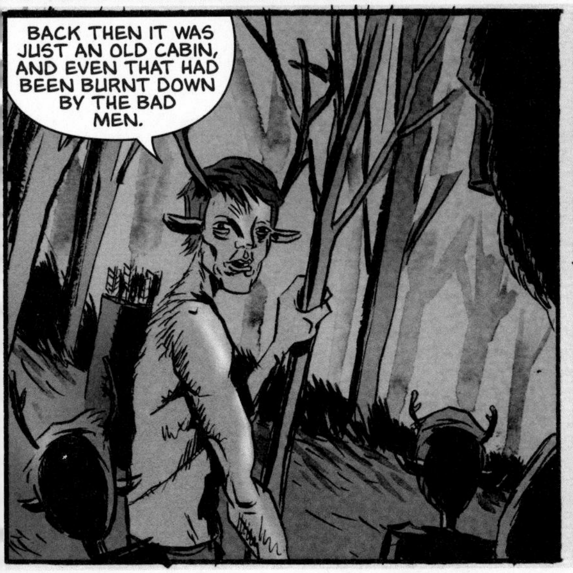
BACK THEN IT WAS JUST AN OLD CABIN, AND EVEN THAT HAD BEEN BURNT DOWN BY THE BAD MEN.

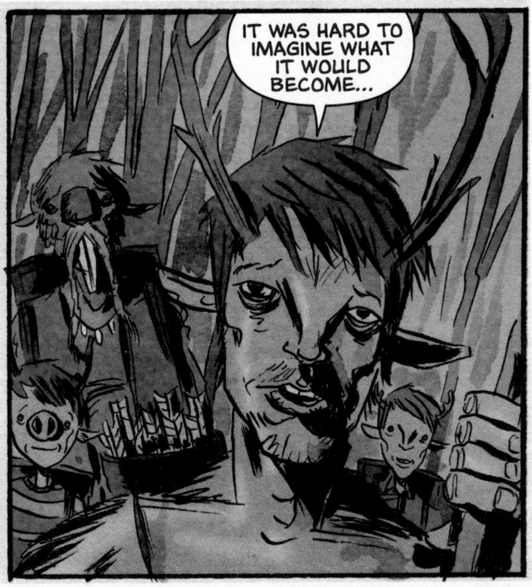
IT WAS HARD TO IMAGINE WHAT IT WOULD BECOME...

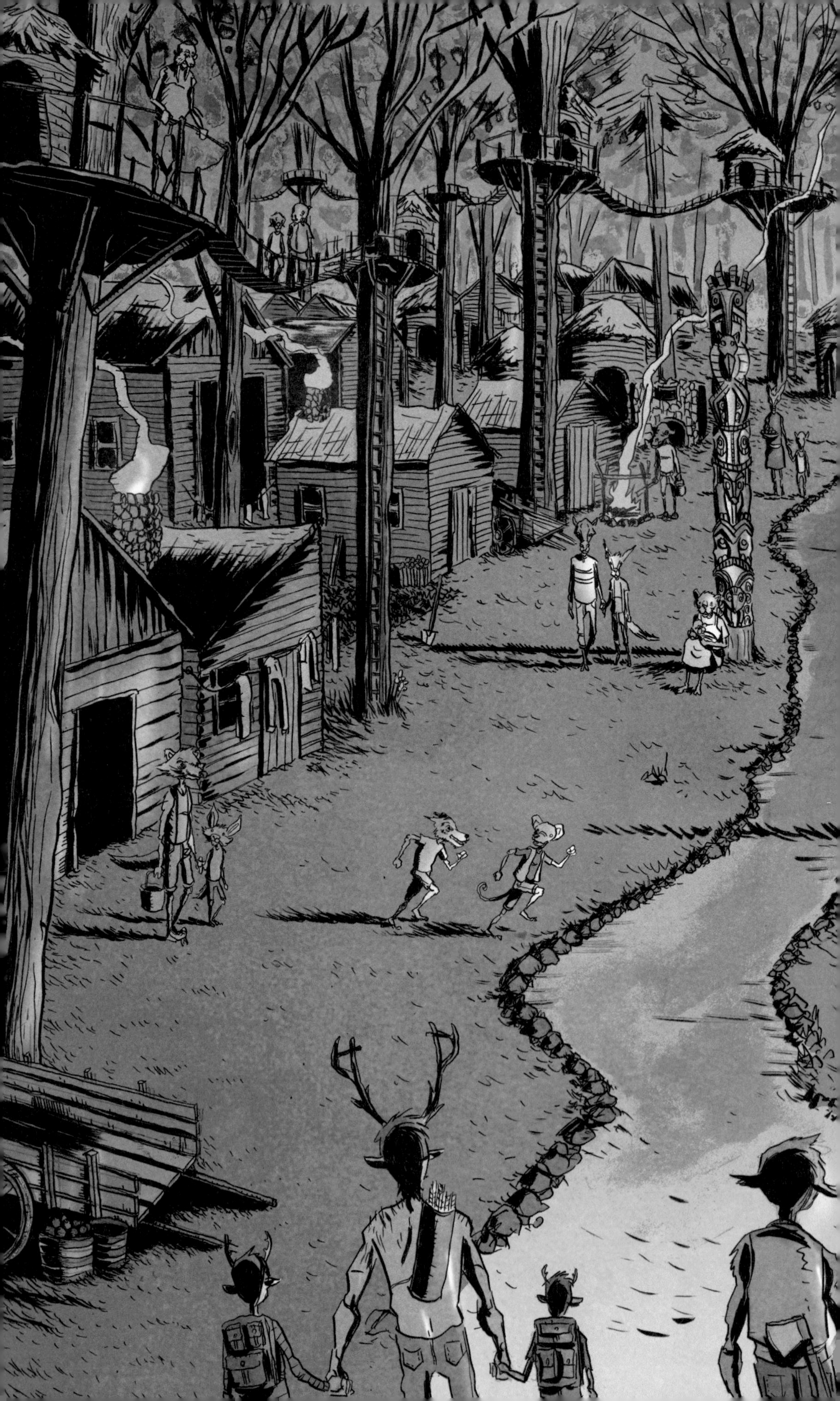

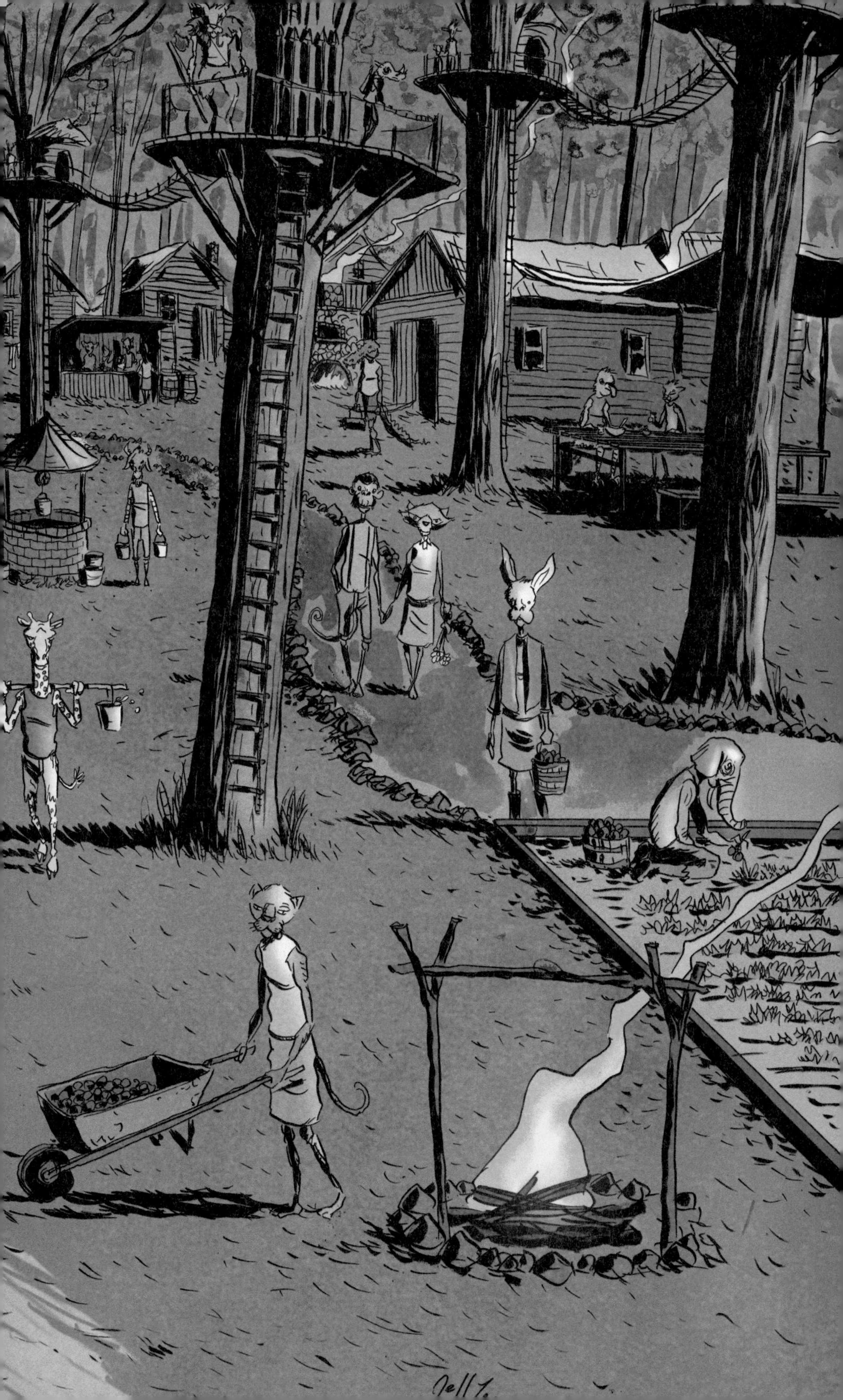

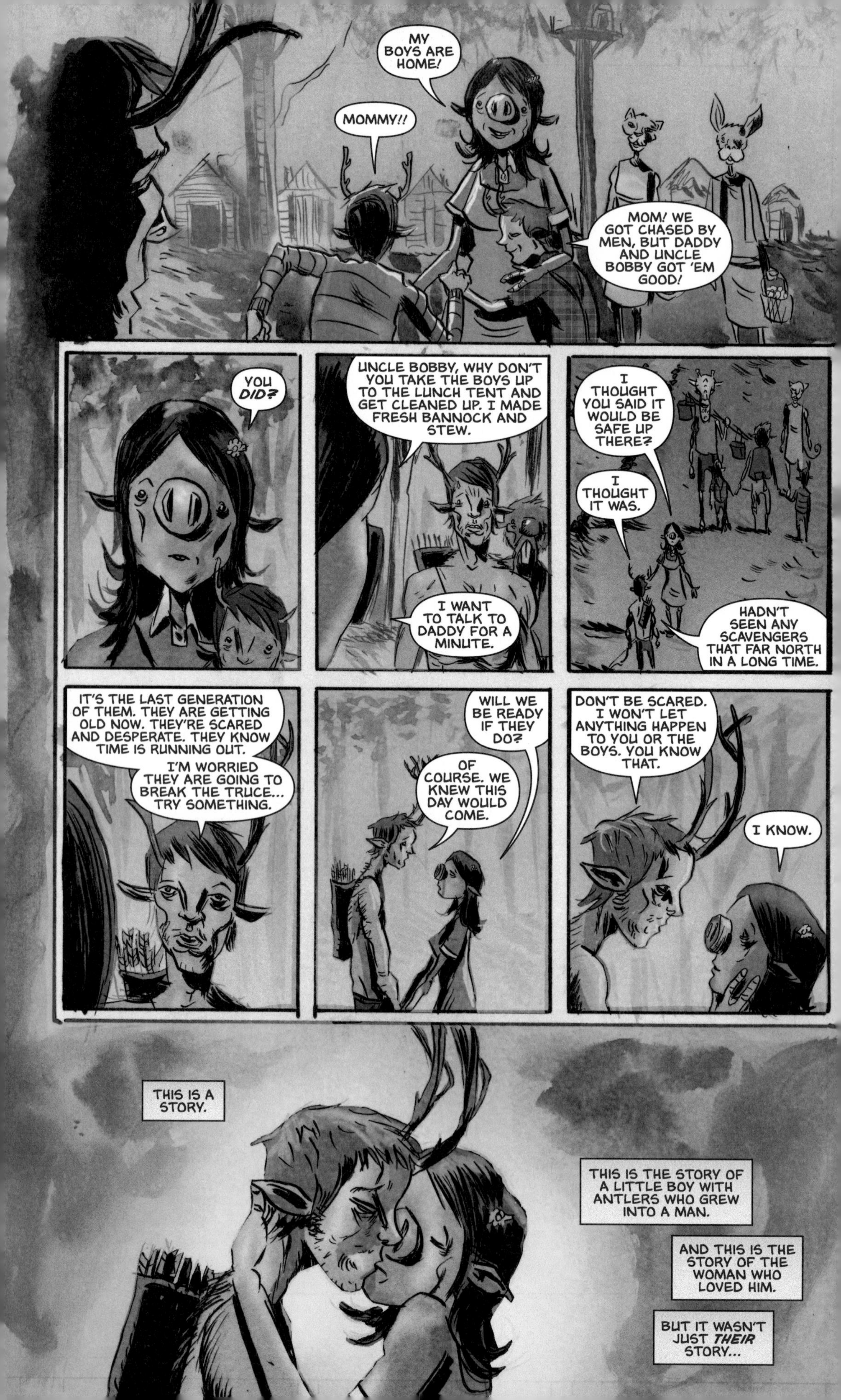
MY BOYS ARE HOME!
MOMMY!!
MOM! WE GOT CHASED BY MEN, BUT DADDY AND UNCLE BOBBY GOT 'EM GOOD!
YOU *DID?*
UNCLE BOBBY, WHY DON'T YOU TAKE THE BOYS UP TO THE LUNCH TENT AND GET CLEANED UP. I MADE FRESH BANNOCK AND STEW.
I WANT TO TALK TO DADDY FOR A MINUTE.
I THOUGHT YOU SAID IT WOULD BE SAFE UP THERE?
I THOUGHT IT WAS.
HADN'T SEEN ANY SCAVENGERS THAT FAR NORTH IN A LONG TIME.
IT'S THE LAST GENERATION OF THEM. THEY ARE GETTING OLD NOW. THEY'RE SCARED AND DESPERATE. THEY KNOW TIME IS RUNNING OUT.
I'M WORRIED THEY ARE GOING TO BREAK THE TRUCE... TRY SOMETHING.
WILL WE BE READY IF THEY DO?
OF COURSE. WE KNEW THIS DAY WOULD COME.
DON'T BE SCARED. I WON'T LET ANYTHING HAPPEN TO YOU OR THE BOYS. YOU KNOW THAT.
I KNOW.
THIS IS A STORY.
THIS IS THE STORY OF A LITTLE BOY WITH ANTLERS WHO GREW INTO A MAN.
AND THIS IS THE STORY OF THE WOMAN WHO LOVED HIM.
BUT IT WASN'T JUST *THEIR* STORY...

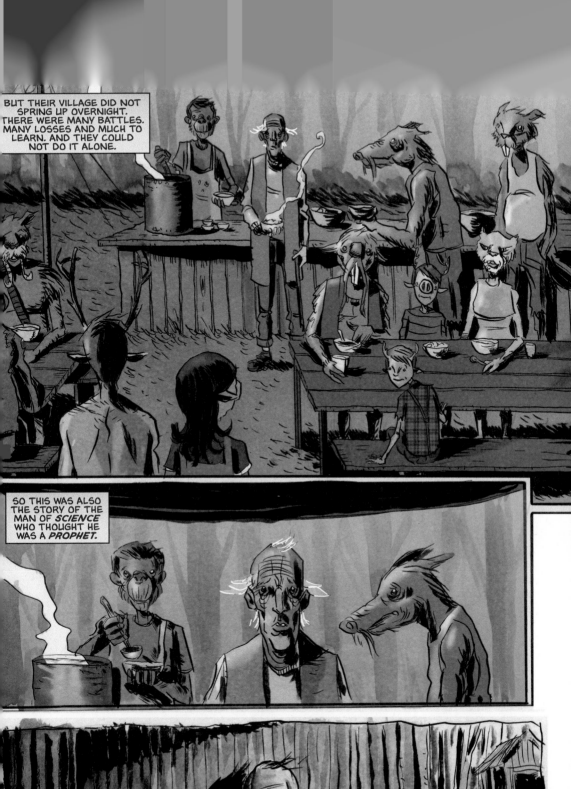

BUT THEIR VILLAGE DID NOT SPRING UP OVERNIGHT. THERE WERE MANY BATTLES. MANY LOSSES AND MUCH TO LEARN. AND THEY COULD NOT DO IT ALONE.

SO THIS WAS ALSO THE STORY OF THE MAN OF *SCIENCE* WHO THOUGHT HE WAS A *PROPHET.*

IN MANY WAYS THE DOCTOR HAD ALWAYS BEEN A LOST SOUL. BUT NEVER MORE SO THAN IN THOSE EARLY DAYS AFTER THEY ARRIVED IN THE DEEP WOODS.

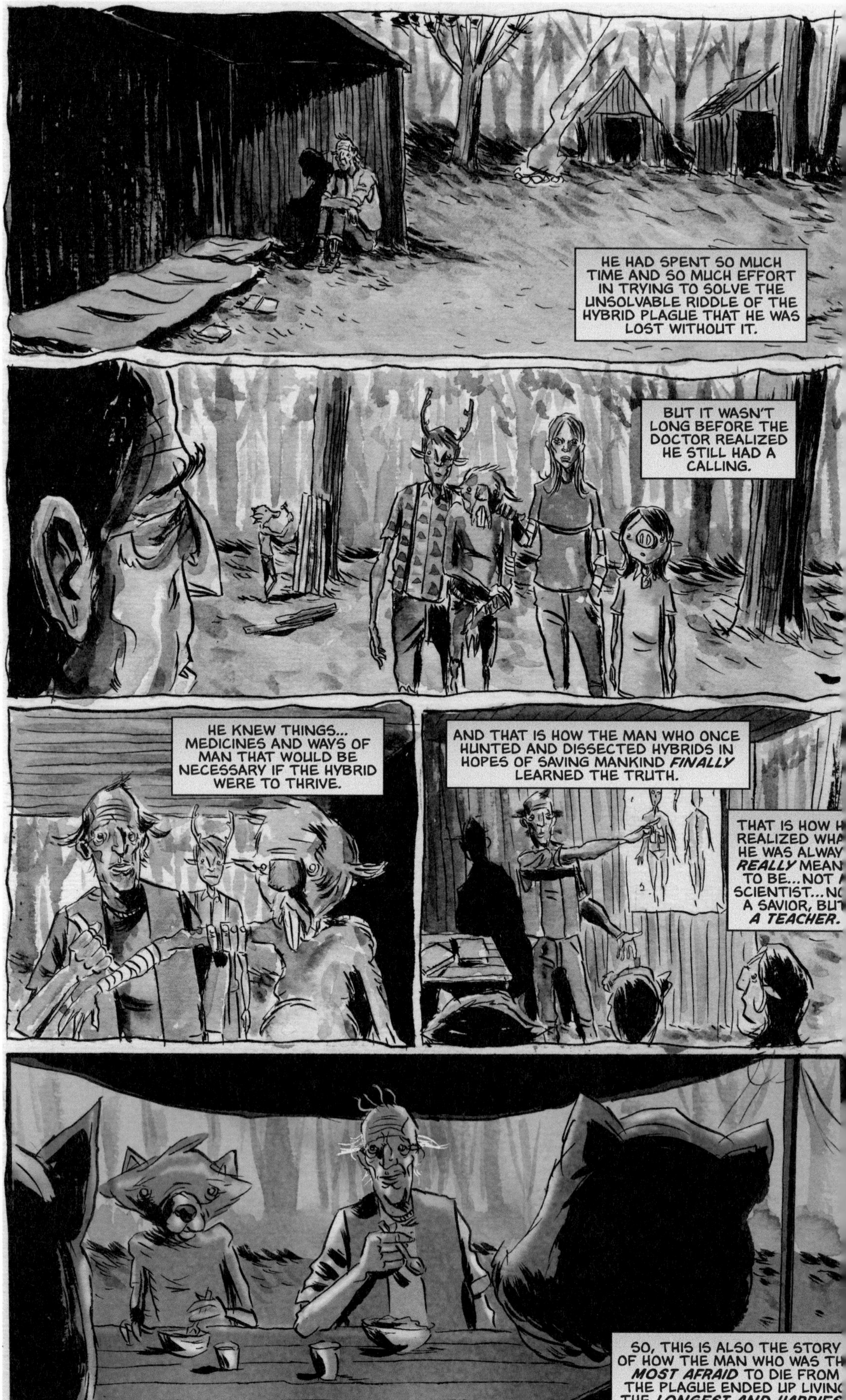
HE HAD SPENT SO MUCH TIME AND SO MUCH EFFORT IN TRYING TO SOLVE THE UNSOLVABLE RIDDLE OF THE HYBRID PLAGUE THAT HE WAS LOST WITHOUT IT.
BUT IT WASN'T LONG BEFORE THE DOCTOR REALIZED HE STILL HAD A CALLING.
HE KNEW THINGS... MEDICINES AND WAYS OF MAN THAT WOULD BE NECESSARY IF THE HYBRID WERE TO THRIVE.
AND THAT IS HOW THE MAN WHO ONCE HUNTED AND DISSECTED HYBRIDS IN HOPES OF SAVING MANKIND *FINALLY* LEARNED THE TRUTH.
THAT IS HOW H REALIZED WHA HE WAS ALWAY *REALLY* MEAN TO BE...NOT SCIENTIST...NO A SAVIOR, BUT *A TEACHER.*
SO, THIS IS ALSO THE STORY OF HOW THE MAN WHO WAS TH *MOST AFRAID* TO DIE FROM THE PLAGUE ENDED UP LIVIN THE *LONGEST AND HAPPIES* LIFE OF THEM ALL.

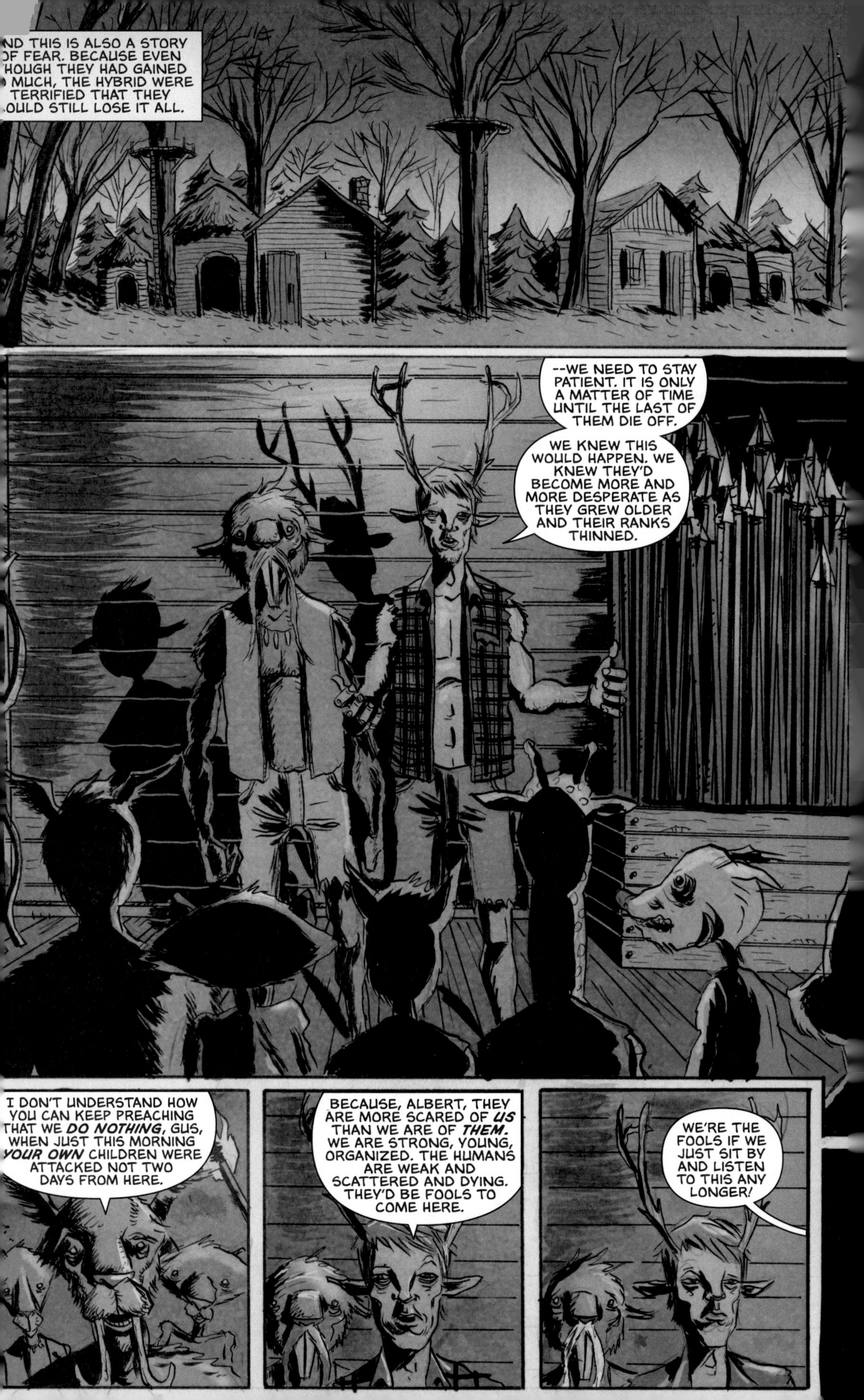
ND THIS IS ALSO A STORY OF FEAR. BECAUSE EVEN THOUGH THEY HAD GAINED SO MUCH, THE HYBRID WERE TERRIFIED THAT THEY COULD STILL LOSE IT ALL.
--WE NEED TO STAY PATIENT. IT IS ONLY A MATTER OF TIME UNTIL THE LAST OF THEM DIE OFF.
WE KNEW THIS WOULD HAPPEN. WE KNEW THEY'D BECOME MORE AND MORE DESPERATE AS THEY GREW OLDER AND THEIR RANKS THINNED.
I DON'T UNDERSTAND HOW YOU CAN KEEP PREACHING THAT WE *DO NOTHING*, GUS, WHEN JUST THIS MORNING *YOUR OWN* CHILDREN WERE ATTACKED NOT TWO DAYS FROM HERE.
BECAUSE, ALBERT, THEY ARE MORE SCARED OF *US* THAN WE ARE OF *THEM*. WE ARE STRONG, YOUNG, ORGANIZED. THE HUMANS ARE WEAK AND SCATTERED AND DYING. THEY'D BE FOOLS TO COME HERE.
WE'RE THE FOOLS IF WE JUST SIT BY AND LISTEN TO THIS ANY LONGER!

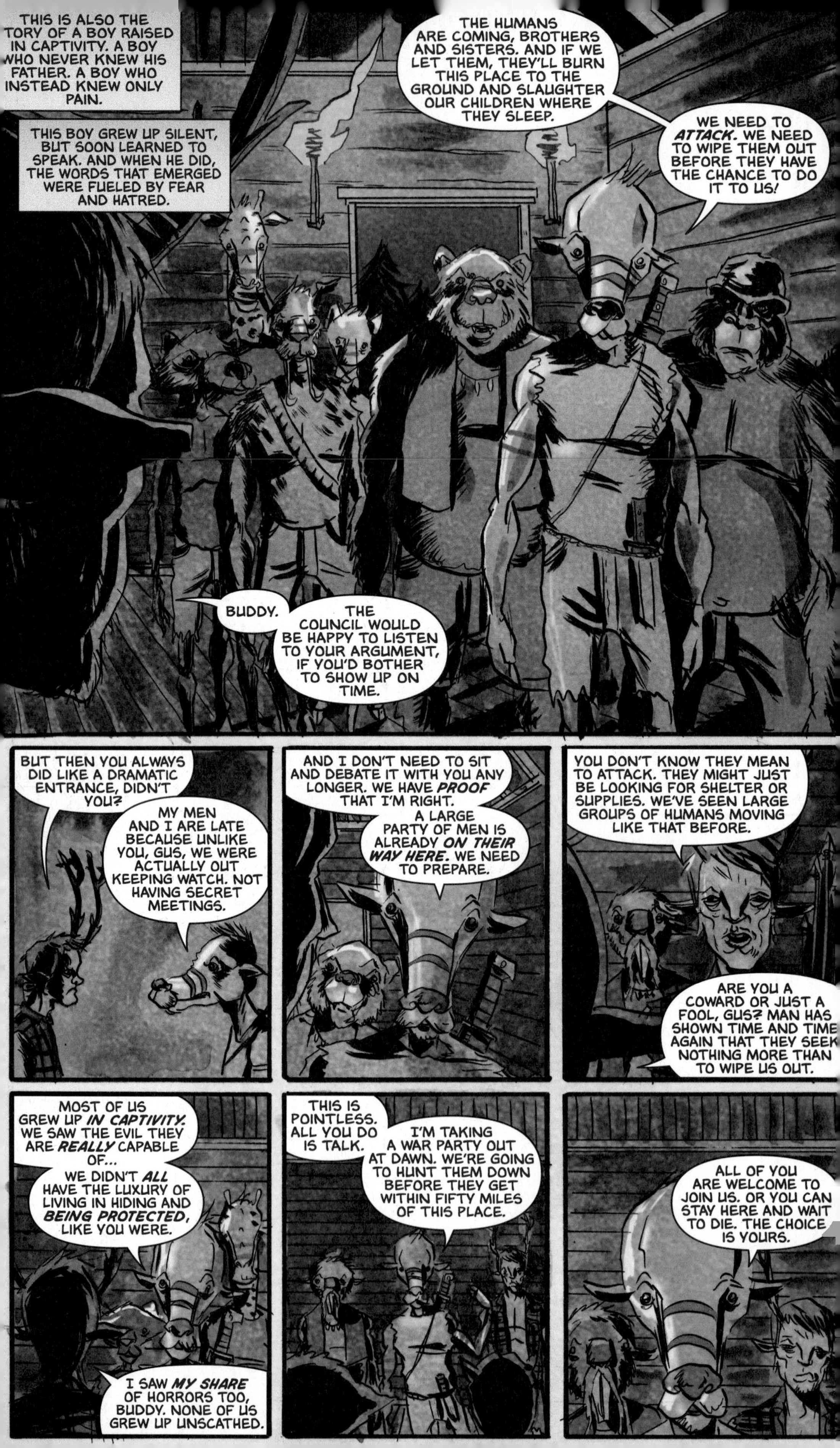
THIS IS ALSO THE STORY OF A BOY RAISED IN CAPTIVITY. A BOY WHO NEVER KNEW HIS FATHER. A BOY WHO INSTEAD KNEW ONLY PAIN.
THIS BOY GREW UP SILENT, BUT SOON LEARNED TO SPEAK. AND WHEN HE DID, THE WORDS THAT EMERGED WERE FUELED BY FEAR AND HATRED.
THE HUMANS ARE COMING, BROTHERS AND SISTERS. AND IF WE LET THEM, THEY'LL BURN THIS PLACE TO THE GROUND AND SLAUGHTER OUR CHILDREN WHERE THEY SLEEP.
WE NEED TO ATTACK. WE NEED TO WIPE THEM OUT BEFORE THEY HAVE THE CHANCE TO DO IT TO US!
BUDDY.
THE COUNCIL WOULD BE HAPPY TO LISTEN TO YOUR ARGUMENT, IF YOU'D BOTHER TO SHOW UP ON TIME.
BUT THEN YOU ALWAYS DID LIKE A DRAMATIC ENTRANCE, DIDN'T YOU?
MY MEN AND I ARE LATE BECAUSE UNLIKE YOU, GUS, WE WERE ACTUALLY OUT KEEPING WATCH. NOT HAVING SECRET MEETINGS.
AND I DON'T NEED TO SIT AND DEBATE IT WITH YOU ANY LONGER. WE HAVE PROOF THAT I'M RIGHT.
A LARGE PARTY OF MEN IS ALREADY ON THEIR WAY HERE. WE NEED TO PREPARE.
YOU DON'T KNOW THEY MEAN TO ATTACK. THEY MIGHT JUST BE LOOKING FOR SHELTER OR SUPPLIES. WE'VE SEEN LARGE GROUPS OF HUMANS MOVING LIKE THAT BEFORE.
ARE YOU A COWARD OR JUST A FOOL, GUS? MAN HAS SHOWN TIME AND TIME AGAIN THAT THEY SEEK NOTHING MORE THAN TO WIPE US OUT.
MOST OF US GREW UP IN CAPTIVITY. WE SAW THE EVIL THEY ARE REALLY CAPABLE OF...
WE DIDN'T ALL HAVE THE LUXURY OF LIVING IN HIDING AND BEING PROTECTED, LIKE YOU WERE.
I SAW MY SHARE OF HORRORS TOO, BUDDY. NONE OF US GREW UP UNSCATHED.
THIS IS POINTLESS. ALL YOU DO IS TALK.
I'M TAKING A WAR PARTY OUT AT DAWN. WE'RE GOING TO HUNT THEM DOWN BEFORE THEY GET WITHIN FIFTY MILES OF THIS PLACE.
ALL OF YOU ARE WELCOME TO JOIN US. OR YOU CAN STAY HERE AND WAIT TO DIE. THE CHOICE IS YOURS.

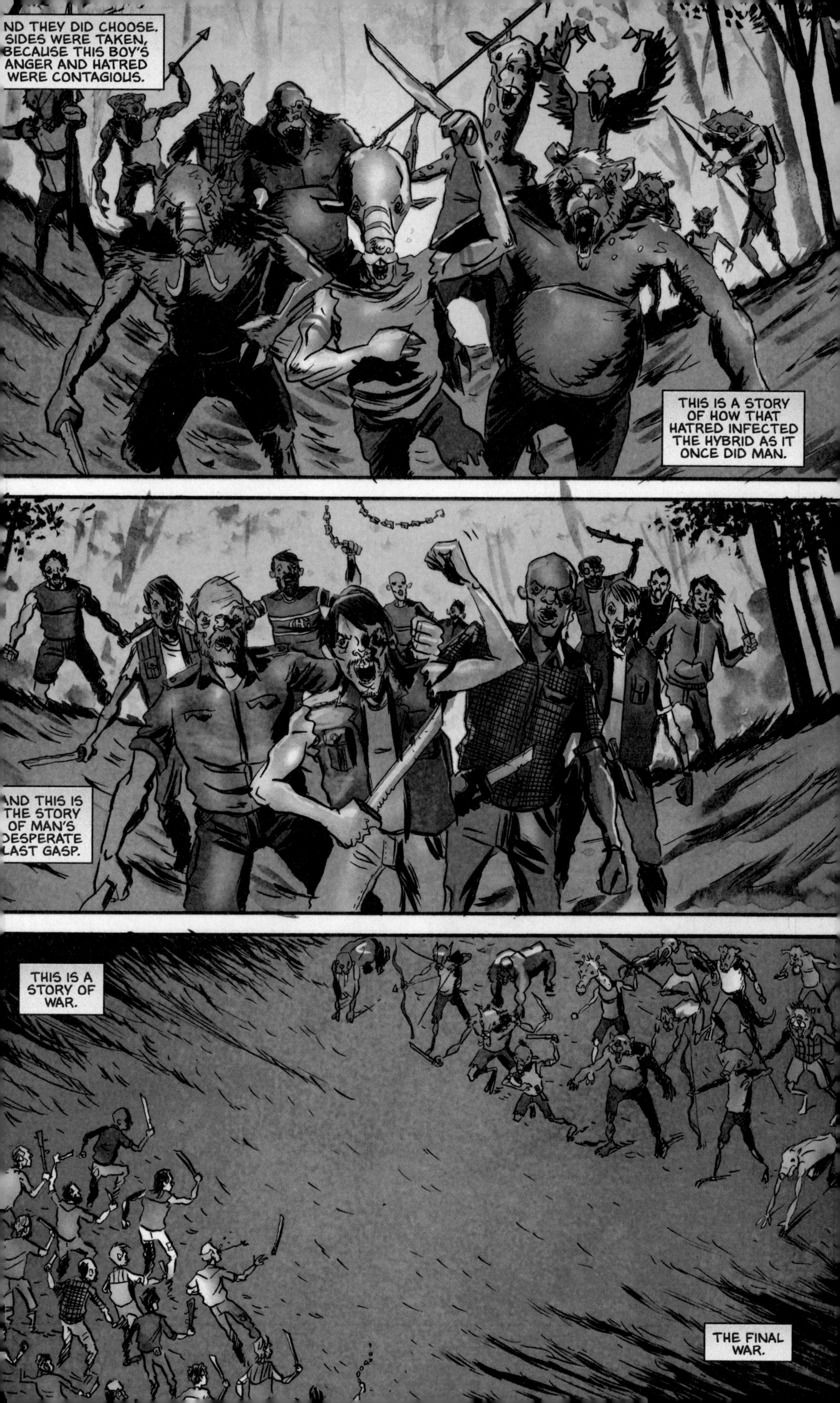
ND THEY DID CHOOSE. SIDES WERE TAKEN, BECAUSE THIS BOY'S ANGER AND HATRED WERE CONTAGIOUS.
THIS IS A STORY OF HOW THAT HATRED INFECTED THE HYBRID AS IT ONCE DID MAN.
AND THIS IS THE STORY OF MAN'S DESPERATE LAST GASP.
THIS IS A STORY OF WAR.
THE FINAL WAR.

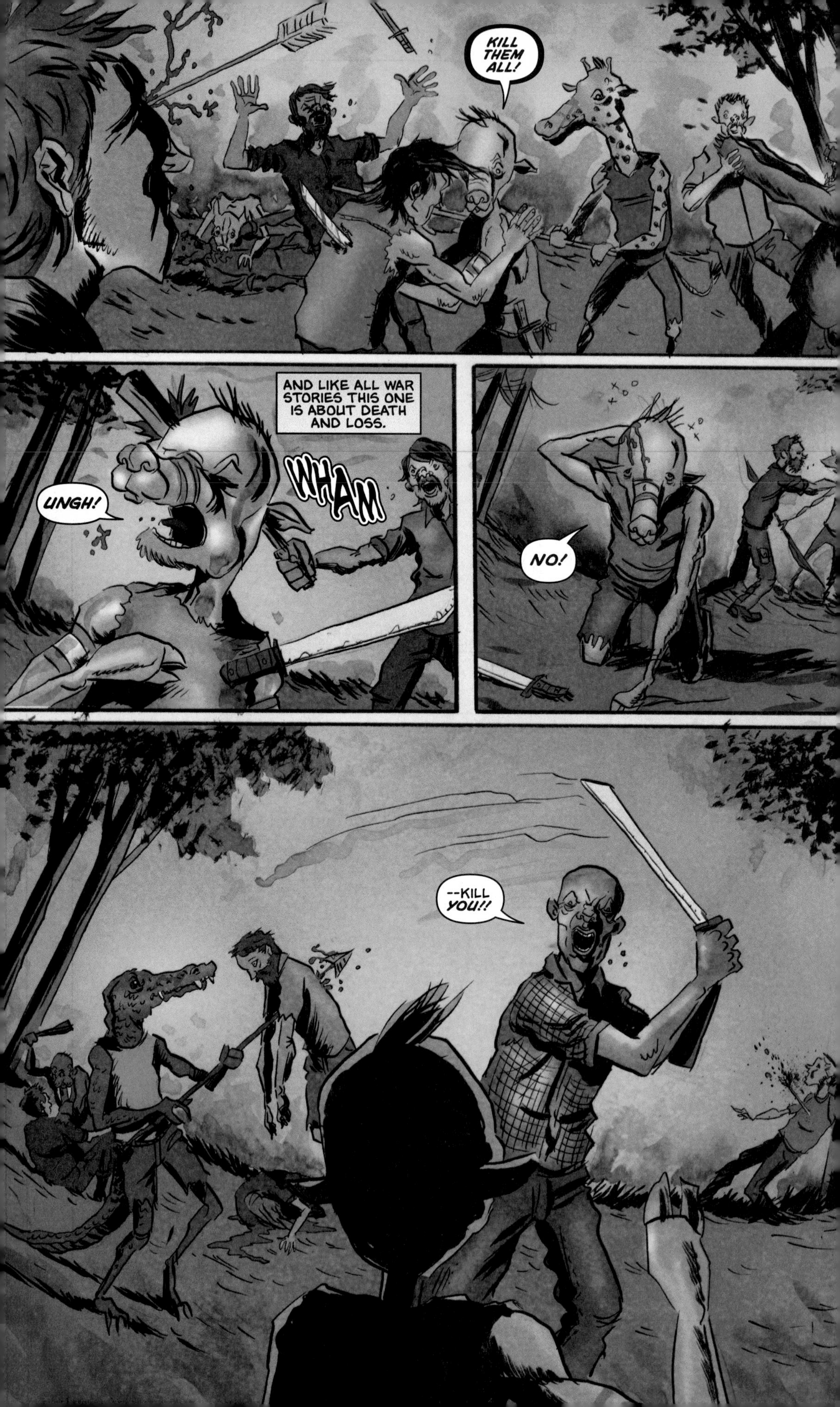
KILL THEM ALL!
AND LIKE ALL WAR STORIES THIS ONE IS ABOUT DEATH AND LOSS.
WHAM
UNGH!
NO!
--KILL YOU!!

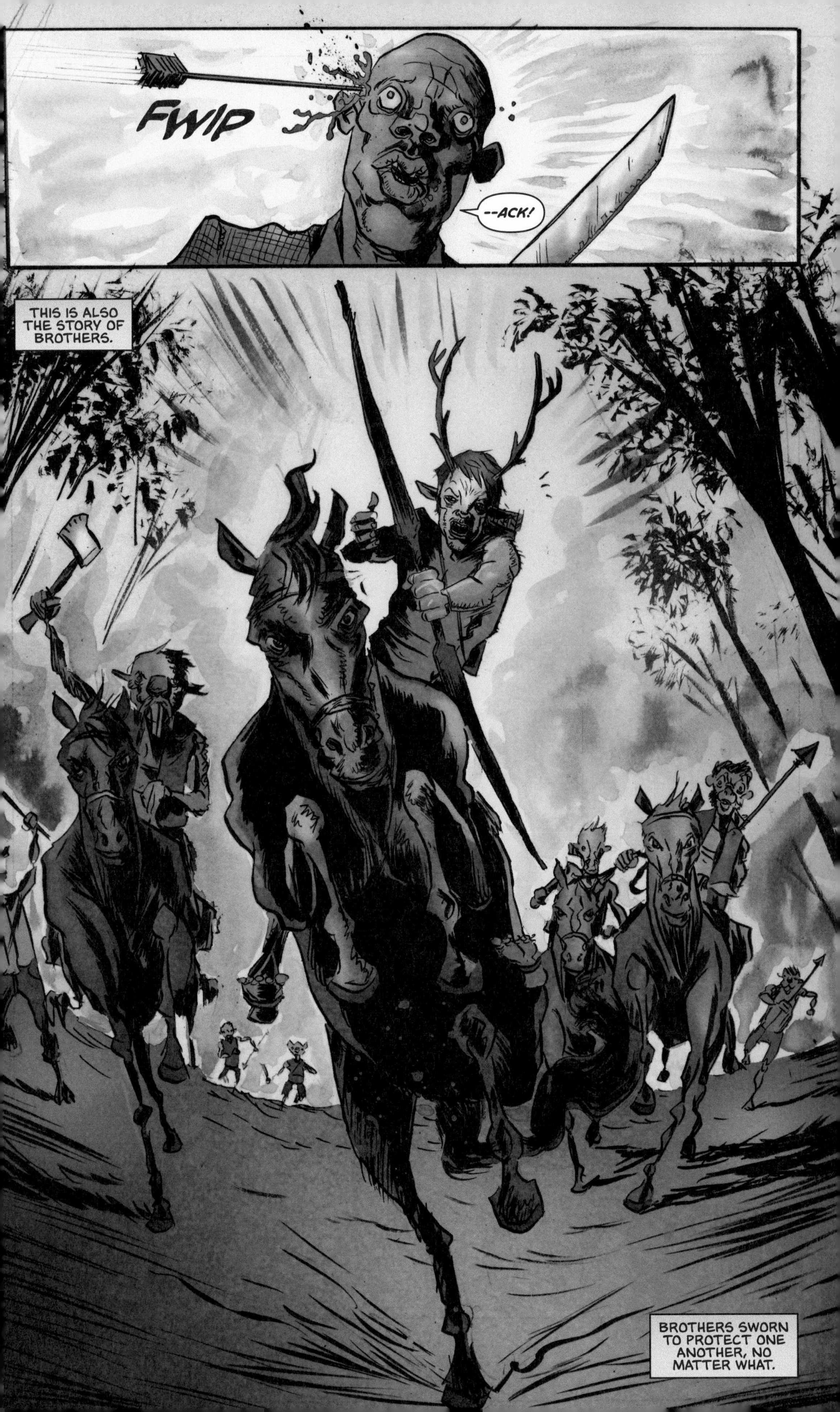
FWIP
--ACK!
THIS IS ALSO THE STORY OF BROTHERS.
BROTHERS SWORN TO PROTECT ONE ANOTHER, NO MATTER WHAT.

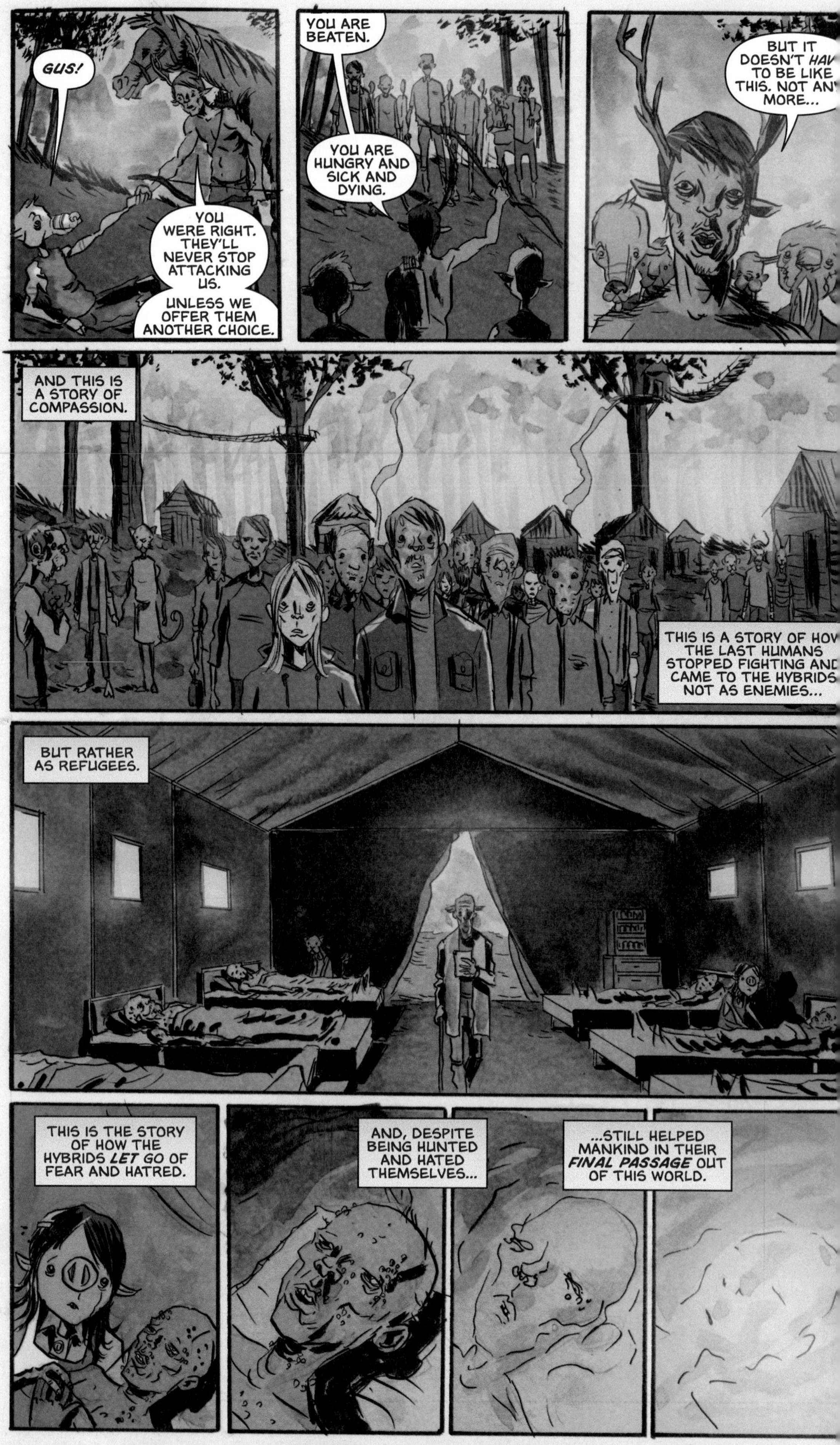
GUS!
YOU WERE RIGHT. THEY'LL NEVER STOP ATTACKING US.
UNLESS WE OFFER THEM ANOTHER CHOICE.
YOU ARE BEATEN.
YOU ARE HUNGRY AND SICK AND DYING.
BUT IT DOESN'T HAV TO BE LIKE THIS. NOT AN MORE...
AND THIS IS A STORY OF COMPASSION.
THIS IS A STORY OF HOV THE LAST HUMANS STOPPED FIGHTING ANC CAME TO THE HYBRIDS NOT AS ENEMIES...
BUT RATHER AS REFUGEES.
THIS IS THE STORY OF HOW THE HYBRIDS LET GO OF FEAR AND HATRED.
AND, DESPITE BEING HUNTED AND HATED THEMSELVES...
...STILL HELPED MANKIND IN THEIR FINAL PASSAGE OUT OF THIS WORLD.

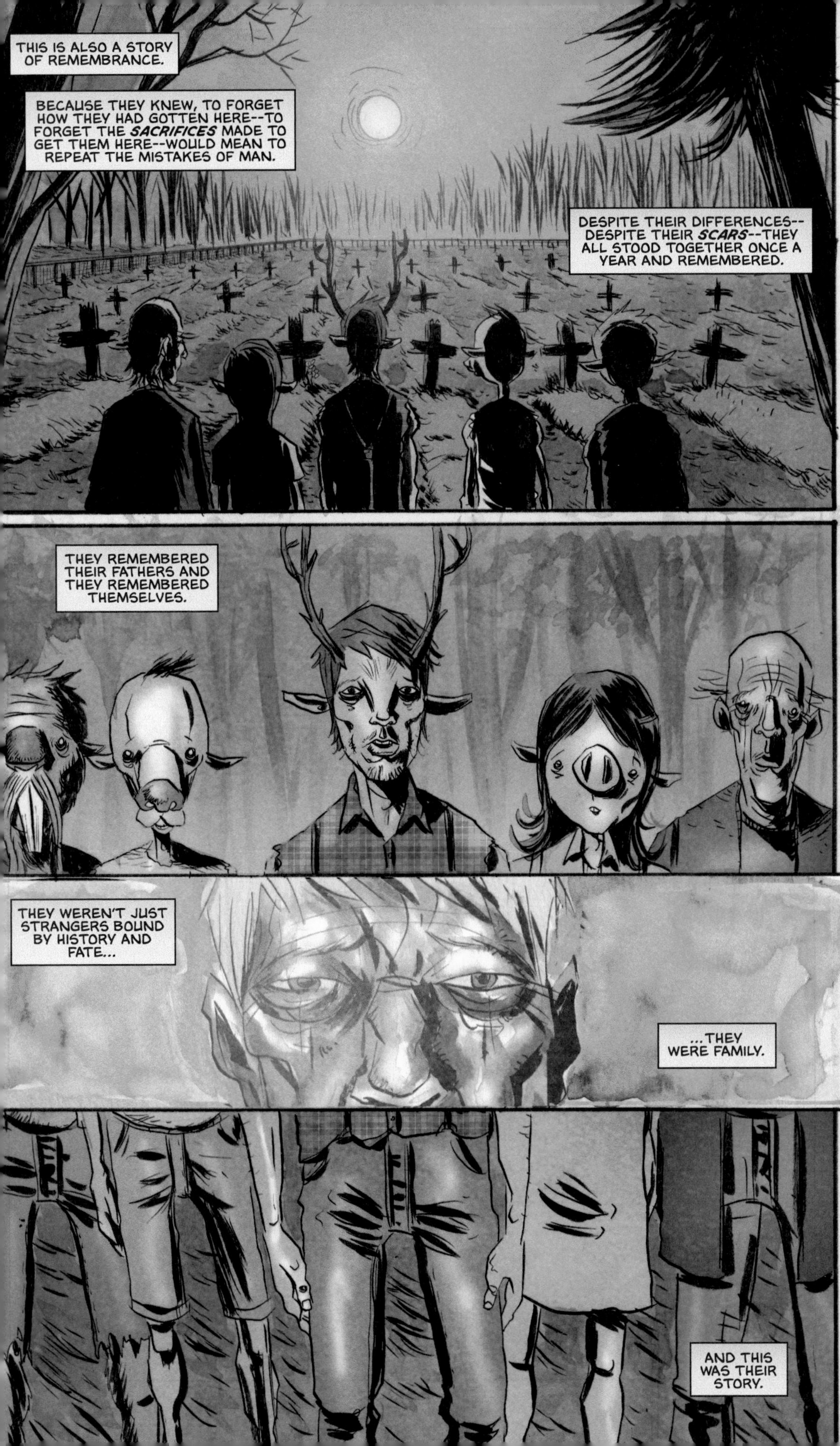
THIS IS ALSO A STORY OF REMEMBRANCE.
BECAUSE THEY KNEW, TO FORGET HOW THEY HAD GOTTEN HERE--TO FORGET THE SACRIFICES MADE TO GET THEM HERE--WOULD MEAN TO REPEAT THE MISTAKES OF MAN.
DESPITE THEIR DIFFERENCES--DESPITE THEIR SCARS--THEY ALL STOOD TOGETHER ONCE A YEAR AND REMEMBERED.
THEY REMEMBERED THEIR FATHERS AND THEY REMEMBERED THEMSELVES.
THEY WEREN'T JUST STRANGERS BOUND BY HISTORY AND FATE...
...THEY WERE FAMILY.
AND THIS WAS THEIR STORY.

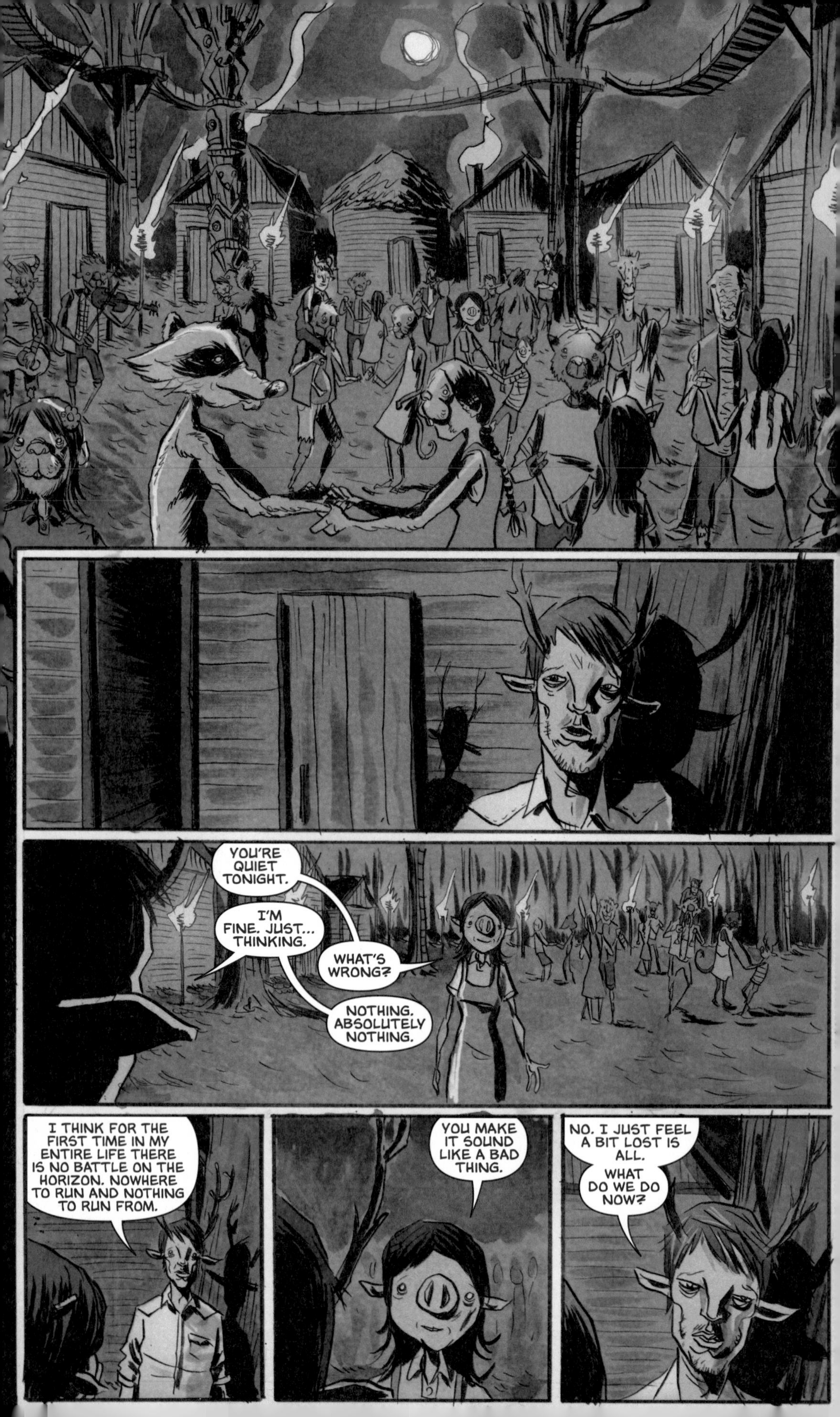
YOU'RE QUIET TONIGHT.
I'M FINE. JUST... THINKING.
WHAT'S WRONG?
NOTHING. ABSOLUTELY NOTHING.
I THINK FOR THE FIRST TIME IN MY ENTIRE LIFE THERE IS NO BATTLE ON THE HORIZON. NOWHERE TO RUN AND NOTHING TO RUN FROM.
YOU MAKE IT SOUND LIKE A BAD THING.
NO. I JUST FEEL A BIT LOST IS ALL.
WHAT DO WE DO NOW?

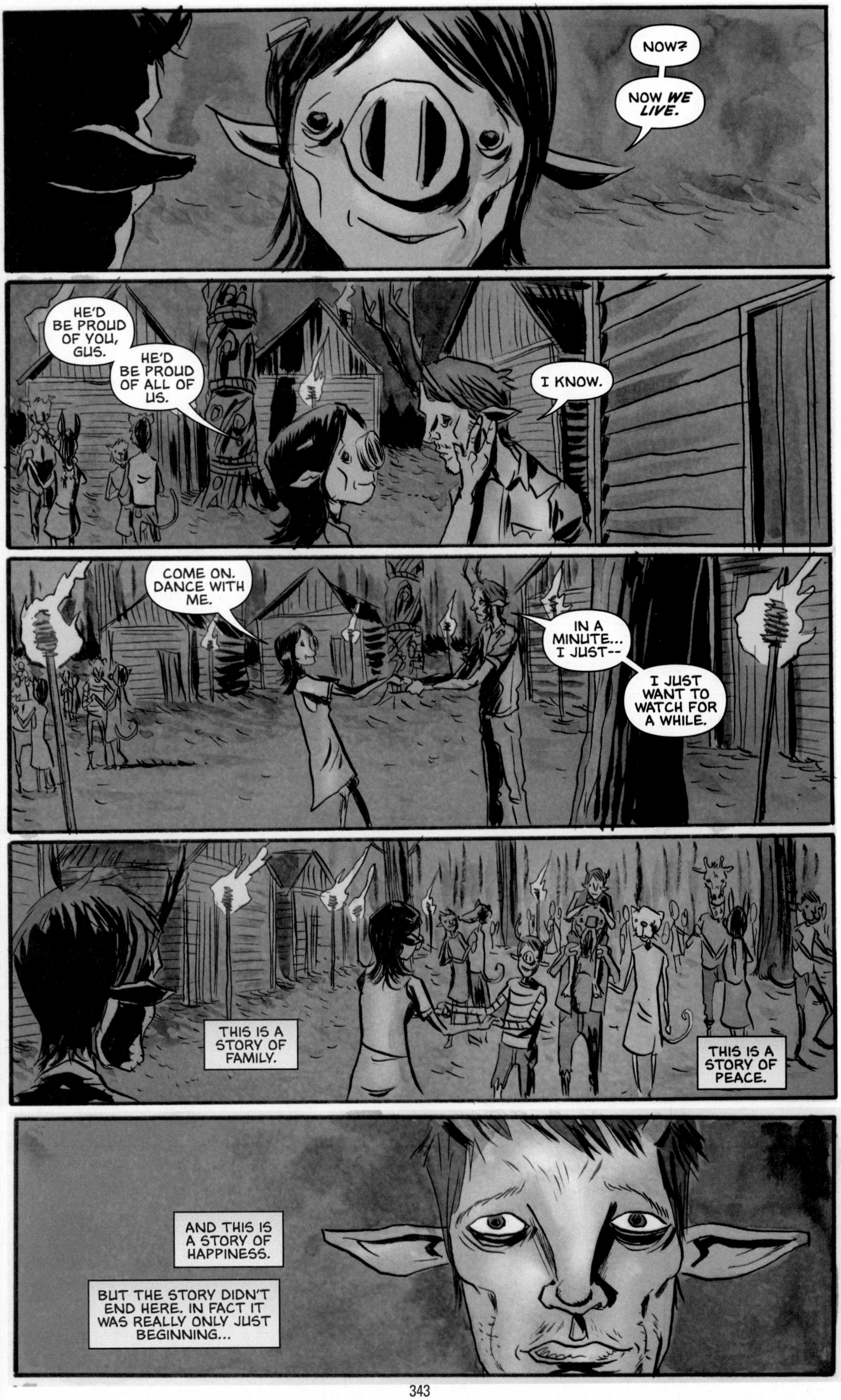
NOW?
NOW WE LIVE.
HE'D BE PROUD OF YOU, GUS.
HE'D BE PROUD OF ALL OF US.
I KNOW.
COME ON. DANCE WITH ME.
IN A MINUTE... I JUST--
I JUST WANT TO WATCH FOR A WHILE.
THIS IS A STORY OF FAMILY.
THIS IS A STORY OF PEACE.
AND THIS IS A STORY OF HAPPINESS.
BUT THE STORY DIDN'T END HERE. IN FACT IT WAS REALLY ONLY JUST BEGINNING...

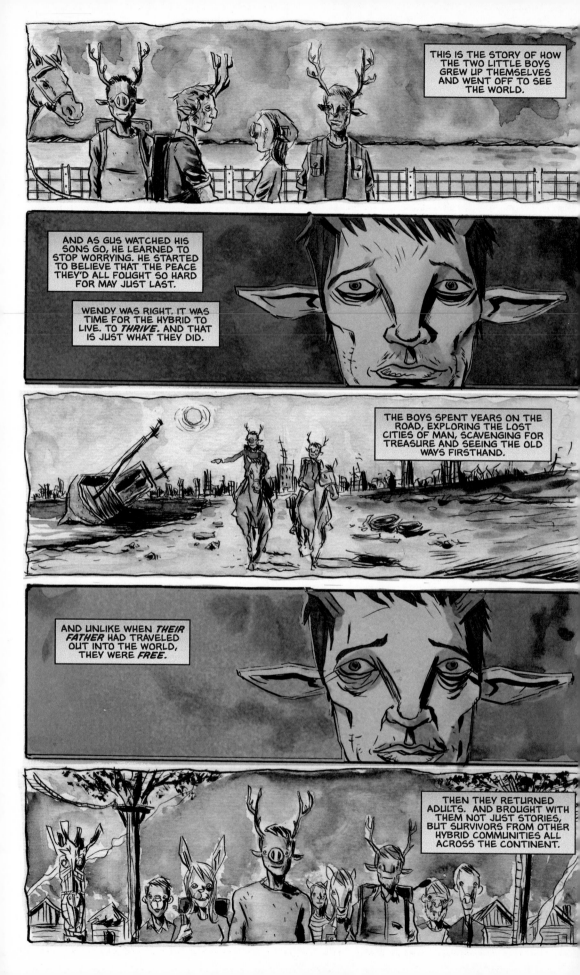

THIS IS THE STORY OF HOW THE TWO LITTLE BOYS GREW UP THEMSELVES AND WENT OFF TO SEE THE WORLD.

AND AS GUS WATCHED HIS SONS GO, HE LEARNED TO STOP WORRYING. HE STARTED TO BELIEVE THAT THE PEACE THEY'D ALL FOUGHT SO HARD FOR MAY JUST LAST.

WENDY WAS RIGHT. IT WAS TIME FOR THE HYBRID TO LIVE. TO *THRIVE*. AND THAT IS JUST WHAT THEY DID.

THE BOYS SPENT YEARS ON THE ROAD, EXPLORING THE LOST CITIES OF MAN, SCAVENGING FOR TREASURE AND SEEING THE OLD WAYS FIRSTHAND.

AND UNLIKE WHEN *THEIR FATHER* HAD TRAVELED OUT INTO THE WORLD, THEY WERE *FREE*.

THEN THEY RETURNED ADULTS. AND BROUGHT WITH THEM NOT JUST STORIES, BUT SURVIVORS FROM OTHER HYBRID COMMUNITIES ALL ACROSS THE CONTINENT.

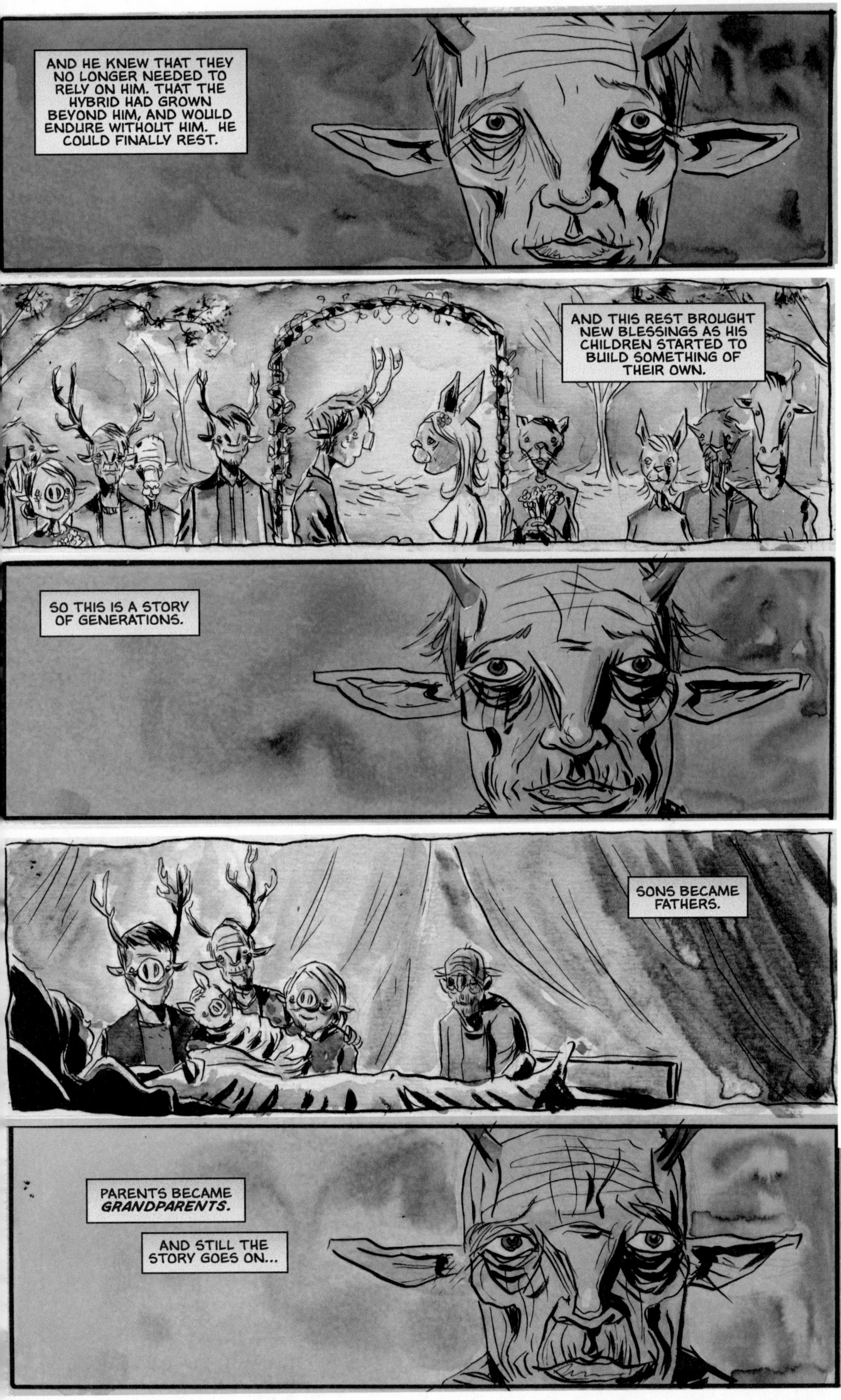
AND HE KNEW THAT THEY NO LONGER NEEDED TO RELY ON HIM. THAT THE HYBRID HAD GROWN BEYOND HIM, AND WOULD ENDURE WITHOUT HIM. HE COULD FINALLY REST.
AND THIS REST BROUGHT NEW BLESSINGS AS HIS CHILDREN STARTED TO BUILD SOMETHING OF THEIR OWN.
SO THIS IS A STORY OF GENERATIONS.
SONS BECAME FATHERS.
PARENTS BECAME *GRANDPARENTS.*
AND STILL THE STORY GOES ON...

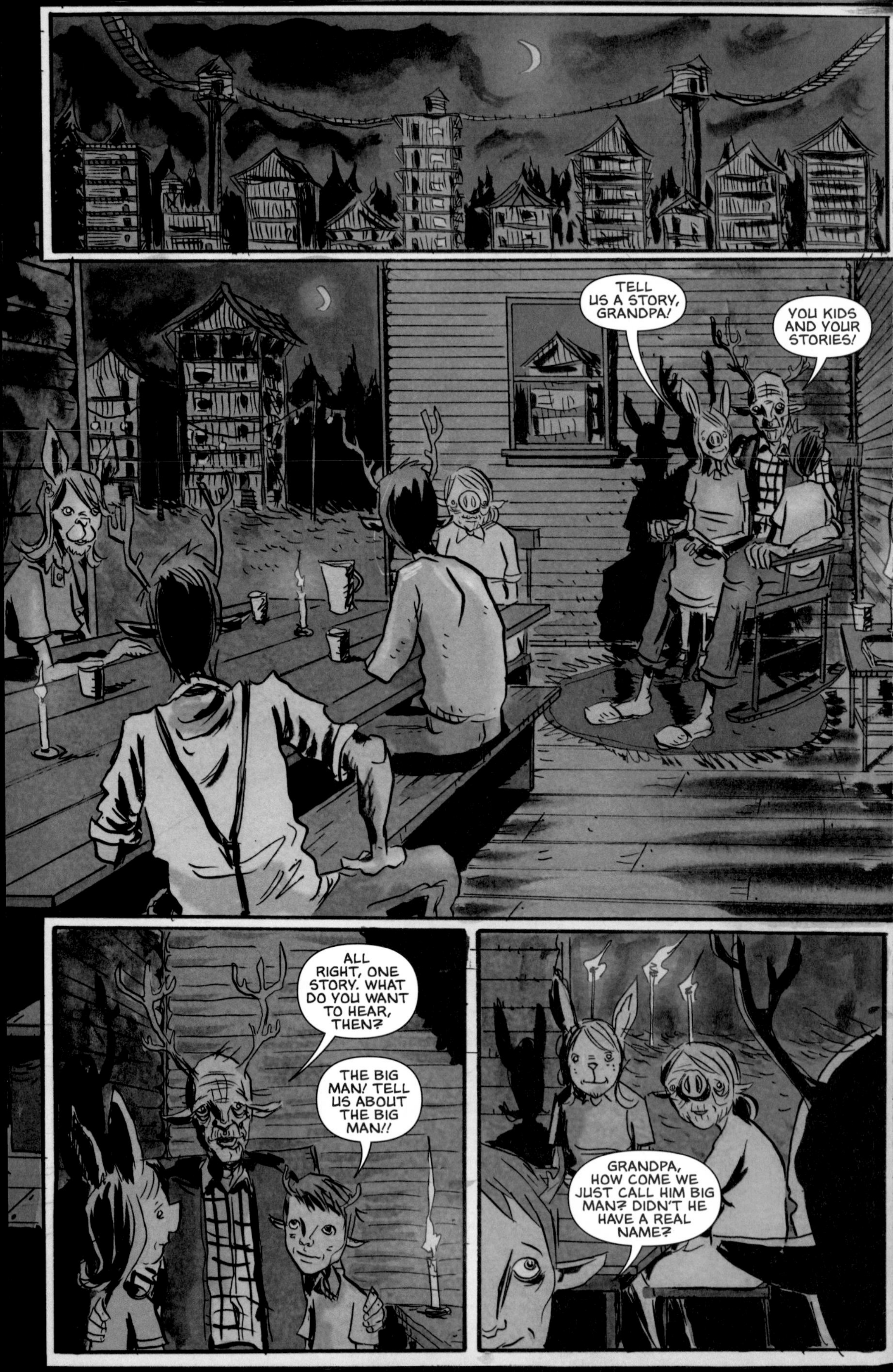
TELL US A STORY, GRANDPA!
YOU KIDS AND YOUR STORIES!
ALL RIGHT, ONE STORY. WHAT DO YOU WANT TO HEAR, THEN?
THE BIG MAN! TELL US ABOUT THE BIG MAN!!
GRANDPA, HOW COME WE JUST CALL HIM BIG MAN? DIDN'T HE HAVE A REAL NAME?

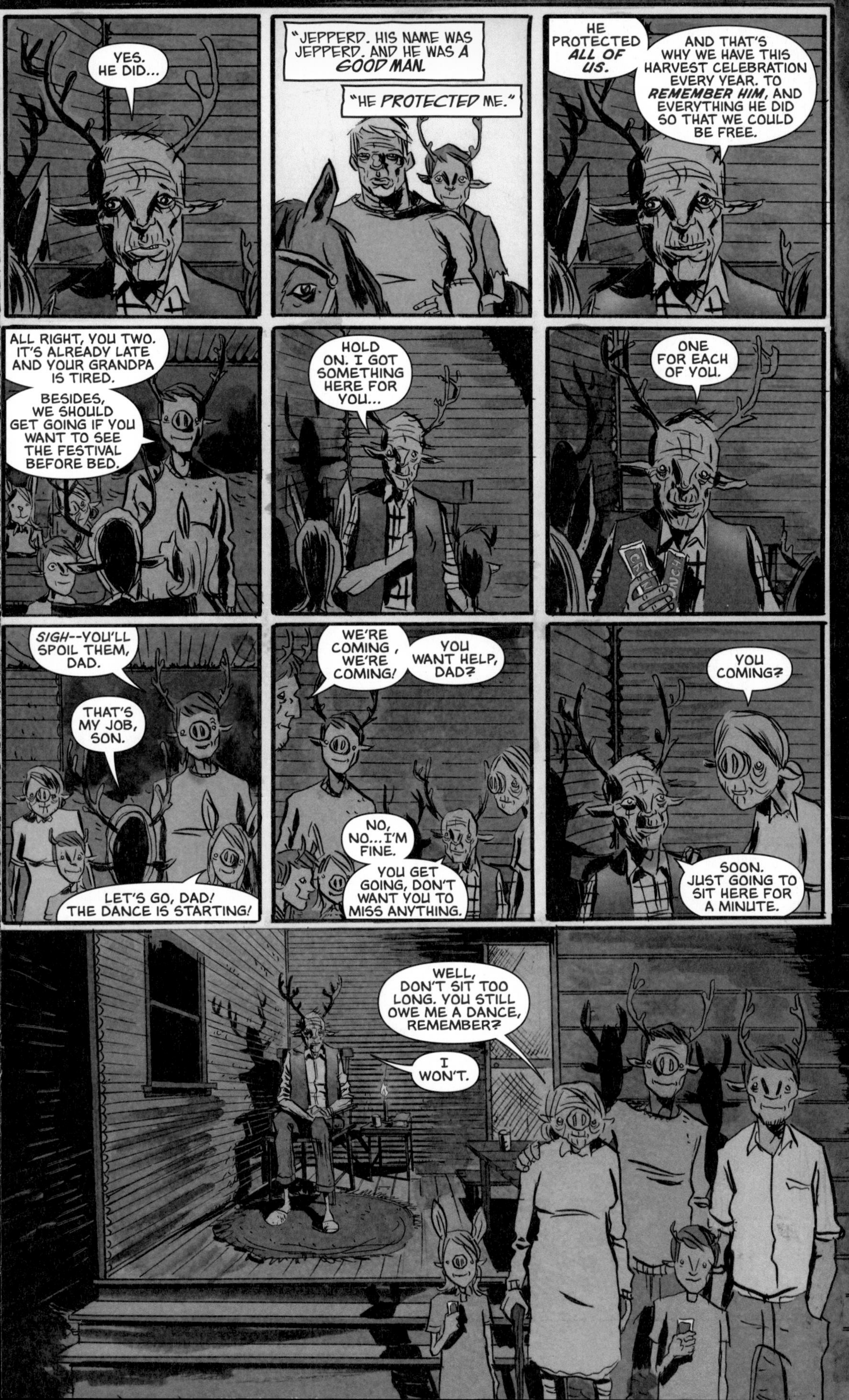
YES. HE DID...
"JEPPERD. HIS NAME WAS JEPPERD. AND HE WAS A GOOD MAN.
"HE PROTECTED ME."
HE PROTECTED ALL OF US.
AND THAT'S WHY WE HAVE THIS HARVEST CELEBRATION EVERY YEAR. TO REMEMBER HIM, AND EVERYTHING HE DID SO THAT WE COULD BE FREE.
ALL RIGHT, YOU TWO. IT'S ALREADY LATE AND YOUR GRANDPA IS TIRED.
BESIDES, WE SHOULD GET GOING IF YOU WANT TO SEE THE FESTIVAL BEFORE BED.
HOLD ON. I GOT SOMETHING HERE FOR YOU...
ONE FOR EACH OF YOU.
SIGH--YOU'LL SPOIL THEM, DAD.
THAT'S MY JOB, SON.
LET'S GO, DAD! THE DANCE IS STARTING!
WE'RE COMING, WE'RE COMING!
YOU WANT HELP, DAD?
NO, NO... I'M FINE.
YOU GET GOING, DON'T WANT YOU TO MISS ANYTHING.
YOU COMING?
SOON. JUST GOING TO SIT HERE FOR A MINUTE.
WELL, DON'T SIT TOO LONG. YOU STILL OWE ME A DANCE, REMEMBER?
I WON'T.

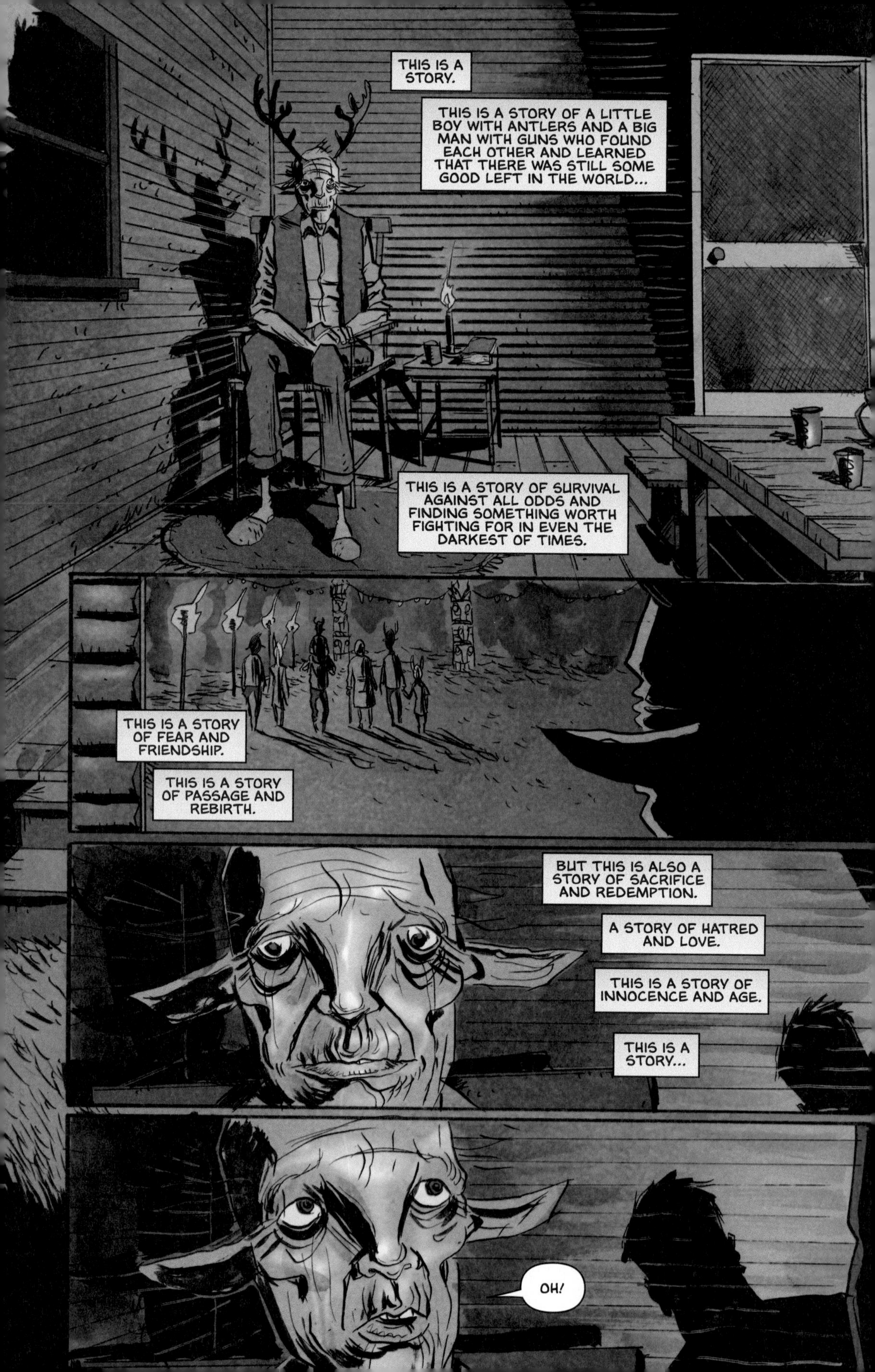
THIS IS A STORY.
THIS IS A STORY OF A LITTLE BOY WITH ANTLERS AND A BIG MAN WITH GUNS WHO FOUND EACH OTHER AND LEARNED THAT THERE WAS STILL SOME GOOD LEFT IN THE WORLD...
THIS IS A STORY OF SURVIVAL AGAINST ALL ODDS AND FINDING SOMETHING WORTH FIGHTING FOR IN EVEN THE DARKEST OF TIMES.
THIS IS A STORY OF FEAR AND FRIENDSHIP.
THIS IS A STORY OF PASSAGE AND REBIRTH.
BUT THIS IS ALSO A STORY OF SACRIFICE AND REDEMPTION.
A STORY OF HATRED AND LOVE.
THIS IS A STORY OF INNOCENCE AND AGE.
THIS IS A STORY...
OH!

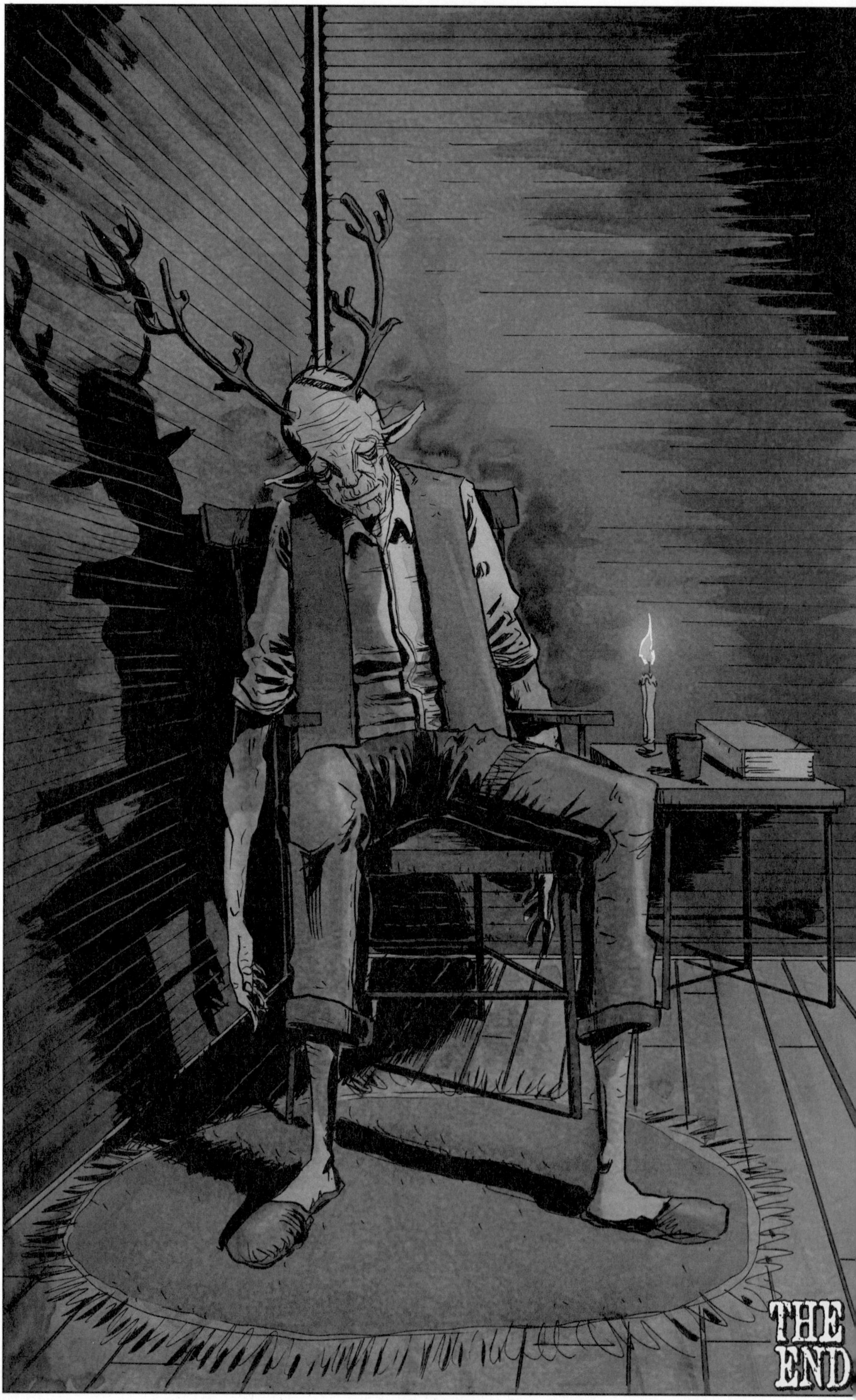
THE END

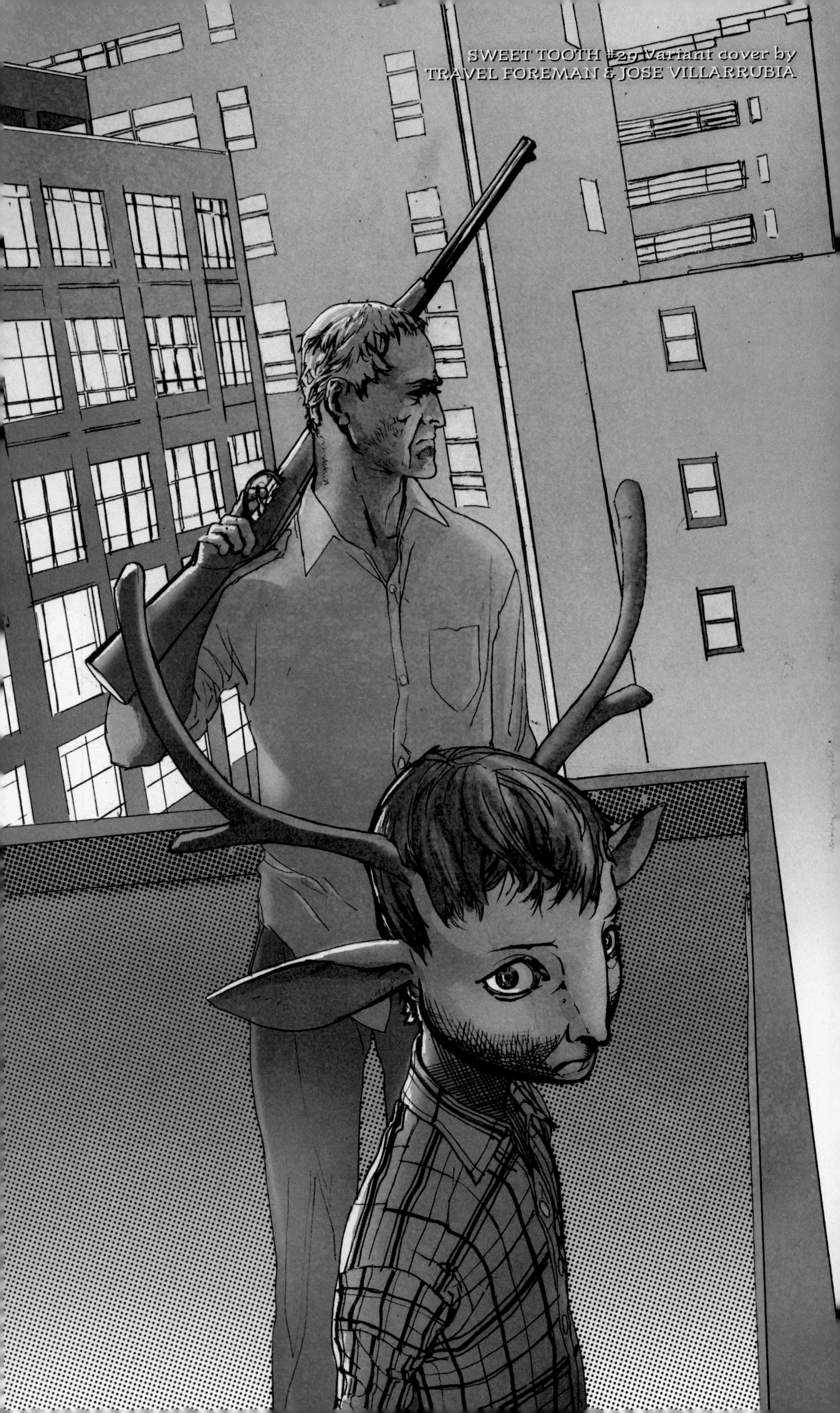

SWEET TOOTH #29 Variant cover by
TRAVEL FOREMAN & JOSE VILLARRUBIA

SWEET TOOTH #40
Variant cover by TIMOTHY TRUMAN

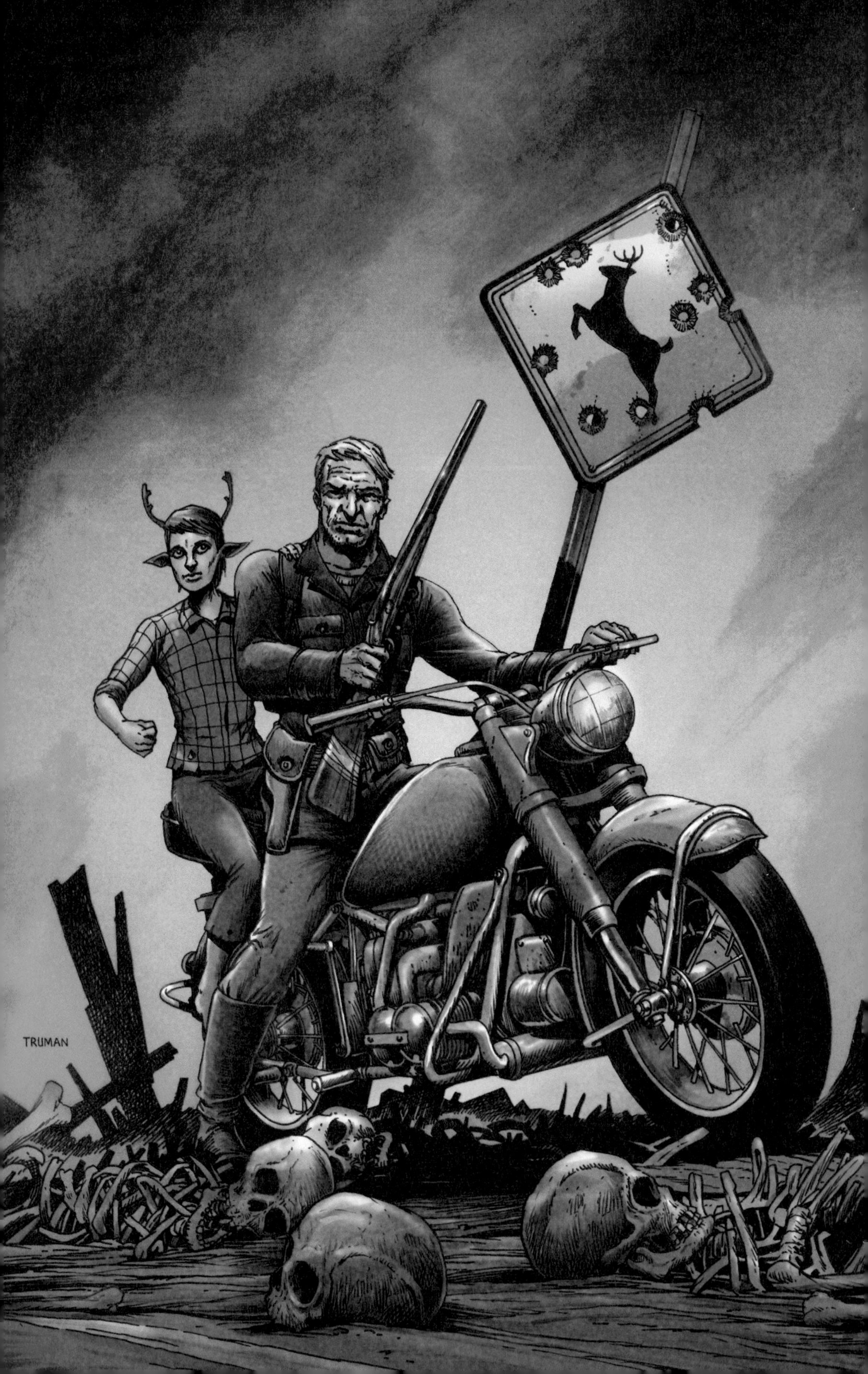
TRUMAN

SWEET TOOTH SKETCHBOOK
Art and text by Jeff Lemire
unless otherwise noted

Original illustration of Gus and
Jepperd, later used as part of the
"storybook" issue

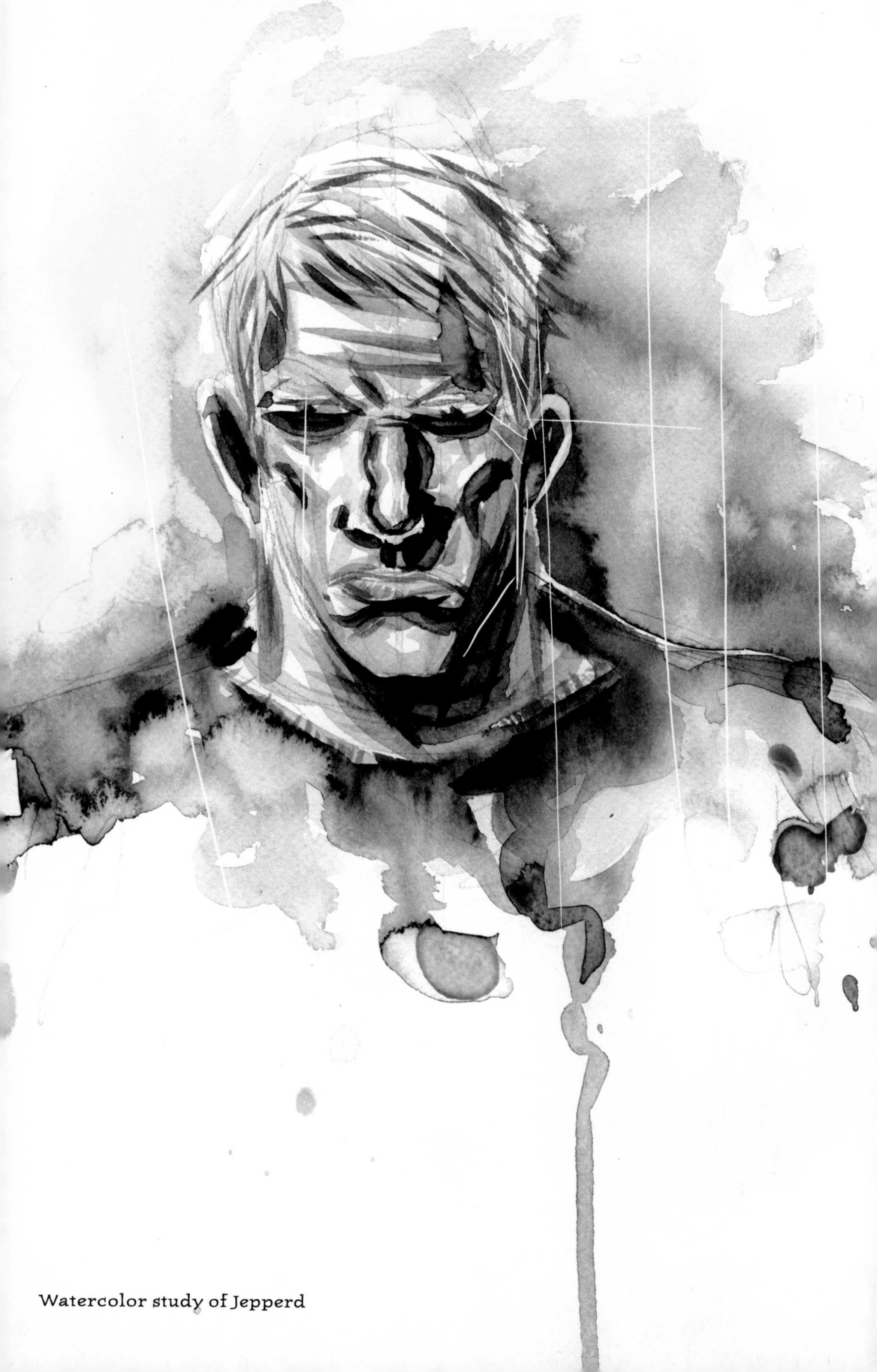

Watercolor study of Jepperd

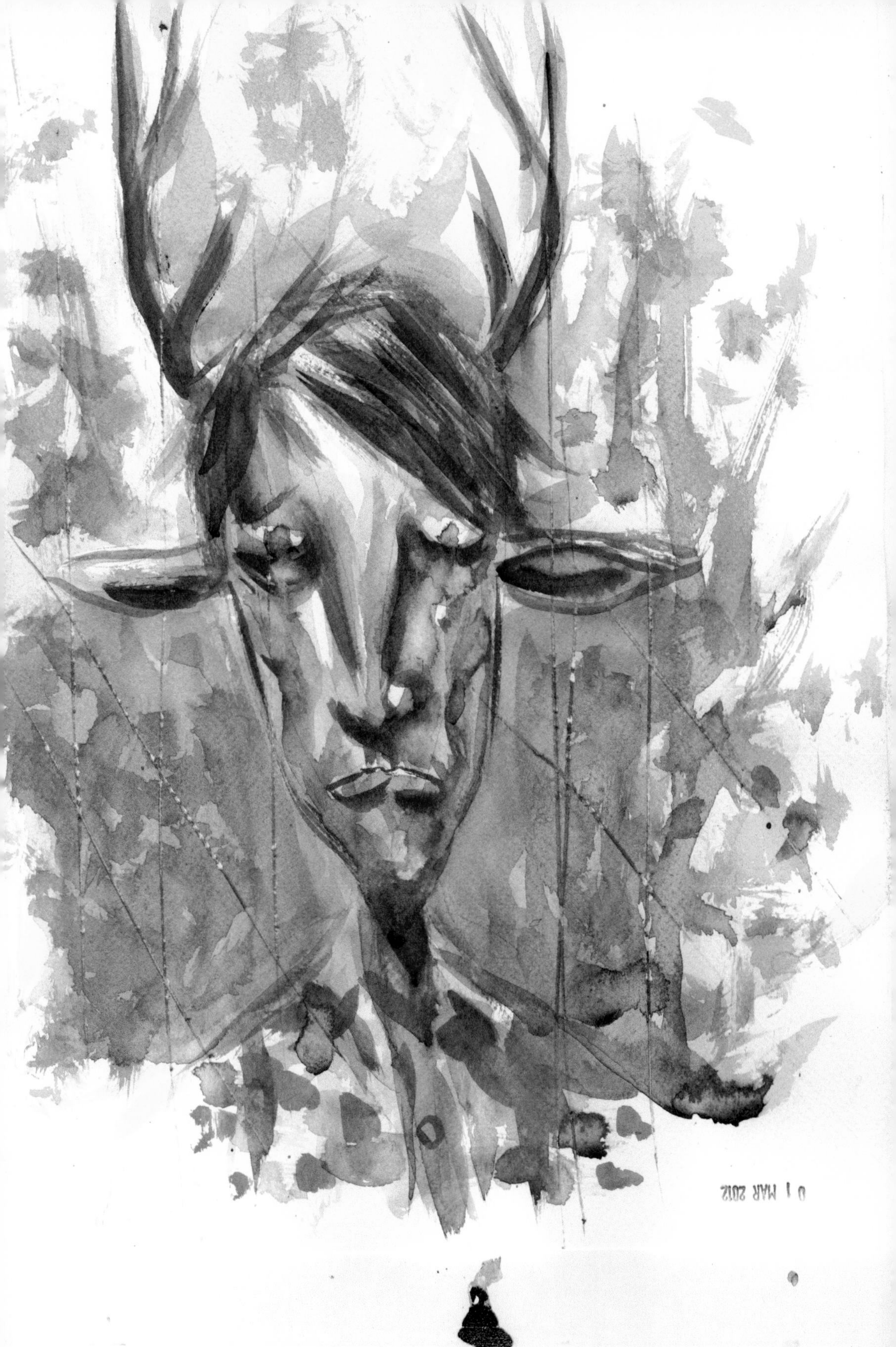

Watercolor study of Gus

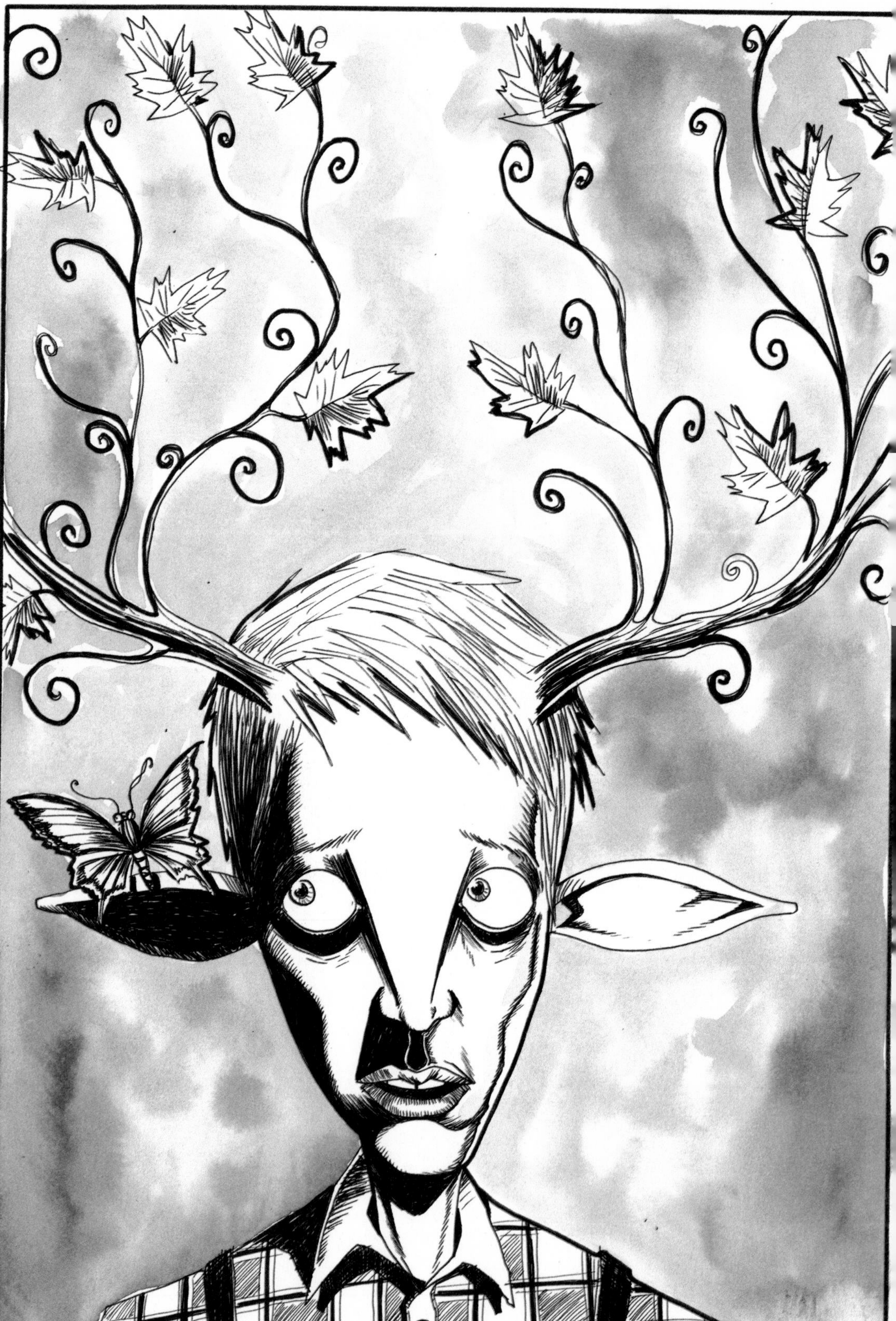

Original illustration done as part of the Comic Book Legal Defense Fund art auction at San Diego Comic-Con in 2012

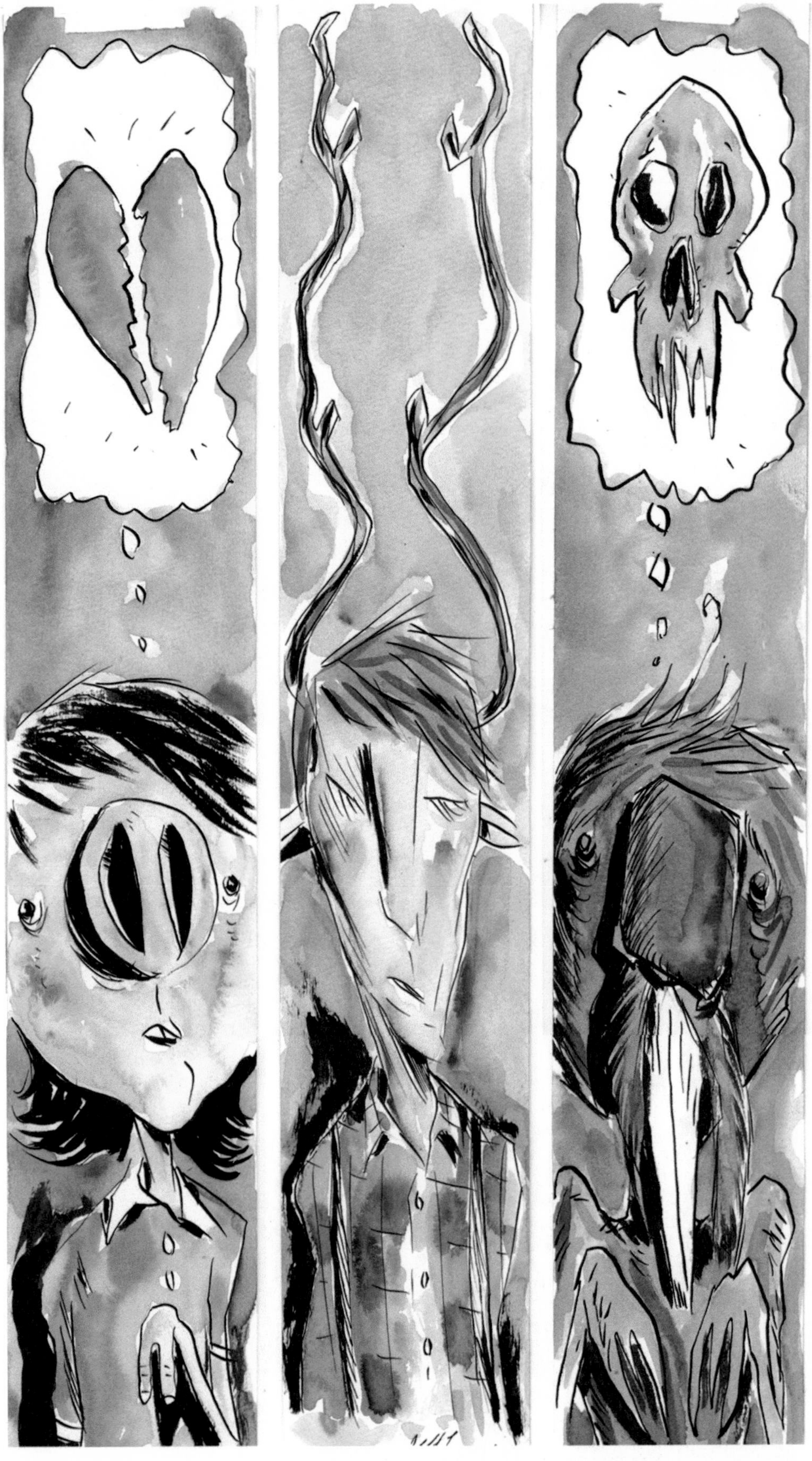

Painting of Gus, Wendy, and Bobby, later
turned into a limited-edition print

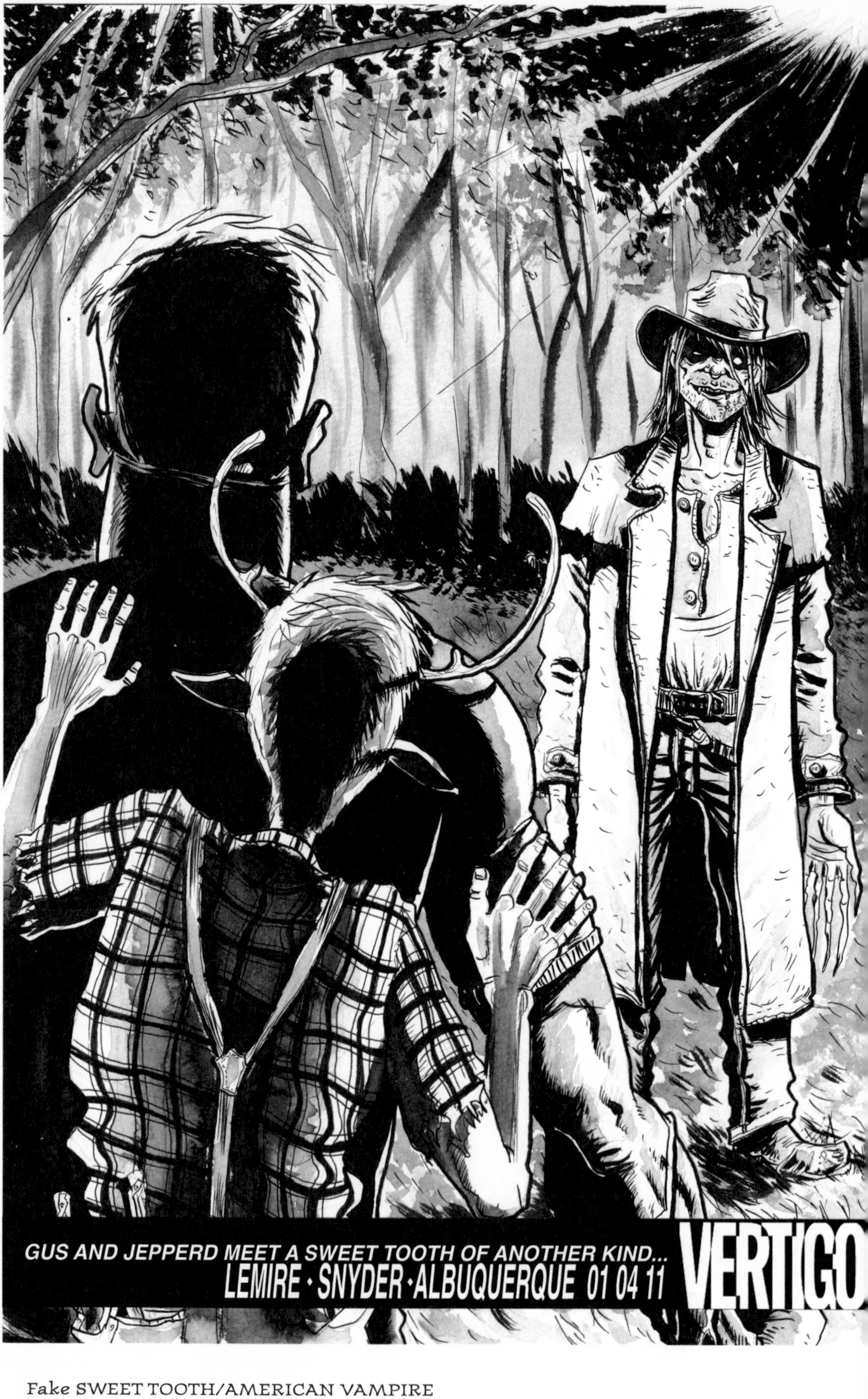
GUS AND JEPPERD MEET A SWEET TOOTH OF ANOTHER KIND...
LEMIRE · SNYDER · ALBUQUERQUE 01 04 11
VERTIGO

Fake SWEET TOOTH/AMERICAN VAMPIRE advertisement made as a Christmas gift for Scott Snyder

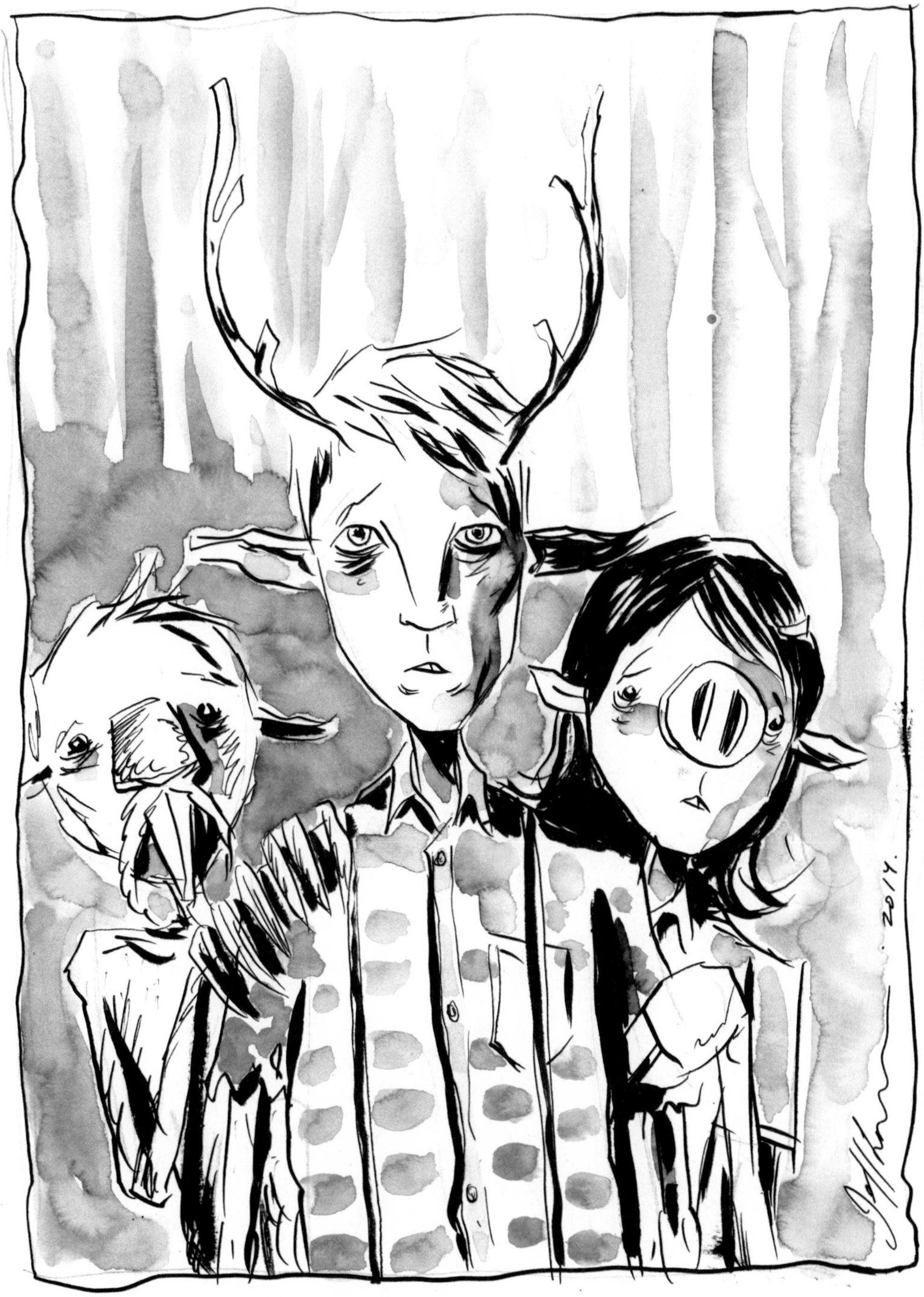
2014.

A rare convention commission

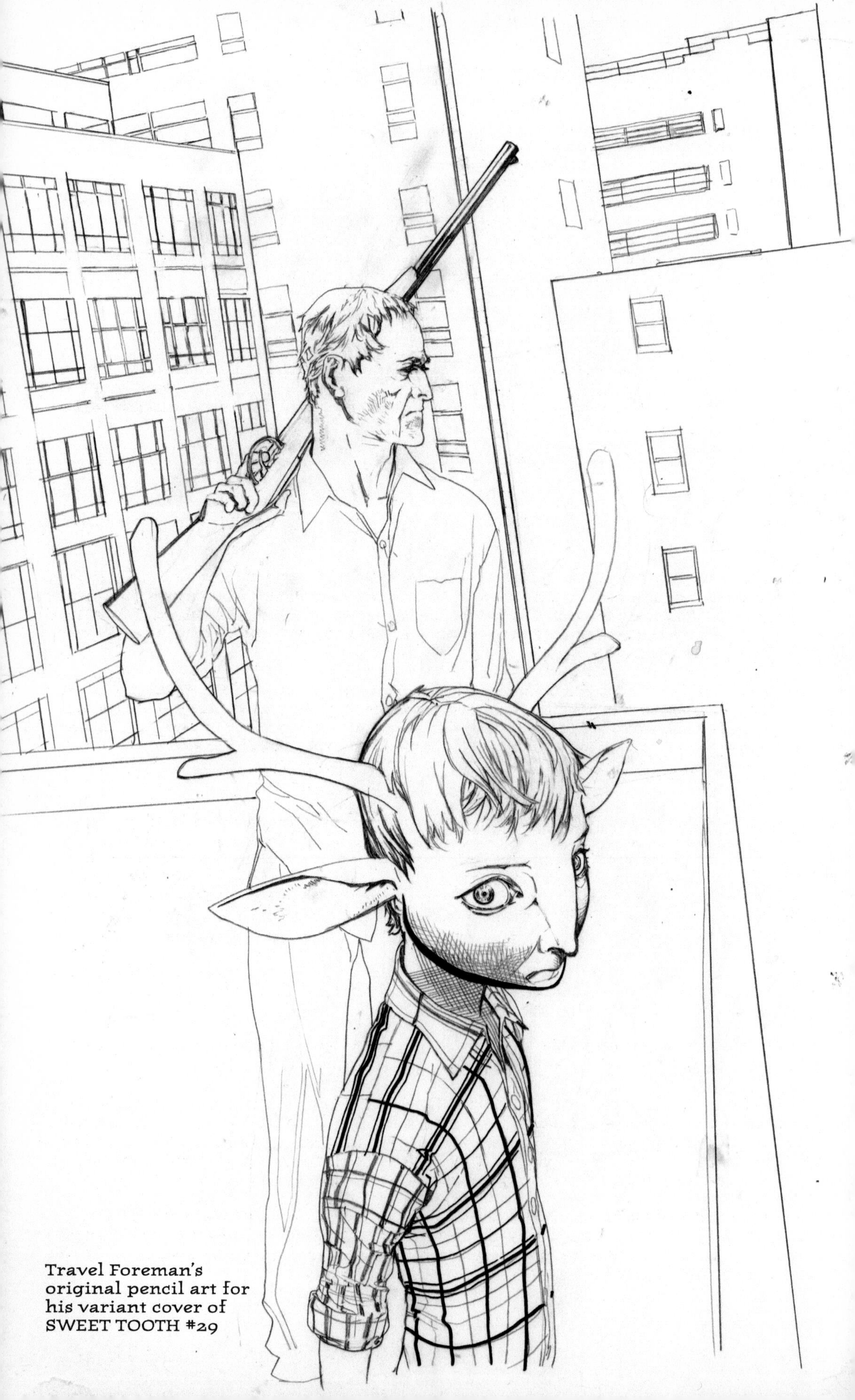

Travel Foreman's
original pencil art for
his variant cover of
SWEET TOOTH #29

INTERVIEW WITH JEFF LEMIRE AND DAMON LINDELOF

To commemorate the final issue of SWEET TOOTH, popular industry website Comic Book Resources asked Jeff Lemire's friend and collaborator Damon Lindelof (co-creator of Lost *and* The Leftovers) *to interview the author about the series' end. The following is reprinted from CBR with permission.*

Damon Lindelof: I will start by saying that I read the final issue yesterday, and I've read it a couple of times since. I don't want that to take on the sort of cold, antiseptic feeling of objective journalist interviewing subject, because that is the opposite of what this is, but Jeff, you know that I've been a huge fan of SWEET TOOTH—it was actually the first thing that I read of yours and it became a portal to all of your other stuff that preceded and the stuff that followed it—so it was obviously an emotionally fraught process just getting the final issue and reading it on my computer, as opposed to having a physical copy in my hands, but I just thought that it was perfect.

And that's not a word I use lightly. I just feel it accomplished everything that I feel a final issue of a story like this would—and then went far beyond any expectations I might have had. I just found myself feeling both enormously happy and enormously jealous that you had executed at such a high level and I offer my sincerest congratulations, because I feel like you stuck the landing perfectly. There is no splash going into the water, and I think this is the final nail in the coffin of a book that is going to live on for decades to come.

Jeff Lemire: Wow. Thank you. That's obviously very flattering. It's funny, because the series has taken on a lot of different directions as it went along that I didn't see coming, but the ending and the final issue, I pretty much always knew it.

Right from when I started writing the pitch, for whatever reason, that whole last issue was there right away. For me, it was just a matter of getting through all the other stuff so I could get to it.

That's an interesting jumping-off point, because I've read a number of interviews with you over the years—I'll be referring to them in some of my other questions—but I think one of the first interviews that I read about the book, I don't know if it was in *USA Today* or something like that, but you actually said that. This was 2009 and we were still writing *Lost*, and you said that you had a very specific idea of exactly how [SWEET TOOTH] was going to end.

But then you also said, "But I don't know how long I am going to have to do that." It depended on whether or not people were going to read it, I think. If memory serves me right, the original plan that you had was somewhere in the neighborhood of 20 to 30 issues. That's how much story you had in your head. So, I do wonder, if people hadn't been buying the book—let's say it was a huge critical success, but you weren't moving issues and you had to end SWEET TOOTH at #12, would this have still been the ending or at least some version of it?

I had this plan, but like you said, when you launch a new series, you never know how long it's going to last. You could get nine issues, you could get 100 issues, but, yes, this was always the ending. It would have been everything else that would have changed. My fallback plan would have been, at the end of #5, Jepperd leaves Gus at the militia camp, he kind of betrays him, and then #6 to #10 would have been Jepperd changing his mind and coming back and saving Gus, and then the final issue would jump ahead to basically what we see in the final issue, or some variation of that. I obviously just kept expanding on that when it became 20 issues, 24 issues, and then 40 issues.

I kind of fell in love with the supporting cast more than I expected. The length of the series gave me room to develop the supporting cast, especially the other kids and Dr. Singh and people like that, so it just kept getting bigger from there.

Really, the whole Dam storyline was tacked on in the middle to expand the story into the 40-issue range. So yes, it went through various versions, the overall story, but that last issue was always going to be the ending.

You can probably understand this from *Lost*—SWEET TOOTH was never about the secret of how the hybrid children came to be or the secret of what the plague was or any of that stuff. That was all way down on my priority list. It was always about where Gus ended up, and the characters ended up. Much like you did on *Lost*, revealing the secret of the plague and all that was never really something that I cared all that much about. It was more of a plot device to keep certain characters, mostly Dr. Singh, in the mix.

That being said, and I want to ask you about that a little later, I do like the way you handled that mythology. Detouring and doing the period Thacker story in its entirety was really clever and something that I thought was ballsy and gutsy at the time that I was reading it. I also feel like the series as a whole would be diminished if that wasn't there.

If they just went to Alaska and found the empty casket and the journal and you had two pages to explain it. "Here's what happened here..." But by grounding it in one guy's emotional journey, it felt like it was grafted into the larger tale and it became really integral to the storytelling as opposed to filler.

I think it's funny, because the whole Thacker flashback story was never something I had in mind at all. That was never a part of any of my original plans. That really came about because I had to finish *The Underwater Welder* and I just didn't have time. It was really stressing me out, because my monthly book was taking up all the time that I really needed, obviously, so my editor Mark Doyle and I started thinking of ways that I could build in some time where I could take three or four months to work on *The Underwater Welder*. We came up with this idea of Matt Kindt drawing some issues.

My thought was that if Matt was going to draw something, I should kind of remove it somehow from the main storyline just because I would have felt weird having someone else drawing the main storyline. It kind of came out of that. But like you said, as soon as I started writing it, I realized, "Oh, my God. This is so important to the overall story." I can't imagine what it would have been without it, now, and how I would have revealed stuff in Alaska without it. It really was crucial, like you said, but it was one of those things that came about organically out of need really.

It's so interesting that you say that, because I think that whatever is going on in a creator's life when they are bringing a story like this to a close directly impacts the way that they do it. It's not just what they're thinking or doing or reading or if they just had a kid or if they're going through a divorce. Those things are obviously usually impactful, but just the sheer magnitude of what their creative life is and the other projects that they're working on and how much workload that puts on their shoulders—the audience never takes any of that into account. It's like, "Okay, Kerri Strug: You've sprained your ankle, but you better do this vault because it's the Olympics. We have an expectation."

It's a wonderful story in hindsight, if you get the gold. But if she doesn't, nobody says, "Well, she did sprain her ankle."

This is my roundabout way of saying, in spite of the sheer workload on *The Underwater Welder*, it being as magnificent as it is, in addition to all the other DC books that you were doing as [SWEET TOOTH] was wrapping up, it never feels like you neglected any of your children along the way, which is pretty extraordinary. So again, well done.

It is tough balancing different things. I'm sure you know that, too. It honestly doesn't take that long to write an issue of ANIMAL MAN or GREEN ARROW. Once it's plotted out, it takes maybe a day or two to write one of those scripts, whereas drawing an issue of SWEET TOOTH takes three or four weeks. I always spend more time with that book. I would catch myself some days, going through the motions a bit when I was drawing it, and I would always try to catch myself and make sure my priorities were in line and become reinvested in the book in some way.

It's not like you're just writing a script for SWEET TOOTH for three or four months and moving on to the next project. It was a three- or four-year thing, so I fell in and out of love with it a few times. I got sick of it a few times, but always managed to come back fresh in different ways. That's why I think when I took that break in the middle, with Matt coming on, it was a really good thing for me creatively, where I could come back and have fresh eyes. It reinvigorated me in a lot of ways.

Awesome. I was reading this interview with Vince Gilligan this morning. Do you watch *Breaking Bad*?

Yeah.

Well, he's basically in the process of writing their final three episodes, and they are asking him a lot of the same questions that I am sure you are being asked—some of which I will have to ask, because people want to know the answers to them, which I will dodge, because I hated being asked them myself. [Laughs]

He was kind of quoting Henry Mancini, the composer, in saying that whether these are movies—or long-form sagas, in the case of SWEET TOOTH—they should have a certain degree of inevitability around them. There is comfort in embracing the obvious. It's not really about twists and turns at this point. I guess the question buried in all this is, you said you've known that this was the ending, but along the way, did you ever consider an aberration from that or changing it or even maybe having someone who was originally going to make it, not make it?

Not really. I think it's exactly like you said, where you get to the end of something and the readers have been with you for a long time and you've been with the story for a long time. Almost every story can be boiled down to a couple sentences when you ask, what is it about?

I think SWEET TOOTH is about Gus and Jepperd. It's about Gus coming of age, and it's about Jepperd learning to love again and opening his heart again. That's what the book is about, so that's what the ending should be about. To throw in a big twist would be false. As far as the idea that someone might make it that didn't or vice versa, I pretty much stuck with everything that I had planned. The only thing, and this is a spoiler, but my original plan was that Gus would end up with Becky, the human girl, and not Wendy. But I realized as I got closer to the end that people really wanted to see Gus and Wendy together. Plus, I really wanted to draw little kids with pig noses and antlers. [Laughs]

But it feels like you gave us our cake and let us eat it, too, because there is this moment where he's asked, "Are you going to tell them about Becky?" And Gus acknowledges, "No, I'm not going to complicate things. They really only have one mom." And then, in just a number of panels, you very briefly kind of show us—if the story that you're telling is that human life is coming to an end and the plague is still out there—the original ending, so I feel like we got both.

Thanks. I wanted to make sure that you had that moment where you know he had this thing with Becky, but in the long run, it was about this new race of creatures and humans were going away.

Is it the idea that his older son, Tommy, is his son with Wendy and his younger son, Richard, is his and Becky's?

That's not a question that I would like to answer. I know in my mind what the answer is, but...

Good, because I don't want to know.

[Laughs] It's just one of those fun things that you don't answer.

They're fun for a while until somebody gets really, really angry about it! But I stand by your decision. Sorry, I can't help but put my fanboy cap on and speculate.

Just to get off-plot for a second, because I think we'll weave in and out of that, one of the things that was sort of a recurring talking point, whenever I heard you talking about SWEET TOOTH or read you speaking about it, is this idea of Gus' journey and this notion of innocence. Starting him in this very innocent, literally sheltered place, and we are going to take him out of this place as he's exposed to Jepperd. What was always really cool about Jepperd, in the Joseph Campbell-ian myth-making style, is that he is the mentor. He's Obi-Wan. He's the one that shows Gus how the world works. But he's not Obi-Wan. He's not Mr. Miyagi. [He has] this very grizzled, savage approach to the world, which actually kind of turns out to be right. It saves Gus a number of times.

In SWEET TOOTH #40, there is a time lapse, and we are reintroduced to Gus and he is very Jepperd-like in many ways. But there are a couple of turns in the issue where we learn that he hasn't become totally and completely savage like Jepperd. There is still compassion there. I'm curious if you're saying—when we meet him at the beginning of the story in SWEET TOOTH #1, Gus is totally innocent, he's tabula rasa. Where is he at the end?

To me, at the outset, Gus is a total innocent and Jepperd is a total savage. As the book goes on, as they're exposed to one another, they both start going the other way. At the end, Gus becomes the best of both of them. He becomes a hybrid of what he was at the beginning and what Jepperd was. He's just enough of each to survive, and he's better than each of them on their own. He has the parts of Jepperd he needs to survive and he needs to lead this new breed and help them survive, but he also has those important things that he's always had that make him better than mankind, which is his innocence and his heart—an ability to love people and let them in, which Jepperd couldn't always do.

I feel like you articulated that really beautifully with Buddy. Taking these ideas, it's easy for characters to espouse philosophy, but you have to choose representatives to carry the water of different ideas, and that was one of the big surprises of the book for me, was Buddy. "Oh right, of course—he's here too." The fact that he had become more representative of being war-like and conflict-driven in terms of his attitude and approach to man, which makes absolute and total sense if you were Buddy, because he really didn't have Jepperd as an active, ongoing participant in his life.

I think, clearly, that he was resenting Gus for that because Gus got the father he was supposed to have.

Sure, and then there is this very powerful moment where Buddy is about to be killed for going to war, for taking on this group of humans, and Gus comes riding in to save him. And it says, something along the line of, "But they were brothers." That idea of looking after someone that you fundamentally disagree with was really powerful without being preachy.

Like I said, Gus is the best of everything, so he would be so forgiving of that. With everything that happened to Buddy, he would see a reason why. And he would overlook that. He would always be there. And also he would be because that's what Jepperd asked him to do in SWEET TOOTH #39.

That's good that you thought that and bought that cover. [Laughs] Because, again, I don't think there was ever a period where I even considered killing Gus off. "Make sure you take care of Buddy, no matter what."

When you first started talking about the ending of SWEET TOOTH, you were asked if you were going to give it a happy ending. And your answer was some version of: "No comment." And I remember when I read that, thinking, "Oh, no. Terrible, terrible things are going to happen." Now that everybody has read it, can you answer that question? It is a yes or no question, but can you answer it now?

Yes. For me, it's a very happy ending. At least to me it is. When I was writing it, it was very joyous kind of ending. I felt like all the bad things that happened and the wringer that you put the characters through for 39 issues, it would be pointless and just cruel to have that be the way that it ends without a reason, without a greater purpose. To me, it's probably the happiest ending I've ever put on a book. [Laughs] To me, the last page is really happy.

Speaking of unhappy, you've said you've always known where this was going, you've known what this last issue was, and again, circling back to the inevitability idea, it always felt like Jepperd was not going to make it. It always felt like he had to die in order for Gus to evolve to sort of move forward. Even knowing, from the word go, that Jepperd is not going to make it, can you just talk about, a little bit, what it was like emotionally to draw those specific pages from the story when he died?

It's tough. I always knew he was going to die, but I also always knew I was going to miss that character—drawing him and being with him on a day-to-day basis. It's pretty emotional when you draw things like that. When you draw that last page, it's really hard and really weird thinking that would be the last time I draw Jepperd in any meaningful way other than pinups or commissions for people at shows.

For me, I worried a bit at the end that I'd made Jepperd too soft. I didn't know if I went too far. There is always that worry. We'll see. One thing that did change in the last issue was that in the last couple pages of SWEET TOOTH #40, Jepperd was never going to be on those pages until right before I did them, but I realized that he needed to have a presence in that last issue. The book needed to end in some way with Gus and Jepperd together, even in a symbolic way.

We'll get to that choice because obviously, I found it incredibly moving. It's similar to the kind of spiritual inevitability of a life and what happens when a life ends, reuniting with other lives that impacted it, etc. But I will say that when I went into the comic book store and saw the cover of SWEET TOOTH #39, and kind of knowing you and knowing the kind of storyteller that you are, and it has Jepperd clutching a piece of Gus' shirt and there is blood all around—the feeling in my heart was that this had to be a mislead—I thought you actually had the balls to kill Gus.

As inevitable as it felt to me that Jepperd was going to die, I was so sure, but when I saw that cover, I felt like, "Oh my god. This could go the other way entirely." And what a rare thing that is to be feeling, one issue away from the end of a story that you're dealing with an artist and a writer that is willing to go into that territory. I guess I want to make sure that everyone reading this doesn't think that I had it all figured out.

That was never really an option for me. I did consider killing Bobby at one point, but I thought everyone would have hated me.

I wouldn't have hated you. I would have strongly disliked you, but it would have passed.

••••

I know you've mentioned *The Punisher: The End* by Garth Ennis and Richard Corben as an inspiration in the past, but how did the end of other TV shows, movies, comics, or graphic novels affect how you handled the end of SWEET TOOTH? Or, absent of that, what endings do you hold up as endings that you really loved? And that is non-inclusive of *Lost*, because if you say you love the ending of *Lost*, I won't believe you, so let's just leave that off the table.

First off all, *Lost* is a big inspiration for SWEET TOOTH, and I'm not just saying that because you are on the phone. It's funny, because when I was writing and drawing some of the issues right before the Dam story arc, I was re-watching *Lost* on DVD. I watch TV shows while I draw, and I think that was right around the same time we had our Twitter introduction. *Lost* is a huge inspiration for SWEET TOOTH—the whole idea of a serialized story with a central mystery and how to handle that. I totally ripped off the Dharma Initiative with the people in the Dam and the Evergreen Project.

And the ending to *Lost* was very inspirational to me. It's hard to have a sincere conversation, because people will just think that I am sucking up to you because we're on the phone together, and you probably won't believe me, but I loved the ending of *Lost*. I know not everyone does, but I thought it was perfect and a really beautiful ending. That was really the guide for me, or at least one of the guides for me in the end, for creating an ending that was more concerned with an emotional truth than a big reveal about the mystery.

Another big one was *Six Feet Under*, which is one of my favorite shows. I really, really liked *Six Feet Under*. I just finished watching it again for, like, the fifth time a week or two ago. The ending of *Six Feet Under*, where they flash forward to all the main characters in the future, was definitely an influence on how to end SWEET TOOTH.

I can't think of a particular comic that influenced the ending of SWEET TOOTH. It was mostly *Six Feet Under* and *Lost*. Those two [shows], really. *The Punisher: The End* was more an inspiration for how Jepperd would look, so that wasn't really [an influence]. I also really liked the ending of *The Sopranos*, but I don't think that influenced SWEET TOOTH all that much.

I don't want to use the word "emotional" as something that is manipulative or purposeful, but I think it's something that infuses your writing, whether you like it or not. I think, clearly, that *Six Feet Under* was a show that—Alan Ball very much wove emotion into its tapestry. That's not to say *The Sopranos* was absent of emotion, but it wasn't the kind of show where—let's just say, I am hard-pressed to think of any moment of any episode where I said that I cried when I watched *The Sopranos*. Or even, "Wasn't that sad?" Whereas for *Six Feet Under*, I could name 15 of those moments off the top of my head. A show has to die as it lives in that regard, and I think you did that with SWEET TOOTH. Any mistakes? Regrets? Things that you wish you had done differently? Is there a story point or an issue, even artistically speaking, that you would call a do-over on?

As a writer, and as far as the story itself, no, there are not that many regrets. I guess there might be little things here and there, little tweaks, but nothing big. But I am very hard on myself in terms of my drawing. I can't even look at something I drew a month ago. I see only mistakes. I can't look at the first trade of SWEET TOOTH. I just cringe. That's a tough thing, and a different thing. But from a story point of view, I don't really have any regrets.

That said, I did reach a point during the first half of the last issue, when Gus and Bobby are grown up with the kids by the campfire and everything, and there was a really serious point there when I thought, maybe I shouldn't be ending SWEET TOOTH. Maybe there is a whole other series of these characters at that age. I actually considered calling my editor and asking if we could end SWEET TOOTH here and then bring it back as SWEET TOOTH Vol. 2, a brand-new series based on them at that age. It would inevitably lead to the ending that I had in mind anyway! What stopped me was that no matter what I did with Sweet Tooth and his kids, it would just be repeating what I did with Sweet Tooth and Jepperd. I just didn't want to let go. I had to stop myself from doing that.

That's great, and I'm glad that you did that. I did have a question planned for near the end, but now that you mentioned it, I will ask you a version of that question. Is this a world you would ever want to revisit? You've told the story of these characters, but generationally speaking, does finding nooks and crannies that you haven't explored before, does that interest you at all?

You never say never. I'm sure you know that. When you finish something, you think you'll never come back to it, but 10 years from now, I may get some brilliant idea that I just fall in love with revolving around [Gus'] grandchildren, totally unique from what I have already done and something that I really want to tell. But at this point, I feel like this ending was exactly what I wanted and I can't see myself returning to the world. Again, I feel like I would just be repeating themes and the same stories that I've already told, just with a different generation, which seems pointless.

I want to talk a little bit about the world, because I certainly had this experience when I was growing up and reading Stephen King's books, where there is nothing that precluded them from happening in the same world. Obviously, when you read *The Stand*, everybody dies, but I think *The Stand* is significant to the point that I am going to try and make.

Books that [King] wrote subsequent to *The Stand* can't be happening if the superflu basically killed everybody. But then he started writing the Gunslinger books. He had been writing them for quite some time, and he started really tying some of those worlds together. And I will say that, to the exclusion of your DC books, which are based on an entirely different continuity and are not drawn by you, the books that are the "Lemire" books, the *Essex County* trilogy and SWEET TOOTH and *The Underwater Welder*—though *The Underwater Welder* has a supernatural subtext to it, it's not overtly supernatural—it does feel like they all take place in the same world. I wonder if you view it that way when you're writing them?

Yeah, they do. They all do. I kind of alluded to it as much in an earlier issue, when Gus and Jepperd basically find Lester's bedroom from *Essex County*.

Oh yeah, right.

It can't really be Lester's bedroom, because they are in Nebraska and *Essex County* is supposed to be in Essex County, but it really kind of is. [Laughs] In my mind, yes, it is all the same universe. I don't know if it's actually all been connected like a "Dark Tower" kind of thing, but definitely, I always feel like they are people existing in the same world. Jepperd probably played hockey against Jimmy at one point.

It's interesting, because I read *Essex County* after SWEET TOOTH. I don't remember exactly where I was in the continuing story of SWEET TOOTH when I was reading *Essex County*, because *Essex County* is a deep read, so I didn't do it all in one sitting. I was reading them both simultaneously, but I was getting that feeling, because you have a specific mood when you do that thing you do.

This is a nice segue into my next question, which is one of the things that I think is very unique to what you do, which is that everything has a very deep thematic resonance without ever openly talking about it. Even though inside *Essex County*, one of the stories might be about imagination and another one might be about regret, or *The Underwater Welder* may be more specific in terms of saying, "This is about fatherhood and the fear of becoming a father and the fear of becoming your own father." I felt this tense thematic resonance hanging around SWEET TOOTH, too. Then, there is this scene in #40 where they are about to eat this rabbit and Gus recites this amazing prayer, which kind of sums up the entire series beautifully, and he does it in a way where he is saying, "Here is the mythology of the series." But actually, he's talking entirely about theme. I'm curious, can you talk a little bit about writing that speech?

I think you're going to be very disappointed in my answer. It's one of those things that just kind of came out. It's not 'til after, when you go back and reread, when you understand the resonance that it has. But yes, it did sum up the series quite well.

I'm the opposite of disappointed—I love it. It goes to what I just said: It's kind of effortless for you. You're not trying to hit us over the head with it.

I don't want it to sound like it's so easy for me or whatever. But I will say that, when I am writing, I'm not often aware of what the themes are in that kind of way, until much later or until someone else starts talking about the book. For me, it is a much more organic or natural thing. It sounds silly, but I'm just writing stories and letting characters talk. I figure out what the book is about as they do, as it goes along. I don't sit down and say, "The themes of this project will be..."

But again, I don't remember everything that he says, and I don't have it right in front of me. I am paraphrasing and thusly butchering your words, but he says that everything bad that happened is a result of the fact that we've lost the faces of our fathers and mankind has lost touch with their natural symbiosis. That's how we got to where we are, but now, when we're eating these animals, they are us and we are them so we're basically thanking the gods and remembering the faces of our fathers.

But we look like man, too, so we can't forget about the mess that they fucking got us into. And that's our cross to bear. And I was like, "Oh yeah, that's what this book is about." It had never really occurred to me directly, but you couching it as a grace, I thought that was very clever. The fact that you didn't put that much thought into it makes me want to hit you with a brick.

[Laughs] Obviously, I did the Thacker story and the stuff at the end, but I've been reading a lot of Native American or First Nations literature, and I think a lot of that has been seeping into my work, the second half of SWEET TOOTH especially. Really, a lot of that stuff comes from the idea of returning to nature.

For me, SWEET TOOTH #40 was really about finding a better way of living and not making the same mistakes.

This is a great segue for the other thing that I wanted to talk to you about, which is, I think there has been a lot of post-apocalyptic stuff out there, probably for the last three decades or so. You've talked about *Mad Max* being an inspiration for this, but especially now, in the pop culture landscape, beyond the silliness of the Mayan apocalypse and all that stuff, shows like *The Walking Dead* and *Revolution* are really connecting with audiences. One of the keystones of the apocalypse in these stories is that they are a cautionary tale. I guess what I want to ask you is, now that you've written SWEET TOOTH, I'm curious: Do you, the individual Jeff, buy into this? I mean, where is mankind in 50 to 100 years? Do we deserve to be the dominant species? SWEET TOOTH seems to say no.

I don't think we do. I feel like the reason post-apocalyptic stuff is so popular right now, and maybe I am wrong, but I feel it's because we all look around and see what a fucking mess the world is in, and the terrible things that we're doing to one another. We know what's coming—and it may be some variation of this. It might not be cool and dramatic like *The Walking Dead* or SWEET TOOTH, but we're not heading in a good direction. We see that, and maybe these types of stories provide a little escape.

But yes, for me, I really feel like we're fucking up right now. And yes, that's what SWEET TOOTH is basically about. I don't hide that at all. I think we've messed up, and I think it's too late. I know that's a sadistic thing to say, but at the end of the day, if things are getting so bad and they're only going to get worse, what do we have? What we really have is each other, and that's also what SWEET TOOTH is about. I guess that's just how I feel about the world.

I couldn't agree with you more.

You were talking about where you took some of these issues, particularly in the back half of the series, and their connection to certain Native American spirituality. I'd written this question before you talked about it, but I am interested in going a little bit deeper. SWEET TOOTH is obviously a spiritual book, and it uses religious themes regularly from the outset, in terms of what Gus' relationship is to his father who is taking care of him at the cabin. But is this something that you do consciously? Because I do feel like, especially now, and speaking from personal experience while working on *Lost*, I actually believe the world is a lot more religious than it wants to take credit for. In our particular pop culture sphere and the comic book sphere and the genre television sphere, it's very unpopular to say that you are a religious person, or that you have spiritual beliefs. Where are you on the religious spectrum? I know it's a very personal question, but how do you use it in your work?

Well, I think it's a big part of everything that I do. I was raised in a Roman Catholic home and church. It was a really big part of my upbringing, but I don't know if I ever felt comfortable with it. My parents are very, very religious and very into that stuff, but as soon as I got away from home, when I was 19, I just completely separated myself from any kind of religion because I didn't really believe in organized ideas of Christianity. At the same time, I think I am spiritual in the way that I do believe in something; I just don't know what it is, exactly.

I think SWEET TOOTH and whatever else I'm working on right now, in large part, it's all probably about me looking around at different things in different ways as a reaction to me not buying into the religion that I was raised in.

Right. It's a reaction to, as opposed to an endorsement of.

Exactly. It's more of me looking for some sort of, like all of us, spirituality or some sort of greater meaning when you don't really believe in the thing that you were raised with anymore. You're looking for a common thread of many different religions, which we kind of draw from.

What's so interesting to me about that sort of disconnect between what I would view as a comic book-consuming audience and their sort of rejection of religion or that idea is how those entire worlds and the whole construct of a superhero is so mythic. It skews, obviously, much closer to Greco-Roman mythology, where you've got the God of the Sun and the God of the Earth and the God of the Underworld, but all of those figures are represented in these stories. The only difference is that we just don't believe they're real. But a good story is a good story, right? The Bible is a perennial bestseller for a reason. [Laughs] I'd like to see you adapt it one of these days.

[Laughs] I'm working on it right now.

I can't wait to see how you end that one. [Laughs] Speaking of story, again, the words "This is a story" become almost like a song lyric in this final issue. They're the first words and the last words. As you've said, you knew what was going to happen, but did you know that those words were going to become such a huge motif, or did that kind of surprise you?

If I look at my original outlines that I have for SWEET TOOTH or my original pitch, that was always there, and it even repeated at the end. Originally, that came from the idea that, in some of the earlier issues, there were stories about the deer and the rabbit that were following him around, the Disney kind of characters. Then I did those couple of issues where they were sideways format—those were supposed to feel like children's books or whatever, so the idea was that this book is about stories and then maybe they were part of a bigger story, too. That was always a part of it. Gus' stories are informing the next generation after that. It just seemed to flow through everything and then, it sets up the last, the end, of course. It just seemed like the best way to end it.

I have to close by asking some obvious questions, because if I don't, someone else will, and if I don't ask them, readers will say, "How can you not have asked him...?" We've already asked one, which is, would you ever consider revisiting this world, but the second one is about the adaptation of SWEET TOOTH. Where is SWEET TOOTH in those terms? Has it been optioned? Would you prefer it to be a movie or a TV show or neither? Do you want it just to live in the form in which you created it?

It's a tricky question, and I'll try to answer it in a way that won't get me in trouble with DC, but when you do a book for Vertigo, the contracts get kind of complicated. Warner Bros. controls the properties more than a book that I might have done for, let's say, Top Shelf. So in terms of being optioned, it's a lot harder for that to happen because of Vertigo's contracts than I would like, maybe. There's a lot of interest, but it's very complicated, so it hasn't been optioned yet.

But yes, I would love to see it adapted. I think maybe more as a movie than a TV show. I think it could be really boiled down to the original idea I had, which was that the first 10 or 11 issues of the series could almost be the whole movie or the whole series. Everything else could be cut out. I just don't have the luxury of sitting around and thinking about that happening because it's out of my control, really.

I have some friends over at Warner Bros. Features, so I'll crack the whip and make sure they get working on it. [Laughs]

[Laughs] That would be great. Have you seen *The Grey* with Liam Neeson?

I have, yes.

After seeing that, I can't imagine anyone else playing Jepperd except for Liam Neeson now.

That would be awesome. He'd be fantastic. I actually love that movie. That movie is not at all what I expected but—spoiler alert on *The Grey*—when I ask people if they've seen that movie, and they go, "Is that the one where Liam Neeson makes the glove with the glass on it and he's punching wolves?" I go, "Would you be surprised if I told you that shot was the last 40 seconds of the movie?" They always look at me like, "What?" And I'm like, "You need to see it, because it's not the movie that you think it is."

It doesn't surprise me that you liked that movie. I saw that movie with Michael Giacchino, who did all the music for *Lost*, and I'll say, because I don't want to be arrested, that we were under the influence, and we ended up talking for two hours afterwards about the meaning of life and how fleeting it is and how much we wanted to have sex with Liam Neeson even though we're both straight men. But we could still be straight because it's Liam Neeson. [Laughs]

Since we're now clearly delving into more comedic territory, I do have one final question for you. I read SWEET TOOTH monthly, but I also get the trades so I have it as reference material, because I don't keep individual issues or my house would be overwhelmed by comic books. I remember seeing one of the trades and Jason Aaron had been blurbed on it, who in addition to you and Brian K. Vaughan are part of my holy trinity of comic writers right now. Not to say that there aren't other guys like Mark Millar, who I have just loved forever, but Jason said something along the lines of, "I would crawl over broken glass to read this." [Laughs] And I was just wondering, is there any way to put him through the test?

That's a really good question. [Laughs] Let me send him an email!